D1522873

A Companion to
Biological Anthropology

The *Blackwell Companions to Anthropology* offers a series of comprehensive syntheses of the traditional subdisciplines, primary subjects, and geographic areas of inquiry for the field. Taken together, the series represents both a contemporary survey of anthropology and a cutting edge guide to the emerging research and intellectual trends in the field as a whole.

1. *A Companion to Linguistic Anthropology* edited by Alessandro Duranti
2. *A Companion to the Anthropology of Politics* edited by David Nugent and Joan Vincent
3. *A Companion to the Anthropology of American Indians* edited by Thomas Biolsi
4. *A Companion to Psychological Anthropology* edited by Conerly Casey and Robert B. Edgerton
5. *A Companion to the Anthropology of Japan* edited by Jennifer Robertson
6. *A Companion to Latin American Anthropology* edited by Deborah Poole
7. *A Companion to Biological Anthropology* edited by Clark Spencer Larsen

Forthcoming

A Companion to Medical Anthropology edited by Merrill Singer and Pamela I. Erickson

A Companion to Cognitive Anthropology edited by David B. Kronenfeld, Giovanni Bennardo, Victor de Munck, and Michael D. Fischer

A Companion to Biological Anthropology

Edited by
Clark Spencer Larsen

WILEY-BLACKWELL

A John Wiley & Sons, Ltd., Publication

This edition first published 2010

Blackwell Publishing was acquired by John Wiley & Sons in February 2007. Blackwell's publishing program has been merged with Wiley's global Scientific, Technical, and Medical business to form Wiley-Blackwell.

Registered Office
John Wiley & Sons Ltd, The Atrium, Southern Gate, Chichester, West Sussex, PO19 8SQ, United Kingdom

Editorial Offices
350 Main Street, Malden, MA 02148–5020, USA
9600 Garsington Road, Oxford, OX4 2DQ, UK
The Atrium, Southern Gate, Chichester, West Sussex, PO19 8SQ, UK

For details of our global editorial offices, for customer services, and for information about how to apply for permission to reuse the copyright material in this book please see our website at www.wiley.com/wiley-blackwell.

Library of Congress Cataloging-in-Publication Data

A companion to biological anthropology / edited by Clark Spencer Larsen.
    p.   cm.—(Blackwell companions to anthropology)
  Includes bibliographical references and index.
  ISBN 978-1-4051-8900-2 (hardcover : alk. paper)   1. Physical anthropology.   I. Larsen, Clark Spencer.
  573—dc22
                                                2009052087

A catalogue record for this book is available from the British Library.

Set in 10/12.5pt Galliard by SPi Publisher Services, Pondicherry, India
Printed and bound in Singapore by Fabulous Printers Pte Ltd

01   2010

Dedicated to Phillip L. Walker (1947–2009), biological anthropologist and friend

Contents

List of Illustrations

List of Tables

Notes on Contributors

Barry Bogin is Professor of Biological Anthropology at Loughborough University, United Kingdom. His current research interests are physical growth and health between ethnically Maya children living in Guatemala and Mexico versus the USA; the evolution of the pattern of human growth, especially in childhood and adolescence; the use of relative leg length as an indicator of healthy growth; and intergenerational influences on health. He is the author of *The Growth of Humanity* (2001).

David R. Begun is Professor of Anthropology at the University of Toronto. A paleoanthropologist with twenty-five years of experience in the study of Miocene hominoids, he has excavated fossils in Spain and Hungary and surveyed for new sites in Spain, Hungary, Croatia, Romania, Turkey, and Kenya. His primary research interests are in functional anatomy, phylogeny reconstruction, and the biogeography of hominid origins. He is the co-editor of the *Journal of Human Evolution*.

Anne V. Buchanan is Research Associate in the Department of Anthropology at the Pennsylvania State University. She has a long-standing interest in complex traits, including disease, and has worked on many projects in genetic epidemiology and developmental genetics.

Jane E. Buikstra is Regents' Professor of Bioarchaeology and director of the Center for Bioarchaeological Research at Arizona State University. Her research focuses on the changing human condition over time, as documented through human remains recovered from archaeological contexts. She is a former president of the American Association of Physical Anthropologists and of the American Anthropological Association; a Fellow of the American Association of the Advancement of Science; and a member of the National Academy of Sciences. She is the co-author of *The Bioarchaeology of Tuberculosis: A Global View on a Reemerging Disease* (2003).

Rachel Caspari is Associate Professor of Anthropology at Central Michigan University. Her current research and recent publications focus on demographic changes associated with the origin of modern humans, especially changes in adult survivorship and longevity. Co-author of *Race and Human Evolution* (1997), she also has a long-standing interest in the concept of race, its history, and its ongoing relationship with, and influence on, the anthropological and biomedical sciences.

Douglas E. Crews is Professor of Anthropology and Public Health at The Ohio State University. His research interests include the evolutionary biology of human senescence, physiological aspects of stress across populations and in the development of chronic degenerative diseases and senescence, and cross-population responses to senescence and aging. He has studied a wide range of populations, including those in Samoa, Japan, Slovenia, and central Ohio. He is the author of *Human Senescence: Evolutionary and Biocultural Perspectives* (2003).

David J. Daegling is Associate Professor of Anthropology at the University of Florida. His research interests include the biomechanics of the primate skull, with particular emphasis on the modeling of stress and strain in the cranium and mandible in comparative applications.

Darna L. Dufour is Professor of Anthropology at the University of Colorado, Boulder. She is the author of publications that focus on diet and energy expenditure in Amerindians in the northwest Amazon and in economically disadvantaged women in Cali, Colombia. She is Chair of the Biological Anthropology Section of the American Anthropological Association and Associate Dean for Faculty and Administrative Affairs in the College of Arts and Sciences of the University of Colorado, Boulder.

Dean Falk is Senior Scholar, School for Advanced Research, Santa Fe, New Mexico, and Honorary Professor of Human Biology at the University of Vienna. She is the author of numerous publications that focus on early hominids, brain evolution, comparative neuroanatomy, primate behavior, and cognitive evolution. She is a Fellow of the American Association for the Advancement of Science. Falk collaborates with colleagues from the Mallinckrodt Institute of Radiology in St Louis, most recently on the virtual endocast of "Hobbit" (*Homo floresiensis*). She is the author of *Primate Diversity* (2000), *Braindance: Revised and Expanded Edition* (2004), and *Finding Our Tongues: Mothers, Infants, and the Origins of Language* (2009).

Timothy B. Gage is Professor of Anthropology and of Epidemiology and Biostatistics at the University of Albany, SUNY. He is the author of a number of publications concerning various demographic estimation procedures. His recent research examines the role of birth weight as a "cause" of infant mortality. He is currently director of the Center for Social and Demographic Analysis, the NICHD-funded population center at the University of Albany.

Daniel L. Gebo is currently Board of Trustees Professor and has held Distinguished Teaching and Research Professorships at Northern Illinois University, where he has worked in the Department of Anthropology for more than two decades. He has conducted field research in North, South and Central America, Africa, and Asia and is currently working in China, on topics related to primate and anthropoid origins.

James H. Gosman is Adjunct Professor of Anthropology at The Ohio State University. His research interests encompass skeletal biology and bioarchaeology. Recent publications and presentations focus on human trabecular bone ontogeny and locomotor development. In a parallel career path, he serves as a consulting physician, being supported by an MD and board certification in orthopedic surgery. He is an elected member of the American Society for Bone and Mineral Research and of the American Academy of Orthopedic Surgeons.

Debbie Guatelli-Steinberg is Associate Professor of Anthropology at The Ohio State University, with a courtesy appointment in the Department of Evolution, Ecology, and Organismal Biology. She is a former president of the Dental Anthropology Association. Much of her work focuses on questions relating to the growth of teeth in primates – human and non-human, fossil and living – and on its implications for life history and evolutionary biology.

Gregg F. Gunnell is Vertebrate Collection Coordinator and Associate Research Scientist in the Museum of Paleontology at the University of Michigan. His research focuses on the origin and diversification of modern mammalian groups, with a primary interest in insectivores, primates, bats, and carnivores. For more than thirty years he has conducted fieldwork in the North American West; he has also worked extensively in Pakistan, Kazakhstan, Indonesia, Thailand, Myanmar, Egypt, and Tanzania. His bibliography of over 100 publications includes a research monograph, two edited books, and more than eighty papers in peer-reviewed scientific journals. He has served as associate editor for the *Journal of Human Evolution* and is currently serving as associate editor of *Palaios*.

D. Ann Herring is Professor of Anthropology at McMaster University, Hamilton, Canada. Her research centers on the anthropology of infectious disease. She has a special interest in emerging infections and the social circumstances that permit them to flourish; aboriginal health in Canada; and nineteenth and twentieth-century epidemics (particularly influenza and tuberculosis). In collaboration with Lisa Sattenspiel, she has studied the spread of the 1918–19 influenza epidemic among aboriginal groups in northern Canada.

Gary D. James is Professor of Nursing, Anthropology, and Bioengineering and director of the Institute for Primary and Preventative Health Care at Binghamton University in Binghamton, New York. His research interests include physiological and endocrine adaptations to the dynamic stresses of everyday life, the relation of these responses to the development of chronic disease, the health effects of modernization, women's health, and ambulatory blood pressure technology.

Frederika A. Kaestle is Associate Professor of Anthropology and Fellow of the Institute of Molecular Biology at Indiana University, Bloomington. She is an anthropological geneticist whose research has centered on using ancient and modern DNA to understand regional population movements and to reconstruct prehistoric behavior in the Americas, the Pacific, and Central Eurasia. She is also interested in the co-evolution of humans and their diseases, and has focused on ancient DNA approaches to understanding the origin and evolution of tuberculosis in the Americas. She has conducted fieldwork in the Great Basin, the Midwest, Brazil, Germany, and Siberia and has worked with ancient samples from around the globe.

Clark Spencer Larsen is Distinguished Professor of Social and Behavioral Sciences and Chair of the Department of Anthropology at The Ohio State University. His research focuses on bioarchaeology, examining long-term adaptive transitions in a range of Old and New World settings. He co-directs the Global History of Health Project, a study of worldwide trends in health based on the study of skeletal remains over the last 10,000 years of human evolution. He is a Fellow and Chair-Elect of the Anthropology Section of the American Association for the Advancement of Science; a former vice president and president of the American Association of Physical Anthropologists; and a former editor of the *American Journal of Physical Anthropology*. He is the author of *Bioarchaeology: Interpreting Behavior from the Human Skeleton* (1997).

Michael A. Little is Distinguished Professor of Anthropology at Binghamton University, State University of New York. He has conducted high-altitude research in the Peruvian Andes on Quechua speaking Native Americans and ecological research in the Kenya savanna on nomadic Turkana pastoralists. His current research centers on the history of biological anthropology and human biology, where his fieldwork is in the library and in archives. He has served as president of the Human Biology Association and of the American Association of Physical Anthropologists. He is a Fellow in the American Association for the Advancement of Science.

Peter W. Lucas is Professor of Anthropology at George Washington University, Washington DC. His research focuses on feeding and food choice in mammals, particularly in humans and other primates, and on anatomical and physiological adaptations that have evolved in relation to such processes. This theme stems from a long-term interest in dentistry and the evolution of masticatory anatomy. It has broadened from an initial focus on dental function, chewing, and swallowing to the consideration of any other physical and chemical factors that influence food preference. He is the author of *Dental Functional Morphology: How Teeth Work* (2004).

Lorena Madrigal is Professor of Anthropology at the University of South Florida. Her interests lie in the study of microevolution in recent or living populations, conducted by using demographic and genetic approaches. She is particularly interested in the diaspora of African and East-Indian people in the Caribbean, and looks into how these people have contributed to the formation of new populations. She is also interested in the study of the genetic basis of longevity and of the way in which maternal and grand maternal longevity affects women's genetic fitness. She is a former vice president of the American Association of Physical Anthropologists.

W. Scott McGraw is Professor of Anthropology at The Ohio State University. He has carried out field studies on primates in the Democratic Republic of Congo, Ghana, and on the Ivory Coast. His research interests include the intersection between anatomy and behavior, feeding ecology, predator–prey dynamics, and conservation. He is the co-director of the Taï Forest Monkey Project, Ivory Coast.

Martin K. Nickels is Professor Emeritus of Anthropology at Illinois State University and Adjunct Professor of Anthropology at Illinois Wesleyan University. He chairs the Education Committee of the American Association of Physical Anthropologists. His scholarly interests include the history of human evolutionary studies and human evolution education. He was twice selected as the Outstanding University Teacher at Illinois State University (1991–2, 1996–7). He is a co-author of *The Study of Physical Anthropology and Archaeology* and a former Sigma Xi National Distinguished Lecturer. He was a co-recipient of three National Science Foundation Teacher Enhancement Grants.

Dennis H. O'Rourke is Professor of Anthropology at the University of Utah. An anthropological geneticist, he has conducted fieldwork in primate and human population biology in the former Soviet Union, Mexico, Belize, the Great Basin, the Aleutian Islands, and the North Slope of Alaska. For the past twenty years, his research has focused on the use of ancient DNA to reconstruct regional population histories and patterns of colonization and dispersal in the Americas. He has served as vice president and president of the American Association of Physical Anthropologists and is a former editor of *Human Biology*. He is a Fellow of the American Association for the Advancement of Science.

John H. Relethford is SUNY Distinguished Teaching Professor at the Department of Anthropology, State University of New York College at Oneonta. His research and teaching interests are human population genetics, human biological variation, and human evolution. Much of his research has focused on global patterns of craniometric variation, the population history of Ireland, and the origin of modern humans. He is a former vice president and president of the American Association of Physical Anthropologists, and currently a Fellow of the American Association for the Advancement of Science. He is the author of *Genetics and the Search for Modern Human Origins* (2001).

G. Philip Rightmire is Research Associate in the Department of Anthropology at Harvard University and Distinguished Professor of Anthropology at Binghamton University (SUNY). He is a Fellow of the American Association of the Advancement of Science. He is a paleoanthropologist with interests in the evolution of the genus *Homo*, in the morphology and systematics of *Homo erectus*, in speciation in the Middle Pleistocene, and in the emergence of modern humans. He has worked in Africa and the Far East and currently participates in an ongoing program of research and excavations at the Plio-Pleistocene locality of Dmanisi in Georgia. He is the author of *The Evolution of* Homo erectus (1990).

Lisa Sattenspiel is Professor of Anthropology at the University of Missouri, Columbia. She uses archival data and mathematical and computer models to understand the geographic spread and the impact of infectious diseases. In collaboration with Ann Herring, she has spent over a decade studying how the community structures and movement patterns of fur trappers helped to carry the 1918–19 influenza epidemic to communities in central Manitoba and northern Ontario. In 2006 she began a new project in Newfoundland and Labrador, with the ultimate goal of understanding the long-term impact of simultaneous and successive infectious disease outbreaks in that province during the first half of the twentieth century.

Margaret J. Schoeninger is Professor of Anthropology and co-director of the Center for Academic Research and Training in Anthropogeny (human origins) at the University of California, San Diego. Her research centers on subsistence strategies in humans and nonhuman primates and intends to address the social, behavioral, and ecological aspects of human uniqueness. She has participated in archaeological, paleontological, and ethnographic fieldwork projects in North America, Mesoamerica, Peru, Pakistan, India, Kenya, and Tanzania. Her laboratory analyzes carbon, nitrogen, and oxygen stable isotope ratios in various biological materials, including hair, bone collagen, and bone carbonate. She is a Fellow of the American Association for the Advancement of Science.

Mary T. Silcox is Associate Professor of Anthropology at the University of Winnipeg, Canada. Her research program is focused on understanding the evolutionary relationships of primates to other mammals and on characterizing and interpreting the earliest phases of primate evolution both from a phylogenetic and from an adaptive perspective. In addition to doing fieldwork in the western part of North America, her research program involves the use of ultra-high resolution x-ray computed tomography to uncover previously unavailable aspects of anatomy.

Scott W. Simpson is Associate Professor in the Department of Anatomy at the Case Western Reserve University School of Medicine in Cleveland, Ohio. His current research is focused on human evolution, with an emphasis on the context and anatomy of the earliest hominins. This research complements his ongoing paleontological field research, first with the Middle Awash Project and more recently with the Gona Project, in the Miocene to Pleistocene sedimentary deposits in the Afar, Ethiopia.

Fred H. Smith is Professor of Anthropology and Biological Sciences and Chair of the Department of Sociology and Anthropology at Illinois State University. His interests focus on the paleobiology of European Neandertals and on the origin of modern humans. He has conducted field research in Europe, West Asia, and Africa for nearly forty years. In 2009 he received the Dragutin Gorjanović-Kramberger Medal from the Croatian Academy of Science for his contributions to science. He is a former secretary–treasurer and president of the American Association of Physical Anthropologists. He is the co-author of *The Human Lineage* (2009).

Samuel D. Stout is Professor of Anthropology at The Ohio State University. His research and teaching interests are in skeletal biology, particularly envisaged from a microscopic (histomorphological) perspective, and in its applications in bioarchaeology and forensic anthropology. He is a Fellow of the American Academy of Forensic Sciences.

Karen B. Strier is Hilldale Professor of Anthropology at the University of Wisconsin-Madison. Her main research interests are in understanding the behavioral ecology of primates from a comparative perspective and in contributing to conservation efforts on their behalf. One of the current priorities of her long-term field study on the critically endangered northern muriqui in South America is to understand how stochastic demographic fluctuations and individual life histories affect population viabilities and behavior. She is a Fellow of the American Association for the Advancement of Science, a member of the National Academy of Sciences, and a member of the American Academy of Arts and Sciences. She is the author of *Primate Behavioral Ecology* (2007).

Robert W. Sussman is Professor of Anthropology and Environmental Science at Washington University, St Louis. His research interests include the behavioral ecology, evolution, and conservation of human and non-human primates and the history of biological anthropology. He has conducted field research in Madagascar, Mauritius, and Central and South America. He is a Fellow and secretary of the Anthropology Section of the American Association for the Advancement of Science, a former editor of the *American Anthropologist*, and the current editor of the *Yearbook of Physical Anthropology*. He is the co-author of *Man the Hunted* (2009).

Douglas H. Ubelaker is Curator of Physical Anthropology and Senior Scientist at the Smithsonian Institution's National Museum of Natural History. He has published extensively in the general field of human skeletal biology, placing an emphasis on bio-archaeological and forensic applications. He has directed numerous field projects in bioarchaeology and forensic anthropology in North America, the Caribbean, South America, and Europe. Since 1978 he has served as the primary consultant in forensic anthropology for the Federal Bureau of Investigation. In this capacity he has reported on more than 800 cases and has testified in numerous legal proceedings. He is a Fellow of the American Association for the Advancement of Science and a Diplomate in the American Board of Forensic Anthropology. He is the co-author of *Bones: A Forensic Detective's Casebook* (2000).

Peter S. Ungar is Distinguished Professor and Chair of the Department of Anthropology at the University of Arkansas. His research interests include the evolution of diet in early hominins, relationships between diet and the size, shape, and wear of teeth in primates and other mammals, and the feeding ecology of living primates. His current work focuses on using new technologies to tease evidence of diet from the teeth of fossil forms. He has studied fossil species spanning the past twenty-five million years, and has logged thousands of hours of direct observation of the feeding ecology of apes and monkeys.

Phillip L. Walker was Professor of Anthropology at the University of California, Santa Barbara. A pioneer in the field of bioarchaeology, he was interested in, and published on, a wide range of topics relating to the human condition and the interaction between people and the environment. At the time of his death in 2009, he was directing bioarchaeological projects in California, Iceland, and China and was co-director of the Global History of Health Project, documenting the history of human health in the Holocene. He was a Fellow of the American Association for the Advancement of Science, and had served as vice president and president of the American Association of Physical Anthropologists.

Kenneth M. Weiss is Evan Pugh Professor of Anthropology at Pennsylvania State University. His research is on evolution as a process generally, and specifically on how it generates the genetic basis of complex morphological traits such as the teeth and the skull. He has written widely on how simple biological principles, which go beyond the basic Darwinian ones, produce complexity on both the developmental and evolution-ary timescales; these publications include a regular column in the journal *Evolutionary Anthropology*. He is a Fellow of the American Association for the Advancement of Science and the author of *Genetic Variation and Human Disease: Principles and Evolutionary Approaches* (1995).

Jessica Willoughby completed her undergraduate work in anthropology at the University of South Florida and is currently pursuing nursing studies. She is a member of the staff at All Children's Hospital in St Petersburg, Florida.

Bernard A. Wood is University Professor of Human Origins at the George Washing-ton University and Adjunct Senior Scientist at the National Museum of Natural His-tory, Smithsonian Institution. His research centers on increasing our understanding of human evolutionary history by developing and improving the ways we analyze the hominin fossil record, and on using the principles of bioinformatics to improve the ways we store and collate data about this record. He is the editor of the forthcoming *Wiley-Blackwell Encyclopedia of Human Evolution*. He is a Fellow in the American Association for the Advancement of Science.

Acknowledgments

I extend my gratitude and thanks to the authors for their contributions to the volume. All eagerly agreed to write overviews dealing with their areas of expertise in biological anthropology. Their excellent writing made my job as editor an easy one. I thank Daniel Temple, Tracy Betsinger, Haagen Klaus, Patricia Lambert, and Leslie Williams for their input and advice. I thank Rosalie Robertson at Wiley-Blackwell for her invitation to edit the book, and to her and her associate, Julia Kirk, for overseeing the many details involved in the process of production and publication. I am grateful to Manuela Tecusan and Joanna Pyke who oversaw the copy editing and management of page proof corrections.

Introduction

Clark Spencer Larsen

The genius of Franz Boas, the founder of the discipline of anthropology in the United States, was rooted in his holistic approach to understanding the human condition, both from cultural and from biological perspectives. His strong interest in the biology of humanity played a key role in the rise of biological (physical) anthropology, the study of human evolution and variation.[1] It was Boas's vision that laid the foundation for the growth and development of biological anthropology as a distinctive and successful scientific discipline. But it was also the vision and leadership of two other key players that made the field what it is today: Aleš Hrdlička of the Smithsonian Institution and Earnest Albert Hooton of Harvard University (see Little and Sussman, Chapter 1). Hrdlička founded the professional journal – *American Journal of Physical Anthropology* – and was the driving force in the organization of the professional society – American Association of Physical Anthropologists. Hooton taught and trained nearly all the first generation of PhDs, who would in turn educate the next generation of professional biological anthropologists. Between the two of them, Hrdlička and Hooton dealt with virtually every subject area in biological anthropology. Simply put, it was their collective intellectual visions that lay the foundation for the diverse and growing enterprise of biological anthropology as we see it thriving in the early twenty-first century.

The contributors to this book are the direct beneficiaries of these earlier, remarkable individuals – Boas, Hrdlička, and Hooton – who pioneered areas outlined by Michael Little and Robert Sussman in their opening chapter to this book. Space limitations prevent the presentation of a truly comprehensive history of the discipline, but Little and Sussman cover quite a lot of ground, which introduces the beginnings and the history of biological anthropology and many of the areas discussed in this book.

While this is a highly diverse field of study, all of its various areas of interest are unified by the focus on evolution. That, I believe, is what gives biological anthropology such a unified approach to the study of humankind. A century and a half ago, the central mechanism underlying evolution – natural selection – was first described by Charles Darwin and Alfred Wallace (Weiss and Buchanan, Chapter 2). It was this mechanism that has given such a profound insight into what explains biological variation and evolution. In order to make sense of the complexity of past and present living forms, the development of systematics and taxonomy were well under way by the time Darwin and Wallace thought about evolution. While taxonomy in particular was originally built on the notion that life is static, Darwin's and Wallace's pioneering work showed that life is dynamic and that earlier ancestral species give rise to later descendant species. Today the reconstruction of phylogeny – evolutionary trees showing ancestral–descendant relationships – serves as the framework for interpreting the biology of past and present organisms (Wood, Chapter 3).

The mechanisms that drive evolution are few – natural selection, mutation, genetic drift, and gene flow (Weiss and Buchanan, Chapter 2; Relethford, Chapter 4; and others in the book). But, as Relethford points out, these forces interact in many different combinations and often in complex ways. It is the interaction of these evolutionary forces that determines genetic variation both within and between populations. As the implications of these evolutionary forces came to be realized in the first half of the twentieth century, a group of early geneticists, especially Sewall Wright, Ronald Fisher, and J. B. S. Haldane, tackled key issues by using mathematics and founded the new area of study called population genetics (Relethford, Chapter 4).

As applied to humans, population genetics is fundamental to explaining patterns of genetic change, and biological anthropologists have been at the forefront of the continued development of this area of study. More than any other discipline, biological anthropology recognized the importance of variation in DNA markers for interpreting evolutionary change in primates, including humans. The DNA revolution transformed the field of genetics, occasioning the development of molecular genetics. New genetic markers provided an essential supplement to the rough maps of genetic variation identified by using traditional markers (e.g. blood group polymorphisms, PTC tasting, and lactase deficiency: see O'Rourke, Chapter 5). In addition, the application of genetics to the study of dental and skeletal variation has extended back in time our understanding of the operation of evolutionary forces in earlier human populations. These analyses have also shown that to compartmentalize human variation into discrete groups called "races" is incorrect (Caspari, Chapter 6). While biological anthropologists have long recognized that biological variation in humans cannot be categorized, the race concept is alive and well, both in the public sphere and in various areas of scientific investigation.

Boas recognized very early in his career that the study of growth and development provides special insight into understanding human variation. Ever since his early studies, biological anthropologists have studied the entirety of the human life span, from conception through to senescence and death (Crews and Bogin, Chapter 7). Humans are unique in the way they mature, both prior to birth and after. For example, humans are the only primates to have menopause. Moreover, health in later stages of life is profoundly affected by negative environments. It is now recognized that poor health in the youngest stages of growth and development – well prior to birth – predicts poor health in adulthood and earlier death.

Biological anthropologists are learning that adaptation to extreme environments and the spread of humans into a remarkably wide spectrum of terrestrial habitats in later human evolution have been key to understanding variation in today's populations (James, Chapter 8). The origin of *Homo sapiens* was in an equatorial setting in

Africa. The descendants of those populations rapidly spread throughout Europe and Asia, including in regions with extreme conditions – cold, heat, high altitude, low ultraviolet radiation, and other such factors. Biological anthropologists have been at the forefront of showing how and under what circumstances these adaptations have shaped body and limb proportions, facial morphology, nutrition, skin pigmentation, and many other features that characterize the biology of living and past humans.

The evolution of humans has also been shaped in many ways by the myriad of infectious diseases that have plagued humanity since the earliest hominins first appeared (Sattenspiel and Herring, Chapter 9). The kinds of infectious diseases have changed dramatically over time, especially with regard to the interaction between various pathogens and the social and behavioral structures of human populations. We know, for example, that population concentration and size is a crucial factor in explaining the timing and degree of spread of disease-causing pathogens. The mechanisms associated with the spread of pathogens have been a focus of study by biological anthropologists for a range of infectious diseases in historic and modern populations. Anthropologists are especially well positioned to contribute to the growing discussion of the epidemiology of infectious disease, owing to their insights into the relationship between pathogens and social and behavioral factors.

Fundamental to the study of populations carried by anthropologists is the demographic structure, which includes especially mortality (death rates), fertility (birth rates), and age structure – as well as the way age structures change over time (Gage, Chapter 10). Methods of study in anthropological demography, including the study of past populations (paleodemography), have developed in dramatic ways. One challenge in the study of small-scale societies and past populations is that of age determination: the data set for demographic analysis are, after all, only as good and accurate as the representation of age in the population. New advances are helping to address long-standing issues in demographic structure. Gage makes it clear that we have learned much about age structure in the anthropological settings.

The study of diet and nutrition has had a central role in biological anthropology for a long time (Dufour, Chapter 11). Humans, like primates generally, are omnivorous and have nutritional requirements that are derived from a wide range of foods, including fruits and vegetables. Humans have adopted a remarkable variety of technologies and means of acquiring and processing food that provide the necessary nutritional requirements. Although humans share common nutritional needs and capacities, there is nonetheless an astonishing diversity in the foods we eat. This diversity suggests that human dietary adaptations have emerged rapidly, and many of them in the recent past. For example, overnutrition – leading to obesity – is recent in human history. While its causes are multifactorial, the availability of an abundance of food, combined with low physical effort needed to acquire these foods, is central to understanding the current global epidemic of obesity. In the big picture, adequate food intake and the energy it provides are essential for normal reproductive and work functions. In this regard nutrition plays an important part in our evolutionary past.

The study of living populations in these previous chapters reveals that evolution is ongoing, and perhaps even accelerating. Contrary to many popular perceptions, evolution did not stop once humans achieved a certain level of cultural and social complexity. Madrigal and Willoughby (Chapter 12) provide wonderful examples of how key forces of evolution are operating in recent and living societies. One fascinating example is the CCR5-Δ 32 gene. The gene controls a receptor for the human immu-nodeficiency (HIV) virus. When the gene is present, the receptor is missing. Even if they are infected with the HIV virus, homozygous individuals with the gene do not develop the disease AIDS, and heterozygous individuals only develop a mild form of the disease. It turns out that the gene, which probably started as a mutation, has a high frequency in northern Europe. There may have been a selective advantage to having the gene, perhaps beginning prior to the Middle Ages and in the context of other infectious diseases derived from other regions of Europe.

The study of non-human primates has a central place in biological anthropology and in developing our understanding of the behavior, adaptation, and evolution of both non-human and human primates. McGraw (Chapter 13) emphasizes that, while anthropologists and others have debated the characteristics of the order primates – and few diagnostic traits stand out – it is the presence of specialized combinations of features that define the order, making primates distinctive from other mammals. The growing consensus is that the central complex of features that marks the primates as an order relates to the visual/neural system, appendicular skeleton, and life history. Primates also show a number of trends in anatomy, physiology, and behavior that are either minimized or absent in other mammals. Key to understanding primates are the evolutionary trends, especially in relation to arboreal adaptation.

The study of behavior in non-human primates offers possible insights into the ori-gins and evolution of human sociality (Chapter 14, Strier). Virtually all primates spend their time in the company of other members of their social group: generally speaking, primates are highly social. Why are primates social? While a variety of answers to this question have been forthcoming in primate studies over the last half century, the key reasons seem to be protection from predation and competition for food resources. In large part, the size and kind of the social unit is a compromise between safety and subsistence issues. Regardless of the characteristics of the social group, social behavior is closely tied to evolutionary success.

Evolutionary changes in the brains of primates (including humans) provide insights into social and other behaviors. Advanced cognition and intelligence are defining characteristics of the primates, and to understand the evolution of the brain and nervous system generally is to understand the broader picture of primate and human evolution – including sociality, manipulative skills, language, and intelli-gence. Numerous analytical methods have been developed in the study of the evolu-tion of the brain and cognitive functions of primates: comparative methods, endocasts from fossils, communication (for instance language in humans), and the-ory of mind are some of them. As Falk discusses in Chapter 15, central to debates about neurological evolution is the role of brain size versus brain organization in the cognitive function. While much is yet to be learned, several key observations stand out – for example about the similarity of organization among primates in general, although this organization has greater complexity in humans. Other traits characteristic of primates that are now mapped out include areas relating to the ocular convergence for stereoscopic vision and to the reduction in smell. Only humans have speech, and the evolution of the neurological pathways leading to it is an exciting area of investigation. New findings strongly suggest that the neurologi-cal basis for language derives from areas of the brain which have evolved in order to serve reaching and grasping functions.

Retracing various stages in the history of the brain is one aspect of the new developments in the study of primate and human evolution. In the next five chapters, the *Companion* contributors outline the details of this remarkable evolutionary record. Primate paleontologists identify the record for the origins and evolution of the first primates, focusing on the Paleocene and Eocene epochs (roughly 65 million years ago [mya] to 37 mya). While the molecular record has provided important insights into key phylogenetic developments, the burgeoning fossil record gives us a picture of what these early ancestors looked like. Gunnell and Silcox (Chapter 16) make the argument that the first primates are the plesiadapiforms, a very diverse and abundant group found throughout Europe, Asia, and North America. They suggest that the origin of the order primates can be traced to North America, the order itself having evolved from an arboreal ancestor. The first modern-looking primates endowed with the hallmark characteristics of orbital closure, ocular convergence, and nails (instead of claws) rapidly diversify in the Eocene, laying the ground for all later primate evolution.

Out of this proliferation of Eocene primates come the higher primates of the Old World, the catarrhines (Begun, Chapter 17). This fascinating record is a rich one; it largely focuses on the sequence of late Eocene and Oligocene fossil primates recovered from the Fayum, Egypt. The origin of hominoids is unclear, but the record is derived from geological deposits in East Africa dating from at least 20 mya (early Miocene) in the fossil primate, *Proconsul*. This is followed by a new adaptive radiation and proliferation of ape-like taxa, which are found in Africa, Europe, and Asia. The spread of apes to Europe and Asia about 17 mya sets the foundation for the evolution of apes and, later, for the appearance of human-like hominins, traditionally called hominids (see Simpson, Chapter 18).

Arguably, one of the most interesting and controversial records of evolution is that of humans and human-like ancestors (Simpson, same chapter). Twenty years ago, the record of hominin evolution extended back to just over 4 mya. In the last 10 years, this record has been extended back to at least 7 mya. The record of the first hominins derives from Africa and contains a phylogenetic succession of preaustralopithecines, early australopithecines, and late australopithecines over a time frame of some 6 million years. Much of the record appears to involve one lineage, evolving and diversifying in an adaptive radiation in later australopithecines. The hallmark attribute of the origin and evolution of early hominins is increasingly efficient obligate bipedality associated with shift from part-time to full-time terrestrial adaptation. It is clear that the origin of hominins occurred in a wooded habitat, which refutes the long-held notion that this event in primate evolution was associated with open grasslands.

During the evolution of the later australopithecines, there is a concurrent appearance of the genus *Homo*, a larger-brained, smaller-toothed hominin by comparison with the australopithecines. It is also during this time that we see the origins of stone tool manufacture and use. These tools represent the earliest record of human material culture. Whatever the causes, this material culture – together with brain expansion and dedication to full-time terrestriality – signals the beginning of the rise of humans and of their remarkable evolutionary success.

The appearance of the *Homo* lineage is the foundation for all of the anatomical and behavioral developments linked with humans and humanness (see Rightmire,

Chapter 19). Beginning with brain expansion, reduction in tooth size and in the masticatory complex, and appearance of increasingly complex tools, the course is set for the eventual domination achieved by humans over most of the landscapes they occupy. Soon following the appearance of *Homo erectus* in Africa, hominins migrate out of Africa to Asia and Europe. This hominin was the first so dramatically to expand its adaptive niche, geographically and ecologically, from a tropical setting to temperate locations where climates were severe, at least on a seasonal basis. The key to this remarkable success lies in the increasing focus on intelligence, dependence on culture, and ability to adapt to novel circumstances.

It is out of the evolution of the earliest *Homo erectus* in Europe and Asia that we see the rise, about 400,000 years ago, of distinctive morphological variation, especially in the craniofacial complex (Chapter 20, Smith). Commitment to culture as an adaptive strategy, brain size increase, and reduction in masticatory size unifies these descendants as a lineage. Predictably, increased habitat diversity is associated with morphological diversity. Post-*Homo erectus* evolution sees the rise of what some authorities call the archaic *Homo sapiens* and what Smith calls *Homo heidelbergensis* (the "Heidelbergs"). Relative to earlier hominids, these show marked brain size expansion and skeletal features indicating tropical adaptation. In Europe, craniofacial changes seen in later developments of the genus *Homo* foreshadow the ones seen in the Neandertals. In Africa the Heidelbergs evolve; but, in contrast to developments in Europe and Asia, the facial characteristics are decidedly modern. Documented from the site of Herto (Ethiopia), this early modern anatomy was present at least 160,000 years ago. The record – both fossil and molecular – shows that these humans left Africa and migrated to Asia, then to Europe. By the very late Pleistocene, these early specimens of the modern *Homo sapiens* occupied a new frontier. Some authorities believe there was as complete replacement of the indigenous Neandertals by these newcomers, whereas others regard the phenomenon as an example of migration and gene flow, a kind of multiregional rise of modern humans. Smith argues that assimilation is the more likely development, whereby much of the anatomical variation we see in living humans in Europe and Asia derives from an African ancestor.

The final section of the book focuses on key areas that inform our understanding mostly of Holocene human populations and skeletal and dental biology. Larsen and Walker (Chapter 21) outline bioarchaeology, the study of human remains from archaeological settings – mostly the last 10,000 years of human evolution. The large samples of skeletal remains provide key insights at population level for the understanding of lifestyle and quality of life through a variety of recently developed methods. Similarly, the expanding understanding of human health in recent populations via paleopathology offers new tools for disease diagnosis. Buikstra (Chapter 22) makes the strong case that the study of ancient pathogens has direct application to the study of disease in living humans. Paleopathologists have made extraordinary progress in the development of tools for the diagnosis of disease and its placement in interpreting health conditions in regional and global settings. Indeed, it is the population perspective that has made the study of ancient disease such an important part of modern biological anthropology.

The study of human remains and the application of the knowledge and methods of biological anthropologists have contributed enormously to the legal community in the arena of forensic anthropology (Ubelaker, Chapter 23). While most of the focus has been on identification, forensic anthropologists have developed new and compelling approaches to putting flesh on the bones of the recently deceased. As with a number of areas discussed by authors in this book, a central focus is on accuracy in age identification, on methods that are most reliable, and on handling the variation in age and senescence in older adults. It is now well understood that older adults age at different rates and express increase variation in physical manifestations of senescence (see Crews and Bogin, Chapter 7). New methods and approaches are rapidly contributing to more accurate means of age estimation, especially for older adults. Ancestry is fundamental at least to an initial identification of remains of the deceased.

Biological anthropologists have been especially sensitive to the issue of "race" (see Caspari, Chapter 6). They are well aware of the public perceptions of the social dimensions of race, and they address this issue and the focus on the identification of ancestry. While the term "race" is not always appropriate, forensic anthropologists have contributed to understanding the underlying biological variation for ancestral identification. New methods are providing important tools for the identification of geographical origins, for instance stable isotope analysis and inferences drawn about the origins of the food and water ingested by the deceased (see this application in Chapter 21).

All of these areas strongly overlap with, and complement, the discussions in the final chapters of the book. Individual identifications through analysis of DNA from bones, teeth, and other tissues obtained from ancient settings open a window onto a range of issues that interest biological anthropologists. The new subdiscipline of paleogenetics or molecular archaeology uses a range of techniques developed for the study of living populations and applies it to past populations (Chapter 24, Kaestle). This part of the molecular revolution is possible because of the remarkable advances in molecular biology generally. And, like so many areas discussed in this book, paleogenetics has been successfully used by biological anthropologists to address long-standing issues about humans, primates, and the evolutionary record. Much of this paleogenetic record pertains to mtDNA, but new advances make possible the study of the nuclear DNA, including the Y chromosome sequences, for a range of important issues such as sex identification, familial relationships and social organization, movement of persons, continuity of lineages, and identification of pathogens. While preservation and contamination issues continue to make the enterprise a challenging one, the developments in sampling and analysis are beginning to allow kinds of studies that were not possible even a few years ago.

Similarly, advances in bone and tooth chemistry – especially stable isotope analysis – have developed in rapid progression in the last several decades (Schoeninger, Chapter 25) in ways that have provided unprecedented insight into diet and dietary ecology (and see also Larsen, Chapter 21). Analysis of some key isotopes of carbon, nitrogen, hydrogen, strontium, and oxygen has given a remarkably detailed picture of the relative consumption of specific dietary plants as well as glimpses into major shifts in diet – such as the one associated with the transition from foraging to farming – amounts of meat in diet, and trophic interpretations – for instance the age-of-weaning and interpretations concerning the social behavior of mothers and their offspring. Bone chemistry is beginning to tell far more than diet about the human past, especially with respect to forensic identification, migratory history and residential movement, environment, gender, and long-term trends in ecological adaptation in a range of non-human primates.

The study of the biology of bones and teeth is a crucial endeavor in biological anthropology. In regard to bone biology, Gosman and Stout (Chapter 26) make clear the importance of understanding the biology of bone for many of the areas addressed in the book, including paleoanthropology, bioarchaeology, forensic anthropology, and paleopathology. Without an understanding of the underlying growth, development, and dynamic processes in bone growth and maintenance, these areas of research become in part mere description. While growth, development, and process may not be included in any one particular study in bioarchaeology or paleopathology, the biological anthropologist who studies past or present skeletons understands the biology. That is, they understand the dynamic nature of bone as manifested over the course of life: the skeleton grows, adapts itself to various factors, and maintains itself. This chapter focuses on mechanobiological concepts currently used for understanding the biology of bone, focusing especially on the latter as a living tissue.

Similarly, the study of teeth has had a central role to play in the study of past and present populations. As is so well emphasized by Guatelli-Steinberg (Chapter 27), the enamel of teeth has a very specific developmental biology, different from any other. Unlike bone, the enamel, once formed via a process of enamel matrix deposition and mineralization, is minimally dynamic. Teeth are almost like a living fossil, in that only about 4 percent of the tissue is non-mineral. Thus, it comes as no surprise that this tissue tends to endure even severe taphonomic processes, which result in the disappearance of bone in many archaeological and paleontological contexts where teeth are preserved. Fortunately, the information packed into teeth with regard to their growth is hugely valuable to the biological anthropologist. In particular, the incremental growth of teeth provides a diary of growth and of disturbances during growth, and even insight into the pace of growth. The applications of dental growth and biology provide a fund of data concerning the time when physiological stress occurs and the duration of stress episodes.

As the next three chapters so well emphasize, function is a highly significant area of study in biological anthropology. Built on the premise that "form follows function," this general area of inquiry provides perspective on a range of issues for addressing questions about functional and evolutionary adaptation in primates and humans. With respect to the skull, Daegling (Chapter 28) places function within the context of protection of the brain and sensory functions, mastication, respiration, and speech production. Much of the focus in biological anthropology is on functional morphology, especially in relation to mastication, in large part because of the central role of diet and dietary reconstruction in a range of areas of the discipline.

Dentition is central to the study of the masticatory function. It is the teeth that come into contact with food, and the teeth provide a record of the kinds of foods eaten and of how they are initially processed prior to digestion. In Chapter 29, Ungar and Lucas provide an overview of the various approaches to understanding the role, function, and process of diet and mastication in primate diets, and they also discuss issues that biological anthropologists deal with in regard to tooth size, shape, and structure, and nongenetic dietary indicators.

As a number of chapters point out, one of the most significant contributions of biological anthropology is the understanding of function as it pertains to the postcranial skeleton. And function, as it relates to everything below the neck, is dominated by locomotion (Gebo, Chapter 30). The primate arboreal adaptation discussed by

McGraw (Chapter 13) guides our understanding of the general bauplan of postcranial skeletal structure; yet it is the range of specializations and adaptations in this general structure that provides perspective on the evolution of primates over the past 65 million years. Primates are dominated by their hindlimbs, but this feature is coupled with a remarkable mobility of the joints for movement in trees and ability to grasp, with varying degrees of opposability, for holding on to curved surfaces such as branches. Moreover, all primates climb, including the terrestrial ones. The study of locomotor function in primates provides an important perspective for understanding the very specialized adaptation of perhaps the most terrestrial primates: bipedality in humans. This adaptation is likely to have arisen quickly; it involved a complete reorientation of the lower limb and back, and a reduction from four to two limbs used for support.

Nickels concludes the book with some good news and same bad news about biological anthropology (Chapter 31). The good news: biological anthropology has provided a remarkable record for understanding primate evolution and variation in particular, and evolution in general. The bad news: despite the availability of this remarkable record for understanding ourselves, public knowledge of it is exceptionally low. This unacceptable situation is not due to lack of evidence from which biological anthropologists (and others) might teach their students. Nickels appeals to the notion that facts supporting evolution are not enough to break the education barrier. Rather, we need to focus on increasing the general levels of science literacy in order to help the public to acquire, through education, an understanding of how science works. How should biological anthropologists accomplish the goal of educating the public more broadly about science? Nickels argues that teachers of biological anthropology should use evolution – including the remarkable record of primates – in order to place students in a context appropriate for understanding why evolution is such an important and strong theory. By focusing on the process of science and by placing evolution in its context, students will be far better prepared to understand the meaning of evolution – and, ultimately, of themselves – in the natural world.

Note on the Organization of the Book

I have long felt that the understanding of the biology of the past – derived largely from the fossil record – is informed by an understanding of the biology of the present. Indeed the founders of evolutionary theory in the nineteenth century had little fossil record from which to reconstruct and interpret biological change, and their ideas were derived from the study of living variation. Therefore, much of the book is organized along the line that studying the present can inform our understanding of the past. Following the historical overview in Chapter 1, Chapters 2 through to 14 discuss key aspects of the living, ranging from genetics and phylogeny to behavior and the ongoing evolution in humans and primates generally. We then follow with a series of chapters on the fossil record (Chapters 16 to 20), and then with chapters presenting syntheses of other areas that are broadly applicable to past and living humans – especially regarding variation in health and lifestyle, forensic applications, population history and ancient DNA, dietary reconstruction, and biology and function of the skeleton and dentition (Chapters 21 to 30). The broader public arena of biological anthropology and evolution is then discussed in the final chapter.

NOTE

1 The traditional disciplinary phrase is 'physical anthropology,' used by its founders and commonly in textbooks and curricula in the United States. However, the discipline is also commonly referred to as 'biological anthropology.' Both phrases – physical anthropology and biological anthropology – are used interchangeably throughout this book, depending on the preference of individual chapter authors.

PART I

History

CHAPTER **1**

History of Biological Anthropology

Michael A. Little and Robert W. Sussman

THE EIGHTEENTH AND NINETEENTH-CENTURY ORIGINS OF PHYSICAL ANTHROPOLOGY

The fundamental subject matter of physical (or biological) anthropology is an interest in, and an exploration of, human origins and human variation. This interest dates back to antiquity, but professional writing on such topics might be said to have begun with the Enlightenment of the eighteenth century. The Enlightenment was also a time when the concept of 'race' was formalized and various racial classification systems were proposed (Brace 2005: 22ff.). 'Race' as a typological characterization of human variation was to become a dominant theme in physical anthropology until the mid-twentieth century. Classification, an elemental building block of all sciences, was first conducted for humans by the great Swedish taxonomist Carl von Linné (also known as Linnaeus) (1707–78). He identified the close relationships between humans and non-human primates; classified *Homo sapiens* as a member of this primate category (*Anthropomorpha* then, later, *Primates*); and identified several 'racial' varieties, both known and mythical (Broberg 1983, Mielke et al. 2006: 5). Johann Friedrich Blumenbach (1752–1840), the German physician and anatomist, followed Linné's geographic four-fold classification system of human varieties from America, Asia, Africa, and Europe, but later added a fifth variety, Malay, to represent Pacific populations (Gould 1996: 401ff.). Some identify Blumenbach as one of the founders of physical anthropology because of his interest in 'human varieties' and in human craniology (Burns 2003: 29–30; Mielke et al. 2006: 7; Shapiro 1959).

In the United States the Enlightenment was represented by a number of important scholar–scientists (e.g. Benjamin Franklin), and the one most closely linked to physical anthropology was Samuel Stanhope Smith (1751–1819). Smith was on the faculty of Princeton University and later became president of this institution. His view of human diversity was one according to which all groups are members of the same species, having continuous variation and being subjected to environmental modification.

This view was similar to that of Blumenbach's, but differed from the 'fixed-race' (and even 'separate species') typologies of many of his contemporaries.

A very significant figure from Philadelphia who has been deconstructed in recent years is Samuel G. Morton (1799–1851; Gould 1996: 82ff.). Morton was, in his days, a highly respected physician and scientist who made many contributions to paleontology, geology, and anatomy (Brace 2005: 80). His principal contribution to anthropology was his work on cranial studies: he collected more than 700 crania, which he identified as Blumenbach's five racial varieties. A major work on Native Americans, *Crania Americana* (Morton 1839), was pronounced by Brace (2005: 82) "a monumental piece of scholarship." Aleš Hrdlička (1869–1943), who held Morton in the highest esteem, chose Samuel Morton's photograph as the frontispiece of his book on the history and status of physical anthropology and called him the "father of American physical anthropology" (Hrdlička 1919). Hrdlička was himself a major figure in the development of physical anthropology in the United States and will be discussed below.

Stephen Jay Gould's (1996) critique of Samuel Morton in his book *The Mismeasure of Man* was based on his conviction that Morton's calculations of cranial capacity were unconsciously biased – not only because of Morton's belief that some races were innately inferior to others, but also because of Morton's belief in *polygenism*. Polygenism was the idea that God had created the races separately and that the observed differences were a reflection of a hierarchy of quality in intelligence and ability. Polygenism explained human varieties as resulting from multiple origins. *Monogenism*, on the other hand, asserted a single human origin or creation by God. Polygenism was also linked to the belief that races were fixed entities, whereas monogenism allowed that races were capable of change, as some of the earlier Enlightenment thinkers believed. Both polygenism and monogenism could carry racist implications, since many monogenists believed that some races or varieties other than the European (or Caucasian) had degenerated over time to their present inferior state (Stocking 1988).

In the latter half of the nineteenth century, physical anthropology was dominated by studies of anatomy, craniology, skeletal biology, human origins, and race. Most of the physical anthropologists were trained as physicians or anatomists, and their primary data were gathered by anthropometric and osteometric measurements and morphological observations. There was little interest in evolution; races or human varieties were seen as fixed and unchanging; typological approaches were applied to concepts of race; studies seldom applied scientific methods of hypothesis testing; and knowledge of the impact of the environment on humans was limited. Much of the scientific activity during this period was taking place in Europe, particularly in England, France, and Germany. Charles R. Darwin's (1809–82) publication of the *Origin of Species* in 1859 and his ideas about evolution brought about changes within the community of ethnologists and physical anthropologists. In England a rift developed between the Ethnological Society of London (ESL), founded in 1843, and the Anthropological Society of London (ASL), founded in 1862 largely by physicians, anatomists, and physical anthropologists (Stocking 1987: 248ff.). The former was represented by ethnologists and Darwinian evolutionists (including Alfred Wallace (1823–1913), Thomas Huxley (1825–95), John Lubbock (1834–1913), and E. B. Tylor (1832–1917)), while the latter was characterized by interests in craniology and race, by a resistance to evolution, and by widespread support for polygenist views (Stocking 1987). This conflict was carried over to the British Association for the Advancement of Science and is probably at the origin of the separation of physical anthropology from both ethnology and evolution in the UK and in the US throughout the latter half of the nineteenth century and into the first part of the twentieth. The ESL and the ASL combined to form the Anthropological Institute of Great Britain and Ireland in 1871, with Thomas Huxley as its first president.

As Brace (2005: 144) noted, "the appearance of Darwin's *Origin of Species* and the outbreak of the American Civil War – combined to demolish the American School of Anthropology [essentialist, polygenist, craniological] as a recognizable entity." And "[f]or the remainder of the nineteenth century there were no acknowledged representatives of the American School on the western side of the Atlantic."

In the mid to late 1800s, physical anthropology (or 'anthropology,' as it was known in Europe) was most highly developed in France and Germany (Stocking 1988), where the majority of the physical anthropologists were trained in medicine and the physical anthropology training was done through medical studies (Proctor 1988). In France 'anthropology' was established by Paul Broca (1824–80), a celebrated physician and anatomist who, together with Claude Bernard, founded the Association Française pour l'Avancement des Sciences in 1872. Earlier on he had founded the Société d'Anthopologie de Paris (SAP) in 1859, the Laboratoire d'Anthropologie of the Ecole Practique des Hautes Etudes (LA-EPHE) in 1867, and the Ecole d'Anthropologie in 1876 (Spencer 1997a). As Brace (2010) suggested, Paul Broca had a great admiration for Samuel Morton's ideas, which he incorporated into his own, in turn influencing Aleš Hrdlička when he went to Paris in 1896, to study at the Laboratoire d'Anthropologie with Broca's student, Léonce-Pierre Manouvrier (1850–1927). Throughout much of Hrdlička's life, he hoped to develop a research/teaching institute of physical anthropology according to the French model (Stewart 1981).

In Germany, physical anthropology was badly tarnished by the extreme racism, 'racial cleansing,' and anti-Semitism which began in late nineteenth-century Germany (although these phenomena had earlier roots) and by the 'scientific racism' of the twentieth century (Barkan 1992; Proctor 1988, Spencer 1997b). As in France, physical anthropology was taught in medical schools. The founder of American anthropology, Franz Boas (1858–1942), was trained in physics and geography in Germany during a period of relative liberalism and experienced little anti-Semitism during his school days – that is, before anti-Semitism began to rise and liberalism declined after 1879 (Cole 1999: 58, 87). His basic training in physical anthropology took place in 1881–3, under the direction of Rudof Virchow (1821–1902); then later, after his fieldwork on Baffin Island, he studied ethnography with Adolf Bastian (1826–1905) in Berlin. Both Virchow's and Bastian's anti-Darwinian views probably influenced Boas's early ideas on evolution. Virchow's liberal views on race and the unity of mankind certainly influenced Boas (Massin 1996). As Spencer (1997b: 428) stated: "It was during this time [the 1880s] that anthropology finally secured a permanent foothold in German academia." Academic chairs in physical anthropology were established in Munich in 1886 and in Berlin in 1888. Prior to and after World War I, Germany had the strongest scientific establishment in the world and the largest number of physical anthropologists.

In England, interests in physical anthropology were held by many outside the realm of medicine and often in conjunction with paleontology, evolution, and archaeology. Aside from its author's fame as Darwin's friend and supporter, Thomas Huxley's book *Evidence as to Man's Place in Nature* (1863) might be considered the first text in physical anthropology. It included a synthesis of the information available on the comparative anatomy of human and non-human primates; a summary of fossil evidence up to that time; and a review of the natural history of non-human primates.

However, little information was available on the last two subjects mentioned. Huxley also conducted studies of living human populations after 1863. In 1873 the great biometrician Francis Galton (1822–1911), Darwin's cousin, began conducting body measurements on children (among other contributions). Arthur Keith (1866–1955) survived the transition from nineteenth-century to post-World War II twentieth-century physical anthropology, although he upheld values that were largely derived from the nineteenth century. Keith, who spent most of his career at the Royal College of Surgeons in London and was widely respected in the UK and US, had interests in the comparative anatomy of primates, in non-human primate and human paleontology, in primate locomotion, and in human evolution. However, despite his professed commitment to Darwinian evolution, he was neither a believer in natural selection nor a believer in the Darwinian mechanistic model (Spencer 1997c).

TWENTIETH CENTURY BEGINNINGS AND THE RISE OF PROFESSIONALISM

Physical anthropology in Europe

There was in Europe a number of major figures who were active at the turn of the twentieth century. Léonce-Pierre Manouvrier, as noted, played an important role in Aleš Hrdlička's training, but he was also the first to demonstrate that male and female cranial capacities were simply a function of differences in body size, and he established a number of skeletal indices which are still in use today (Spencer 1997d). Rudolph Martin (1864–1925), who was Swiss, joined the faculty as a physical anthropologist at the University of Zurich in 1899. He later published the *Lehrbuch der Anthropologie* [*Handbook of Physical Anthropology*] (Martin 1914), which became the classic reference and textbook during the early decades of the twentieth century. In Germany, Martin took the Chair in Anthropology at the University of Munich in 1918, and in the 1920s he conducted anthropometric surveys of Munich schoolchildren. Prior to World War I there was a number of German anthropologists who actively conducted research. Spencer (1997b) identified multiple centers of physical anthropology in Germany at the end of the Weimar Period (1918–33). The National Socialist Period (1933–45), which saw the rise of Adolf Hitler and Nazism, was, of course, marked by an obsession with 'race' and racial purity as well as by its own atrocities. One of the most influential anthropologists during this period was Eugen Fischer (1874–1964), who was the Rector of the University of Berlin and a strong proponent of the policy of 'racial hygiene.'

English scientists made substantial contributions to comparative primate anatomy in the early part of the twentieth century, including Arthur Keith (above) in London and Grafton Elliot Smith (1871–1937) in Manchester. In fact both played an important role by training scientists who later left their mark on physical anthropology in the United States. Smith had worked with T. Wingate Todd (1885–1938) at Manchester, and Keith recommended Todd for a position at Western Reserve University (now Case Western Reserve University) in Cleveland, which the latter took in 1912. Todd established a skeletal collection of several thousand individuals (now the Hamann–Todd Collection) and did substantial research on skeletal development in humans. Earnest A. Hooton (1887–1954) was also influenced by Arthur Keith, with whom he had close contacts when he was a Rhodes Scholar at Oxford University, from 1911 to 1913. Little was done in the United Kingdom in the early 1900s on

Figure 1.1   Franz Boas posing in Inuit garb in Minden, Germany, after his return from Baffin Island in 1885/86. Courtesy of the American Philosophical Society

primate behavior, except for Keith's observations on gibbons in Thailand in the late 1890s and the publication of Solly Zuckerman's (1904–93) book on *The Social Life of Monkeys and Apes* later, in 1932. Considerable work was done by UK scientists in what is now known as paleoanthropology; this work included the Piltdown fraud, from its discovery in 1912 to its refutation in 1953 (Weiner 1955).

Physical anthropology in the United States
Three individuals were instrumental in founding physical anthropology during the first half of the twentieth century in the United States: Franz Boas, Aleš Hrdlička, and Earnest A. Hooton.

Franz Boas was a founder of American anthropology, but he is less well known for his contributions to physical anthropology – perhaps because the ones he made to other areas of anthropology were so great. Boas had a broad vision of anthropology as a four-field science, and contributed to each of these fields. His research in physical anthropology and biometrics alone led to the publication of more than 180 works, which ranged from anthropometrics and osteometrics to race and racial origins, to environmental influences, and to human growth and the development of children (Little 2010). He is best known in anthropology for his study of migrants from Europe to the United States (Boas 1912), but his most significant and lasting research was in child growth (see Figure 1.1). Boas's contributions in physical anthropology

Figure 1.2 The Department of Anthropology at the US National Museum in 1904. Aleš Hrdlička is third from the left. Courtesy of the US National Museum, Smithsonian Institution

were, in many ways, ahead of their times, and because of this they were seldom embraced by mainstream physical anthropologists. However, the term 'culture,' as defined by Boas, was an immediate and seminal contribution to cultural anthropology (Degler 1991). Boas served as one of the assistant editors of *Science* in the late 1880s, as president of the American Anthropological Association in 1907–8, and as president of the American Association for the Advancement of Science in 1931.

Aleš Hrdlička was committed to physical anthropology and determined to move it forward as a recognized science in the United States. He single-handedly founded the *American Journal of Physical Anthropology* (*AJPA*) in 1918 and kept it going in the early years with his own money. He was also the principal organizer and first president of the American Association of Physical Anthropologists in 1930. His energy and enthusiasm were instrumental in "securing the discipline's identity" and a continuing place for it within the broader field of anthropology (Spencer 1982a: 6). Franz Boas, from his positions at the American Museum of Natural History and then at Columbia University, and Hrdlička, from his position at the Smithsonian Institution in Washington, DC, trained very few professional physical anthropologists during their long careers, but both of them were instrumental in building physical anthropology in many other ways, and especially its disciplinary identity (see Figure 1.2).

Earnest Hooton, who was considerably junior to Boas and Hrdlička, spent his entire professional career at Harvard University, beginning in 1913. He had been trained in classics at Wisconsin (PhD in 1911), then received a diploma in anthropology at Oxford in 1912. During his long career he supervised more than twenty-five PhD students (see Figure 1.3). Hooton's students dominated the profession and played important leadership roles in the American Association of Physical Anthropologists through the 1970s and early 1980s. In sum, Boas's primary contributions were in creative and forward-looking research design; Hrdlička's contributions were in the resolute and persistent promotion of the profession; and Hooton's contributions were in training the first generation of physical anthropologists, to fill an expanding faculty at universities around the US. In fact the majority of active American physical anthropologists were trained within the academic lineage leading directly back to Hooton (Kelley and Sussman 2007).

Three other important figures from this period were Raymond Pearl (1879–1940), T. Wingate Todd (above), and Adolph Schultz (1891–1976). Pearl was a Michigan-trained biologist with broad interests in human population biology and strong mathematical formation, who worked at Johns Hopkins University (Kingsland 1984). Pearl not only contributed to the development of ideas in human population biology, but he founded two journals that would define the field, namely the *Quarterly Review of Biology* (1926) and *Human Biology* (1929). Todd was a Manchester-trained anatomist influenced by two prominent anthropologists in England; subsequently he went to Western Reserve University in the US, to fill a chair in anatomy (Kern 2006). He made substantial contributions to skeletal age assessment. Both Pearl and Todd were presidents of the American Association of Physical Anthropologists in the 1930s. Schultz was a comparative anatomist trained at the University of Zürich, but he went to the US after completing his PhD (Erikson 1981). Later on he secured an appointment at Johns Hopkins University in anatomy, but as a physical anthropologist. His principal contributions were in comparative primatology. He was also a founding editor of *Folia Primatologica*.

Figure 1.3 Earnest A. Hooton in 1926, about the time when he trained his first PhD student. Courtesy of the Peabody Museum, Harvard University

Formative areas of physical anthropology were beginning to emerge from studies already underway and from perspectives just beginning to form: child growth and development from Boas's research in the 1880s and 1890s and from his later migrant design; centers of bone growth and formation and child development from Todd's work in the 1920s and 1930s; nineteenth-century anthropometrics and osteometrics from Manouvrier, Hrdlička, and Martin; primatology and paleoanthropology from Keith and Hooton in the early 1920s and 1930s; and demography, genetics, epidemiology, and statistics from Pearl's work throughout the early 1900s. Human population biology had not yet arisen as a defined area of study at the beginning of the century, yet Franz Boas's early studies and Pearl's involvement in physical anthropology and his editorship of *Human Biology* helped to define the field. Boas and Pearl were major figures in the development of scientific approaches to inquiry. Field primatology was yet to emerge as an interest on the part of physical anthropologists (Sussman 2007).

Physical anthropology as a profession

At the turn of the twentieth century there were virtually no physical anthropologists in academia in the United States, despite its institutional development in Europe. The oldest anthropology program in the United States had been established at Harvard University in 1888 by Frederic Ward Putnam (1839–1915; see Spencer 1982a). Putnam was an archaeologist who believed in a broad anthropology program, which included physical anthropology; yet only three PhDs in physical anthropology were produced at Harvard through to 1925. Up until the same date, only two other PhDs in the subject existed: one at the University of Pennsylvania, another under Boas at

Columbia University (Louis R. Sullivan, who died of tuberculosis at the age of 33). During the same period (1900–25), there were thirty-four PhDs awarded in archaeology and ethnology at the four PhD degree-granting institutions – Harvard, Penn, Columbia, Berkeley (Spencer 1981). Hence physical anthropology had rapidly fallen behind other branches of the field because of limited PhD training. Up until that time, most of the research in physical anthropology was carried out in museums, institutes, and medical schools. Boas was at the American Museum of Natural History in New York City before moving to Columbia University in 1905, and Hrdlička was at the US National Museum of Natural History (USNM – Smithsonian Institution) from 1903. Boas trained a handful of other students after Sullivan, but Hrdlička had no graduate program at the USNM.

It was not until Earnest Hooton began training students at Harvard that more professional physical anthropologists began to take academic positions. Between 1926 and the beginning of World War II Hooton trained about twenty PhDs in physical anthropology, many of whom began to fill academic positions throughout the United States. He trained eight more PhDs before his death in 1954. Other pre-war physical anthropologists who went on to distinguished careers were trained at Berkeley – Theodore D. McCown (1908–69), who worked with Alfred Kroeber and Arthur Keith; at the University of Chicago – Wilton M. Krogman (1903–87), who worked with Fay Cooper Cole; and at Western Reserve University – W. Montague Cobb (1903–90), who worked with T. Wingate Todd.

Founding of the *American Journal of Physical Anthropology* (*AJPA*) and of the American Association of Physical Anthropologists (AAPA)

The *American Journal of Physical Anthropology* was Hrdlička's brainchild, and he rightly believed that the publication would serve as a forum both to disseminate ideas in physical anthropology and to provide a base for identifying the field as an appropriate science among the others. Hrdlička edited the journal from 1918 until his retirement in 1941, and he published in it many of his own articles. The original editorial board included a number of anatomists, but also Franz Boas and two of his students – Alfred Kroeber and Clark Wissler – who were not, strictly speaking, physical anthropologists; an executive from the Prudential Life Insurance Company; the superintendent of the Battle Creek Sanitarium; the President of Clark University; and Earnest Hooton. It was a highly respected editorial board and it gave the journal the stature that Hrdlička felt it merited. The *AJPA* was originally published independently, but then it was acquired by Wistar Press in Philadelphia, where it remained for many years.

In December 1928, at the Section H (Anthropology) meeting of the American Association for the Advancement of Science (AAAS), Hrdlička presented the proposal to form a new professional society in physical anthropology. The proposal was approved, an organizing committee was formed, and a group of more than eighty charter members was solicited by Hrdlička. More than half of these first members were anatomists and physicians, and only eight were physical anthropologists. The first formal meeting of the AAPA was held in Charlottesville, Virginia, in April 1930, in conjunction with that of the American Association of Anatomists. The charter membership and linkage with the American Association of Anatomists reflected the close ties that Hrdlička and many physical anthropologists had, at the time, with anatomical sciences. The distinguished Mexican physical anthropologist Juan Comas (1900–79) published a history of the AAPA from 1928 to 1968 that includes detailed descriptions of the annual meetings during that period (Comas 1969). A translation of this Spanish-language work is now available (Alfonso and Little 2005).

Basic themes of inquiry

There are several basic areas or themes of inquiry that characterize the early decades of the twentieth century. These include studies of race, eugenics, human origins, primates, and human osteology/skeletal biology. *Race* was a preoccupation which offered an essentialist or typological framework for viewing human population variation; it was largely discarded, but only after World War II (Washburn 1984). The *eugenics* movement began in the nineteenth century, was developed by Francis Galton in England, and declined in its impact on human population studies in the United States during the late 1930s. Studies of *human origins* were more highly developed among European scientists, while some work was done in the US by Hrdlička and others, particularly on the origins of New World populations. Research on *primates* began as the comparative anatomy of primates and humans in the nineteenth century and continued into the twentieth century. The first behavioral studies of non-human primates were done in zoos, whereas early research on naturalistic behavior began in the 1930s; but this early work was done by psychologists. *Genetics* was developed largely outside of physical anthropology. Interest in *human osteology* in the US dates back to Samuel Morton in the nineteenth century. Hooton had an interest in osteology and *skeletal biology*, and trained a number of physical anthropologists who began their careers under work relief programs during the Great Depression in the 1930s (Larsen in press).

Race   Areas of interest during the early 1900s and between the two world wars were the identification of races through careful anthropometric measurements and morphological observation; determining the effects of mixture on behavior and biology; and ascertaining the origins and history of different racial groups. There was a sense that races were fixed entities which could be identified as pure groups, and that some races were clearly superior to others in biology and intelligence. These ideas were carry-overs from nineteenth-century beliefs linked to slavery in the United States and to contacts with Native Americans. There were exceptions to these beliefs; people's views ran the whole gamut, from extreme positions on racial inferiority to egalitarian and liberal ideas. A proponent of views of the latter kind was Franz Boas, who had long been interested in the environmental plasticity or flexibility built into the growth of children (Boas 1897, 1930, 1940). His famous migration study was designed to test the assertion, made by many, that the cephalic index was fixed by race and unchanged by the environment. This assertion had also influenced public views about US immigration policy. Boas found, from the measurement of thousands of immigrants from Europe, that there were generational differences in cephalic index which were statistically significant (Boas 1912). He also found that the children of immigrants were taller, and that children from large families with limited resources were shorter than their counterparts from small families. Although Boas's carefully designed studies of growth and of migrants demonstrated the plasticity of race, the impact of these ideas was generally felt only after World War II (Little 2010).

Eugenics   The term 'eugenics' was coined by Francis Galton, and it represented his late nineteenth-century Victorian view that 'good breeding' would give the 'better' races an advantage over the 'poorer' ones (Brace 2005: 178). More broadly, eugenics centers on the problem of improvements to the human species (Marks 1997). Eugenics beliefs are reviled today, largely because of the Holocaust atrocities committed by the Nazis during World War II. Other examples of extreme eugenics, including forced sterilization and 'racial cleansing,' are documented in Gould (1996). The eugenics movement in the United States developed during the 1920s, when many geneticists and physical anthropologists participated in the movement. Hrdlička (1919) believed that the growing science of eugenics would essentially be transformed into a form of *applied* anthropology. Charles B. Davenport (1866–1944), later president of the AAPA (1943–4), was an early proponent of eugenics. He established the Carnegie Institution-funded Eugenics Record Office at Cold Spring Harbor. Davenport, along with Henry Fairfield Osborn (1857–1935) and Madison Grant (1865–1937), founded the Galton Society in 1918 (Gregory 1919). Osborn's nephew, Frederick Osborn, was one of the early directors of the American Eugenics Society and was instrumental in the society's transformation to a post-war 'new' eugenics, which was largely concerned with family planning, human population demography, and medical genetics (Osborne and Osborne 1999). This post-war 'eugenics' rejected the earlier racist and racial improvement emphases that characterized the late nineteenth century and early twentieth century eugenics in England and the United States.

Human origins   United States anthropologists tended to focus on New World populations, particularly Native Americans from North America. European anthropologists were active in England, France, other parts of Europe, and Asia. Important work was also done in Africa, especially in South Africa, by Raymond A. Dart (1893–1988), the discoverer of *Australopithecus* (Dart 1925). Hrdlička devoted considerable effort to exploring the Neandertal origins problem and argued that Neandertals were unilineal ancestors to the modern *Homo sapiens* (Hrdlička 1927; Spencer and Smith 1981). His major interest, however, was in the origin and prehistory of Native Americans (Hrdlička 1912).

Primatology   Considerable work was done before World War II in comparative anatomy, paleontology, and the naturalistic behavior of primates. William King Gregory (1876–1970), a dedicated evolutionist, wrote on fish, birds, and mammals, but also on fossil primates and on human dentition. Adolph Schultz's contributions to comparative primate anatomy have already been mentioned. An important publication from the late 1920s was the *The Great Apes* (Yerkes and Yerkes 1929), a compilation of knowledge up to that time, although almost nothing was known of primate natural history. Robert M. Yerkes (1876–1956) was a psychologist and avid eugenicist who stimulated the study of the naturalistic behavior of primates in the wild (Sussman 1997, 2007). He sponsored Henry Nissen's (1901–58) two-month study of chimpanzees in the Congo. C. Raymond Carpenter (1905–75), also trained as a psychologist, after working with Robert Yerkes as a post-doctoral fellow at Yale, studied Howler monkeys on Barrow Colorado Island in Panama. Several years later, in 1937, Carpenter participated in the famous multidisciplinary study of gibbons in Thailand. Adolph Schultz and a young Sherwood. L. Washburn (1911–2000) were the physical anthropologists on the expedition. Carpenter was the only scientist before the late 1950s to do extensive research on primate natural history in the wild. His early writings were reprinted in a 1964 collection (Carpenter 1964).

Human osteology/skeletal biology   Hooton's interests in human variation extended to archaeological populations, resulting in a number of key monographs (for instance Hooton 1930). While the work was largely typological and descriptive, a number of Hooton's students were central players in the description and publication of large series of human remains recovered in the 1930s, especially in the American southeast. Out of this work there developed methods and interests in population biology in a range of archaeological settings in North America (Larsen n.d.).

The Science Matures: Post-World War II

World War II markedly reduced any scientific activity not associated with the war effort in the United States. The annual meeting of the AAPA was suspended in 1943 and 1944, and younger members of the profession were teaching, or were in the military, or were working in some sort of governmental capacity. Carleton Coon (1904–81) was a member of the Office of Strategic Services and worked in North Africa and in the Near East on account of his knowledge of these areas. Earnest Hooton and others assisted in the design of military clothing and equipment on account of their training in anthropometrics and human engineering. C. Raymond Carpenter assisted in making army training films. Gabriel W. Lasker (1912–2002) and William S. Laughlin (1919–2001) were conscientious objectors who worked on a variety of government projects. Following the war, there was an upsurge in under-graduate and, later, graduate enrollments in colleges and universities because of the GI-Bill to support veterans' education.

Before World War II began in the US in 1941, a private foundation was established that same year, with substantial funding, to support anthropological research and other activities. The Viking Fund Foundation was endowed by Axel Wenner-Gren and directed by Paul Fejos (1897–1963) during the first twenty-two years of its exist-ence. Now known as the Wenner-Gren Foundation for Anthropological Research, it was, during the 1940s and 1950s, a vital source of financial and organizational sup-port for anthropology. In 1945, the Viking Fund/Wenner-Gren Foundation spon-sored the Summer Seminars in Physical Anthropology, which were 'state of the art' occasions to bring together younger and more senior anthropologists to discuss the most current and exciting research in the profession (Little and Kaplan 2010). Held in New York City, they were organized largely by Sherwood Washburn, who had completed his PhD degree under Hooton in 1940. Washburn along with Gabriel Lasker, a brand new PhD under Hooton, initiated the *Yearbook of Physical Anthropology* that same year, both to report on the Summer Seminars and to review the important research which had been conducted during the previous year (Lasker was the *Yearbook* editor). The Summer Seminars continued through 1955, whereas the *Yearbook* con-tinues to be published to the present day as an annual supplement to the *AJPA*.

In June 1950, a watershed symposium was held at the Cold Spring Harbor Institute for Quantitative Biology on Long Island, New York. This was the same institute where Charles Davenport had housed the Eugenics Record Office, but the perspectives of the institute had changed dramatically after the war. Organized by Sherwood Washburn and by the distinguished population geneticist Theodosius Dobzhansky (1900–75), the 15th Cold Spring Harbor Symposium on Quantitative Biology was entitled "The Origin and Evolution of Man" (Warren 1951). The meeting was attended by more than 100 of the most influential anthropologists, geneticists, and evolutionary biologists, as well as by scientists from the Institute. Both the Viking Fund/Wenner-Gren Foundation and the Carnegie Corporation funded the conference. In many ways the symposium signaled the end of the old era of a descriptive science, while ushering in modern concepts of evolutionary biology. The talks at the symposium focused more on population as a unit of evolution than on fixed races, and there was a sense of scientific problem-solving and breadth of inquiry that suggested a change in perspectives and directions for physical anthropology.

The 'new physical anthropology' of Washburn

About a year after the Cold Spring Harbor Symposium, Washburn published a seminal paper on the 'new physical anthropology' (Washburn 1951), on which he elaborated in a chapter published in the Kroeber compendium *Anthropology Today* (Washburn 1953). Washburn's ideas were formative and original, but they were built on the Summer Seminars in New York City during the 1940s and on the Cold Spring Harbor Symposium in 1950. Washburn's 'new physical anthropology' was to focus on primate and human evolution and human variation, but with a return to Darwinian evolutionary theory and with genetics as an important unifying perspective (Stini 2010). Also, races were to be studied as populations rather than as essentialist 'types,' and the more common descriptive studies were to shift to studies employing scientific design and hypothesis testing. These ideas were both a driving force in transforming the profession of physical anthropology and a reflection of changes that were already taking place. A few physical anthropologists had traditionally employed hypothesis-driven research design, particularly Franz Boas and Raymond Pearl, but this was not the norm until the post-war period.

'Race' in the 1950s and 1960s

Despite Washburn's contention that the concept of 'race' was inappropriate as a means of studying human variation and that the broader concept of 'population' was more productive, the concept of 'race' as a more or less concrete and identifiable unit was still fixed in people's minds, including many scientists' minds. A new book on race was published in 1950 by three of Earnest Hooton's former students: Carleton S. Coon (above), Stanley M. Garn (1922–2007), and Joseph B. Birdsell (1908–94). They presented a six-fold geographical classification, divided the major races into thirty subpopulations, and then identified several micropopulations and hybrid populations. In the classifications of race there were concepts of adaptation to the environment and of natural selection that attempted to explain the bases for these variations. Boyd (1950) produced a classification of six races according to their blood group genetics.

About a decade later, Garn (1961) refined these classifications and identified geographical and local races as well as microraces, in a hierarchy of populations and subpopulations. These three works were different from previous efforts at classification in that they attempted to apply contemporary evolutionary, genetic, and ecological principles to the identification of racial variation (or population variation) around the world. They were transitional in the sense that they applied modern theory to an outdated typological system, in which the boundaries between populations were fixed. They were hierarchical classifications of human populations, but they differed from pre-war classifications in that evolutionary processes were considered.

In 1949, Julian Huxley, Thomas Huxley's grandson and former director general of UNESCO (United Nations Educational, Scientific and Cultural Organization), supported a recommendation that a committee be convened to study and report on the current status of race (Shipman 1994: 158–159; Marks 2010). The raporteur for the committee was Ashley Montagu (1905–99), who was well known for having written a book on race called *Man's Most Dangerous Myth: The Fallacy of Race* (1942) in which he argued against concepts of race, claiming that race was a social concept, not a biological one. Only one other physical anthropologist was on the committee: the Mexican Juan Comas. Montagu largely wrote the 1950 UNESCO document, but there was substantial criticism. On the basis of this criticism of the first document, UNESCO convened a second committee, composed largely of biologists. The second document tended to be more hereditarian and weakened the statements of the first document concerning equality among the races. A modern revised statement of the UNESCO document was prepared by an AAPA committee chaired by Solomon Katz in 1993 (AAPA Statement 1996; see also Cartmill 1998).

Another significant event was the controversy over Carleton Coon's book on *The Origin of Races* (1962). In it he asserted that there were five races – Congoid, Mongoloid, Caucasoid, Capoid, and Australoid – and that all of them, evolved as they were from *Homo erectus*, had crossed the threshold to *Homo sapiens*, but some had developed into our modern species earlier than others. This assertion caused a storm of controversy. As Relethford (2010) observed, the book was data-rich and detailed, but the evolutionary model was weak and not well defined. Stimulated by the controversy over Coon's book, several papers were published in the international journal *Current Anthropology* by established evolutionary scientists and physical anthropologists (Theodosius Dobzhansky, Ernst Mayr, Loring Brace, Juan Comas, and Frank Livingstone) who argued for and against the concept of race as a biological unit of study. In some cases the older concept of a fixed race was conflated with a more recent view of race-as-population, which confused some of the arguments. Controversies over race did not end in the 1960s. They continue up to the present, but there is a general sense in physical anthropology that the earlier use of race as a unit of study or as a conceptual unit is no longer viable and that this transition came in the 1960s (Harrison 1998; Brace 2005).

Increasing specialization and development in the 1960s, 1970s, and 1980s

The period from the 1960s through to the 1980s was one of considerable research and training of doctoral students in physical anthropology. The National Science Foundation (NSF) had been established in 1950 and science was being promoted in the United States, partly as a result of competition with the Soviet Union. Before World War II physical anthropologists could, in some sense, be generalists and conduct studies of skeletal biology, measure living populations, deal with the prehistory, and understand the current research in human paleontology. That picture began to change after the war, and during the 1960s graduate training started to incorporate increasing specialization and focus on a number of subareas of physical anthropology. These areas included genetics, living population biology, child growth and development, primatology, paleoanthropology, skeletal biology, and forensic science.

Genetics   Theodosius Dobzhansky was extremely influential within post-war physical anthropology up his death in 1975. When Washburn was teaching at Columbia University during the 1940s, the two became friends, which led to their co-organization of the Cold Spring Harbor Symposium in 1950. It is probably this friendship that led Dobzhansky to know other physical anthropologists during that time. A center of human population genetics was the University of Michigan, with James V. Neel (1915–2000), the founder of the Department of Human Genetics, and with James Spuhler (1917–92) and Frank B. Livingstone (1928–2005) in the Department of Anthropology. This was a powerful group of scientists, who were engaging in innovative research and were training students in what later became known as anthropological genetics. Livingstone's work on malaria and sickle-cell prevalence in Liberia became a classic example of culture influencing evolution via changes in gene frequencies (Livingstone 1958). As Weiss and Chakraborty (1982: 383) pointed out: "The major thrust of Livingstone's synthesis, namely, the *ongoing* effect of culture in molding human evolution, is a point still largely misunderstood or ignored by many researchers without anthropological training." One might add that the point is also misunderstood by anthropologists with no genetics training.

There were some former students of Hooton who had developed professional expertise in population genetics. Alice Brues (1913–2007) was marvelously creative and innovative in the modern sphere of physical anthropology. She published a paper of the ABO blood groups, one of the polymorphic systems thought to be neutral – that is, not under strong selective pressure (Brues 1954). She demonstrated that the worldwide distribution of these blood groups was not uniform and strongly suggested selection. Spuhler (1951) conducted original research on Native American origins and genetic variations.

James Neel also made substantial contributions to anthropological population genetics through his studies of South American tropical forest natives in Brazil and Venezuela, and particularly through his work with the Yanomama (Neel and Salzano 1966). This pioneering multidisciplinary research was done under the aegis of the International Biological Programme (IBP) Human Adaptability (HA) projects.

By the late 1970s, population genetics was in a state of transformation. New laboratory methods permitted the DNA to be studied directly, so that the time-honored method of determining the genotype from protein separation (that is, from the phenotype) was becoming less important. Both nuclear and mitochondrial DNA studies were being used to establish 'precise' phylogenic relationships among the primates, including humans, and the 'mitochondrial Eve' hypothesis on modern human origins was first presented a decade or so later (Cann et al. 1987). The culmination of the new DNA research was the completion of the Human Genome Project shortly after the turn of the new millennium.

Human population biology   The 1950s and 1960s were a period of scientific maturation for those anthropologists interested in human population biology. J. B. Birdsell
was one of the pioneers of ecology in the 1950s (Mai et al. 1981). The period during
the 1960s was unusual by being one of the few times when some anthropologists
from the subfields of sociocultural anthropology, archaeology, and physical anthropology were united in the pursuit of a common theoretical perspective: adaptation
to the environment in the context of human ecology (Vayda and Rappaport 1968).
There was also receptivity to integrated, collaborative research. In the physical anthropology of living populations, topics in genetics, child growth, demography, nutrition,
and disease were all being explored within evolutionary and adaptive frameworks.
There was also a rise in international exchange and communication that enriched the
advancement of the research.

In 1964 several distinguished British human biologists published a new text
(Harrison et al. 1964). Nigel A. Barnicott (1914–75) and Geoffrey A. Harrison (1927–)
wrote sections on genetics and phenotypic variation; James M. Tanner (1920–) wrote
on human growth; and Joseph S. Weiner (1915–82) wrote on human ecology and
adaptation. This important book coincided with the initiation if the International
Biological Programme (IBP), which was to continue from 1964 through to 1976 and
to focus on the worldwide study of ecology and human welfare. The human study
component of this program was called 'human adaptability,' and the international head
was Joseph Weiner of the UK (Weiner 1965). A planning meeting in 1964 was sponsored by the Wenner-Gren Foundation and held in Austria at the Burg Wartenstein
castle; it outlined the basic plan for the human adaptability research (Baker and Weiner
1966). Later studies (Collins and Weiner 1977; Little et al. 1997) centered on a great
deal of multidisciplinary and multinational research (Andean Natives, Circumpolar
Inuit and Saami, Tokelau Island Migrants, Yanomama Natives, Papua New Guineans),
which moved human population biology forward in a quantum leap. One of the leaders of IBP Human Adaptability in the United States was Paul T. Baker (1927–2007),
who also directed pioneering high-altitude research in Peru (Baker 1978). In addition,
at Pennsylvania State University, Baker trained more than twenty-five PhD students in
human population biology through the early 1990s.

When the IBP came to a close in the early 1970s, a new international program was
established through UNESCO, in order to continue some of the worldwide ecological research initiated by IBP projects. There was a number of single-population,
multidisciplinary projects that were either conducted under the aegis of this UNESCO
program – called The Man and the Biosphere Program – or were independently conceived; these projects studied Andean Aymara, Samoan Migrants, Ituri Forest Pygmies,
Central American Garafuna, and Turkana Pastoralists. Several of them were continued
into the 1990s.

Growth and development   Interests in human growth in anthropology arose from
several sources in the late nineteenth and early twentieth centuries. First, Franz Boas's
studies, which served as a basis for modern growth investigations, were derived from
his interest in human plasticity and the characteristics of populations. Boas also had
concerns with child health and welfare and initiated the practice of longitudinal
growth studies (sequential measurements of the same children). There was considerable long-term survey of child growth in the United States from the 1920s through to

the 1950s, in response to the child welfare movement (Tanner 1981: 299ff.). Another source was the anthropological, cross-cultural interest in child and adolescent behavior and socialization, as displayed in Margaret Mead's early work. A third source has an anatomical and skeletal origin in interests in skeletal growth and maturation, such as shown in T. Wingate Todd's research in Cleveland. And a fourth source was the clinical research dealing with everything from craniofacial growth and orthodontics to pediatrics and childhood diseases.

Major post-war figures in human growth studies were James M. Tanner, who was conducting innovative studies of adolescent growth in the UK, and Wilton M. Krogman, who established the Philadelphia Center for Research in Child Growth and Development at the University of Pennsylvania in 1947 (named the Krogman Center later, in 1971). Stanley M. Garn was the leading anthropologist at the University of Michigan Center for Human Growth and Development from 1968 until his retirement. In the 1960s, one of the major areas of worldwide study as a part of the IBP was the comparative research on child growth. Hundreds of studies were conducted around the globe and synthesized in a major compilation by Eveleth and Tanner (1976). The field of human growth was expanding considerably, with students being trained at the University of Pennsylvania and elsewhere during the 1960s and 1970s. New research demonstrated that growth can be saltatory; that a 'lifetime approach' is a productive way to explore adult disorders; and that birth weight variation can profoundly influence adult health in middle age and beyond.

Primatology There was a remarkable expansion of primate studies during the late 1950s and 1960s. As early as 1942, Earnest Hooton had argued for the importance of primate studies (Hooton 1942, 1954), which were only beginning to flourish at the time of his death in 1954. The earliest post-war research was conducted by biologists on the Barro Colorado howler monkeys originally studied by Carpenter, and the Japanese set up a colony of Japanese macaques to begin longitudinal studies of this native species. Sherwood Washburn led the resurgence of interest in primatology in the US after observations of baboons in the wild made in the mid-1950s (Haraway 1988; Ribnick 1982). The first study of the social behavior of baboons was carried by Washburn and DeVore (1961) at the Amboseli Game Reserve in Kenya. Following his move to Berkeley, Washburn began training a whole generation of students in primatology. Between 1962 and 1974 more than thirty Berkeley students completed a PhD degree in primate behavior, comparative primate anatomy, and paleoanthropology under his supervision. By the mid-1950s and early 1960s, many conferences and books focused on the relationship between primate behavior and human evolution. By the 1960s, conferences on free-ranging primates were held and related books began to appear. These included the first intensive studies of the great apes. Washburn was the major catalyst of many of these meetings and his influence on primate field biology cannot be overestimated. In fact, by 2007, over 60 percent of the field primatologists active in the US were derived from Washburn's academic lineage (Kelley and Sussman 2007).

What stimulated these interests in primate behavior toward the study of non-human primates was the realization that living populations might serve as models for human ancestral populations (Sussman 1997). Knowledge of primate ecology was linked to concerns about the growing number of endangered primate species both in the Old World and in the New World tropics. Conservation then became an important issue, which led to a practical need to gather information on primate ecology, habitats, diets, and declining land resources (Wolfheim 1983; Cowlishaw and Dunbar 2000). A major trend that began in the 1980s was the reclassification of numerous primate species on the basis of the DNA.

Paleoanthropology   By the late 1950s, after the discovery that Piltdown was a fraud (Weiner 1955), Australopithecines became accepted as the earliest ancestors of humans, and a more modern view of human evolution emerged (Sussman 2000). By this time discoveries of fossil hominids shifted from Europe and Asia to East and South Africa. Mary D. Leakey's (1913–96) and Louis Leakey's (1903–72) discovery of *Zinjanthropus* (*Australopithecus*) in 1959 and of *Homo habilis* in 1964 at Olduvai Gorge in Tanzania placed the Leakeys and East African hominids in the spotlight of paleoanthropology. Australopithecines, *Homo habilis*, and *Homo erectus* specimens were found at a number of sites in East Africa throughout the 1960s to 1980s. Work in the Omo Valley in southern Ethiopia began in 1967 with a team of French, American, and Kenyan investigators headed by F. Clark Howell (1925–2007) and led to many fossil discoveries. Around that time, Richard Leakey discovered the hominid fossil-bearing site of Koobi Fora, on the eastern shore of Lake Turkana in northwest Kenya, and in 1972 Donald Johanson began working with French scientists in Hadar, Ethiopia. Also in Ethiopia, the Awash River Valley project was begun in 1981 and produced specimens from pre-Australopithecines up to specimens of early modern *Homo*. In 1974 Mary Leakey's Laetoli discoveries, including those of Australopithecine footprints, added to the accumulating evidence for an early hominid evolution in East Africa. All of these sites were highly productive. Two major new sites opened up during the 1970s and 1980s. Atapuerca in northern Spain has produced rich fossils of archaic specimens of *Homo*, dated as early as 800,000 years ago. Dmanisi in the Republic of Georgia has produced hominids dated to 1.8 mya.

With the exception of F. Clark Howell, whose PhD in 1953 was under Washburn's direction, few physical anthropologists had been trained in paleoanthropology in the US until the 1960s. Theodore D. McCown (1908–69) was trained by Alfred Kroeber at Berkeley, but his real training in paleoanthropology came through his associations with Arthur Keith and the Mount Carmel (Israel) studies. During this decade Sherwood Washburn trained several paleoanthropologists at Berkeley who took positions at the University of Chicago, at the University of Pennsylvania, and at Columbia University. These Washburn students then began training their own students, to add to the pool of American paleoanthropologists. When John T. Robinson (1923–2001) moved to the University of Wisconsin from South Africa in 1963, another center of training was established. Most of the current generation of senior US paleoanthropologists were trained either at these universities or abroad.

Early research in non-human primate evolution was conducted by vertebrate paleontologists or by general mammalian anatomists. Since the 1960s, however, Elwyn Simons (1930–), of Yale and Duke Universities, has had the greatest influence on paleoprimatology in anthropology. Simons was trained by G. L. Jepson (1903–74), a vertebrate paleontologist at Princeton University, and by Wilfrid E. Le Gros Clark (1895–1971) at Oxford University. Simons revived the discipline in the early 1960s with his reviews of the primate fossil record. He is responsible for training a vast majority of primate paleontologists in the field since that time (Fleagle and Hartwig 1997; D. T. Rasmussen, personal communication).

Skeletal biology, bioarchaeology, and forensic science   Craniology and skeletal biology have been traditional pursuits of physical anthropologists. Up until the 1960s, much effort was devoted to what Armelagos et al. (1982) referred to as the 'racial–typological model' of skeletal analysis, where the research focused on cranial and morphological types or races that were particularly associated with New World and other human origins. By the 1970s papers in skeletal biology had increased to more than half of the published papers in the *American Journal of Physical Anthropology*, and half of these articles were classified as descriptive rather than analytical in scope (Lovejoy et al. 1982). However, by the 1960s and 1970s papers were dealing increasingly with paleodemography, biomechanics, growth, and skeletal maturation rather than with anatomical description. In addition to these developing areas, there were new methods of analysis of the bone material for dating purposes; dietary analyses (^{12}C to ^{13}C ratios); trace-element analyses; behavioral reconstruction; and biomechanics (Ubelaker 1982; Larsen 1997). Studies of craniofacial growth expanded during the 1960s and 1970s, as did work in bone density, through the use of a variety of x-ray and physical methods (Baker 1961; Garn 1981). The shift from description to understanding past populations in relation to lifestyle, behavior, and health in biocultural perspective was a fundamental development (Buikstra and Beck 2006; Larsen 1997).

Forensic anthropological skeletal analyses probably began with Wilton Krogman's (1939) guide on skeletal identification for the FBI and with its application in identifying war dead from World War II. Another physical anthropologist who participated in war dead identification was Mildred Trotter (1899–1991), who developed stature estimates from long bones. These activities further stimulated forensic publications by T. Dale Stewart (1901–97), Harry L. Shapiro (1902–90), J. Lawrence Angel (1915–86), and Wilton Krogman (Thompson 1982). The 8th Wenner-Gren Summer Seminar in 1955 was devoted to forensic anthropology and held at the Smithsonian Institution in Washington at the end of the Korean War. After Krogman's seminal *The Human Skeleton in Forensic Medicine* was published in 1962, forensic anthropology began to be recognized in anthropology as an appropriate applied science. The American Academy of Forensic Sciences, founded in 1948, established a new section on physical anthropology in 1972. Following this, there was an increasing professional identification of many physical anthropologists as forensic anthropologists.

Currently, with DNA analysis techniques serving the classic purpose of victim identification, forensic anthropology is in the process of developing a new conceptual framework. Forensic anthropologists are now increasingly involved in the interrelated fields of forensic taphonomy, forensic archaeology, and forensic trauma analysis, fields concerned with the reconstruction of events surrounding death (Dirkmaat et al. 2008).

NEW JOURNALS AND PROFESSIONAL SOCIETIES

At the end of World War II there were two journals – the *American Journal of Physical Anthropology* and *Human Biology* – that published papers in physical/biological anthropology and one professional society – the American Association of Physical

Anthropologists. The quarterly journal *Human Biology* had been founded by Raymond Pearl in 1929 and had survived the war, although Pearl's death in 1940 had left the journal in a precarious position. The annual *Yearbook of Physical Anthropology*, established in 1945, reprinted articles, but served to broaden the topical coverage of the profession. It was not until 1972 that the next new journal was founded: the *Journal of Human Evolution*. The Human Biology Council, affiliated with the journal *Human Biology*, was established in 1974 (later, in 1994, it became the Human Biology Association). In 1981, the American Society of Primatologists was founded and its associated *American Journal of Primatology* began to be published. The Dental Anthropology Association was founded in 1986, the Paleoanthropology Society in 1992, and the American Association of Anthropological Genetics in 1994. Three new journals were initiated during that period: the *American Journal of Human Biology* in 1989 (affiliated with the Human Biology Association), *Evolutionary Anthropology* in 1992, and *PaleoAnthropology* in 2003 (affiliated with the Paleoanthropology Society). This proliferation of professional societies and specialized journals reflects the continuing division of physical anthropology into subfields that require increasingly specialized training programs.

Into the Twenty-First Century: Contemporary Trends and Approaches

Research, discoveries, and the expansion of professionals in physical anthropology in the late twentieth and early twenty-first centuries are testimony to the health and importance of our science. The important tools that physical anthropologists have traditionally had and that maintain the viability of the science are: (1) a biocultural/biobehavioral approach capable of solving scientific problems that are intractable for unidisciplinary social or biological scientists; (2) a theoretical perspective and process applied to humans, *evolution*, whose explanatory power is truly remarkable; (3) an ability to view humans and their biobehavior in deep time and in evolutionary perspective and to use this information to foresee problems in contemporary societies, and the reverse; (4) the exploration of human biology and behavior within a population perspective; and (5) the application of the comparative approaches to human societies, to non-human primate relatives, and to our evolutionary antecedents. Use of these valuable tools, along with the application of the scientific method, has enabled physical anthropologists to make substantial progress in a number of our subfields in the years bracketing the millennium.

In anthropological and molecular genetics, DNA research, the Human Genome Project, and its expansion toward the exploration of the variation associated with the human genome have revolutionized human population genetics in anthropology (Crawford 2000). Multidisciplinary and interdisciplinary science has expanded over the past few decades, the National Science Foundation being much more receptive to multi-year and integrated research projects. Arising from a detailed knowledge of skeletal anatomy and variation, forensic science in anthropology has literally exploded in the past two decades. Diplomate membership (by examination) in the American Board of Forensic Anthropology has grown to more than 80 physical anthropologists, and training capabilities at United States universities have expanded to fill increasing demands. A new area of exploration is Darwinian medicine, where applications of evolutionary theory are leading to insights into the bases of human health and welfare. At the same time, biomedical anthropology is drawing on epidemiological and anthropological principles and placing trained students in various health-care contexts. Research in primatology, especially studies of naturalistic behavior and of the ecology of non-human primates in the wild, has expanded substantially (Kelley and Sussman 2007). This is partly because of our interest in our closest relatives among mammals, but also because of habitat loss and the need to preserve threatened and endangered species of primates. Finally, in paleoanthropology, new discoveries are providing a finer resolution to non-human primate and human origins and to the web of our ancestors' evolutionary pathways – one of the earliest objectives of our science.

Archival and Published Sources

Some of the important bibliographic sources for the history of physical anthropology have been cited in earlier sections of this chapter. However, it is useful to summarize them here. By far the most significant historical research has been done by the late Frank Spencer (1982b, 1997e; Boaz and Spencer 1981). His teacher, C. Loring Brace (2005), has done substantial work on race, as have Ashley Montagu (1942, 1961), Stephen Jay Gould (1996), and Pat Shipman (1994). Other sources of biographical information on physical anthropologists can be found in: (1) several autobiographical prefatory articles in the *Annual Review of Anthropology*; (2) *Biographical Memoirs* of the National Academy of Sciences; (3) *Festschriften* published by students and colleagues; (4) autobiographical memoirs; (5) obituaries; and (6) archived unpublished letters, papers, photographs, and other documents (Little et al. 1995). Finally, there are several published histories of professional organizations and journals. These include the American Association of Physical Anthropologists (Comas 1969; Alfonso and Little 2005), the Human Biology Association (Little and James 2005), the *Annals of Human Biology* (Tanner 1999), and *Human Biology* (Crawford 2004).

Conclusions

The history of physical anthropology in the western world has its roots in the eighteenth-century *Age of Enlightenment*. Interest was focused on race typology and craniology in the United States and Europe during the early nineteenth century. Physical anthropology only began to achieve professional recognition in the US after the first quarter of the twentieth century, when students began to be trained in larger numbers, principally at Harvard under Hooton. The younger generation of post-World War II physical anthropologists largely discarded typological ideas of race, embraced evolutionary theory, and began applying the scientific method to research designs. During the 1950s and 1960s these perspectives transformed the profession, such that the subfields of genetics, human population biology, human osteology, paleoanthropology, and primatology could begin to move into the rapidly developing world of science. Since that time, physical anthropology has grown in breadth of research interests and in numbers of professionals, and it continues to make unique contributions to science that are not possible in other scientific realms.

REFERENCES

AAPA Statement (1996) AAPA Statement on the Biological Aspects of Race. *American Journal of Physical Anthropology* 101: 569–570.

Alfonso, M. P., and Little, M. A. (eds and transl.) (2005) Juan Comas's Summary History of the American Association of Physical Anthropologists (1928–1968). *Yearbook of Physical Anthropology* 48: 163–195.

Armelagos, G. J., Carlson, D. S., and Van Gerven, D. P. (1982) The Theoretical Foundations and Development of Skeletal Biology. In F. Spencer (ed.), *A History of American Physical Anthropology, 1930–1980* (pp. 305–328). New York: Academic Press.

Baker, P. T. (1961) Human Bone Mineral Variability and Body Composition Estimates. In J. Brožek and A. Henshel (eds), *Techniques for Measuring Body Composition* (pp. 69–75). Washington, DC: National Academy of Sciences–National Research Council.

Baker, P. T. (ed.) (1978) *The Biology of High-Altitude Peoples.* Cambridge: Cambridge University Press.

Baker, P. T., and Weiner, J. S. (eds) (1966) *The Biology of Human Adaptability.* Oxford: Clarendon Press.

Barkan, E. (1992) *The Retreat of Scientific Racism: Changing Concepts of Race in Britain and the United States between the World Wars.* Cambridge: Cambridge University Press.

Boas, F. (1897) The Growth of Children. *Science* 5: 570–573.

Boas, F. (1912) *Changes in the Bodily Form of Descendants of Immigrants.* New York: Columbia University Press.

Boas, F. (1930) Observations on the Growth of Children. *Science* 72: 44–48.

Boas, F. (1940) Age Changes and Secular Changes in Anthropometric Measurements. *American Journal of Physical Anthropology* 26: 63–68.

Boaz, N. T., and Frank Spencer (eds) (1981) 1930–1980: Jubilee Issue. *American Journal of Physical Anthropology* 56 (4): 327–557.

Boyd, W. C. (1950) *Genetics and the Races of Man.* Boston: Little, Brown.

Brace, C. L. (2005) *'Race' Is a Four-Letter Word: The Genesis of the Concept.* New York: Oxford University Press.

Brace, C. L. (2010) 'Physical' Anthropology at the Turn of the Last Century. In M. A. Little and K. A. R. Kennedy (eds), *Histories of American Physical Anthropology in the Twentieth Century* (pp. 25–53). Lanham MD: Lexington Books.

Broberg, G. (1983) *Homo sapiens*: Linnaeus's Classification of Man. In T. Frängsmyr (ed.), *Linnaeus: The Man and His Work* (pp. 156–194). Berkeley: University of California Press.

Brues, A. M. (1954) Selection and Polymorphism in the ABO Blood Groups. *American Journal of Physical Anthropology* 12: 559–597.

Buikstra, J. E., and Beck, L. A. (eds) (2006) *Bioarchaeology: The Contextual Analysis of Human Remains.* Burlington MA: Academic Press.

Burns, W. E. (2003) *Science in the Enlightenment: An Encyclopedia.* Santa Barbara: ABC-CLIO.

Cann, R. L., Stoneking, M., Wilson, A. C. (1987) Mitochondrial DNA and Human Evolution. *Nature* 325: 31–36.

Carpenter, C. R. (1964) *Naturalistic Behavior of Nonhuman Primates.* University Park PA: The Pennsylvania State University Press.

Cartmill, M. (1998) The Status of the Race Concept in Physical Anthropology. *American Anthropologist* 100: 651–660.

Cole, D. (1999) *Franz Boas, The Early Years: 1858–1906.* Seattle: University of Washington Press.

Collins, K. J., and Weiner, J. S. (1977) *Human Adaptability: A History and Compendium of Research*. London: Taylor and Francis.

Comas, J. (1969) *Historia Sumaria de la Asociación Americana de Antropólogos Físicos (1928–1968)*. Mexico: Instituto Nacional de Antropologia e Historia.

Coon, C. S. (1962) *The Origin of Races*. New York: Knopf.

Coon, C. S., Garn, S. M., and Birdsell, J. B. (1950) *Races: A Study of the Problems of Race Formation in Man*. Springfield IL: C. C. Thomas.

Cowlishaw, G., and Dunbar, R. (2000) *Primate Conservation Biology*. Chicago: University of Chicago Press.

Crawford, M. H. (2000) Anthropological Genetics in the Twenty-First Century: Introduction. *Human Biology* 72: 3–13.

Crawford, M. H. (2004) History of Human Biology (1929–2004). *Human Biology* 76: 805–815.

Dart, R. (1925) *Australopithecus africanus*, the Man–Ape of South Africa. *Nature* 115: 195–199.

Darwin, C. R. (1859) *The Origin of Species by Means of Natural Selection, or the Preservation of Favoured Races in the Struggle for Life*. London: John Murray.

Degler, C. N. (1991) *In Search of Human Nature: The Decline and Revival of Darwinism in American Social Thought*. New York: Oxford University Press.

Dirkmaat, D. C., Cabo, L. L., Ousley, S. D., and Symes, S. (2008) New Perspectives in Forensic Anthropology. *Yearbook of Physical Anthropology* 51: 33–52.

Erikson, G. E. (1981) Adolph Hans Schultz, 1981–1976. *American Journal of Physical Anthropology* 56: 365–371.

Eveleth, P. B., and Tanner, J. M. (eds) (1976) *Worldwide Variation in Human Growth. International Biological Programme 8*. Cambridge: Cambridge University Press.

Fleagle, J., and Hartwig, W. C. (1997) Paleoprimatology. In F. Spencer (ed.), *History of Physical Anthropology: An Encyclopedia*, 2 vols (pp. 796–808). New York: Garland.

Garn, S. M. (1961) *Human Races*. Springfield IL: C. C. Thomas.

Garn, S. M. (1981) The Growth of Growth. *American Journal of Physical Anthropology* 56: 521–530.

Gould, S. J. (1996) *The Mismeasure of Man, Revised and Expanded*. New York: Norton.

Gregory, W. K. (1919) The Galton Society for the Study of the Origin and Evolution of Man. *Science* 49: 267–268.

Haraway, D. J. (1988) Remodelling the Human Way of Life: Sherwood Washburn and the New Physical Anthropology, 1950–1980. In G. W. Stocking, Jr (ed.), *Bones, Bodies, Behavior: Essays on Biological Anthropology* (pp. 206–259). Madison: University of Wisconsin Press.

Harrison, F. V. (ed.), 1998 Contemporary Issues Forum: Race and Racism. *American Anthropologist* 100: 607–715.

Harrison, G. A., Weiner, J. S., Tanner, J. M., and Barnicot, N. A. (1964) *Human Biology: An Introduction to Human Evolution, Variation, and Growth*. Oxford: Oxford University Press.

Hooton, E. A. (1930) *The Indians of Pecos Pueblo: A Study of Their Skeletal Remains*. New Haven: Yale University Press.

Hooton, E. A. (1942) *Man's Poor Relations*. New York: Doubleday.

Hooton, E. A. (1954) The Importance of Primate Studies to Anthropology. *Human Biology* 26: 179–188.

Hrdlička, A. (1912). Early Man in South America (in collaboration with W. H. Holmes, B. Willis, F. E. Wright, and C. N. Fenner). *Bulletin of the Bureau of American Ethnology* No. 102: 1–405. Washington DC: Smithsonian Institution.

Hrdlička, A. (1919) *Physical Anthropology: Its Scope and Aims; Its History and Present Status in the United States*. Philadelphia: Wistar Institute.

Hrdlička, A. (1927) The Neanderthal Phase of Man. *Journal of the Royal Anthropological Institute* 57: 249–274. (The Thomas Huxley Memorial Lecture, 1926.)

Huxley, T. H. (1863) *Evidence as to Man's Place in Nature*. London: Williams and Norgate.

Kelley, E. A., and Sussman, R. W. (2007) An Academic Genealogy on the History of American Field Primatology. *American Journal of Physical Anthropology* 132: 406–425.

Kern, K. F. (2006) T. Wingate Todd: Pioneer of Modern American Physical Anthropology. *Kirtlandia* (Cleveland) 55: 1–42.

Kingsland, S. (1984) Raymond Pearl: On the Frontier in the 1920s. Raymond Pearl Memorial Lecture, 1983. *Human Biology* 56: 1–18.

Krogman, W. M. (1939) A Guide to the Identification of Human Skeletal Material. *FBI Law Enforcement Bulletin* 3: 3–31.

Krogman, W. M. (1962) *The Human Skeleton in Forensic Medicine*. Springfield IL: Thomas.

Larsen, C. S. (1997) *Bioarchaeology: Interpreting Behavior from the Human Skeleton*. Cambridge: Cambridge University Press.

Larsen, C. S. (n.d.) History of Paleopathology in the American Southeast: From Pox to Population. In J. E. Buikstra and C. A. Roberts (eds), *A History of Paleopathology*.

Little, M. A. (2010) Franz Boas's place in American Physical Anthropology and Its Institutions. In M. A. Little and K. A. R. Kennedy (eds), *Histories of American Physical Anthropology in the Twentieth Century* (pp. 58–85). Lanham MD: Lexington Books.

Little, M. A., and James, G. D. (2005) A Brief History of the Human Biology Association: 1974–2004. *American Journal of Human Biology* 17: 41–154.

Little, M. A., and Kaplan, B. A. (2010) The Post-War years: The *Yearbook of Physical Anthropology* and the Summer Seminars. In M. A. Little and K. A. R. Kennedy (eds), *Histories of American Physical Anthropology in the Twentieth Century* (pp. 155–172). Lanham MD: Lexington Books.

Little, M. A., Buikstra, J., and Spencer, F. (1995) The Records of Biological Anthropology. In S. Silverman and N. J. Parezo (eds), *Preserving the Anthropological Record*, 2nd edn (pp. 107–121). New York: Wenner-Gren Foundation.

Little, M. A., Leslie, P. W., and Baker, P. B. (1997) Multidisciplinary Research of Human Biology and Behavior. In F. Spencer (ed.), *History of Physical Anthropology: An Encyclopedia* (pp. 695–701). New York: Garland.

Livingstone, F. B. (1958) Anthropological Implications of the Sickle Cell Gene Distribution in West Africa. *American Anthropologist* 60: 533–562.

Lovejoy, C. O., Mensforth, R. P., and Armelagos, G. J. (1982) Five Decades of Skeletal Biology as Reflected in the *American Journal of Physical Anthropology*. In F. Spencer (ed.), *A History of American Physical Anthropology, 1930–1980* (pp. 329–336). New York: Academic Press.

Mai, L. L., Shanklin, E., and Sussman, R. W. (eds) (1981) *The Perception of Evolution: Essays Honoring Joseph B. Birdsell*. Los Angeles: UCLA Publication Services.

Marks, J. (1997) Eugenics. In F. Spencer (ed.), *History of Physical Anthropology: An Encyclopedia*, 2 vols (pp. 362–366). New York: Garland.

Marks, J. (2010) The Two Twentieth Century Crises of Racial Anthropology. In M. A. Little and K. A. R. Kennedy (eds), *Histories of American Physical Anthropology in the Twentieth Century* (pp. 187–206). Lanham MD: Lexington Books.

Martin, R. (1914) *Lehrbuch der Anthropologie in systematischer Darstellung: Mit besonderer Berücksichtigung der anthropologischen Methoden: Für Studierende, Ärzte, und Forschungreisende*. Jena: Fischer.

Massin, B. (1996) From Virchow to Fischer: Physical Anthropology and 'Modern Race Theories' in Wilhelmine Germany. In G. W. Stocking, Jr (ed.), *Volksgeist as Method and Ethic: Essays on Boasian Ethnography and the German Anthropological Tradition* (pp. 79–154). Madison: University of Wisconsin Press.

Mielke, J. H., Konigsberg, L. W., and Relethford, J. H. (2006) *Human Biological Variation*. New York: Oxford University Press.

Montagu, A. (1942) *Man's Most Dangerous Myth: The Fallacy of Race*. New York: Columbia University Press.

Montagu, A. (1961) UNESCO Statements on Race. *Science* 133: 1632–1633.

Morton, S. G. (1839) *Crania Americana: or, a Comparative View of the Skulls of Various Aboriginal Nations of North and South America; to which Is Prefixed an Essay on the Varieties of the Human Species*. Philadelphia: J. Dobson.

Neel, J. V., and Salzano, F. (1966) A Prospectus for Genetic Studies on the American Indian. In P. T. Baker and J. S. Weiner (eds), *The Biology of Human Adaptabilty* (pp. 245–274). Oxford: Clarendon Press.

Osborne, R. H., and Osborne, B. T. (1999) The History of the Journal *Social Biology*, 1954 (Vol. 1) Through 1999 (Vol. 46). *Social Biology* 46: 164–178.

Proctor, R. (1988) From *Anthropologie* to *Rassenkunde* in the German Anthropological Tradition. In G. W. Stocking, Jr (ed.), *Bones, Bodies, Behavior: Essays on Biological Anthropology* (pp. 138–179). Madison: University of Wisconsin Press.

Relethford, J. H. (2010) Race and the Conflicts within the Profession of Physical Anthropology during the 1950s and 1960s. In M. A. Little and K. A. R. Kennedy (eds), *Histories of American Physical Anthropology in the Twentieth Century* (pp. 207–219). Lanham MD: Lexington Books.

Ribnick, R. (1982) A Short History of Primate Field Studies: Old World Monkeys and Apes. In F. Spencer (ed.), *A History of American Physical Anthropology, 1930–1980* (pp. 49–73). New York: Academic Press.

Shapiro, H. L. (1959) The History and Development of Physical Anthropology. *American Anthropologist* 61: 371–379.

Shipman, P. (1994) *The Evolution of Racism: Human Differences and the Use and Abuse of Science*. New York: Simon and Schuster.

Spencer, F. (1981). The Rise of Academic Physical Anthropology in the United States (1880–1980); A Historical Overview. *American Journal of Physical Anthropology* 56: 353–364.

Spencer, F. (1982a) Introduction. In F. Spencer (ed.), *A History of American Physical Anthropology, 1930–1980* (pp. 1–10). New York: Academic Press.

Spencer, F. (ed.) (1982b) *A History of American Physical Anthropology, 1930–1980*. New York: Academic Press.

Spencer, F. (1997a) Broca, Paul (Pierre) (1824–1880). In F. Spencer (ed.), *History of Physical Anthropology: An Encyclopedia*, 2 vols (pp. 221–222). New York: Garland.

Spencer, F. (1997b) Germany. In F. Spencer (ed.), *History of Physical Anthropology: An Encyclopedia*, 2 vols (pp. 423–434). New York: Garland.

Spencer, F. (1997c) Keith, (Sir) Arthur (1866–1955). In F. Spencer (ed.), *History of Physical Anthropology: An Encyclopedia*, 2 vols (pp. 560–562). New York: Garland.

Spencer, F. (1997d) Manouvrier, Léonce-Pierre (1850–1927). In F. Spencer (ed.), *History of Physical Anthropology: An Encyclopedia*, 2 vols (pp. 642–643). New York: Garland.

Spencer, F. (ed.) (1997e) *History of Physical Anthropology: An Encyclopedia*, 2 vols. New York: Garland.

Spencer, F., and Smith, F. H. (1981) The Significance of Aleš Hrdlic̆ka's 'Neanderthal Phase of Man': A Historical and Current Assessment. *American Journal of Physical Anthropology* 56: 435–459.

Spuhler, J. N. (1951) Some Genetic Variations in American Indians. In W. S. Laughlin (ed.), *The Physical Anthropology of the American Indian* (pp. 177–202). New York: Viking Fund.

Stewart, T. D. (1981) Aleš Hrdlička, 1869–1943. *American Journal of Physical Anthropology* 56: 347–351.

Stini, W. A. (2010) Sherwood L. Washburn and the 'New Physical Anthropology.' In M. A. Little and K. A. R. Kennedy (eds), *Histories of American Physical Anthropology in the Twentieth Century* (pp. 173–185). Lanham MD: Lexington Books.

Stocking, G. W., Jr (1987) *Victorian Anthropology*. New York: The Free Press.

Stocking, G. W., Jr (1988) Bones, Bodies, Behavior. In G. W. Stocking, Jr (ed.), *Bones, Bodies, Behavior: Essays on Biological Anthropology* (pp. 3–17). Madison: University of Wisconsin Press.

Sussman, R. W. (1997) Primate Field Studies. In F. Spencer (ed.), *History of Physical Anthropology: An Encyclopedia*, 2 vols (pp. 842–848). New York: Garland.

Sussman, R. W. (2000) Piltdown Man: The Father of American Field Primatology. In S. C. Strum and L. F. Fedigan (eds), *Primate Encounters: Models of Science, Gender, and Society* (pp. 85–103). Chicago: University of Chicago Press.

Sussman, R. W. (2007) A Brief History of Primate Field Studies. In C. J. Campbell, A. Fuentes, K. MacKinnon, M. Panger, and S. K. Bearder (eds), *Primates in Perspective* (pp. 6–10). New York: Oxford University Press.

Tanner, J. M. (1981) *A History of the Study of Human Growth*. Cambridge: Cambridge University Press.

Tanner, J. M. (1999) The Growth and Development of the *Annals of Human Biology*: A 25-Year Retrospective. *Annals of Human Biology* 26: 3–18.

Thompson, D. D. (1982) Forensic Anthropology. In F. Spencer (ed.), *A History of American Physical Anthropology, 1930–1980* (pp. 357–369). New York: Academic Press.

Ubelaker, D. H. (1982) The Development of American Paleopathology. In F. Spencer (ed.), *A History of American Physical Anthropology, 1930–1980* (pp. 337–356). New York: Academic Press.

Vayda, A. P., and Rappaport, R. A. (1968) Ecology, Cultural and Noncultural. In J. A. Clifton (ed.), *Introduction to Cultural Anthropology: Essays in the Scope and Methods of the Science of Man* (pp. 476–497). Boston: Houghton Mifflin.

Warren, K. B. (ed.) (1951) *Origin and Evolution of Man. Cold Spring Harbor Symposia on Quantitative Biology*, Vol. 15. Cold Spring Harbor, New York: The Biological Laboratory.

Washburn, S. L. (1951) The New Physical Anthropology. *Transactions of the New York Academy of Science* 13: 298–304.

Washburn, S. L. (1953) The Strategy of Physical Anthropology. In A. L. Kroeber (ed.), *Anthropology Today: An Encyclopedic Inventory* (pp. 714–727). Chicago: University of Chicago Press.

Washburn, S. L. (1984) Review of *A History of Physical Anthropology: 1930–1980*, edited by Frank Spencer, Academic Press, New York, 1982. *Human Biology* 56: 393–410.

Washburn, S. L., and DeVore, I. (1961) The Social Life of Baboons. *Scientific American* 204 (6): 63–71.

Weiner, J. S. (1955) *The Piltdown Forgery*. London: Oxford University Press.

Weiner, J. S. (1965) *International Biological Programme Guide to the Human Adaptability Proposals*. London: International Council of Scientific Unions, Special Committee for the IBP.

Weiner, J. S. (1977) History of the Human Adaptability Section. In K. J. Collins and J. S. Weiner (eds), *Human Adaptability: A History and Compendium of Research* (pp. 1–31). London: Taylor and Francis.

Weiss, K. M., and Chakraborty, R. (1982) Genes, Populations, and Disease, 1930–1980: A Problem-Oriented Review. In F. Spencer (ed.), *A History of American Physical Anthropology, 1930–1980* (pp. 371–404). New York: Academic Press.

Wolfheim, J. H. (1983) *Primates of the World: Distribution, Abundance, and Conservation*. Seattle: University of Washington Press.

Yerkes, R. M., and Yerkes, A. W. (1929) *The Great Apes*. New Haven: Yale University Press.

Zuckerman, S. (1932) *The Social Life of Monkeys and Apes*. New York: Harcourt, Brace.

PART II

The Present and the Living

CHAPTER **2**

Evolution: What It Means and How We Know

Kenneth M. Weiss and
Anne V. Buchanan

A MATTER OF TIME

Evolution is change over time, a process that generates a history of relatedness among all living things. The connectedness of life on Earth had been noticed for centuries, but, 150 years ago, Charles Darwin and Alfred Russel Wallace suggested a mechanism, natural selection, to explain how that connectedness, and the functional traits of organisms, could come about. Their brilliantly simple insight made their theory of evolution both new and enduring. Many aspects of evolution are still debated, including the nature and relative importance of selection, but no evolutionary biologist doubts that individuals who can't survive don't survive and that species today have their ancestry in ancient species.

Evolution happens on a vast time scale, but evolutionary changes usually start small and on a much shorter scale. Changes are passed from the cells in which they first arise to their descendant cells, in a process of *inheritance with memory*: what you and your individual cells are today depends on their immediate cellular ancestors. This is because inherited control involves the nucleotide-sequence nature of genes. Cellular memory is encoded by the functional elements in the DNA, and changes in DNA are transmitted to descendant cells. This is memory because organisms and cells die and their traits must be regenerated by their descendants – dramatically so in organisms like humans, who begin life as a single cell, a fertilized egg. It is the accumulated changes from cell to cell, in an unbroken chain that stretches back four billion years to the origins of life on Earth, that has produced the Tree of Life, whose branch tips comprise the species that are alive today.

Organisms as well as genes evolve, and an objective of biology is to understand how the functions and diversity of organisms, as well as their genes, have evolved. The modern theory of evolution has been formulated around genes, on the assumption that traits are due to, and made by, genes, even if it is organisms that are born, live, and die. If this assumption is right, then the processes that change genes also change organisms. But this does mean that we need to pay particular attention to the relationship between genotypes and phenotypes.

Traditionally, the means of genetic change are grouped into four categories. Together they provide a formal mathematical theory of evolution, called *population genetics*. This theory is presented at various levels in many fine textbooks (for instance Ridley 2004; Templeton 2006; Hartl and Clark 2007) and with special focus on humans (Relethford 2003; Jobling et al. 2004; Boyd and Silk 2006). However, these categories are not as distinct or discretely different as their traditional treatment suggests, and they also depend on the reality of populations as biological units. While the following description keeps the standard categories, we put their names in quotes, to indicate that they are not so neat – an issue to which we will return later.

1 'Mutation': change in the DNA sequence itself, the ultimate source of new variation. Because of inheritance with memory, a mutational change that arises in a cell is (if viable and lucky enough) transmitted to the descendant cells. But other changes, including modifications that affect the way in which DNA is used without changing its sequence, also occur and are inherited. And many non-DNA aspects of a cell are transmitted as well.

2 'Gene flow': the movement of genes over space from one generation to the next, as individuals choose mates or produce offspring in places other than those where they were born. Typically, most humans and other primates reproduce near their own birthplace, with the fraction diminishing as the distance between natal locales increases. Long-distance migration by land or water mainly seems to have occurred in incursions into areas that were uninhabited by other humans, especially in post-agricultural times beginning roughly 10,000 years ago. Migration on a very large scale is even more recent, but of course it has larger and more immediate effects, especially when the indigenous population is decimated as a result of the immigrant colonization.

3 'Genetic drift': countless factors, including Mendelian parent–offspring transmission, that introduce probabilistic effects on each individual's reproductive success. The factors can be intentional (for instance choosing to be celibate for cultural reasons), or purely due to environmental happenstance. They are called 'chance' because they occur independently of the genotypes they affect. The frequency of a genetic variant (an 'allele') from one generation to the next in a given population is always susceptible to change for such probabilistic reasons, which are a predominant source of reproductive variation in any generation. And, since each generation is the foundation for the succeeding ones, chance is important in long-term evolution as well.

    Some forms of chance are unique events, like lightning strikes. But many involve repeatable events, for which one can assign probabilities. For example, under most circumstances, an *Aa* heterozygote has a 50 percent chance of transmitting its *a* allele to a given offspring. Thus even among genetically identical individuals in the same environment, who have the same *chance* of reproducing, there can – and usually there will – be differences in their *achieved* reproductive output or their completed family size.

    Thus change in allele frequency does not by itself imply that anything other than chance is involved. Indeed reproduction always has stochastic aspects.

When the observed amount of change is not unusually large in relation to its probabilistic likelihood, we characterize the change as genetic drift. 'Unusually' is a subjective term, but it is important because the core of Darwin's and Wallace's theory was about systematic change – change that, by some criterion, is *not* due to chance alone.

4 'Natural selection': when one genetic variant reproduces systematically more than another *because* of some causal factor(s), we say that the variant has higher Darwinian fitness and that natural selection occurs. The phrase 'natural selection' implies differences not simply due to chance. From Darwin to the present, natural selection invokes force-like notions of relative inherent value attached to genetic variants. Darwin's basic rationale for his view was that populations typically over-reproduce, forcing a competition among contemporaries that provides opportunity for the worst of them to be weeded out through early mortality or failure to acquire mates or to reproduce, and for the favored to advance through a better survival or reproduction.

Selection can act in various ways. Most commonly, it seems, new mutations that disrupt existing function are usually harmful and removed from the population through 'purifying' or 'negative' selection. Occasionally, a mutation confers an advantage in the environment in which it arises, and it increases in frequency through 'positive' or 'directional' selection. If more than one variant in a system are harmful by themselves, yet their combination in individuals confers some relative advantage, the variants can be maintained in the population through 'balancing' selection, also known as 'heterosis' or heterozygote advantage. Many or even most traits may, for example, be harmful at the extremes (for instance low and high birthweight) and, to the extent that these trait-values are genetically based, balancing selection maintains genetic variation in the population.

Identifying selecting factors in the environment is usually much more difficult than identifying statistical evidence of selection from genetic variation data. Like reproduction, a selective factor can act probabilistically: individuals with the same *expected* reproductive output (which is greater, say, than that of a competing variant) can have a different number of *achieved* offspring. Again, the individuals are probabilistically equal. Only if, in this sense, genotypes retain their unequal, if probabilistic, fitness values do we attribute the differences to selection. Variants that are probabilistically equivalent are said to be selectively 'neutral.'

Because selection and drift are both probabilistic, and especially since selection seems generally to be very slow and weak, the distinction between the two is often subjectively based on our judgment of the relative likelihood of an observed change, which is based on some chosen statistical significance test.

When selective differences are very small, the expected offspring sizes between variants would be difficult to detect with statistical significance under most circumstances, even in large samples and especially in small ancestral human demes. A further complication is that natural selection is inherently *relative*. Fitness is not an inherent property of an allele. If conditions change – and they often do – selective differences among the same set of competing alleles can also change: a favored variant may find itself disfavored, or in competition with new mutations that are better than the former competitors. To the extent that conditions are unstable in relation to weak selective differences, selection is much less force-like and deterministic, less certain to drive a population in a predictable direction, more likely to be but one out of several equally 'fit' alternatives, and on the whole much closer to the effects of chance alone (for some similar ideas from a population genetics viewpoint, see Lynch 2007).

Contrary to the usual and sometimes unspoken assumption, Malthusian overpopulation does not imply that selection will occur or will be important. Overpopulation provides one way for competing variants to *be* favored by selection; but they may not be. There may not be particularly advantageous variants in the population. Overpopulation could just cause misery for everyone. However, experimental situations in the laboratory or in agriculture show that in most populations there is enough standing genetic variation for deliberate, strong selection to produce a response in the favored direction. Presumably environments could do the same. Antibiotic and pesticide resistance are somewhat artificially accelerated, but rapid major climate change, infectious epidemics, and the like could also produce change that fits the usual Darwinian model well. However, even then, the selective effect may not just favor a single adaptive genotype.

Darwin thought of evolution by natural selection as a very slow, gradualistic, quantitative, force-like deterministic process, which molds organisms to their circumstances. There were problems reconciling this view with the large, sometimes qualitative variation within or among species, like the number of vertebrae or of teeth. These discrete differences didn't seem possible under Darwinian gradualism, where one would expect intermediate states to occur during the process: one cannot have 6 ½ fingers – which raised a problem for evolutionary explanations of closely related species with different numbers of fingers. Evolutionary ideas were made more perplexing by Gregor Mendel's demonstration, in plants, that inheritance worked through stable, discrete particles (eventually to be called 'genes'). In principle, that could explain discontinuous inheritance, for instance different colored peas, or even different numbers of fingers; but it was hard to relate to the evolution of continuously varying traits that Darwin thought mostly about.

* * *

These ideas were reconciled by the 1940s in what was known as the 'modern evolutionary synthesis.' Quantitative traits were understood to be compatible with small contributions from large numbers of discrete Mendelian genes. Such many-gene, or polygenic, traits could also be affected by the environment. This could generate quantitative variation. But it is also possible that, when the quantitative levels of some factor(s) exceed a threshold, a state change – such as in the number of cusps, teeth, or vertebrae – would occur.

On the basis of the understanding that genes control traits, the modern synthesis defined evolution, theoretically, as change in the frequency of genetic variation, and early theorists developed the four basic evolutionary phenomena. The theory was centrally Darwinian in its outlook, stressing the formative power of selection. This view acknowledged chance, mutation, and gene flow – but mainly as statistical noise or as modifiers around the true, selective signal. Then as now, biologists said such things as "when I see order, I see selection," or "selection fine-tunes" a trait, or "if this had no function, it would have been removed by selection, because it has an energy cost to the organism."

These notions are, at best, overstatements of the ubiquity and power of natural selection. The idea that other factors, including drift of various kinds, could be quite important too has arisen and has been debated; it even prevails when it comes to 'non-functional' elements in the DNA, which, by definition, must change through chance alone (since there is no function for selection to work on), or through 'hitch-hiking' along with variation on the same chromosome that is being driven by selection. With a steady march of new knowledge in genetics, it has become less clear just what is functional in the DNA and what isn't. However, many or even most biologists resist challenges to the sacrosanct principle – or rather *assumption* – that anything with a function has to have selective value.

Even under this view, however, we are facing new levels of unexpected complexity in the phenogenetic relationships associated with most biological traits, that is, the relationships between genotypes and phenotypes. The indications are that future knowledge will place more emphasis on drift, and less on selection at the level of *individual* genetic elements, even when selection is molding the net result – the phenotypes of individuals. Phenotypic variation that is of no interest to natural selection can change by chance alone – a process called phenotypic drift.

Genotypes are only transmitted by individuals with successful phenotypes, whether they succeeded by luck or with selection's help. Competition and drift jointly produce successful function in organisms, which goes by the name 'adaptation.'

On the shorter time scale of the trees of cellular descent *within* an organism, a rather different kind of evolution occurs. The somatic (body, or non-germline) cells of an organism contain essentially the same genotype, which was inherited in the single fertilized egg cell with which the organism's life began. Mutations do occur and are transmitted from cell to cell. But change in function within an organism is largely based on change in gene *usage*, not in gene sequence; that is, different tissues use different subsets of the same set of available genes (the others being inactive in that cell). To be differentiated into a tree-like relationship among organs and tissues, gene usage is based on cooperation rather than competition among cells with similar genomes but different gene usage. Cells respond to their environment, which, in an individual, largely involves signaling molecules coded by genes and sent from one type of cell to other cells (hormones are an example). These signals are produced by the sending-cell's gene usage, and received by receptor molecules coded by genes used by the receiving cells. An organism functions only to the extent that its thousands of genes and their action interact successfully in such ways during embryogenesis, homeostasis, detection, and response to the outer and inner world.

The distinction is important. Cooperation is what most life, on a continuing and daily basis, is all about. Competition is only a part of the evolutionary story, applying mainly to the accumulation of long-term effects. But, since Darwin, and perhaps due to the transformative nature of his dramatic theory and to the role of social competition in our culture, the appeal of a competitive perspective typically obscures the more important, more prevalent, and at least as vital, cooperative nature of life in the short term.

Population genetics is a rigorous mathematical theory, and it is key to understanding patterns of genetic variation that we observe today, to designing experimental breeding for the improvement of agriculture, to understanding the ecology and history of infectious diseases, and to much more. But it works by extrapolating events at any given time over long periods of time, under its particular assumptions; and, to the extent that such an extrapolation is imprecise, deviation from the theory will occur, and the amount of error – usually unknown – will be proportional to the imprecision. This makes it difficult to interpret the *why* and *how* of the evolutionary histories of organisms, even if the *what* can be reconstructed from fossils, present morphology, biology, and genetics.

The four traditional categories of the evolutionary process are not as different as an itemized list would suggest, because the theory depends on the definition (and reality) of 'population.' As we said earlier, even when a population can be concisely defined, selection and drift are part of a probabilistic spectrum of change. In a similar way, mutation is not the only source of new variation, only of variation in DNA sequences. Recombination and intrusion from outside the population, as well as epigenetic modification of the DNA, which changes its use but not its sequence, also introduce new variation into a population.

Gene flow is not just a sometime process among distinct, isolated populations. Almost all transition from one generation to the next includes the movement of genes from the parents' birthplace to where their children are born. This is true even if the 'flow' is between adjacent demes, or lineages within demes; and most demes are not water-tight, with stable discrete boundaries. The diffusion of variation is more or less continuous across space, without rigid population boundaries and hence without rigid populations (there are some exceptions, like truly isolated populations). With more gradual change in frequency over space and time, gene flow, and even mutation, are seen as aspects of the same spectrum of change. This is one reason why categories related to humans – 'races' for example – are not as rigid, as discrete, or even as easy to define as is often uncritically believed. They are culturally defined concepts designed to chop the more continuous variation into categories.

A gene-centered theory of evolution largely rests on the tacit assumption that genes are closely connected to phenotypes. But phenogenetic connections often prove to be very complex and indirect, weakening simplified notions of evolutionary change and determinism. Categorical concepts can lead to oversimplified thinking and to correspondingly inaccurate conclusions. A more fluid view of evolution and of phenogenetic relationships can help to explain a number of important issues.

THE GENE AS ICON AND METAPHOR

The working assumption in biology, that genes 'cause' traits, can have two basic meanings. The first is the mechanistic one, according to which genes code for proteins, and proteins make traits. The second is the meaning related to population, whereby genetic variation is associated with variation in relevant traits.

Under this assumption, genes have become iconic metaphors for ultimate causation in life. One hears of genes for language, for upright posture, and so on. But we don't really know what the genetic basis of – or genes 'for' – language or upright posture are. In fact we don't know the genetic basis of most traits, especially traits more complex than those dominated by a single protein – for instance melanin production related to skin color; hemoglobin genes that may be associated with malarial resistance; or the lactase enzyme that digests milk sugar. We *do* know, however, that, even in these instances, our understanding is incomplete, while environment, chance, and other unidentified contributory factors (including genes) affect the trait.

Similarly, reconstructing evolutionary origins is necessarily indirect, since we can't observe the past. The degree of indirectness is almost always such that our reconstructions are much more problematic than we would like to admit or be aware of if we didn't recognize the metaphoric use of evolutionary language. Often, without really convincing evidence, we assign selective advantage to present function: "thumbs evolved to manipulate tools" is implicitly intended to mean "hominids with variation in genes for thumbs had more children than hominids without those variants, *because* they were able to use tools." There is a big difference between these sentences and the actual evidence, which is that "thumbs can be used to manipulate tools." The difference is easy to see: given thumbs, we *design* tools that can be manipulated by thumbs. Because we don't know the genetic basis of complex traits like thumbs, when we use evolutionary–genetic rhetoric we are almost forced to explain such traits metaphorically, or worse, to commit the sin of circularity, *assuming* what we want to prove.

Genes-for and selection-for evolutionary stories may get media attention, but they can be poor science. Understanding real evolution is much more challenging. Most of the genetic evidence we actually have is comparative. We compare DNA sequences among individuals within species or between species, and both genetic causation and fitness are statistical in nature, as described earlier. We look for parts of the genome in which the amount of variation statistically suggests that natural selection played a role in its evolution. We can either search the whole genome for such regions, identify the functional elements, and try to determine what their evolutionary history may have been, or we can look for such evidence in candidate genes that we think are involved in a trait of interest. Bioinformatic methods for computer-based analysis of DNA sequence data are rapidly advancing, and we have many tests for statistical signatures of the result of natural selection, such as unusually little or unusually large amounts of change between species, or variation within species, the former perhaps reflecting purifying selection, and the latter, positive directional selection. But building a solid selective explanation is still problematic, especially in terms of a specific selective 'force.'

THE CENTRAL DOGMA: IT IS NOT A DOGMA ANY MORE, BUT IS IT CENTRAL?

Of the many roads that might have been taken, discovery in genetics has gone where the territory is paved. Mendel started us down the genetics road, and a series of focused studies, building on his discoveries, gradually led by the mid-twentieth century to an understanding of genes that became known as 'the central dogma' of biology: the DNA codes for protein via a messenger RNA (mRNA) intermediate, and this information flows from DNA to protein, but not the other way.

It turns out that, like any dogma, this is an incomplete understanding, a consequence of the road taken. There are other roads on the genetic map. For example,

DNA has many other functions beyond coding for proteins, including in DNA packaging, protection, and copying, and in the differential usage of genes (gene expression) referred to earlier. Because of the expanding understanding of what DNA does, the definition of a 'gene' itself has been dissolving into fuzziness under the microscope of modern molecular technology (e.g. Gerstein et al. 2007). Protein coding remains an important function of DNA, to be sure, but whether it is 'central' is debatable. So, when we speak of genes 'for thumbs,' we need to be careful what we mean.

ANOTHER DOGMA THAT IS NOT

Evolution by competition is a watchword of our times, but, as noted earlier, biology is predominantly about cooperation, about components interacting at the proper time and place. Internally and externally, cells work through the interaction of proteins with each other and with non-protein substrates, including the RNA and the DNA. These interactions are not incidental. Gene expression is based on cascades of regulatory factors (coded by other genes), on cells interacting with each other via cell-surface receptor molecules detecting external signal molecules, and so on. Similar mechanisms at the gene and cell level are involved in ecological interactions among species and between organisms and their environments on the basis of sensory and neural systems. Since contemporary mechanisms set the stage and determine branch-points for the future legacy, cooperation is much more important – even on the evolutionary time scale – than is generally credited.

This is not a reference to cooperation in the sense of social behaviors, sharing, and altruism. They are real parts of nature, but a competition-centered evolutionary worldview demands an individual-based selective explanation in terms of (metaphoric or real) genes. Strong Darwinians object to words like 'cooperation' as referring to nothing but competition in disguise ("I share only because there's something in it for me"). According to that view, cooperation is a socially loaded term, which seems to be a wishful thinking retreat from cold Darwinian materialism. But 'competition' is equally loaded culturally, and has at least as much potential to mislead.

THE CONSEQUENCES OF EVOLUTION BY PHENOTYPE

Whole organisms are born, compete, reproduce, and die. It is the traits borne by organisms that are screened through selection. The genetic basis of a trait is only affected indirectly. The slippage between genotype and phenotype adds statistical noise in evolutionary systems. Since most traits are the result of the aggregate contributions of many genes, many genotypes yield similar phenotypes. The effect of natural selection working on phenotypes, on any one of the contributing genes, may be very small. Individually, each allele may essentially be evolving by drift, or nearly so.

With this type of redundancy, a trait can be conserved by selection; but, over time, different genes or alleles can come to be responsible. This is called phenogenetic drift (Weiss and Fullerton 2000). There are many examples. The presence of teeth has been maintained in vertebrates for hundreds of millions of years, but the genetic basis of teeth has changed (Kawasaki et al. 2005).

Some Controversies that Are not

People, including scientists, enjoy controversy. Whether it's good for good science can be debated. But we can look at some current controversies involving evolution, to see the extent to which they are real or exaggerated.

Is speciation adaptive? Darwin felt that his main contribution was the idea that species arise because of *adaptation*: due to natural selection, populations of organisms diverged in the details of their functionality or ecological niche. Leaving aside the problems with the definition of species itself, the basic requirement is reproductive isolation, because that is what allows divergent adaptation to take place.

Darwin essentially felt that adaptation came first, but speciation can occur initially through isolation (individuals never meet to mate, so they never do the latter), with traits diverging subsequently. Chromosomal or other genetic change that interferes with fertilization can lead to the required isolation as much as geographic barriers or distance can, among groups whose other traits and behavior are identical. These changes can arise by chance and by drift, especially in small populations, and need not involve natural selection or new adaptation. Divergent adaptation to environmental conditions may occur later but need not be part of the speciation process itself.

What is 'orderly' life? It is widely argued that the orderly appearance of organisms is due to adaptation through natural selection, on the grounds that otherwise only religious explanations could account for such traits. There is some truth to that. For example, really *disorderly* traits seem to be eliminated through natural selection (organisms bearing them simply can't survive). But there are other ways for orderliness to evolve that are not due to natural selection, or at least not to a simple version of it.

We discussed above how both drift and selection launch one generation probabilistically into the next. Phenotypic drift can occur among variations in which selection has no interest. But, even under the watchful eye of selection, at any given time there may be a range of phenotypes that are equally advantageous. Such traits, and the genes that affect them, are neutral and will change by drift *in relation to each other*. Anthropological examples of phenotypic drift include head shape differences among related primate species (Ackermann and Cheverud 2000); these may not demand adaptive explanation.

Organisms are not just passively screened by the environment and judged more or less fit. They are adaptable and usually exploratory, responding to circumstances; they seek, or *construct*, the circumstances they like. Choosing favorable circumstances is called organismal selection when it is genetically based: organisms which like a given environment from among the ones available to them will aggregate there and mate. Over time, it will appear as if the genes responsible for the preference have been favored by selection; but they need not have had any competitive advantage relatively to the genotypes that aggregated elsewhere as a result of different preferences. The building of suitable microenvironments is called niche construction. Bird nests and human houses are examples.

Now there is a curious fact. Those who hold a strongly selectionist world view rely on the fact that evolutionary time periods are long in order to argue that highly organized traits, like eyes or brains, could have been – *were* – produced through gradual selection. This is because, without long time periods, we would have to accept saltational evolution – the sudden appearance of new, organized traits – which seems implausible. When the weak nature of most selection and the consequent relative importance of drift are raised as a challenge to strong selectionism, a common response is as follows: yes, today's organized traits might be modified slightly here and there by drift, but they must have been driven to their current, highly organized state by the ever-present, always-acting, fine-tuning systematic force of selection. The flaw in this argument is that it assumes that we are living a special time in the history of life. Instead, selection may *always* have been weak and slow; and, if viewed at *any* given time in the past, then-current traits would have seemed highly organized and adapted. The importance of drift can, and perhaps must, apply back to the history of life, leaving adaptation to be the result of chance much more than is generally believed.

Is life adaptive? In a similar vein, it is said that organisms are obviously suited to their circumstances, and this is supposed to show the truth of adaptive–evolutionary explanations. How else could they have gotten here? Yet the truth of the statement is not as obvious as it may seem. Adaptation is a kind of tautology. If an organism (or at least its ancestors) were not suitable for life, it would not be here today. We can see the reasons why it survives today; but this is not the same as the reasons why it *is* here today. To equate present function to past adaptive selection is a mistake known as the naturalistic fallacy.

We usually cannot know what selective reasons (if any) applied in the past. Classically, Darwinian adaptive evolution certainly occurs and may even be a part of the story most of the time. But selection of a specific type need not have been the key agent, and much less the only one. Enumerating the reasons why an adaptation is good is to make the same mistake as the proponents of the 'intelligent design' view in religion make. Not all of an organisms' functions need work all that well – all we know is that they have worked *well enough* in the past.

How deterministic is evolution? Darwin was very clear that he viewed natural selection in essentially Newtonian deterministic terms, as a force, or as a law of nature. He said several times that selection detects the 'smallest grain in the balance' (meaning the smallest grain on the scale) of competition (Weiss 2004). Yet, when we try to identify the genetic basis of a trait or to detect selection in real time, there is always variation, noise, and subtlety. If selection is typically weak, its existence may be undetectable at *any* given time – and perhaps at *every* time – in the course of a trait's evolution.

Adaptation occurs, but less determinedly, requiring less precision in the screening ability of nature; and it occurs with greater flexibility and tolerance. More organisms have a chance to do well, and populations are not as threatened with poor fitness as they might otherwise be. Chance is *part* of that process. This is a more sanguine and epistemologically more sound view of evolution than an argument about determinism versus chance – selection versus drift – would imply (see for instance Lynch 2007).

What is the source of adaptive variation? Over the years, there have been many debates about the source of new variation – numerous enough to serve as fuel for the idea of a 'creative' (not creationist!) evolution. In the early twentieth century there were debates as to whether an existing variation, variation plus recombination, or a new mutation was most important. Mutation was thought to be too rare to drive response to changing environments (if those changed rapidly – another unstated assumption?). However, standing variation and its rearrangement or recombination through sexual reproduction readily and steadily present new *combinations* of existing variants to nature; and selection screens whole organisms, not individual genes.

There has been a growing recognition that chromosomal duplication events of various kinds have produced new genes. A duplicate gene is a redundant one, and it is the potential source of a new function. Correlations between the time of gene duplication events and the appearance of new traits such as body plans have been attributed to this process.

Another debate is about whether adaptive evolution occurs through selected change in the protein-coding regions of the genome or in regions affecting the genes' regulation: this is a function versus expression debate (see for instance Carroll et al. 2005; Hoekstra and Coyne 2007). Many, if not most, proteins are *pleiotropic*: they have many different functions. One idea is that, if the DNA code for a protein suffers mutation, the protein will not function well in all (if in any) of its many uses, and the likely result will be a very unhappy organism. On the other hand, the *expression* of a gene is controlled by numerous short DNA sequences (only a few nucleotides long) near its protein-coding region. When these regulatory sequences are physically bound by other proteins called *transcription factors*, the binding event causes the gene to be used – transcribed into mRNA – or its expression level is altered. Short regulatory sites can arise easily in random sequence among the tens of thousands of bases flanking protein-coding regions, and hence they can come and go by mutation. In any cell that is producing the transcription factor protein itself, such modifications in the regulatory region of other genes could change the time or place of expression of those genes.

Many transcription factors are needed to induce (or repress) the expression of a gene, and the cooperative nature of life is such that many different proteins must interact with each other and with the flanking DNA to accomplish gene expression. This means that *those* genes must already be expressed earlier in the cell in question. This is cooperation in action. But, either by altering the expression of the transcription factor gene itself or by those genes which the transcription factor protein activates, phenotypic change can evolve, and fairly rapidly.

Variation arises in all of these ways. Which one is 'more important' is rather a non-question – like what is more important, food or water?

Is there too *much evidence for selection?* Finally, the argument over whether evolution happens by selection or drift, which is sometimes couched as Darwinian versus non-Darwinian evolution, is misplaced. From a neutralist perspective, selected variation is quickly lost or fixed in the population, while neutral variation can stay – drift – around for a long time before being fixed or lost. If so, then most of the variation one sees at any given time, for example in current genetic data, has been evolving neutrally. The argument is important as a way to explain the total *amount* of variation observed among individuals within a species, or accumulated between species. If all the observed variation were being maintained in the population through balancing selection, the amount of over-reproduction needed to compensate for individuals who are eliminated through selection (called the 'genetic load') could be beyond sustaining. Individuals would simply be unable to have enough children to ensure that one could survive to replace each parent. But the weak nature of selection in which most variation is evolving neutrally (or nearly so) at any given time relieves this argument, since change due to drift requires no excess reproduction.

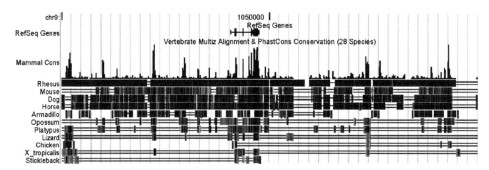

Figure 2.1   Widespread conservation of non-protein-coding sequence in the human genome. This is a random selection of 100,000 basepairs (0.003 percent) of the human genome starting 1,000,000 nucleotides from the end of chromosome 9. From the UCSC Genome browser (http://genome.ucsc.edu)

Key:
topline shows basepair position;
RefSeq represents exons and introns of known gene (a transcription factor called DMRT2);
Mammal Cons shows degree of sequence conservation among mammals;
final lines show positions of conservation in each of many species going back to fish (stickleback).

Yet one question does still pertain, though it is little noticed. If one aligns the genomes of related species, even distant vertebrate species, there is a huge amount of conserved sequence, *in addition to* protein-coding sequence, across the genome. A randomly chosen segment of just 0.003 percent of the human genome is shown in Figure 2.1. The figure shows the extensive amount of sequence that has been very deeply conserved, even between humans and fish. If not natural selection, then what could conserve this sequence for so long? But how is the selective burden, the genetic load, being maintained? This remains a major question for the future.

PHENOGENOMIC VS PHENOGENETIC EVOLUTION: A RECONCEPTUALIZATION OF EVOLUTION?

The usual idea of evolution is that, if a new mutation helps the organism to outcompete its peers, it steadily rises to high frequency. Yet the fundamentally cooperative aspect of nature seems to be at odds with such a world view. When we examine the evidence for genetic contributions to biological traits, we find that a substantial fraction of variation seems heritable (that is, is passed from parent to offspring, so that relatives resemble each other more than would be expected to happen by chance). Yet intensive searches of the genome identify only modest numbers of genes influencing traits of interest, and variation in those genes accounts for only a fraction of the total heritability (Weiss 2008). It seems that traits are affected by many genes whose individual variation from person to person contributes too little to be identified by available methods, amidst the sea of contributing factors.

A view on the nature of life has been growing under the name of 'systems biology.' It is a recognition that much of life is about interaction – cooperation – among large numbers of gene products. Networks have alternate pathways and, in systems thinking, it is the *network* of interactions as a whole that is functionally important. This could be the case for complex traits like the mammalian skull or social behavior, to which many genes contribute and each one may contribute in multiple ways.

If a network has a great many factors, hundreds or even thousands, selection's impact on any one of them could be so slight that the variant evolves basically by drift – a point we made earlier. The *trait* could evolve adaptively, being driven in some particular direction – such as towards upright posture, language ability, or useful thumbs. Overall, the genome as a whole will have changed so as to accumulate the variation in the many genes responsible for the trait, but the individual underlying genetic variants may have changed mainly by drift; it would suffice that at any time there was an appropriate mix of them to respond to selection. This could be called *phenogenomic* rather than the usual *phenogenetic* evolution. If accurate, it is a picture of evolution very different from the one that has been in place since the discovery of the protein-coding nature of genes, in which the focus on function has perhaps inaccurately resulted in a focus on the importance of individual genes as the main factors in evolution.

THE COLLAPSE OF POSSIBILITIES AND OVERSIMPLIFIED VIEWS OF EVOLUTION

Looking forward from any given time to the future, there will usually be many comparably viable ways in which a species or an ecosystem can change. Chance will be an essential, even a major part in the mix of possibilities. Indeed the mix changes every generation. This greatly limits the power of long-term prediction, but it accurately reflects the nature of life.

Looking backward in time from the present, evolution seems to have taken a much simpler, more direct, or even environmentally directed path. The reason is that all the possibilities have collapsed into one – what actually happened. With a long-term retrospective viewpoint, evolution and its processes can look much simpler, and it may seem easier to assert the values that nature has placed upon the traits of organisms. This, then, leads to a state of confidence about those values today, with all the societal dangers associated with it when the subject is our own species.

SOCIAL MISUSES OF DARWINIAN REFLEXES

Darwinian evolution is a concept so simple and generic as to be easy to invoke, without technical knowledge, as if to assume it were the same as to prove it. Major and sometimes catastrophic consequences have resulted from an uncritically 'Darwinian' assertion that life is made of inherently good and bad things engaged in vital competition with each other and that the inherent characteristics of individuals are written in their genes. The ideas of inherent worth, deterministic selection, and identifiable, discrete populations are all abstractions that derive from an assumed theory, and the consequences of that theory may subtly depend on assumptions.

In the case of humans, the obvious and historically ample examples relate to racism and eugenics, in which a group of people in power decide what is good and bad, attribute the same judgment to natural selection, and justify engineering society and interfering with people on the basis of these people's presumed inherent worth. Behavioral traits, especially intelligence and deviant behavior, are among the favorite targets of these value judgments. Genocide has been a result, and a wise person would always keep in mind the dangers of equating personal views with nature's views, theory with reality, and determinism with probabilism. The temptation to be armchair Darwinians is great; the news media, and even scientists, routinely indulge in drawing speculative value-laden scenarios. So, if evolution has been a transformative idea in modern thought, it has also had its downside.

FINALLY, DO GENES MATTER?

If evolution is driven by genetic changes, we can ask, what does it mean, then, to 'understand' the evolution of a trait? Do we need to identify every gene? Or every variant in every gene in every population of every species? Is it enough to know just the pattern of gene-by-gene interactions and how they are conserved among species or not, or do we need to identify the specific genotype in each individual? There are no objective answers to these questions, although complete enumeration seems literally impossible. Perhaps, for many purposes, we don't need to know.

Not every question we want to answer, not even every functional or evolutionary question, is a genetic question, even though everything about life involves genes and inheritance in one way or another. For geneticists, understanding the contribution of genes to any given trait may be fascinating and relevant. But, for understanding many aspects of evolution, function, adaptation, and the like, making lists of genes that contribute to a trait may be as irrelevant as enumerating bricks would be for understanding the purpose for which a building was built. In their own place, genes are irreplaceable. But in our evolution not everything of interest is best explained in terms of genes. This is especially true of human behavior, which is largely, if not predominantly, molded by culture.

Darwin was interested in embryology, the way fertilized eggs 'evolve' – the earlier use of the term – into adults. But he used comparative embryology to reinforce his main interest: the long-term evolution of adaptations and species. His theory was about phenotypes and it worked, even though his genetic ideas were thoroughly incorrect. Today, too, unless one is a geneticist or interested in mechanism, the phenotypes of organisms are still the most important aspect of evolution.

However, ever since Darwin changed the focus of biology, the notion of evolutionary change has been restricted to the long term. But as we have described, evolution also occurs on the shorter developmental and ecological time scales (Weiss and Buchanan 2009). There the processes are substantially different from the canon of four factors that have occupied evolutionary thinking for the last century. The picture has been changing because of advances in molecular technologies which have greatly enhanced what can be learned about these time scales of life.

Since long-term evolution is the accumulation of short-term changes that occur from cell to cell, a perspective that includes the understanding of those short-term changes should illuminate traditional evolutionary studies. In fact, when we look at life on all of its time scales, a set of simple, general principles emerges (Weiss and Buchanan 2009). Beyond Darwin's processes for species evolution, these general principles reflect the many ways in which functional change, the branching divergence of function and species, communication and cooperation, and other characteristics of life operate on scales ranging from those of cells to those of ecosystems. With a broader perspective, an understanding of change and variation in life will continue to challenge and excite our interest for generations to come.

REFERENCES

NOTE 'Evolution' and the points discussed in this chapter comprise a vast subject. We cite only a few references, because an exhaustive bibliography would be impossible. These topics and ideas can most profitably be pursued by searching the many sources on the internet.

Ackermann, R. R., and Cheverud, J. M. (2000) Phenotypic Covariance Structure in Tamarins (Genus *Saguinus*): A Comparison of Variation Patterns Using Matrix Correlation and Common Principal Component Analysis. *American Journal of Physical Anthropology* 111 (4): 489–501.

Boyd, R., and Silk, J. (2006) *How Humans Evolved*. New York: Norton.

Carroll, S. B., Grenier, J. K., Weatherbee, S. (2005) *From DNA to Diversity: Molecular Genetics and the Evolution of Animal Design*. Malden MA: Blackwell.

Gerstein, M. B., Bruce, C., Rozowsky, J. S., Zheng, D., Du, J., Korbel, J. O., Emanuelsson, O., Zhang, Z. D., Weissman, S., Snyder, M. (2007) What is a Gene, Post-ENCODE? History and Updated Definition. *Genome Res* 17 (6): 669–681.

Hartl, D., and Clark, A. G. (2007) *Principles of Population Genetics*. Sunderland MA: Sinauer.

Hoekstra, H. E., and Coyne, J. A. (2007) The Locus of Evolution: Evo Devo and the Genetics of Adaptation. *Evolution* 61 (5): 995–1016.

Jobling, M., Hurles, M., Tyler-Smith, C. (2004) *Human Evolutionary Genetics: Origins, Peoples and Disease*. New York: Garland.

Kawasaki, K., Suzuki, T., Weiss, K. M. (2005) Phenogenetic Drift in Evolution: The Changing Genetic Basis of Vertebrate Teeth. *Proceedings of the National Academy of Sciences, USA* 102 (50): 18063–18068.

Lynch, M. (2007) *The Origin of Genome Architecture*. Sunderland MA: Sinauer Associates.

Relethford, J. (2003) *The Human Species: An Introduction to Biological Anthropology*. New York: McGraw-Hill.

Ridley, M. (2004) *Evolution*. Malden MA: Blackwell.

Templeton, A. (2006) *Population Genetics and Microevolutionary Theory*. Hoboken NJ: J. Wiley.

Weiss, K. M. (2004) The Smallest Grain in the Balance. *Evolutionary Anthropology* 13 (4): 122–126.

Weiss, K. M. (2008) Tilting at Quixotic Trait Loci (QTL): An Evolutionary Perspective on Genetic Causation. *Genetics* 179 (4): 1741–1756.

Weiss, K. M., and Buchanan, A. V. (2009) *The Mermaid's Tale: Four Billion Years of Evolution in the Making of Living Things*. Cambridge MA: Harvard University Press.

Weiss, K. M., and Fullerton, S. M. (2000) Phenogenetic Drift and the Evolution of Genotype–Phenotype Relationships. *Theoretical Population Biology* 57 (3): 187–195.

CHAPTER 3

Systematics, Taxonomy, and Phylogenetics: Ordering Life, Past and Present

Bernard A. Wood

INTRODUCTION

Systematics includes *all* of the activities involved in the study of the diversity and origins of living and extinct organisms. This chapter focuses on: (A) identification and comparison; (B) species-level classification; (C) phylogeny reconstruction; and (D) classification above the level of the species. These activities have to be carried out in the order in which they are listed, thus (A) must precede (B); (A) and (B) must precede (C); and so on. The first two activities, 'identification and comparison' and 'species-level classification,' constitute what Mayr et al. (1953) referred to as 'alpha taxonomy,' and the fourth activity, 'classification above the level of the species,' corresponds to the way these authors define 'beta taxonomy' (ibid., p. 19).

In physical anthropology, 'identification' means working out what region of the body a specimen comes from and making sure that the specimen itself is a primate. 'Comparison' involves recording its morphology as thoroughly and objectively as possible, comparing the specimen with appropriate extant and fossil taxa, and then assigning it either to an existing and phenetically coherent group or to a novel group. 'Phenetic coherence' implies that the distributions of the observed morphological characteristics of a group of organisms are sufficiently non-overlapping with those of other groups for it to be possible to use those observations to assign individual specimens securely to the correct group. The second activity, species-level classification, involves the formal recognition of those phenetically coherent groups as species, and then the formal attribution of names for them. The third activity, phylogeny reconstruction, uses either all of the phenetic evidence or a subset of it, as in cladistic analytical methods, to generate either relatively simple hypotheses about the relationships among the taxa (for instance a cladogram) or more complex hypotheses, which include specifying ancestors and descendants (for instance a phylogenetic tree). Phylogeny reconstruction aims to recover what some researchers refer to as the 'natural' relationships among taxa (in other words, the branching pattern of the 'tree of life'). The fourth activity, classification above the level of the species, involves using the results of phylogenetic reconstruction to allocate species to a genus, tribe, and so on and then to assemble these various taxa into a hierarchical classification.

Taxonomy is the study of the principles and theory that inform the process of classification. *Nomenclature*, which straddles classification and taxonomy, includes both the principles that should be used when formal names (such as a Linnaean binomial) are assigned to taxa, and the rules (priority, synonymy, and the like) and recommendations that govern the use of those principles in taxonomic research.

The classification system used by contemporary biologists was developed by Carolus Linnaeus (he was not raised into the ranks of nobility, as Carl von Linné, until the 12th edition of his *Systema naturae*) in the late eighteenth century, and it is referred to as 'Linnaean taxonomy.' It is also called the 'binomial system,' because two (bi-) of the categories, the genus and the specific name, make up the Latin name given to each species (*Homo sapiens, Pan troglodytes*).

The system introduced by Linnaeus recognized five basic levels or categories: kingdom, class, order, genus, and species. Since the introduction of the binomial system, biologists have found that more than five categories are needed to reflect the complexity of the living world. Consequently, Linnaeus's original categories have been supplemented by adding new ones (for instance the tribe has been inserted between the genus and family), and by adding the prefixes 'super-' ('above'), or 'sub-' and 'infra-' ('below') to some categories. These additions increase the potential number of taxonomic categories below the level of order to a total of twelve (see the list in the diagram below). The heart of the Linnaean hierarchy is its least inclusive category, the 'species,' which is at origin a Latin word derived from *specio, -ere* ('to look'), together with words like *specimen* and *spectio* (etymologically, the English 'inspection' comes from the same root).

List of the categories used in a Linnaean taxonomy. Higher taxa are in bold type:

Kingdom
Phylum
Subphylum
Superclass
Class
Subclass
Infraclass
Cohort
Superorder
Order
Suborder
Infraorder
Superfamily
Family

Subfamily
Tribe
Subtribe
Genus
Subgenus
Species
Subspecies

A group at any level in the Linnaean hierarchy is called a 'taxon' (plural 'taxa'). Thus the species *Homo sapiens* is a taxon, but so is the order Primates. Taxa must be distinguished from 'categories' in the Linnaean hierarchy. Taxa are the actual groups in nature to which we give names (*Homo sapiens*, Primates) and which we then classify at the appropriate categorical rank in the hierarchy (species, genus, family). The names of taxa function like the names of people; they are a kind of shorthand reference system for the identification of an individual biological entity (species, person). Taxa are also divided into lower and higher taxa. Lower taxa comprise species and genera; higher taxa are all those above the level of the genus. When the system is applied to a group of closely related organisms, the resulting scheme is called a 'classification.'

There is confusion about the proper use of the terms 'diagnosis' and 'definition' in relation to taxonomy. Diagnosis is what your medical doctor does when she/he discriminates among the likely causes of your illness; the doctor uses your symptoms and signs to identify the correct cause of your illness. Diagnosis in taxonomy is a similar exercise. Thus a diagnosis is a list of the features that (1) permit one taxon to be distinguished from another, and (2) facilitate the correct assignment of individual organisms (or specimens) to a taxon. A definition, on the other hand, concentrates on the morphology the members of a taxon have in common. A definition is a list of the features that bind the organisms of a taxon together; it does not necessarily discriminate the taxon from others (so modern humans are bipeds, but without further qualification this attribute does not distinguish us from species in the extinct genus *Australopithecus*).

IDENTIFICATION AND COMPARISON

Identification

The first duty of anyone claiming to have found a fossil primate is to make sure the specimen really belongs to a primate and is not the hard-tissue evidence of another type of non-primate mammal.

The first step is to identify the specimen anatomically as precisely as the preserved morphology allows and to determine its ontogenetic status. For example, a complete femur is difficult to confuse with a complete humerus, but an undiagnostic piece of long-bone shaft or a fragment of tooth enamel may not be so easy to locate on the skeleton. For parts of the body that are serially homologous, like teeth or vertebrae, researchers must use whatever evidence they can to locate a mandibular molar in the tooth row, or a thoracic vertebra to the upper, middle, or lower part of the thoracic spine. Precise anatomical identification is important because it determines which other fossils and which components of the extant comparators should be used to help make decisions about whether the new fossil belongs to an existing species or not. It is important to determine the specimen's ontogenetic status because a newly discovered juvenile fossil primate mandible should be compared with other juvenile mandibles and not with adult mandibles.

The next all-important step is to compare the correctly identified anatomical part with the same part from appropriate comparative groups, to make sure that the taxon (in this case, a primate) is correctly identified using relevant diagnostic criteria. If the specimen is very scrappy, this can be a difficult and sometimes inconclusive process; better preserved or more complete specimens are more likely to result in a correct taxonomic assignment than poorly preserved or fragmentary ones.

Consolidation, reassembly and reconstruction

Some fossils are so fragile that they are little better than bone-shaped or tooth-shaped collections of powder that crumble when touched (the newly described *Ardipithecus ramidus* associated skeleton, *ARA-VP-6/500*, is an example; see White et al. 2009), and if they are to be preserved care must be taken to consolidate such fossils with hardening compound, as they are exposed. Bones and teeth that are undistorted but fragmented can be *reassembled*; researchers sit down with the original pieces and fit them together by hand. If only part of an undistorted fossil bone or tooth has been preserved, the whole can be *reconstructed*. Reconstruction may involve duplication if the missing piece is a bilateral structure and the other side (called the antimere) is preserved, or it may involve extrapolation if there is no antimere, or if only part of a structure is preserved. In general, the more complete a bone or tooth is and the more contact points there are between the fragments, the more reliable the reconstruction is. More difficult problems arise when cracks run through a fossil and they are filled with matrix, or if the fossil has been affected by *plastic deformation* (i.e. the bone has behaved like a viscous material). If the deformation has affected only one side of a bilateral structure, then the undeformed side can be used to reconstruct the deformed side. If both sides are deformed, then researchers must either painstakingly remove the matrix between the fragments and then physically reassemble them, or digitally image the fossil and use software programs to estimate and restore the undeformed shape (Zollikofer et al. 2005). However, the problem with creating 'virtual fossils' is that it can be difficult to determine which parts of a virtual fossil are 'real' and which are reconstructed, and it is all too easy to begin to assume that a reconstructed virtual fossil has the same value as a well preserved 'real' fossil (but see Gunz et al. 2009 for a defense of the value of virtual fossils).

Relatively few fossil specimens totally escape damage from breakage, loss, erosion and/or deformation, processes that result in the loss or distortion of information. Recognizing lost or distorted information and, where possible, maximizing its recovery through reassembly, restoration, and reconstruction are the most important early steps in the analysis of a fossil.

Capturing morphology for comparison

The morphological characteristics of fossils need to be captured as comprehensively and as objectively as possible. The morphology of a fossil can be divided into two overlapping sets of categories: *external* and *internal*, and *macroscopic* and *microscopic*.

Information about internal morphology and microstructure can be obtained *non-destructively* or *destructively*. Non-destructive techniques employ X-rays (high-energy photons with a very short wavelength), other forms of invisible radiation, and ultrasound (acoustic frequencies above the range audible to the modern human ear – that is, over 20,000 hertz). Researchers are beginning to exploit the sophisticated imaging techniques that are used in clinical medicine such as Computed Tomography (CT) and micro-CT. These techniques allow researchers to visualize structures such as the bony labyrinth (Spoor et al. 2000), hidden from naked-eye view within bones, and to determine the thickness of dense cortical bone and the internal structure of cancellous bone (Ohman et al. 1997). Bromage et al. (2005) pioneered the use of confocal microscopy to study the microstructure of fossil hominins. A confocal microscope, which uses a system of discs to shut out any light that is not coming from the part of the specimen the researcher wants to concentrate on, allows researchers to look beneath the surface of a bone or tooth. More recently, synchrotron radiation microtomography (SR-μCT) has been used to recover information about dental microstructure in intact teeth (Tafforeau and Smith 2007).

Most of the destructive studies of the microstructure of fossils have involved the dentition (for instance Dean et al. 1993). These researchers used a diamond saw to take very thin slices through a tooth, then they re-cemented the parts of the tooth crown, adding a thin layer of acrylic cement to make sure that the tooth had the same dimensions as it did before the thin section was removed.

Metrical and non-metrical methods for capturing morphology

Two systems of recording morphology are commonly in use. One, called *metrical* or *morphometric* analysis, uses measurements; the other, called *non-metrical* analysis, records morphology by using presence/absence criteria, by comparing the fossil with a series of standards, or by characterizing morphology qualitatively. Examples of non-metrical traits include the numbers of cusps or roots on a tooth and the presence or absence of markings for cranial venous sinuses.

Measurements are traditionally made between standardized locations, called *landmarks*. Many of these are defined as the places where sutures meet on bones, or where fissures meet on teeth, or they are points that can be located with the minimum of ambiguity (for example the width of the shaft of a long bone at 50 percent of its total length); but not all such landmarks are homologous. The measurements taken are usually the shortest distance between the points; these are known as chord distances. If the surface between the landmarks is curved, a tape laid between the two points will record the arc distance, and the difference between the chord and the arc reflects the degree of curvature. It is also possible to use angles to record morphology. These record the orientation of a structure relative to the sagittal or coronal planes, or to a reference plane such as the Frankfurt Horizontal or the Orbital Plane.

Recently introduced techniques usually referred to as geometric morphometrics collect data in three dimensions, and thus they capture more of the original morphology than is possible using traditional linear measurements. The position of each reference point is recorded using a three-dimensional coordinate system, and the distances between any two of the recorded points can be recovered if needed. Initially the three-dimensional coordinates of landmarks were captured mostly by using machines called 'digitizers.' These machines have a mobile arm with a fine point at the end. The tip is placed on the reference point and the machine automatically records its location in three dimensions (3D). Newer techniques capture data from complex surfaces using laser beams, CT scans, or other technologies. Because many laser or CT scans can be made, these latter methods capture 3D data even more densely than is possible with digitizers. They also have the advantage that researchers do not have to decide in advance what landmarks to use. Traditional landmarks can be located in 3D on the virtual fossils, and semi-landmarks (these are landmarks specified by placing a fixed number of equidistant points along homologous curves) can be used to capture the shape of curved surfaces and ridges between traditional landmarks. Special software programs (for instance *Morphologika*, http://hyms.fme.googlepages.com/resources) can be used to remove overall size, so that researchers can focus on shape differences (see below).

Comparing specimens

Observations can be compared one at a time – *univariate analysis* – or by plotting two variables against each other – *bivariate analysis*. It is also possible to analyze many variables simultaneously – *multivariate analysis*. The last two methods compare known groups by summarizing multiple variables in the form of a smaller number of factors or axes. One type of multivariate analysis allows researchers to compute the distance between individuals in multivariate space, and this 'multivariate distance' can be used to compare differences between fossils with the differences observed within, and between, samples from comparative groups. Other multivariate methods are designed to identify clusters of similar fossils by simplifying the patterns of correlation and variance, and a subgroup of multivariate methods allows the form of a structure to be broken down into components of size and shape.

When analyses are based on traditional linear measurements between reference points, the morphological information they capture is only a small part of the potential information available, and conventional multivariate techniques provide no visual image of how organisms differ in size and shape. The new generation of 3D geometric morphometric analytical methods uses grids or arrows to show how the reference specimen needs to be deformed, or warped, in order to assume the shapes of the specimens with which it is being compared.

Morphological differences can be resolved into differences in *size* and differences in *shape*. Comparative analyses have been consistent in showing that differences in shape are consistently more valent taxonomically than differences in overall size, so a common aspect of many metrical methods is the scaling of the data through the use of a surrogate for overall size such as the geometric mean. There is, however, a difference between correcting for overall size and removing the 'effects' of size. Size and shape are seldom independent, for most of the relationships among metrical variables in organisms are *allometric*. In such a relationship, a change in overall size results in a predictable difference in shape. Thus, in these circumstances, even if overall size is removed from an analysis, the *effect* of overall size differences on shape will not necessarily be removed.

SPECIES-LEVEL CLASSIFICATION

Individual fossils cannot be classified. A fossil has to be assigned to a group, and then the group can be classified. If a new fossil is within the inferred limits of variation of an existing species, then it can be added to the *hypodigm* of that species – that is, to the list of specimens assigned to that species. However, if the specimen falls outside the range of variation of known species, then it *may* warrant the erection of a new species. The new species has to be given an appropriate name; a *holotype* (the *type specimen*) needs to be designated; and then the classification needs to be modified to accommodate the new species.

What is a species?

It may seem counter-intuitive, but biologists have devised many different ways of defining species. Smith (1994) divides contemporary, non-typological, species concepts into *process-related* and *pattern-related*. The former emphasize the processes involved in the generation and maintenance of species' boundaries, whereas the latter emphasizes the operations biologists use to demarcate species' boundaries.

The three main species concepts in the process category are: the *biological species concept* (BSC); the *evolutionary species concept* (ESC); and the *recognition species concept* (RSC). The BSC, as promulgated by Mayr (1942, 1982), defined the species as "groups of interbreeding natural populations reproductively isolated from other such groups." There are two problems with the BSC. First, it is a relational definition, in the sense that, to delimit one species, reference has to be made to at least one other species; and, second, it stresses mechanisms for maintaining reproductive (and hence genetic) isolation, rather than emphasizing the factors that bind the individuals within a species together.

The ESC was an attempt by Simpson (1961) to add a temporal dimension to the BSC. Wiley (1978) developed Simpson's concept and defined the ESC as "a single lineage of ancestor–descendant populations which maintains its identity from other such lineages and which has it own evolutionary tendencies and historical fate." Some use the term 'chronospecies' to refer to a segment of the type of evolving lineage implied in the ESC definition. The boundaries of the segment can be defined by discontinuities in the fossil record, or a lineage can be subdivided because the fossil sample exceeds the degree and/or the pattern of variation within closely related living species. A problem with the ESC is that it assumes pre-existing knowledge of phylogeny, which logically should follow and not precede alpha taxonomy.

The third concept in the process category, the RSC, focuses on the factors that promote interbreeding. Paterson (1985) suggested that under the RSC a species is "the most inclusive population of individual, biparental organisms which shares a common fertilization system." The latter, which he termed 'the specific mate recognition system' or SMRS, comprises the mechanisms which organisms use to recognize potential mates and to ensure fertilization; this may be a distinctive external morphological feature (see below), a characteristic coloration, a distinctive call, or even an odor. Paterson claims that the RSC is, at least potentially, applicable to the fossil record as long as a species' SMRS fossilizes.

The three main pattern-based species concepts are: the *phenetic species concept* (PeSC); the *phylogenetic species concept* (PySC); and the *monophyletic species concept* (MSC). When applied to the fossil record, all three are *morphospecies* concepts in that they emphasize different aspects of an organism's morphology. The PeSC, as interpreted by Sokal and Crovello (1970), gives equal weight to *all* aspects of the phenotype and uses multivariate analysis to detect clusters of individual specimens that share a similar phenotype. Under the PySC introduced by Cracraft (1983), the emphasis is on those aspects of the phenotype that are diagnostic. According to Nixon and Wheeler (1990), a PySC species is "the smallest aggregation of populations diagnosable by a unique combination of character states." Lastly, under the MSC the morphological emphasis is narrower still, species being defined not on the basis of unique combinations of characters but only on the basis of uniquely derived characters. The problem with the MSC is that it assumes researchers know which characters are uniquely derived. But in order to know this you must have performed a cladistic analysis (see below), and to do that you must have already decided on the taxa to include in the analysis. The MSC is thus undermined by circular reasoning.

What happens in practice?

Most primatologists use either the phylogenetic species concept (although often without specifically acknowledging it) or the evolutionary species concept. If they use the former, then they search for the smallest cluster of individual organisms that is diagnosable on the basis of the preserved morphology. Because in the primate fossil record most of that morphology is craniodental, most diagnoses of fossil primate taxa inevitably emphasize craniodental morphology.

Eldredge (1993) developed Ghiselin's (1972) proposal that a species taxon should be regarded as an 'entity.' Eldredge suggested that an individual species taxon has the equivalent of a 'life,' with a beginning (the result of a speciation event), a middle (which lasts as long as the species persists), and an end (either extinction or participation in another speciation event). On this interpretation, when we observe living species we are looking at the equivalent of a snapshot taken during the course of its life. Physical anthropologists must decide whether a collection of fossils spanning perhaps several hundred thousand or even a million years consists of samples of several different taxa or of several samples of the same taxon. One of the many factors which physical anthropologists must take into account in addition to the time represented in their sample is that they have to work with a fossil record which is confined to remains of the hard tissues (bones and teeth). We know from living animals that many uncontested species are difficult to distinguish by using bones and teeth (for example *Cercopithecus* or *Hylobates* species). Thus there are reasons to suspect that a hard-tissue-bound fossil record is always likely to underestimate the number of species.

In Eldredge's formulation, all species begin at the point of speciation when they and their sister taxon – that is, the other taxon that arose at the same speciation event – arise from a common ancestor. A species may then change during the course of its history (a process called anagenesis), but its existence will come to an end when it either becomes extinct or becomes the common ancestor of two daughter taxa. Eldredge also acknowledges the fact that the morphological characteristics of a living, or neontological, species, or of an evolutionary lineage, are never uniformly distributed across its range; and he follows Sewall Wright in recognizing the existence of distinctive local populations or 'demes.' Related demes would share the same SMRS, and Eldredge suggests that their morphological distinctiveness could, in some cases, justify their being regarded as separate species. He also acknowledges that the same logic could be applied to the chronospecies which make up a lineage, because the incompleteness of the fossil record suggests that splitting events are more likely to be underestimated than overestimated. Thus within the fossil record it may be possible to identify several paleospecies (*sensu* Cain 1954) within the equivalent of a neontological biological species, or within a species based on the recognition concept (that is, a species made up of all the demes that share the same species recognition system). De Queiroz (2007) includes a useful figure (Fig. 1, p. 882), emphasizing that the various properties researchers have suggested as criteria for recognizing species may arise at different stages in the speciation process.

What are the most appropriate comparators?

How different does a new fossil have to be from specimens in the existing fossil record before a researcher can reasonably assume that it represents a new species? Once a researcher has satisfied him/herself that observed differences are not due to the fossil's state of preservation (the effects of plastic deformation, or of an increase or decrease in size due to matrix-filled cracks or erosion, respectively), to ontogeny (comparing a young individual with an old individual), to sex (comparing a male with a female), and to within-species geographical variation, the decision rests on the range of morphological variation which the researcher in question is prepared to tolerate within a species. In practical terms, paleontologists usually take the extent of size and shape variation within closely related living species as the criterion for judging whether the amount of variation within a collection of fossils justifies their being divided into more than one species (see for instance Wood 1991). However, the museum collections used as samples of these contemporary species capture variation at what is effectively an instant in geological time, whereas fossil taxa are usually sampled across geological time. No one knows what 'extra' variation, if any, needs to be added to that observed in the museum collections to make them more comparable to a fossil taxon.

A very different interpretation: Reticulate evolution

All the species concepts considered thus far subscribe to a common model of evolution. According to it, speciation is a bifurcating hierarchy: one species splits into two, each of these species in turn bifurcates, and so on. On this model, speciation is a process in which new species arise in geographically isolated subpopulations. This is called 'allopatric' speciation, which means speciation in another terrritory. These subpopulations gradually develop distinctive combinations of genes, which eventually result in their carriers' reproductive isolation from the parent population. Proponents of the recognition species concept would argue that this phenomenon occurs when the new species develops a distinctive specific mate recognition system in allopatry.

In reticulate evolution, new species arise when two existing species undergo *hybridization*. On this model species are seen as components of a complex network, hence

Table 3.1 Terminology for the higher taxonomic categories immediately involved in the classification of the species *Homo sapiens*

Category	Ending	Homo	Informal name
Superfamily	-oidea	Hominoidea	hominoid
Family	-idae	Hominidae	hominid
Subfamily	-inae	Homininae	hominine
Tribe	-ini	Hominini	hominin
Subtribe	-ina	Hominina	hominan

the term reticulation. This model of evolution is close to the way in which some researchers interpret evolution in geographically widespread groups like baboons. There are peaks of morphological distinctiveness in contemporary baboons; these differences are equivalent to those which, in other taxa, are interpreted as species differences. The location and nature of these peaks will change over time and new species will form in the hybrid zones between the peaks (Jolly 2001).

Nomenclature

The steps involved in naming a new species, genus, or higher taxon are collectively referred to as 'nomenclature', and the process is controlled by rules and recommendations set out in the International Code of Zoological Nomenclature, otherwise known as the ICZN, or just 'the Code' (Ride et al. 1999). The stipulations in the Code are designed to ensure that everyone who takes part in discussions about issues involving classification and nomenclature does so with a common understanding. They are also designed to make sure that: (a) the names given to new taxa are appropriate; (b) the proposed name has not already been used for an existing taxon (in other words, there is no homonymy); and (c) only one name is given to a taxon (in other words synonymy is satisfied), namely on a principle of *priority* (other than in exceptional circumstances, the name that was used first cannot be replaced).

The Code also sets out the conventions used when writing about taxa. Genus and species names are both italicized. The genus name always begins with a capital letter, but in print it can be abbreviated to the initial after its first mention. Thus for our own species, *Homo sapiens*, the abbreviated form is *H. sapiens*. However, when the genus name is used alone, it must always be given in full (*Homo*, not *H.*). The names of the taxa in all the ranks above the genus are never italicized, but they always begin with a capital letter. Such taxa usually take the root of the name of the earliest validly named genus included within it, and an ending is added that reflects the rank of the taxon. The informal way to describe the classification of the species *Homo sapiens* in the scheme used here is, in order of decreasing inclusivity, 'hominoid' (superfamily), 'hominid' (family), 'hominine' (subfamily), 'hominin' (tribe), and 'hominan' (subtribe) (see the diagram below).

Thus *Homo sapiens* is one of several species in the genus *Homo*; the genus *Homo* is the only genus in the subtribe Hominina and one of several genera in the tribe Hominini. An example of a contemporary classification that reflects molecular (Bradley 2008) and other evidence, which points to a close relationship between chimpanzees/bonobos and modern humans, is given in the diagram below. Represented here is a typical taxonomy that recognizes the close genetic links between *Pan* and *Homo*. This consensus classification is unsatisfactory in that *Australopithecus* is almost certainly paraphyletic, but it must suffice until we can resolve relationships among hominin taxa more reliably than is presently the case. In the diagram, the fossil-only taxa are in bold type:

Superfamily Hominoidea
  Family Hylobatidae
       Genus *Hylobates*
  Family Hominidae
   Subfamily Ponginae
      Genus *Pongo*
   Subfamily Gorillinae
      Genus *Gorilla*
   Subfamily Homininae
    Tribe Panini
      Genus *Pan*
    Tribe Hominini
      Subtribe Australopithecina
        Genus *Ardipithecus*
        Genus *Australopithecus*
        Genus *Kenyanthropus*
        Genus *Sahelanthropus*
        Genus *Orrorin*
        Genus *Paranthropus*
     Subtribe Hominina
      Genus *Homo*

PHYLOGENY RECONSTRUCTION

Relationships among taxa

No matter how many species are recognized in the primate fossil record, researchers must tackle the task of working out how primate species are related. This is because a well supported hypothesis of relationships is necessary in order to reconstruct most of the important details of primate evolutionary history.

Hypotheses about the relationships among fossil taxa can be divided into three categories on the basis of their complexity (Tattersall and Eldredge 1977). The least complex statement about relationships groups taxa together according to whether they share any novel characteristics or not. This enables them to be located as 'sister taxa' in a hierarchical branching diagram. Such diagrams are called 'cladograms' (from the ancient Greek word for branch, *klados*). Note that a cladogram is free of absolute time, unlike a phylogenetic tree (see below). At the nodes linking two sister taxa, common ancestors are implied but not specified. Cladograms are generated using a method called 'phylogenetic analysis' or 'cladistics.' Remember that, even though phylogenetic analysis is often used as a synonym for cladistics, cladistic methods generate cladograms, *not* phylogenetic trees. The methods for generating hypotheses concerning relationships, together with the specialized terminology linked with those methods, were set out by Willi Hennig in the 1950s, but they were not widely adopted until they were published in English (Hennig 1966).

The intermediate category expresses hypotheses about relationships in the form of *phylogenetic* or *phyletic trees*. Phylogenetic trees contain more information than clado-grams do. As well as specifying the hierarchy of the relationships (in the form of sets of nested taxa), these trees place the taxa in ancestor–descendant sequences in abso-lute time. This category of hypotheses goes beyond the one generated by using cla-distic methods, and it requires reliable information about the age of the fossils. Several different phylogenetic trees may be consistent with a single cladogram.

The most complex category of hypotheses about evolutionary relationships is the *evolutionary scenario*. It not only specifies a particular phylogenetic hypothesis, but it also furnishes process-level explanations of how evolution came to take a particular course. Some of these explanations involve factors intrinsic to the taxa themselves (for example developmental constraints). Others involve factors external to the organism, and these may be biological (they are also known as 'biotic') or non-biological ('abi-otic'). Examples of the former include the effects of competition with other animals for resources. Global and regional climate change, or changes in paleoenvironments, are interrelated examples of potential abiotic influences on human evolutionary history.

Principles of cladistics

The intrinsic resemblances between any two species can be crudely resolved into three elements, called 'patristic,' 'cladistic' and 'homoplasic' (Cain 1954).

Patristic similarities are those that reflect relatively remote evolutionary history. In the case of modern humans and chimpanzees, these would include discrete parts of the phenotype, called 'character states,' which make them vertebrates, mammals, and primates. These patristic features (also called 'primitive' or 'symplesiomorphic') are useful for generating a hypothesis about the nature of the relationships between a modern human, a chimpanzee, and a snail; but they are incapable of resolving the relationships among, say, modern humans, chimpanzees, and gorillas. In the example given above, the cladistic element of the phenotype is the part that is expressed differ-ently in modern humans, chimpanzees, and gorillas. The shared possession of cladistic character states (also called 'shared–derived,' or 'synapomorphic') can then be used to develop hypotheses about the evolutionary relationships among those taxa. Taxa linked on the grounds that they share these sorts of characters are called 'sister taxa.' A pair of sister taxa is the minimum size of a 'monophyletic group,' or 'clade.' However, a monophyletic group can comprise any number of pairs of sister taxa, as long as they can all be traced back to a common ancestor from which they inherited at least one shared–derived character state that is not present in a closely related clade. A 'polyphyletic group' is a group that includes taxa belonging to more than one clade. For example, savannah (*Papio*), forest (*Mandrillus*) and mountain (*Theropithecus*) baboons appear, at least from genetic evidence, to be a polyphyletic group, for they did not inherit their long muzzles from their most recent common ancestor. A 'para-phyletic group' is a taxonomic grouping that *omits* one or more member(s) of a monophyletic group.

The third type of resemblance is referred to as 'homoplasy,' and the characters involved are called 'homoplasic' or 'homoplastic.' The three causes of homoplasy are *convergent evolution, parallel evolution*, and *character reversal*. Convergent and parallel evolution represent one and the same in principle. Both generate parts of the phenotype that look similar in two taxa, yet those similarities were not inherited from the most recent common ancestor of the taxa. Convergent homoplasies evolve independently in relatively distantly related taxa, whereas parallel homoplasies evolve independently in more closely related taxa. A character reversal occurs when a character in a taxon reverts to its more primitive condition, and this also gives the false impression that the two taxa are more closely related than they really are.

There is a fourth, potentially confusing, component to adult morphology. This comprises phenetic features that can alter in size and shape according to how active an individual organism is. For example some of the phenotype linked with mastication will be modified if the teeth are lost on one side, so that chewing is concentrated on the remaining teeth. Likewise, the thickness of the shafts of long bones will increase if activity levels are chronically high (for instance the cortical bone of the humerus of the dominant arm/hand of tennis players is thicker than that of the non-dominant side). These are examples of *epigenetic* effects. Some have claimed that these function-related morphological differences (also known as 'homoiologies') represent one of the sources of the *character conflict* (the presence of characters consistent with a cladogram different from the most parsimonious one) that occurs in many cladistic analyses (see below).

Cladistic analysis: Where to begin?

The first decision is what taxa to include in a cladistic analysis (the cladistic phrase for each of the taxa included in a cladistic analysis is 'operational taxonomic unit' or OTU). These taxa make up the *ingroup*. The next step is to determine the morphology whose expression will be compared among the OTUs. The cladistic method requires that the phenotype be broken down into morphological units which are uncorrelated. This means that each morphological unit should provide information which is independent of all the others. This requirement is, in practice, difficult to comply with. It is also, in some ways, counter-intuitive; for, as we shall see below, cladistic analysis depends on the fact that a particular branching pattern is supported by more than one character. However, the desirable correlations are those that are due to shared phylogenetic history; the correlations to be avoided are the ones that are due to other reasons than the shared recent common ancestry (for instance descriptive redundancy, homoplasy, or homoiology).

The morphological units are called 'characters,' and their different morphological expressions, which must vary among at least some of the taxa included in the analysis, are called 'character states.' Character states must be 'homologous' – that is, they must have the same developmental basis and they must be capable of being assessed objectively. This can be achieved by careful description, but some claim that the only objective way of doing it is to use measurements.

Determining character polarity

The next task in a cladistic analysis is to determine the sequence of the states of each character, ranging from its most 'primitive' expression – that is, its expression in the common ancestor of all the ingroup taxa – to the most 'derived,' or specialized, expression of that character. This ordination process is known as 'polarization.' Two criteria, the 'ontogenetic' one and the 'outgroup' one, may be used to establish which of the character states is the most primitive and which is the most derived, as well as the sequence of state changes that connects them. In the case of the ontogenetic criterion, it is assumed that a character state which resembles more closely the early stages of the ontogeny of an animal will range towards the primitive end of the morphocline. For example, no matter how complex the morphology of a tooth root eventually becomes, early in ontogeny all teeth had a single root. Thus the ontogenetic criterion suggests that a single root is the primitive condition for the teeth of primates.

The outgroup criterion is based on the assumption of parsimony. This assumption takes the form that, if any of the character states seen in the ingroup taxa is also seen in one or more closely related outgroup taxa, then the state in question is likely to have been the primitive condition for the ingroup. Outgroup taxa are chosen because of their previously determined and close phylogenetic relationship to the OTUs, and not on the basis of their phenetic resemblance to the taxa under investigation. Thus the proper outgroup for a study of cetaceans (whales, dolphins, and porpoises) would be another mammal, not a bony fish; and the proper outgroup for a cladistic analysis of the living great apes would be one of the taxa in the clade that contains the extant gibbons and siamangs.

Generating and comparing cladograms

Once the character states are recorded and their polarity determined, the 'topology' or shape of the cladogram can be determined. The two ways to do this are the Hennig Method, in which cladograms are based on a single character's expression across all the taxa, and the Wagner Method, in which cladograms are generated by comparing the distributions of all the characters, taxon by taxon. As a practical matter, most cladistic studies focus on analyses of all of the characters at once.

There are two main methods for assembling a 'consensus cladogram' from the individual character cladograms for the suite of characters used in an analysis of morphology (other methods exist, too, which are applied typically to genetic data). The 'maximum parsimony' method minimizes the independent acquisition of character states (or homoplasy) and the number of times when character states have to be reversed, so the consensus cladogram will be the cladogram with the fewest character state changes. According to the second method – which is the 'compatibility method' – the consensus cladogram is the one supported by the largest group of compatible characters (that is, characters that result in the same cladogram). Most modern cladistic studies focus on parsimony analysis when dealing with anatomical data.

Cladograms are conventionally compared by using indices: either the 'consistency index' (CI), or the 'retention index' (RI). The consistency index is calculated so as to represent the minimum number of steps (or character state changes) necessary to explain the distribution of character states in the taxa being analyzed, divided by the observed number of steps in a cladogram. The retention index is calculated to be the maximum number of steps possible on a tree minus the observed number of steps, divided by the maximum number of steps possible on a tree minus the minimum number of steps calculated from the data. The RI contains additional information about homoplasy compared to the CI, and is not inversely related to tree length, as is the CI; but both indices have their uses (Farris 1989). The third commonly used measure of the quality and information content of a cladogram, the 'rescaled consistency index' (RCI), is the product of the RI and the CI. An index value of 1 suggests a 'perfect' fit (that is, one with no character conflict), and an index of 0.5 would mean that half of the character appearances on the cladogram are due to reasons other than inheritance from the most recent common ancestor (reasons such as homoplasy or homoiology).

Once the shape of a cladogram has been determined, the distribution of the character states can be assessed. Those that lie at the base of the cladogram are the shared primitive characters, or, in Hennigian terminology, the 'symplesiomorphies.' Those that are limited to the smaller, terminal, clades are called shared–derived characters or 'synapomorphies.' Both synapomorphy and symplesiomorphy are rank-specific. That is, a synapomorphy that unites three taxa in a monophyletic group will be symplesiomorphic for any monophyletic taxa *within* the group. Character states that only appear in one taxon are called 'uniquely derived characters'; they are also known as 'autapomorphies.' As mentioned earlier, character states that arise independently (in other words, they appear in more than one clade, but they are not present in the most recent common ancestor of those clades) are known as 'homoplasies.'

A 'total group' is a monophyletic group that includes every taxon which is more closely related to a living taxon than it is to any other living taxon. Fossil hominins are a total group, for they contain all the taxa which are more closely related to modern humans than to chimpanzees and bonobos. A 'crown group' is the smallest monophyletic group that includes the living taxon in a clade. In the case of hominins, this will be a subset of the genus *Homo*, probably *H. sapiens* and *H. neanderthalensis*. A 'stem group' is a total group minus its crown group. For hominins, this would be all the species included in hominin genera, except *Homo sapiens* and its sister taxon.

Classification

Once hypotheses about the relationships among taxa have been generated – and these days most of them are generated by using cladistic methods or by applying phenetic methods to 3D data – they can be used to inform the way in which species are grouped into genera and into higher taxa.

What is a genus?

Ideally, a genus should be both a *clade* and a *grade*. To be a clade, a species grouping must consist of all the members of a monophyletic group – not of more and not of less. For a species grouping to be a grade, all the species in it must share the same adaptive regime. A clade is analogous to the *make* of a car: all Ford cars share a recent common ancestor, the 'Model T,' which is not shared with any other make of car; whereas a grade is analogous to the *type* of a car: the SUVs made by Lexus, Porsche, and Land-Rover are functionally similar, yet they have different evolutionary histories and therefore have no recent exclusive common ancestor. But not all the species in the same grade have to be in the same genus; for a grade may contain species belonging to more than one monophyletic group or clade. Comparable stipulations should apply to more inclusive taxonomic categories (tribe, family). Others have suggested that genera should be defined by a certain time depth, but this would mean that genera would be prone to additional and external causes of instability.

How should higher taxa be defined?

Higher taxa should also be both clades and grades, and the same criteria that were used to define genera can be used to sort the genera into higher taxa. Some researchers insist that cladistic hypotheses should be rigidly reflected in any classifications above the species level. But the problem with this approach is that the results of cladistic analyses *are* hypotheses, and if a new classification had to be generated every time a new cladistic hypothesis was generated, it would result in classifications which are unhelpfully unstable. A particularly difficult classification problem concerns stem taxa, which are notoriously resistant to sorting into groups that are both grades and clades. To accommodate these taxa, some researchers have proposed using the category of 'plesion,' which allows taxa to be placed within a taxonomic hierarchy without assigning it a formal rank.

DIFFERENT PERSPECTIVES CAN AFFECT TAXONOMIC HYPOTHESES

It is obvious that, at each stage in the complicated process just described, researchers can quite legitimately make different decisions and judgments, which result in different conclusions about how many species should be recognized and how these species should be assembled into genera and higher taxa. It is often difficult to tell whether disagreements about classification among physical anthropologists are due to genuine differences in the way they interpret a particular part of the primate fossil record, or whether they reflect different perspectives about what a species or a genus is.

Usually, close textual analysis of such wrangles reveals that both types of reason play a part. Researchers who favor a more 'anagenetic' or gradualistic interpretation of the primate fossil record generally stress the importance of continuities in it and tend to opt for fewer species. They are referred to informally as 'lumpers.' Researchers who favor a more 'cladogenetic' – or punctuated, equilibrium-based – interpretation of the primate fossil record generally tend to stress the importance of discontinuities within the fossil record and will generally opt for more speciose taxonomic hypotheses. These are called 'taxic' interpretations, and the researchers who favor them are referred to informally as 'splitters.'

But, when all is said and done, phylogenetic reconstructions and classifications are hypotheses that will inevitably be tested and corroborated or revised as new evidence accumulates and as more effective analytical methods are developed. This is the nature of science.

REFERENCES

Bradley, B. J. (2008) Reconstructing Phylogenies and Phenotypes: A Molecular View of Human Evolution. *Journal of Anatomy* 212: 337–353.

Bromage, T. G., Perez-Ochoa, A., and Boyde, A. (2005) Portable Confocal Microscope Reveals Fossil Hominid Microstructure. *Microsocopy and Analysis* 19 (3): 5–7.

Cain, A. J. (1954) *Animal Species and Evolution*. Princeton: Princeton University Press.

Cracraft, J. (1983) Species Concepts and Speciation Analysis. *Current Ornithology* 1: 159–187.

De Queiroz, K. (2007) Species Concepts and Species Delimitation. *Systematic Biology* 56 (6): 879–886.

Dean, M. C., Beynon, A. D., Thackeray, J. F., and Macho, G. A. (1993) Histological Reconstruction of Dental Development and Age at Death of a Juvenile *Paranthropus robustus* Specimen, SK 63, from Swartkrans, South Africa. *American Journal of Physical Anthropology* 91: 401–419.

Eldredge, N. (1993) What, If Anything, Is a Species? In W. H. Kimbel and L. B. Martin (eds), *Species, Species Concepts, and Primate Evolution* (pp. 3–20). New York: Plenum Press.

Farris, J. S. (1989) The Retention Index and Homoplasy Excess. *Systematic Zoology* 38: 406–407.

Ghiselin, M. T. (1972) Models in Phylogeny. In T. J. M. Schopf (ed.), *Models in Paleobiology* (pp. 130–145). San Francisco: Freeman, Cooper.

Gunz, P., Mitteroecker, P., Neubauer, S., Weber, G.W., and Bookstein, F. L. (2009) Principles for the Virtual Reconstruction of Hominid Crania. *Journal of Human Evolution* 57: 48–62.

Hennig, W. (1966) *Phylogenetic Systematics*. Chicago: University of Illinois Press.

Jolly, C. J. (2001) A Proper Study for Mankind: Analogies from the Papionin Monkeys and Their Implications for Human Evolution. *Yearbook of Physical Anthropology* 44: 177–204.

Mayr, E. (1942) *Systematics and the Origin of Species*. New York: Columbia University Press.

Mayr, E. (1982) *The Growth of Biological Thought: Diversity, Evolution and Inheritance*. Cambridge MA: Harvard University Press.

Mayr, E., Linsley, E. G., and Usinger, R. L. (1953) *Methods and Principles of Systematic Zoology*. New York: McGraw-Hill Book Company, Inc.

Nixon, K. C., and Wheeler, Q. D. (1990) An Amplification of the Phylogenetic Species Concept. *Cladistics* 6: 211–233.

Ohman, J. C., Krochta, T. J., Lovejoy, C. O., Mensforth, R. P., and Latimer, B. (1997) Cortical Bone Distribution in the Femoral Neck of Hominoids: Implications for the Locomotion of *Australopithecus afarensis*. *American Journal of Physical Anthropology* 104: 117–131.

Paterson, H. E. H. (1985) The Recognition Concept of Species. In E. S. Vrba (ed.), *Species and Speciation* (pp. 21–29). Pretoria: Transvaal Museum, Monograph 4.

Ponce De Léon, M. S. (2002) Computerized Paleoanthropology and Neanderthals: The Case of Le Moustier 1. *Evolutionary Anthropology* (Suppl.) 11: 68–72.

Ride, W. D. L., Cogger, H. G., Dupuis, C., Kraus, O., Minelli, A., Thompson, F. C., and Tubbs, P. K. (eds) (1999) *International Code of Zoological Nomenclature*, 4th edn. London: The Natural History Museum (also available at http://www.iczn.org/iczn/index.jsp).

Simpson, G. G. (1961) *Principles of Animal Taxonomy*. New York: Columbia University Press/ OUP.

Smith, A. B. (1994) *Systematics and the Fossil Record: Documenting Evolutionary Patterns*. Oxford: Blackwell.

Sokal, R. R., and Crovello, T. J. (1970) The Biological Species Concept: A Critical Evaluation. *American Naturalist* 104: 127–153.

Spoor, F., Jeffery, N., and Zonneveld, F. (2000) Using Diagnostic Radiology in Human Evolutionary Studies. *Journal of Anatomy* 197: 61–76.

Tafforeau, P., and Smith, T. M. (2007) Nondestructive Imaging of Hominoid Dental Microstructure Using Phase Contrast X-Ray Synchrotron Microtomography. *Journal of Human Evolution* 54: 272–278.

Tattersall, I., and Eldredge, N. (1977) Fact, Theory and Fantasy in Human Paleontology. *American Scientist* 65: 204–211.

White, T. D., Asfaw, B., Beyene, Y., Haile-Selassie, Y., Lovejoy, C. O., Suwa, G., and Wolde-Gabriel, G. (2009) *Ardipithecus ramidus* and the Paleobiology of Early Hominids. *Science* 326: 75–86.

Wiley, E. O. (1978) The Evolutionary Species Concept Reconsidered. *Systematic Zoology* 27: 17–25.

Wood, B. A. (1991) A Palaeontological Model for Determining the Limits of Early Hominid Taxonomic Variability. *Palaeontologica Africana* 28: 71–77.

Zollikofer, C. P. E., Ponce de León, M. S., Lieberman, D. E., Guy, F., Pilbeam, D., Likius, A., Mackaye, H. T., Vignaud, P., and Brunet, M. (2005) Virtual Cranial Reconstruction of *Sahelanthropus tchadensis*. *Nature* 434: 755–759.

CHAPTER 4

The Study of Human Population Genetics

John H. Relethford

INTRODUCTION

Genetics can be studied at three different levels. Molecular genetics is concerned with the structure and function of DNA and RNA in cells. Mendelian genetics, named after the nineteenth century Austrian priest Gregor Mendel, is concerned with the process of genetic inheritance from one generation to the next. The third level is population genetics, the mathematical theory of genetic changes in a population from one generation to the next (a process known as microevolution). Like Mendelian genetics, population genetics is concerned with the transmission of genetic information from one generation to the next – but for the entire breeding population, and not just for some specific pair of mates.

   Population genetics looks at genetic change in a population by focusing on the frequency of different alleles (the different forms of a gene or DNA sequence), and on the way these frequencies change over time. Imagine, for example, that you are looking at the frequencies of two alleles, *A* and *B*, for a hypothetical genetic locus. You visit a population and you note that the frequency of the *A* allele is 60 percent and the frequency of the *B* allele is 40 percent. Assume that you come back a generation later to find that the frequencies of these alleles are now 58 percent and 42 percent. A small amount of evolution has taken place – the frequency of *A* has gone down and the frequency of *B* has gone up. The study of population genetics looks at the mechanisms by which this type of allele frequency change could take place. The purpose of the present chapter is to review the application of population-genetic theory and methods to the study of genetic variation in human populations.

ELEMENTS OF POPULATION GENETICS

Before looking more closely at how genetic change takes place within populations, it is useful to consider what is meant by a 'population.' In an idealized sense, a population corresponds to a breeding population. The population in this context is usually defined as the local unit within which most mating takes place. For many organisms, including humans, distinct geographic units are often used to delineate populations – for example different towns or villages. This works well in most contexts because, as in the case of many bisexual species, much of human mating is constrained by geography; you are more likely to choose a mate from nearby than one from farther away. Human mate choice can often be more complex, however, and the definition of a population may often have to be reconsidered if one has to deal with other influences on mate choice such as ethnicity, religion, and social class (among others).

What causes genetic change in populations? A principle of population genetics known as the Hardy-Weinberg equilibrium states that, *under certain conditions*, allele and genotype frequencies will remain constant from one generation to the next. When these conditions are not met, then change can occur. One of the conditions of the Hardy-Weinberg equilibrium is random mating within the population. When this condition is violated, as for instance when significant inbreeding occurs within a population, the genotype frequencies are changed in the next generation. Specifically, inbreeding increases the frequencies of homozygotes and decreases the frequency of heterozygotes relative to the case of complete random mating. It is important to remember that deviations from random mating affect only the genotype frequencies, but not the actual allele frequencies.

From a microevolutionary perspective, evolution is defined as a change in allele frequencies over time. There are four mechanisms that cause evolutionary change, and they are known as the evolutionary forces:

1   mutation: random change in the genetic code, which is the ultimate source of all new genetic variation (where new alleles come from);
2   natural selection: differences in the survival and reproduction of different genotypes, causing changes in allele frequencies;
3   genetic drift: random change in allele frequency due to sampling effect (the allele frequencies of an offspring generation are not likely to be the same as the parent generation). Smaller populations show the effect of genetic drift than larger populations;
4   gene flow: the mixing of gene pools from different populations as a function of migration between them.

It is important to remember that these forces can interact in many different and often complex ways. For example, a new mutation will often be lost in a small population because of genetic drift, but in some cases a mutation can actually increase dramatically due to genetic drift. To consider another example, genetic differences between populations may increase as a result of genetic drift, but are reduced by gene flow, which leads to little net change.

The interaction of evolutionary forces affects the level of genetic variation within a population. Mutation increases diversity within a population through the introduction of something new (the mutation itself), which was not there before. Gene flow can also increase diversity in a population when new alleles enter it from another population (for instance a mutation appears in one group, and then spreads to another group via gene flow). On the other hand, genetic drift reduces variation because drift will lead over time to allele frequencies becoming fixed (= 100 percent) or lost (= 0 percent). Either way, genetic diversity will tend to decline over time in a population due to genetic drift. Finally, natural selection can act to increase or decrease genetic variation, depending on initial allele frequencies and on the specific direction of natural selection.

The interaction of the evolutionary forces also affects the level of variation *between* populations (the differences in allele frequencies between them). In general, gene flow reduces the genetic difference between populations because, as populations mix, they become more similar to each other, by analogy with the mixing of different colors of paint. Although gene flow tends to reduce genetic differences between populations, genetic drift tends to increase genetic differences over time, as drift occurs randomly in each population. Natural selection can act toward increasing or decreasing genetic differences between populations, depending on the nature of selection and on differences in environments. In human populations, for example, differences in skin color have increased between different continents because, in our past, darker skin has been selected for in populations at or near the equator, whereas lighter skin has been selected in populations further away from the equator.

It is mathematically and pedagogically useful to learn about the different evolutionary forces one at a time. We need to remember, however, that the genetic makeup of a population, and the genetic relationship between populations within a species, are the net effect of *all* of the evolutionary forces acting at the same time. As demographic and/or environmental conditions change, the net balance of the evolutionary forces can also change. Changes in human cultural adaptations can also affect this balance, as is illustrated in several examples later in this chapter.

A BRIEF HISTORY OF HUMAN POPULATION GENETICS

The mathematical theory of population genetics developed in the early twentieth century due largely to the work of Sewall Wright, Ronald Fisher, and J. B. S. Haldane (Provine 1971). These theoretical developments, combined with field studies and laboratory experiments on microevolution, led to the evolutionary synthesis that combined evolutionary insights from a variety of fields, including zoology, botany, ecology, and paleontology. As population genetics developed, application to human populations also became more common.

Many initial studies of human populations focused on red blood cell groups, which are genetic markers defined by antibody–antigen reactions, including well known systems such as the ABO, Rhesus, and MN blood groups, as well as many others. By the early 1950s, blood group analysis was being used to address questions of population affinity and history (see for instance Boyd 1950).

By the early 1970s, the use of laboratory methods such as electrophoresis (the separation of proteins on the basis of molecular size and electrical charge) had led to a large number of red blood cell proteins and enzymes showing variation among human populations, a rich data set that was being compiled for a variety of questions in human variation and evolution (Crawford 1973). At the same time, the anthropological nature of studies of human population genetics became more widely apparent, and the phrase 'anthropological genetics,' first coined by Derek Roberts (1965), became more widespread. The scope of investigations in human population genetics was then outlined by the classic edited volume *Methods and Theories of Anthropological Genetics* (Crawford and Workman 1973).

Several other key works show the continued growth of human population genetics and the vast array of studies resulting from an expanding body of data on red blood cell and white blood cell genetic markers. Mielke and Crawford's (1980) edited volume collected a number of chapters describing progress in old (and new) areas of study that had developed since the 1973 Crawford and Workman volume. One topic, the study of population structure (described below), was elaborated on in detail by researchers in a separate volume edited by Crawford and Mielke (1982).

By the late 1980s, the development of new methods in molecular biology (such as the polymerase chain reaction) opened up a more precise view on human genetic variation (Crawford 2007). Literally millions of new genetic markers are now being described, and our species' entire genome is being compared with those of our close relatives, the African apes. In addition, the ability to extract ancient DNA from fossils has opened up the potential data set on human genetic variation even further, including by addressing questions concerning our evolutionary relationship to other human ancestors such as the Neandertals. Of course, the analysis of DNA markers that are not subject to recombination, such as mitochondrial DNA (inherited only from one's mother) and Y-chromosome DNA (inherited only from father to son), has revolutionized studies of human migration and ancestry. DNA markers can provide unique information on patterns of human ancestry and migration (Jobling et al. 2004).

THE SCOPE OF HUMAN POPULATION GENETICS RESEARCH TODAY

There is a number of different areas of study within the field of human population genetics. One area is the study of population structure, which looks at the effect of geographic, demographic, and cultural influences on the genetic relationship between individuals and populations. That is, how is a population structured? Human populations are frequently structured by geographic location, social class, ethnicity, language differences, and other factors, and the study of population structure seeks to determine the genetic impact of these factors.

Another related area of study is the analysis of population origins and history. That is, what is (are) the ancestral origin(s) of a population? How are populations related to one another over time? Which populations are most closely related to each other, and what are the historical reasons for these relationships? Our focus here is on the origin and evolution of populations, and quite often such studies are used to help answer historical questions.

Studies of population structure and history focus on overall patterns of genetic similarity that reflect the interaction between mutation, gene flow, and genetic drift. Where possible, the objective is to get an estimate of genetic similarity averaged over as many different loci as possible, and to look at neutral traits – those not affected by natural selection (or presumed to be unaffected, or minimally affected, by it). Natural selection in this context is 'noise' interfering with the ability of the researcher to discover the 'signal,' which is a picture of population structure or history. For example, one would not want to base interpretations of population affinity on the frequency of the lactase persistence allele, which has been selected for in populations with a history of dairy farming. If we find two populations which have a high and similar frequency of the lactase persistence allele and we do not take into account the action of natural selection, we might incorrectly infer that the two populations are related. As another example, consider skin color. Both sub-Saharan Africans and Melanesians have very dark skin color, but this common phenotype cannot be used to argue for a close historical connection between the two, because both populations have dark skin color because of adaptation to a similar environment: they live near the equator, where dark skin helps protect against the damaging effects of ultraviolet radiation.

In studies of human population structure and history, we want to exclude such traits because they would distort the signal of population relatedness that we were looking for. In other cases, however, the situation will be reversed, and the objective will be to detect and analyze natural selection. In such cases, what counts as 'signal' and what counts as 'noise' is reversed. Studies of natural selection are interested in the history of a specific trait and in how it originated and evolved.

A focus on single genes or traits is also the concern of studies of genetic epidemiology that seek to unravel the interaction between genetic and environmental (in the broadest sense) factors affecting phenotypes. Much research today is geared toward understanding genetic correlates of disease and physiology and the way these genes vary across populations.

All of the areas of study in human population genetics have benefited enormously from the ongoing revolution in molecular genetics. It is important to realize, however, that these newer markers have supplemented, but not replaced, the earlier massive data sets on genetic markers based on red and white blood cell polymorphisms (these are often referred to collectively as 'classical genetic markers'). Although the newer DNA markers are preferable in many kinds of analyses, much information can still be gleaned from the analysis of classical genetic markers, particularly given the much larger number of populations for which data has been collected (see for example Roychoudhury and Nei 1988). An excellent example of the use of classical genetic markers is the comprehensive volume of L. L. Cavalli-Sforza and colleagues, *The History and Geography of Human Genes* (Cavalli-Sforza et al. 1994), which examines global and regional studies of the relationship of genetic variation to geographic distance and population history.

It is important to note that much progress has also been made in the area of using information on quantitative traits such as craniofacial, dental, and anthropometric measures in a population-genetic context. Analysis of such traits is sometimes ignored in studies of population genetics, because these traits are affected by environmental and developmental factors. Although classical genetic markers and DNA markers are preferred for many studies, analysis of quantitative traits can also be valuable (Relethford 2007). Comparison of patterns of variation of quantitative traits and genetic markers provides information on the relative influence of genetics and environment on quantitative traits. A number of studies have shown that, although quantitative traits *are* affected by environmental and developmental factors, this influence does not erase patterns of genetic relationship between populations (Relethford 2004a). Thus, quantitative traits can be used successfully in studies of population structure and history. A growing number of studies of skeletal biology have used these principles to address questions of prehistoric population history (for instance Steadman 2001).

All of these areas of research in human population genetics are clearly anthropological in nature, and not just because the species of interest are human beings. The anthropological nature of human population genetics is apparent in every avenue of study. Mate choice, for example, is something that is affected by cultural factors. Marriage preferences and rules affect levels of inbreeding, and sociocultural variables such as ethnicity, religion, and social class (among others) can have a direct genetic impact in terms of inbreeding and gene flow. Culture also effects demography, specifically the size and growth of the population, which in turn affects genetic drift. Cultural adaptations can affect the nature of genetic adaptations, thus having a direct effect on patterns of natural selection; as humans change their cultural and physical environment, they can change the rate and direction of natural selection. In short, human population genetics is yet one more way of looking at the traditional anthropological view of interactions between culture, biology, and nature.

Although much of the underlying genetic and mathematical basis of human population genetics is the same as that of any other organisms, be they fruit flies or guinea pigs, there are also models and methods that apply specifically to humans. Gene flow, for example, is often much easier to study in human populations because one can simply ask a person about the birthplace of one's parents, whereas tracking gene flow in other species is more complicated. A number of demographic measures (births, deaths, population size) are easier to track in human populations, at least ones that keep records.

Thus, some population genetic methods are often more useful in the study of human populations. One example is migration matrix analysis, where predictions of the balance between gene flow and genetic drift are made on the basis of migration patterns and population size (see Rogers and Harpending 1986). This method allows for the comparison between patterns of genetic variation which are based on recent demographic patterns and those observed from genetic data (Jorde et al. 1982). Genealogical data are also useful in studies of human population genetics, providing insight into patterns of inbreeding and genetic drift (Cavalli-Sforza et al. 2004). An additional source of data on human population genetics that is uniquely human is surnames, which can be used to reconstruct inbreeding and population affinities (see Lasker 1985; Relethford 1988).

EXAMPLES OF STUDIES OF HUMAN POPULATION STRUCTURE

The remainder of this chapter focuses on selected examples of some of the past and current studies of human population genetics conducted by anthropologists. These examples are not meant to provide either a comprehensive review of the literature or a detailed examination of selected case studies. Instead, the purpose here is to give a flavor of some of the major avenues of research in human population genetics.

As noted above, human populations are not homogenous randomly mating units, but are instead divided into a number of subpopulations. Two primary measures are of interest in studies of subdivided populations. One is the *degree* of genetic differentiation among the subpopulations, F_{ST}, where higher values of F_{ST} indicate greater genetic impact of subdivision. The second measure of interest is the *pattern* of genetic differentiation, usually assessed using a measure of genetic distance that tells us which subpopulations are most closely related to each other, and by how much.

As noted above, subdivision can occur because of sociocultural factors. For example, studies of human populations have looked at religion (Crawford et al. 1995), social class (Harrison 1995), and language differences (Friedlaender 1975) among other factors. By far the most widely studied aspect of population structure has been the effect of geographic distance. As shown in numerous studies, geographic distance limits gene flow, such that human populations in many cases tend to be genetically most similar to their geographic neighbors and less similar to populations farther away – a phenomenon known as 'isolation by distance,' which is also seen in many other organisms (it is not exclusive to humans). Greater amounts of geographic isolation result in greater levels of genetic differentiation (F_{ST}) among populations. Isolation by distance also results in a correlation between measures of geographic and genetic distance. Some of the many studies of isolation by distance in human populations are referenced in Jorde (1980), Crawford and Mielke (1982), and Cavalli-Sforza et al. (1994).

EXAMPLES OF STUDIES OF HUMAN POPULATION HISTORY

Studies of human population structure were frequent in the 1970s and 1980s. Although population structure remains an important focus area of human population genetics, a major focus in recent years has been on the study of human population history. Genetic data have been used to investigate questions of historical origin for local, regional, continental, and global levels of analysis (see Olson 2002 and Relethford 2003 for general surveys). Many early studies of population history have used classical genetic markers and quantitative traits, most often drawing inferences regarding population origins and affinities from analyses of genetic distance. New methods of analyzing DNA markers have allowed even greater precision in answering questions of ancestral origin because of their ability to track mutations across time and space, providing a record of past migrations.

Many studies of population history focus on the initial origin of populations. One example is the origin of the first Americans. For decades, biological data – including cranial measures, dental measures, classical genetic markers – and archaeological evidence have pointed to an origin in Northeast Asia (Crawford 1998). DNA markers have confirmed this hypothesis (Schurr 2000). At present, genetic and archaeological studies continue to seek greater resolution of the movement of humans into the New World, including on questions concerning the number, route(s), and timing of migration events. Much current work on the level and pattern of genetic diversity among Native Americans suggests that the initial settlement of the New World may have resulted from a single migration event, although this hypothesis is not yet conclusively proved (Goebel et al. 2008).

Another example of analysis of origins is the case of the origin of Polynesians. Archaeological evidence shows that humans began dispersing out of South/Southeast Asia eastward into the Pacific starting about 3,330 years ago. Seafaring skills and outrigger canoes allowed the ancestors of modern-day Polynesians to spread rapidly across the Pacific Ocean, settling as far away as New Zealand, Hawaii, and Easter

Island. Because the early Polynesians expanded past Melanesia, a region settled tens of thousands of years earlier, the question has arisen as to exactly how fast the Polynesians expanded and if they interbred with Melanesian populations during their expansion. The origin of Polynesians has often been discussed in terms of a rapid expansion with little, if any, interbreeding ('the express train model') versus a slower expansion with more Melanesian gene flow ('the slow boat model'). Early genetic studies were difficult to resolve, as analyses of mitochondrial DNA supported the express train model and analyses of Y-chromosome DNA supported the slow boat model. One difficulty of mitochondrial DNA and Y-chromosome DNA studies is that they each rely on a single locus and may not always provide a clear picture of overall genetic affinity. A recent study of a very large number of DNA markers (687 microsatellites and 203 insertion/deletion loci) provides a much clearer picture of population relationships and supports the view that Polynesian ancestors moved quickly past Melanesia, with little intermixture (Friedlaender et al. 2008).

Genetic analysis of population history has also been used to investigate archaeological hypotheses. An example is the nature of the spread of agriculture into Europe. The archaeological record shows that agriculture began spreading out of the Middle East into Europe about 9,000 years ago, moving in a northwest direction over the next several thousand years. What was less clear, however, was exactly *how* this happened. One model ('demic diffusion') proposes that farming populations expanded out of the Middle East into Europe, spreading both agriculture and their genes as they mixed with pre-existing populations in Europe. Another model ('cultural diffusion') suggests that *only* agriculture spread as a new idea adopted by more and more populations over time. Both models account for the spread of agriculture as a new cultural idea, but under the demic diffusion model, *both* genes and culture spread across Europe, whereas under cultural diffusion only the idea spread. Therefore, the demic diffusion model predicts that genetic traits should show the same geographic pattern (a gradient from southeast to northwest), whereas there would be no correlation with genetics under cultural diffusion. Spatial analysis of allele frequencies of classical genetic markers has been used to test these hypotheses. The primary geographic pattern across dozens of loci shows a clear gradient from southeast to northwest, paralleling the spread of agriculture and supporting the demic diffusion model (see for instance Cavalli-Sforza et al. 1993).

Studies of human population history often look at the intermixture of different human groups that come together for a variety of historical reasons; these include, but are not limited to, colonization, slavery, warfare, and trade. The result is admixed populations with complex patterns of ancestry, often from source populations that are widely scattered geographically. Events following the contact of Europeans with native populations in the New World led to varying degrees of mixture between Native American, European, and African populations. Genetic admixture studies have been conducted in Mexico (Crawford 1976), Belize (Crawford 1984), and African American populations (Parra et al. 1998, 2001).

One example of admixture analysis has been the study of the population genetics of African American populations. The enslavement and transportation of Africans to the New World led to gene flow between African and European populations. Admixture studies have long used genetic data to estimate the approximate percentage of European ancestry in African American populations. One of the most comprehensive analyses of European admixture in African Americans was conducted by Parra et al. (1998, 2001), who looked at the frequency of DNA markers in twelve African American populations compared with frequencies in European and African populations representative of ancestral source populations. Given these frequencies, the total amount of accumulated ancestry since the founding of the African American gene pool can be estimated (this is the total amount of ancestry over many generations). Parra and colleagues found that there was considerable variation in European ancestry, ranging from 4 percent in the Gullah of South Carolina to 23 percent in New Orleans. These figures are averages for the entire sample. Ancestry of individuals within each sample also varied: some African Americans had almost no European ancestry, whereas others had over half of their ancestry from Europe. Such results show that a culturally defined group such as that of African Americans actually encompasses a wide range of genetic ancestry, and that treating African Americans or any other group as biologically homogeneous is an error.

GLOBAL PATTERNS OF GENETIC VARIATION AND THE ORIGIN OF MODERN HUMANS

An increasing number of studies have looked at the relationship between genetic variation, history, and geography on a *global* basis, using the findings to make inferences regarding the origin and dispersal of our species. Many anthropologists interpret the fossil record as also showing an African origin, as the earliest known anatomically modern human forms are found in Africa 200,000 years ago, much earlier than elsewhere in the world. Although the idea of an initial African origin is accepted by most, there is still uncertainty about what happened after modern humans began expanding out of Africa and encountered archaic humans outside of Africa, such as the Neandertals of Europe. Some argue for complete replacement; others, for some degree of interbreeding whereby archaic genes were assimilated into the gene pool of modern humans (Smith et al. 2005). Over the past two decades, population genetic analyses have produced several lines of evidence that support an African origin of our species. Analytic methods have been developed that use DNA sequences to reconstruct a gene tree, which shows evolutionary relationships between genetic variants and can be used to estimate information on the time and geographic origin of the most recent common ancestor. A number of studies have looked at common ancestry for different genes and DNA sequences. To date, most gene trees show an African root, which is compatible with the idea of an African origin of our species; but the issue of possible intermixture outside of Africa is still debated (Relethford 2008).

An African origin is also compatible with the observation that many genetic markers (and quantitative traits) show higher levels of diversity in Africa than elsewhere. These regional differences in diversity have been interpreted as a reflection of the history of our species. Under an African origin model, human populations existed for a longer time in Africa than elsewhere, and these populations had more time to accumulate mutations, which led to an increase in genetic diversity over time. Later, when modern human populations began expanding out of Africa, the initially small group of founders who dispersed out of Africa would have had reduced diversity, as smaller founding groups usually lose diversity because of genetic drift. Thus, modern human populations outside of Africa would have had less time to accumulate as many mutations, and therefore the pattern would be the one we see today, of higher diversity in Africa. Further, there is a geographic pattern of diversity in our species, with levels of genetic diversity decreasing with geographic distance from Africa. This pattern might be due to a series of sequential founding events, whereby new populations split off from older populations as the species dispersed (Ramachandran et al. 2005). It is not clear, however, how much of the regional differences in diversity might reflect instead the possibility of larger population size in Africa in the past, as population size also affects levels of diversity (Relethford 2008).

Globally, there is a strong relationship between genetic distance and geographic distance, particularly after adjusting for known routes of migration of early humans (for instance the geographic distance associated with movement from Asia to the New World via Siberia rather than a straight-line distance across the oceans. The correlation between genetics and geography is seen in classical genetic markers, DNA markers, and craniometric traits. It is not clear to what extent this relationship is due to the limiting effect of geographic distance on gene flow (isolation by distance) and/or to a geographic pattern structured by the dispersal of modern humans out of Africa (Relethford 2004b).

Although genetic and fossil evidence both point to an African origin, the debate over replacement versus assimilation continues, particularly in prehistoric Europe, where Neandertals and modern humans overlapped in time before the Neandertals disappeared. Did Neandertals become extinct through replacement, or did they disappear by being assimilated into a larger gene pool (Smith et al. 2005)? Ancient DNA recovered from Neandertal fossils has been used to answer this question. To date, small sequences of mitochondrial DNA have been recovered from fifteen Neandertal fossils (Hodgson and Disotell 2008), and an entire mitochondrial DNA sequence has been recovered from one Neandertal (Green et al. 2008). Preliminary nuclear DNA sequences have also been recovered (Hodgson and Disotell 2008). All of these results show that Neandertal DNA is different from that of living humans, and there is no evidence of Neandertal ancestry in a modern human fossil dating back 28,000 years ago (Caramelli et al. 2008). To date, the evidence is consistent with an early divergence of the Neandertal line (about 500,000 years ago) and little, if any, interbreeding (Hodgson and Disotell 2008), although further work will be needed to rule out the possibility of small levels of interbreeding and genetic drift leading to loss of Neandertal DNA in living humans.

STUDIES OF RECENT NATURAL SELECTION IN HUMAN POPULATIONS

Studies of the history of specific genes often focus on the role of natural selection, particularly in recent human evolution, where population dispersals, adaptations to widely different environments, and cultural revolutions such as the origin and spread of agriculture and civilization could lead to genetic changes in human populations. For example, the dispersal of humans into different environments has led to major differences in human skin color because of varying levels of ultraviolet radiation. In populations at or near the equator, selection has favored darker skin for protection against the damaging effects of too much ultraviolet radiation, such as folate deficiency, sunburn, and skin cancer. For populations whose ancestors dispersed far from the equator, where ultraviolet radiation levels are lower, the problem was that they had too little exposure to ultraviolet radiation, which would have led to a reduction in vitamin-D levels; hence the selection for lighter skin (Jablonski and Chaplin 2000).

Genetic responses to changing cultural conditions have also been a focus of studies of natural selection in human populations. The classic example is Livingstone's (1958) analysis of the distribution of the sickle cell hemoglobin allele (S) in West Africa. Higher frequency of the sickle cell allele is found in populations that have experienced frequent malaria, because individuals with one copy of this allele are resistant to malarial infection and have higher fitness than individuals with either no S alleles (normal hemoglobin) or two S alleles (sickle cell anemia). The case of the sickle cell and malaria is a classic example of balancing selection, where having *one* copy of an allele gives higher fitness than having none or two copies. Livingstone went further in his analysis, outlining the way in which humans changed the environment by bringing horticulture into the area several thousand years ago: this created more favorable conditions for the spread of the mosquito population that carried the malaria parasite. As malaria spread, people with one copy of the S allele were selected for, leading to an increase in the frequency of S. Thus, cultural change led to environmental change, which in turn led to genetic change.

Another example of recent human evolution through natural selection is the selection for lactase persistence in populations with a history of dairy farming. As mammals, humans produce the enzyme lactase to digest milk sugar from breastfeeding. The normal pattern is to cease production of lactase early in life after weaning. In human populations that have become reliant on dairy farming, there has been selection for an allele that allows for the production of lactase throughout adult life, as the ability to digest milk ensures additional nutrition and water. Recent analyses show that different mutations leading to lactase persistence have been selected for in different parts of the world over the past 7,000 years, which is the estimated age of these mutations (Tishkoff et al. 2007).

As research on molecular genetics continues, we are likely to see an increasing number of examples of recent selection in human evolution. Statistical analysis of the human genome suggests that more of our genome has been shaped by natural selection than was thought to be the case several decades ago. Contrary to the oft-stated view that human evolution no longer occurs, it seems likely that natural selection will continue and, given the huge size of our species, the potential for new mutations with every generation is higher than ever (Hawks et al. 2007).

Conclusion

The study of human population genetics has grown considerably in the last fifty years, as has our knowledge of the cultural, demographic, geographic, and ecological factors that affect genetic variation at different levels, ranging from the local population to the entire species. New sources of data have continued to provide new windows on genetic variation, as have new analytic methods and advances in the mathematical theory of genetic change. At present, the field is increasingly focused on the immense amount of data becoming available from the revolution in molecular genetics. The challenge for future generations is to find new and efficient ways of analyzing these data and not drown in them.

REFERENCES

Boyd, W. C. (1950) *Genetics and the Races of Man.* Boston: Little, Brown and Company.

Caramelli, D., Milani, E., Vai, S., Modi, A., Pecchioli, E., Girardi, M., Pilli, E., Lari, M., Lippi, B., Ronchitelli, A., Mallegni, F., Casoli, A., Bertorelle, G., and Barbujani, G. (2008) A 28,000 Years Old Cro-Magnon mtDNA Sequence Differs from All Potentially Contaminating Modern Sequences. *PLoS One* 3(7): e2700. doi: 10.1371/journal.pone.0002700.

Cavalli-Sforza, L. L., Menozzi, P., and Piazza, A. (1993) Demic Expansions and Human Evolution. *Science* 259: 639–646.

Cavalli-Sforza, L. L., Menozzi, P., and Piazza, A. (1994) *The History and Geography of Human Genes.* Princeton: Princeton University Press.

Cavalli-Sforza, L. L., Moroni, A., and Zei, G. (2004) *Consanguinity, Inbreeding, and Genetic Drift in Italy.* Princeton: Princeton University Press.

Crawford, M. H. (1973) The Use of Genetic Markers of the Blood in the Study of the Evolution of Human Populations. In M. H. Crawford and P. L. Workman (eds), *Methods and Theories of Anthropological Genetics* (pp. 19–38). Albuquerque: University of New Mexico Press.

Crawford, M. H. (ed.) (1976) *The Tlaxcaltecans: Prehistory, Demography, Morphology, and Genetics.* University of Kansas Publications in Anthropology No. 7. Lawrence: University of Kansas.

Crawford, M. H. (ed.) (1984) *Current Developments in Anthropological Genetics,* Vol. 3. *Black Caribs: A Case Study in Biocultural Adaptation.* New York: Plenum Press.

Crawford, M. H. (1998) *The Origins of Native Americans: Evidence from Anthropological Genetics.* Cambridge: Cambridge University Press.

Crawford, M. H. (ed.) (2007) *Anthropological Genetics: Theory, Methods and Applications.* Cambridge: Cambridge University Press.

Crawford, M. H., Koertvlyessy, T., Huntsman, R. G., Collins, M., Duggirala, R., Martin, L., and Keeping, D. (1995) Effects of Religion, Economics, and Geography on Genetic Structure of Fogo Island, Newfoundland. *American Journal of Human Biology* 7: 437–451.

Crawford, M. H., and Workman, P. L. (eds) (1973) *Methods and Theories of Anthropological Genetics.* Albuquerque: University of New Mexico Press.

Crawford, M. H., and Mielke, J. H. (eds) (1982) *Current Developments in Anthropological Genetics,* Vol 2. *Ecology and Population Structure.* New York: Plenum Press.

Friedlaender, J. S. (1975) *Patterns of Human Variation: The Demography, Genetics, and Phenetics of Bougainville Islanders.* Cambridge: Harvard University Press.

Friedlaender, J. S., Friedlaender, F. R., Reed, F. A., Kidd, K. K., Kidd, J. R. Chambers, G. K., Lea, R. A., Loo, J.-H., Koki, G., Hodgson, J. A., Merriwether, D. A., and Weber, J. L. (2008) The Genetic Structure of Pacific Islanders. *PLoS Genetics* 4 (1): e19 (doi: 10.1371/journal.pgen.0040019).

Goebel, Ted, Waters, M. R., and O'Rourke, D. H. (2008) The Late Pleistocene Dispersal of Modern Humans in the Americas. *Science* 319: 1497–1502.

Green, R. E., Malaspinas, A. S., Krause, A., Briggs, W., Johnson, P. L. F., Uhler, C., Meyer, M., Good, J. M., Maricic, T., Stenzel, U., Prüfer, K., Siebauer, M., Burbano, H. A., Ronan, M., Rothberg, J. M., Egholm, M., Rudan, P., Brajković, P., Kućan, Ž., Gušic, I., Wikström, M., Laakkonen, L., Kelso, J., Slatkin, M., and Pääbo, S. (2008) A Complete Neanderthal

Mitochondrial Genome Sequence Determined by High-Throughput Sequencing. *Cell* 134: 416–426.

Harrison, G. A. (1995) *The Human Biology of the English Village*. Oxford: Oxford University Press.

Hawks, J., Wang, E. T., Cochran, G. M., Harpending, H. C., and Moyziz, R. K. (2007) Recent Acceleration of Human Adaptive Evolution. *Proceedings of the National Academy of Sciences, USA* 104: 20753–20758.

Hodgson, J. A., and Disotell, T. R. (2008) No Evidence of a Neanderthal Contribution to Modern Human Diversity. *Genome Biology* 9: 206 (doi: 10.1186/gb-2008-9-2-206).

Jablonski, N. G., and Chaplin, G. (2000) The Evolution of Human Skin Coloration. *Journal of Human Evolution* 39: 57–106.

Jobling, M. A., Hurles, M., and Tyler-Smith, C. (2004) *Human Evolutionary Genetics: Origins, Peoples and Disease*. New York: Garland.

Jorde, L. B. (1980) The Genetic Structure of Subdivided Human Populations: A Review. In J. H. Mielke and M. H. Crawford (eds), *Current Developments in Anthropological Genetics*, Vol. 1. *Theory and Methods* (pp. 135–208). New York: Plenum Press.

Jorde, L. B., Workman, P. L., and Eriksson, A. W. (1982) Genetic Microevolution in the Åland Islands, Finland. In J. H. Mielke and M. H. Crawford (eds), *Current Developments in Anthropological Genetics*, Vol. 1. *Theory and Methods* (pp. 333–366). New York: Plenum Press.

Lasker, G. W. (1985) *Surnames and Genetic Structure*. Cambridge: Cambridge University Press.

Livingstone, F. B. (1958) Anthropological Implications of Sickle Cell Gene Distribution in West Africa. *American Anthropologist* 60: 533–562.

Mielke, J. H., and Crawford, M. H. (eds) (1980) *Current Developments in Anthropological Genetics*, Vol. 1. *Theory and Methods*. New York: Plenum Press.

Olson, S. (2002) *Mapping Human History: Genes, Race, and Our Common Origins*. Boston: Mariner Books.

Parra, E. J., Marcini, A., Akey, J., Martinson, J., Batzer, M. A., Cooper, R., Forrester, T., Allison, D. B., Deka, R., Ferrell, R. E., and Shriver, M. D. (1998) Estimating African American Admixture Proportions by Use of Population-Specific Alleles. *American Journal of Human Genetics* 63: 1839–1851.

Parra, E. J., Kittles, R. A., Argyropoulos, G., Pfaff, C. L., Heister, K., Bonilla, C., Sylvester, N., Parrish-Gause, D., Garvey, W. T., Jin, L., McKeigue, P. M., Kamboh, M. I., Ferrell, R. E., Pollitzer, W. S., and Shriver, M. D. (2001) Ancestral Proportions and Admixture Dynamics in Geographically Defined African Americans Living in South Carolina. *American Journal of Physical Anthropology* 114: 18–29.

Provine, W. B. (1971) *The Origins of Theoretical Population Genetics*. Chicago: University of Chicago Press.

Ramachandran, S., Deshpande, O., Roseman, C. C., Rosenberg, N. A., Feldman, M. W., and Cavalli-Sforza, L. L. (2005) Support from the Relationship of Genetic and Geographic Distance in Human Populations for a Serial Founder Effect Originating in Africa. *Proceedings of the National Academy of Sciences, USA* 102: 15942–15947.

Relethford, J. H. (1988) Estimation of Kinship and Genetic Distance from Surnames. *Human Biology* 60: 475–492.

Relethford, J. H. (2003) *Reflections of Our Past: How Human History is Revealed in Our Genes*. Boulder: Westview Press.

Relethford, J. H. (2004a) Boas and Beyond: Migration and Craniometric Variation. *American Journal of Human Biology* 16: 379–386.

Relethford, J. H. (2004b) Global Patterns of Isolation by Distance Based on Genetic and Morphological Data. *Human Biology* 76: 499–513.

Relethford, J. H. (2007) The Use of Quantitative Traits in Anthropological Genetic Studies of Population Structure and History. In M. H. Crawford (ed.), *Anthropological Genetics: Theory, Methods and Applications* (pp. 187–209). Cambridge: Cambridge University Press.

Relethford, J. H. (2008) Genetic Evidence and the Modern Human Origins Debate. *Heredity* 100: 555–563.

Roberts, Derek F. (1965) Assumption and Fact in Anthropological Genetics. *Journal of the Royal Anthropological Institute of Great Britain and Ireland* 95: 87–103.

Rogers, A. R., and Harpending, H. C. (1986) Migration and Genetic Drift in Human Populations. *Evolution* 40: 1312–1327.

Roychoudhury, A. K., and Nei, M. (1988) *Human Polymorphic Genes: World Distribution.* New York: Oxford University Press.

Schurr, T. G. (2000) Mitochondrial DNA and the Peopling of the New World. *American Scientist* 88: 246–253.

Smith, F. H., Janković, I., and Karavanić, I. (2005) The Assimilation Model, Modern Human Origins in Europe, and the Extinction of Neandertals. *Quaternary International* 137: 7–19.

Steadman, D. W. (2001) Mississippians in Motion: A Population Genetic Analysis of Interregional Gene Flow in West–Central Illinois. *American Journal of Physical Anthropology* 114: 61–73.

Tishkoff, S. A., Reed, F. A., Ranciaro, A., Voight, B. F., Babbitt, C. C., Silverman, J. S., Powell, K., Mortensen, H. M., Hirbo, J. B., Osman, M., Ibrahim, M., Omar, S. A., Lema, G., Nyambo, T. B., Ghori, J., Bumpstead, S., Pritchard, J. K., Wray, G. A., and Deloukas, P. (2007) Convergent Adaptation of Human Lactase Persistence in Africa and Europe. *Nature Genetics* 39: 31–40.

5 Human Molecular Genetics: The DNA Revolution and Variation

Dennis H. O'Rourke

INTRODUCTION

Anthropological geneticists have been documenting patterns of genetic variation in the study of population history and human adaptability for over seventy-five years (Crawford 2007; O'Rourke 2003). Until recently, this research effort was focused on classical markers typed in human blood samples (O'Rourke 2006). But the field has been transformed in the last twenty years by what has come to be known as the molecular revolution. The earlier reliance on primary (proteins) or secondary (blood groups) gene products has given way to a direct assessment of variation in DNA sequences that underlie both the downstream products of genes, as well as documenting variation in regions of the genome not involved in protein coding.

SOME MOLECULAR BASICS

In a practical sense, the molecular revolution began with Watson and Crick's (1953) discovery of the double-helical structure of DNA (Figure 5.1). This structural insight made sense of the previously observed equality among the four bases (adenine, thymine, guanine and cytosine) that were components of DNA. In any DNA preparation, the amount of adenine always equaled thymine, while the concentrations of guanine and cytosine were equally equivalent. Given the new insight regarding DNA structure, it became clear that guanine and cytosine were complementary and existed in a paired form, as did adenine and thymine. Subsequently, the fact that three adjacent nucleotide bases in a DNA sequence determined a specific amino acid, which are the building blocks of proteins, helped reveal the molecular and biochemical dynamics of protein synthesis. By the 1980s, more efficient molecular and biochemical methods had been developed to isolate DNA from tissue and blood samples, and technological innovations were introduced to facilitate the generation of DNA sequence data, and therefore the documentation of sequence diversity among individuals.

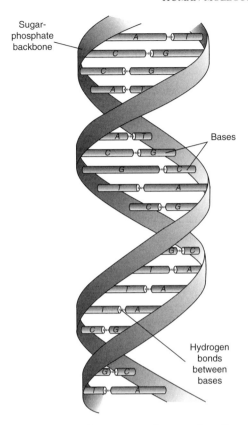

Figure 5.1   Double-stranded DNA indicating complementarity of bases, G-C and T-A. Figure by R. W. O'Rourke

A development that had a particularly important impact on anthropological genetics was the introduction of the Polymerase Chain Reaction (PCR) by Mullis in 1984. PCR emulates a normal cellular function. During cell division, DNA molecules need to be duplicated in order for each new daughter cell to contain the full complement of chromosomes required for normal cellular function. This duplication is accomplished by the 'unzipping' of double-stranded DNA into single strands and, under the influence of an enzyme (a polymerase), the complementary nature of DNA bases (A-T and C-G) results in the generation of a new, synthetic strand of DNA, complementary to the original strand. This new strand and the original template strand then re-establish the double-stranded structure of the original molecule. PCR performs a very similar series of reactions, first by using heat denaturation to dissolve the bonds holding the DNA double helix together, which yields single-stranded DNA. By designing short DNA fragments of around twenty bases (oligonucleotides) that are complementary to known DNA sequences, the addition of an appropriate polymerase will result in the creation of a new, synthetic strand, complementary to an existing single strand.

The PCR process is achieved in three separate steps, each taking place at a specific temperature. The first one, as already noted, is denaturation, designed to produce single-stranded DNA templates. The second step is annealing, which takes place at a lower temperature that allows the short oligonucleotide fragments, known as 'primers,' to bind to their complementary sequences on the template strand. The final step, termed 'extension,' involves the introduction of the appropriate polymerase to catalyze the synthesis of the new, complementary strand from the sites of the existing primers. Careful primer design results in the production of two double-stranded DNA molecules that contain the same specific sequence, bounded by the primers. Repeating this three-step procedure through multiple cycles results in a geometric increase in the amount of DNA sequence of interest.

This procedure became the workhorse of molecular genetic labs around the world starting in the 1980s and helped make the molecular revolution accessible to anthropological genetic labs. It also made it possible to manipulate and study specific DNA sequences extracted from prehistoric source material (Hofreiter et al. 2001; Gilbert et al. 2004; O'Rourke 2007). Although this DNA (now known as ancient DNA or aDNA) is routinely degraded to small size and is often acquired in conjunction with enzymatic inhibitors and contaminants, the sensitivity of PCR has made it possible to study the genetic variation in prehistoric populations directly, rather than relying on indirect methods.

PATTERNS OF VARIATION

Each individual actually possesses two independent genomes. One, the nuclear genome, is located in the nucleus of each cell, is comprised of DNA packaged into twenty-three pairs of linear structures called 'chromosomes' (Figure 5.2), and is biparentally inherited, with half of the genome coming from each parent. It is also quite large, being comprised of approximately 3 billion base pairs. The second genome is located within the mitochondria – small organelles responsible for cellular metabolism in the cytoplasm of each cell that contain their own unique genome. The mitochondrial genome differs from the nuclear genome in important ways. It is a comparatively small, circular molecule of just over 16,500 base pairs (bp) (Figure 5.3). It is exclusively maternally inherited, and is comprised almost entirely of coding sequence. This contrasts sharply with the nuclear genome, where the majority of the sequence is not involved in coding for protein product. The mitochondrial genome contains genes involved in electron transport and oxidative phosphorylation (which are important steps in oxidative metabolism), as well as in the ribosomal and transfer RNA genes required to synthesize those proteins. It should be noted, however, that most of the genes required for the oxidative metabolism are found in the nuclear genome, are synthesized outside the mitochondria, and are later imported in.

Two important aspects of the mitochondrial genome that have made it so useful to human population geneticists are its high copy number per cell and the fact that there exists no molecular editing machinery in the mitochondria. Although the nuclear genome is much larger than the mitochondrial genome, there is only one diploid copy of it in each cell. But each cell may contain many mitochondrial organelles, each with multiple copies of its genome, such that there are typically hundreds of copies of the mitochondrial genome per cell. This high copy number helps explain why the mitochondrial genome (mtDNA) has been so widely used in ancient DNA studies (see Kaestle's chapter in this volume). Like all organic material, nucleic acids degrade postmortem. However, the very high number of mtDNA molecules per cell makes it

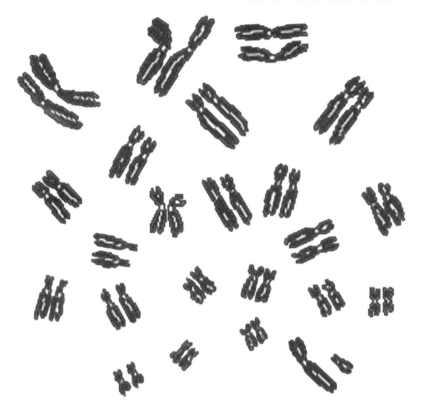

Figure 5.2   Normal human karyotype showing the full complement of chromosomes in the nucleus during cell division. Each chromosome has already been duplicated, hence the 'X' shapes of each chromosome. Figure by R. W. O'Rourke

much more likely that a target sequence of interest will persist for some time after the death of the organism. The likelihood that it can be accessed, amplified via PCR, and sequenced is greater than is true for the single cellular copy of the nuclear genome. The second important property of mtDNA, the lack of an editing function in the mitochondria, means that molecular copy errors, mutations, are not corrected as they occur, as is usually the case in the nuclear genome. Rather, they accumulate rapidly, generating a greater degree of mtDNA diversity in a shorter time period than is possible in the nuclear genome. As a result, mtDNA sequences provide insight into population dynamics and evolutionary events in a comparatively recent period of the past. The temporal window into which we can look with mtDNA sequence data is approximately the same as that afforded by archaeology – on the order of centuries or a few millennia. The slower evolutionary rate of much of the nuclear genome provides instead a window into the deeper past.

The uniparental inheritance of mtDNA also means that diversity in this molecule only informs us about the history of maternal lineages. Fortunately, there is an analog in the nuclear genome for paternal lineages: the Y-chromosome. Among other things, Y-chromosome genes are involved in sex determination during embryogenesis and are transmitted from fathers to sons. Thus, while everyone possesses mtDNA inherited from their mothers, only males possess a Y-chromosome in the nuclear genome

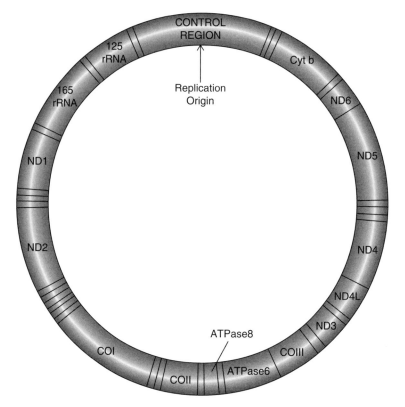

Figure 5.3   The circular structure of mitochondrial DNA. Figure by R. W. O'Rourke

inherited from their fathers. These two uniparentally inherited genomes, then, permit historical tracking of maternal and paternal lineages, respectively, over time. Because the Y-chromosome is part of the nuclear genome, with its sophisticated molecular editing machinery, the two genomes evolve at different rates, occasionally leading to inferred disparities in male and female evolutionary histories.

In addition to being much larger in size than the mtDNA genome, the nuclear genome is also more complex in other ways. The 3-billion plus bases that constitute the nuclear genome are arrayed in forty-six linear chromosomes: twenty-three pairs of autosomes and two sex chromosomes (X and Y). The traditional view is that the DNA sequences that comprise each chromosome define a series of genes that determine the production of protein, or other gene products, important for normal cellular function. On this view, genes are thought of as being arrayed along the chromosomes like 'beads on a string.' Moreover, the genes are considered to be unitary entities of DNA sequence, with variation arising through changes in nucleotide sequences. The modern view of the genome differs substantially from this historical, traditional characterization (Human Genome Project Information, www.genomics.energy.gov).

The structure of genes is more complex than it was once thought. Genes are DNA sequences that contain both sequences involved in the translation of proteins, called 'exons,' and stretches of intervening sequence, called 'introns,' which are not involved in the translation of DNA sequence to protein (Figure 5.4). The average gene in the human genome has just over eight exonic regions and a comparable number of

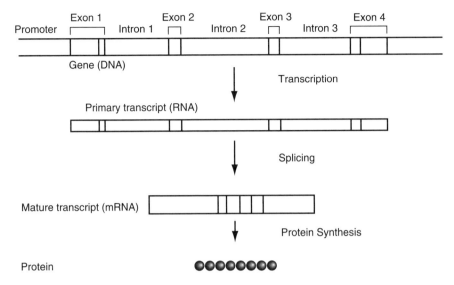

Figure 5.4 Gene structure illustrating placement of promoter, exons and introns in a DNA strand, and schematic relationship to protein synthesis. Figure by R. W. O'Rourke

introns. Both exons and introns are translated during protein synthesis, but the intronic sequences are spliced out of the transcripts prior to translation. Indeed, alternative splicing sites within genes and between exons and introns likely provide much of the genetic diversity we see in the constellation of proteins produced. This helps explain, in part, why the human genome appears to have only 20,000–25,000 genes, rather than the 100,000 genes hypothesized prior to the sequencing of the human.

Of the known genes, the function of nearly 50 percent remain unknown. Moreover, genes tend to be clustered in apparently random sections in the genome, being separated by large tracts of non-coding DNA. Indeed, less than 2 percent of the nuclear genomic sequence codes for protein products. A large fraction of the genome (about 50 percent) is composed of non-coding repeat sequences. The repeats may be characterized by short (2–6 bases, microsatellites), medium (10–70 bases, minisatellites) or long (hundreds to thousands of bases, SINES (Short Interspersed Elements) and LINES (Long Interspersed Elements) repeat motifs. The shorter repeat motifs are usually repeated in tandem fashion, while the longer repeat motifs are dispersed thoughout the genome. Although most of the non-coding sequence, including repeat sequences, is of unknown function, it is becoming clear that it is likely to be involved in gene regulation and expression. For example, there are substantial stretches of DNA sequence in non-coding regions that are known to be conserved across species. Such conservation of DNA sequences across large segments of evolutionary time is typically associated with important cellular functions to the organism. Thus, these conserved non-coding regions (CNRs) are generally thought to be involved in some fundamental regulatory pathway that we have yet to identify. It is known that areas of the genome where coding regions are clustered tend to be bounded by long tracts of guanine–cytocine (GC) repeats. The repeated guanine–cytosine base pairs (called 'CpG islands') are subject to chemical modification or methylation. Methylation is important in turning genes on and off during periods of development, and therefore it is clearly involved in gene regulation and expression. Thus, many of the non-coding regions, repeats and CNRs alike, may be involved in basic regulatory functions that we are only beginning to appreciate. Such regulatory activity by non-coding regions would contribute to the phenotypic diversity we see as a result of alterations in, for example, growth and development that would not be reflected in protein diversity.

GENOMICS, ADAPTABILITY AND ANTHROPOLOGY

Genes, language, and geography

Anthropological geneticists have long been interested in using patterns of genetic variation to more clearly discern population histories, particularly the population and demographic details of colonization (for instance Tishkoff and Gonder 2007; Arredi et al. 2007; O'Rourke and Raff in press). A major question that has occupied the time and efforts of geneticists interested in reconstructing population histories is whether geography or language plays a greater role in structuring population genetic variation. A strong case for either one can be made, *a priori*, as a significant force in patterning genetic variation.

There is a rich, quantitative area of population genetic theory which predicts that geography should be a dominant factor in the distribution of genetic variation. The logical basis of this is clear. Many demographic studies have demonstrated that individuals tend to select mates who live nearer to them rather than farther away. If this is generally true and is a practice followed over time, then individuals residing in geographic proximity will tend to be more closely related, genetically, than those residing at greater distances. This principle is known as isolation by distance in population genetics, and it predicts that geography should be a primary factor in the distribution of genetic variation. A similar, logically obvious case can be made for language as a factor in the patterning of genetic variation. It seems intuitively obvious that individuals are more likely to select mates with whom they can easily communicate – that is, who speak the same, or a similar, language. If this is true, then language and related cultural aspects of mate selection may be important modifiers in the distribution of genetic variation, independently of geography. Since languages and language families also exhibit geographic structure, it has been difficult to document unequivocally the relative importance of either.

In an early study of classical marker variation in Native American populations, Spuhler (1972) argued that the pattern of variation between tribal groups reflected geographic distances between them better than did the distribution of genetic variation between languages or language groups. With the advent of molecular markers, it has become possible to investigate the relative contributions of geography and language on a finer scale. In most instances, geography does seem to have a greater effect than language on the distribution of genetic variation, but the latter is not without effect.

Hunley and Long (2005) investigated mitochondrial DNA variation in many Native American populations distributed throughout the Americas. They found that, irrespective of the language classification system used, language was a worse predictor of genetic affinity than was geography. More recently, Novembre and colleagues (2008) studied the distribution of variation at over 500,000 single nucleotide polymorphisms (SNPs) distributed across the genome in almost 3,200 individuals across Europe. Not all of the single nucleotides assayed were equally informative or polymorphic, and the final analysis focused on over 197,000 loci. Similarly, the final sample size of individuals was reduced to just fewer than 1,400 individuals after controlling for those with ancestry outside Europe and with grand-parental ancestry from more than one European location. Despite the reduction in the number of markers and individuals analyzed, this study was far larger than any that could have been done using older, classical markers. The results show clearly that the pattern of genetic variation in Europe replicates the geography of Europe. The use of a Principal Components Analysis, which reduces the large data array to a smaller set of independent factors, resulted in observed correlations between the first two principal components and latitude and longitude greater than 0.85. Indeed, using multiple regression methods to predict geographic origin from the genetic data resulted in over 50 percent of individuals being placed within 310 kilometers of their actual place of origin and over 90 percent being placed within 700 kilometers of their point of origin. This is remarkable geographic precision from genetic data on a continental scale.

In a simultaneous and independent study, Lao and colleagues (2008) reached similar conclusions. These authors also used the Affymetrix 500K SNP chip to assay genetic variation in over 2,500 individuals distributed across twenty-three European subpopulations. The result of this study was to find strong correlations between geographic and genetic distances among the European subpopulations, reflecting the strong influence of geography on the genetic structure of the European continent. As Lao and his team (2008), as well as others, have observed, Europe is characterized by reduced genetic variation relative to some other continental populations. That the effects of geography are so evident here, despite the lack of overall genetic variation, suggests that the effects of geography on patterns of genetic variation might be even more easily documented in other regions (Africa, Asia) once large-scale genetic surveys are completed for multiple populations in these continental areas.

It is important to note that the strong role of geography in structuring genetic variation in Europe does not mean that other factors are completely unimportant. In a worldwide survey of 377 microsatellite loci, Belle and Barbujani (2007) found that, while genetic differences between populations reflect geographic distances more closely than linguistic differentiation between them does, linguistic diversity did have an observable, although small, effect, independently of geography. In the European survey of Novembre and colleagues (2008), reducing the scale of analysis from continental to a more regional scale resulted in the observation that the distribution of variation in Switzerland corresponded to the distribution of linguistic areas within the country – areas which, of course, were also correlated with geography.

In comparing studies such as those described above, several issues should be kept in mind. First, scale of analysis is of considerable import. It makes a difference whether the geographical scale is regional, continental, or global. Second, the type of molecular genetic marker studied can also be important. For example, Lao and colleagues (2008) and Novembre and colleagues (2008) assayed variation in a large number of SNPs in European populations. Belle and Barbujani (2007) studied microsatellite (STR) variation. The latter evolve much more rapidly than the former, due to different mutational mechanisms. Thus, the nature of the variation being studied and the evolutionary history of the markers may be quite different and may need to be accommodated in any population level analysis. Nevertheless, analytical methods have been developed to accommodate the different types of molecular markers in population genetic studies, and the scope, volume, and level of resolution afforded by molecular marker data is substantially greater than anything that could have been imagined by earlier workers studying genetic variation in classical marker systems.

Molecular genetics, human adaptability, and diet

Human biologists have long known that most human populations follow the general mammalian pattern of losing the ability to digest lactose shortly after weaning. However, a few populations of the world, notably European and some African groups, maintain their ability to digest lactose into adulthood. Exactly how and when this dietary adaptation arose has been of critical interest to those interested in human adaptation and dietary evolution (Simoons 1978; Holden and Mace 1997).

Lactose is a disaccharide found in milk. It is digested to monosaccarides (simple sugars) more useable by the gut by the enzyme lactase-phlorizin hydrolase (LPH). In most human populations the production of LPH declines following weaning, such that after about the age of 5 most people can no longer digest the lactose in milk. It has long been observed that the ability to consume milk into adulthood is correlated with a history of herding and dairying (Holden and Mace 1997). Although it seemed obvious that the genetic basis of the ability to continue to digest lactose after childhood must involve variation in the gene encoding lactase (*LCT*, located at 2q21), no such polymorphism had been identified. With the advent of molecular screening, the genetic basis of this important adaptive trait has been clarified (Wooding 2007).

Enattah and colleagues (2002) demonstrated that, while variation in *LCT* sequences was not obviously associated with LPH persistence, a single nucleotide polymorphism in a neighboring gene, *MCM6*, was strongly associated with lactase persistence. This SNP is a C-to-T transition (that is, a a change from cytocine to thymine in the base sequence of DNA) in intron 13 of the *MCM6* gene (C/T-13910), and it is located 14kb (kb = a thousand bases) from *LCT*. Although not located in the *LCT* gene itself, this remote polymorphism appears to have a regulatory effect on *LCT* promoter activity. Curiously, this strong association between marker and lactase persistence is only predictive of the lactose digestion phenotype in Europeans, but not in lactase persistent populations elsewhere. In a subsequent study of molecular diversity and lactose absorption phenotypes in East African populations, Tishkoff and colleagues (2007) identified three additional SNPs (G/C-14010, T/G-13915, and C/G-13907), also in the 13th intron of *MCM6*, associated with LPH persistence in African populations. Out of these three SNPs, only the G/C-14010 variant is widely distributed at appreciable frequency in multiple African populations. None of the forty-three African populations studied by Tishkoff and colleagues possessed the C/T-13910 SNP predictive of lactase persistence in Europeans.

The result of these molecular analyses indicates that the genetic basis for lactase persistence and for the adaptation to adult consumption of the nutritionally rich milk of domesticated animals has arisen at least twice. The European and African forms of lactase persistence are the result of separate and independent mutations, brought to high frequency by natural selection. Both mutations appear to have regulatory roles on *LCT*, although they are not found within the lactase gene (*LCT*) itself. Indeed, both mutations are found within intronic sequences of a neighboring gene. The simple story of selection for persistent lactase production via *LCT* variants in herding populations is now known to be more complex, with at least two separate molecular bases for the trait in different geographic regions. The picture may be even more complicated, as Enattah and colleagues (2008) have recently identified yet a third genetic variant: a compound allele of two different SNPs (also occurring in *MCM6* introns), which is associated with lactase persistence in Middle Eastern populations. Thus similar but distinct molecular mechanisms may account for three separate and independent origins for lactase persistence in humans.

Another example of the molecular underpinnings of dietary evolution is the salivary enzyme amylase and its role in starch hydrolysis. Starch is a significant, and increasing, component of diet in agricultural populations and in some populations of hunter–gatherers in arid environments, but it is of lesser significance in tropical forest or arctic populations. Salivary amylase is responsible for starch hydrolysis and is controlled by the gene *AMY1* known to be characterized by variable copy number in humans (Groot et al. 1989).

Perry and colleagues (2007) demonstrated that the number of *AMY1* copies in individual genomes correlated strongly with amylase protein level in human saliva, and that individual populations characterized by high starch diets have, on average, more copies of the *AMY1* gene than individuals in populations characterized by low starch diets. These investigators studied three populations with high starch diets (European Americans, Japanese, and Hadza hunter-gatherers) and four populations with low starch diets (Biaka and Mbuti tropical forest hunter–gatherers, Datog pastoralists, and Yakut pastoralist/fishers). Results of the *AMY1* copy number analysis across these populations indicated that the high starch diet populations had significantly more copies of the *AMY1* gene than the low starch populations. The proportion of individuals in the high starch diet populations that had at least six copies of the *AMY1* gene was 70 percent, whereas the comparable figure for the low starch populations was only about 35 percent. Since both the high and the low starch diet populations were widely distributed, with both including African and Asian populations, the result is unlikely to be due to simple models of geography or shared ancestry. Rather, it appears that diet predicts *AMY1* copy number better than geography, which suggests that selection based on dietary starch has driven up *AMY1* copy number in high starch diet populations.

Perry and colleagues (2007) extended their analysis to chimps and bonobos to clarify the origin of the increased copy number observed in some human populations. In a sample of fifteen wild chimpanzees, all exhibited two diploid copies of *AMY1*. Among bonobos, a gain in *AMY1* copy number was observed, but the sequence data suggest that the copies may not be functional. Thus, among the great apes tested – which consume only small amounts of starch in their diets – *AMY1* copy number has apparently not expanded as it has in humans, and this fact strengthens the inference that copy number expansion is a result of dietary selection. Moreover, sequence diversity in *AMY1* gene sequences suggests that the copy number expansion has occurred in humans within the past 200,000 years or so (Perry et al. 2007). If this is true, then it means that the expansion process may be an example of direct selection acting during the time of the evolutionary transition to modern humans.

Finally, the ability to taste phenylthiocarbamide (PTC) has long intrigued biological anthropologists and geneticists. This synthetic compound was found to taste bitter to some individuals, but seemed tasteless to others as a result of a laboratory accident (Fox 1932). The taste sensitivity to the compound appeared to be familial, and the phenotypes of tasting and non-tasting led to the inference of a simple, single, biallelic locus for control of the sensory polymorphism (Wooding 2006). At first, the existence of a genetic system controlling the ability to taste a synthetic compound was puzzling, but in the end it became clear that the compound resembled compounds found in the Brassica family of plants, which occasionally act as thyroid stressors. Thus, the system was viewed as another case of dietary adaptation at the genetic level.

Although R. A. Fisher and colleagues documented at an early date that the taste polymorphism for PTC also existed in the great apes (Fisher et al. 1939) and inferred an ancient origin for the polymorphism and for any adaptation associated with it, the genetic basis for the taste sensitivity remained elusive. The general model was one of a single locus with two alleles, where one allele conferred the ability to taste PTC (and closely related compounds), while the alternative allele, presumably damaged or non-functional, resulted in an inability to taste the compounds. The molecular genetic architecture of the trait was finally elucidated by Kim and colleagues (2003) and Drayna and colleagues (2003), who demonstrated that 50–80 percent of the variation in PTC taste sensitivity is accounted for by molecular variation at the *TAS2R38* locus. Most of the variation at this locus accounting for PTC taste sensitivity derives from two haplotypes, a 'taster' and a 'non-taster' haplotype.

Knowing the molecular genetic basis for PTC taste sensitivity has led to a change in perspective on this sensory polymorphism. Molecular characterization of each haplotype revealed that the 'non-taster' variant was not simply a damaged or non-functional version of the 'taster' haplotype. Rather, the 'taster' and 'non-taster' haplotypes differ by only three amino acids, and both appear to be fully functional. The 'non-taster' haplotype may be the basis for a functional receptor of some family of compounds that does not contain PTC. While no specific ligand for the 'non-taster' haplotype has been identified, some plant compounds have been identified that are 'tasted' by PTC non-tasters, but not by PTC tasters. Further functional studies of a variety of plant compounds and of their relationships to taste sensitivity and molecular characterization are required to elucidate more fully the evolutionary history of this interesting sensory and dietary polymorphism.

One additional component to the PTC story has also been clarified by the newer molecular genetic studies. Fisher and colleagues (Fisher et al. 1939), having documented PTC taste sensitivity in the great apes, concluded that the PTC taste polymorphism was of ancient origin, predating the human–ape differentiation. Molecular analysis has again refined our understanding of the evolution of this system. While the molecular genetic analysis of *TAS2R38* sequence variation in human populations has led to the inference of balancing selection as the origin of the observed variation (Wooding et al. 2004), it cannot account for the PTC taste sensitivity pattern observed in chimpanzees. Like humans, chimps have two PTC taste sensitivity alleles at *TAS2R38*. However, the two alleles are much more similar in chimps than in humans. In chimps, the 'non-taster' allele derives from a single SNP in the start codon, changing it from ATG to AGG and resulting in a non-functional protein. This origin of the 'non-taster' allele in chimps is quite different from that of the functional, but still 'non-taster,' allele in humans, which differs by three amino acid substitutions from the 'taster' allele. Thus Wooding and colleagues (2004) have demonstrated that, while humans and chimps both possess 'taster' and 'non-taster' alleles at *TAS2R38* in roughly equivalent frequencies, the non-taster alleles are quite different in structure and in molecular mechanism and indicate that, in the primate lineage, 'non-tasting' alleles at this locus have evolved twice, independently (Wooding et al. 2004; Wooding 2006).

Population genomics and morphological variation

The role of morphological variation in documenting human population history and evolution is the subject of other chapters in this volume, so little time and space need be allotted to it here. However, it is worth observing that the metric and meristic variation which has for over a century characterized physical anthropological investigations of human diversity and evolution are now being augmented by molecular analyses. It has long been assumed that the metric variation exhibited by human populations (stature, weight, cranial and dental metrics), as well as the discrete traits (meristic variants in the crania and dentition) reflected variation in underlying genes affecting morphological development, and therefore were informative analogs for genetic variation. On the basis of heritability estimates, for example, 80 percent of the variation in adult stature may be genetically determined (Silventoinen et al. 2003). Certainly human stature is a complex multifactorial trait, which results from the interaction of alleles at multiple loci along with environmental variation in diet, prenatal environment, and disease exposure, among others. Recently, the molecular technology afforded by large-scale marker screening and by the use of Genome Wide Association Studies (GWAS) has begun to identify some of the specific genes responsible for adult stature.

The first GWAS study of adult stature, by Weedon and colleagues (2007), indicated that common variants in the *HMGA2* gene were associated with variation in stature in both adults and children, but that they accounted for very little of the observed variation in stature. Sanna and colleagues (2008) examined over 2 million SNPs in over 6,500 individuals in Finland and Sardinia, to investigate additional sources of genetic variation for stature. These authors identified two linked genes on chromosome 20: *GDF5* (growth differentiation factor 5) and *UQCC* (a ZIC-binding protein suppressed by a fibroblast growth factor); these genes were found to contribute to variation in adult stature in the samples (Sanna et al. 2008). Both genes have functional roles in growth, such that alterations in them could plausibly have effects not only on growth rates and trajectories, but also on human height. The variants identified by Sanna and colleagues are also important in the risk of osteoarthritis. Their effects were estimated to add up to 0.44 cm of stature – a fairly small effect on the overall variation in human stature.

More recently, three research groups (Gudbjartsson et al. 2008; Weedon et al. 2008; Lettre et al. 2008) published three additional GWAS on human height that added at least forty new genomic variants with significant effects on the variation in stature. The sample sizes employed in these studies are daunting, ranging from nearly 15,000 to over 30,000 individuals in the initial screening phase (which identified 95 promising variants), to approximately half those sample sizes in the validation stage. Using a SNP chip array to screen over 500,000 markers in each individual, the 54 variants ultimately identified have an average effect size of 0.4 cm on stature (Visscher 2008). Collectively, these newly identified variants account for only a small proportion of variation in adult stature. Although helping confirm the traditional view of stature as a complex character with many underlying genes, the identification of such genomic variants for complex traits is important in speeding up the discovery of the functional gene products involved in the developmental pathways contributing to height and other complex phenotypes of interest.

Large genomic scans on large samples is an expensive enterprise, which takes such projects beyond the scope of most individual investigators. It is worth noting, however, that the GWAS for height described in the above studies was not actually undertaken to investigate the genetic architecture of stature. Rather, the samples were pooled from earlier studies, where genomic screens had been performed to identify disease susceptibility genes for various diseases (Visscher 2008). But in each of these studies height had been recorded, permitting a subsequent meta-analysis of the genomic data, combined with the recorded statures. This emphasizes for our discipline the potentially fruitful nature of collaborative research with investigators of diverse interests and the importance of training in statistical and quantitative analyses in the future of biological anthropology. These studies also emphasize the developing capacity to screen rapidly large population samples for ever larger arrays of molecular markers, making it likely that the genetic architecture of complex morphological traits like stature, among others (such as BMI, Willer et al. 2009; obesity, Thorleifsson et al. 2009), will succumb to molecular genetic analysis in the foreseeable future, thus providing greater precision and resolution to the historical data on human morphological variation.

REFERENCES

Arredi, B., Poloni, E. S., and Tyler-Smith, C. (2007) The Peopling of Europe. In M. H. Crawford (ed.), *Anthropological Genetics: Theory, Methods, and Applications* (pp. 380–408). Cambridge: Cambridge University Press.

Belle, E. M. S., and Barbujani, G. (2007) Worldwide Analysis of Multiple Microsatellites: Language Diversity Has a Dectectable Influence on DNA Diversity. *American Journal of Physical Anthropology* 133: 1137–1146.

Crawford, M. H. (ed.) (2007) *Anthropological Genetics: Theory, Methods, and Applications.* Cambridge: Cambridge University Press.

Drayna, D. H., Coon, Kim, U. K., Elsner, T., Cromer, K., Otterud, B., Baird, L., Peiffer, A. P., and Leppert, M. (2003) Genetic Analysis of a Complex Trait in the Utah Genetic Reference Project: A Major Locus for PTC Taste Ability on Chromosome 7q and a Secondary Locus on Chromosome 16p. *Human Genetics* 112: 567–572.

Enattah, N. S., Sahi, T., Savilahti, E., Terwilliger, J. D., Peltonen L., and Jarvela, I. (2002) Identification of a Variant associated with Adult-Type Hypolactasia. *Nature Genetics* 30: 233–237.

Enattah, N. S., Jensen, T. G. K., Nielsen, M., Lewinski, R., Kuokkanen, M., Rasinpera, H., El-Shanti, H., Seo, J. K., Alifrangis, M., Khalil, I. F., Natah, A., Ali, A., Nateh, S., Comas, D., Mehdi, S. Q., Groop, L., Vestergaard, E. M., Imtiaz, F., Rashed, M. S., Meyer, B., Troelsen, J., and Peltonen, L. (2008) Independent Introduction of Two Lactase-Persistence Alleles into Human Populations Reflects Different History of Adaptation to Milk Culture. *American Journal of Human Genetics* 82: 57–72.

Fisher, R. A., Ford, E. B., and Huxley, J. (1939) Taste-Testing the Anthropoid Apes. *Nature* 144: 750.

Fox, A. L. (1932) The Relationship between Chemical Constitution and Taste. *Proceedings of the National Academy of Sciences, USA* 18: 115–120.

Gilbert, M. T. P., Wilson, A. S., Bunce, M., Hansen, A. J., Willerslev, E., Shapiro, E., Higham, T. F. G., Richards, M. P., O'Connell, T. C., Tobin, D. J., Janaway, R. C., and Cooper, A. (2004) Ancient Mitochondrial DNA from Hair. *Current Biology* 14: R463–R464.

Groot, P. C., Bleeker, M. J., Pronk, J. C., Arwert, F., Mager, W. H., Planta, R. J., Eriksson, A. W., and Frants, R. R. (1989) The Human Alpha-Amylase Multigene Family Consists of Haplotypes with Variable Numbers of Genes. *Genomics* 5: 29–42.

Gudbjartsson, D. F., Walters, G. B., Thorleifsson, G., Steffansson, H., Halldorsson, B. V., Zusmanovich, P., Sulem, P., Thorlacius, S., Gylfason, A., Steinberg, S., Helgadottir, A., Ingason, A., Steinthorsdottir, V., Olafsdottir, E. J., Olafsdottir, G. H., Jonsson, T., Borch-Johnsen, K., Hansen, T., Andersen, G., Jorgensen, T., Pedersen, O., Aben, K. K., Witjes, J. A., Swinkels, D. W., den Heijer, M., Franke, B., Verbeek, A. L. M., Becker, D. M., Yanek, L. R., Becker, L. C., Tryggvadottir, L., Rafnar, T., Gulcher, J., Kiemeney, L. A., Kong, A., Thorsteinsdottir, U., and Stefansson, K. (2008) Many Sequence Variants Affecting Diversity of Adult Human Height. *Nature Genetics* 40: 609–615.

Hofreiter, M., Serre, D., Poinar, H. N., Kuch, M., and Pääbo, S. (2001) Ancient DNA. *Nature Reviews Genetics* 2: 353–359.

Holden, C., and Mace, R. (1997) Phylogenetic Analysis of the Evolution of Lactose Digestion in Adults. *Human Biology* 69: 605–628.

Human Genome Project Information. www.genomics.energy.gov.

Hunley, K., and Long, J. C. (2005) Gene Flow across Linguistic Boundaries in Native North American Populations. *Proceedings of the National Academy of Sciences, USA* 102: 1312–1317.

Kim, U. K., Jorgenson, E., Coon, H., Leppert, M., Risch, N., and Drayna, D. (2003) Positional Cloning of the Human Quantitative Trait Locus Underlying Taste Sensitivity to Phenylthiocarbamide. *Science* 299: 1221–1225.

Lao, O., Lu, T. T., Nothagel, M., Junge, O., Freitag-Wolf, S., Caliebe, A., Balascakova, M., Bertranpetit, J., Bindoff, L. A., Comas, D., Holmlund, G., Kiouvatsi, A., Macek, M., Mollet, I., Parson, W., Palo, J., Ploski, R., Sajantila, A., Tagliabracci, A., Gether, U., Werge, T., Rivadeneira, F., Hofman, A., Uitterlinden, A. G., Gieger, C., Wichmann, H.-E., Rüther, A., Schreiber, S., Becker, C., Nürnberg, P., Nelson, M. R., Krawczak, M., and Kayser, M. (2008) Correlation between Genetic and Geographic Structure in Europe. *Current Biology* 18: 1241–1248.

Lettre, G., Jackson, A.U., Gieger, C., Schumacher, F. R., Berndt, S. I. Sanna, S., Eyheramendy, S., Voight, B. F., Butler, J. L., Guiducci, C., Illig, T., Hackett, R., Heid, I. M., Jacobs, K. B., Lyssenko, V., Uda, M., The Diabetes Genetics Initiative, FUSION, KORA, The Prostate, Lung Colorectal and Ovarian Cancer Screening Trial, The Nurses' Health Study, SardiNIA, Boehnke, M., Chanock, S. J.,Groop, L. C., Hu, F. B., Isomaa, B., Kraft, P., Peltonen, L., Salomaa, V., Schlessinger, D., Hunter, D. J., Hayes, R. B., Abecasis, G. R., Wichmann, H.-E., Mohlke, K. L., and Hirschhorn, J. N. (2008) Identification of Ten Loci Associated with Height Highlights New Biological Pathways in Human Growth. *Nature Genetics* 40: 584–591.

Novembre, J., Johnson, T., Bryc, K., Kutalik, Z., Boyko, A. R., Auton, A., Indap, A., King, K. S., Bergmeann, S., Nelson, M. R., Stephens, M., and Bustamante, C. D. (2008) Genes Mirror Geography within Europe. *Nature* 456: 98–101.

O'Rourke, D. H. (2003) Anthroplogical Genetics in the Genomic Era: A Look Back and Ahead. *American Anthropologist* 105: 101–109.

O'Rourke, D. H. (2006) Classical Marker Variation in Native North Americans. In D. H. Ubelaker (ed.), *Handbook of North American Indians*, Vol. 3. *Environment, Origins and Population* (pp. 762–776). Washington DC: Smithsonian Institution.

O'Rourke, D. H. (2007) Ancient DNA and Its Application to the Reconstruction of Human Evolution and History. In M. H. Crawford (ed.), *Anthropological Genetics: Theory, Methods and Applications* (pp. 210–231). Cambridge: Cambridge University Press.

O'Rourke, D. H., and Raff, J. (in press) A Genetic Perspective on American Colonization. *Current Biology.*

Perry, G. H., Dominy, N. J., Claw, K. G., Lee, A. S., Fiegler, H., Redon, R., Werner, J., Villanea, F. A., Mountain, J. L., Misra, R., Carter, N. P., Lee, C., and Stone, A. C. (2007) Diet and the Evolution of Human Amylase Gene Copy Number Variation. *Nature Genetics* 39: 1256–1260.

Relethford, J. H. (2008) Geostatistics and Spatial Analysis in Biological Anthropology. *American Journal of Physical Anthropology* 136: 1–10.

Sanna, S., Jackson, A. U., Nagaraja, R., Willer, C. J., Chen, W.-M., Bonnycastle, L. L., Shen, H., Timpson, N., Lettre, G., Usala, G., Chines, P. S., Stringham, H. S., Scott, L. J., Dei, M., Lai, S., Albai, G., Crisponi, L., Naitza, S., Doheny, K.F., Pugh, E. W., Ben-Shlomo, Y., Ebrahim, S., Lawlor, D. A., Bergman, R. N., Watanabe, R. M., Uda, M., Tuomilehto, J., Coresh, J., Hirschhorn, J. N., Shuldiner, A. R., Schlessinger, D., Collins, F. S., Smith, G. D., Boerwinkle, E., Cao, A., Boehnke, M., Abecasis, G. R., and Mohlke, K. L. (2008) Common Variants in the GDF5–UQCC Region are Associated with Variation in Human Height. *Nature Genetics* 40: 198–203.

Silventoinen, K., Sammalisto, S., Perola, M., Boomsma, D. I., Cornes, B. K., Davis, C. Dunkel, L., de Lange, M., Harris, J. R., Hjelmborg, J. V. B., Luciano, M., Martin, N. G., Mortensen, J., Nisticò, L., Pedersen, N. L., Skytthe, A. Spector, T. D., Stazi, M. A., Willemsen, G., and Kaprio, J. (2003) Heritability of Adult Body Height: A Comparative Study of Twin Cohorts in Eight Countries. *Twin Research* 6: 399–408.

Simoons, F. J. (1978) The Geographic Hypothesis and Lactose Malabsorption. A Weighing of the Evidence. *American Journal of Digestive Diseases* 23: 963–980.

Spuhler, J. N. (1972) Genetic, Linguistic, and Geographical Distances in Native North America. In J. S. Weiner and J. Huizinga (eds), *The Assessment of Population Affinities in Man* (pp. 72–95). Oxford: Clarendon Press.

Thorleifsson, G., Walters, G. B., Gudbjartsson, D. F., Steinthorsdottir, V., Sulem, P., Helgadottir, A., Styrkarsdottir, U., Gretarsdottir, S., Thorlacius, S., Jonsdottir, I., Jonsdottir, J., Olafsdottir, E. J., Olafsdottir, G. H., Jonsson, T., Jonsson, F., Borch-Johnsen, K., Hansen, T., Andersen, G., Jorgensen, T., Lauritzen, T., Aben, K. K., Verbeek, A. L. M., Roeleveld, N., Kampman, E., Yanek, L. R., Becker, L. C., Tryggvadottir, L., Rafnar, T., Becker, D. M., Gulcher, J., Kiemeney, L. A., Pedersen, O., Kong, A., Thorsteinsdottir, U., and Stefansson, K. (2009) Genome-wide association yields new sequence variants at seven loci that associate with measures of obesity. *Nature Genetics* 41: 18–24.

Tishkoff, S. A., Reed, F. A., Ranciaro, A. Voight, B. F., Babbitt, C. C., Silverman, J. S., Powell, K., Mortensen, H. M., Hirbo, J. B., Osman, M., Ibrahim, M., Omar, S. A., Lema, G., Nyambo, T. B., Ghori, J., Bumpstead, S., Pritchard, J. K., Wray, G. A., and Deloukas, P. (2007) Convergent Adaptation of Human Lactase Persistence in Africa and Europe. *Nature Genetics* 39: 31–40.

Tishkoff, S. A, and Gonder, M. K. (2007) Human Origins Within and Out of Africa. In M. H. Crawford (ed.), *Anthropological Genetics: Theory, Methods, and Applications* (pp. 337–379). Cambridge: Cambridge University Press.

Visscher, P. M. (2008) Sizing up Human Height Variation. *Nature Genetics* 40: 489–490.

Watson, J. D., and Crick, F. H. C. (1953) Molecular Structure of Nucleic Acids: A Structure for Deoxyribonucleic Acid. *Nature* 171: 964–969.

Weedon, M. N., Lettre, G., Freathy, R. M., Lindgren, C. M., Voight, B. F., Perry, J. R. B., Elliott, K. S., Hackett, R., Guiducci, C., Shields, B., Zeggini, E., Lango, H., Lyssenko, V., Timpson, N. J., Burtt, N. P., Rayner, N. W., Saxena, R., Ardlie, K., Tobias, J. H., Ness, A. R., Ring, S. M., Palmer, C. N. A., Morris, A. D., Peltonen, L., Salomaa, V., The Diabetes Genetics Initiative, The Wellcome Trust Case Control Consortium, Smith, G. D., Groop, L. C., Hattersley, A. T., McCarthy, M. I., Hirschhorn, J. N., and Frayling, T. M. (2007) A Common Variant of HMGA2 Is Associated with Adult and Childhood Height in the General Population. *Nature Genetics* 39: 1245–1250.

Weedon, M. N., Lango, H., Lindgren, C. M., Wallace, C., Evans, D. M., Mangino, M., Freathy, R. M., Perry, J. R. B., Stevens, S., Hall, A. S., Samani, N. J., Shields, B., Prokopenko, I. Farrall, M., Dominiczak, A., Diabetes Genetics Initiative, The Wellcome Trust Case Control Consortium, Johnson, T., Bergmann, S., Beckmann, J. S., Vollenweider, P., Waterworth, D. M., Mooser, V., Palmer, C. N. A., Morris, A. D., Ouwehand, W. H., Cambridge GEM Consortium, Caulfield, M., Munroe, P. B., Hattersley, A. T., McCarthy, M. I., and Frayling, T. M. (2008) Genome-Wide Association Analysis Identifies 20 Loci that Influence Adult Height. *Nature Genetics* 40: 575–583.

Willer, C. J., Speliotes, E. K., Loos, R. J. F., Li, S., Lindgren, C. M., Heid, I. M., Berndt, S. I., Elliott, A. L., Jackson, A. U., Lamina, C., Lettre, G., Li, N., Lyon, H. N., McCarroll, S. A., Papadakis, K., Qi, L., Randall, J. C., Roccasecca, R. M., Sanna, S., Scheet, P., Weedon, M. N., Wheeler, E., Zhao, J. H., Jacobs, L. C., Prokopenko, I., Soranzo, N., Tanaka, T., Timpson, N. J., Almgren, P., Bennett, A., Bergman, R. N., Bingham, S. A., Bonnycastle, L. N., Brown, M., Burtt, N. P., Chines, P., Coin, L., Collins, F. S., Connell, J. M., Cooper, C., Smith, G. D., Dennison, E. M., Deodhar, P., Elliott, P., Erdos, M. R., Estrada, K., Evans, D. M., Gianniny, L., Gieger, C., Gillson, C. J., Guiducci, C., Hackett, R., Hadley, D., Hall, A. S., Havulinna, A. S., Hebebrand, J., Hofman, A., Isomaa, B., Jacobs, K. B., Johnson, T., Jousilahti, P., Jovanovic, Z., Khaw, K., Kraft, P., Kuokkanen, M., Kuusisto, J., Laitinen, J., Lakatta, E. G., Luan, J., Luben, R. N., Mangino, M., McArdle, W. L., Meitinger, T., Mulas, A., Munroe, P. B., Narisu, N., Ness, A. R., Northstone, K., O'Rahilly, S., Purmann, C., Rees, M. G., Ridderstra, M., Ring, S. M., Rivadeneira, F., Ruokonen, A., Sandhu, M. S., Saramies, J., Scott, L. J., Scuteri, A., Silander, K., Sims, M. A., Song, K., Stephens, J., Stevens, S., Stringham, H. M., Tung, Y. C. L., Valle, T. T., Van Duijn, C. M., Vimaleswaran, K. S., Vollenweider, P., Waeber, G., Wallace, C., Watanabe, R. M., Waterworth, D. M., Watkins, N., The Wellcome Trust Case Control Consortium, Witteman, J. C. M., Zeggini, E., Zhai, G., Zillikens, M. C., Altshuler, D., Caulfield, M. J., Chanock, S. J., Farooqi, I. S., Ferrucci, L., Guralnik, J. M., Hattersley, A. T., Hu, F. B., Jarvelin, M.-R., Laakso, M., Mooser, V., Ong, K. K., Ouwehand, W. H., Salomaa, V., Samani, N. J., Spector, T. D., Tuomi, T., Tuomilehto, J., Uda, M., Uitterlinden, A. G., Wareham, N. J., Deloukas, P., Frayling, T. M., Groop, L. C., Hayes, R. B., Hunter, D. J., Mohlke, K. L., Peltonen, L., Schlessinger, D., Strachan, D. P., Wichmann, H.-E., McCarthy, M. I., Boehnke, M., Barroso, I., Abecasis, G. R., & Hirschhorn, J. N. for the GIANT Consortium (2009) Six New Loci Associated with Body Mass Index Highlight a Neuronal Influence on Body Weight Regulation. *Nature Genetics* 41: 25–34.

Wooding, S., Kim, U., Bamshad, M. J., Larsen, J., Jorde, L. B., and Drayna, D. (2004) Natural Selection and Molecular Evolution in PTC, a Bitter-Taste Receptor Gene. *American Journal of Human Genetics* 74: 637–646.

Wooding, S. (2006) Phenylthiocarbamide: A 75-Year Adventure in Genetics and Natural Selection. *Genetics* 172: 2015–2023.

Wooding, S. (2007) Following the Herd. *Nature Genetics* 39: 7–8.

6 Deconstructing Race: Racial Thinking, Geographic Variation, and Implications for Biological Anthropology

Rachel Caspari

INTRODUCTION

Over the last century, anthropological discourse about race has changed dramatically. Once a core concept in anthropology, it is now said to be a 'myth,' a moniker coined by Ashley Montagu (1942) to denote that race was a social construction with no basis in biology. Although the decline of the race concept in biological anthropology has been slow (Lieberman et al. 1992; 2003a, 2003b) and vestiges of the race concept persist (Armelagos et al. 1982; Brown and Armelagos 2001; Caspari 2003; Gravlee 2009), most anthropologists, though by no means all, claim to accept its demise (Lieberman et al. 2003a; 2003b; Kaszycka et al. 2009). Despite this, typological thinking about human variation persists in science and society. As biological anthropologists continue to debate whether there is a human taxonomy below the species level, and diseases (and pharmaceuticals) are ascribed (and prescribed) to specific racial groups, science continues to reify race, reinforcing the popular notion that races are natural, homogeneous biological subdivisions of the human species and that race is synonymous with geographic variation.

In fact, race continues to be important to biological anthropologists in a number of ways. This paper explores three of them. First, the race concept is not dead. Racial thinking persists in the public mind and in various scientific studies. In fact, racial thinking may be a part of the human condition, like essentialism itself, and therefore can only be eradicated (or mitigated, if eradication is impossible) through education.

Since race and geographic variation are so often conflated, race should be directly addressed when teaching biological variation.

Second, the question still remains of whether races exist (or whether the pattern of human geographic variation is consistent with racial thinking). The ongoing discussions about the apportionment of geographic variation in the human species are far from being over. Lewontin's seminal work (1972) showed minimal average population structure in the human species, and subsequent studies likewise showed relatively little variation among groups (Nei and Roychoudhury 1982; Barbujani and Belle 2006; Barbujani et al. 1997; Jorde et al. 2000; Rosenberg et al. 2002). This work appeared to drive the final nails in the coffin of the race concept. Recent work, however raises questions about the validity of the statistics used in some studies, and about the nature of human population structure (Long and Kittles 2003; Long et al. 2009; Hunley et al. 2009). Anthropological geneticists have yet to reach consensus on this issue (Serre and Pääbo 2004; Ramachandran et al. 2005; Risch et al. 2002).

Finally, while social races are not genealogical entities, they have biological dimensions. There are many negative health outcomes associated with race and inequality which are of increasing importance to biocultural anthropologists. Unfortunately, because of the primacy of racial thinking, these biological attributes of social groups help to reify race.

THE RACE CONCEPT IS NOT DEAD

Challenges to the race concept are not recent

There has been debate about race in American anthropology since the inception of the modern discipline in the late nineteenth century. By the time of the founding of the American Anthropological Association in 1902 and of the American Association of Physical Anthropologists in 1930, the race concept had already been challenged by factions within the anthropological community (Caspari 2003, 2009). Franz Boas published against racial determinism of culture as early as 1894 (Boas 1894a), and continued to undermine the race concept by demonstrating the instability of types and the complexities of human variation (see for example Boas 1894b, 1911, 1912, 1918). He was interested in the lack of concordance in the geographic distribution of different features, and by 1918 mapped clines of different traits in attempts to understand human variation (Boas 1918). Presaging Lewontin (1972) by sixty years, he wrote in *The Mind of Primitive Man* (Boas 1911: 94) that "differences between different types of man are, on the whole, small as compared to the range of variation within each type." He also clearly understood that patterns of variation were variable – some populations were more homogeneous than others (Boas 1918) – and, by implication, that a universal pattern of diversity was unlikely. He pointed out that such patterns were best determined locally: "as far as anthropological method is concerned […] data from small political units and […] family groups are indispensible." (Boas 1918: 425). Therefore many elements of the arguments against race that emerged in the 1960s and 1970s (Livingstone 1962; Brace 1964; Lewontin 1972) were present a century ago, and were perpetuated within American anthropology by Boas, his students, and those influenced by them (Kroeber 1923; Mead et al. 1968; Montagu 1964; Washburn 1963).

However, other factions within the American anthropological community, especially those in physical anthropology, maintained race as a core concept. The most influential figures in the development of American physical anthropology as a separate discipline were Harvard's Earnest Hooton, the first to train PhDs specifically in physical anthropology (Giles 1997), and Aleš Hrdlička, the Czech born and Smithsonian based physical anthropologist who founded the *American Journal of Physical Anthropology* (*AJPA*) and the American Association of Physical Anthropologists (Spencer 1997). Races were important to them as units of study, and the race concept shaped the way they thought about human variation (Blakey 1987; Caspari 2003, 2009). Thus, despite the ongoing critique of race in American anthropology, a critique that seems very compelling to modern sensibilities, race remained a core concept in physical anthropology until the challenges to race in the 1960s.

The criticisms of race in the 1960s developed out of earlier critiques, raised both by Boasians in America (Montagu 1942) and by Europeans motivated by the rise of Nazism and the Holocaust (Huxley and Haddon 1935). Seminal papers were published against the essentialism, and particularly against the biological determinism, inherent in the race concept – for instance those in Mead and colleagues (1968) and in Montagu (1964). Others were published on the non-existence of human races themselves (Livingstone 1962; Brace 1964). Ultimately, this phase in the movement of antiracial sentiment in the field was widely adopted, so that today many textbooks in biological anthropology discuss race as an antiquated way of viewing human variation and teach that races are invalid scientific categories, which only exist as social constructs (Lieberman et al. 2003a, 2003b). Many factors contributed to the demise of race in the 1960s (Caspari 2003; Jackson 2001), some scientific (for instance the growth of evolutionary thought, population genetics and the modern synthesis) and some social (such as the rise of the civil rights movement). The result is that many anthropologists believe that race is dead; however, among some biological anthropologists and others in the biomedical sciences, this is not so clear. While there is consensus that races as large homogeneous subspecies do not exist (Edgar and Hunley 2009), there is considerable debate about the pattern of human genetic and morphological variation. Simply put, racial thinking still persists and influences understandings of human variation (Brown and Armelagos 2001; Caspari 2003; Gravlee 2009).

Questions about the reality of the demise of the race concept in American anthropology have been addressed for decades (Kaszycka and Štrkalj 2002; Kaszycka and Strzałko 2003a, 2003b; Kascycka et al. 2009; Lieberman 2001; Lieberman et al. 1992, 2003a, 2003b, 2004; Littlefield et al. 1982). Studies have demonstrated a lack of consensus about the existence of race in textbooks and among working anthropologists. However, in general, there has been a trend over time showing a decline in the number of American anthropologists who accept the existence of biological races, so that currently 70–80 percent of American anthropologists claim to reject the biological race concept (Kaszycka et al. 2009). This corresponds to the increasing representation of anti-race sentiment in American anthropology textbooks over the last quarter century (Lieberman et al. 1992; 2003a; 2003b). In Europe and Asia, the number of anthropologists rejecting race is lower; in some countries, significantly lower (Lieberman et al. 2004).

Recent studies indicate a resurgence of the race concept in the newest generation of biological anthropologists in Europe, contrasting with the post-war generation, who had largely rejected the race concept (Kaszycka et al. 2009). This may not be the result of a resurgence of racism in European academia, but rather of a lack of critical thinking about race. Despite a long history of challenges and increasingly compelling evidence against race, the concept is surprisingly resistant. If people are not actively taught that races don't exist, the race concept re-emerges. This may be because race is much more than a bad idea about geographic variation; it has psychological and social dimensions which make it a bad idea about geographic variation that is exceptionally difficult to depose. It may be that, left to their own devices, humans think racially because they think taxonomically.

Why won't race die? Essentialism and the psychology of taxonomy

It may be part of the human condition to construct naïve taxonomies of the natural and social world, which predispose us to racial thinking (Atran 1990, 1994, Atran et al. 2002; Hirschfeld 1996, 1998; Hirschfeld and Gelman 1994; Gil-White 2001; Prentice and Miller 2007). Essentialism is a critical component of all such taxonomies. Moreover, the western race concept, by conflating biological and social taxonomies, by fiat 'biologizes' social categories (Blakey 1999) and may make the western race concept more insidious than other forms of social classification.

Humans create taxonomies of the biological, social, and physical world in similar ways, cross-culturally (Atran 1990, 1994, Atran et al. 2002; Hirschfeld 1996, 1998; Hirschfeld and Gelman 1994; Gil-White 2001; Prentice and Miller 2007). These taxonomies are knowledge structures that allow many inferences to be made (beyond the information given) about constituent categories. Some categories are more inferentially rich than others, allowing stereotypes to form without an empirical basis. These categories have been termed 'natural kinds,' because people believe them to be part of the natural world – 'real'; they do not recognize them as mental or cultural constructions (Hirschfeld and Gelman 1994).

'Natural kinds' are produced through cognitive mechanisms that are specific to particular domains (and perhaps based on different mental modules); some domains allow people subconsciously to construct naïve theories (and associated inferences) about aspects of the physical world, while competence in another domain governs living things. 'Natural kinds' that reflect the biological world have been termed 'living kinds,' which people learn through different cognitive processes from those used to learn inanimate things or the processes that relate to them (naïve physics). Hirschfeld (1996, 1998) notes that, in addition to a cognitive domain that governs 'living kinds,' humans have a separate domain, which allows them to learn easily 'human kinds' and the traits that make up the essence of a particular kind. These 'human kinds' are social categories that are particularly important to a culture; they are thought by members of that culture to be intrinsic to a person's identity. Just as biological categories carry information about the essence of a species, genus or class, 'human kinds' carry information about the 'essence' of a type of person – what the persons belonging to that type are supposed to look like, think like, or act like. The fact that many members of a category don't conform to the stereotype does not dispel the stereotype: this is a hallmark of essentialism.

'Human kinds,' then, are groups whose members are believed to share some fundamental essence, considered to be inheritable and relatively unchangeable. In western society – and to some extent globally, because of cultural interconnection, western dominance and the legacies of colonialism – 'race' is a 'human kind,' and therefore has a psychological dimension (Hirschfeld 1996, 1998; Gil-White 2001; Prentice and Miller 2007). We may be psychologically and evolutionarily disposed to racial thinking.

But races are also 'living kinds.' The western race concept is based loosely on ideas about geographic variation, variation which has great social meaning because of the history of colonialism and slavery, which continues to link differences in power and privilege to geographic ancestry. It developed in part through science, in the age of discovery, as racial classifications were used to make sense of new social groups, effectively 'biologizing' relationships between Europeans and other people they encountered, and even relationships between different European groups (Blakey 1999). Incorporated into the natural history tradition, race was a taxonomy of 'living kinds,' even as it was simultaneously a taxonomy of 'human kinds.' While race is clearly social, its 'naturalness' has been validated by incorporating racial categories into a biological taxonomy.

It is likely that this psychological dimension of race contributes to the persistence of the race concept; in addition to sociopolitical factors, it explains why stereotypes are so difficult to dispel and why racial thinking remains so dominant in science and society. Anthropology's long struggle with the race concept underscores this. In the nineteenth century, Topinard himself, disciple of the polygenist Paul Broca and a major influence on the founders of American physical anthropology, struggled with the idea of types. Although he was a pre-eminent student of types and a staunch promoter of the type concept, Topinard recognized that the concept of racial 'essence' was undermined by the lack of homogeneity of populations, and that any continuity with supposedly once pure racial types was at best "a hypothesis […] convenient for study, impossible to demonstrate" (Topinard 1892). Yet, while he considered races to be an abstraction, Topinard was simultaneously convinced of their reality and of the reality of racial assumptions underlying human variation. As cited by Stocking (1968: 59):

> we cannot deny them, our mind sees them, our labor separates them out; if in thought we suppress the intermixtures of peoples, their interbreedings, in a flash we see them stand forth – simple, inevitable, a necessary consequence of collective heredity. (Topinard 1885 p. 202, cited in Stocking 1968, p. 59)

Topinard's dilemma (Caspari 2009), the conflict between the type concept he believed in and the reality he observed, is one shared by many workers and continues to be an obstacle to reconciling race within biological anthropology; racial thinking may be so entrenched that anthropological work which refutes the race concept may be unrecognized even by the workers themselves. Brown and Armelagos (2001) point out a modern example of the same conflict: while Nei and Roychoudhury's 1982 paper undermined racial categorization (they found only 9–11 percent of the total genetic heterozygosity at 86 loci attributable to racial classifications), they nevertheless discuss the evolution of Mongoloid, Caucasoid, and Negroid racial groups. As Brown and Armelagos (2001: 36) put it: "This speaks to the logical disconnect shown by many researchers who simultaneously prove the irrelevance of genetic race and then proceed to discuss the genetic evolution of races."

This psychological dimension of race is of interest to biological anthropologists in several ways. The evolutionary basis of essentialism and race, as a product of mind, is an interesting issue for evolutionary psychologists, and has implications for human evolution. It also explains why the race concept does not die and why, even when race seems dead, it is so easily resurrected. Therefore, although 'races' are no longer objects of study, race remains an important topic within biological anthropology that affects us as scientists and educators. Our students may arrive on campus with naïve taxonomies which are at odds with current understandings of human variation, and, perhaps more importantly, our understandings of human variation may be influenced by our own naïve taxonomies.

Does Race Exist?

Race does not equal geographic variation

Of course, there may be a much simpler reason for the persistence of the race concept. Perhaps biological races exist. There is still considerable debate over the existence and meaning of race within biological anthropology, as shown in a recent special issue of the *AJPA* (Edgar and Hunley 2009). Resolution of this issue depends on what anthropologists mean by race. Certainly, all anthropologists recognize geographic variation, which is sometimes conflated with race; yet the question addressing race is not whether variation exists, but whether the pattern of human variation can be explained taxonomically. Is the relationship between human groups at any level, from continental regions to local populations, phylogenetic?

In his 1962 paper on the non-existence of human races, Livingstone eloquently laid out why race or any subspecific taxonomy is misleading:

> The causes of intraspecific biological variation are different from those of interspecific variation and to apply the term subspecies to any part of such variation is not only arbitrary or impossible but tends to obscure the explanation of that variation. (Livingstone 1962: 279)

Recognizing the non-concordance of many traits, he was a strong proponent of non-racial clinal studies, arguing that "there are no races, only clines" (ibid., p. 279). Human variation, he felt, was best studied through the distribution of individual traits.

Others, however, argued that the biology of the groups themselves was also a valid target of inquiry. In the *Current Anthropology* discussion following the Livingstone paper, Dobzhansky, one of the foremost scientific voices *against* racism, argued *for* the existence of human races. This is not as incongruous as it first appears. For Dobzhansky (1962) as for many others, 'race' referred to any group that varied from another in terms of allele frequencies. Dobzhansky was not a racial thinker; he did not express the underlying essentialist assumptions of race. He used 'race' as a term for population and recognized the importance of gene flow and the fluidity of groups. His argument was basically that populations could differ significantly from one another and were valid objects of study. Like many, he conflated the idea of race with that of differences between populations.

But race is not simply geographic variation, or differences between populations; because of the history of the concept and of the psychology of racial thinking, race is a taxonomic way of viewing human variation. Because of the relationship between taxonomy and phylogeny, the existence of race in a scientific sense implies that racial differences are phylogenetic. If they are genealogical entities, there are implications about the biological processes that form and maintain races; isolation and independent histories are important aspects of the race concept.

Components of race: Essentialism, biological determinism, and isolating mechanisms

The eighteenth-century natural history tradition was largely descriptive, and the western race concept developed within it to delineate and describe the primary divisions of humankind (Marks 1995; Brace 2005). While there were debates within science about the number and constituents of the divisions (three, five, or more), there was little question about what they represented: subspecies, or perhaps species. The races defined by the western race concept were codified by Linnaeus and by the definitive 10th edition of his *Systema naturae*. He described five subspecies of humans, listing both the morphological and the behavioral characteristics of each type. These traits were considered a part of the essence of the category and were implicitly (and explicitly) understood to be part of the intrinsic biology of the race. European prejudices were clearly incorporated into Linnaean typology (Marks 1995; Blakey 1999), so that Africans (*Homo sapiens afer*) were described as impassive and lazy, and Europeans (*Homo sapiens europus*) as very smart. Thus, from its very inception, the race concept embodied both essentialism and biological determinism, the linking of behavioral traits such as intelligence, criminality, industriousness, and other personality traits to the essences of racial categories. The categories and their essences, with both physical and behavioral components believed to be stable and unchanging, were defined by science as natural groups, even as they were part of a stratified social system. While the Linnaean taxonomy applied to continental groupings as subspecies of humans, racial taxonomies could extend to groups lower in the taxonomic hierarchy. A major goal of anthropology in the nineteenth century and through much of the twentieth century was the determination of the number and types of races (Coon et al. 1950). Many workers recognized a few primary races (subspecies), each with multiple subdivisions. For example, Topinard devoted his career to racial identification (Ferembach 1997), ultimately recognizing nineteen 'types' within three primary races.

Race was the core concept in anthropology as it emerged at the turn of the nineteenth century (Brace 2005; Stanton 1960; Stocking 1968); and biological determinism, a long-standing part of the anthropological tradition through the first half of the twentieth century, represented its value as an applied science. Anthropology could reinforce the underlying assumption of the inferiority of non-dominant racial groups and provide evidence to support social policy, from slavery and immigration restrictions to genocide (Blakey 1987; Gasman 1971; Hrdlička 1918a, 1918b, 1918c; Proctor 1988; Paul 1998; Stein 1988). Biological determinism applied to the evolutionism that explained cultural variation in the nineteenth century, and was a core concept of the eugenics movement of the twentieth century. Following World War II, however, it was the component of the race concept that was most ardently addressed by the field, because of its obvious social implications (Mead et al. 1968; Montagu 1964). From the 1960s to the present, anthropology has presented a strong voice against the biological determinism embedded in the race concept (Caspari 2003).

Isolation, the third component of the race concept, has implications for how human variation is apportioned. This *is* the issue when the question of the existence of race is debated in biological anthropology today (Edgar and Hunley 2009). Can biological differences between populations be explained phylogenetically? There are two issues here. First, do the races of the western race concept exist, in that there are continental groups that can be considered human subspecies? Second lies the deeper issue of whether *racial thinking* is supported by patterns of geographic variation – is there *any* human taxonomy below the species level – can tree structures validly be used to model human population relationships?

Historically, tree models have been important components of race; races have been depicted as clades on an evolutionary tree. While race concepts held by members of society are rarely deconstructed, scientific explanations of human variation need to be consistent with the type concept for races to be valid. Trees, as the way in which taxonomic hierarchies are conceived and depicted, express how types can exist – they embody an explanation for the concordance of physical and behavioral traits that are believed to make up race. Historically, this has rendered thinking about race very similar to thinking about biological species. This was exemplified in the polygenism prevalent in the American and French schools of thought that dominated much of anthropology for the first half of the nineteenth century (Stanton 1960; Stocking 1968; Brace 1982).

After the widespread acceptance of evolution and of many of the elements of Darwinian theory, a form of polygenism continued to thrive (Caspari 2003; Wolpoff and Caspari 1997). Taxonomic categories, including subspecific ones, continued to be conceptualized as discrete groups, while the essences of the categories were explained as products of separate evolutionary histories. Races, like species categories, were depicted as branches on an evolutionary tree, whose differences could now be explained through their independent evolution, and inequality, through different selection pressures and rates of evolutionary change. Frequently (for example Haeckel 1883), evolutionary histories were truncated for 'primitive' races, while the longer branches of 'advanced' races indicated a 'more evolved' (and therefore better) group. This approach provided phylogenetic explanations for human differences; human groups were effectively species on a smaller scale, whose differences could be accounted for through independent evolution.

Human evolutionary literature is filled with examples of evolutionary polygenism – from Carl Vogt (1864), who suggested that different races arose from different great apes, to Haeckel (1883, 1905), who suggested that there were larger differences between racial groups than between some species; to Hermann Klaatsch (1910, 1923), whose model of convergent evolution included the idea that Aboriginal Australians were ancestral to all great apes and humans; or to Arthur Keith (1936), who felt that interracial competition accounted for the parallel evolution intrinsic to polygenic models. Earnest Hooton believed that pure races had a common ancestor as far back as the Miocene (Hooton 1931). His student, Carlton Coon, developed a polygenic model of racial origins where races shared a common ancestor in the middle Pleistocene (Coon 1962). In all these interpretations, races were lineages transcending species;

their common ancestor lived long ago and the different races effectively achieved their humanity separately, just as the older polygenic ideas suggested.

'Minor races' within racial hierarchies were also depicted as smaller branches within major ones (Coon 1939, 1965), and, while the people cited above believed in long separate evolutionary histories accounting for big differences between continental racial groups, short branches represented the same assumptions on a smaller scale. Branches, whatever their length, imply divergence and isolation, a pattern that does not depict relationships between human populations interconnected by gene flow. While tree models in themselves do not necessarily represent racism (for instance, short branches have been used to underscore human similarities and the 'brotherhood of man,' depicting a recent common ancestor of all populations), they are completely in accord with the essentialism of the race concept and with the hierarchical structure of folk taxonomies. Phylogenetic models are an intuitive way to account biologically for discrete essences. It is telling that the phylogenetic assumption has largely been used, yet untested, throughout the history of anthropology. Because of the power and prevalence of the race concept, phylogenetic relationships among human populations have often been simply assumed. Recently, however, there has been a more complex discussion of the kinds of models best used to represent human genetic diversity (for instance Hunley et al. 2009).

Therefore the biological race concept is not equivalent to human variation; it has three components that make it a specific way of interpreting variation: essentialism (which, as discussed earlier, is intrinsic to taxonomies and itself may have a biological basis); biological determinism; and the assumption that human intraspecific relationships are phylogenetic. Biological determinism, as a link between race and racism, has been ardently and effectively addressed by the field since the 1960s, partially in reaction to expressions of racism from the scientific community and to the ways in which they were politically used (Coon 1962; Gates 1944; Garrett 1961; George 1962; Putnam 1962). However, the essentialism of the race concept is more difficult to dispel, and this fact would be made even more difficult if the pattern of human relationships really is phylogenetic.

Apportionment of human diversity: Can differences between human groups be understood phylogenetically?

Today the most cited and influential challenges to the existence of race derive from genetic studies showing minimal population structure in humans (Lewontin 1972; Serre and Pääbo 2004). However, there was an earlier challenge. The modern synthesis brought focus on subspecific evolutionary processes that challenged the validity of subspecific taxonomies. Studies of clines were introduced and the term 'population' replaced 'race' as a focus of study.

With renewed focus on systematics during the synthesis (Mayr 1942), the question of the usefulness of taxonomy below the species level was debated. Wilson and Brown's much cited 1953 paper laid out the problems of 'subspecies' and the inadequacies of race. They grappled with potential non-phylogenetic causes of subspecific taxonomy, concluding that subspecies were difficult to define and delimit despite the expectation that a co-adapted system would lead to a distinguishable entity. They noted that, despite this expectation, in practice there was non-concordance of independent genetic characters and therefore that any 'useful' subspecific or racial categories were by necessity based on very few traits; further, they pointed to numerous examples of the same characteristic traits typifying several geographic regions. Turning to phylogenetic notions of subspecies, they made two further points: that the degree of population divergence necessary to recognize subspecies was arbitrary; and, perhaps most importantly, that in many cases the population structure below the subspecies level was greatest. They argued that the large geographic races that subspecies were supposed to represent should be more heterogeneous than the small local populations or demes. This is especially the case in sedentary taxa like snails, which have very homogeneous local populations. Therefore they concluded that the naming of subspecies, or races, actually obscures the real nature of geographic variation.

In biological anthropology, two alternatives to race emerged from the problems of subspecies: a focus on clines and a focus on populations. The study of the clinal distribution of traits became an alternative to race, and the focus on population directly addressed the importance of local groups that may have more biological integrity than large geographic races. Because of the non-concordance of genetically independent features, clines came to be seen as an alternative to race. As Brace (1964) pointed out, races, and even populations, are inadequate for the study of human variation. Instead he advocated the study of individual traits – the study of their distribution and the selection that causes their variation. Promoted by Livingstone (1962), the study of clines, the distribution of individual morphological and genetic traits, came to replace race as a focus of analysis for many workers. Livingstone argued against using subspecific taxa, not only because they were arbitrary and difficult to define, but also because the phylogenetic assumption inherent in taxonomy obscured the complex causes of their variation: migration and gene flow represent intraspecific evolutionary processes, which were such a critical component of the modern synthesis.

Others, however (for instance Brues 1972), accepted the importance of clines, but argued that the biology of groups themselves was also a valid target of inquiry. With the 'populational thinking' of the modern synthesis that formed the basis of Washburn's 'new physical anthropology' (Haraway 1988), 'populations' replaced 'races' as groups of study. By emphasizing intraspecific evolutionary processes, populational thinking focuses on variation and on the fluidity between populations – on all the processes that reduce or increase variation within and between populations. Gene flow is critical to populational thinking; its action, combined with other evolutionary forces, explains the distribution of variation within species. Gene flow undermines racial thinking. Mayr himself suggests that the populational thinking he promoted helped cause the demise of the race concept, as essentialism is the antithesis to Darwinian approaches to variation.

However, populational thinking does not necessarily go hand-in-hand with the study of populations. Many anthropologists, whether studying genes (Boyd 1950) or morphology, thought of populations as races: they were breeding populations, isolated from other groups. Some recognized this implicitly; some explicitly, as Garn wrote (1962: 6): "the contemporary approach to race stems from population genetics, where a race is viewed as a breeding population, neither more nor less." He identified small 'local races' like the 'Bushmen' of South Africa as more or less *isolated* breeding populations (Garn 1962). In spite of Washburn's (1963) admonition that races or populations were open systems, populations were thus conceptualized as closed. Therefore the existence of types was implicit, even if the scientific focus was on their adaptations. Moreover, as Armelagos and colleagues pointed out, many studies in skeletal biology and genetics continued to employ typological methods to typological ends: the recognition and delineation of populations. Their conclusion in 1982 was that, whether using skeletal or genetic traits, many studies of populations are just as typological as the studies of race (Armelagos et al. 1982).

Despite the typological assumptions of some genetic studies, genetics had a strong influence on the changing race concept, especially the population genetics of the modern synthesis, which focused on the dynamics of intraspecific evolution. Population geneticists through the years have provided compelling evidence for human unity. Perhaps the most cited scientific challenge to the race concept is Lewontin's 1972 paper emphasizing that very little human genetic variation is attributable to racial or even populational differences. Using Sewall Wright's F-statistic, originally developed to assess inbreeding, Lewontin showed that an assumed hierarchical population structure explained very little of the genetic variation in humans. F_{ST}, the proportion of the total variation attributable to between-group genetic differences, was very low: about 6 percent for regional differences and 8 percent at the subpopulation level. The vast majority, about 85 percent, of the variation was found within subpopulations. These low levels of interpopulational diversity have been supported by a large number of studies since then (for instance Barbujani and Belle 2006; Barbujani et al. 1997; Jorde et al. 2000; Manica et al. 2005; Nei and Roychoudhury 1982; Prugnolle et al. 2005; Rosenberg et al. 2002; Serre and Pääbo 2004). By showing minimal population structure on several levels, this work undermines the phylogenetic assumption not only at the level of subspecies, but also at level of population. This has been underscored by Templeton (1998), who has argued that human populations have such little structure that 'treeness' is not demonstrated and phylogenetic models are invalid. A number of more recent studies have underscored the fluidity of populations, showing strong correlations between genetic variation and geographic distance (Prugnolle et al. 2005; Manica et al. 2005), some conforming to an isolation by distance model, with few discrete boundaries between populations (Serre and Pääbo 2004). By challenging the phylogenetic assumption, these studies refute not only the western race concept, but also racial thinking in general.

However, there remains debate about whether there is a taxonomic pattern to population relationships. While some workers interpret the correlation of genetic variation with geography as clinal (Serres and Pääbo 2004), other studies have found such correlations consistent with a nested hierarchical pattern (Ramachandran et al. 2005). This underscores a problem pointed out by Long and colleagues (2009), that the choice of model used in an analysis biases the results. This is the core of the recent critique of F_{ST}, which has been challenged as an oversimplification of the apportionment of human genetic diversity (Long and Kittles 2003; Long et al. 2009). These authors have argued that, contra Lewontin (1972), population structure may still explain human diversity, but not the very simple structure assumed in Wright's F_{ST} model as used by Lewontin. They highlight several problems. Because F_{ST} expresses *average* diversity found between subpopulations, it does not adequately express variation in diversity: some populations may vary a lot, while others very little. Thus population structure may better explain the diversity among some populations than among others. Moreover, it has been argued that aspects of F_{ST} may be circular – that the actual deviance from the population structure assumed in the model affects the apportionment of diversity estimated by F_{ST}. Long and Kittles (2003) point out that the violated assumption of the evolutionary independence of populations (intrinsic to population structure models – that is, trees) may have the consequence of increasing the gene identity estimation (the probability of homozygosity) for the total population. Since F_{ST} measures the gene identity of subpopulations relative to the total population, this would serve to depress F_{ST} measures artificially.

Nevertheless, the conclusions of most studies using various approaches to the assessment of genetic diversity agree that human subspecies don't exist, mostly on the basis of low levels of diversity and of the geographic patterning of that diversity (Serres and Pääbo 2004; Relethford 2002, 2009; Rosenberg et al. 2002). Some workers have also argued against the taxonomic validity of race on the grounds that 'races' occupy different levels of a genetic diversity hierarchy; so, for example, if the basic division was between Africans and everyone else, sub-Saharan Africans (a supposed subrace) would occupy a higher level in the taxonomy than Asians or Europeans (Hunley et al. 2009). All recent studies underscore the complexity of human population relationships and the problems of continental races.

For some, the claim against race has been taken to mean that there is no geographically structured biological variation and that any genetic clustering of populations (or of classically defined races) indicates that races exist (Risch et al. 2002), or that it is valid to model them phylogenetically. This is a straw man argument: there clearly are biological differences between myriad human groups. This has always been clear; even the low levels of intergroup variation suggested by Lewontin are significant (Hunley et al. 2009). At issue for the race concept is how significant population structure is in characterizing relationships between local populations, and whether those relationships should be considered taxonomic.

Recent studies have underscored the complexities of the causes of human genetic diversity, complexity caused by variation in gene flow and selection which undermines the taxonomic assumption. Since the genetics of populations are based on population histories (including large-scale migrations, population fissioning and reticulation, marriage patterns and an assortment of other social variables) and, perhaps most importantly, on natural selection, the apportionment of diversity is extremely variable. This was underscored in a recent study where the genetic diversity at a number of neutral microsatellite loci was compared to computer simulations of the genetic variation predicted for different demographic models: isolation by distance, independent regions, serial fissions and nested regions (Hunley et al. 2009). Results indicate that none of these models completely fits the data and that a combination of isolation by distance and nested regions seemed to fit the data best. Moreover, while most genetic studies involving the apportionment of human variation have focused on neutral loci, the pattern of spread of recent alleles under selection may also contribute to our understanding of population relationships (Hawks et al. 2007; Coop et al. 2009), including the evolution and spread of mutations of regional adaptive significance. The genetic data to date indicate that there is a clinal pattern for both neutral and adaptive genetic variation, which is affected by variable population expansions and population structure. This complexity undermines the taxonomic assumptions of the race concept.

Biological Dimensions of Social Races

Links between biological and social race

While social races are constantly redefined and now appear to be only loosely tied to the impugned biological races of the western race concept, they cannot be truly separated from them; they are linked through the psychological dimensions of race and through the role that race has played historically in western culture. Social races are treated as though they are biological races, and this is evident in the relationship between race and ancestry. Race and ancestry are not the same, although there are elements of ancestry associated with race, and races are presumed to be based on ancestry. Race can be thought of as that aspect of ancestry (either real or imagined) that is most important to identity (either self identity or socially imposed identity). There is often a phenotypic component to race that people recognize, and this underscores the 'naturalness' or presumed biological basis of the category. People scrutinize each other for clues of racial identity; hence the slightest African feature could prevent a person from 'passing for white' in highly racialized early twentieth-century US society. Students sometimes ask why subordinate racial features are 'dominant' in mixed-race people: they aren't. We just are good at looking for them. It may be a part of the human condition that we seek biological cues of social identity.

Race, in fact, obscures ancestry. Weidenreich once argued against race, describing human groups as having multiple ancestors and multiple descendents (Caspari and Wolpoff 1996; Wolpoff and Caspari 1997). However, perhaps because of the psychological properties of taxonomies discussed earlier, people think about their ancestry in terms of 'pure races.' Thus a person might speak of her ancestry as "half Black, a quarter White, and a quarter Native American" speaking of the social races of her grandparents. Of course each grandparent may also have had mixed ancestry, but this is obscured by the system of racial classification in society. This racial view of ancestry may have consequences, particularly regarding research into health disparities among different racial groups.

Health consequences

Among the ways in which race is relevant to biological anthropology, the biomedical implications of race may have the largest social importance (Gravlee and Sweet 2008). While races do not exist as genealogical entities, there are significant biological differences between social groups caused by a variety of factors and their interrelationships. A few factors relate to genetics and ancestry; there is endogamy within social groups (although this is highly variable), and there are some elements of a partially shared, complex ancestry that may result in observable phenotypic differences between social groups, including ones affecting health. Most importantly, however, there are the biological consequences of shared social factors, especially income disparity and discrimination, which result in disparate health outcomes for members of different racial groups.

There is a significant literature on health inequalities among different racial groups in the US and globally. As recently reviewed in Gravlee (2009), in the US, African Americans are most disadvantaged. They present significantly higher age-adjusted death rates than whites do, from a variety of disorders such as kidney disease, hypertension, diabetes, cardiovascular disease, some forms of cancer, infections and trauma. These have been linked to a number of environmental variables. An increasing number of anthropologists and epidemiologists are focusing on the importance of biocultural interactions, including the biological consequences of poverty, to explain many of these disparities (see for example Dressler et al. 2005; Goodman and Leatherman 1998; Gravlee 2009; Gravlee et al. 2005; Schell 1997). Residential and environmental discrimination have been shown to have serious health consequences, including obesity, cardiovascular disease, hypertension, low birth-weight, some forms of cancer, tuberculosis, and poisoning from environmental pollutants including heavy metals (Schell 1997; Williams and Collins 2001). In addition, the psychosocial effects of racism and discrimination have been associated with negative mental and physical conditions, including some of the ones listed above (hypertension, cardiovascular disease, and obesity) (Krieger 2004). Insidiously, in a process that mimics genetic heredity, these conditions may be perpetuated across generations through development; adult chronic conditions negatively impact the fetal and early post-natal environment, resulting in poor birth outcomes. These, in turn, are linked to the development of adult chronic conditions (Kuzawa 2008). Therefore, while races may not be biological categories, there are serious biological ramifications of race. As Gravlee (2009: 51) put it: "Epidemiological evidence shows that, in a very certain sense, race *is* biology."

Despite the fact that racial disparities in health may be best understood as the biological consequences of social conditions, they are often presumed to be the result of genetic factors (Braun 2006; Duster 2005; Frank 2007; Schwartz 2001), a consequence of the primacy of racial thinking. Because the taxonomic meanings of race are so entrenched, many health workers and researchers assume without evidence that racial differences in health are the consequence of (untested) genetic differences between groups; and, for some, the fact that there are racial differences *is* the evidence for a genetic basis for a condition (Gravlee 2009). There are dangers in uncritically applying a racial–genetic model in medicine. It can obscure the actual genetic factors; because of the dominance of racial thinking, those aspects of ancestry which are not a part of social identity may be unrecognized or ignored. The application of this model also overlooks the cultural factors of stress associated with negative health outcomes. Because race and variation are so often conflated, any biological differences between racial groups can serve to reify the race concept.

CONCLUSION

While many anthropologists consider race to be an outmoded and irrelevant concept, race remains a critical part of biological anthropology in particular and of science in general. The race concept is not dead, and is unlikely to die soon. Racial thinking may be a part of the human condition, like essentialism itself, and so it is difficult to eradicate. Race and geographic variation continue to be conflated, influencing understandings of biological diversity. While there are clearly differences among populations, the pattern of morphological and genetic variation within our species is not phylogenetic, and genetic studies continue to undermine both the concept of large geographic races and the basis of racial thinking by revealing the complexities of human genetic relationships. Nevertheless, race models remain prevalent in science and society, influencing, among other things, the interpretation and treatment of health disparities among racially defined social groups.

Because of the primacy of racial thinking, the study of populational variation itself may serve to reify race. In the public mind, when the biology of race is discussed, or when race (or ancestry) is scientifically identified by using biological cues, this reinforces the taxonomic assumptions and the biological determinism that are part of the race concept. Since races are unequal social categories, the assumptions that underlie race – biological determinism and separate biological histories – subtly 'explain' the social inequality. Since races are 'biologized' social categories, social inequality becomes the consequence of inferior biology in the minds of many. It has thus been argued that the reification of race gives rise to biological determinism and is, in itself, racist (Blakey 1999). This is a conundrum that faces physical anthropologists and other human biologists today; since the assumptions of race are so deeply embedded, the recognition of the biological attributes of social categories, from the health risks associated with poverty to those associated with aspects of an individual's ancestry, may serve to reify race (Duster 2005). Although the study of population disparities is of critical importance, the reification of race may make social equality even more difficult to achieve. This underscores the importance of an understanding of race, in all its many dimensions, to the study of human variation.

ACKNOWLEDGMENTS

I thank Clark Larsen for the invitation to contribute to this volume, and to the students and colleagues, too many to name, who have helped me formulate the ideas on race and racism expressed here.

REFERENCES

Armelagos, G. J., Carlson, D. S., and Van Gerven, D. P. (1982) The Theoretical Foundations and Development of Skeletal Biology. In Frank Spencer (ed.), *A History of American Physical Anthropology 1930–1980* (pp. 305–328). London: Academic Press.

Atran, S. (1990) *Cognitive Foundation of Natural History.* New York: Cambridge University Press.

Atran, S. (1994) Core Domains vs. Scientific Theories: Evidence from Systematics and Itza-Maya Folk Biology. In L. Hirschfeld and S. Gelman (eds), *Mapping the Mind* (pp. 316–340). Cambridge: University of Cambridge Press.

Atran, S., Medin, D. I., and Ross, N. (2002) Thinking about Biology. Modular Constraints on Categorization and Reasoning in the Everyday Life of Americans, Maya, and Scientists. *Mind and Society* 3 (2): 31–63

Barbujani, G., and Belle, E. M. S. (2006) Genomic Boundaries between Human Populations. *Human Heredity* 61: 15–21.

Barbujani, G., Magagni, A., Minch, E., and Cavalli-Sforza, L. L. (1997) An Apportionment of Human DNA Diversity. *Proceedings of the National Academy of Sciences, USA* 94: 4516–4519.

Blakey, M. (1987) Skull Doctors. Intrinsic Social and Political Bias in the History of American Physical Anthropology. With Special Reference to the Work of Aleš Hrdlička. *Critique of Anthropology* 7: 7–35.

Blakey, M. (1999) Scientific Racism and the Biological Concept of Race. *Literature and Psychology* 45: 29–43.

Boas, F. (1894a) Human Faculty as Determined by Race. *Proceedings of the American Association for the Advancement of Science* 43: 301–327.

Boas, F. (1894b) The Half-Blood Indian, an Anthropometric Study. *Popular Science Monthly* 45: 761–769.

Boas, F. (1911) *The Mind of Primitive Man*. New York: Macmillan.

Boas, F. (1912) Changes in the Bodily Form of Descendents of Immigrants. *Am Anthropol* 14 (ns): 530–562.

Boas, F. (1918) Note on the Anthropology of Sweden. *American Journal of Physical Anthropology* 1: 415–426.

Boyd, W. C. (1950) *Genetics and the Races of Man*. Boston: Little, Brown.

Brace, C. L. (1964) A Nonracial Approach towards the Understanding of Human Diversity. In M. F. Ashley Montagu (ed.), *The Concept of Race* (pp. 103–152). New York: The Free Press.

Brace, C. L. (1982) The Roots of the Race Concept in Physical Anthropology In Frank Spencer (ed.), *A History of American Physical Anthropology 1930–1980* (pp. 11–29). London: Academic Press.

Brace, C. L. (2005) *Race Is a Four-Letter Word. The Genesis of the Concept*. New York: Oxford University Press.

Braun, L. (2006) Reifying Human Difference: The Debate on Genetics, Race and Health. *International Journal of Health Services* 36: 557–573.

Brown, R. A., and Armelagos, G. J. (2001) Apportionment of Human Genetic Diversity: A Review. *Evolutionary Anthropology* 10: 34–40.

Brues, A. (1972) Models of Clines and Races. *American Journal of Physical Anthropology* 37: 389–399.

Caspari, R. (2003) From Types to Populations: A Century of Race, Physical Anthropology and the American Anthropological Association. *American Anthropologist* 105: 65–76.

Caspari, R. (2009) 1918: Three Perspectives on Race and Human variation. *American Journal of Physical Anthropology* 139 (1): 5–15.

Caspari, R., and Wolpoff, M. H. (1996) Coon and Weidenreich. *Human Evolution* 11: 203.

Coon, C. S. (1939) *The Races of Europe*. New York: Macmillan.

Coon, C. S. (1962) *The Origin of Races*. New York: Knopf.

Coon, C. S. (1965) *The Living Races of Man*. New York: Knopf.

Coon, C. S., Garn, S. M., and Birdsell, J. B. (1950) *Races: A Study of the Problems of Race Formation in Man*. Springfield: C. C. Thomas.

Coop, G., Pickerell, J. K., Novembre, J., Kudaravalli, S., Li, J., Absher, D., Myers, R. M., Cavalli-Sforza, L. L., Feldman, M. W., Pritchard, J. K. (2009) The Role of Geography in Human Adaptation. *Public Library of Science Genetics* 5 (6): e1000500. doi: 10.1371/journal pgen.1000500.

Dressler, W. W., Oths, K. S., Gravlee, C. C. (2005) Race and Ethnicity in Public Health Research: Models to Explain Health Disparities. *Annual Review of Anthropology* 34 (1): 231–252.

Dobzhansky, T. (1944) On Species and Races of Living and Fossil Man. *American Journal of Physical Anthropology* 2: 251–265.

Dobzhansky, T. (1962) Comment to: On the Non-Existence of Human Races by F. Livingstone. *Current Anthropology* 3: 535–544.

Dobzhansky, T. (1963) Possibility that Homo sapiens Evolved Independently 5 Times is Vanishingly Small. *Current Anthropology* 4: 360–366.

Duster, T. (2005) Race and Reification in Science. *Science* 307: 1050–1051.

Edgar, H. J. H., and Hunley, K. L. (2009) Race Reconciled? How Biological Anthropologists View Human Variation. *American Journal of Physical Anthropology* 139: 1–4.

Ferembach, D. 1997. *Topinard, Paul (1830–1911)*. In F. Spencer (ed.), *History of Physical Anthropology: An Encyclopedia*, Vol. 2 (pp. 1040–1041). New York: Garland Publishing.

Frank, R. (2007) What to Make of It? The (Re)Emergence of a Biological Conceptualization of Race in Health Disparities Research. *Social Science and Medicine* 64: 1977–1983.

Gasman, D. (1971) *The Scientific Origins of National Socialism: Social Darwinism in Ernst Haeckel and the German Monist League*. New York: Elsevier.

Garn, S. M. (1957) Race and Evolution. *American Anthropologist* 59: 218–224.

Garn, S. M. (1962) *Human Races*, rev. edn. Springfield: C. C. Thomas.

Garrett, H. E. (1961) The Equalitarian Dogma. *Perspectives in Biology and Medicine* 4: 480–484.

Gates, R. R. (1944) Phylogeny and Classification of Hominids and Anthropoids. *American Journal of Physical Anthropology* 2: 279–292.

George, W. C. (1962) *The Biology of the Race Problem*. Washington, DC: National Putnam Letters Committee.

Gil-White, F. (2001) Are Ethnic Groups Biological Species to the Human Brain? *Current Anthropology* 42 (4): 515–553.

Giles, E. (1997) Hooton, E(arnest) A(lbert) (1887–1954). In Spencer F. (ed.), *History of Physical Anthropology: An Encyclopedia*, Vol. 1 (pp. 499–500). New York: Garland Publishing.

Goodman, A. H., and Leatherman, T. L. (1998) *Building a New Biocultural Synthesis: Political–Economic Perspectives on Human Biology*. Ann Arbor: University of Michigan Press.

Gravlee, C. C. (2009) How Race Becomes Biology: Embodiment of Social Inequality. *American Journal of Physical Anthropology* 139: 47–57.

Gravlee, C. C., and Sweet, E. (2008) Race, Ethnicity and Racism in Medical Anthropology, 1977–2002. *Medical Anthropology Quarterly* 22: 27–51.

Gravlee, C. C., Dressler, W. W., Bernard, H. R. (2005) Skin Color, Social Classification and Blood Pressure in Southeastern Puerto Rico. *American Journal of Public Health* 95: 2191–2197.

Haeckel, E. (1883) *The History of Creation, or the Development of the Earth and Its Inhabitants by Natural Causes. A Popular Exposition of the Doctrine of Evolution in General, and that of Darwin, Goethe, and Lamark in Particular*. New York: Appleton.

Haeckel, E. (1905) *The Wonders of Life*. New York: Harper.

Haraway, D. (1988) Remodeling the Human Way of Life: Sherwood Washburn and the New Physical Anthropology, 1950–1980. In G. W. Stocking, Jr (ed.), *Bones, Bodies, and Behavior: Essays on Biological Anthropology* (pp. 206–259). Madison: University of Wisconsin Press.

Hawks, J., Wang, E. T., Cochran, G. M., Harpending, H. C., and Moyzis, R. K. (2007) Recent Acceleration in Human Adaptive Evolution. *Proceedings of the National Academy of Sciences, USA* 104: 20753–20758.

Hirschfeld, L. A. (1996) *Race in the Making: Cognition, Culture and the Childs Construction of Human Kinds*. Cambridge MA: MIT Press.

Hirschfeld, L. A. (1998) Natural Assumptions: Race, Essence and Taxonomies of Human Kinds. *Social Research* 65 (2): 331–350.

Hirschfeld, L. A., and Gelman, S. A. (eds) (1994) *Mapping the Mind: Domain Specificity in Cognition and Culture*. New York: University of Cambridge Press.

Hooton, E. A. (1931) *Up from the Ape*. New York: MacMillan.

Hrdlička, A. (1918a) Physical Anthropology: Its Scope and Aims; Its History and Present Status in America. A. Physical Anthropology, Its Scope and Aims. *American Journal of Physical Anthropology* 1: 3–23.

Hrdlička, A. (1918b) Physical Anthropology: Its Scope and Aims; Its History and Present Status in America. B. History. *American Journal of Physical Anthropology* 1: 133–182.

Hrdlička, A. (1918c) Physical Anthropology: Its Scope and Aims; Its History and Present Status in America. C. Recent History and Present Status of the Science in North America. *American Journal of Physical Anthropology* 1: 267–304; 377–414.

Hulse, F. S. (1962) Race as an Evolutionary Episode. *American Anthropologist* 64: 929–945.

Hulse, F. S. (1963) Review of *The Origin of Races. American Anthropologist* 65: 685–687.

Hunley, K., Healy, M. E., and Long, J. C. (2009) The Global Pattern of Gene Identity Variation Reveals a History of Long-Range Migrations, Bottlenecks and Local Mate Exchange: Implications for Biological Race. *American Journal of Physical Anthropology* 139: 35–46.

Huxley, J. S., and Haddon, A. C. (1935) *We Europeans: A Survey of 'Racial' Problems.* London: Jonathan Cape.

Jackson, J. P., Jr. (2001) 'In Ways Unacademical': The Reception of Carleton S. Coon's *The Origin of Races. Journal of the History of Biology* 34: 247–285.

Jorde, L. B., Watkins, W., Bamshad, Dixon, M., Ricker, C., Seielstad, M., and Batzer, M. (2000) The Distribution of Human Genetic Diversity: A Comparison of Mitochondrial, Autosomal, and Y-Chromosome Data. *American Journal of Human Genetics* 66: 979–988.

Kaszycka, K. A., and Štrkalj, G. (2002) Anthropologists' Attitudes towards the Concept of Race: The Polish Sample. *Current Anthropology* 43 (2): 329–335.

Kaszycka, K. A., and Strzałko, J. (2003a) 'Race' – Still an Issue for Physical Anthropology? Results of Polish Studies Seen in the Light of the US Findings. *American Anthropologist* 105 (1): 116–124.

Kaszycka, K. A., and Strzałko, J. (2003b) Race: Tradition and Convenience or Taxonomic Reality? More on the Race Concept in Polish Anthropology. *Przegląd Antropologiczny – Anthropological Review* 66: 23–37.

Kaszycka, K. A., Štrkalj, G., and Strzałko, J. (2009) Current Views of European Anthropologists on Race: Influence of Educational and Ideological Background. *American Anthropologist* 111 (1): 43–56.

Keith, A. (1936) *History from Caves. A New Theory of the Origin of Modern Races of Mankind.* London: British Speleological Association Publication.

Kevles, D. J. (1985) *In the Name of Eugenics: Genetics and the Uses of Human Heredity.* Berkeley: University of California Press.

Klaatsch, H. (1910) Menschenrassen und Menschenaffen. *Correspondenzblatt der Deutschen Gesellschaft für Anthropologie, Ethnologie, und Urgesichte* 41: 91–99.

Klaatsch, H. (1923) *The Evolution and Progress of Mankind.* New York: Stokes.

Krieger, N. (ed.) (2004) *Embodying Inequality: Epidemiologic Perspectives.* Amityville, NY: Baywood Publishing Company.

Kroeber, A. L. (1923) *Anthropology.* New York: Harcourt-Brace.

Kuzawa, C. W. (2008) The Developmental Origins of Adult Health: Intergenerational Inertia, Adaptation and Disease. In W. Trevathan and J. McKenna (eds), *Evolutionary Medicine and Health: New Perspectives* (pp. 325–349). New York: Oxford University Press.

Lewontin, R. C. (1972) The Apportionment of Human Diversity. *Evolutionary Biology* 6: 381–398.

Lieberman, L. (2001) How 'Caucasoids' Got Such Big Heads and Why They Shrank: From Morton to Rushton. *Current Anthropology* 42: 69–95.

Lieberman, L., Kirk, R. C., and Corcoran, M. (2003a) The Decline of Race in American Physical Anthropology. *Przegląd Antropologiczny – Anthropological Review* 66: 3–21.

Lieberman, L., Kirk, R. C., and Littlefield, A. (2003b) Perishing Paradigm: Race – 1931–1999. *American Anthropologist* 105 (1): 110–113.

Lieberman, L., Hampton, R. E., Littlefield, A., and Hallead, G. (1992) Race in Biology and Anthropology: A Study of College Texts and Professors. *Journal of Research in Science Teaching* 29 (3): 301–321.

Lieberman, L., Kaszycka, K. A., Martinez Fuentes, A. J., Yablonsky, L., Kirk, R. C., Štrkalj, G., Wang, Q., and Sun, L. (2004) The Race Concept in Six Regions: Variation without Consensus. *Collegium Antropologicum* 28 (2): 907–921.

Linnaeus, C. (1758) *Systema Naturae*, 10th edn. Stockholm: Laurentii Salvii.

Littlefield, A., Lieberman, L., and Reynolds, L. T. (1982) Redefining Race: The Potential Demise of a Concept in Physical Anthropology. *Current Anthropology* 23 (6): 641–655.

Livingstone, F. B. (1962) On the Non-Existence of Human Races. *Current Anthropology* 3 (3): 279–81.

Long, J. C., and Kittles, R. A. (2003) Human Genetic Diversity and the Non-Existence of Human Races. *Human Biology* 75: 449–471.

Long, J. C., Li, J., and Healey, M. E. (2009) Human DNA Sequences: More Variation, Less Race. *American Journal of Physical Anthropology* 139: 23–34.

Manica, A., Prugnolle, F., and Balloux, F. (2005) Geography is a Better Determinant of Human Genetic Differentiation than Ethnicity. *Human Genetics* 118: 366–371.

Marks, J. (1995) *Human Biodiversity: Genes, Race, and History*. New York: Aldine de Gruyter.

Mayr, E. (1942) *Systematics and the Origin of Species*. New York: Columbia University Press.

Mead, M., Dobzhansky, T., Tobach, E., and Light, R. E. (eds) (1968) *Science and the Concept of Race*. New York: Columbia University Press.

Montagu, A. (1942) *Man's Most Dangerous Myth: The Fallacy of Race*. New York: Columbia University Press.

Montagu, A. (ed.) (1964) *The Concept of Race*. New York: The Free Press.

Nei, M., and Roychoudhury, A. K. (1982) Evolutionary Relationships and the Evolution of Human Races. *Evolutionary Biology* 14: 1–59.

Paul, D. B. (1998) *The Politics of Heredity: Essays on Eugenics*. Albany: SUNY Press.

Prentice, D. A., and Miller, D. T. (2007) Psychological Essentialism of Human Categories. *Current Directions in Psychological Science* 16 (4): 202–206

Proctor, R. (1988) From *Anthropologie* to *Rassenkunde* in the German Anthropological Tradition. In G. W. Stocking, Jr (ed.), *Bones, Bodies, and Behavior: Essays on Biological Anthropology* (pp. 138–179). Madison: University of Wisconsin Press.

Prugnolle, F., Manica, A., and Balloux, F. (2005) Geography Predicts Neutral Genetic Diversity of Human Populations. *Current Biology* 15: R159–R160.

Putnam, C. (1962) *Race and Reason: A Yankee View*. Washington, DC: Public Affairs Press.

Ramachandran, S., Deshpande, O., Roseman, C. C., Rosenberg, N. A., Feldman M. W., and Cavalli-Sforza, L. L. (2005) Support from the Relationship of Genetic and Geographic Distance for a Serial Founder Effect Originating in Africa. *Proceedings of the National Academy of Sciences, USA* 102: 15942–15947.

Relethford, J. H. (2002) Apportionment of Global Human Genetic Diversity Based on Craniometrics and Skin Color. *American Journal of Physical Anthropology* 73: 629–636.

Relethford, J. H. (2009) Race and Global Patterns of Phenotypic Variation. *American Journal of Physical Anthropology* 139: 16–22.

Risch, N., Burchard, E., Ziv, E., and Tang, H. (2002) Categorizations of Humans in Biomedical Research: Genes, Race and Disease. *Genome Biology* 3 (7): Comment 2007.1–2007.12.

Rosenberg, N. A., Pritchard, J. K., Weber, J. L., Cann, H. M., Kidd, K. K., Zhivotovsky, L. A., and Feldman, M. W (2002) Genetic Structure of Human Populations. *Science* 298: 2381–2385.

Schell, L. M. (1997) Culture as a Stressor: A Revised Model of Biocultural Interaction. *American Journal of Physical Anthropology* 102: 67–77.

Schwartz, R. S. (2001) Racial Profiling in Medical Research. *The New England Journal of Medicine* 344: 1392–1393.

Serre, D., and Pääbo, S. (2004) Evidence for Gradients of Human Genetic Diversity within and among Continents. *Genome Research* 14: 1679–1685.

Spencer, F. (1997) Hrdlička, Aleš (1869–1943). In F. Spencer (ed.), *History of Physical Anthropology: An Encyclopedia*, Vol. 1 (pp. 503–504). New York: Garland Publishing.

Stanton, W. (1960) *The Leopard's Spots: Scientific Attitudes toward Race in America 1815–59.* Chicago: University of Chicago Press.

Stein, G. J. (1988) Biological Science and the Roots of Nazism. *American Scientist* 76: 50–58.

Stocking, G. W., Jr. (1968) *Race, Culture, and Evolution: Essays on the History of Anthropology.* New York: Free Press.

Templeton, A. R. (1998) Human Races: A Genetic and Evolutionary Perspective. *American Anthropologist* 100: 632–650.

Topinard, P. (1885) *Eléments d'anthropologie générale.* Paris: Delahaye et Lecrosnier.

Topinard, P. (1892) On Race in Anthropology. In E. Count (ed.), *This is Race: An Anthology Selected from the International Literature on the Races of Man* (pp. 171–176). New York: Henry Schuman.

Vogt, C. (1864) *Lectures on Man: His Place in Creation and in the History of the Earth.* London: Longman, Green, Longman and Roberts.

Washburn, S. L. (1963) The Study of Race. *American Anthropologist* 65: 521–532.

Williams, D. R., and Collins, C. (2001) Racial Residential Segregation: A Fundamental Cause of Racial Disparities in Health. *American Journal of Public Health* 93: 200–208.

Wilson, E. O., and Brown, W. L., Jr. (1953) The Subspecies Concept and Its Taxonomic Implications. *Systematic Zoology* 2: 97–111.

Wolpoff, M. H., and Caspari, R. (1997) *Race and Human Evolution.* New York: Simon and Schuster.

Growth, Development, Senescence, and Aging: A Life History Perspective

CHAPTER 7

Douglas E. Crews and
Barry Bogin

Life history theory is the study of the evolution and function of life stages and of behaviors related to these stages (Stearns 1992).

> The life history of a species may be defined as the evolutionary adaptations used to allocate limited resources and energy toward growth, maintenance, reproduction, raising offspring to independence, and avoiding death. Life history patterns of species are often a series of trade-offs between growth versus reproduction, quantity versus quality of offspring, and other biological possibilities given the limited time and resources available to all living things. (Bogin 2009)

Biological anthropologists and human biologists have long been interested in how human growth, development, senescence, and aging differ from the corresponding processes in other apes, our closest phylogenic relatives, other non-human primates, and mammals. It is easy to document these differences, such as altricial offspring, slow, prolonged growth including childhood and adolescence stages, late start to reproduction, menopause, survival into the eighth and ninth decades, and maximum life span over 122 years (Arking 2006; Bogin 1999; Crews 2003). Determining the evolutionary forces that produced these and other aspects of life history has not been as easy. We begin with a review of the general patterns of human growth and development and follow it with a review of reproductive adulthood and of patterns of human senescence and aging. We follow it, in turn, with a review of theoretical models for why humans came to be slowly maturing, reproductively successful, and long-lived large-bodied primates.

Arking (2006) proposed a general model of the human life span that is useful to structure this review. He divided the human life span into three phases: the development, the health, and the senescence spans (p. 501). The 'development span' (ages 0–19.9 years) is characterized by the building up and integration of tissues and structures to develop a fully functional and reproductively capable organism. It ends at the point where individuals are fully developed and nutritionally self-supporting, at about 20 years of age. At the end of development, the 'health span' phase of life commences. During the health span (between 20 and about 49.9 years), humans are at their maximum levels of physical fitness and physiological health and show their lowest adult mortality rates. From the age of 20 through the remainder of life, mortality rates double about every 7–10 years. Beginning at a low rate, at the age of 20–30 (about 0.001), mortality goes up very slowly in early adulthood (reaching about 0.002 at 40 and .004 at 50). The health span ends when age-dependent mortality increases significantly, roughly at the age at which 10 percent of the population is deceased (Arking 2006: 24). The 'senescent span' begins when the reproductive effort is declining and when systematic deterioration across the soma (that is, the body and its systems) becomes obvious; it lasts from about the age of 50 until death. These phases are general enough to be usefully applied across multiple species, including humans, and to allow us to structure our views of human life history.

Our definition of life history theory mentioned the importance of trade-offs due to limited energy resources and time for all of life's demands. In an important paper, Gadgil and Bossert (1970: 3) stated: "An organism's life history may be looked upon as resultant of three biological processes, namely, maintenance, growth, and reproduction. Any organism has limited resources of time and energy at its disposal. The three component processes of the life history compete for these limited resources." During the growth span, there are some life history trade-offs (LHTOs) between amount of growth and rate of maturation. In humans, for example, growth rate in length and weight slows quickly between birth and the age of 2.9 years, and then it remains slow, or even declines, until puberty (Figure 7.1). However, brain growth remains rapid and maturation of motor control systems and of the teeth is rapid as well. Throughout most of human history there was not enough food, hence energy, to support rapid growth and maturation simultaneously.

During the development span there are few LHTOs between somatic survival and reproductive effort, as virtually all available energy is directed toward growth and maintenance. Once body growth and sexual maturation are complete and the point of maximum reproductive potential (MRP; see Crews 2003) is attained, competition between reproduction and maintenance ensues. To the degree that an organism is able to build a body that is stronger, endowed with somatic resources that are more integrated, is physiologically more resilient, and has more reserve capacity (RC; see Crews 2003, which is discussed more fully in a later section), its likelihood of survival through the health span and well into the senescent span is greater (Bogin 2009; Crews 2003, 2008; Crews and Stewart in press; Larke and Crews 2006). Aspects of senescence initiated in the development or health spans often express themselves during the senescent span. In the following sections of this chapter we explore the spans of human development, health, and senescence in greater detail.

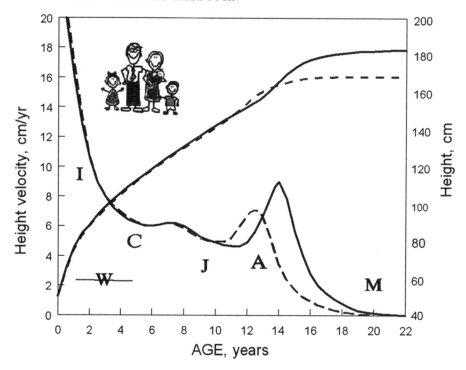

Figure 7.1 Distance and velocity curves of growth for healthy, well-nourished human beings. These are modal curves based on height data for the western European and North American populations. The stages of post-natal growth are abbreviated as follows: I = infancy, C = childhood, J = juvenile, A = adolescence, M = mature adult. W = range of weaning age, centered on the mean age of 3.0 years. Modified from Bogin 1999

Key:
Dashed line = girls
Solid line = boys

THE DEVELOPMENT SPAN

Humans show unique patterns of growth within different tissues and dimensions (neurological, reproductive, somatic, dental, immunological, height, and weight), both *in utero* and post-natally (Figure 7.2). Height distance shows the sigmoid pattern of growth already mentioned (Figure 7.1). During uterine development, the soma develops rapidly until the beginning of the third trimester, but then slows, as the brain and neurological system show rapid development. This pattern of rapid neurological development is maintained through the first 5–6 years of life, as the brain completes 95 percent of its total lifetime growth (see Figure 7.2, and also Figure 5.7 in Larsen 2008, p. 126). However, the skull does not completely seal its multiple sutures till the early twenties, when the final integration of its neurons, via dendrite growth and final/additional synaptic connections, is achieved. Growth in the dentition is complete around age 15, with only the third (or 18-year) molars remaining to erupt. Reproductive development is the most delayed among these patterns, showing a slow steady growth till about the twelfth year of life and then rising rapidly in a geometric fashion to arrive at its endpoint at about the same time as stature growth is

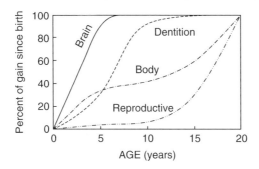

Figure 7.2   Scammons curves for the proportion of growth of various tissue types, from birth to their adult maximums. Note the differences in patterns, rates, and timing of attainment of adult size. Modified from Bogin 1999

complete (Figures 7.1 and 7.2). The immune system develops rapidly from birth to about the age of 15, when the thyroid begins decreasing in size and decreasing its output of naïve t-cells, till it completely involutes by about the age of 20.

During intrauterine growth, the developing individual responds to the environment that is conveyed to it by maternal physiology via the placenta. The human placenta separates the fetal and maternal blood supplies by just a single cell, which makes it one of the most 'intimate' of all mammalian placentas. Due to this intimacy, the fetus is exposed to much of what the mother experiences. Stresses encountered by the mother at this time may be imprinted upon the developing fetus and permanently alter its future physiology and risks for disease in adulthood and old age (Barker 1998; Cameron and Demerath 2002). This has been termed the 'fetal programming hypothesis' (Kuzawa 2005; Kuzawa and Sweet 2009), and sometimes the 'Barker effect.' Clearly, events occurring at the earliest stages of human growth and development are imprinted upon the developing organism *in utero* and alter all later aspects of that individual's life history (LH; see also the figure and box on p. 124 in Larsen 2008). Such fetal programming may even last over three generations of individuals (Price and Coe 2000; Drake and Walker 2004), because the ova that will form a mother's grandchildren are laid down while the developing fetus of her child is still in her womb. Multiple additional modifications of fetal development appear to have characterized the evolution of modern humans.

In contrast with living people, the large-bodied apes, such as chimpanzees and gorillas, have a pattern of rapid fetal development and of physically precocial newborns. Over hominin evolutionary history, the ape pattern was altered such that hominin newborns became less physically developed – or 'secondarily altricial' (Smith 1989). Altricial mammals are very dependent on maternal care at birth, in contrast to precocial mammals, who are independent of most maternal care, except for feeding by lactation. While less developed than apes in most respects, newborn humans are the brainiest of primates; human brain weight at birth averages 366 grams, and in chimpanzees it averages 136 grams (Robson et al. 2006). Human brains grow more rapidly than the brains of apes, so that, at 18 months of age, human brains weigh more than 1,000 grams and chimpanzee brains average about 300 grams.

Human newborns remain physically altricial for a very long period, while the brain and neurological tissues show rapid rates of development (Figure 7.2). This trade-off between precocial and altricial development may be very ancient in the hominin line (Rosenberg and Trevathan 2002). Moreover, this ape–human being difference points to important distinctions in life history patterns. Sometime during hominin life history evolution, two new, uniquely human, stages were inserted into the human life cycle. These are the stages of childhood and adolescence.

Primate life history stages

All mammals have, at minimum, two life history stages between birth and death. These are infancy, defined as the period of feeding by lactation from the mother, and adulthood, defined as the period of reproduction and care for offspring. Some species of mammals live in social groups, in which individuals of the group recognize each other, interact both cooperatively and antagonistically according to individual recognition, and maintain these relationships for relatively long periods of time. Wolves, hyenas, lions, some marine mammals such as whales and porpoises, and most primate species are examples of social mammals. These social species stand in contrast to species of herd mammals such as wildebeest and deer, which form groups mainly out of each individual's selfish fear of predators (Hamilton 1971) or desire to maximize reproductive effort.

The social mammals, including most species of non-human primates have three post-natal life history stages – infant, juvenile, and adulthood (Pereira and Fairbanks 2003; Bogin 1999). Terms such as 'juvenile,' 'child,' and 'adolescent' are often used interchangeably in the biological and sociological literature. In this chapter we define these terms more precisely, using measurable biological characteristics and observable behaviors, especially methods of feeding. Infant mammals are defined as being administered all their nourishment or some of it via lactation. Juvenile mammals are weaned, which means that they no longer receive food via lactation. Juveniles must find their own food and must be able to eat and digest an adult-type diet. This requires adult-type teeth, and one marker for the transition from infancy to juvenility is the eruption of the first permanent molar teeth. In addition, juveniles are still growing and not yet sexually mature (a trade-off between growth and reproduction). Inserted between infancy and adulthood, evolution of mammalian juvenility is an important problem in life history research, but it will not be discussed further here (see Pereira and Fairbanks 2003; Kappeler and Pereira 2003; Evans and Harris 2008).

The Primate life history stages of infant, juvenile, and adult were originally modeled by Shultz (1947, Smith 1989, 1991) using a linear model, suggesting a gradual progressive alteration in life stages. Schultz and his followers considered human life history to be a prolongation of the three stages found in non-human primates. By the late 1980s, evidence had accumulated to indicate that human life history included new stages between infancy and adulthood, which are defined as childhood and adolescence (Bogin 1988, 1993, 1997, 1999; Bogin and Smith 1996). The five-stage LH of modern humans is illustrated in Figure 7.1 (from Bogin 1999) and in Figure 7.3. Those of several other primate and mammal species are illustrated in Figures 7.4 and 7.5. These clearly illustrate that something different occurs during human growth and development, which is not observed in other species. The differences are revealed not only in modes of feeding, but also in rates of growth (growth velocity). In brief, and as is shown in Figure 7.1, human infancy spans the first three years of life and is characterized by a rapid rate of growth, which is declining precipitously. Infancy is followed by a childhood phase of relatively steady growth, from 36 months through to about 6.9 years. The juvenile stage commences around age 7,

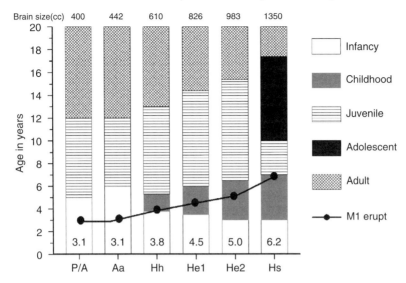

Figure 7.3   The evolution of hominin life history during the first 20 years of life. Abbreviations are: P/A., *Pan* (Chimpanzee)/ *Australopithecus afarensis*, Aa, *Australopithecus africanus*; Hh, *Homo habilis*; He1, early *Homo erectus*; He2, late *Homo erectus*; Hs, *Homo sapiens*. The dating of the fossil hominin species is *Australopithecus afarensis*, 3.8–3.2 million years ago (MYA); *A. africanus*, 3.0–2.5 MYA; *Homo habilis*, 2.2–1.6 MYA; early *H. erectus*, 1.8–1.0 MYA; late *H. erectus*, 1.0 MYA–150,000 years ago; *H. sapiens*, 200,000–present. The numbers across the top indicate the known or estimated brain sizes for each species. The numbers along the bottom indicate the age in years for the eruption of the first permanent molar teeth, M1. From Bogin 1999

and it shows a declining rate of growth. This stage ends with puberty, which is a set of neuroendocrine changes that begin in the brain and eventually stimulate the hypothalamic–pituitary–gonadal axis toward sexual maturation. In terms of growth, puberty begins a new acceleration in growth rate, leading to the adolescent growth spurt. In modern cosmopolitan settings with good nutrition, the spurt begins at about 10 in girls and 12 in boys and extends till the reproductive adulthood stage, at about 20 years of age (18–19 for girls and 20–22 for boys) (for additional details, see Bogin 1999, 2006, in press).

Human life history from womb to tomb

Intrauterine development   As the name suggests, intrauterine development is the LH phase prior to birth. It is easily determined as occurring from conception till birth. It is the phase of life during which the *Anlagen* for all later aspects of somatic development are initiated. All mammals have an intrauterine phase of life. Among most non-human primates, growth, development, and integration of somatic and physiological systems form the main goal of intrauterine development. Among humans, neurological growth and development take center stage at least during the later trimester of intrauterine life. All extant large-bodied apes show a similar gestation length: humans 266 days, chimpanzees 237 days, gorillas 257 days, and orangutans 260 days. These similarities suggest that an eight to nine month gestation period was the ancestral

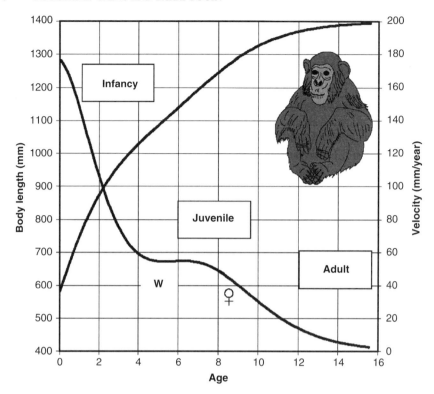

Figure 7.4   Chimp growth. A model of distance and velocity curves for chimpanzee growth in body length (growth of the summed length of crown to rump, thigh, and leg). This is based on the longitudinal study of captive chimpanzee growth conducted by Hamada and Udono (2002). In the wild, weaning (W) usually takes place between 48 and 60 months of age (Pusey 1983). Original figure from Bogin 2006, reprinted by permission from *The Evolution of Human Life History,* edited by Hawkes and Paine. © 2006 by the School for American Research, Santa Fe, New Mexico, USA.

condition for the last common ancestor of living hominoids. This is due possibly to constraints on the length of intrauterine life among large-bodied apes. There may be a pleisomorphic limit (that is, in taxonomy, an ancestral trait shared by descendants from a common ancestor) to the period during which large-bodied apes may provide an adequate environment for their developing offspring. This limit may have imposed a constraint upon fetal development, and for modern humans it may represent a trade-off between somatic and neurological growth *in utero.*

Infancy   A period of almost total dependence on parents for sustenance and protection, infancy is observed across not only mammalian, but also multiple avian, reptilian, and insect species. As noted above, mammalian infancy is characterized by feeding via maternal lactation. Among humans, infancy is the LH stage lasting from birth to 36 months, and it is characterized by dependence upon lactation, or some imitation of lactation, for sustenance. By one year of age, or earlier in modern well fed populations, an infant's body size and energy needs are greater than what may be supplied by mother's milk alone. Some form of complementary feeding of supplementary foods

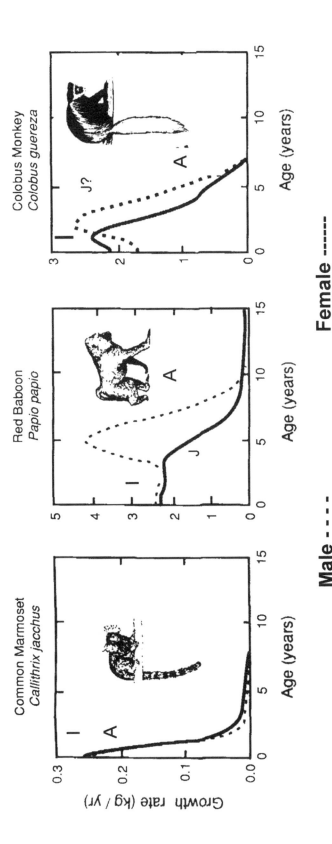

Figure 7.5 Non-human primate growth. Three primate species showing different patterns of post-natal growth in weight. Abbreviations are; I = infancy, J = juvenile, A = Adult. Marmosets are weaned at 63 days and can breed at one year or age (Harvey et al. 1986). Marmoset growth rate shows no post-natal growth spurt and no change in growth rate typical of a juvenile growth stage. Baboons are weaned by 18 months and begin puberty at about 3.5 years for females and 4.5 years for males (ibid.). Baboons have a juvenile growth stage for both males and females, but only males have a clear weight growth spurt. Colobus monkeys are weaned at about 13 months, and females have their first birth at about 4.6 years of age. Colobus monkeys show a post-natal spurt for both sexes, but it is not clear if there is any juvenile growth stage. The velocity curves are fit to cross-sectional data collected from captive animals. The curves are fit using the statistical estimates based on lowest regression (see the text for details). From Bogin 1999.

© Cambridge University Press

is needed to meet the demands of growth, immune function, body maintenance, and physical activity (Bogin 1988, 1999, 2006, in press; Sellen 2006). The deciduous teeth erupt during this period and allow the infant to consume complementary foods, but breast-feeding continues to a mean age of 2.8 years in a wide variety of human societies (modern industrial societies with little or no lactation are unusual 'outliers' is this regard).

Among most primates, infants are able to cling to their parents within hours or days of their birth; they swing about on their own within a couple of weeks; and they begin foraging by the age of 1 or 2 years. Human infants cannot do these things at these ages; but, even so, humans terminate infancy much sooner than the other apes. Anthropologists usually take the end of lactation, also defined as weaning, as a criterion for the termination of infancy. By this criterion, in the wild, chimpanzee infancy lasts on average to 4–4.5 years, gorilla infancy lasts to 3.5 years, and orangutan infancy lasts to 6–7 years (see Figures 7.3 and 7.4). Weaning is associated with several behavioral changes, one being that infant primates tend to spend more of their time with age-mates rather than under the watchful eye of their parents. Throughout infancy human offspring show rapid neurological growth, as the brain continues to grow at the same pace it achieved during the final intrauterine trimester. At the same time, the body continues to increase slowly in size and integration, as the infant develops its ability to control its soma, vocalize its thoughts and needs, and process environmental stimuli (see Bogin 1988, 1999, 2006, in press).

Childhood   Childhood is a period of steady growth in length and weight (about 5–6 cm per year in length), but of relatively rapid development of neurological and motor control systems, cognitive capacities, language usage, and emotional expression. The childhood life history stage spans from the end of infancy (about 2.9 years) until about 6.9 years, which is about the time of the eruption of the first permanent molar teeth (Bogin 1988, 1999, 2006, in press). While children are maturing and gaining increasing independence in many tasks, the childhood stage is primarily characterized by dependence on older people for care and feeding. Until the age of 7, the youngster does not have the ability to feed itself, due to the lack of permanent teeth, muscular strength, motor control, and cognitive capacity to realize its own needs for survival. Childhood dependency is well studied by developmental psychologists such as Jean Piaget, who has produced classic work on cognitive abilities (Piaget 1954; Piaget and Inhelder 1969), and by school systems around the world, which structure learning objectives and physical education by grades, according to average degrees of independence. Also telling is the observation that so-called 'street children' are not, in fact children, but juveniles or older. The present authors are not aware of any study showing that youngsters under 6.5 years of age are living 'on the street,' that is, independently of some type of home and dependency on adults. This is so even in cases when the 'home' is a place of abuse and/or neglect. Until about the age of 7, youngsters cannot break the emotional/cognitive/physical attachments to caregivers, which were developed in infancy and early childhood.

As mothers wean their infants to childhood, other people play an ever increasing role in their care and feeding. These people include older siblings, aunts and grandmothers, fathers and other men from the family, as well as other adult members of the social group. These people provision the children with nutrient-dense, easy to chew, and easy to digest foods obtained and processed by themselves or others. Children may acquire some foods and do some other chores, but they are not usually positive contributors to the subsistence of their social group. Rather, they remain dependent upon others for sustenance. Resource sharing within human social groups provides food and other items for children to continue their growth and development, while they also learn behavioral, social, and life skills for their future survival and reproductive effort.

Human biocultural reproduction

Biologists call this type of behavior 'cooperative breeding,' and it is found in some species of insects, birds, and mammals (for instance wolves and hyenas). Cooperative breeding works to increase the net reproductive output (Bergmüller et al. 2007). In those species, and in many but not all human groups, the cooperative breeders are close genetic relatives of the mother (Clutton-Brock 2002). By assisting the mother to care for her offspring, the helpers increase their own inclusive fitness, which means that they help to ensure that their genetic kin survive to reproductive age (Hawkes et al. 1998; Hawkes and Paine 2006).

   Human societies define kinship relations on the basis of genetic and social ties. Humans are the only species to use language and the cultural institution of marriage to define kinship categories. The overarching importance of kinship for the human species is that, in traditional societies (foragers, horticulturalist, pastoralists, and pre-industrial agriculturalists), kinship is the central organizing principle for economic production, social organization, and ideology (moral codes, religious behavior). Industrial western societies make use of fictive kinship – that is, the application of kin-ship names to people unrelated by marriage or descent – to enhance social relations, including their rights and their responsibilities towards each other's offspring. An example is calling the close friend of one's mother by the name 'Aunt Maria' instead of Mrs Smith. 'Aunt Maria' may provide food, supervision, protection, gifts and other types of parental investment to her 'niece,' and the 'niece' is expected to behave in accordance with the rules of interaction between family members. Human coopera-tive breeding, therefore, is bicultural in nature – it can be explained both by genetic and by fictive kinship. The human condition may better be called 'biocultural repro-duction,' as human cooperative reproduction enhances the social, economic, political, religious, and ideological 'fitness' of the social group members as much as, or even more than, it contributes to the genetic fitness of any individual.

   The provisioning of human children by social group members also frees mothers from the sole/primary care and feeding of their offspring and allows them to rebuild their own reserve capacity (RC), while also sequestering additional resources for self-maintenance and additional reproductive effort (Bogin 1999, 2009; Crews 2003; Larke and Crews 2006). Reserve capacity includes all available resources and energy for somatic maintenance that are not currently needed to sustain the soma (see Figure 3.2 in Crews 2003, p. 77). RC includes energy stores, excess lung, kidney, immune and heart function above that needed for current survival, and retention of cellular func-tion over the life span (see Crews 2003; Weinstein and Ciszek 2002). The building of RC begins in childhood and continues throughout life in settings with low external stressors, a surfeit of nutrients and opportunities to achieve one's growth potential (Bogin 2009; Crews 2003, 2007, 2008; Larke and Crews 2006). These are provided in humankind's bioculturally constructed niches. RC also aids in explaining the balance between cellular tissue repair and tumor suppression in cells (Weinstein and Ciszek 2002). A childhood phase of life does not seem to characterize any other primates or mammals, which mature from infant to adult or from infant to juvenile to adult. Thus the insertion of this phase into human LH over evolutionary time must have occurred through some selective advantage that improved the reproductive fitness of the off-spring or their parents. A childhood phase of life spreads growth and development across an extended timeframe, thereby reducing the day-to-day caloric needs of off-spring and the amount that must be provided daily by others (Gurven and Walker 2006). Both infancy and childhood phases also allow opportunities for non-mothers, fathers, uncles, aunts, siblings, and grandparents to contribute to the development of their offspring, nephews/nieces, brothers/sisters, and grand-offspring through alloparental care, provisioning, and carrying of children. These contributions all lead to improved survival in mothers and offspring and enhance the RC and fertility of mothers (see Bogin 1988, 1999, 2006, 2009, in press).

Juvenile   Humans, like most social mammals and non-human primates, show a phase of life typified by sexual immaturity and slow growth, during which they are capable both mentally and physically of providing some resources for themselves in terms of feeding, locomotion, and self-care. During this juvenile LH phase, the immature are generally not involved in direct reproductive effort, male–male competition, or estrous/menstrual cycling. Among humans, the juvenile phase occurs between the age of about 7 and the beginning of the adolescent growth spurt (Bogin 1988, 1999, 2006, in press). This spurt ends the juvenile period in humans and occurs around the age of 10 in girls and of 12 in boys. Much of the adult dentition erupts during the human juvenile period; the eruption of the first permanent molar occurs at the begin-ning of the period, as does that of the central incisors, while eruption of the second permanent molar marks the end of the juvenile period. In other large-bodied apes and non-human primates, the same period occurs after the infant stage and leads directly into reproductive adulthood. For humans, it is sandwiched between the two phases of LH not observed in these other species – childhood and adolescence. During the juvenile period the human growth rate declines slowly before taking off at puberty and at the beginning of adolescence. This slowed-down growth during the human juvenile period probably represents a LH trade-off between current growth and developing a soma of higher quality, endowed with greater RC and greater physical and neurological integration.

In more traditional cultural settings (foraging, horticulture, pastoralism, pre-industrial agriculture), human juveniles begin to practice and take on many adult roles, including those of producing and obtaining some of their own foods, gardening, herd-ing, hunting, foraging, infant-child-care, and traveling without the oversight of adult members of their social group. In some traditional societies, human juveniles may even achieve energy balance in terms of their own calorie acquisition (Walker et al. 2006). Juveniles in modern cosmopolitan settings are trained in formal school settings to take on future adult roles and are enculturated with the skills (reading, arithmetic, and sci-ence), behaviors and ideologies (manners, social customs, rules) for participating and achieving in their sociocultural environments. Non-human primate juveniles learn the lifeways of their natal group, how to forage for themselves, and the behaviors needed to perform adequately within their social groups also. Some non-human primate males even seem to have evolved a physiological ability to delay further maturation until they are physically prepared for the male–male competition that ensues upon maturation.

Adolescence   A new phase of human LH, not presaged among the non-human primates, not even the large-bodied apes, follows the human juvenile phase of growth and development. Termed 'adolescence,' this LH phase begins with the pubertal growth spurt and ends with the eruption of the third molar (when present at all) or with the end of skeletal growth and the attainment of maximum adult height (see Bogin 1988, 1999, 2006, in press). Adolescence encompasses the years of rapid growth commonly referred to as the post-pubertal growth spurt, and is easily observed in height velocity and distance curves (Figure 7.1). For girls, the period commonly includes the period between 10 and 18 years, and for boys, the period between 12 and 21 years of age. During adolescence, the slow stable growth velocity of the childhood and juvenile phases is replaced by a very rapid phase of growth in virtually all skeletal dimensions.

During adolescence most humans become sexually mature and capable of providing for their own sustenance and energy requirements (Kaplan et al. 2000), but they are still not sufficiently mature socioculturally to achieve their maximum reproductive potential (MRP: this is similar to Fischer's reproductive value, but modified in order to account for the need to achieve sociocultural maturity for maximum reproductive success in humans; for further details see Crews 2003, 2008, Larke and Crews 2006). Girls and boys become reproductively mature adult men and women at about the end of their adolescent stage (Bogin 1988, 1999, 2006, in press). In modern, highly constructed environments with well nourished and healthy adolescents, girls achieve physiologically defined fecundity at a median age of 18 years, when 80 percent of their menstrual cycles lead to the release of a mature ovum. Boys may produce fertile sperm by the age of 13.5 years, but they do not have the physical body size, social skills, or economic power to be attractive as fathers. In general, in most modern settings boys do not father offspring until they are 20 or older; nor do most girls give birth to children until they are about 19 (Bogin 2001). In more traditional societies and remote settings, these ages may be several years higher (Himalayas) or lower (Amazon; see Larke and Crews 2006).

Adolescents are generally capable not only of producing, extracting, or foraging for their own energy requirements, but also of attaining a surplus, to share with others in their social group. They are also able to participate in most economic, social, and ideological activities within the realm of their natal sociocultural systems. Insertion of an adolescence phase into human LH is a trade-off that further delayed the onset of human reproductive effort, but allowed additional years not only for attaining MRP, but also for building a higher RC and greater somatic stability before reproducing one's offspring.

One interesting aspect of the childhood, juvenile, and adolescence phases is their association with mortality rates. During these LH phases, mortality rates are at the lowest they will ever attain over the human life course; a 10–12-year-old girl in the USA is about as immortal as a human can ever be, with a mortality risk of 0.00015. One positive aspect of slow growth over multiple LH phases is humankind's uniquely high survivorship among primates. This is in part due to living in culturally constructed, built environmental niches, which produce benign and cushy life styles (Crews 2008;

Crews and Stewart in press). These changes, in addition to the evolution of slowed-down growth, have produced a selective advantage to humankind and have contributed to decreased child mortality, improved survival, and increased fertility among human populations.

Evolutionary pressures

Evolution operates through differential fertility and mortality. Additional life history phases of human growth and development evolved in our ancestors, either to maintain levels of reproductive success and survival or to enhance reproductive success and to reduce mortality. Otherwise additional phases of growth and development would not have been inserted into the human LH, as the trade-off associated with the new phases is too energetically expensive to have arisen by mutation or genetic drift. To understand why the stages of childhood and adolescence evolved, it is necessary to understand evolutionary pressures on early hominin and human LH.

Compared to other large-bodied hominids (living apes and their direct ancestors), hominins (living humans and their ancestors) are habitually bipedal. Bipedalism altered the arrangement of the human female pelvis and birth canal, changing all aspects of obstetrics among modern humans as compared to other large-bodied apes (Rosenberg and Trevathan 2002). Bipedalism seems to have promoted multiple alterations to human growth, including secondarily altricial newborns due to slow physical development *in utero*, and delayed maturation during the entire growth phase. The addition of childhood and adolescent phases must have followed alterations in earlier phases that produced individuals in need of additional development time in order to increase their ultimate survival and eventual reproductive fitness. The apes also have a relatively slow rate of growth and development compared with other mammals, even with other primates such as monkeys, lemurs, tarsiers, and lorises (Figure 7.5). Apes deal with slow infant growth and development via a prolonged infancy, feeding by lactation, and maternal protection while the young mature and learn to survive on their own. Most mammals stop nursing their young when the first permanent molar, or M1, erupts (Smith 1991, Smith et al. 1994). The chimpanzee infant's M1 erupts at a mean age of 3.1 years (Anemone et al. 1996; Smith et al. 1994), but the mother continues to nurse for about another two years as the infant learns how to acquire and process foods (Pusey 1983). Because of the chimpanzee infant's dependency on the mother, the average period between successful births for chimpanzee females is about five years.

Human infants are weaned early relative to M1 eruption, at a median age of 30–36 months in traditional human societies (Dettwyler 1995), and much earlier in agricultural and early industrial societies of the past 200 years. The human M1 erupts at about 6 years of age. Even at the age of 6, human offspring have much to learn before they can survive on their own. The relatively early weaning of human infants is therefore quite unexpected when compared with that of other primates and mammals. Early weaning means that women can have a short birth interval, which gives them a distinct advantage over the apes. Women can produce and rear two offspring through infancy during the time it takes chimpanzees or orangutans to produce and rear one offspring. The weaned infant, though, must survive to adulthood if the short human birth spacing is to result in a true reproductive advantage. How is it possible that human beings trade off early weaning for increased reproductive frequency and still ensure offspring survival? Humans use biocultural reproduction, as described above, and this new type of social behavior evolved along with the evolution of childhood as a life history stage. Elsewhere we propose that the earliest evidence of childhood may date from about 2.2 million years ago, that is, with the appearance of *Homo habilis* and of stone tools in the paleontological record (Bogin 1999).

Childhood, which may have evolved as a reproductive adaptation for the mother to reduce her birth intervals, seems to be linked with other defining features of human evolution, such as stone tool manufacture. The stone tools of *Homo habilis* may have been used to obtain bone marrow of long bones scavenged from the killings of predatory cats. As a nutrient, bone marrow is dense, soft, and readily digestible, which makes it an ideal food for children.

Additional selective pressure for bipedalism may have come from the value of childhood. Bipedal locomotion involves many costs and trade-offs in anatomy, physiology, and behavior and its evolutionary value has not been easy to explain. One traditional explanation proposes that bipedalism freed the upper limbs, allowing our ancestors to manipulate their environments in ways that other large-bodied apes could not. Hominins could carry infants, large quantities of food, and ultimately tools over long distances. But why would they do these things when no other animal does them? Perhaps it was the reproductive advantages of the evolution of childhood and of biocultural reproduction that gave the impetus to sustain and intensify bipedal locomotion, tool use, and food carrying for provisioning for children. Once started, the way of life represented by bipedalism, stone tools, and provisioning could lead to newer technologies and improved abilities to modify the environment and produce ever safer constructed niches, in which offspring could survive and thrive.

As mental and cultural abilities to manufacture implements and tools improved over evolutionary time, hominins and, ultimately, modern humans were able to engage in ever greater niche modification and in new niche construction (see Odling-Smee et al. 2003). Today humans live in a highly constructed biocultural niche. Even the most isolated human groups live in artificially constructed shelters, use fire, cloth, and metal tools, and have knowledge of western biomedicine and life ways. All humans have complex economic, social, political, and religious systems. Biocultural evolution in such niches has allowed many modern populations to face fewer stresses from disease, injury, and climatic factors and has promoted a reduced mortality at all ages and, particularly, improvements in sanitation and immunization that increase the survival of infants and children. More recently, medical and social investments in adults and the elderly are reducing mortality in these age groups, allowing more individuals to survive sufficiently long to express their innate long-lived propensities.

HEALTH SPAN

Reproductive effort

The health span is the period of maximum reproductive effort. This includes mating effort (searching for, finding/attracting, and keeping (a) mate(s)); reproductive effort (siring, gestating, and birthing offspring); and parental investment (PI: all expenditures of the parents' time, energy, and future reproductive effort on one offspring, at a cost to those parents' abilities to invest in their own somas or in other possible offspring and to enhance their own fitness (see Hamilton 1964, 1966). Parental investment includes gestation, lactation, and provisioning, protecting, acculturating, and teaching offspring. During the health span, evolutionarily successful organisms must complete the necessary tasks of life (Weisman 1889; Crews 2008; Crews and Stewart in press), which include reproducing and fledging offspring who themselves reproduce. Such reproductive success is the *sine qua non* of Darwinian fitness; but it is slightly different from fertility (number of children ever born to a female).

Human reproductive effort is most substantial between the ages of 20–50 in most societies. During this period, women reproduce their first offspring at about the age of 19, and they achieve their maximum fecundity at about the age of 30 (Bogin 1999, 2006; Larke and Crews 2006). After about 35 years, fecundity begins a slow decline until menopause (that is, the cessation of monthly menstrual cycling and the absence of menses in adult women) and until reproductive senescence in women, at about 45–50 years. Men's reproductive success follows closely that of women in the same population, although in many traditional settings a larger variance in their total fitness is observed due to cultural behaviors (Alexander et al. 1979; Chagnon 1979; Crews 2007; Marlowe 2000). In so-called 'natural fertility' societies (which have no use of modern contraception), fertility rates may be over 15.0 per women; in modern cosmopolitan settings with wide use of birth control, they fall below 2.0 (Larke and Crews 2006). Parental investment (PI) in human offspring is extensive and long-lasting in all societies (ibid.). Extensive, high-quality PI is a hallmark of human reproductive effort that sets us apart from all other mammals and other large-bodied apes (Lancaster and Lancaster 1983). Besides investing in offspring, humans share food with and provision biological relatives, non-relatives, infirm and frail members of their populations, and the infants and children of relatives and non-relatives (Crews 2005). It is the quality and quantity of such investments that allow women, among all large-bodied apes, to express the highest fertility and shortest interbirth intervals of all the apes (Bogin 1999).

Menopause   Women who survive after the age of 35 experience waning fecundity (the biological capability for producing offspring) with increasing age; then they experience a complete cessation of reproductive capability around the age of 50. Apparently almost all mammals who survive beyond 35 years show a decline in reproduction, then loss of it after about 50 years. Evolutionary and allometric constraints on the size of ovaries and on the number of available primary oocytes may lead to reproductive decline with increasing age among all large-bodied mammals (Austad 1994; Graham et al. 1979; Jones 1975; Leidy 1994; Packer et al. 1998). Although some have attempted to make a special case for human reproductive decline and menopause by suggesting that they are uniquely human (Hawkes et al. 1997, 1998; Pavelka et al. 1991), oocyte depletion over the life course appears to be universal among female mammals (Austad 1994, 1997a; Graham et al. 1979; Leidy 1994; Packer et al. 1998). Austad (1994, 1997a) describes reproductive decline with increasing age among mammalian females in such a fashion that one must conclude it is a pleisomorphic LH trait (see also Packer et al. 1998). The main reason why few female mammals show menopause as currently defined is that few commonly survive past their fifth decade of life, at which age almost all women are post-menopausal (see Figure 3.5 in Crews 2003, p. 114). Recent reports on chimpanzee populations suggest that some females reproduce into their mid-fifties (Thompson et al. 2007), and some whale species may also reproduce through their sixth and later decades of life. But these are unusually long-lived individuals within their species, and most chimps and whales die in their third or fourth decade of life (see also Hawkes et al. 2009).

Menopause not only marks the end of the reproductive and health span for women, it also appears to be a precursor to senescent change across physiological systems. With menopause comes a decrease in circulating estrogen and progesterone levels and an increase in circulating follicle-stimulating hormone. This decrease in estrogen is associated with increased cardiovascular diseases, hypertension, bone loss, and cancer risks (changes discussed in the next section as part of the senescent span). Multiple tissue and cell types follow closely life-long patterns of reproductive hormones. Vaginal and uterine tissues show hyperplasia during puberty and hypoplasia following menopause (Arking 2006). In addition, women show greater susceptibility to several circulatory conditions and reproductive tissue cancers after menopause. Also, women who experience early natural menopause (before the age of 44) experience higher mortality rates than those whose natural menopause is between 50–54 years of age (Snowden et al. 1989). Senescent degeneration of the reproduction function may promote a general loss of homeostatic control, promoting a cascade of senescent alterations throughout the soma. For example, prior to menopause, women have a rate of bone loss that is slightly higher than that of men. After menopause, women lose bone mass at two to three times the rate of bone mass loss in men of the same age (Stini 1990). Women in traditional societies who remain physically active may show less physical decline with age and may not progress as rapidly to morbidity as do less physically active women in richer nations. High physical activity throughout life may ameliorate many of the apparent detrimental impacts associated with menopause.

Chronic degenerative conditions

Reproductive human adults, aged 20–50 years, generally are in the health span of their lives. Although physiological function declines over the health span, the majority of adults living in modern, culturally constructed niches (Crews 2008; Crews and Stewart in press) retain sufficient reserve capacity across all somatic systems to survive through about eight decades of life. However, some find themselves at risk from many degenerative processes, at earlier ages, as a result of multiple inherent factors, lifestyles and environmental risks. Physiological variation across individuals leads to a series of chronic degenerative conditions (CDCs) affecting some in their middle age and almost all in their later years (Crews 2003, 2007; Crews and Gerber 2003; Gerber and Crews 1999; Ossa and Crews 2006).

Propensities to CDCs vary across different individuals within families, different families within populations, different ethnic groups and subpopulations within nations, and different nations across the world (see Harper and Crews 2000; Crews and Ice in press). CDCs are the leading causes of morbidity and mortality in cosmopolitan settings. Mortality and morbidity rates for CDCs – coronary artery diseases, hypertension, cerebrovascular diseases, diabetes, cancers, and chronic infectious diseases (including for example HIV) – vary widely across populations. Research has documented genetic propensities, segregating within families and within subgroups of populations, for each of these CDCs (see Crews and Williams 1999). In fact, multiple loci within the human genome contribute to most CDCs. Today such quantitative trait loci (QTL) have been identified for most CDCs, as have single nucleotide polymorphisms (SNP) and insertion/deletion polymorphisms (indels: where a segment of DNA is added to, or lost from, a sequence) for many of our common CDCs. Among the 'high risk' allelic variants are the BRCA 1 and 2 loci and breast cancer; the apolipoprotein E*4 allele/protein and hyperlipidemia, cardiovascular disease, and late onset of Alzheimer's disease; mutated mismatch repair genes and Lynch syndrome; and LDL-receptor mutations and familial hypercholesterolemia. However, such major genetic predispositions account for only a minority of all CDCs – perhaps as little as 10–20 percent. Most of the risk for an adult onset of CDCs is derived from lifestyle and from environmental and culturally related exposures and activities, and is termed sporadic. The most obvious example of a lifestyle risk association is the one between lung cancer and cigarette smoking. Smokers have a multifold increased risk for lung cancer compared to non-smokers. Such genetic and lifestyle propensities generally express themselves during the latter part of the health span and throughout the senescent span of life.

Transitions

Early in life and during the period of maximum reproductive effort, natural selection (NS) favors somatic maintenance in iteroparous species (species that reproduce multiple times) or in those that provide PI to their offspring after birth/hatching (Crews 2003, 2005, 2008; Larke and Crews 2006; Hamilton 1964, 1966). As life continues, investment in reproductive effort eventually takes priority over somatic maintenance and senescent processes may not be eliminated, because additional somatic investments yield trivial reproductive benefits. Eventually, the net effect of NS declines to zero. Metazoans have complex, interrelated, and interdependent cells, organs, and systems within their somas. Senescence of cells begins early in the life span, as strategic resources are directed toward replicating the immortal germline at the expense of the soma (Austad 2005; Kirkwood 1977, 1990; Drenos and Kirkwood 2004). Among species with high PI and multiple reproductive cycles, NS works to maintain the parental soma, because it is the sole reproductive organ and source of continued investment in reproductive effort and PI. When extrinsic mortality is high, there is little selection against senescent processes, because few organisms survive long enough for senescence to reduce their fitness. However, when extrinsic mortality is reduced, selection against senescent processes is stronger, as longer life may improve fitness. NS may not exert strong influences on the length of life, because older organisms retain little to no reproductive value and have little influence over their own or others' fitness (Crews and Stewart in press; Stearns 1992), but it will act against senescent processes that reduce total fitness. This means that all sexually reproducing organisms will eventually die. Although death cannot be precisely timed by natural selection, the building of RC in early life (before reproduction begins) can lead to a longer adult lifespan. The evolution of childhood and adolescence allows for the building of greater RC in the human species if and when the needed physical and social resources are available, as they often are in bioculturally constructed settings. These new life history stages account for much of the extended longevity observed in modern humans (Bogin 2009; Crews 2003, 2007, 2008; Larke and Crews 2006).

The Senescent Span

The later part of the life span commences at about the same time as most women become post-reproductive. It is not likely that this stage of life was achieved by any large portion of individuals in hominin species prior to the evolution of modern *Homo sapiens* (Caspari and Lee 2004), and it is seldom achieved by non-human hominoids in their natural environments today. The large number of humans who survive into their fifth decade of life in recent generations (and since the Neolithic revolution) are a modern phenomenon based upon recent biocultural evolution in highly constructed niches (Crews 2007, 2008; Crews and Stewart in press). There are few skeletal remains or fossils of persons who could be ascribed ages over 35 in the fossil record (Caspari and Lee 2004), which suggests that extended life spans beyond 50 years have only become common since the advent of modern humans, around 250,000 years ago. Even among these populations, few individuals are likely to have survived the struggles of life so as to achieve their fiftieth birthday. Average life span in the United States only increased from 48 to 75 years during the twentieth century, being due in large part to an improved survival of infants and children. However, the expectation of life at ages 20 and 40 has also increased during this period, which suggests improvements in life expectancy at all ages (Harper and Crews 2000; Crews and Ice in press). At the end of the twentieth century, 75 percent of men in Japan and 65 percent of men in the USA could expect to survive to the age of 70, while 88 percent of women in Japan and 79 percent of women in the USA could; but only 41 percent of men and 47 percent of women in India could (Crews 2005). On the basis of estimated ages and survival patterns observed in living foraging/hunting populations, some suggest that, once people survive childhood and their second decade of life (up to 20 years) in such settings, they are likely to live into their fifth or sixth decade of life (that is, until 40–50 years; Carey and Judge 2001; Hawkes et al. 1997, 1998). Since the late Paleolithic, it is likely that in most human groups some individuals survived to complete 50–60 years of life or more. Nevertheless, it is unlikely that many survived up to 70 or 80 years – ages that few survive to today in many populations. Among pre-agricultural groups of foragers, gatherers, and hunters of the Paleolithic with small local populations (around 500), it is not probable that many survived even to their sixties. Estimates of survival probabilities based upon estimated birth and death rates among today's foraging populations may not be reliable. Actual birthdates seldom are known, and data for constructing stable life tables are not available for recent generations. Multiple external factors influence such estimates. In contemporary cosmopolitan settings, life expectancy exceeds 85 years among women in only a couple of settings (Sweden and Japan; see Crews 2005; Larke and Crews 2006). Such observations indicate that biocultural modifications, lifestyles and constructed niches have had greater influences on human survival than genetic modifications have.

The senescent span of life is characterized by an increasing probability of death, a decreasing probability of reproduction among men, the loss of reproductive capability among women, and an increasing loss of function across most physiological systems, as cells are lost to intrinsic and extrinsic stressors and damage (Arking 2006; Austad 1997a; Ben-Porath and Weinberg 2005; Crews 2003, 2007; Crews and Ice in press; Rose 1991, 2005; Weinstein and Ciszek 2002). Senescence is a biological process of loss of cellular, tissue, and organ function that reduces the ability of an individual to mount allostatic responses to intrinsic and extrinsic stressors; these push the soma out of its homeostatic equilibria, thereby increasing the probability of death and decreasing the likelihood of additional reproductive effort (Arking 2006; Crews 2003, 2007; Crews and Ice in press). Aging is the visible process of becoming older; it also represents the outward somatic signs of underlying senescent alterations at the cellular, tissue, and organ levels that lead to CDCs, frailty, and an increasing allostatic load (Crews 2005a, 2007; Walston 2005). Included among aging changes are social, cultural, behavioral, and physiological changes that occur over an individual's life but that do not themselves increase the probability of death (Crews 2003, see also Larsen 2008, p. 129).

As with all organisms, senescent changes in humans tend to be cumulative (there is increasing vulnerability to challenge over time), progressive (losses are gradual), intrinsic (they do not result from modifiable environmental factors), and deleterious (reduced function increases mortality risks in the next time interval; see Arking 2006). Senescence is not measured in days, months and years, but rather in biological time (Arking 2006; Crews 2003, 2007; Hayflick 2004). Ideally, one would use a series of physiological biomarkers or cascades of metabolic events that produced the dysfunction or disintegration of physiological pathways, cell doublings or DNA transcription cycles, or changes in gene expression patterns and cellular proteomes to measure the rate of senescence (see Arking 2006). Senescence is not dependent upon the passage time, but rather upon cell cycles and activities, which are fundamental units of biological time (ibid.).

As in the case of growth and development, senescence follows upon current competencies, organism-wide integration via messenger molecules, and the ability of receptors to receive various signals and to modulate cellular functions (Finch and Rose 1995). Human senescence is based upon the same processes and mechanisms that lead to senescent changes in all living organisms, including worms, insects, rodents, large-bodied mammals and primates. A major difference between these species and humans is humankind's unique biocultural adaptations and ability to contemplate its own demise.

Cellular senescence A number of processes occurring within cells have been identified as senescent. Reactive oxygen species (ROS: highly reactive oxygen molecules with an unpaired electron, such as superoxide and singlet oxygen) are generated particularly during oxidative phosphorylation (OXPHOS) within mitochondria. Over biological time, mitochondrial DNA (mtDNA) incurs numerous alterations due to damage by ROS. ROS also damage nuclear DNA (nDNA), proteins, and cellular structures (Aviv 2002; Ben-Porath and Weinberg 2005). When they are sufficiently damaged, cells are removed by apoptosis (programmed cell death). Over the life span, both senescent and damaged cells may not be removed efficiently enough, as a result of damage in the apoptosis system (Aviv 2002); thus they remain in tissues and reduce the functional RC. At the same time, healthy cells may be inappropriately marked for apoptosis and lost from tissues, which leads to loss of functional cells and dysfunction. Mitochondria with damaged DNA often cease producing ATP and may show more rapid reproduction than do wild-type mitochondria within cells. Mutant mitochondria eventually may overwhelm the functioning mitochondria, causing the cell no longer to produce sufficient energy for its survival.

Dividing cells may be lost to apoptotic death, because their telomeres shorten to lengths incompatible with continued cell cycling, thus contributing to senescence of tissues (Aviv 2002; Blasco 2005; Olovnikov 1996). During each round of cell division, telomeres that cap the ends of human chromosomes (tandem repeats of TTAGGG) are reduced; loss of telomeric DNA is about 31–3 base pairs (bp)/year (Hastie et al. 1990; Slagboom et al. 1994). The shortening of telomeres limits cellular replicative life spans and leads to the Hayflick limit of human fibroblasts *in vitro* (Aviv 2002; deLange 1998, 2002; Olovnikov 1996; Shay 1997). Telomere shortening is associated significantly with heart failure, immunosenecence, digestive tract atrophies, infertility, reduced viability of stem cells, reduced angiogenic potential, reduced wound-healing, and loss of body mass (Aviv 2002; Blasco 2005). Dividing cells that reach their replicative limit *in vivo* become senescent and tend to accumulate in somatic tissues. Such data suggest that chromosome shortening measures or represent intrinsic cellular senescence, an internal biological clock in the dividing cell. Still, cell replicative capacity is not closely associated with individual life spans, nor do other biomarkers of senescence correlate closely with telomere shortening (Blasco 2005). Interestingly, at birth, women's telomeres are longer then men's (Aviv 2002). Men also show senescence-related changes earlier than women do (Anderson-Ranberg et al. 1999; Foley 1986), although this may not always be true (Graves et al. 2006). Men may require more cell doublings to accommodate their 15–20 percent larger body sizes, thus exhausting their shorter telomeres earlier in life. Attrition of telomeres of cells *in vitro* correlates with the replicative history of primate cells, including human cells; however, a similar association is not observed for rodent cells (Aviv 2002).

The senescence of the immune system begins early in human LH; the involution of the thyroid gland starts in the twenties. This limits the numbers of circulating t-lymphocytes and naive lymphocytes, leading to slower immune responsiveness with increasing age. Elders show reduced immunocompetence, sluggish responses to both old and new infections, and they often fail to produce circulating antibodies in response to vaccinations. This is in part due to cumulative loses within the immune system. A compromised immune system leads to more infectious diseases and related damages, increased risk for neoplastic disease, and more frequent parasitism, all of which cause in turn greater wear-and-tear on the aging soma. Elders also show higher frailty due to increasing sarcopenia (loss of muscle cells) with advanced age. Loss of muscle cells is associated with greater infiltration of fat into the myocardium and skeletal muscle and with reduced oxidative metabolism due to the loss of mitochondria. Sarcopenia also results in greater frailty and increased risk of disease and mortality (Walston et al. 2005, 2006).

Physiological senescence

Most, if not all, physiological systems and tissues show senescent alterations due to these multiple cellular processes of senescence (Arking 2006; Austad 1994). Relationships between biological aging and age-related pathologies in humans are not as tight as would be expected if senescence were an age-dependent process or the sole cause of CDCs (see Hayflick 2004). As already mentioned, after menopause women lose bone mass at two to three times the rate among men of the same age (Stini 1990). Consequently, elderly women suffer from osteoporosis and hip fractures at three to four times the rate of same-age elderly men. Bone mineral loss over the senescent span is one of the best examples, along with atherosclerosis, of a senescent change in humans (Arking

Table 7.1 Activities of daily living (ADLs) and instrumental activities of daily living (IADLs)

Physical ADLs	Instrumental ADLs
Bathing	Using telephone
Dressing	Transportation
Grooming	Laundry
Transferring (moving from chair to bed or chair to toilet and vice versa)	Shopping
Feeding	Taking medicine
Ambulating	Managing money

2006; Crews 2008). Because many human beings now live long enough to develop many diseases specific to aging, it is instructive to review briefly several of the most common causes of loss of active life span and of morbidity in late life.

Osteoporosis and osteoarthritis   Bones lose both calcium and minerals with increasing age. As bone mineral density (BMD) decreases, bones become more brittle and prone to breaks. Loss of BMD and of matrix leads to osteoporosis, which is associated with increased risks of hip fractures and may in turn lead to muscular atrophy, fractures, bed sores, secondary infections, and ultimately death (Cummings and Nevitt 1989). Subsequent to the decreased BMD and to osteoporosis, the spinal column compresses as the vertebrae collapse, producing more porous bone with less interstitial matrix. Degenerative joint disease (DJD) affects all joints, but most particularly knee joints, where articular cartilage is lost first, and eventually bone. Calcification and build-up of bone spurs may also occur. This is associated with loss of lean body mass (muscle, bone). As height decreases due to the loss of BMD in the spine and knees, joints become inflamed and stiff, which results in osteoarthritis.

Osteoarthritis, particularly of weight-bearing joints, often occurs in concert with osteoporosis, leading to loss of mobility and of the ability to care for oneself. Subsequently, abilities to complete the required activities of daily living (ADLs) and the instrumental activities of daily living (IADLs: Table 7.1) become impaired (see Table 1 in Katz et al. 1963; also Brock et al. 1990; Crews and Ice in press; Miles and Brody 1994). After about the age of 50, osteoarthritis is common; by the age of 70, it is almost universal. Osteoarthritis of the knees begins with the loss of cartilage. As cartilage is lost in joints, bones start to articulate with other bones and bony spurs may form; previous injuries enhance these processes. Osteopenia, osteoporosis and osteoarthritis form a continuum of progressive change from decreased mass and loss of RC to disease and senescent change. Loss of BMD increases the likelihood of fractures and falls, magnifying the risks of death from accidents – the fifth leading cause of death in the US (www.cdc.gov).

Arteriosclerosis/Atherosclerosis   Atherosclerosis or arteriosclerosis is a chronic degenerative condition characterized by yellowish plaques of highly cross-linked collagen, frayed elastin, calcium, cholesterol, lipids, amyloid, and cellular debris on the walls of arteries. Humankind has suffered from atherosclerosis since at least the times when the ancient Egyptians were mummifying their dead. Atherosclerosis is so common that some consider it among the best examples of senescent phenotypes (Arking 2006). Atherosclerosis has been reported in both captive and feral chimpanzees, as well as in other non-human primates, and has been suggested to be a process of senescence in all long-lived primates. With increasing age, the thickening consequent upon atherosclerosis leads to thicker elongated and dilated arterial walls and to loss of elastic response, as collagen cross-links, calcium amyloid and lipid are deposited, elastin fragments and vascular compliance is lost. Vascular resistance and aortic independence increase and baroreceptor responses become blunted, which leads to higher systemic blood pressure. In the USA, over 50 percent of the persons aged 70 and over show amyloid deposits in their arteries. Atherosclerosis progresses over the life span; it is cumulative, debilitating, and to a large degree intrinsic. Atherosclerosis results from a combination of genetic predispositions, environmental exposures and cultural modulators. It affects many members of cosmopolitan societies and leads to a variety of complications: elevated blood pressure, cardiovascular diseases, and stroke. Arterial compliance decreases with age, as arteries lose elasticity due to the cross-linking of macromolecules from non-enzymatic glycation, causing blood pressure to increase. Atherosclerosis contributes fundamentally to two out of the three leading causes of death in the US – heart disease at number 1 and stroke at number 3 – and is an outcome of the sixth leading cause, diabetes (ibid.). Both high blood pressure and elevated cholesterol are leading risk factors in cardiovascular diseases.

Dementias The dementias are a heterogeneous assortment of diseases affecting the brain and the central nervous system. Most well known are senile dementia of the Alzheimer's type (SDAT), Parkinson's dementia (PD), vascular dementias, pharmacological and alcohol-induced dementias, and non-Alzheimer's types of senile dementias. Patients with dementia of all types tend to show loss of cognitive function, loss of orientation in time and space, loss of muscular control, loss of long-term and short-term memory, and impaired neurological functions. Most affected are language abilities, attention, memory and higher-order executive functions. Dementias likely represent a dysfunctional endpoint consequent upon life-long neurological alterations that occur in the brains of all primates. As with strokes, the site of a vascular or neurological change due to dementia processes determines whether the dysfunctional endpoint is specific to certain tasks or generalized across functions.

   Although there are some specific genetic risks for familial forms of SDAT – Apolipoprotein *E*4* (Chromosome 19), mutated presenilins *1* and *2* (Chromosomes 14 and 1), and mutated amyloid precursor proteins (Chromosome 21) – most of the risk of dementia is thought to come from environmental exposures, lifestyles, and biological fragility. There are both late-onset forms of SDAT (at the age of 65 and later) and early-onset forms (before the age of 65), and familial forms appear to be of both types. Because dementia, and particularly SDAT, shows a continual increase with age, it is likely that all persons who live sufficiently long will suffer from it. The 2000 US census indicates that among people aged 65–74, 1.6 percent suffered from SDAT; this rate increased to 19 percent among people aged 75–84 and to 42 percent in people of 84 years and older (Herbert et al. 2003). The dementias are a leading cause of morbidity and mortality among older adults and show an ever-increasing frequency. Alzheimer's disease is currently the seventh leading cause of death in the US population

(Leading Causes of Death: www.cdc.gov). Although some may suggest that we will all suffer SDAT if we survive, Jeanne Calment, who died at almost 122.5 years, did not express SDAT prior to her death. Understanding how the oldest documented person ever to live avoided dementia may help the rest of us to do so as well.

CONCLUSION

The opportunity to build excess somatic capacity (or reserve capacity: see Figure 3.2 in Crews 2003, p. 77) during human childhood and adolescence, capacity which may be relied upon in later times of need, combined with biocultural reproduction in a bioculturally constructed niche, explains in large part why a greater percentage of young humans survive to adulthood than among the young of any other primate species. The need to grow and develop through two new life history stages helps to account for the greater RS and greater longevity of human adults among other primates. Having proper nutrition and an extended period of growth in a bioculturally enhanced setting allows humans to build better, healthier bodies, while they also develop biological, behavioral, and cultural resilience prior to sexual maturity (Bogin 2009; Crews 2003, 2008). Early investments in reserves produce improved adult health, fitness, and longevity in today's constructed niches. A significant period of postreproductive life for women and late-life survival for men derives from early-life selective propensities to build RC during an extended prereproductive life span. Today this reserve is available for maintaining the soma over late life. In the environment of evolutionary adaptation, opportunities to build such reserves were probably hampered by a higher extrinsic mortality in early life, low energetic inputs for maintaining stores, and a lack of survival beyond the fourth decade of life (Caspari and Lee 2004). Since the advent of modern human life histories, opportunities for attaining extensive reserve capacity during growth and development as well as the health span within constructed niches have expanded, since human environments have become much more benign.

At older ages, health and illness are strongly determined by inherent biological stability (genetic and cellular propensities), life-long and ongoing biological modifications (wear-and-tear, senescence), environmental factors (stressors), history (age, period, cohort effects), and physiological function (allostatic load (AL), metabolic RC, frailty; see Table 7.2). Growth and development represent a co-adapted and allometrically related series of events, which begin at conception and proceed through the completion

Table 7.2   Determinants of health and illness during older ages

Domain	Measurable components
Biological stability	Genetic predispositions/Growth and Development
Biological modifications	Senescent alterations/Illness/Stress responses
Environment	Stressors/Exposures/Climate
History	Age/Period/Cohort
Physiological function	Allostasis/Frailty/Homeostasis/Reserve capacity

Reprinted with permission from Crews 2007.

of the adult soma (Arking 2006; Bogin 1999; Crews 2003). This produces a complex web of causation, which we assess through change and disease as senescent processes that are individualized, progressive, multifactorial, and deleterious (Arking 2006). Senescence occurs at the genetic, protein, cellular, tissue, organ, and organ system levels, involving complex and multiple interactions across levels. Senescence may usefully be viewed as an event-driven process of damage and loss, which affects all organs and bodily systems and continually increases the probability of death (Arking 2006; Austad 1997a; Crews 2003). Living in protected environments, with fewer extrinsic risks, reduces the frequency and slows the rate of such events, allowing for greater investments in somatic stability over the life span. Although senescence is not time-dependent, senescent changes accumulate over an organism's life span, making it age-related (Arking 2006; Crews 2003). This is partly because early LH events pace the timing of senescence (Crews 2003), and partly because loss of function is dependent upon cellular processes of replication and differentiation that occur over biological time (Arking 2006). Variable patterns and timing of senescence are its hallmarks (Crews 2003). Biocultural reproduction, added phases of the development span, and living in niches that allow the building and retention of reserve capacity alter the timing and patterning of senescence by reducing stressors and by increasing the RC available during the senescent span, and they decrease the extrinsic mortality of young and old alike.

REFERENCES

Alexander, R. D., Hoogland, J. L., Howard, R. D., Noonan, K. M., and Sherman, P. W. (1979) Sexual Dimorphisms and Breeding Systems in Pinnipeds, Ungulates, Primates and Humans. In N. Chagnon and W. Irons (eds), *Evolutionary Biology and Human Social Behavior: An Anthropological Perspective* (pp. 402–435). North Scituate MA: Duxbury Press.

Anderson-Ranberg, K., Christensen, K., Jeune, B., Skytthe, A., Vasegaard, L., and Vaupel, J. W. (1999) Declining Physical Abilities with Age: A Cross-Sectional Study of Older Twins and Centenarians in Denmark. *Age and Ageing* 28: 373–377.

Anemone, R. L., Mooney, M. P., and Siegel, M. I. (1996) Longitudinal Study of Dental Development in Chimpanzees of Known Chronological Age: Implications for Understanding the Age at Death of Plio-Pleistocene Hominids. *American Journal of Physical Anthropology* 99 (1): 119–133.

Arking, R. (2006) *The Biology of Aging: Observations and Principles*, 3rd edn. New York: Oxford University Press.

Arking, R., Novoseltseva, J., Hwangbo, D. S., Novoseltseva, V., and Lane, M. (2002) Different Age-Specific Demographic Profiles are Generated in the Same Normal-Lived Drosophila Strain by Different Longevity Stimuli. *Journals of Gerontology: Biological Sciences* 57: B390–B398.

Austad, S. N. (1994) Menopause – An Evolutionary Perspective. *Experimental Gerontology* 29: 255–263.

Austad, S. N. (1997a) Comparative Aging and Life Histories in Mammals. *Experimental Gerontology* 32: 23–38.

Austad, S. N. (1997b) *Why We Age: What Science Is Discovering about the Body's Journey through Life*. New York: Wiley–Liss.

Austad, S. N. (2005) Diverse Aging Rates in Metazoans: Targets for Functional Genomics. *Mechanisms of Ageing and Development* 126: 43–49.

Aviv, A. (2002) Telomeres, Sex, Reactive Oxygen Species, and Human Cardiovascular Aging. *Journal of Molecular Medicine* 80: 689–695.

Barker D. J. P. (1998) *Mothers, Babies, and Health in Later Life*, 2nd edn. Edinburgh: Churchill Livingston.

Bergmüller, R., Johnstone, R. A., Russell, A. F., and Bshary, R. (2007) Integrating Cooperative Breeding into Theoretical Concepts of Cooperation, *Behavioral Processes* 76 (2): 61–72.

Ben-Porath, I., and Weinberg, R. (2005) The Signals and Pathways Activating Cellular Senescence. *International Journal of Biochemistry & Cell Biology* 37: 961–976.

Blasco, M. A. (2005) Telomeres and Human Disease: Ageing, Cancer and Beyond. *Nature Reviews Genetics* 6: 611–622.

Bogin, B. (1988) *Patterns of Human Growth*. Cambridge: Cambridge University Press.

Bogin, B. (1993) Why Must I Be a Teenager at all? *New Scientist* 137: 34–38.

Bogin, B. (1997) Evolutionary Hypotheses for Human Childhood. *Yearbook of Physical Anthropology* 40: 63–89.

Bogin, B. (1999) *Patterns of Human Growth*, 2nd edn. Cambridge: Cambridge University Press.

Bogin, B. (2001) *The Growth of Humanity*. New York: Wiley–Liss.

Bogin, B. (2006) Modern Human Life History: The Evolution of Human Childhood and Adult Fertility. In K. Hawkes and R. Paine (eds), *The Evolution of Human Life History* (pp. 197–230). Santa Fe NM: School of American Research Press.

Bogin, B. (2009) Childhood, Adolescence, and Longevity: A Multilevel Model of the Evolution of Reserve Capacity in Human Life History. *American Journal of Human Biology* 21: 567–577.

Bogin, B. (in press) Evolution of Human Growth. In M. Muehlenbein (ed.), *Human Evolutionary Biology*. Cambridge: Cambridge University Press.

Bogin, B., and Smith, B. H. (1996) Evolution of the Human Life Cycle. *American Journal of Human Biology* 8: 703–716.

Brock, D. B., Guralnik, J. M., and Brody, J. A. (1990) Demography and Epidemiology of Aging in the United States. In E. L. Schneider and J. W. Rose (eds), *Handbook of the Biology of Aging* (pp. 3–23). San Diego CA: Academic Press.

Cameron, N., and Demerath, E. (2002) Critical Periods in Human Growth and Their Relationship to Disease of Aging. *Yearbook of Physical Anthropology* 45: 159–184.

Carey, J. R., and Judge, D. S. (2001) Life Span Extension in Humans Is Self-Reinforcing: A General Theory of Longevity. *Population and Development Review* 27: 411–436.

Caspari, R., and Lee, S. H. (2004) Older Age Becomes Common Late in Human Evolution. *Proceedings of the National Academy of Sciences, USA* 101: 10895–10900.

Chagnon, N. A. (1979) Is Reproduction Success Equal in Egalitarian Societies? In N. A. Chagnon and W. Irons (eds), *Evolutionary Biology and Human Social Behavior: An Anthropological Perspective* (pp. 374–401). North Scituate MA: Duxbury Press.

Clutton-Brock, T. H. (2002) Breeding Together: Kin Selection and Mutualism in Cooperative Vertebrates. *Science* 296: 69–72.

Crews, D. E. (2003) *Human Senescence: Evolutionary and Biocultural Perspectives*. New York, NY: Cambridge University Press.

Crews, D. E. (2005a). Evolutionary Perspectives on Human Longevity and Frailty. In J. R. Carey, J. M. Robine, and Y. Christen (eds), *Longevity and Frailty* (pp. 57–65). New York: Springer-Verlag.

Crews, D. E. (2005b). Artificial Environments and an Aging Population: Designing for Age-Related Functional Loss. *Journal of Physiological Anthropology and Applied Human Sciences* 24: 103–109.

Crews, D. E. (2007) Senescence, Aging, and Disease. *Journal of Physiological Anthropology* 26: 365–372.

Crews, D. E. (2008) Co-Evolution of Human Culture, Mating Strategies and Longevity. In C. Susanne and E. Bodzsar (eds), *Aging Related Problems in Past and Present Populations* (pp. 9–29). Budapest: Eötvös University Press.

Crews, D. E., and Gerber, L. J. (2003) Reconstructing Life History of Hominids and Humans. *Collegium Anthropologicum* 27: 7–22.

Crews, D. E., and Ice, G. J. (in press) Aging, Senescence, and Human Variation. In S. Stinson, B. Bogin, and D. O'Rourke (eds), *Textbook of Human Biology: Evolutionary and Biocultural Perspectives*, 2nd edn. New York: Wiley–Liss.

Crews, D. E., and Stewart, J. (in press) Human Longevity and Senescence. In M. P. Muehlenbein (ed.), *Human Evolutionary Biology*. New York: Cambridge University Press.

Crews, D. E., and Williams, S. L. (1999) Molecular Aspects of Blood Pressure Regulation. *Human Biology* 71: 475–503.

Cummings, S. R., and Nevitt, N. C. (1989) A Hypothesis: The Cause of Hip Fractures. *Journals of Gerontology* 44: M107–M111.

de Lange, T. (1998) Telomeres and Senescence: Ending the Debate. *Science* 249: 334–335.

de Lange, T. (2002) Protection of Mammalian Telomeres. *Oncogene* 21: 532–540.

Dettwyler, K.A. (1995) A Time to Wean: The Hominid Blueprint for the Natural Age of Weaning in Modern Human Populations. In P. Stuart-Macadam and K. A. Dettwyler (eds), *Breastfeeding: Biocultural Perspectives* (pp. 39–74). New York: Aldine de Gruyter.

Drake, A. J., and Walker, B. R. (2004) The Intergenerational Effects of Fetal Programming: Non-Genomic Mechanisms for the Inheritance of Low Birth Weight and Cardiovascular Risk. *Journal of Endocrinology* 180: 1–16.

Drenos, F., and Kirkwood, T. B. L. (2004) Modeling the Disposable Soma Theory of Ageing. *Mechanisms of Aging and Development* 126: 99–103.

Drenos, F., Westendorp, R., and Kirkwood, T. B. L. (2006) Trade-Off Mediated Effects on the Genetics of Human Survival Caused by Increasingly Benign Living Conditions. *Biogerontology* 7: 287–295.

Evans, K. E., and Harris, S. (2008) Adolescence in Male African Elephants, Loxodonta Africana. *Animal Behaviour* 76: 779–787.

Finch, C. E., and Crimmins, E. M. (2004) Inflammatory Exposure and Historical Changes in Human Life-Spans. *Science* 305: 1736–1739.

Finch, C. E., and Rose, M.R. (1995) Hormones and Physiological Architecture of Life History Evolution. *Quarterly Review of Biology* 70: 1–52.

Foley, C. J. (1986) Aging – A Coming of Age. *New York State Journal of Medicine* 86: 617–618.

Gadgil, M., and W. H. Bossert (1970). Life Historical Consequences of Natural Selection. *American Naturalist* 104, 1–24.

Gerber, L. M., and Crews, D. E. (1999) Evolutionary Perspectives on Chronic Diseases: Changing Environments, Life Styles, and Life Expectancy. In W. R. Trevathan, J. J. McKenna, and N. Smith (eds), *Evolutionary Medicine* (pp. 443–469). New York: Oxford University Press.

Graham, C. E. (1986) Endocrinology of reproductive senescence. In W. R. Dukelow and J. Erwin (eds), *Comparative Primate Biology*, Vol. 3. *Reproduction and Development* (pp. 93–99). New York: Alan R. Liss, Inc.

Graham, C. E., Kling, O. R., and Steiner, R. A. (1979) Reproductive Senescence in Female Non-Human Primates. In D. M. Bowden (ed.), *Aging in Non-human Primates* (pp. 183–209). New York: Van Nostrand Reinhold.

Graves, B. M., Strand, M., and Lindsay, A. R. (2006) A Reassessment of Sexual Dimorphism in Human Senescence: Theory, Evidence, and Causation. *American Journal of Human Biology* 18: 161–168.

Gurven, M., and Walker, R. (2006) Energetic Demand of Multiple Dependents and the Evolution of Slow Human Growth. *Proceedings of the Royal Society* B 273: 835–841.

Hamilton, W. D. (1964) The Genetical Evolution of Social Behavior: I. *Journal of Theoretical Biology* 7: 1–16.

Hamilton, W. D. (1966) The Moulding of Senescene by Natural Selection. *Journal of Theoretical Biology* 12: 12–45.

Hamilton, W. D. (1971) Geometry for the Selfish Herd. *Journal of Theoretical Biology* 31: 295–311.

Harper, G. J., and Crews, D. E. (2000) Aging, Senescence, and Human Variation. In S. Stinson, B. Bogin and D. O'Rourke (eds), *Textbook of Human Biology: An Evolutionary and Biocultural Perspectives* (pp. 465–505). New York: Wiley–Liss.

Harvey, P. H., Martin, R. D., and Clutton-Brock, T. H. (1986) Life Histories in Comparative Perspective. In B. B. Smuts, D. L. Cheney, R. M. Sayfarth, R. W. Wrangham, and T. T. Struthsaker (eds), *Primate Societies* (pp. 161–171). Chicago: University of Chaigo Press.

Hastie, N. D., Dempster, M., Dunlop, M. G., Thompson, A. M., Green, D. K., and Allshire, R. C. (1990) Telomere Reduction in Human Colorectal Carcinoma and with Ageing. *Nature* 346: 866–868.

Haussmann, M., and Mauck, R. (2008) Telomeres and Longevity: Testing an Evolutionary Hypothesis. *Molecular Biology and Evolution* 25: 220–228.

Hawkes, K., and Paine, R. (eds), *The Evolution of Human Life History*. Santa Fe NM: School of American Research Press.

Hawkes, K., O'Connell, J. F., and Blurton Jones, N. G. (1997) Hazda Women's Time Allocation, Offspring Provisioning, and the Evolution of Long Postmenopausal Life Span. *Current Anthropology* 48: 551–577.

Hawkes, K., O'Connell, J. F., Blurton Jones, N. G., Alvarez, H., and Charnov, E. L. (1998) Grandmothering, Menopause, and the Evolution of Human Life Histories. *Proceedings of the National Academy of Sciences, USA* 95: 1336–1339.

Hawkes, K., Smith, K. R., and Robinson, S. L. (2009) Mortality and Fertility Rates in Humans and Chimpanzees: How Within-Species Variation Complicates Cross-Species Comparisons. *American Journal of Human Biology* 21 (4): 578–586.

Hayflick, L. (2004) The Not-So-Close Relationship between Biological Aging and Age-Related Pathologies in Humans. *Journals of Gerontology Series A: Biological Sciences and Medical Sciences* 59A: 547–550.

Herbert, L. E., Scherr, P. A., Bienias, J. L., Bennett, D. A., and Evans, D. A. (2003) Alzheimer Disease in the US Population: Prevalence Estimates Using the 2000 Census. *Archives of Neurology* 60: 1119–1122.

Jones, E. C. (1975) The Post-Fertile Life of Non-Human Primates and Other Mammals. In A. A. Haspels and H. Musaph (eds), *Psychosomatics in Peri-Menopause* (pp. 13–39). Baltimore: University Park Press.

Kaplan, H., Hill, K., Lancaster, J., and Hurtado, M. A. (2000) A Theory of Human Life History Evolution: Diet, Intelligence, and Longevity. *Evolutionary Anthropology* 9: 158–185.

Kappeler, P. M., and Pereira, M. E. (2003) *Primate Life Histories and Socioecology*. Chicago: University of Chicago Press.

Katz, S. A., Ford, A. B., Moskowitz, R. W., Jackson, B. A., and Jaffee, M. W. (1963) Studies of Illness in the Aged. The Index of ADL: A Standardized Measure of Biological and Psychosocial Function. *Journal of the American Medical Association* 185: 94–101.

Kirkwood, T. B. L. (1977) Evolution of Ageing. *Nature* 270: 301–304.

Kirkwood, T. B. L. (1990) The Disposable Soma Theory of Aging. In D. E. Harrison (ed.), *Genetic Effects on Aging II* (pp. 9–19). New Jersey: Teaford Press.

Kuzawa, C. W. (2005) Fetal Origins of Developmental Plasticity: Are Fetal Cues Reliable Predictors of Future Nutritional Environments? *American Journal of Human Biology* 17: 5–21.

Kuzawa, C. W., and Sweet, E. (2009) Epigenetics and the Embodiment of Race: Developmental Origins of US Racial Disparities in Cardiovascular Health. *American Journal of Human Biology* 21: 2–15.

Lancaster, J. B., and Lancaster, C. S. (1983) Parental Investment: The Hominid Adaptation. In D. J. Ortner (ed.), *How Humans Adapt* (pp. 33–65). Washington DC: Smithsonian Institution Press.

Larke, A., and Crews, D. E. (2006) Parental Investment, Late Reproduction, and Increased Reserve Capacity Are Associated with Longevity in Humans. *Journal of Physiological Anthropology* 25: 119–131.

Larsen, C. S. (2008) *Our Origins: Discovering Physical Anthropology.* New York: W. W. Norton and Company, Inc.

Leading Causes of Death: www.cdc.gov/nchs/FASTATS/lcod.htm.

Leidy, L. E. (1994) Biological aspects of Menopause: Across the Lifespan. *Annual Review of Anthropolgy* 23: 231–253.

Leigh, S. R. (1994) Ontogenetic Correlates of Diet in Anthropoid Primates. *American Journal of Physical Anthropology* 94: 499–522.

Marlowe, F. (2000) The Patriarch Hypothesis: An Alternative Explanation of Menopause. *Human Nature* 11: 27–42.

Miles, T., and Brody, J. (1994) Aging as a Worldwide Phenomenon. In D. E. Crews and R. M. Garutto (eds), *Biological Anthropology and Aging: Perspectives on Human Variation Over the Life Span* pp. 3–15. New York: Oxford University Press.

Odling-Smee, F. J., Laland, K. N., and Feldman, M. W. (eds) (2003) *Niche Construction.* Princeton: Princeton University Press.

Olovnikov, A. M. (1996) Telomeres, Telomerase and Aging: Origin of the Theory. *Experimental Gerontology* 31: 443–448.

Ossa, K., and Crews, D. E. (2006) Biological and Genetic Theories of the Process of Aging throughout Life. In C. Sauvain-Dugergil, H. Leridon, and N. Mascie-Taylor (eds), *Human Clocks: The Bio-Cultural Meanings of Age* (pp. 61–84). Liège, Belgium: International Union for the Scientific Study of Population.

Packer, C., Tatar, M., and Collin, A. (1998) Reproductive Cessation in Female Mammals. *Nature* 392: 807–810.

Pavelka, M., McDonald, S., and Fedigan, L. (1991) Menopause: A Comparative Life History Perspective. *Yearbook of Physical Anthropology* 34: 13–38.

Pereira, M. E., and Fairbanks, L. A. (2003) *Juvenile Primates: Life History, Development and Behavior.* Chicago: University of Chicago Press.

Perls, T. T. (2006) The Different Paths to 100. *The American Journal of Clinical Nutrition* 83: 84–7S.

Piaget, J. (1954) *The Construction of Reality in the Child.* New York: Basic Books.

Piaget, J., and Inhelder, B. (1969) *The Psychology of the Child.* New York: Basic Books.

Price, K. C., and Coe, C. L. (2000) Maternal Constraint on Fetal Growth Patterns in the Rhesus Monkey (*Macaca mulatta*): The Intergenerational Link between Mothers and Daughters. *Human Reproduction* 15: 452–457.

Pusey, A. E. (1983) Mother–Offspring Relationships in Chimpanzees after Weaning. *Animal Behaviour* 31: 363–377.

Robson, S. L., van Schaik, C. P., and Hawkes, K. (2006) The Derived Features of Human Life History. In K. Hawkes and R. Paine (eds), *The Evolution of Human Life History* (pp. 17–44). Santa Fe NM: School of American Research Press.

Rose, M. R. (1991) *Evolutionary Biology of Aging.* New York: Oxford University Press.

Rose, M. R., Rauser, C. L., and Mueller, L. D. (2005) Late Life: A New Frontier for Physiology. *Physiological and Biochemical Zoology: PBZ* 78: 869–78.

Rosenberg, K., and Trevathan, W. (2002) Birth, Obstetrics and Human Evolution. *BJOG-an International Journal of Obstetrics and Gynaecology* 109: 1199–1206.

Schultz, A. H. (1960) Age Changes in Primates and Their Modifications in Man. In J. M. Tanner (ed.), *Human Growth* (pp. 1–20). Oxford: Pergamon Press.

Sellen, D. W. (2006) Lactation, Complementary Feeding and Human Life History. In K. Hawkes and R. Paine (eds), *The Evolution of Human Life History* (pp. 155–196). Santa Fe NM: School of American Research Press.

Shay, J. W. (1997) Molecular Pathogenesis of Aging and Cancer: Are Telomeres and Telomerase the Connection? *Journal of Clinical Pathology* 50: 799–800.

Slagboom, P. E., Droog, S., and Broomsma, D. I. (1994) Genetic Determination of Telomere Size in Humans: A Twin Study of Three Age Groups. *American Journal of Human Genetics* 55: 876–882.

Smith, B. H. (1989) Growth and Development and Its Significance for Early Hominid Behaviour. *OSSA* 14: 63–96.

Smith, B. H. (1991) Age at Weaning Approximates Age of Emergence of the First Permanent Molar in Non-Human Primates. *American Journal of Physical Anthropology* Suppl. 12: 163–164.

Smith, B. H., Crummett, T. L., and Brandt, K. L. (1994) Ages of Eruption of Primate Teeth: A Compendium for Aging Individuals and Comparing Life Histories. *Yearbook of Physical Anthropology* 37: 177–231.

Snowden, D. A, Dane, R. L., Beeson, G. L., Sprafka, M., Bitter, J., Iso, H., Jacobs, D. R., and Philips, R. L. (1989) Is Early Natural Menopause a Biologic Marker of Health and Aging? *American Journal of Public Health* 79: 709–714.

Stearns, S. C. (1992) *The Evolution of Life Histories.* Oxford: Oxford University Press.

Stini, W. A. (1990) Changing Patterns of Morbidity and Mortality and the Challenge to Health Care Delivery Systems of the Future. *Collegium Anthropologicum* 14: 189–195.

Thompson, M. E., Jones, J. H., Pusey, A. E., Brewer-Marsden, S., Goodall, J. Marsden, D., Matsuzawa, T., Nishida, T., Reynolds, V., Sugiyama, Y., and Wrangham, R. W. (2007) Aging and Fertility Patterns in Wild Chimpanzees Provide Insights into the Evolution of Menopause. *Current Biology* 17: 2150–2156.

Walker, R., Hill, K., Burger, O., and Hurtado, A. M. (2006) Life in the Slow Lane Revisited: Ontogenetic Separation between Chimpanzees and Humans. *American Journal Physical Anthropology* 129: 577–583.

Walston, J. D. (2005) Biological Markers and the Molecular Biology of Frailty. In J. R. Carey, J. M. Robine., J. P. Michel, and Y. Christen (eds), *Longevity and Frailty* (pp. 39–56). New York: Springer-Verlag.

Walston, J., Hadley, E. C., Ferrucci, L., Guralnik, J. M., Newman, A. B., Studenski, S. A., Ershler, W. B., Harris, T., and Fried, L. P. (2006) Research Agenda for Frailty in Older Adults: Toward a Better Understanding of Physiology and Etiology: Summary from the American Geriatrics Society/National Institute on Aging Research Conference on Frailty in Older Adults. *Journal of the American Geriatrics Society* 54: 991–1001.

Weinstein, B., and Ciszek, D. (2002) The Reserve-Capacity Hypothesis: Evolutionary Origins and Modern Implications of the Trade-Off between Tumor-Suppression and Tissue-Repair. *Experimental Gerontology* 37: 615–627.

Weismann, A. (1889) *Essays upon Heredity and Kindred Biological Problems*, Vol. 2, edited by E. B. Poulton and A. E. Shipley, translated by Selmar Schonland (authorized translation). Oxford: Clarendon Press.

CHAPTER 8

Climate-Related Morphological Variation and Physiological Adaptations in *Homo sapiens*

Gary D. James

Since *Homo sapiens* evolved, populations have dispersed across the planet, inhabiting niches that span the spectrum of available terrestrial habitats. Many of these populations survived for millennia in extreme environments, developing adaptations which have contributed significantly to the phenotypic and to some extent genotypic variation found among present day people. That this variation might be partly related to environmental adaptability was not obvious to physical anthropologists through the first half of the twentieth century, when cultural perspectives led most researchers to focus on the description of racial types (Johnson and Little 2000). The questions of how and why particular characteristics arose and flourished in particular populations appeared as an important area of inquiry only after World War II, with the emergence of the 'new physical anthropology' and its emphasis on human variation resulting from natural selective processes (Coon et al. 1950; Washburn 1951; Hanna et al. 1989).

At present it is accepted that *Homo sapiens* evolved from equatorial, sea-level populations in Africa who then spread across the planet over the past 100,000 to 200,000 years, although debate remains as to the timing and nature of the species dispersion (Conroy 2005; Young et al. 2005). Nonetheless, Newman (1970) described our migrating species as a "sweaty and thirsty naked ape"; and, given the point wherefrom our evolutionary roots emanated, it is reasonably clear that all modern human populations are descended from tropical 'heat adapted' ancestors (Hanna and Brown 1979; Hanna et al. 1989). So, in evaluating adaptations of 'indigenous' human populations living in various extreme environments, the focus is really on how these populations evolved so as to survive and reproduce under conditions that would seem unfavorable for a tropical, sea-level species (Baker 1984). Such conditions would include low temperature, decreased barometric pressure at high altitude and variation in ultraviolet (UV) radiation. The purpose of this brief overview is to present and discuss research regarding possible morphological and physiological adaptations in humans that relate to variation in climatic factors beyond our tropical ancestry: specifically, adaptation to cold temperature, high-altitude hypoxia, and low ultraviolet radiation. The impact of some of these adaptations with regard to the risk of chronic health conditions in presentday populations will also be discussed.

HUMAN MORPHOLOGY AND ECOGEOGRAPHIC RULES

In the nineteenth century, naturalists Karl Bergmann (1847) and Joel Asaph Allen (1877) noted relationships between climate, adult body size, and morphology in homeothermic species; their observations are codified today as Bergmann's and Allen's rules. Bergmann's rule states that, within a wide-ranging homeothermic species, body mass increases with latitude and with decreasing ambient temperature. The presumed reason for Bergmann's rule is that animals with greater mass have a lower ratio of surface area to volume than smaller animals and therefore, in the cold, will radiate less body heat and stay warmer. Similarly, in warmer climates body heat generated by metabolism needs to be dissipated, hence animals with smaller mass and a greater ratio between surface area and volume will radiate more body heat and stay cooler. The relationship between body size and latitude is related to the fact that there is an inverse temperature cline with an increasing latitude. Allen's rule states that, in homeotherms from colder climates, the limbs are shorter than in equivalent animals from warmer climates. This limb-length relationship is attributed to the same factors of heat dissipation and conservation that operate in Bergman's rule. That is, shorter appendages offer less surface area and are more effective in maintaining body heat, while longer appendages offer more surface area, and thus greater opportunity to dissipate the heat.

Physical anthropologists have examined whether these rules apply to humans – specifically, whether adaptation to ambient temperature partially explains morphological variation in human populations that inhabit different ecosystems. As previously noted, systematic study into the possible role of climate in human variation only began after World War II, and was prompted in large part by the work of Coon and colleagues (1950), who devoted several chapters of their book to body size and climate relationships (Hanna et al. 1989).

Roberts (1953) was among the first to test Bergmann's rule in humans using a distributional approach. He focused on weight as the critical measure of body size, and included in his analysis only groups that offered measurements on more than twenty subjects of the same sex (Bindon and Baker 1997). From the literature, he assembled morphometric data on 116 indigenous populations of males and on 33 populations of females from Africa, Asia, Europe, East Asia, North America, and South America. He found strong negative relationships between weight and mean annual temperature. He showed that Bergmann's rule was applicable both between and within continents and in all the groups combined. This latter point is illustrated in his analysis of weight and mean annual temperature among the adult male samples, which showed a substantial and significant inverse correlation (r = −.6). Of particular interest in Robert's study is the fact that the anthropometry on which it is based was taken on population groups predominantly studied prior to World War II: this suggests that there was minimal western contact and influence on the measurements (Bindon and Baker 1997). Roberts later expanded his analysis (see Roberts 1978) and showed that Allen's rule also applied to human populations. In an examination of 370 population samples, he found that arm span as a percentage of stature was negatively correlated with mean annual temperature (Hanna et al. 1989). In his original series, Roberts found that Polynesian populations (island samples) did not adhere too well to the morphological ecogeographic rules, in that they tended to have much higher average weight than expected. Bindon and Baker (1997) have suggested that this anomaly is due to their thrifty genotype, which probably arose as a consequence of the need for energy efficiency during the voyaging that the Polynesians needed to undertake in order to colonize the remote Pacific islands they now inhabit.

Ruff (1994) later confirmed Robert's earlier findings regarding Bergmann's rule, by correlating human body breadth as reflected in the bi-iliac diameter, weight, and body surface area/body mass ratio with latitude in 56 living populations. In this series, correlations were equally strong (r = .87, r = .61 and r = −.65) for each of the body form/mass measures. Finally, a more recent comprehensive distributional study undertaken by Katzmarzyk and Leonard (1998) evaluated the data on body weight, body mass index (BMI: weight (kg)/stature (m)^2), body surface area/body mass ratio, and relative sitting height (sitting height/stature) in relation to the mean annual temperature in 223 male and 195 female population samples from studies published since Roberts's landmark work in 1953. This analysis showed that, while body weight, BMI and the ratio between body surface area and body mass continued to show consistent associations with the mean annual temperature (r = −.27; r = −.22; r = .29 in male sample groups respectively), the degrees of association were substantially attenuated by comparison with the earlier studies. These differences appear to be related to a secular trend in weight, particularly among tropical populations. In these groups average weight and BMI have increased, while the ratio of surface area to body mass has decreased by comparison with findings from earlier studies. Katzmarzyk and Leonard (1998) suggest that the associational decline is due to the impact of acculturation, lifestyle and nutritional change and to improvements in health in tropical populations. While there is some evidence that there is a genetic basis for the climate–morphology relationships in humans (Katzmarzyk and Leonard 1998; Serrat et al. 2008), a growing body of data suggests that the associations arise from a developmental acclimatization which results, for example, in a shortening of the limbs when growth occurs in cold ambient temperatures (Newman and Munro 1955; Frisancho 1993; Katzmarzyk and Leonard 1998; Serrat et al. 2008).

Physiological–functional studies have shown that a low ratio of surface area to mass may reduce heat loss, regardless of underlying subcutaneous fat (Hanna et al. 1989; Beall and Steegmann 2000; Tilkens et al. 2007). However, there is also some evidence suggesting that the body mass/body surface ratio may be irrelevant to maintaining thermal homeostasis (Steegmann 2007). More recent experimental research regarding Allen's rule reveals that individuals with longer limbs, particularly a long proximal segment (for instance the femur), do indeed have greater heat dissipation (Tilkins et al. 2007).

Another ecogeographic rule, Thomson's rule, involves the human nose, which becomes relatively narrower when climate is cooler and dryer (Beall and Steegmann 2000). Using a geographically dispersed sample, Weiner (1954) noted that there was a high inverse correlation ($r = -.82$) between the nasal index (nose width/nose height) and vapor pressure (the amount of water vapor suspended in the air). Later studies also showed that average nose protrusion is similarly related (Beall and Steegmann 2000). Cold and dry air holds little water vapor, but the respiratory system must remain warm and moist in order to function properly. It is postulated that a narrow, beak-like nose improves the turbulence of cool dry air when this is inspired, heating and moistening it so that it will not damage lung tissues. There are, however, no experimental data to support this postulate (Beall and Steegmann 2000).

Finally, a number of studies also suggest that populations living in cold and dry climates tend to have more rounded heads, while those from hot climates have long heads (Steegmann 1975). This morphological cline may also be an adaptation associated with the need for heat conservation or loss.

THERMOREGULATION AND TEMPERATURE ACCLIMATIZATION IN ADULT HUMANS

Thermoregulation in humans is entirely about maintaining the core body temperature in the range of 98.6/99.7 °F or 37/37.6 °C (Beall and Steegmann 2000). Temperature elevated or decreased much beyond this range is lethal. For example, if body temperature rises above 104–7 °F (40–2 °C), there is organ failure, tissue hemorrhage and ultimately death (Beall and Steegmann 2000). Conversely, if body temperature drops to 87.8–89.8 °F (31–2 °C), the physiological mechanisms designed to elevate core temperature fail, stupor sets in and, if the person is not externally warmed, death from hypothermia will ensue (Beall and Steegmann 2000).

There is a variety of physiological mechanisms that work to insure the maintenance of core body temperature. These include sweating, peripheral vasoconstriction and dilation, shivering, and increasing or decreasing basal metabolic rate (BMR) (Frisancho 1993; Beall and Steegmann 2000). In addition, there are passive traits, such as subcutaneous fat, which can act both as a body insulator and as a source of energy stores, which also help with body temperature maintenance. It is beyond the scope of this brief review to discuss the complex feed-back systems that maintain thermal homeostasis; Frisancho (1993) and Beall and Steegmann (2000) provide useful in-depth discussions. However, it is important to understand that humans, like all homeotherms, must maintain a particular core temperature in the face of external temperature challenges. This principle forms the basis of the research that has focused on the effects of environmental temperature on the human body form.

Finally, there is considerable developmental and physiological acclimation and acclimatization that occurs in response to short-term and long-term exposure to hot and cold external temperatures, and these processes significantly affect the ability of humans to adapt to such temperatures (Hanna et al. 1989; Frisancho 1993; Beall and Steegmann 2000). These acclimatizations improve functional ability and survival, primarily allowing individuals to work without overheating or initiating excessive metabolic responses, and they are more or less common to all populations (Hanna et al.

1989). Plasticity and acclimatization are hallmarks of our species, and probably not features that developed as part of the adaptive radiation beyond the tropics. Again, the details of hot and cold acclimatization are beyond the scope of this brief review, but they are extensively described in more comprehensive works such as Frisancho (1993) and Beall and Steegmann (2000).

ADAPTATIONS TO COLD CLIMATE

To function in the cold, core temperature must be maintained at a level high enough for mental and physiological processes to continue. Appendages (feet and hands) are particularly vulnerable to cold injury, as they can develop frostbite. As human populations left the African tropics and colonized areas of colder climate, some have evolved unique biological protections. However, survival in the cold also requires substantial behavioral adaptations, which have probably attenuated the extent of genetic selection in cold-climate populations.

Present evidence suggests that modern humans were the first hominid species to settle permanently circumpolar environments (latitudes ≥ 55° N), which occurred in two stages of settlement, between about 46,000 and 20,000 years ago (Snodgrass et al. 2007). During the first stage (beginning around 46,000 years ago) populations inhabited the subarctic regions of Siberia and Eurasia, while during the second (beginning around 20,000 years ago) populations expanded into circumpolar Europe and Asia, and later into North America and Greenland. The North American Arctic was inhabited only in the last 7,000 years (Snodgrass et al. 2007).

As with Bergmann's and Allen's rule, there appears to be a temperature-related cline in basal metabolic rate (BMR) such that average BMR increases with the decreasing mean annual temperature in geographically dispersed populations (Roberts 1978). Subsequent studies have tended to confirm this cline, as they show that many tropical populations have a lower average BMR, while northern and artic populations have, on average, an elevated BMR (Leonard et al. 2002). However, one aspect of the physiology of high-latitude populations that has received increased attention is the long-term up-regulation of basal metabolic rate (BMR). Several studies indicate that indigenous circumpolar populations – including the Inuit, Chippewa, and Athapascan North American populations and the Evenki, Buryat, and Yakut populations of Siberia – show distinctive metabolic adaptations to their cold environment. In these populations average BMRs are systematically higher than expected on the basis of the average body mass, fat free mass, or surface area of the populations (Leonard et al. 2002; Snodgrass et al. 2007). Recent studies among the Siberian populations suggest that thyroid hormones play an important role in structuring this metabolic adaptation and that, moreover, this cold-related adaptation may have a genetic basis, since BMR continues to be elevated even when the weather is warm (Leonard et al. 2002; Snodgrass et al. 2007).

There also occurs a clear difference among populations in their response to the cooling of peripheral extremities and, specifically, to cold-induced vasodilation (CIVD); this response is known as the 'hunting response' or 'Lewis waves' (Frisancho 1993). External cooling induces a sympathetically driven immediate constriction of the blood vessels in the extremities, which conserves body heat by cutting down the peripheral flow of blood. CIVD is a pulsatile, relatively rapid, and periodic release of this constriction, so that the tissues of the hand or foot are not subjected to frostbite or damage from the chronically low temperature (James and Baker 1995).

Studies of frostbite in US soldiers during military service in Korea revealed that having African ancestry was the single best predictor of frostbite injury (Schuman 1953; Steegmann 1975). Subsequent studies (Rennie and Adams 1957; Newman 1967) have shown that this was likely to occur because people with African ancestry show a markedly reduced and hence inadequate CIVD response. Specifically, these people show a more intense peripheral vasoconstriction in response to cold stress (such as hand immersion in ice water), and there is a high frequency of individuals who fail to show any CIVD. While groups with African ancestry display an inadequate response, virtually all other populations from geographically dispersed areas around the globe demonstrate some degree of CIVD (Steegmann 1975; Frisancho 1993; Beal and Steegmann 2000), and high-latitude populations seem to have the best developed CIVD responses (Steegmann 1975; Frisancho 1993). It is reasonably clear that this population difference in peripheral response to cold is genetically based, and most probably has evolved after early *Homo sapiens* migrated out of Africa, given that our tropical African ancestors were rarely exposed to chronically low or freezing temperatures (Steegmann 1975; James and Baker 1995).

Finally, studies of Australian Aborigines suggest that these populations may have developed a unique response to moderate cold stress. Specifically, the aborigines of central Australia live in a desert, with extreme changes in temperature between day and night: excessive heat during the day, moderate cold at night. Traditionally they do not wear clothing, except for genital covering, and so there is little cultural buffering of the temperature extremes (Frisancho 1993). Studies evaluating sleeping for an eight-hour period in temperature ranging from $3°$ to $5°C$ show that aboriginal subjects were able to sleep better than comparative European white controls, while their metabolic rate, core temperature, and skin temperature dropped. There was a 30 percent reduction in heat conductance from their body core to the skin (Scholander et al. 1958). These data suggest that aborigines appear to adapt to whole-body cold stress by increasing the insulation of their body core through a generalized vasoconstriction and by tolerating moderate hypothermia without increasing basal metabolism (Frisancho 1993). It has been suggested that this response probably has both genetic and acclimatizational components (Steegmann 1975).

ADAPTATIONS TO HIGH-ALTITUDE HYPOXIA

Hypoxia can be defined as a less than normal sea-level amount of oxygen in the inspired air, or a reduction in the physiologically available oxygen (Beall and Steegmann 2000; Beal 2001). High-altitude hypoxia is a severe physiological stress caused by a decrease in available oxygen, which results from decline in barometric pressure with an increasing altitude. That is, a liter of air contains 21 percent oxygen at all altitudes; but at 4,000 meters (13,200 feet) that same liter contains only 63 percent of the number of oxygen molecules in a liter of air taken at sea level (Beall 2001). So, in order to survive in high-altitude environments, the body, starting from a reduced inspired oxygen supply, must develop mechanisms to mobilize sufficient oxygen for cellular metabolism. High-altitude hypoxia is unavoidable, and from the perspective of our migrating, tropically adapted ancestors who colonized high-altitude ecosystems, a biological response was the only available survival option, since it was not possible for them to create a non-hypoxic microenvironment by using behavioral or cultural means (Beall 2001).

The effects of high-altitude hypoxia generally begin at around 2,500 meters (8,250 feet) above sea level (Pawson and Jest 1978). When sea-level natives sojourn to high altitudes, several physiological acclimatizations occur which enhance oxygen delivery to tissues. One physiological measure of the hypoxic stress is oxygen saturation (SaO_2), or change in the percentage of arterial hemoglobin that carries oxygen. At sea level, SaO_2 is greater than 95 percent; but, when sojourners first arrive at altitude, SaO_2 will fall as low as to a level around 80 percent, and then it will increase over the next two to three weeks (Beall and Steegmann 2000). This increase, however, does not rise to the same level as sea-level values. To increase oxygen intake and thus SaO_2, sojourners elevate their rate and depth of breathing (a hyperventilatory response, HR). This elevated HR diminishes after a week or so at altitude. Oxygen transport to the tissues is also improved by an increase in heart rate and by an increase in the volume of blood pushed by the heart with each ventricular contraction. As a consequence of the increase in heart rate, the BMR is also increased. The amount of oxygen in the blood is further increased by elevating hemoglobin-carrying red blood cell concentration. This increase is accomplished at first through a decrease in plasma volume and later through an increased production of red blood cells (Beall and Steegmann 2000). Finally, because of the lower oxygen, maximal work capacity is attenuated in sojourners to altitude. This loss does not improve, even after months of acclimatization (Beall and Steegmann 2000). There are other physiological adjustments of low-altitude populations to short-term and long-term high-altitude exposure, which are further detailed in more comprehensive works (Moore et al. 1998; Beall and Steegmann 2000; Beall 2001).

The effect of high altitude on lowland people has been of interest to biomedical science for well over a century. However, up until the late 1950s and early 1960s, knowledge of the biology of indigenous populations living at altitude was mostly fragmentary and limited to a series of studies of populations living in the Andean highlands in Peru (Baker 1978). Research on the biology of high-altitude populations significantly expanded with the International Biological Programme in the early 1960s (Baker and Little 1976; Baker 1978). Studies of human adaptation to high altitude have been conducted on indigenous populations residing above 2,500 meters in the Andean highlands of South America, in the Tibetan Plateau of Central Asia, and in the Semien Plateau in the Ethiopian highlands of Africa (Baker 1978; Beall 2001).

From the perspective of migration out of Africa, the Andean and the Tibetan populations offer a contrasting evaluation of population adaptation to high-altitude hypoxia. It should be noted first that the responses to altitude in both these populations differ substantially from those of low-altitude sojourners and acclimatized lowlanders living at altitude. The indigenous populations of the Andean and Tibetan plateaus are descendants of migrants who colonized these areas 11,000 and approximately 25,000 years ago respectively (Beall 2007). As Beall (2001, 2007) has noted, evidence accumulated over the past thirty years demonstrates that the descendant populations of the two high plateaus differ quantitatively in respiratory, circulatory, and haematological traits which ameliorate the stress of life-long hypoxia. What has occurred in these populations is an extraordinary natural experiment, in which populations with the same low-altitude hypoxic response settled permanently, for millennia, in high-altitude areas different from their original ones, allowing natural selection to operate independently on each population's genome. Beall (2001, 2007) has summarized several of the functional adaptational differences between the two populations, which are as follows. First, the Tibetans retain the high-resting ventilation of acute exposure of lowlanders, while the Andeans ventilation rates are similar to those of sea-level populations. Second, the Tibetans maintain a sea-level hypoxic ventilatory response (HVR), while the Andeans have a very low HVR. Third, the Tibetans maintain hemoglobin concentration near sea-level values up to 4000 meters, but have elevated concentrations above that altitude, while the Andeans maintain substantially elevated hemoglobin levels in proportion to the altitude, starting at elevations as low as 1,600 meters. Fourth, the Andeans have higher average SaO_2 than the Tibetans. Fifth, there is a difference in pulmonary blood flow, whereby the Tibetans maintain a lower pulmonary arterial pressure than the Andeans. Sixth, the two populations employ different mechanisms to deliver oxygen to the fetus during pregnancy, although each one maintains sufficiently heavy babies at birth. Seventh, the Tibetans may have a denser capillary network than the Andeans, which may give them an easier dissociation of oxygen at the tissue level. Finally, Erzurum and colleagues (2007) have recently reported that the Tibetans have a ten-fold increase of nitric oxide (NO) and of bioactive NO products by comparison to low-altitude residents. NO is a potent vasodilator that increases blood flow – another adaptation that would enhance oxygen delivery. This finding suggests that NO products are regulated differently in Tibetans and implies another functional pathway through which altitude adaptation is operating. Lastly, genetic analyses reveal that the Tibetans have higher genetic variance for oxygen transport traits than the Andeans (Beall 2001; 2007). A major gene for oxygen saturation was also discovered in the Tibetan population (Beall et al. 1994). Further details of the possible role of genetics in the functional adaptations of these high-altitude populations, as well as more in-depth description of their functional differences, are documented elsewhere (Beall 2001, 2007).

Finally, recent studies of indigenous groups living on the Semien Plateau of Ethiopia suggest that there may be a third successful pattern of functional adaptation to high-altitude hypoxia (Beall et al. 2002). Specifically, the Ethiopian population, even at 3,500 meters, retains sea-level SaO_2, by contrast with both the Tibetan and the Andean populations, who exhibit a decrease in saturation compared to sea-level values. The Ethiopians also show no increase in hemoglobin concentration – which is similar to the Tibetan adaptive pattern but different from the Andean one, in which hemoglobin concentrations increase. The functional mechanisms underlying the Ethiopian pattern – a pattern of high SaO_2 with no increase in hemoglobin concentration – are currently unknown (Beall et al. 2002).

ADAPTATIONS TO VARIATION IN ULTRAVIOLET RADIATION

Adaptation to ultraviolet radiation (UVR: wave lengths between about 280 and 400 nanometers) is focused on the effect of UVR on skin color. This is primarily determined by the amount, type, and distribution of melanin, which is a pigment in the epidermis (Beall and Steegmann 2000; Jablonski 2004; Parra 2007). UVR varies with latitude, season of the year, cloud cover, and other environmental factors such as atmospheric ozone; its greatest intensity is at the Equator, its lowest is at the highest latitudes (Jablonski 2004). It is clear that human populations which migrated from Africa and colonized the rest of the Earth were darkly pigmented (Rodgers et al. 2004; Jablonski 2004); thus the variation in skin pigmentation seen among indigenous populations in Europe, Asia, North America, South America, Australia, and the Pacific is a product of natural selection (Jablonski 2004).

There is latitudinal variation in skin pigmentation among indigenous populations, more darkly pigmented populations generally living near the Equator and tropical areas (for instance in sub-Saharan Africa, South Asia, Australia, and Melanesia in the Pacific), while more lightly pigmented populations live nearer the poles (Relethford 1997, 2005; Jablonski 2004). In-between populations have an enhanced ability to develop facultative pigmentation according to seasonal UVR levels (Jablonski 2004). According to Jablonski (2004), this geographic pattern of pigment variation has resulted from two overlapping and opposing clines driven by natural selection. The first is a cline of photoprotection, which ranges from the heavily pigmented populations at the Equator to the lightly pigmented populations at higher latitudes. The second is a cline of vitamin D_3 synthesis, which ranges from the lightly pigmented populations at higher latitudes to the more heavily pigmented groups at the Equator.

The selection of increasing melanin levels in the first cline is related to the ability of melanin to protect the skin from (1) sunburn and skin cancer caused by excess UVB (UVR wavelengths around 300 nanometers) and (2) the destruction (photolysis) of folate caused by excess UVA (UVR wavelengths around 340 to 360 nanometers; see Jablonski 2004 and Parra 2007). The darker skin of populations in areas of high UVR such as the tropics would militate against skin damage and folate loss.

The importance of folate in understanding the skin color cline has only recently been understood. Folate is a nutrient necessary for DNA synthesis, repair, and expression and for all the processes involved in cell division and homeostasis (Jablonski 2004; Parra 2007). Folate deficiency also constitutes a risk factor for neural tube defects, early pregnancy loss, and other pregnancy complications in women, and folate is important in spermatogenesis in men (Jablonski 2004; Parra 2007). Several studies have shown that serum folate concentrations are decreased significantly after short-term and prolonged exposure to near-UVA and UVA radiation (Jablonski 2004; Parra 2007).

The selection against melanin levels in the second cline is related to the role of UVB in the photosynthesis of vitamin D_3 in the skin. Vitamin D_3 has important effects in bone growth and development, but recent research suggests that it may also play a significant role in the prevention of autoimmune diseases, in the control of invading pathogens and in the regulation of cell growth and differentiation (Parra 2007). Melanin is very effective at absorbing and scattering UVB; thus high concentrations of melanin in the skin will decrease the efficiency of the production of D_3 and subsequently the amount of D_3 available for metabolism (Jablonski 2004). As dark-skinned humans moved out of the high UVR tropics to low UVR higher latitudes, their exposure to UVR in general and to UVB in particular was markedly reduced, which rendered them unable to produce adequate amounts of D_3 to meet physiological demand. As a consequence, there was a strong selective pressure for depigmentation in these populations (Jablonski 2004).

The genetics of skin pigmentation are complicated, and as many as sixty genes or more are involved, although the highly polymorphic melanocortin-1 receptor gene (MC1R) appears to be a major gene (Jablonski 2004; Parra 2007). Emerging genetic evidence indicates that the evolution of pigmentation genes has been driven by purifying and diversifying selection. This evidence also indicates that similar skin pigmentations have evolved independently in populations who settled in similar environments (Jablonski 2004). Further details of the biology of melanin and human skin and of its variation in human populations relative to UVR are extensively reviewed by Jablonski (2004) and Parra (2007).

CLIMATIC ADAPTATIONS AND HEALTH

As previously noted, all modern human populations are descended from tropical 'heat adapted' ancestors, and it is also true that modern sub-Saharan African populations retain that heat-adapted physiology, or, more precisely, a physiology adapted to a predominantly hot and wet environment (Hanna and Brown 1979; Young et al. 2005). An important aspect of that physiology aside from a decrease in body hair and the ability to sweat copiously is an ability to retain salt (sodium) as there is limited salt availability in hot, tropical environments (James and Baker 1995; Young et al. 2005). Recently, Young and colleagues (2005) have reported a geographic cline, from the Equator to higher latitudes, of 'heat adapted' alleles from five functional genes that affect salt retention and blood vessel tone. The team has found that populations living within ten degrees of the Equator have an average 74 percent 'heat adapted' allelic variants at these genes, while populations within ten degrees of the Arctic have only 43 percent 'heat adapted' variants. Comparative data from fifty-three populations, geographically dispersed between the Equator and the poles, suggest that the frequency of 'heat adapted' alleles declined as our African ancestors colonized environments which were cooler and rich in salt, and then it rose again among groups who migrated from those areas back to tropical climates poorer in salt. It is estimated that these changes in 'heat adapted' genes occurred over a time frame of 12,000 to 30,000 years (Young et al. 2005). The same researchers have suggested that, since the 'heat adapted' alleles help to retain salt and since excessive dietary salt intake is a major risk factor in hypertension, populations with the 'heat adapted' alleles are probably more susceptible to hypertension, particularly if they have migrated in more recent times (either forcibly or by choice) to cooler environments rich in salt, or if they have substantially increased the element of salt in their diet *in situ* (Young et al. 2005). This scenario may partially explain the higher prevalence of hypertension and cardiovascular morbidity found today in African American populations.

It has also been suggested that the ancestral African 'heat adapted' physiology, which is also characterized by an inadequate vasodilatory response induced by cold, may further contribute to the development of hypertension and cardiovascular morbidity in African American populations (James and Baker 1995). Specifically, peripheral cold stress that induces sympathetically driven vasoconstriction will increase blood pressure (Pickering and Gerin 1990), and chronic vasoconstriction is likely to lead to hypertension (Kaplan 1978). African Americans living in the temperate and freezing climates of North America are likely to experience chronic cold stress through the winter months, being potentially exposed to chronic vasoconstriction (James and Baker 1995). It should also be noted that sympathetic hormone receptors among African Americans appear to be more sensitive than among European Americans. In addition, it appears that the blood pressure of African Americans is much more sensitive to changes in epinephrine, a vasoactive sympathetic hormone (van Berge-Landry et al. 2008). Whether this difference in sympathetic tone among groups with African ancestry is related to climate is at present unknown.

The migration of equatorial, darkly pigmented populations to higher latitudes has also lead to an increase in vitamin D_3 deficiency in migrant groups due to the diminishing of UVB at higher latitudes (Jablonski 2004). As a consequence of the diminished D_3 synthesis, vitamin D-related pathologies and the altered function of the vitamin D endocrine system are more prevalent among populations in this category (Jablonski 2004). Conversely, migration of higher-latitude populations to equatorial regions with extremely high UVB has lead to an increase in the incidence of skin cancers in the migrant populations, particularly among Australians, despite the ability to darken the skin by tanning (Jablonski 2004).

Finally, diet has also played a part in developing pathologies in climatically adapted populations – a phenomenon well illustrated among the Eskimo-Aleut peoples of northeast Asia and of the North American Arctic. These populations exhibit a darker pigmentation than would be predicted from models by using UVB levels alone (Jablonski and Chaplin 2000). There are several reasons for this phenomenon, including the relatively recent colonization of the area from lower-latitude regions in Asia (Jablonski 2004). However, while UVB is very low in the Arctic, UVA levels are high, which might also favor darker skin (Jablonski 2004, Parra 2007). The ability of these relatively dark-skinned populations to survive in this low UVB environment rests on a high vitamin-D rich diet consisting largely of fish, marine mammals and caribou, which have an abundance of vitamin D_3 (Jablonski 2004). This synergy between diet and climate is dramatically demonstrated by the increased prevalence of vitamin D-related pathologies (such as rickets) in Eskimo-Aleut populations who have abandoned their traditional diet in favor of a more westernized one – high in refined carbohydrates and saturated fats (Jablonski 2004; Snodgrass et al. 2007).

CONCLUSIONS AND FUTURE DIRECTIONS

Research over the last sixty years has demonstrated that the diversity of the climate across our planet has directly influenced the morphological, physiological, and genetic variation within our species. This variation occurs through a process of acclimatization, both in the short term and developmentally, and through the process of natural selection. Genetically related adaptations have also led to adverse health consequences, not only in populations who have migrated to different environments from the ones in which the adaptation occurred, but also in populations who have undergone behavioral change *in situ*.

While this brief overview has discussed separately the adaptations to cold, to low barometric pressure, and to ultraviolet radiation, there are populations who experience all of these climatic stresses simultaneously (Baker 1984). Adaptations in these populations might be seen as a compromise that allows survival in the face the multiple stresses.

Finally, there are still many unknown factors in the study of climatic adaptations in humans. First, many of the functional differences found to be associated with climatic stresses are based on a very few studies with small sample sizes. Thus a lot of the findings need to be more fully verified. In fact, as Steegmann has noted (2007), studies of adaptation to the physical environment have diminished markedly after about 1975 in favor of studies on nutrition, disease and stress; and Steegmann argues that several topics – for instance "How important is muscle tissue as an insulator?" and "Do thermally protective behaviors make special biological adaptations unnecessary?" – are still not well understood. While many functional–physiological differences between populations have been identified, the genetic basis of those functional traits is for the most part unknown. There may be other, as yet undiscovered, climate-related variants in human populations, and the health implications of climatic adaptations need to be more fully explored. There is still much to learn about the way in which humans have adapted to climate.

REFERENCES

Allen, J. A. (1877) The Influence of Physical Conditions in the Genesis of Species. *Radical Review* 1: 108–140.
Baker, P. T. (1978) IBP High-Altitude Research: Development and Strategies. In P. T. Baker (ed.), *The Biology of High-Altitude Peoples* (pp. 1–15). London: Cambridge University Press
Baker, P. T. (1984) The Adaptive Limits of Human Populations. *Man* NS 19: 1–14.
Baker, P. T., and Little, M. A. (eds) (1976) *Man in the Andes: A Multidisciplinary Study of High Altitude Quechua.* Stroudsburg, PA: Dowden, Hutchinson & Ross.
Beall, C. M. (2001) Adaptation to Altitude: A Current Assessment. *Annual Review of Anthropology* 30: 423–456.
Beall, C. M. (2007) Two Routes to Functional Adaptation: Tibetan and Andean High Altitude Natives. *Proceedings of the National Academy of Science, USA* 104 (Suppl. 1): 8655–8660.
Beall, C. M., and Steegmann, A. T., Jr (2000) Human Adaptation to Climate: Temperature, Ultraviolet Radiation and Altitude. In S. Stinson, B. Bogin, R. Huss-Ashmore and D. O'Rourke (eds), *Human Biology: An Evolutionary and Biocultural Perspective* (pp. 163–224). New York: Wiley–Liss Inc.
Beall, C. M., Blangero, J., Williams-Blangero, S., and Goldstein, M. C. (1994) A Major Gene for Percent of Oxygen Saturation of Arterial Hemoglobin in Tibetan Highlanders. *American Journal of Physical Anthropology* 95: 271–276.
Beall, C. M., Decker, M. J., Brittenham, G. M., Kushner, I., Gebremedhin, A., and Strohl, K. P. (2002) An Ethiopian Pattern of Human Adaptation to High-Altitude. *Proceedings of the National Academy of Science, USA* 99 (26): 17215–17218.
Bergmann, K. (1847) Über die Verhältnisse der wärmeökonomie der Thiere zu ihrer Grösse. *Göttinger Studien* 3 (1): 595–708.
Bindon, J. R., and Baker, P. T. (1997) Bergmann's Rule and the Thrifty Genotype. *American Journal of Physical Anthropology* 104: 201–210.
Conroy, G. C. (2005) *Reconstructing Human Origins*, 2nd edn. New York: W. W. Norton Company, Inc.

Coon, C. S., Garn, S. M., and Birdsell, J. B. (1950) *Races: A Study of the Problem of Race Formation in Man*. Springfield, IL: Charles C. Thomas.

Erzurum, S. C., Ghosh, S., Janocha, A. J., Xu, W., Bauer, S., Bryan, N. S., Tejero, J., Hemann, C., Hille, R., Stuehr, D. J., Feelisch, M., and Beall, C. M. (2007) Higher Blood Flow and Circulating NO Products Offset High-Altitude Hypoxia Among Tibetans. *Proceedings of the National Academy of Science, USA* 104 (45): 17593–17598.

Frisancho, A. R. (1993) *Human Adaptation and Accommodation*. Ann Arbor: University of Michigan Press.

Hanna, J. M., and Brown, D. A. (1979) Human Heat Tolerance: Biological and Cultural Adaptations. *Yearbook of Physical Anthropology* 22: 163–186.

Hanna, J. M., Little, M. A., and Austin, D. M. (1989) Climatic Physiology. In M. A. Little and J. D. Haas (eds), *Human Population Biology: A Transdisciplinary Science* (pp. 132–151). New York: Oxford University Press.

Jablonski, N. G. (2004) The Evolution of Human Skin Color. *Annual Review of Anthropology* 33: 585–623.

Jablonski, N. G., and Chaplin, G. (2000) The Evolution of Skin Coloration. *Journal of Human Evolution* 39: 57–106.

James, G. D., and Baker, P. T. (1995) Human Population Biology and Blood Pressure: Evolutionary and Ecological Considerations and Interpretations of Population Studies. In J. H. Laragh and B. M. Brenner (eds), *Hypertension: Pathophysiology, Diagnosis and Management* (pp. 115–126). New York: Raven Press Ltd.

Johnson, F. E., and Little, M. A. (2000) History of Human Biology in the United States of America. In S. Stinson, B. Bogin, R. Huss-Ashmore and D. O'Rourke (eds), *Human Biology: An Evolutionary and Biocultural Perspective* (pp. 27–46). New York: Wiley–Liss Inc.

Kaplan, N. M. (1978) Stress, the Sympathetic Nervous System and Hypertension. *Journal of Human Stress* 4: 29–34.

Katzmarzyk, P. T., and Leonard, W. R. (1998) Climatic Influences on Human Body Size and Proportions: Ecological Adaptations and Secular Trends. *American Journal of Physical Anthropology* 106: 483–503.

Leonard, W. R., Sorenson, M. V., Galloway, V. A., Spencer, G. J., Mosher, M. J., Osipova L., and Spitsyn, V. A. (2002) Climatic Influences on Basal Metabolic Rates among Circumpolar Populations. *American Journal of Human Biology* 14: 609–620.

Moore, L. G., Niermeyer, S., and Zamudio, S. (1998) Human Adaptation to High Altitude: Regional and Life Cycle Perspectives. *Yearbook of Physical Anthropology* 41: 25–64.

Newman, R. W. (1967) A Comparison of Negro and White Responses to a 5°C Water Bath (Abstract). *American Journal of Physical Anthropology* 49: 249.

Newman, R. W. (1970) Why Is Man such a Sweaty and Thirsty Naked Animal: A Speculative Review. *Human Biology* 42: 12–27.

Newman, R. W., and Munro, E. H. (1955) The Relation of Climate and Body in US Males. *American Journal of Physical Anthropology* 13: 1–17.

Parra, E. J. (2007) Human Pigmentation Variation: Evolution, Genetic Basis, and Implications for Public Health. *Yearbook of Physical Anthropology* 50: 85–105.

Pawson, I. G., and Jest, C. (1978) The High-Altitude Areas of the World and Their Cultures. In P. T. Baker (ed.), *The Biology of High-Altitude Peoples* (pp. 17–45). London: Cambridge University Press.

Pickering, T. G., and Gerin, W. (1990) Cardiovascular Reactivity in the Laboratory and the Role of Behavioral Factors in Hypertension: A Critical Review. *Annals of Behavioral Medicine* 12: 3–16.

Relethford, J. H. (1997) Hemispheric Difference in Human Skin Color. *American Journal of Physical Anthropology* 104: 449–457.

Relethford, J. H. (2005) *The Human Species*, 6th edn. New York: McGraw–Hill.

Rennie, D. W., and Adams, T. (1957) Comparative Thermoregulatory Responses of Negroes and White Persons to Acute Cold Stress. *Journal of Applied Physiology* 11: 201–204.

Roberts, D. F. (1953) Body Weight, Race and Climate. *American Journal of Physical Anthropology* 11: 533–558.

Roberts, D. F. (1978) *Climate and Human Variability*, 2nd edn. Menlo Park: Cummings.

Rodgers, A. R., Iltis, D., and Woodling. S. (2004) Genetic Variation at the MC1R Locus and the Time since Loss of Human Body Hair. *Current Anthropology* 45: 105–107.

Ruff, C. B. (1994) Morphological Adaptation to Climate in Modern and Fossil Hominids. *Yearbook of Physical Anthropology* 37: 65–107.

Scholander P. F., Hammel, H. T., Hart, J. S., LeMessurier, D. H., and Stern, J. (1958) Cold Adaptation in Australian Aborigines. *Journal of Applied Physiology* 13: 211–218.

Schuman, L. M. (1953) Epidemiology of Frostbite, Korea 1951–1952. In *Cold Injury-Korea (1951–1952)*. US Army Medical Research Laboratory (Ft. Knox, Kentucky), Report 113: 205–568.

Serrat, M. A., King, D., and Lovejoy, C. O. (2008) Temperature Regulates Limb Length in Homeotherms by directly Modulating Cartilage Growth. *Proceedings of the National Academy of Science, USA* 105 (49): 19348–19353.

Snodgrass, J. J., Sorenson, M. V., Tarskaia, L. A., and Leonard, W. R. (2007) Adaptive Dimensions of Health Research among Indigenous Siberians. *American Journal of Human Biology* 19: 165–180.

Steegmann, A. T., Jr. (1975) Human Adaptation to Cold. In Albert Damon (ed.), *Physiological Anthropology* (pp. 130–166). New York: Oxford University Press.

Steegmann, A. T., Jr. (2007) Human Cold Adaptation: An Unfinished Agenda. *American Journal of Human Biology* 19: 218–227.

Tilkens, M. J., Wall-Scheffler, C., Weaver, T. D., and Steudel-Numbers, K. (2007) The Effects of Body Proportions on Thermoregulation: An Experimental Assessment of Allen's Rule. *Journal of Human Evolution* 53: 286–291.

Van Berge-Landry, H. M., Bovbjerg, D. H., and James, G. D. (2008) The Relationship between Waking-Sleep Blood Pressure and Catecholamine Changes in African American and European American Women. *Blood Pressure Monitoring* 13: 257–262.

Washburn, S. L. (1951) The New Physical Anthropology. *Transactions of the New York Academy of Science* 13: 298–305.

Weiner, J. S. (1954) Nose Shape and Climate. *American Journal of Physical Anthropology* 12: 1–4.

Young, J. H., Chang, Y. C., Kim, J. D., Chretien, J.-P., Levine, M. A., Ruff, C. B., Wang, N. Y., and Chakravarti, A. (2005) Differential Susceptibility to Hypertension Is Due to Selection during the Out-of-Africa Expansion. *PLoS Genetics* 1(6): e82.

CHAPTER 9

Emerging Themes in Anthropology and Epidemiology: Geographic Spread, Evolving Pathogens, and Syndemics

*Lisa Sattenspiel and
D. Ann Herring*

In 2003 a new disease, severe acute respiratory syndrome (SARS), rapidly spread throughout the world. Initial reports of the disease reached the World Health Organization in February 2003, and within the next five months cases were noted from twenty-six different countries on five continents. From its apparent beginning in China, the epidemic spread to Hong Kong, Vietnam, Singapore, Canada, and elsewhere, and by the end of the epidemic nearly 800 people died, although the bulk of these deaths occurred in only a handful of countries. During the epidemic, the western world was gripped by fear that a new and deadly worldwide pandemic would devastate populations everywhere, but the collaborative efforts of many different types of scientists and medical professionals and the actions of various governments, coupled with the unique biology of the SARS virus, ensured that the epidemic was relatively short-lived and limited in scope. Epidemiologists, whose work centers on understanding how, when, where, and why diseases occur, worked closely with other investigators to help contain the SARS pandemic.

The roots of the field of epidemiology most likely extend back into prehistory, but the modern discipline really got its start during the latter part of the nineteenth century, after the acceptance of the germ theory of disease. Much of the credit for this theory is given to Pasteur, who showed in the 1860s that disease could be produced after certain microorganisms (germs) were introduced into the body. His theory was the culmination of several earlier ideas, including the ancient Hippocratic belief that health is strongly influenced by climate and by the environment. Modern epidemiology was also influenced by the concept of contagion – the idea that diseases can be transferred from person to person via invisible particles in the air, an idea formalized by Girolamo Fracastoro in the sixteeenth century.

Modern epidemiology itself is said to have begun with the work of John Snow, who conducted one of the first detailed studies linking a particular environmental risk factor to the development of disease. Snow plotted all deaths from cholera on a map of London and was able to show convincingly that these deaths were linked to water coming from one particular source. He was not able to isolate the real cause of cholera, however. That had to wait until 1883, when Robert Koch proved that the microorganism *Vibrio cholerae* was causally linked to the disease. Koch's work solidified the role of Pasteur's germ theory of disease in modern epidemiology.

As its name suggests, epidemiology was initially centered on the study of infectious disease epidemics. However, as the application of germ theory and improved sanitation led to more effective control of epidemics, emphasis shifted to the study of more chronic and non-infectious health conditions, such as cancer or heart disease. For a while, at least in the western world, infectious diseases were thought to be a thing of the past, so active research on infectious diseases declined in the last quarter of the twentieth century, until the HIV/AIDS pandemic emerged. Although it is clearly recognized that infectious diseases are still with us and still capable of causing much suffering for humans everywhere, most epidemiology programs continue to place more emphasis on chronic diseases, since these are the most common causes of death in western societies.

Life in the twenty-first century is marked by a significant increase in overall rates of worldwide travel and by increased interactions among individuals who were once isolated from one another by distance and by cultural barriers. As a result, diseases like SARS are able to spread through global networks in a matter of weeks, or even days; and, in addition, there are many new opportunities for the evolution and spread of emerging pathogens. Thus scientists studying infectious diseases are playing an increasingly important role in modern endeavors to continue improving the health and wellbeing of all populations.

Anthropologists and epidemiologists have worked in parallel and in collaboration for much of the twentieth and twenty-first centuries, sharing conceptual and theoretical affinities, qualitative and quantitative methods, and an interest in international health; but at the same time they have retained boundaries and some healthy skepticism about each others' research (Janes et al. 1986; Trostle 2006). In this chapter we focus on some of the ways in which physical anthropologists have used epidemiological theory and methods to address questions of interest to anthropologists.

Although the study of disease in prehistoric populations falls almost entirely within the purview of physical anthropology, since the primary source of evidence used in such studies is skeletal remains, epidemiological studies based on skeletal analyses are described in several other chapters of this book, so we center our discussion on disease in historical and modern populations. It is worth noting, however, that through the study of skeletal remains in an archaeological context physical anthropologists have expanded Omran's (1971) classic model of the epidemiological transition. In the original formulation of his theory, Omran focused on data from pre-industrial western Europe. Physical anthropologists have addressed a number of weaknesses in the model and extended it to the Paleolithic in order to offer a framework of how major shifts in social and demographic conditions – for instance the progressive reliance on food production; increased social complexity and social stratification; larger population size and density; growing sedentism; and widening trade networks associated with the Neolithic – shaped human disease patterns from prehistory to the present (Barrett et al. 1998). Social inequalities have mediated all the epidemiological transitions in human history, resulting in higher burdens of disease and death among relatively less affluent people – within as well as between societies.

A growing number of physical anthropologists focus on epidemiology in more recent historical and modern populations. Some study the epidemiology of chronic diseases. For example James Neel, Emöke Szathmáry, Kue Young, and colleagues produced a number of studies of diabetes in native communities in North America (see for example Neel 1962; Szathmáry 1994; Young et al. 1990). Nevertheless, much of the recent research using epidemiological approaches within physical anthropology (including our own) has focused on infectious diseases (see for instance Inhorn and Brown 1997). In a historical context, Hauteniemi and colleagues conducted an intensive analysis of mortality in two eighteenth-century New England communities (Hauteniemi et al. 1999); Mielke and colleagues studied the spread of smallpox and other infectious diseases in the Åland Islands, Finland (Mielke 2003); Madrigal and Koertvelyessy looked at epidemic cycles in Costa Rican, Hungarian, and US agricultural populations (Madrigal and Koertvelyessy 2003); Scott and Duncan performed detailed analyses of epidemic patterns for a number of diseases in pre-industrial and early industrial England and Wales (Scott and Duncan 1998, 2001); Swedlund and colleagues studied scarlet fever as part of a long-term study of the disease history of the Connecticut Valley (Swedlund and Donta 2003); Sawchuk analyzed a series of cholera epidemics within the changing demographic fabric of the civilian population of Gibraltar (Sawchuk 2001); and we studied the impact of the 1918–19 influenza epidemic in central Canadian fur trapping populations (Herring and Sattenspiel 2007; Sattenspiel and Herring 1998). Examples of epidemiological studies in contemporary human groups include studies of tuberculosis and helminths in the Ache of Paraguay undertaken by Hurtado and colleagues (Hurtado et al. 2003, 2008); Littleton and King's (2008) analysis of the political ecology of tuberculosis in New Zealand; research on HIV among Peruvian men who have sex with men, pursued by Goodreau and colleagues (2005); and a study of mortality among the Tsimane Amerindians of Bolivia conducted by Gurven and colleagues (2007).

Given our interest and expertise, and because a complete overview of both chronic and infectious disease epidemiology is beyond the scope of this chapter, we focus here on three important areas of infectious disease research that have recently received attention within anthropology: the geographic distribution and spread of infectious diseases; emerging infectious diseases; and the interaction between multiple pathogens and social and behavioral factors in epidemics – a growing emphasis in epidemiology, which is coming to be known as 'syndemics'.

THE GEOGRAPHIC DISTRIBUTION AND SPREAD OF INFECTIOUS DISEASES

Identifying and predicting the distribution and geographic spread of infectious diseases is a topic of major importance in today's world, and a number of methods are being used to aid in this endeavor. We illustrate here one major approach: the use of mathematical and computer modeling to predict patterns of epidemic spread.

The process of using mathematical or computer models to describe the geographic spread of infectious diseases requires a rigorous representation of the disease process within an individual. Two overlapping sets of terms are used to describe this process: one set focuses on the transmission process (the transmission framework) and the other focuses on symptomatic illness (the symptoms framework) (see Figure 9.1). Both frameworks begin with a susceptible person, who is at risk of a disease. Upon infection with a disease-causing pathogen, in the symptoms framework the person enters the incubation period (that is, the time period between infection and the development of symptoms), while in the transmission framework the person enters the latent period (the time period between infection and the ability to pass on the pathogen to someone else). After the incubation period, the person enters the period of symptomatic illness, and this is followed by a state of recovery. After the latent period (in the transmission framework), the person enters the infectious period, which ends when that person can no longer transmit the pathogen to others. The incubation period is often somewhat longer than the latent period, and in such cases infected persons can begin to transmit the pathogen before they are aware of being infected. The infectious period may end before, at the time, or after symptoms subside, depending on the particular disease. Finally, many (but not all) infectious diseases result in either temporary or permanent immunity after the infection. Death may occur at any time during this process, with the probability of death dependent on the particular disease, on the underlying health of the infected person, and on contributing environmental or genetic risk factors.

The use of mathematical and computer models to describe the geographic spread of infectious diseases has grown exponentially over the last twenty-five years (see Sattenspiel 2009 for an extensive overview of this topic). Because the question of geographic spread involves understanding how a disease is transmitted from one

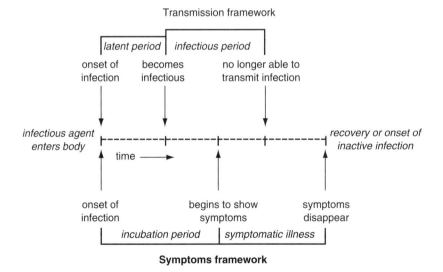

Figure 9.1   The progress of infection from the clinical (symptomatic) perspective and from the transmission process perspective. Note that the symptomatic period overlaps with, but is not the same as, the infectious period. Also, depending on the biological characteristics of the disease of interest, the infectious period may end before, at, or occasionally after the time at which symptoms disappear.

person to another, such models rely on the transmission framework rather than on the symptoms framework. Essentially, most models of this process divide a population into subgroups representing the stages of disease specific to the condition of interest (for instance influenza models typically divide a population into susceptible, infectious, and recovered individuals, although they may also include an exposed stage). Models can be designed either at the population level (here variation among individuals within a population or subpopulation is ignored) or at the individual level (in this approach the activities of different individuals are explicitly modeled). The models generally consist of a representation of the disease process as individuals progress through different stages, combined with a representation of the process of interaction among individuals that serves to spread the disease across space.

Mathematical and computer models are now regularly included among the tools used to control outbreaks of infectious diseases. For example, mathematical models were used from the beginning of the 2003 SARS epidemic to help in predicting how serious the epidemic might become, to explore the effectiveness of different proposed control strategies, and, perhaps most importantly, to estimate critical disease-related variables such as the pathogen reproductive rate (see for example Chowell et al. 2004; Lipsitch et al. 2003; Riley et al. 2003). Because SARS was a new disease, data on such variables did not exist and mathematical models provided important information that helped to limit the spread of the epidemic.

Models have also been used extensively in studies of the spread of influenza epidemics, both for understanding past epidemics and for predicting the impact of future ones. Influenza models have included both population-based and individual-based approaches and offer some of the earliest and most influential studies of the geographic spread of infectious diseases. Almost all of the population-based models are adaptations of a model initially developed by O. V. Baroyan, L. A. Rvachev, and their colleagues in the Soviet Union, from the late 1960s through to the late 1970s (Baroyan and Rvachev 1967; Baroyan et al. 1969). Rvachev and Longini (1985) developed the model further, ending up with the basic form that is widely used in modern epidemiological modeling. What is really interesting about this body of work is that it was based on estimates of actual transportation data, initially derived from rail travel, later extended to bus travel, and then to air travel data. This work has stimulated several other influenza studies as well as studies of a few other diseases; in addition, much recent effort has been directed at finding more sophisticated ways to determine exactly which features of the highly complex transportation networks present in the modern world are most important for the spread of infectious diseases.

In response to a recognition that individual variability is of great importance in disease transmission processes, several individual-based models of influenza transmission have been developed recently and used in attempts to predict how, when, and where the next influenza epidemic might spread and how such an epidemic might be controlled (see for example Ferguson et al. 2005, 2006; Germann et al. 2006; Longini et al. 2005). In general these models focus more on spread within a particular population than on spread among populations across space, but they do try to assess how an epidemic might be kept from spreading to other regions.

How can physical anthropologists contribute to the study of the geographic spread of infectious diseases? We shall take here our own work to illustrate the value of anthropological approaches to such research. We have used both population-based models (Sattenspiel and Herring 1998, 2003) and individual-based models (Carpenter and Sattenspiel 2009; Herring and Sattenspiel 2007) to study the spread of the 1918–19 influenza epidemic among fur trapping populations in central Manitoba. Initially we focused simply on how the traditional travel patterns of the trappers, displayed during the course of their business with the Hudson's Bay Company, helped to spread the epidemic across the region. Simulations of our initial (population-based) models indicated that the overall impact of mobility was limited to changes in the timing of epidemics in different communities, but that other factors, in particular rates of contact between individuals, were primary forces influencing the overall extent and severity of the epidemics. These results caused us, as anthropologists, to think much more carefully about the specific cultural activities of people within the communities we studied – for instance about how families were structured at different times in the seasonal cycle of subsistence activities; who was interacting with whom; and how those activities helped to spread the influenza epidemic within and among the communities.

As a consequence of our shift towards modeling specific human activities and behaviors, we began to realize the importance of incorporating variability in those activities and behaviors into our models and, as a result, we have started to use, in our research, more individual-based approaches to modeling. The results of our simulations have confirmed the importance of rates of contact within and between groups for the spread of epidemic diseases. They also indicate that including variability in human activities and behaviors is essential if we are to understand the impact infectious diseases have upon human groups.

Our research on the spread of the 1918–19 influenza epidemic in central Manitoba has several dimensions that make it anthropological in addition to epidemiological. First, the communities we studied – Aboriginal fur trappers in central Canada – allowed us to examine the global effects of an international business, the fur trade, on the introduction and circulation of diseases in these local communities. Second, as anthropologists, we have always emphasized the importance, along with biological factors, of human activities and cultural behaviors in influencing the spread of infectious diseases; and we have been aware of, and sensitive to, the importance of variability in these areas rather than thinking that all humans are alike. This is not to say, however, that epidemiologists and other modelers never do what anthropologists do. Like anthropology, epidemiology as a discipline tries to address the interaction between biology and behavior, and hence there is much overlap. But considerations of individual variability in human behavior and of diversity in social organization and in subsistence activities are more central to anthropological approaches; in the field of epidemiology they constitute a real contribution. Finally, the underlying question that has framed much of this research relates to long-standing anthropological questions: How have introduced pathogens affected the indigenous people of the Americas? How and why have the effects of those pathogens varied from community to community?

Emerging Infectious Diseases

The phrase 'emerging infectious disease' refers to diseases that either are new to a population or show an increase in the number of cases, in association with a rapid expansion of their range (Morse 1993). While media attention to emerging infections has generated panic and a tendency to connect this phrase with exotic and frightening viruses such as Ebola, the phrase is appropriately applied to many seemingly mundane diseases such as influenza, which have ebbed and flowed over the course of human history. The phrase came into fashion in the 1990s, in the wake of the HIV/AIDS epidemic, which demonstrated that infectious disease was not a feature of the past (according to Omran's classic epidemiologic transition theory discussed earlier), but an inevitable aspect of ordinary life. And, while HIV/AIDS was initially believed to be a 'new disease' caused by a frightening 'new microorganism', phylogenetic analysis of its genome indicates that it is likely to be at least 100 years old. Furthermore, the family of viruses to which it belongs is ancient (Grmek 1990).

Diseases emerge, in fact, when they become visible, and thus it is rare for a truly new disease to be discovered. Hantavirus – a member of a family of viruses classified as haemorrhagic fevers – is considered to have 'emerged' in the southwestern USA in 1993. Hantaviruses, however, have a global distribution, were known for centuries in Asia, and may have existed for millions of years (Schmaljohn and Hjelle 1997). The Hantaan virus, which causes Korean haemorrhagic fever, is believed to have been carried by rodents across the Bering land bridge from Asia into the Americas as early as the Oligocene. Arenaviruses, another (probably) ancient family of haemorrhagic fever-causing viruses, are found in the Americas. The antiquity of these pathogens opens up new questions for physical anthropologists interested in disease history and in the demographic history of the Americas. For instance, some researchers have asked whether some of the sixteenth-century Mesoamerican epidemics usually attributed to pathogens introduced from Europe (such as smallpox and typhus) were caused instead by an indigenous haemorrhagic virus carried by a rodent host (Marr and Kiracofe 2000; Acuna-Soto et al. 2002).

It is a central premise of contemporary epidemiological theory that zoonoses – animal pathogens which occasionally infect humans – are an important source of epidemics in human populations and played a significant role in the major epidemiological transitions in human history (Barrett et al. 1998). It is therefore important for physical anthropologists to incorporate zooarchaeological evidence – the remains of non-human animal species found at archaeological sites – into their studies of ancient human disease. Dogs, for instance, may have been transferring diseases to humans for some 15,000 years (Mitchell 2003).

Human–primate contact in contemporary settings has also been the focus of research on disease transmission by physical anthropologists, because primates have been discovered to be a reservoir of infection for a number of human diseases such as HIV. Primates and humans often have overlapping ranges and interact in predator/prey settings, exotic pet settings, zoo and laboratory settings, religious settings and so on. Several infectious agents have been transmitted from primates to human (for example retroviruses, herpesviruses, cytomegalovirus), either directly or through intermediate hosts (Engel and Engel 2008). Concentrating on the potential for the cross-species transmission of pathogens represents an important direction in the study of infectious disease in human history.

Human–primate contact is not, however, the only type of present-day human–animal contact that provides opportunities for new pathogens to enter human groups. Pathogens are undoubtedly transmitted between humans and their pets, and many of the common human childhood diseases are thought to have derived originally from domesticated animals (although transmission can also go the other way, as recent genetic evidence on tuberculosis is suggesting (Wirth et al. 2008)). Ebola haemorrhagic fever, whose mode of transmission is suspected to be connected to human contact with fruit bats (Hewlett and Hewlett 2008), draws our attention to the fact that much remains to be learned about infectious disease and its effects on human societies.

In the last few years much research has been devoted to understanding the transmission of avian influenza to humans, because it is widely believed that new influenza pandemics are likely to evolve from presently circulating avian influenza strains. Anthropologists are playing an important role in understanding this process. Domesticated fowl in Asia are becoming infected with strains carried by wild fowl, and the cultural practices related to the care of infected domesticated fowl – such as keeping birds in shelters within or near houses or having children or young women care for flocks – are likely to be important components influencing the risk of transmission of the flu to humans and the possible evolution of a new human strain from avian strains. Avian influenza, however, is not simply an infectious disease problem or an interesting issue in evolutionary biology. Chicken is often the cheapest animal protein in the developing countries in which avian influenza is most often found and it has been an important feature of development initiatives in southeast Asia. Policies aimed at controlling avian influenza, therefore, have broader anthropological implications, because they have an impact on the nutritional status, livelihoods, and health of rural farm families whose flocks are culled in the interests of global safety (Lockerbie and Herring 2008).

SYNDEMICS

The bulk of physical anthropological research on infectious disease discussed so far has focused on the determinants, dynamics, and distribution of single diseases in past and present populations. There is growing recognition, however, of the importance of studying interactions between pathogens. For example the potential influence of other sexually transmitted diseases (STDs) and of tuberculosis on the transmission of HIV has been a long-standing focus of AIDS research. Severe influenza pneumonia in humans, too, is often caused by concurrent viral–bacterial infections. Complicated respiratory tract infections frequently characterized the 1918–19 pandemic, contributing to the excess mortality that typified this outbreak. In particular, co-infections with tuberculosis presumably predisposed many people to die from influenza during the pandemic (Noymer 2009), exemplifying how endemic and epidemic diseases can interact synergistically to increase a community's burden of morbidity and mortality and underlining the importance of widening the analytic lens beyond individual infectious diseases.

Yet social influences play an equally vital role in molding the risks of disease transmission as well as the differential impact of disease on members of a society (Goodman and Leatherman 1998). Not only do pathogens interact, but the prevalence of several diseases in particular groups, such as the co-occurrence of HIV/AIDS and other sexually transmitted diseases, can be driven and sustained by deleterious social conditions (Singer et al. 2006). The term 'syndemic' is a useful extension of the biocultural concept. Researchers are asked to consider whether a particular epidemic is, in fact, part of a larger set of interactive and mutually accelerating epidemics involving disease interactions at the biological level, which develop and persist in a community because of harmful social conditions (Singer and Clair 2003). The syndemics perspective seeks to discover and chart the pathways through which diseases and other health conditions work together within individual bodies and within populations. The concept facilitates a more complex discussion of co-circulating pathogens in different social contexts, helping physical anthropologists to address one of the central questions of our subdiscipline: that of explaining diversity in human biosocial experience – including the differential impact of epidemics of infectious disease.

Numerous syndemics have been described (for a review, see Singer et al. 2006). In Latin America, for instance, the prevalence of congestive heart failure (CHF), both as a cause and as a consequence of the epidemiologic transition, is on the rise. Among the major contributors to the growing rates of CHF are two infectious diseases: Chagas disease, caused by infection with *Trypanosoma cruzi*, and rheumatic heart disease, due to a *Streptococcus pyogenes* infection. Both of these diseases are more often observed in rural areas, where access to basic health care is limited. Their prevalence among poor, rural children, coupled with the lack of adequate treatment, is likely to result in a large proportion of these children progressing to CHF over the next twenty to forty years of their lives, which in turn might lead to death from CHF at a relatively young age (Cubillos-Garzon et al. 2004). This illustrates how the experience of infectious diseases in childhood, acting in conjunction with poor or non-existent health care, creates a chronic, non-infectious health condition – in this case, heart disease – in early adulthood. Another example of a syndemic has been described among 18–25- year old African Americans and Puerto Ricans living in Hartford, Connecticut. Researchers have identified a cluster of epidemics of two sexually transmitted diseases in addition to a third, AIDS. This cluster of epidemics has in turn been linked to health and social disparities manifest in these groups – disparities which have given rise to beliefs and behaviors that favor the spread of these STDs among the members of the groups in question (Singer et al. 2006).

TRENDS IN ANTHROPOLOGICAL EPIDEMIOLOGY

Although physical anthropologists have shared theoretical and methodological approaches with epidemiologists for some time, there are several areas in which our research can be said to be distinctive. The kinds of questions anthropologists ask are often different from those asked by epidemiologists. Our interest in human variability and cultural differences leads us to explore disease in international contexts and among people living in relatively small-scale societies, and to ask how cultural differences have molded susceptibility and resistance to diseases among individuals and societies, and have influenced the ways in which diseases spread. We ask questions not only about the human–pathogen interactions, but also about the cultural activities that bring people into contact with one another and about the ways in which these activities influence how, when, where, and why diseases spread within and among populations.

Our interest in human origins and evolution leads physical anthropologists to ask about the evolution of human disease from the prehistoric past, guiding us to develop a broader temporal framework against which to consider diseases in the present. Emerging infectious diseases, a focus of contemporary epidemiological interest, have raised problems for human societies since the most remote past. Some physical anthropologists specialize in paleopathology and in the analysis of ancient DNA, and some of them are working to identify whether particular pathogens were present in past populations. As such, these scholars provide valuable information for those epidemiologists who are interested in understanding the evolutionary history of the pathogens.

As scholars interested in humans and regarding them as a part of the natural world, we examine changing patterns of human–animal relationships; how these relationships are structured by cultural values, history, and local and global economies; and how they, in turn, influence our vulnerability to zoonotic diseases. Because of our commitment to understanding the biological and social determinants of human health, we try to understand the interactions between these inextricably linked domains. Pathogens alone cannot explain infectious disease; they flourish in particular human settings, which provide the resources they need for reproduction and the circumstances that allow them to spread from animals to people and from person to person. As anthropologists, we are thus interested in the full range of human experience, from the biological to the cultural, as it develops through time; and our unique emphasis on all kinds of human experiences will continue to make significant contributions to understanding human epidemiology in times to come.

REFERENCES

Acuna-Soto, R., Stahle, D. W., Cleaveland, M. K., and Therrell, M. D. (2002) Megadrought and Megadeath in 16th Century Mexico. *Emerging Infectious Diseases* 8 (4): 360–362.

Baroyan, O. V., and Rvachev, L. A. (1967) Deterministic Models of Epidemics for a Territory with a Transport Network. *Cybernetics* [*Kibernetika*] 3: 67–74.

Baroyan, O. V., Genchikov, L. A., Rvachev, L. A., and Schaschkov, V. A. (1969) An Attempt at Large-Scale Influenza Modelling by Means of a Computer. *Bulletin of the International Epidemiological Association* 18: 22–31.

Barrett, R., Kuzawa, C. W., McDade, T., and Armelagos, G. J. (1998) Emerging and Re-Emerging Infectious Diseases: The Third Epidemiologic Transition. *Annual Reviews of Anthropology* 27: 247–271.

Carpenter, C., and Sattenspiel, L. (2009) The Design and Use of an Agent-Based Model to Simulate the 1918 Influenza Epidemic at Norway House, Manitoba. *American Journal of Human Biology* 21 (3): 290–300.

Chowell, G., Castillo-Chavez, C., Fenimore, P. W., Kribs-Zaleta, C. M., Arriola, L., and Hyman, J. M. (2004) Model Parameters and Outbreak Control for SARS. *Emerging Infectious Diseases* 10 (7): 1258–1263.

Cubillos-Garzon, L., Casas, J., Morillo, C., and Bautista, L. (2004) Congestive Heart Failure in Latin America: The Next Epidemic. *American Heart Journal* 147 (3): 412–417.

Engel, L., and Engel, G. (2008) A Multidisciplinary Approach to Understanding the Risk and Context of Emerging Primate-Borne Zoonoses. In C. Panter-Brick and A. Fuentes (eds), *Health, Risk and Adversity. Studies of the Biosocial Society*, Vol. 2 (pp. 52–77). New York/Oxford: Berghahn Books.

Ferguson, N. M., Cummings, D. A. T., Fraser, C., Cajka, J. C., Cooley, P. C., and Burke, D. S. (2006) Strategies for Mitigating an Influenza Pandemic. *Nature* 442: 448–452.

Ferguson, N. M., Cummings, D. A. T., Cauchemez, S., Fraser, C., Riley, S., Meeyai, A., Iamsirithaworn, S., and Burke, D. S. (2005) Strategies for Containing an Emerging Influenza Pandemic in Southeast Asia. *Nature* 437: 209–214.

Germann, T. C., Kadau, K., Longini, I. M., Jr, and Macken, C. A. (2006) Mitigation Strategies for Pandemic Influenza in the United States. *Proceedings of the National Academy of Sciences, USA* 103 (15): 5935–5940.

Goodman, A. H., and Leatherman, T. L. (eds) (1998) *Building a New Biocultural Synthesis: Political Economic Perspectives on Human Biology*. Ann Arbor: University of Michigan Press.

Goodreau, S. M., Goicochea, L. P., and Sanchez, J. (2005) Sexual Role and Transmission of HIV Type 1 among Men Who Have Sex with Men, in Peru. *Journal of Infectious Disease* 191 (Suppl 1): S147–S158.

Grmek, M. D. (1990) *History of AIDS: Emergence and Origin of a Modern Pandemic*, translated by Russell C. Maulitz and Jacalyn Duffin. Princeton: Princeton University Press.

Gurven, M., Kaplan, H., and Zelada Supa, A. (2007) Mortality Experience of Tsimane Amerindians of Bolivia: Regional Variation and Temporal Trends. *American Journal of Human Biology* 19: 376–398.

Hauteniemi, S. I., Swedlund, A. C., and Anderton, D. L. (1999) Mill Town Mortality. *Social Science History* 23: 1–39.

Herring, D. A., and Sattenspiel, L. (2007) Social Context, Syndemics, and Infectious Diseases in Northern Aboriginal Populations. *American Journal of Human Biology* 19: 190–202.

Hewlett, B. S., and Hewlett, B. L. (2008) *Ebola, Culture and Politics: The Anthropology of an Emerging Disease*. Belmont CA: Thomson Higher Education.

Hurtado, A. M., Hill, K. R., Rosenblatt, W., Bender, J., and Scharmen, T. (2003) Longitudinal Study of Tuberculosis Outcomes among Immunologically Naïve Aché Natives of Paraguay. *American Journal of Physical Anthropology* 121 (2): 134–150

Hurtado, A. M., Frey, M. A., Hurtado, I., Hill, K., and Baker, J. (2008) The Role of Helminthes in Human Evolution: Implications for Global Health in the Twenty-First Century. In S. Elton and P. O'Higgins (eds), *Medicine and Evolution: Current Applications, Future Prospects* (pp. 151–178). New York: Taylor and Francis.

Inhorn, M. C., and Brown, P. J. (eds) (1997) *The Anthropology of Infectious Disease: International Health Perspectives*. Australia: Gordon and Breach.

Janes, C. R., with Stall, R., and Gifford, S. M. (eds) (1986) *Anthropology and Epidemiology: Interdisciplinary Approaches to the Study of Health and Disease*. Dordrecht/Boston: D. Reidel.

Lipsitch, M., Cohen, T., Cooper, B., Robins, J. M. Ma, S., James, L., Gopalakrishna, G., Chew, S. K., Tan, C. C., Samore, M. H., Fisman, D., and Murray, M. (2003) Transmission Dynamics and Control of Severe Acute Respiratory Syndrome. *Science* 300: 1966–1970.

Littleton, J., and King, R. (2008) The Political Ecology of Tuberculosis in Auckland: An Interdisciplinary Focus. In J. Littleton, J. Parks, D. A. Herring, and T. Farmer (eds), *Multiplying and Dividing: Tuberculosis in Canada and Aotearoa New Zealand*. Research in Anthropology and Linguistics–3, No. 3 (pp. 43–53). New Zealand: University of Auckland, Department of Anthropology. Electronic document, http://researchspace.auckland.ac.nz/xmlui/handle/2292/2558 (accessed January 26, 2009).

Lockerbie, S., and Herring, D. A. (2008) Global Panic, Local Repercussions: Economic and Nutritional Effects of Bird Flu in Vietnam. In R. Hahn and M. Inhorn (eds), *Anthropology and Public Health: Bridging Differences in Culture and Society*, 2nd edn (pp. 754–778). Oxford: Oxford University Press.

Longini, I. M., Jr, Nizam, A., Xu, S., Ungchusak, K., Hanshaoworakul, W., Cummings, D. A. T., and Halloran, M. E. (2005) Containing Pandemic Influenza at the Source. *Science* 309: 1083–1087.

Madrigal, L., and Koertvelyessy, T. (2003) Epidemic Cycles in Agricultural Populations: A Cross-Cultural Study. *Human Biology* 75: 345–354.

Marr, J. S., and Kiracofe, J. B. (2000) Was the Huey Cocoliztli a Haemorrhagic Fever? *Medical History* 44: 341–362.

Mielke, J. H. (2003) War and Population Composition in Åland, Finland. In D. A. Herring and A. C. Swedlund (eds), *Human Biologists in the Archives: Demography, Health, Nutrition and Genetics in Historical Populations*. Cambridge Studies in Biological and Evolutionary Anthropology Series 35 (pp. 216–233). Cambridge: Cambridge University Press.

Mitchell, P. (2003) The Archaeological Study of Epidemic and Infectious Disease. *World Archaeology* 35 (2): 171–179.

Morse, S. S. (ed.) (1993) *Emerging Viruses*. Oxford: Oxford University Press.

Neel, J. V. (1962) Diabetes Mellitus: A 'Thrifty' Genotype Rendered Detrimental By Progress? *American Journal of Human Genetics* 14: 353–362.

Noymer, A. (2009) Testing the Influenza–Tuberculosis Selective Mortality Hypothesis with Union Army Data. *Social Science and Medicine* 68: 1599–1608.

Omran, A. R. (1971) The Epidemiological Transition. *Millbank Memorial Fund Quarterly* 49: 509–538.

Riley, S., Fraser, C., Donnelly, C. A., Ghani, A. C., Abu-Raddad, L. J., Hedley, A. J., Leung, G. M., Ho, L.-M., Lam, T.-H., Thach, T. Q., Chau, P., Chan, K.-P., Lo, S.-V., Leung, P.-Y., Tsang, T., Ho, W., Lee, K.-H., Lau, E. M. C., Ferguson, N. M., and Anderson, R. M. (2003) Transmission Dynamics of the Etiological Agent of SARS in Hong Kong: Impact of Public Health Interventions. *Science* 300: 1961–1966.

Rvachev, L. A., and Longini, I. M., Jr (1985) A Mathematical Model for the Global Spread of Influenza. *Mathematical Biosciences* 75: 3–22.

Sattenspiel, L., with contributions from A. Lloyd (2009) *Modeling the Geographic Spread of Infectious Diseases: Models and Applications*. Princeton: Princeton University Press.

Sattenspiel, L., and Herring, D. A. (1998) Structured Epidemic Models and the Spread of Influenza in the Norway House District of Manitoba, Canada. *Human Biology* 70: 91–115.

Sattenspiel, L., and Herring, D. A. (2003) Simulating the Effect of Quarantine on the Spread of the 1918–19 Flu in Central Canada. *Bulletin of Mathematical Biology* 65 (1): 1–26.

Sawchuk, L. A. (2001) *Deadly Visitations in Dark Times: A Social History of Gibraltar in the Time of Cholera*. Gibraltar: Gibraltar Government Heritage Publications, Monograph 2.

Schmaljohn, C., and Hjelle, B. (1997) Hantaviruses: A Global Disease Problem. *Emerging Infectious Diseases* 3 (2): 95–104.

Scott, S., and Duncan, C. J. (1998) *Human Demography and Disease*. Cambridge: Cambridge University Press.

Scott, S., and Duncan, C. J. (2001) *Biology of Plagues*. Cambridge: Cambridge University Press.

Singer, M., and Clair, S. (2003) Syndemics and Public Health: Reconceptualizing Disease in Bio-Social Context. *Medical Anthropology Quarterly* 17 (4): 423–441.

Singer, M. C., Erickson, P. I., Badiane, L., Diaz, R., Ortiz, D., Abraham, T., and Nicolaysen, A. M. (2006) Syndemics, Sex and the City: Understanding Sexually Transmitted Diseases in Social and Cultural Context. *Social Science and Medicine* 63 (8): 2010–2021.

Swedlund, A. C., and Donta, A. (2003) Scarlet Fever Epidemics of the Nineteenth Century: A Case of Evolved Pathogenic Virulence? In D. A. Herring and A. C. Swedlund (eds), *Human Biologists in the Archives: Demography, Health, Nutrition and Genetics in Historical Populations*. Cambridge Studies in Biological and Evolutionary Anthropology Series 35 (pp. 159–177). Cambridge: Cambridge University Press.

Szathmáry, E. J. E. (1994) Non-Insulin Dependent Diabetes Mellitus among Aboriginal North Americans. *Annual Review of Anthropology* 23: 457–482.

Trostle, J. A. (2006) *Epidemiology and Culture*. Cambridge: Cambridge University Press.

Wirth, T., Hildebrand, F., Allix-Béuec, C., Wölbeling, F., Kubica, T., Kremer, K., van Soolingen, D., Rüsch-Gerdes, S., Locht, C., Brisse, S., Meyer, A., Supply, P., and Niemann, S. (2008) Origin, Spread, and Demography of the *Mycobacterium tuberculosis* Complex. *PLoS Pathogens* 4 (9): e1000160.

Young, T. K., Szathmáry, E. J. E., Evers, S., and Wheatley, B. (1990) Geographical Distribution of Diabetes among the Native Population of Canada: A National Survey. *Social Science and Medicine* 31: 129–139.

CHAPTER **10** Demographic Estimation: Indirect Techniques for Anthropological Populations

Timothy B. Gage

Demographic estimation is simple and straightforward if accurate census counts and vital statistics for births and deaths are readily available. However, this is only the case in a few modern nations. More often, direct demographic data, when available, are biased and require corrective measures. In addition, among the populations studied by anthropologists, data sets are small and consequently statistically unstable. In some anthropological settings, notably in paleodemography, sufficient data are entirely missing. The problem of bias is difficult to deal with even at the level of modern nations and is generally handled by using either indirect estimation procedures or small-scale intensive sampling in order to assess and correct bias. Small data sets, on the other hand, are readily dealt with by using modern statistical methods. Methods such as Kaplan–Meier life table approaches, Cox regression, and accelerated lifetime models, are now in common use both in the national and in the anthropological literature. Missing data, however, remain a problem, which can only be circumvented through indirect estimation techniques. This review attempts to summarize the indirect methods available for demographic estimation, placing an emphasis on anthropological demography, and particularly on paleodemography. Are estimates of mortality, fertility, and population dynamics possible with anthropological data?

The standard demographic characterization consists of measuring age-specific mortality using census data and deaths by age; of estimating age-specific fertility with census data and births recorded by the age of the mother; and of examining population dynamics by solving the net maternity function (NMF), which is the product of survivorship and reproductivity (that is, fertility based on female births only). Mortality or life table estimates are typically summarized as an expectation of life, while fertility is summarized as a total fertility rate – a cross-sectional view of completed family size.

The Eigen values and vectors of the net maternity function define the intrinsic rate of increase of the population, the stable age structure, the periodicity of waves (caused by baby booms) in the age structure, and the rate at which the age structure approaches the stable age structure (Coale 1972). The tradition of using census and vital registry data was originated by Qutelet in the mid-1800s. These are considered the first accurate life tables (Gage 1997). Keyfitz and Fleiger (1971) provide complete analyses of this type for many national populations, as well as computer programs designed to generate the results.

Recently, attempts to estimate the demography of contemporary anthropological populations have largely followed the same direct methods as national demographic analyses (Howell 1979; Hill and Hurtado 1996; Gurven and Kaplan 2007). The problem here is that anthropological populations typically do not have vital registry systems; therefore the enumeration of births and deaths is based on ethnographic interviews – which may be biased, particularly regarding the deaths. When mortality and fertility estimates are combined to obtain population dynamics, any errors are multiplied. Perhaps this is one reason why few demographic analyses of contemporary anthropological populations have attempted to estimate the dynamics of these populations. Few studies have taken advantage of the indirect methods of demographic estimation based on non-stable population theory, which depend upon data that are likely to be more reliable and simpler to collect.

Attempts to measure demography in the archaeological setting, on the other hand, have depended entirely upon indirect methods. This is largely due to missing data. In particular, archaeological data typically consists of age at death statistics. Census data are not available, because the archaeological record cannot control time with sufficient precision. Consequently many national demographers have written off paleodemography (Petersen 1975), on the basis of Quetelet's argument (among other reasons) that census data are essential to accurate life table estimation. Nevertheless, an interest in paleodemography among national demographers has recently emerged (Hoppa and Vaupel 2002), due to the realization that mortality, particularly viewed in relation to senescence, is a biological phenomenon of human evolutionary history (and see Crews and Bogin, Chapter 7 of the present volume). Thus an understanding of prehistoric mortality patterns may help predict future trends in mortality. This has generated a renewed interest in indirect methods of demographic estimation, specifically for paleodemographic applications.

The primary aim of the present chapter is to review the methods of indirect demographic estimation, especially with respect to populations traditionally studied by anthropologists. Are the tools in place to conduct a complete analysis of demography (mortality, fertility, and population dynamics) in the archaeological and ethnographic settings? Indirect methods of estimation for ethnographic settings are mentioned only briefly. These methods are already well established in the anthropological literature. The methods of estimating age at death from skeletal remains – what is called in the field 'the aging of skeletal remains' – are also only briefly considered. This is an area that has undergone a revolution within the last decade, generating a vast new literature. My assumption here is that the theoretical issue (if not the practical application) of aging skeletal remains has been resolved (Hoppa and Vaupel 2002). Nevertheless, aging is treated briefly, since indirect demographic techniques are a part of the current solution to these issues. My specific aims are:

1   to review the measures of mortality and fertility;
2   to assess population theories, which are the basis of indirect estimation;
3   to analyze developments in model mortality and fertility tables;
4   to assemble a strategy for the indirect analysis of age-at-death data, complete and applicable to archaeological data; and
5   to discuss some of the remaining issues.

Measures of Mortality and Fertility

Age-specific mortality can be represented in three ways: as a hazard (h_a), as survivorship (l_a), and as the distribution of deaths classified by age at death (f_a). All three of these measures are presented in a standard life table and, when one is available, the others can be derived from it. For example, given h_a:

$$1 \quad l_a = e^{-\int_{x=0}^{a} h_x dx}$$

$$2 \quad f_a = h_a l_a$$

$$3 \quad f_a = h_a e^{-\int_{x=0}^{a} h_x dx}.$$

The hazard is the instantaneous death rate; and, when data are available, the hazard is estimated as the number of deaths at age a, divided by the number of individuals exposed to the risk of death at age a. This is the traditional entrance into the life table for national demographers. Survivorship is the proportion of the original birth cohort surviving to age a. This is the approach to life table estimation employed in the Kaplan–Meier life table, although the method uses the exact age of individual deaths rather than data grouped at fixed age intervals, as in the conventional life table. The distribution of deaths classified by age-at-death is traditionally the least commonly used method of estimating a life table. However, it is the standard method in paleo-demography (Moore et al. 1975; Weiss 1973a), since the only data available are those of the distribution of skeletal ages at death. Expectation of life, a summary measure of mortality, is simply the integral of survivorship.

Fertility is measured as a simple age-specific risk of giving birth, similar to the hazard rate in mortality. Total fertility (or completed fertility) is the integral of the age-specific fertility function. Reproductive rates are similar to fertility rates, but only include same-sex births (generally female births).

Population Theories: The Basis for Indirect Estimation

Population theories define the effects of mortality and fertility on age structure and population growth (population dynamics). Since these theories may also include simplifying assumptions, they have traditionally provided methods of estimating demographic rates with incomplete data. Three theories of population dynamics reviewed here are the stationary, the stable, and the variable r (non-stable).

Stationary population theory assumes that mortality and fertility are constant and that the population is not growing or declining (in other words, the number of births each year is constant). Since populations change in size, this is unlikely to be a reasonable assumption. Nevertheless, it is the assumption that underlies indirect life table construction in most anthropological settings. The theory simply states that:

4   $N_a = bl_a.$

N_a is the age structure of the population, b is the size of the birth cohort, and l_a is survivorship. If the age structure can be estimated with a census and an estimate of the number of yearly births is available, then l_a can be estimated and a life table can be derived for ethnographic applications. Similarly, a life table can be generated from the distribution of ages at death (Moore et al. 1975), which is the standard paleodemographic method. However, if either of these methods are used and the population is not stationary, then error is introduced into the life table. Moore and colleagues (1975) illustrate this problem with some examples taken from the paleodemographic perspective.

Stable population theory assumes that mortality and fertility are constant and that the population has achieved its stable age structure. The stable age structure is determined by age-specific mortality and fertility. If mortality and fertility rates remain constant for seventy-five years or so in humans (Keyfitz and Fleiger 1971), then the age structure will approach its stable state and will remain in it until mortality or fertility are perturbed. In stable theory,

5   $N_a = be^{-ra}l_a.$

In this equation, r is the rate of growth or decline of births (and of the population). As with stationary theory, if a census, the number of current births, and the rate of growth (r) can be estimated, then a life table can be derived. Methods are also available to estimate a life table from a distribution of ages at death (Moore et al. 1975), provided that r is also available. Note that, if $r = 0$, then stationary conditions apply. National demographers have not developed an indirect method of estimating fertility on the basis of stable population theory. This is probably because fertility data are considered to be easier to collect and more accurate then mortality data. The explanation is that births occur over a more limited span of ages, are more numerous than deaths in national populations (which are generally growing), and occur to living individuals who are thought to be more likely to report them accurately. Deaths, on the other hand, are reported by third parties and hence may be underrepresented. Nevertheless, Weiss (1973b) has proposed an indirect method of fertility estimation which was published in the anthropological literature, although to my knowledge it has not been widely applied.

The stable assumption is much more reasonable than the stationary assumption, because populations tend naturally toward the stable state (Coale 1972; Keyfitz and Fleiger 1971). If mortality and fertility remain constant, the population will tend toward its stable state (age structure), which is uniquely defined by the mortality and fertility patterns. Populations oscillate around the stable age structure during their approach to the stable state. Stable population theory is commonly used by national demographers and appears to provide reasonable results (Keyfitz and Fleiger 1971).

Non-stable (variable r) population theory is a simple extension of stable population theory (Preston and Coale 1982). It allows r, the rate of growth, to be age-specific. In particular:

$$6 \quad N_a = be^{-\int_{x=0}^{a} r_x dx} l_a.$$

In this equation, r_x are age-specific rates of increase (or decline). Non-stable theory requires no assumptions and provides a number of indirect estimation procedures. The development of non-stable theory led to a realization that the population dynamics and the fertility of a population could also be indirectly estimated. And, in particular, that

$$7 \quad NMF_a = v_a e^{\int^{a} r_x dx}$$

and

$$8 \quad m_a = \frac{v_a e^{\int^{a} r_x dx}}{l_a},$$

where v_a is the age pattern of fertility, NMF_a is the net maternity function, and m_a is age-specific fertility (Preston and Coale 1982). The net maternity function defines the population dynamics of a population. The first Eigen value of the net maternity function is r, the intrinsic rate of increase (growth rate of the stable population), while the first Eigen vector is the stable age structure of the population. The remaining Eigen values and vectors describe the oscillations and rate of approach of age structure to its stable state (Coale 1972; Keyfitz and Fleiger 1971).

A wide variety of indirect methods are implied by non-stable theory. The best developed series of methods depend upon two censuses on the same population, taken a few years apart (Preston and Coale 1982; Preston 1983; Preston and Bennett 1983; Gage et al. 1984a; Gage et al. 1984b). These are ideal methods for ethnographic research, since they depend on data that is routinely collected and likely to be relatively accurate. Unlike the direct methods, they do not depend on a complete collection of births and deaths. Further, they appear to be highly accurate even with relatively small sample sizes (Gage et al. 1986). However, they have only been applied to a few ethnographic populations (Gage et al. 1984a; Gage et al. 1984b; Fix 1989). It is noteworthy here that much of the impetus in the development of non-stable theory was driven by the need to develop methods of checking the accuracy of vital registration data in national populations. An indirect method based on non-stable theory and using only deaths has been proposed (Preston and Coale 1982), but never applied. Unfortunately, it is unlikely that this method will be useful in the archaeological context, since a fine temporal control of deaths would be necessary.

Specification of non-stable population theory also clarified the role of r in demography. For example, equation 6 can be written as

$$9 \quad N_a = be^{-\int_{x=0}^{a} r_x^1 + r_x^2 dx} l_a,$$

where r^1 and r^2 are different effects on the rate of change of the number of individuals age a. For example, r^1 could represent the rate of population growth, while r^2 could represent migration into or out of the population. Further, r^1 and r^2 could represent two different classifications of the cause of death; that is, indirect estimations of a cause-decremented life table (that is, the life table that would result if the cause of death were eliminated). r is isomorphic with mortality! In paleodemographic applications, r^2 could represent age-specific taphonomic processes (that is, loss from the population of skeletal samples, post-mortality, due to cultural deposition or differential preservation). In any event, this is the formal mechanism by which taphonomy and migration could be incorporated into indirect demographic estimation procedures, if a model is available for r^2.

AGE ESTIMATION

Age estimation is a difficult problem in all anthropological settings. In the ethnographic context, populations may be ill numerate, or chronological age may simply not be important to them, so that people would not know their true ages. In such cases age must be estimated, often through the use of event calendars (Howell 1979; Hill and Hurtado 1996). Formal demographic models may also be used. For example Howell (1979) used the Coale and Demeny model of age structures to graduate age estimates for individual !Kung bushmen. She went on to measure mortality using the Coale and Demeny model life tables as well. The modern western bias introduced by using Coale and Demeny model life tables is well recognized by anthropological demographers. On the other and, the potential for bias introduced by using Coale and Demeny model age structures, which are based on the model life tables, in order to arrive at an estimate of age is not widely recognized. However, the potential for bias is likely to be the same using either the Coale and Demeny model life tables or the Coale and Demeny model age structures.

It is clear, and now widely recognized, that traditional methods of aging skeletal materials using type collections has serious flaws (Bocquet-Appel and Masset 1982; Hoppa and Vaupel 2002). In particular, the traditional approach assumes that, given age, a, the probability of a set of skeletal age characteristics, c, is equal to the probability of age, given a set of characteristics. However, this is not normally the case. In general, Bayes's theorem demonstrates that:

$$10 \quad P(a|c) \neq P(c|a).$$

However, Bayes's theorem also provides a solution, but it requires the prior knowledge of the probability density of ages at death (f_a, the distribution of ages at death). The solution proposed at Rostock (Hoppa and Vaupel 2002) is:

$$11 \quad P(c) = \int_0^{\alpha} P(c|a) f_a \, da,$$

where $P(c)$ is the probability density of skeletal age indicators. All that is needed is to select the f_a from a series of model f_a that best reproduces the observed $P(c)$. It remains to be determined if the unusual age patterns of mortality characteristic of traditional paleodemographic life tables (a more rapid increase in mortality with age among adults, compared to that observed in ethnographic or national life tables: see Howell 1982; Gage 1988; Gurven and Kaplan 2007) disappear with these new methods, although a preliminary application suggests that they might (Konigsberg and Herrmann 2006).

MODELS OF AGE-SPECIFIC VITAL RATES

Given the discussion above, it is clear that good models of age-specific vital rates, which can characterize the range of human experience, would be useful (or perhaps essential) aides for indirect demographic estimation, for instance for mortality, fertility, migration, taphonomy, and sex differences. Traditionally these models are also used with direct estimation techniques, to smooth, graduate, and correct these estimates. Only mortality and fertility will be discussed in any detail here.

Mortality models

National demographers had developed a number of empirical models of vital rates for indirect estimation. The best known of these is the Coale and Demeny model life tables (Coale et al. 1983). The Coale and Demeny models are based on a sample of about 350, mostly European, life tables. The oldest of these life tables dates from about 1850. From these tables, the authors generated regression models to predict the age pattern of mortality for expectations of life ranging from twenty to eighty years. They also generated stable age structures for a range of values of r for each life table. Because the age pattern appeared to vary systematically across Europe, four sets of model life tables and stable populations were generated: north, east, south, and west, which were indicative of the pattern in the respective areas of Europe. These empirical models have been immensely useful for indirect estimation in national western demography, and they are frequently applied in anthropological demography as well (Howell 1979; Gage et al. 1984b).

Use of these models in anthropological populations, however, suffers from several problems. First, none of the empirical life tables used to construct the models has an expectation of life which is less than about thirty, although life expectancy in many anthropological settings could be considerably lower. Coale and Demeny did generate models with expectations of life as low as twenty; but most statisticians warn against projecting linear regressions beyond the ranges of observed data. Second, all of the sample life tables came from national populations – almost exclusively from Europe or European-derived populations such as those of Australia, Canada, and the United States. It seems unlikely that these populations represent the range of living conditions (and of age patterns of mortality) of most anthropological populations, particularly given that Coale and Demeny showed that the age patterns of mortality varied systematically within Europe alone. Clearly, post-1850 Europe does not represent the complete range of environmental conditions to which humans have been exposed. Several attempts have been made to extend model life tables to a larger range of the world's environments (United Nations 1982; Gage 1990); however, all have depended upon national life tables. Weiss (1973a) has developed empirical model life tables for anthropological populations. However, there are concerns over the quality of the anthropological data used to construct these models. As a result, attention in the field of anthropology has turned to flexible mathematical models of mortality, which can smooth and improve demographic data without imposing a particular age pattern of mortality.

The simplest mathematical model of mortality is the Siler model (Gage 1988), although models that are more complex have been proposed (see references ibid.). This model treats age-specific mortality as the product of three 'competing' (additive) hazards. In the following equations, the αs and the bs are parameters to be estimated; the additive term subscripted, 1, represents the decline in mortality during infancy; the term subscripted 2 is a constant; and the term subscripted 3 represents the increase in mortality at older ages. The second term (subscripted 2 is the Makeham model, while the third term (subscripted 3) is the Gompertz model. Together they form the Gompertz–Makeham mortality model, which has been used by national demographers to smooth and graduate life tables (over the adult ages) for many years:

12    $h_a = \alpha_1 e^{b_1 a} + \alpha_2 + \alpha_3 e^{b_3 a}$

or

$l_a = e^{-\alpha_1/b_1 (1-e^{-b_1 a})} * e^{-\alpha_2 a} * e^{\alpha_3/b_3 (1-e^{b_3 a})}$.

13

The advantage of models like the Siler model is that they are very flexible and they fit well the mortality patterns of humans as well as of many other organisms, including non-human primates (Gage 1998). Thus they do not impose a European national demography bias on the resulting life table.

Recently, Wood and colleagues (2002) have proposed an alternative mixed model, in which mortality is viewed as a mixture of two subpopulations: one has a high constant risk, and the second is a Gompertz–Makeham subpopulation, where the Makeham constant is lower than that of the high-risk subpopulation. In this case, the subpopulation with the high constant risk accounts for the decline in mortality at the younger ages. This provides similar fits to those of the Siler model; furthermore, it is biologically interpretable – that is, the high constant risk represents a group of births that are constitutionally weaker and prone to early mortality. Thus mortality declines with age until these individuals are eliminated from the population.

Fertility

Models of age-specific fertility have received less attention than models of age-specific mortality. This is probably because, for the reasons mentioned above, (unbiased) fertility data are easier to obtain than age-specific mortality data. This is true of anthropological applications as well as of national applications. Furthermore, the variation in the shape of the age-specific fertility curve is smaller than the variation in the shape of the age-specific mortality curve. Nevertheless, empirical and mathematical models have been developed.

Empirical age-specific fertility models suggest two basic age patterns: a natural fertility pattern, with a slower decline in fertility after the modal age of fertility, and a controlled fertility pattern, with a faster decline in fertility after the modal age of fertility. Several empirically based models have been developed (Coale and Trussell 1974). In addition, a number of mathematical models have been used to smooth and graduate age-specific fertility rates. The simplest of these, the Brass polynomial (Brass 1968), has been shown to fit well the fertility rates of human (natural fertility) and non-human primates, as well as those of several other organisms (Gage 2001). However, it does not fit controlled human fertility well. Nevertheless, for anthropological applications where controlled fertility is unlikely, the Brass polynomial has the same advantages as the Siler model. It is simple, and, since it fits a wide range of age patterns, it does not unduly impose any particular pattern on the data. In addition, all of the parameters represent life history characteristics. In particular,

14    $v_a = c(a - d)(d + w - a)^2,$

where c is the level of fertility, d is the age at which fertility begins, and w is the length of the reproductive period. In human natural fertility populations, d is approximately 15 and w about 35 years. Only the level of fertility, c, varies widely among populations, as mentioned above. If c is scaled so that the area under the curve is equal to 1, then v_a is as defined in equations 7 and 8 above.

COMPLETE INDIRECT METHODS APPLICABLE TO ARCHAEOLOGICAL DATA

Moore and colleagues (1975) described the effect of r on life table estimation. In particular, they described the effects of assuming that $r = 0.0$ when this is not true (the stationary assumption). Similarly, Gage (1988) derived the algebraic equivalent in the context of the Siler model. In this case:

15    $l'_a = e^{-ra} * e^{-\alpha_1/b_1 (1 - e^{-b_1 a})} * e^{-\alpha_2 a} * e^{\alpha_3/b_3 (1 - e^{b_3 a})},$

where l'_a is the misestimated survivorship when the stationary assumption is incorrect, but the population is stable. This simplifies as:

16    $l_a = e^{-\alpha_1/b_1 (1 - e^{-b_1 a})} * e^{-\alpha_2 a} * e^{\alpha_3/b_3 (1 - e^{b_3 a})}.$

Thus the error is incorporated into the Makeham constant, so that the latter becomes the Makeham constant plus the intrinsic rate of increase of the population. A corrected survivorship could be obtained if r were known independently of α_2. This is theoretically possible if the fit is conducted with respect to the distribution of ages at death. In particular, the distribution of ages at death in a stable population with intrinsic rate of increase, r, is:

17    $f'_a = h_a l'_a$

or

18 $\quad f'_a = (\alpha_1 e^{b_1 a} + \alpha_2 + \alpha_3 e^{b_3 a}) * (e^{-\alpha_1 / b_1 (1 - e^{-b_1 a})} * e^{-(\alpha'_2) a} * e^{\alpha_3 / b_3 (1 - e^{b_3 a})}).$

Note that both α_2 and α'_2 are estimated so r can be estimated as the difference, $\alpha'_2 - \alpha_2$. The happy coincidence here is that equation 18 (the distribution of ages at death) is in exactly the form needed in order to estimate simultaneously skeletal age, by using the Rostock procedure. This possibility was first suggested by Holman (unpublished); but, to the author's knowledge, it has never been applied. It will require large skeletal samples to be successfully carried out. How large these samples must be is unknown.

Once r is available, the remaining population dynamics and estimates of age-specific fertility are readily available:

19 $\quad NMF_a = v_a e^{ra}$

20 $\quad m_a = \dfrac{v_a e^{ra}}{l_a},$

following the relations provided by non-stable population theory (Preston and Coale 1982), but assuming stability – that is:

$$\int_0^a r_a dx = ra$$

– which is essentially identical to Weiss (1973b). Note that, in this approach, population dynamics are more directly estimated than fertility (equation 19). In any event, it is theoretically possible to estimate mortality, fertility, and population dynamics from a sample of ages at death, applicable to archaeological settings.

SOME REMAINING ISSUES

The approach presented above for estimating demographic parameters has not, to my knowledge, actually been attempted. While the method is theoretically reasonable, it is not yet clear if the approach is practical. This is largely a data issue. Large data sets will be necessary when attempting to fit equation 18, particularly when in combination with the Rostock approach to age estimation, in order to estimate uniquely the parameters and to obtain acceptable confidence intervals on them. Estimates of population dynamics will depend upon how well r can be estimated. These results are likely to be less reliable than mortality. Similarly, fertility also depends on the accuracy of the remaining Siler parameters, and hence is likely to be even less reliable. To determine how large the data sets should be will require some statistical experiments. It remains to be determined if it is archaeologically feasible to obtain data sets of the necessary sizes. However, there already are attempts to assemble large-scale skeletal data sets in Europe (Steckel 2003). It is clear that mortality, fertility, and population dynamics information is contained in the simple distribution of ages at death, if stable conditions can be assumed.

Indirect methods often require models of age-specific vital rates. As shown above, adequate models of mortality and fertility are available, although there is always room for better models. Models of age-specific sex differences in mortality (Wood et al. 2002), as well as of taphonomy (Walker et al. 1988), have been discussed in the literature. These and other models, such as of migration, will require additional development if they are to be incorporated into applications.

The system of estimation for paleodemography presented above requires that the population is stable. The problem is that in small populations mortality and fertility are not likely to be constant; this is due to environmental factors influencing mortality and fertility, as well as to stochastic factors resulting from small population size. Angel (1969) and Bonneuil (2005) have argued that stable population theory is not applicable to small populations. Bonneuil presents a method of estimating mortality for paleodemographic data without assuming stability. However, this procedure is not statistically identified. Essentially, this means that several statistically reasonable mortality estimates are equally likely, given the data. Either the restrictions – for instance stable theory or something similar – must be agreed upon, or the investigators are free to choose the result they prefer. Clearly this is not a solution. On the other hand, Weiss and Smouse (1976), using simulation studies, have shown that small populations are amenable to the stable assumption if population growth is dependent on density. The issue of the utility of stable theory to small population demography will require additional research and clarification.

One of the assumptions of anthropological demography is the so-called uniformitarian principle, adapted from geology, which states that the processes which occurred in the past are the same as those operating in the present (Howell 1976). In anthropological demography, this has come to mean that the age pattern of mortality in the past should resemble the age pattern of mortality for contemporary populations. After all, we are all genetically similar. As mentioned above, the empirical paleodemographic data currently available do not support this view (Howell 1982; Gage 1988; Gurven and Kaplan 2007), possibly because the paleodemographic data are flawed. Advances in aging may (Konigsberg and Herrmann 2006) or may not resolve some or all of these differences between the observed data and expectation. However, the uniformitarian principle may not be the best analogy for thinking about variation in human vital rates. It might be better to think of the variation in human age patterns of mortality (and or fertility, and so on) as analogous to 'genotype by environmental interaction,' borrowed from the life history literature. In this analogy, the age patterns of mortality are those of a population (not individual level phenomenon), and hence 'genotype' must refer to some general genotype or genetic structure of human populations, for instance conserved phylogenetic characteristics. These might be considered the uniform (or at least slowly changing) processes akin to the uniformitarian principle. However, the environment is also responsible for variation in the age-specific patterns. As reviewed above, very little research has considered how the environment influences the age patterns of mortality, for example why the age patterns of mortality vary within Europe. On the other hand, a great deal of research has examined the environment's effects on the expectation of life, at least since the beginning of the industrial revolution, although no consensus has yet emerged concerning why mortality has declined (Gage 2005). Again, these issues will require further development.

It is useful, however, to turn this issue on its head and ask why age patterns of vital events should differ between contemporary and paleodemographic populations. One reason is that the disease environment has clearly changed. Fenner (1970) has effectively argued that infectious diseases have accumulated as populations evolved from hunter–gatherer to agricultural, then to industrial ones. Many common infectious diseases of the historical period could not have existed (at least in the form they have today) prior to the development of large human populations (ibid.), although the molecular evidence contradicts this view to an extent (Armelagos and Harper 2005). Contemporary ethnographic populations live in an environment where these diseases occur because there are large human reservoirs of disease in the form of national populations, which maintain the illnesses in question. Clearly the disease environments of contemporary ethnographic populations are closer to the conditions of historical national populations than to those of paleodemographic populations. If Fenner (1970) is correct, the disease environments of paleodemographic populations, particularly pre-Neolithic populations, are likely to be considerably different from those of contemporary populations, either with respect to the infectious diseases present or with respect to the virulence characteristics of infectious diseases (if the same 'diseases' were present). In either event, it is not clear why different environments would produce similar age patterns of mortality or similar expectations of life.

On a more mundane level, it is well established that cross-sectional life tables have different age patterns of mortality from longitudinal life tables. This is of course because, at least over the last two hundred years or so, mortality has declined. In a longitudinal life table, infant mortality is measured sixty years earlier than mortality at the age of 60, when mortality is expected to be lower. Similarly, before it declined, mortality varied greatly from one year to the next due to epidemics. Consequently, longitudinal life tables tend not to be smooth from one age to the next. To avoid these issues, national demographers depend upon cross-sectional life tables to define the "age pattern of mortality" (Coale et al. 1983). This is reasonable, in theory, because, if environmental conditions with respect to mortality are constant, then directly estimated cross-sectional and longitudinal life tables should be similar. However, paleodemographic skeletal assemblages are cross-sectional and longitudinal, since in general assemblages are expected to accrue over a number of years. If mortality is cyclical, as in historical populations from before the demographic transition, and if the effects vary by age, then this heterogeneity will bias the age patterns of mortality. The extent of this kind of age-specific bias in paleodemographic life tables depends upon the period over which the data was collected and upon the environmentally induced variation in mortality from one year to the next. Again, it is clear that observed paleodemographic age patterns should be expected to deviate from the patterns, of historical populations after the industrial revolution.

The effects of heterogeneity on the age patterns of mortality have been widely discussed in the national demographic literature (Vaupel et al. 1979; Weiss 1990), in addition to the anthropological and paleodemographic literature (Wood et al. 1992; Wood et al. 2002). In general, the concern has been with individual variation, the differential selection against frail individuals at one age modifying the age-specific mortality rates at older ages because the cohort at the older ages is more robust due to the loss of the frailer members of the cohort. However, the discussion above suggests that heterogeneity over time, and also over space in populations from before the demographic transition, can be expected to influence the shape of the age-specific mortality curve.

CONCLUSIONS

The formal methods available to anthropological demography have come a long way. Accurate indirect methods of estimation that do not require assumptions have been developed for the complete demographic analysis of ethnographic populations on the basis of simple censuses, taken some years apart. Nevertheless, direct methods that are much more data intensive (and hence possibly more subject to bias) remain the rule. In paleodemography, advances have been made in methods of aging skeletal materials, which are beginning to be applied. These might significantly change the observed age pattern of mortality and expectations of life, which were derived from these data in the past. Finally, the theoretical methods are largely in place to conduct a complete demographic analysis based on a simple distribution of ages at death, such as a paleo-demographic skeletal series, assuming a stable population. The method estimates r from the skeletal data. This is a major theoretical advance. However, it remains to be determined if it can be practically applied.

There is much still to do. Additional vital rates need to be modeled and incorporated into estimating procedures – including sex differences, migration, and tapho-nomic considerations. The adequacy of the 'stable' assumption needs to be examined further. Large paleodemographic data sets will need to be assembled, consistently and accurately aged and sexed. Further work is needed concerning the 'devious dynamics of heterogeneity.' National and anthropological demographers have considered individual level heterogeneity, but it appears that environmentally induced temporal and geographic variation (heterogeneity) may also need to be considered in pre-industrial historical populations, as well as in paleopopulations.

ACKNOWLEDGMENTS

I thank Dr Sharon Dewitte for comments on the original manuscript.

REFERENCES

Angel, J. L. (1969) The Basis of Paleodemography. *American Journal of Physical Anthropology* 30: 427–438.

Armelagos, G. J., and Harper, K. N. (2005) Genomics at the Origins of Agriculture, Part Two. *Evolutionary Anthropology* 14: 109–121.

Bocquet-Appel, J. P., and Masset, C. (1982) Farewell to Paleodemography. *Journal of Human Evolution* 11: 321–333.

Bonneuil, N. (2005) Fitting to a Distribution of Deaths by Age with Application to Paleode-mography. *Current Anthropology* 46: S29–S45.

Brass, W. (1968) *The Demography of Tropical Africa*. Princeton: Princeton University Press.

Coale, A. J. (1972) *The Growth and Structure of Human Populations*. Princeton: Princeton Univeristy Press.

Coale, A., and Trussell, J. T. (1974) Model Fertility Schedules: Variations in the Age Structure of Childbearing in Human Populations. *Population Index* 40 (2): 185–258.

Coale, A. J. , Demeny, P., and Vaughan, B. (1983) *Regional Model Life Tables and Stable Populations*. New York: Academic Press.

Fenner, F. (1970) The Effects of Changing Social Organization on the Infectious Diseases of Man. In S. V. Boyden (ed.), *The Impact of Civilization on the Biology of Man* (pp. 48–76). Canberra: Australian National University Press.

Fix, A. G. (1989) Semai Senoi Fertility and Population Dynamics: Two-Census Method. *American Journal of Human Biology* 1 (4): 463–469.

Gage, T. B. (1988) Mathematical Hazard Models of Mortality: An Alternative to Model Life Tables. *American Journal of Physical Anthropology* 76: 429–441.

Gage, T. B. (1990) Variation and Classification of Human Age Patterns of Mortality: Analysis Using Competing Hazards Models. *Human Biology* 62 (5): 589–617.

Gage, T. B. (1997) Demography. In F. Spencer (ed.), *History of Physical Anthropology: An Encyclopedia* (pp. 323–330). New York: Garland Publishing.

Gage, T. B. (1998) The Comparative Demography of Primates: With Some Comments on the Evolution of Life Histories. *Annual Review of Anthropology* 27: 197–221.

Gage, T. B. (2001) Age-Specific Fecundity of Mammalian Populations: A Test of Three Mathematical Models. *Zoo Biology* 20: 487–499.

Gage, T. B. (2005) Are Modern Environments Really Bad for Us? Revisiting the Demographic and Epidemiologic Transitions. *American Journal of Physical Anthropology*, Suppl. 41: 96–117.

Gage, T. B., Dyke, B., and MacCluer, J. W. (1986) Estimating Mortality Rates for Small Populations: A Test of the Non-Stable Two-Census Methods. *Population Studies* 40: 263–273.

Gage, T. B., Dyke, B., and Riviere, P. G. (1984a) Estimating Fertility and Population Dynamics From Two Censuses: An Application to the Trio of Surinam. *Human Biology* 56 (4): 691–701.

Gage, T. B., Dyke, B., and Riviere, P. G. (1984b) Estimating Mortality from Two Censuses: An Application to the Trio of Surinam. *Human Biology* 56 (3): 489–502.

Gurven, M., and Kaplan, H. (2007) Longevity among Hunter–Gatherers: A Cross-Cultural Examination. *Population and Development Review* 33: 321–366.

Hill, K., and Hurtado, A. M. (1996) *Ache Life History*. New York: Aldine de Gruyter.

Hoppa, R. D., and Vaupel, J. W. (eds) (2002) *Paleodemograhy*, Vol. 31. Cambridge: Cambridge University Press.

Howell, N. (1976) Toward a Uniformitarian Theory of Human Paleo-Demography. In R. H. Ward and K. M. Weiss (eds), *The Demographic Evolution of Human Populations* (pp. 25–40). London: Academic Press.

Howell, N. (1979) *Demography of the Dobe !Kung*. New York: Academic Press.

Howell, N. (1982) Village Composition Implied by a Paleodemographic Life Table: The Libben Site. *American Journal of Physical Anthropology* 59: 263–269.

Keyfitz, N., and Fleiger, W. (1971) *Population*. San Francisco: W. H. Freeman and Company.

Konigsberg, L. W., and Herrmann, N. P. (2006) The Osteological Evidence for Human Longevity in the Recent Past. In K. Hawkes and R. R. Paine (eds), *The Evolution of Human Life History* (pp. 267–306). Santa Fe: School of American Research Press.

Moore, J. A., Swedlund, A. C., and Armelagos, G. J. (1975) The Use of Life Tables in Paleodemography. In A. C. Swedlund (ed.), *Population Studies in Archaeology and Biological Anthropology: A Symposium*, Vol. 30 (Memoirs of the Society for American Archaeology) Washington DC: Society for American Archaeology (pp. 57–70). Issued as *American Antiquity*, Volume 40, No2, Part 2.

Petersen, W. (1975) A Demographer's View of Prehistoric Demography. *Current Anthropology* 16 (2): 227–245.

Preston, S. H. (1983) An Integrated System for Demographic Estimation from Two Age Distributions. *Demography* 20 (2): 213–226.

Preston, S. H., and Bennett, N. G. (1983) A Census-Based Method for Estimating Adult Mortality. *Population Studies* 37: 91–104.

Preston, S. H., and Coale, A. J. (1982) Age Structure, Growth, Attrition and Accession: A New Synthesis. *Population Index* 48: 217–259.

Steckel, R. H. (2003) A History of Health in Europe from the Late Paleolithic Era to the Present. *Economics and Human Biology* 1: 139–142.

United Nations (1982) *Model Life Tables for Developing Countries*. New York: United Nations.

Vaupel, J. W., Manton, K. G., and Stallard, E. (1979) The Impact of Heterogeneity in Individual Frailty on the Dynamics of Mortality. *Demography* 16: 439–454.

Walker, P. L., Johnson, J. R., and Lambert, P. M. (1988) Age and Sex Biases in the Preservation of Human Skeletal Remains. *American Journal of Physical Anthropology* 76: 183–188.

Weiss, K. M. (1973a) *Demographic Models for Anthropology*. Memoirs of the Society for American Archaeology, Vol. 27, Washington DC: Society for American Archaeology. (Issued as *American Antiquity*, Volume 38, Number 2, Part 2, April 1973.)

Weiss, K. M. (1973b) A Method for Approximating Fertility in the Construction of Life Tables for Anthropological Populations. *Human Biology* 45: 195–210.

Weiss, K. M. (1990) The Biodemography of Variation in Human Frailty. *Demography* 27 (2): 185–206.

Weiss, K. M., and Smouse, P. (1976) The Demographic Stability of Small Human Populations. In R. H. Ward and K. M. Weiss (eds), *The Demographic Evolution of Human Populations* (pp. 59–74). New York: Academic Press.

Wood, J. W., Holman, D. J., O'Connor, K. A., and Ferrell, R. J. (2002) Mortality Models for Paleodemography. In R. D. Hoppa and J. W. Vaupel (eds), *Paleodemography: Age Distributions from Skeletal Samples* (pp. 129–168). Cambridge: Cambridge University Press.

Wood, J. W., Milner, G. R., Harpending, H., and Weiss, K. M. (1992) The Osteological Paradox. *Current Anthropology* 33 (4): 343–370.

CHAPTER 11 Nutrition, Health, and Function

Darna L. Dufour

INTRODUCTION

Within anthropology, the study of nutrition is a fundamentally biocultural endeavor. It is concerned with the interrelations of biological and cultural–social forces in shaping the nutritional status of individuals and populations in both evolutionary and comparative perspectives (see Table 11.1). On a continuum from purely biological studies of nutrition to purely cultural studies of foods, nutritional anthropology falls somewhere in the middle.

Although anthropologists have always been interested in food and in the behavior related to food in the peoples they have studied, the coalescence of ideas about food and a real focus on nutrition can be traced only to a few sources. Richards's (1939) study "Land, Labour and Diet in Northern Rhodesia" was the first anthropological study to systematically emphasize the interrelationship between food and cultural–social processes. In the 1940s the war effort, both in the USA and in Europe, sparked interest in a better understanding both of food needs and of what people were willing to eat, and so it helped conjoin the biological and social sciences. In the early 1970s, a group of people doing nutritionally and anthropologically related work in the USA formed an interest group within the Society for Medical Anthropology within the American Anthropological Association (Wilson 2002). This initiative was noteworthy, as it demonstrated an emphasis on health-related aspects of nutrition, and not just on food habits. Contemporary scholarship on food and nutrition in anthropology covers a broad range of questions. Their focus is mostly biocultural, but some of them are more biologically, others more socially oriented.

The goal of this chapter is to review some of the current scholarship in nutritional anthropology and to provide ideas for future developments. Given the wide-angle lens typical of anthropology, the discussion will not cover everything. Rather it will focus on scholarship which is of particular interest to biological anthropologists: diet in human evolution; problems of overnutrition and undernutrition in the world today; and functional outcomes.

Table 11.1   Commonly used measures of nutritional status: The biological condition of the organism as it relates to diet

Measure	Examples
Anthropometry	Height, weight, skinfolds, body fat percent
Biochemical parameters	Nitrogen balance, immunocompetence, vitamin A
Hematology	Hemoblobin, hematocrit, serum ferritin
Clinical signs	Edema, night blindness
Dietary intake	24-hr diet recall, diet history

ANCESTRAL DIETS

Anthropologists have had a long-standing interest in the diets of our ancestors. This interest has gone in a number of different directions, but the enduring questions have been, and continue to be, as follows: What did our ancestors eat, and how did that shape the evolution of the genus *Homo*? Are we, physiologically and genetically, what our ancestors ate? These are important but difficult questions to answer, and we may never be able to answer them with the precision desired. We do, however, have clues from a number of different types of information, which, together, can prove the outline of the diets of early hominins – that is, of humans and their ancestors since their divergence from chimpanzees and bonobos.

The fossil record can provide several kinds of clues. The morphology of teeth suggests what an animal is capable of using as food, and the morphology of australopithecine dentition (about 4–1 mya) indicates an omnivorous diet. Dental microwear patterns suggest a diet dominated by soft fruits or other foods of similar texture (Ungar 2007: 396). The analysis of stable carbon isotopes in fossilized tissue indicates that early hominins from South Africa had relatively broad diets, which included both forest-derived foods like fruits and savannah plants like grasses and sedges – and/or the animals themselves ate grasses and sedges (Sponheimer et al. 2007). These data are consistent with our current understanding that early hominins in Africa lived in savannah environments.

The archaeological record contains evidence of the remains of the foods assumed to have been consumed, as well as of the related artefacts. The record provides evidence of the consumption of animals – meat and marrow – as early as 2.5 mya (Blumenschine and Pobiner 2007). Most people, however, associate hunting and meat consumption with the emergence of *Homo erectus* about 1.8 mya, when the evidence is unmistakable. Evidence of plant consumption does not appear until later, around 1.6 mya, in the form of stone tools used to process plants.

The importance of meat in the diet of early hominins is controversial. Paleoanthropologists like Bunn (2007) argue that "meat made us human." That is, the dietary change to increased meat consumption was a driving force behind the appearance of the genus *Homo*. This argument is based on taphonomic evidence (that is, evidence from environmental conditions associated with fossilization) of hominin use of large animals for meat and marrow at the Pleistocene boundary (1.8–1.6 mya) in East Africa. Other researchers (Wrangham et al. 1999) suggest that meat was a smaller part of the diet, and that tubers were instead the key food involved in the transition to *Homo sapiens*. In other words, a dietary change to increased tuber consumption would have been the driving factor/driver/selective force in the evolution of/toward *Homo erectus*.

Studies of living foragers (hunter–gatherers) offer other clues to ancestral diets. Ethnographic evidence from foragers like the Hadza and the !Kung, both of whom live in savannah environments similar to those of the early hominins, indicate broad diets which contain a number of plant foods including underground roots and tubers, as well as a high proportion of meat. By analogy, then, we assume that early hominin diets and early *Homo sapiens* diets might have been similar to those diets up until the time of the agricultural revolution about 10,000 years ago. These analogies are applied broadly, so to cover the period of time in our evolutionary history for which we existed as hunter–gatherers/foragers.

Other approaches to the question of ancestral diets have relied on theoretical considerations. Leonard and colleagues (2007) have approached the question of diet from the perspective of nutrient needs. They asked what kind of diet would have best provided the energy for the evolution of the larger body size and enlarged brains of *Homo sapiens*. They argue that this would have been a higher-quality diet than that of non-human primates like chimps, and that the increase in quality would have come from meat consumption. Why would meat consumption have resulted in a higher-quality diet than one based on fruit and leaves? Because meat is a more concentrated source of energy and nutrients.

Aiello and Wheeler (1995) used a similar line of argument in proposing the "expensive tissue hypothesis." They reasoned that, since brain tissue has a high metabolic rate, a highly encephalized animal should have a higher than expected basal metabolic rate (BMR) for its body size; and, since humans do not have that, something else has to have changed. They posit that a reduction in the size – and hence in the metabolic cost – of the gastrointestinal (GI) tract compensated for the increase in brain size and, further, that size reduction was made possible by the adoption of a high-quality diet. However, subsequent work by Hladik et al. (1999) demonstrated that humans do not appear to be an exception among primates in terms of the relationship between gut size and diet quality, and hence they do not show a trend toward reduced intestinal size which could have allowed for more energy for the brain function. Indeed they showed that, in terms of the total absorptive capacity of the gut, humans fall on the same regression line as frugivores.

Milton (1999) has also argued that the emergence of *Homo* was associated with a higher-quality diet than that found in the other hominoids. She bases her argument on comparative gut anatomy, gut proportions and digestive kinetics in hominoids. Human guts are similar to those of other hominoids at the gross structural level, but their gut proportions are different. In humans, the small intestine accounts for a greater proportion of the total gastrointestinal tract. This proportionality would be the derived condition for, and the indicator of, a higher-quality diet (for instance a diet lower in fiber and lignin), and it would be shared by other, highly omnivorous but distantly related primates such as *Papio* and *Cebus* (Milton 1987). The antiquity of this gut proportionality in our lineage is unknown. Milton also argues that the incorporation of meat into the diets of early humans was a key element in enabling them to maintain a high-quality diet while increasing body size, sociability and levels of physical activity.

Broadhurst and colleagues (2002) also argue for the necessity of a high-quality diet to support the evolution of the large and complex brain in *Homo*, but they go further by proposing that aquatic foods would have been a necessary dietary component. Their argument rests on the fact that the brain is composed almost entirely of two polyunsaturated fatty acids, arachidonic acid (AA) and docosahexaenoic acid (DHA). These are long-chain fatty acids that are not widely available in savannah food chains, but can be synthesized endogenously, albeit slowly, from shorter chain precursors. Hence these researchers hypothesize that AA and DHA could have been limiting factors in the development of a large brain in *Homo*, unless dietary sources for AA and DHA were available. Given that AA and DHA are more abundant in the marine food chain than in the terrestrial one, they argue that the availability of marine resources was critical to encephalization. This is an interesting argument, which relies on some things we know with a good deal of certainty, combined with some questionable assumptions. One of these assumptions is that DHA was a limiting factor in savannah environments because the tissue of local herbivores did not contain DHA. In reality, although herbivore muscle tissue is almost exclusively made of AA, both AA and DHA are prevalent in the neurological tissues which are highly prized by ethnographically known foragers, and they may well have been consumed by early hunters. A second assumption is that the endogenous synthesis of AA and DHA would not have been sufficient to meet the needs of adults; however, adequate data are simply not available to support this assumption (Institute of Medicine 2005). Finally, there is an implicit assumption that brain size is a function of the availability of AA and DHA. Although it is clear that achieving species-typical brain size does require minimum levels of AA and DHA, it does not follow that greater availability of AA and DHA will lead to greater brain size. The availability of both AA and DHA is a necessary, but not a sufficient condition to explain encephalization.

Are we what our ancestors ate?

In 1985, Eaton and Konner made the question of ancestral diets relevant to modern health concerns through an influential paper, entitled "Paleolithic Nutrition: A Consideration of Its Nature and Current Implications." It was the first in a series of papers arguing that:

1 We are genetically adapted to the characteristics of Paleolithic diets.
2 Changes in diet and lifestyle which began with the development of agriculture and animal husbandry some 10,000 years ago were too recent for us to have adjusted to genetically.
3 Our failure to adapt to new dietary conditions is responsible for current problems of chronic disease.

The authors' assessment of pre-agricultural diets was based on the same kind of evidence as the one presented above, but it focused on the essential characteristics of diets based on minimally processed wild resources – as opposed to heavily processed domesticated ones. In a relatively recent paper, Eaton (2006) described the diets of the pre-agricultural *Homo* as being higher in animal protein (on the basis of analogies with modern hunter–gatherer populations); higher in micronutrients (that is, vitamins and minerals); higher in dietary fiber (since wild plant foods are higher in fiber than

Table 11.2 Comparison of ancestral diets and modern US diet. Percentages are calculated out of the total energy intake. Data from Eaton (2006)

Category	Ancestral	Modern USA
Macronutrients		
Fats	35% E	
Carbohydrate	35% E	50% E
Protein	30% E	
Saturated fat	7.5% E	11–12% E
Trans-fat	~ 0	2% E
Polyunsaturated fats	30 g/d	15 g/d
Ratio of n6 to n3 fatty acids	2 : 1	10 : 1
Cholesterol	480 mg/d	260 mg/d
Fruits and vegetables	27–28% E	23% E
Added processed sugars	0	15% E
Fiber	>1000 g/d	15–20 g/d
Vitamins and minerals (except NA)	1.5–8 times more	
Sodium (NA)		
Acid/base balance	Net base	Net acid

domesticated equivalents); lower in saturated fatty acids; and as having a more optimal ratio of sodium to potassium (since processed foods are typically high in sodium) and a more neutral balance between acid and base (whereas most modern diets are metabolically acidic because of the high reliance on cereal grains; see Table 11.2). Lastly, he argued that the diets would have had a lower glycemic load because of the absence of refined grains and sugars. Glycemic load refers to the potential of the diet to raise blood glucose levels, and diets with high glycemic loads are thought to promote insulin resistance and other metabolic changes associated with type 2 diabetes, one of the so-called diseases of civilization.

The argument that humans are genetically adapted to the characteristics of 'Paleolithic' diets has been widely accepted, and the image of 'stone-agers in the fast lane' has taken hold of many people's imaginations. However, the assumption is probably not warranted, as natural selection never sleeps. Indeed, more recent work by Tishkoff and colleagues (2007) on the genetic basis of lactase persistence (the ability to digest milk and other dairy products into adulthood) is a cause for re-thinking. These scholars have identified a number of genetic variants that allow the carrier to digest lactose (milk sugar) into adulthood, and the most common variant originated in the past 3,000 to 5000 years. This is a clear example of recent genetic change due to selective pressure from a dietary element (milk sugar); hence the possibility of adaptation to diets in the past 10,000 years or so should not be discounted.

TODAY'S FAT AND HUNGRY WORLD

Human diets are no longer based on wild food resources, except in very limited instances. In the USA and other developed countries, diets are based largely on industrialized foods, foods that have been produced industrially, morphed into products that bear little resemblance to what was harvested, and injected with preservatives that guarantee a shelf life rivaling that of fossils. In other places, people continue to grow and produce much of the food of their diet. These places are becoming rarer, as forces of globalization introduce industrially processed foods to all corners of the globe. These same forces can make local foods into objects of desire elsewhere. Such is the case of the açai – a palm fruit that forms an important part of the diet of peoples in the Amazon and has now become a 'berry' with almost magical health-related properties in the USA.

The variety of human diets in the modern world is quite astounding. The unevenness of food availability is equally astounding. In some places people do not have enough to eat, in others places they have too much. Anthropologists have been interested in both extremes. Historically, the focus has been on not-enough-to-eat. This problem, and its consequences, are persistent and chronic in some places, episodic in others. People talk of difficulties in getting access to food, of having to eat less and less desirable things, and of not being able to satisfy their hunger (Moreno-Black and Guerrón-Montero 2005). Children suffer from undernutrition, and hunger conspires with disease to take their lives (Hampshire et al. 2009). Adults as well as children succumb to famine (Bearak 2003). In other places food is too available and people suffer from overnutition and obesity. In some places in the developing world, obesity is the companion of undernutrition.

Overnutrition and obesity

Obesity is a new phenomenon in human evolutionary history – new at least in the extent to which it occurs in today's world (Ulijaszek and Lofink 2006). From a purely biological view, obesity is simply the result of a history of positive energy balance – that is, a history of food intake which exceeds energy needs (or expenditure). From an anthropological vantage point, the current situation raises a number of interesting questions. Why are so many people obese at this point in history, and in so many different places? What is it about our current environment that has made this phenomenon possible and/or inevitable? What factors in our evolutionary past may have predisposed us to responding to our current environment in a manner that results in obesity?

A key assumption which has guided the search for answers to these questions is that human evolutionary history has been shaped by adaptation to environments with fluctuations in food availability, and hence by selection for fat storage in times of food abundance. James Neel (1962) has formalized this idea as the 'thrifty' genotype hypothesis. Specifically, he proposed that periods of severe food insufficiency would have been prevalent in the lives of pre-agricultural societies and would have selected a 'thrifty' metabolism, such that in good times food energy would be stored as fat to be used in bad times. This idea has been enormously influential (Lieberman 2003). A recent analysis of the ethnographic record by Benyshek and Watson (2006) indicates, however, that agriculturalists have been just as likely to suffer from periods of food shortage as pre-agricultural societies. This suggests that the selective forces of feast versus famine have been with us forever: they are not just an outcome of our long evolution as foragers.

Our understanding of the underlying genetic basis of a predisposition to obesity has advanced rapidly since Neel (1962) first proposed his thrifty genotype hypothesis.

It is now clear that the genetic predisposition to obesity is complex and that there is significant population variation. It has also become obvious that the environment, pre-natal and post-natal, plays a critical role. During early fetal development, constraints on the uterine environment 'program' the fetus to store fat, so that it may be able to survive in times of famine. If, however, the post-natal environment is good, this fetal programming for fat storage will predispose the individual to obesity (Ulijaszek and Lofink 2006). This kind of selective force would have been the same forever. Undernutrition in childhood can also alter fat metabolism in ways that predispose to obesity in abundant food environments (Frisancho 2003). Hence we need to think in terms of a 'thrifty' phenotype.

During post-natal life, the food environment is equally as important; it needs to be one that allows for consistent positive energy balance. Such is the case in environments where, (1) food is abundant and continuously available, (2) the cost of acquisition is low in terms of physical effort in travel and work, and (3) cultural norms permit, or value, overeating. These three conditions should suffice in accounting for the development of obesity. The first two are assumed to be novel from an evolutionary point of view. Hence, humans are now in novel environments from an evolutionary perspective – environments that have been labeled 'obesogenic.'

Lieberman (2006) has proposed that other aspects of our evolutionary heritage lead to obesity in modern environments. She argues that optimal foraging theory can help make sense of the current obesogenic environment. Optimal foraging theory posits that an organism will forage in a way that maximizes their food energy intake per unit of time (MacArthur and Pianka 1966). If that is our evolutionary heritage, and if access to food in modern environments requires little expenditure of energy to access foods which are dense in energy – in other words, if the foraging costs are low and the caloric return high relatively to prehistoric and historic feeding patterns – it make sense that we are becoming more obese. Indeed, Ulijaszek (2007) has referred to obesity as a "disorder of convenience."

Following this line of reasoning, everyone in the industrialized nations should be obese; but that is not the case. Typically less than 50 percent of the people in any such environment are actually obese. So the real question is, why do some people become obese and others do not? Perhaps we need to reconceptualize the idea of environment as heterogeneous rather than homogenous. Perhaps there are multiple 'environments,' inhabited by people who live in the same geographic space/patch of the earth but are guide by different cultural and economic circumstances. It is, however, clear that some environments are more obesogenic than others for some people. For example, Himmelgreen and colleagues (2004) have documented an increase in obesity with the migration from Puerto Rico to the United States. This indicates that the USA environment would be more obesogenic – all factors being equal. But all factors are never equal.

NUTRITION AND FUNCTION

Nutrition affects function in many ways, from changes in genetic transcription at the cellular level to changes in behavior at the level of the individual. Anthropologists have been most interested in effects on individuals, and particularly in the effects of poor nutritional status on the measurement of functions like work capacity, growth, and reproduction (Table 11.2). Nutritional status refers to the biological condition of the organism with regard to food intake. 'Normal' is a state of equilibrium in which energy needs are balanced by dietary intake. 'Undernutrition' is a state in which energy needs are not being met by the dietary intake, and 'overnutrition' is the opposite – a state in which the dietary intake exceeds the needs. An important assumption is that a dietary intake which is adequate in terms of energy (that is, calories) will be adequate in everything else – protein, vitamins, minerals, essential fatty acids, and so on. This is generally but not always true. For example, energy intake may be adequate, but iron intake not. This occurs in many parts of the world where diets are low in animal products, because there the bioavailability of iron (that is, the ability of dietary iron to be absorbed by the body) is low – though perhaps counterintuitively: energy intake can be excessive, but vitamin and mineral intake inadequate when the diet is based on highly processed non-fortified foods.

Research on nutritional status and function has focused mainly on growth in children, work capacity, and reproductive function (fecundity/fertility).

Growth

Growth velocity and body size are indicators of the quality of the nutritional and health environments of individuals and populations. Genetic endowment sets the potential – a potential that can be reached under optimal conditions of nutrition and health. Under less than optimal conditions, growth velocity is slower and body size smaller. Hence anthropologists and others use body size (weight and stature) as a proxy for environmental quality, and particularly for nutritional quality. For example, Padez (2002) argued that the 8.9 cm increase in the height of Portuguese males between 1904 and 1998 reflected the general improvement in the standard of living, especially after 1960.

Although 'adverse' environments have been conceptualized as environments providing constraints to growth, Cameron (2007) argues that the situation is now more complex, as some adverse environments include both deprivation and abundance. He suggests that this is currently the case in transitional economies like those of South Africa. In this case, constrained physical growth *in utero* leads to physiological changes (a process known as 'fetal programming') which promote fat storage. Such changes would be beneficial in a post-natal environment characterized by food deprivation, but are inappropriate for the food abundance of the actual post-natal environment and consequently predispose the individual to obesity and associated health problems.

Work capacity and productivity

Work capacity refers to the ability to do physical work and is usually measured by a maximal oxygen consumption ($VO_{2\,max}$) or a 'fitness' test, a test done by having the subject run on a treadmill at increasing workloads, until exhausted. This is a measurement of the oxygen-carrying capacity, and it is considered to give the best indication of an individual's ability to do physical work.

Work capacity is negatively affected both by undernutrition and by overnutrition. For example, $VO_{2\,max}$ in undernourished Colombian males ranged from 1 to 2 liters

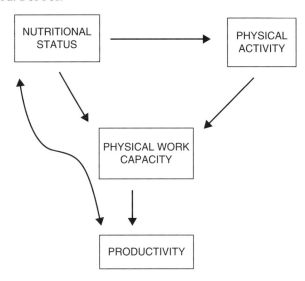

Figure 11.1   Relations among physical activity, nutritional status and work capacity. Adapted from Spurr 1984

of oxygen (O_2) per minute compared to 2.75 in normally nourished controls (Barac-Nieto et al. 1978). This difference can be explained by the lower mass of lean tissue, especially muscle, in the undernourished males. Since the 1970s there has been an interest in the effect of poor nutritional status on work, especially on the physical work done by many in developing countries. The idea is that, unless people are well nourished, they would not be able to do the kinds of physical work demanded of them and necessary for the national economic development.

A simplified sketch of the relations between nutritional status, work capacity, and productivity is shown in Figure 11.1. Some of the classic studies demonstrating these relationships were undertaken by G. B. Spurr and colleagues, with sugar cane cutters in Colombia (Spurr 1984). They demonstrated two important things. The first was that men of normal nutritional status (weight for height, blood hemoglobin, serum albumin), had higher maximal work capacity, as would be expected. The second was that productivity (weight of sugar cane cut per day) was positively correlated to physical work capacity. That is, the men with the higher maximal work capacity cut more sugar cane.

Why might that be so? Maximal work capacity is the maximal effort a person can achieve. No one could sustain work at their maximal capacity for minutes, let alone for an 8-hour work day. Rather, in self-paced work like cane cutting, people tend to work at 35–40 percent of their maximal capacity (Spurr et al. 1977). Hence, if you were to take two individuals working at 40 percent of their maximal capacity over an 8-hour day, the individual with the higher work capacity would produce more – and, in the case of Colombian cane cutters, earn more.

Work capacity is also negatively affected by iron deficiency anemia. Iron deficiency is the most common micronutrient deficiency worldwide, and it affects about two billion people. It can result from inadequate dietary intake, inadequate absorption of dietary iron, or high iron losses. Iron status is assessed in terms of iron stores in the body, which are measured as hemoglobin (Hb) in blood; one or more indicators of iron status are serum ferritin (iron-binding protein) and transferrin (iron transport protein).

The depression of work capacity induced by iron deficiency anemia is assumed to be due to the fact that work capacity is a measure of the oxygen-carrying capacity, and the capacity to transport oxygen depends on iron (Haas and Brownlie 2001). Because iron deficiency depresses work capacity, it also depresses productivity in physically demanding work. Interestingly, a number of studies have shown that productivity is also depressed in less physically demanding jobs, like those of women factory workers (Li et al. 1994; Untoro et al. 1998) and tea-leaf pickers (Edgerton et al. 1979). Two of the studies (Edgerton et al. 1979; Li et al. 1994) demonstrated an increase in physical activity level with iron supplementation in iron deficient women.

The reproductive function

It has long been known that inadequate food intake is associated with the suppression of the reproductive function, both in animals and in humans. The evolutionary explanation is that, under conditions of energy deficiency, animals adjust their energetic priorities – that is, the ways in which they use the available energy – in order to promote individual survival; and, since reproduction is not necessary for individual survival, it receives very low priority (Wade and Jones 2004). Although this argument is theoretically compelling, the actual measurement of the adequacy of food energy intake in free-living humans under natural conditions, carried in order to assess its effect on the reproductive function, is methodologically challenging. Three studies did, however, accomplish it.

Panter-Brick and Ellison (1994) studied rural Tamang women in Nepal who increased their work in subsistence agriculture in the monsoon season. This increase was accompanied by weight loss, which indicates that they were in a negative energy balance (their food energy intake was insufficient to balance the energy expended). Under these conditions, the reproductive function – as measured by the reproductive hormone progesterone in saliva – was lower than normal. Second, Ellison and colleagues (1989) showed that Lese horticulturalists in Zaire had depressed salivary progesterone levels in the pre-harvest season, when food availability was low and body weight declining. Finally, Jasieńska and Ellison (1998) reported that Polish women-farmers showed a loss in body fat and evidence of lowered salivary progesterone levels in response to a 2-month seasonal increase in farm work.

These studies complement research carried on female athletes (recreational and competitive) which demonstrates the suppression of reproductive function with exercise (see Dufour in press). It is not, however, exercise itself that is the cause; rather, it is the inadequacy of food energy intake, which leads to a negative energy balance accompanying the exercise. The suppression of the reproductive function with a negative energy balance strongly suggests the selection of a positive energy balance in our evolutionary past.

FUTURE DIRECTIONS

Research is moving rapidly in several different directions. One is the development of tools like isotopes in order to refine our understanding of early hominin diets as well as of the diets of early members of the genus *Homo*. Another direction is the decoding of the effects of selection on the human genome. This work promises to provide insights into the effects of food as a selective agent. A third area is characterized by a focus on understanding the effects of fetal and early childhood undernutrition on health and function in adulthood.

There are other areas which would benefit significantly from the insights anthropology can offer. Two seem particularly important. The first is the opportunity to collaborate with nutritionists, plant breeders and others so as to integrate nutrition into poverty-reduction and agricultural strategies in culturally appropriate and sustainable ways. The second is to underscore the importance of the 'environment' – that is, of the specific ethnographic contexts of people's lives – in driving increases in overweight mass and obesity at the local level. It is clear that a predisposition to fat storage is the evolutionary heritage of most, if not all, human populations. That predisposition, however, cannot explain the rapid increases in obesity which are occurring recently. These must be due to changes in local 'environments.'

REFERENCES

Aiello, L. C., and Wheeler, P. (1995) The Expensive Tissue Hypothesis: The Brain and the Digestive System in Human and Primate Evolution. *Current Anthropology* 36 (2): 199–221.

Barac-Nieto, M., Spurr, G. B., Maksud, M. G., and Lotero, H. (1978) Aerobic Work Capacity in Chronically Undernourished Adult Males. *Journal of Applied Physiology: Respiratory, Environmental, Exercise Physiology* 44 (2): 209–215.

Bearak, B. (2003) Why People Still Starve. *New York Times*, Section 6: 33, July 13.

Benyshek, D. C., and Watson, J. T. (2006) Exploring the Thrifty Genotype's Food-Shortage Assumptions: A Cross-Cultural Comparison of Ethnographic Accounts of Food Security among Foraging and Agricultural Societies. *American Journal of Physical Anthropology* 131 (1): 120–126.

Blumenschine, R. J., and Pobiner, B. L. (2007) Zooarchaeology and the Ecology of Oldowan Hominin Carnivory. In P. S. Ungar (ed.), *Evolution of the Human Diet: The Known, the Unknown, and the Unknowable* (pp. 167–190). New York: Oxford University Press.

Broadhurst, C. L., Wang, Y. Q., Crawford, M. A., Cunnane, S. C., Parkington, J. E., and Schmidt, W. F. (2002) Brain-Specific Lipids from Marine, Lacustrine, or Terrestrial Food Resources: Potential Impact on Early African *Homo sapiens*. *Comparative Biochemistry and Physiology, B: Biochemistry and Molecular Biology* 131 (4): 653–673.

Bunn, H. T. (2007) Meat Made Us Human. In P. S. Ungar (ed.), *Evolution of the Human Diet: The Known, the Unknown, and the Unknowable* (pp. 191–211). New York: Oxford University Press.

Cameron, N. (2007) Growth Patterns in Adverse Environments. *American Journal of Human Biology* 19 (5): 615–621.

Dufour, D. L. (in press) The Energetic Cost of Physical Activity and Regulation of Reproduction. In C. G. Nicholas Mascie-Taylor and L. Rosetta (eds), *Reproduction and Adaptation*. Cambridge: Cambridge University Press.

Eaton, S. B. (2006) The Ancestral Human Diet: What Was It and Should It Be a Paradigm for Contemporary Nutrition. *Proceedings of the Nutrition Society* 65 (1): 1–6.

Eaton, S. B., and Konner, M. (1985) Paleolithic Nutrition: A Consideration of Its Nature and Current Implications. *New England Journal of Medicine* 312 (5): 283–289.

Edgerton V. R., Gardner, G. W., Ohira, Y., Gunawardena, K. A., and Senewiratne, B. (1979) Iron Deficiency Anemia and Its Effect on Workers Productivity and Activity Patterns. *British Medical Journal* 2 (6024): 1546–1549.

Ellison, P. T., Peacock, N. R., and Lager, C. (1989) Ecology and Ovarian Function among Lese Women of the Ituri Forest, Zaire. *American Journal of Physical Anthropology* 78 (4): 519–526.

Frisancho, A. R. (2003) Reduced Rates of Fat Oxidization: A Metabolic Pathway to Obesity in the Developing Nations. *American Journal of Human Biology* 15 (4): 522–532.

Haas, J. D., and Brownlie, T. (2001) Iron Deficiency and Reduced Work Capacity: A Critical Review of the Research to Determine a Causal Relationship. *Journal of Nutrition* 131 (Suppl. 2): 676S–690S.

Hampshire K. A., Casiday, R., Kilpatrick, K., and Panter-Brick, C. (2009) The Social Context of Childcare Practices and Child Malnutrition in Niger's Recent Food Crisis. *Disasters* 33 (1): 132–151.

Himmelgreen, D. A., Perez-Escamilla, R., Martinez, D., Bretnall, A., Eells, B., Peng, Y., and Bermudez, A. (2004) The Longer You Stay, the Bigger You Get: Length of Time and Language Use in the US Are Associated with Obesity in Puerto Rican Women. *American Journal of Physical Anthropology* 125 (1): 90–96.

Hladik, C. M., Chivers, D. J., and Pasquet, P. (1999) On Diet and Gut Size in Non-Human Primates and Humans: Is There a Relationship to Brain Size? Discussion and Criticism. *Current Anthropology* 40 (5): 695–697.

Institute of Medicine (2005) *Dietary Reference Intakes for Energy, Carbohydrates, Fiber, Fat, Fatty Acids, Cholesterol, Protein and Amino Acids.* Washington DC: National Academies Press.

Jasieńska, G., and Ellison, P. T. (1998) Physical Work Causes Suppression of Ovarian Function in Women. *Proceedings of the Royal Society of London, Series B: Biological Sciences* 265 (1408): 1847–1851.

Leonard, W. R., Robertson, M. L., and Snodgrass, J. J. (2007) Energetic Models of Human Nutritional Evolution. In P. S. Ungar (ed.), *Evolution of the Human Diet: The Known, the Unknown, and the Unknowable* (pp. 344–362). New York: Oxford University Press.

Li, R. W., Chen, X. C., Yan, H. C., Deurenberg, P., Garby, L., and Hautvast, J. G. A. J. (1994) Functional Consequences of Iron Supplementation in Iron Deficient Female Cotton Workers in Beijing, China. *American Journal of Clinical Nutrition* 59 (4): 908–913.

Lieberman, L. S. (2003) Dietary, Evolutionary and Modernizing Influences on the Prevalence of Type 2 Diabetes. *Annual Reviews of Nutrition* 23: 345–377.

Lieberman, L. S. (2006) Evolutionary and Anthropological Perspectives on Optimal Foraging in Obesogenic Environments. *Appetite* 47 (1): 3–9.

Macarthur, R. H., and Pianka, E. R. (1966) On Optimal Use of a Patchy Environment. *American Naturalist* 100 (916): 603–609.

Milton, K. (1987) Primate Diets and Gut Morphology: Implications for Human Evolution. In M. Harris and E. B. Ross (eds), *Food and Evolution: Toward a Theory of Human Food Habits* (pp. 93–116). Philadelphia: Temple Press.

Milton, K. (1999) A Hypothesis to Explain the Role of Meat-Eating in Human Evolution. *Evolutionary Anthropology* 8 (1): 11–21.

Moreno-Black, G., and Guerrón-Montero, C. (2005) Speaking of Hunger and Coping with Food Insecurity: Experiences in the Afro-Ecuadorian Highlands. *Ecology of Food and Nutrition* 44 (5): 391–420.

Neel, J. V. (1962) *Diabetes mellitus*: A 'Thrifty Genotype' Rendered Detrimental by Progress. *American Journal of Human Genetics* 14 (4): 353–362.

Padez, P. (2002) Stature and Stature Distribution in Portuguese Male Adults 1904–1998: The Role of Environmental Factors. *American Journal of Human Biology* 14 (1): 39–49.

Panter-Brick, C., and Ellison, P.T. (1994) Seasonality of Workloads and Ovarian Function in Nepali Women. Human Reproductive Ecology – Interactions of Environment, Fertility and Behaviour. *Book Series: Annals of the New York Academy of Sciences* 709: 234–235.

Richards, A. I. (1939) *Land, Labour and Diet in Northern Rhodesia: An Economic Study of the Bemba Tribe*. New York: Oxford University Press.

Sponheimer, M., Lee-Thorp, J. A., and De Ruiter, D. (2007) Icarus, Isotopes and Australopith Diets. In P. S. Ungar (ed.), *Evolution of the Human Diet: The Known, the Unknown, and the Unknowable* (pp. 132–149). New York: Oxford University Press.

Spurr, G. B. (1984) Physical Activity, Nutritional Status and Work Capacity in Relation to Agricultural Productivity. In E. Pollit and P. Amante (eds), *Energy Intake and Activity* (pp. 207–261). New York: Alan R. Liss–United Nations University.

Spurr G. B., Barac-Nieto M., and Maksud, M. G. (1977) Productivity and Maximal Oxygen Consumption in Sugar Cane Cutters. *American Journal of Clinical Nutrition* 30 (3): 316–321.

Tishkoff, S. A., Reed, F. A., Ranciaro, A., Voight, B. F., Babbitt, C. C., Silverman, J. S., Powell, K., Mortensen, H. M., Hirbo, J. B., Osman, M., Ibrahim, M., Omar, S. A., Lema, G., Nyambo, T. B., Ghori, J., Bumpstead, S., Pritchard, J. K., Wray, G. A., and Deloukas, P. (2007) Convergent Adaptation of Human Lactase Persistence in Africa and Europe. *Nature Genetics* 39 (1): 31–40.

Ulijaszek, S. J. (2007) Obesity: A Disorder of Convenience. *Obesity Reviews* 8 (Suppl. 1): 183–187.

Ulijaszek, S. J., and Lofink, H. (2006) Obesity in Biocultural Perspective. *Annual Review of Anthroplogy* 35: 337–360.

Ungar, P. S. (2007) Limits to Knowledge on the Evolution of Hominin Diet. In P. S. Ungar (ed.), *Evolution of the Human Diet: The Known, the Unknown, and the Unknowable* (pp. 395–408). New York: Oxford University Press.

Untoro, J., Gross, R., Schultink, W., and Sediaoetama, D. (1998) The Association between BMI and Hemoglobin and Work Productivity among Indonesian Female Factory Workers. *European Journal of Clinical Nutrition* 52 (2): 131–135.

Wade, G. N., and Jones, J. E. (2004) Neuroendocrinology of Nutritional Infertility. *American Journal of Physiology – Regulatory, Integrative and Comparative Physiology* 287 (6): R1277–R1296.

Wilson C. S. (2002) Reasons for Eating: Personal Experiences in Nutrition and Anthropology. *Appetite* 38 (1): 63–67.

Wrangham, R. W., Jones, J. H., Laden, G., Pilbeam, D., and Conklin-Brittain, N. L. (1999) The Raw and the Stolen: Cooking and the Ecology of Human Origins. *Current Anthropology* 40 (5): 567–594.

CHAPTER 12

Ongoing Evolution in Humans

Lorena Madrigal and Jessica Willoughby

INTRODUCTION

The synthetic theory of evolution defines evolution as change in gene frequencies from generation to generation, within a breeding population (see Chapter 2 of the present volume). Such change results from four forces, three of which change the frequencies of new genes introduced by mutation. Because the effect of mutation, the fourth force, is standard across populations, we do not discuss it in this chapter. The other three forces of evolution – gene flow, natural selection, and genetic drift – in one way or another change the gene frequencies of a population.

We begin from the understanding that there is overwhelming agreement on a recent African origin of our species – an origin so recent that it has not allowed much variation to accumulate within the species. Indeed most human variation is shared; that is, there are no sharp genetic boundaries between human groups (Balaresque et al. 2007; Jakobsson et al. 2008; Madrigal and Barbujani 2006). Thus the most recent genetic analyses indicate that our species expanded out of Africa and colonized the other continents rather recently. This chapter deals with how natural selection, gene flow, and genetic drift have affected human populations after this expansion.

NATURAL SELECTION

Surely you remember the example of the action of natural selection on moths during the industrial revolution in England. Data indicate that, before industrialization blackened the light tree bark, the light-colored moths escaped predation from birds, whereas the dark-colored moths were preferentially eaten. The gene frequency of the light pigment was high until the trees started turning dark due to pollution, at which point the dark-colored moths became better camouflaged and the frequency of the gene responsible for the dark pigment increased. When pollution was controlled and tree bark became light again, the frequencies of the genes that cause the light and the dark pigment went back to pre-pollution days. This is an excellent example of natural selection, because it shows that a selective force (birds) selects a phenotype (lightly or darkly pigmented moths) by allowing that phenotype to survive and reproduce. Thus we would like to define natural selection as *the differential fertility and mortality of different phenotypes.*

How do we detect if natural selection has acted on the human species? To give an initial answer to the question, we use the classic example of natural selection in humans about which you must have learned before: that of the sickle hemoglobin (Hb S) and malaria. We will only use this example as an introduction to natural selection operating in humans and we will not discuss in depth hemoglobin S, or any of the other polymorphisms associated with malaria (on which see Chapter 4 of this volume): these are very well discussed in other sources (Mielke et al. 2006), whereas we would like to talk about other examples instead.

There are several ways to detect natural selection. Perhaps the most obvious one is offered by the presence of a cline – that is, the differential geographic distribution of a gene. Thus the sickle cell gene is found, at high frequencies, in areas where malaria was, or is, endemic (that is, present in a constant manner). The second way in which we may detect natural selection is by actually measuring if some phenotypes suffer from higher mortality and/or lower fertility than others do. With heterozygotes HbAS (individuals who have one sickle gene and one 'normal' gene), it has been very well established that they have lower mortality from malaria than individuals who only carry the 'normal' gene. Do heterozygotes in malarial environments also have higher fertility, in addition to having lower mortality? This remains controversial, Madrigal indicates that they do not, while Hoff and colleagues indicate that they do, although in a non-malarial environment (Madrigal 1989; Hoff et al. 2001). Finally, in the case of hemoglobin S and malaria, we even have an understanding of the cellular mechanism by which HbAS heterozygotes are able to fight against the malarial infection. It appears that the parasites cause increased sickling of the red blood cell, which in turn causes the host's immune system to remove the sickled cell before the parasite reproduces (Weatherall 2008). Ideally, then, when we are determining if a polymorphism is the result of natural selection, we are looking for a cline, for differential mortality and/or fertility, and for a cellular mechanism for such differential mortality and/or fertility. Here we look at two other human polymorphisms, which are good candidates for having being selected: the ability to drink milk during adulthood, and the CCR5-Δ 32 gene.

Adult lactase persistence

The ability in adults to drink milk is related to an individual's ability to produce the enzyme lactase, which breaks down the sugar in milk (lactose) into easily absorbable sugars. If you drink milk and do not produce lactase, you are setting yourself up for some rather unpleasant gastric problems.

In the USA, many people are surprised to hear that most members of our species cannot drink milk after the age of weaning without suffering ill effects. In other words, the perception that most adults can drink milk and that only a few cannot is incorrect: the ability of adults to drink milk is found only in *some* populations. This should be our first clue that perhaps natural selection is acting to increase the frequency of the gene in some populations, just as it has increased the frequency of hemoglobin S in malarial environments.

Populations whose adults produce lactase are those with a history of pastoralism, which suggests that there was natural selection for the lactase persistence gene in these groups. Just as with Hb S, we observe a cline of the lactase persistence pheno-type. The lactase persistence phenotype is found in as many as 90 percent of the adults of northern Europe, but its frequency decreases towards the south and the east, and it reaches its lowest frequencies in Asian and non-pastoral African popula-tions (Tishkoff et al. 2006).

Why has the lactase persistence gene being selected in pastoral populations? Milk is high in protein, fat, and sugar, and it is an expedient means for obtaining water in dry environments. It was probably an excellent weaning food, one that may even have allowed mothers to start reproducing sooner than they would have been able to, had they continued to breast-feed. If a woman's children have a high probability of surviv-ing because they can drink milk after weaning, her fitness is increased. If that same woman is able to produce more children precisely because she can wean them sooner than other mothers do, she is likely to leave an important genetic contribution to the next generation. This is natural selection at work.

The genetic basis of the lactase persistence phenotype is rather complex, but it has become clearer after the publication of several recent articles (Bersaglieri et al. 2004; Enattah et al. 2008; Tishkoff et al. 2006). These pieces of research show that several mutations have occurred in different parts of the world and have become frequent in pastoral areas. Some authors have even been able to propose a date for the occur-rence of the mutation – a date that coincides with the adoption of dairy farming (Tishkoff et al. 2006).

The case for the high frequency of lactase persistence being a result of natural selec-tion is quite 'tight.' Just like with malaria and Hb S, we have a clear geographical pattern of the phenotype, which overlaps with a plausible selective agent. We also have an understanding of the cellular mechanism at work, since we know that cells which carry chromosomes with the lactase-producing gene produce more lactase than those with-out it (ibid.). Lastly, we know that adult individuals with the lactase persistence gene can drink milk without any ill effects. The only piece of the puzzle we are missing is that we are not able to document differential mortality in the lactase persistent and non-persistent children who were weaned, and who had milk available in the diet, upon the adoption of animal husbandry. However, the genetic signatures of natural selection in lactase persistent populations are so strong that several authors note that this is one of the strongest cases for recent human evolution through the action of natural selection (Beja-Pereira et al. 2003; Bersaglieri et al. 2004; Enattah et al. 2008; Tishkoff et al. 2006). This is a particularly interesting example of natural selection operating in humans, because the selective agent – the fact that the availability of milk in the diet, combined with the capacity to use it, may lead to a higher probability of survival – is a result of human culture. Thus, in this case, human culture has driven human evolution.

The CCR5-Δ 32 polymorphism

We conclude the section on natural selection by examining a polymorphism for which we have the clearest evidence of differential mortality, but whose high frequency remains a matter of intense debate. The CCR5-Δ 32 gene results in the absence of a complex macromolecule on the surface of macrophages: a macromolecule which acts as a receptor to the human immunodeficiency virus (HIV), which in turn causes the disease AIDS. Without this receptor, the virus cannot enter the cell. Individuals who are homozygote for the gene do not get AIDS even if they are infected with HIV. Individuals who are heterozygotes have instead a much more benign disease course than individuals without the mutation do. Since AIDS is a disease with very high mortality rates, individuals with a mild disease course or individuals who do not develop the disease at all, even in the presence of an infection, are clearly favored. Thus in this case we have epidemiological evidence for differential mortality, just as we did for the Hb S polymorphism and malaria – that is, we have a type of evidence we were missing for lactase persistence.

We also have a clear geographical distribution: namely the mutation has a very high frequency in northern Europe, and it is virtually non-existing in non-European populations (Novembre et al. 2005). Why is the mutation so frequent in northern Europe? It has been suggested that the mutation, which now protects against HIV, was protective against some other selective force at some point in the past. In other words, something else drove the gene to its current high frequencies. The gene just came to protect against HIV by chance, many generations after it had achieved its high frequency through another force. What exactly was that force, how strong was it, and when did it act on the European population? This is highly controversial. Whereas some authors propose smallpox or a haemorrhagic infection not too different from the Ebola virus during the Middle ages (Duncan and Scott 2005), others note that the gene is found in bronze-age skeleton samples at frequencies similar to those observed today; so the high frequency of the gene would be due to a force which precedes the Middle Ages (Hedrick and Verrelli 2006). Yet others note that the distribution of the gene can be better understood in a neutral framework (genetic drift) than in a selective evolutionary framework (Sabeti et al. 2005) – a point also made by Hedrick and Verelli (2006). Finally, it has been suggested that the distribution of the gene reflects the expansion of the Roman empire (Faure and Royer-Carenzi 2008). The CCR5-Δ 32 gene is an interesting example of a common evolutionary theme: an organ/trait evolves for one reason, and in later evolutionary times it acquires a different use.

In conclusion, we would like to note that strong signatures of selection at the genetic level have been detected in the human genome (Hawks et al. 2007). However, the example of Hb S and malaria is probably the only one for which we have a clinal distribution, a molecular understanding of the protection afforded by the gene, and epidemiological data of differential survival. For other traits, it is difficult to construct such a 'tight' case of natural selection operating on the trait. In some cases (as in lactase persistence), we lack the epidemiological data. In others (as in the CCR5-Δ 32 gene), we have the epidemiological data and the cellular understanding (in this case, of why HIV does not progress in homozygotes of the gene), but we do not know the evolutionary reason which brought the gene to its high frequencies in some populations but not in others. This is not unexpected. We should not assume that all phenotypes are adaptive nor that evolution proceeds by natural selection primarily (Lewontin 1976).

GENE FLOW

We started the chapter with a clear statement that, in the human species, most genetic variants are shared. That is, all human populations share about 85–95 percent of all the genetic variants. This means that, if there is a terrible catastrophe and only a small group of humans survives, the group will have within it about 85–95 percent of all the genetic variants found in the species.

When gene flow is being studied in humans, the focus is on that 5–15 percent of variation which is not shared among human groups. This makes sense: If we wish to reconstruct the history of human groups, we would gain nothing if we focused on the genes that are shared by all of them. Instead, when we are looking at the history of populations, we focus on that small but informative proportion of human variation which is different among human groups. However, this should not be understood as implying that humans can be classified into distinct, obvious and cross-culturally consistent groups.

Gene flow makes populations similar by allowing the genes to move from one area to another. In humans, the movement of genes may be a result of migration, or even of wars and invasions as a consequence of which people may be displaced out of their homes and moved to different areas. A common term used in gene flow studies is that of 'admixture': if two populations exchange genes, the descendant population is seen as being 'admixed.' Studies which compute admixture estimates must decide which populations to use for representing the 'parental' populations. That is, if we wish to estimate the parental contributions in gene frequency to a descendant population, we will need information on gene frequencies in the parental groups as well as in the descendant group, in order to compute the contribution of the former to the latter.

A review of papers on the microevolutionary effects of gene flow in humans indicates that researchers are frequently interested in either of the following two cases:

1 population movements that colonized large areas;
2 the formation of new populations in more circumscribed regions.

Under the first category, we see papers on topics such as the peopling of Oceania and of the American continent. Under the second, we see papers on small groups such as the Gulah of South Carolina in the USA. We decided to choose two such examples of the microevolutionary effect of gene flow on human populations. The first one deals with the expansion of Neolithic farmers into Europe (a rather large area) from the Middle East, and the second one deals with the formation of a new small population in the New World, specifically in the Atlantic coast of Costa Rica.

The Neolithic expansion into Europe

Perhaps few topics in population genetics have been as hotly debated as the expansion of the Neolithic 'package' – which consisted of cultigens, domesticated animals, and other cultural traits – from the Fertile Crescent in the Middle East into Europe. Because the literature is so large, we refer the reader to comprehensive review articles on the topic (Armelagos and Harper 2005a and b), and we only discuss what, in our opinion, is the emerging consensus. Simply put, the question is whether, upon the adoption of plant and animal domestication, the cultural aspects of the agricultural economy spread to Europe from the Middle East *without* population movements from the Middle East – that is, by cultural diffusion – or *with*/being accompanied by human population expansions – that is, by demic diffusion. According to the former view, called the cultural diffusion model (CD), the current European population would descend mostly from Paleolithic (pre-agricultural) Europeans, since the Neolithic package was adopted through cultural distribution. The view that the Neolithic package spread across Europe because of a population expansion from the Middle East is called the demic diffusion model (DD), and it proposes that the current European population descends mostly from Middle-Eastern farmers. The question, then, is: To what extent is the current European population a result of admixture between Paleolithic Europeans and Middle-Eastern Neolithic farmers?

The proposal that there had been a movement of people stems from the observation of clines spreading from the Middle East into Europe. Do these clines represent evidence of Neolithic farmers moving from the Middle East into Europe? Or could they be evidence of a much earlier population movement, of Paleolithic peoples, into Europe – evidence which was not erased by any subsequent movement of farmers? These questions have been addressed in a large body of literature initiated by the work of Cavalli-Sforza and collaborators (Cavalli-Sforza et al. 1993; Cavalli-Sforza and Piazza 1993); but, because the literature is so long to review, we prefer to refer the reader to the same review papers for a detailed list (Armelagos and Harper 2005a and b) and to focus instead on areas of consensus.

There is emerging agreement that the so-called Neolithic revolution was not so much a revolution as a transformation, which took thousands of years (Twiss 2007). Through this transformation, non-cultivated plants and non-domesticated animals were exploited while humans became more reliant on domesticated plants and animals (Abbo et al. 2006). There is also agreement on the point that there was a large climatological change, which may have prompted the adoption of agriculture at roughly the same time in different areas of the world (Armelagos and Harper 2005a). Indeed, climatic changes appear to have caused a massive population movement out of the Middle East into Europe. According to Turney and Brown, Neolithic farmers were forced to migrate after a flood of the Black Sea about 8,000 years before present times. These authors calculate that the total number of people displaced from the area of the Black Sea could have been as high as 145,000, and they note that, following this sea-level rise, there was a rapid expansion of Neolithic sites, which ultimately lead to the establishment of farming in Europe (Turney and Brown 2007). There is even agreement on the manner in which this expansion took place: apparently the displaced farmers did not move in the steady land-based migratory patterns, as was initially proposed on the demic diffusion model. Instead these farmers followed a maritime route, so that the first Neolithic sites are costal ones, around the Mediterranean Sea (Turney and Brown 2007; Zeder 2008).

What was the genetic effect of this massive movement of people, and how is this effect estimated? Admixture estimates must be computed, where the modern European population is considered the result of admixture between Paleolithic and Neolithic peoples. As stated before, the choice of parental populations is important, as we hope to work with people who accurately represent the parental groups. In this case, there is common agreement that the Basques represent the Paleolithic and the Palestinians and Druze of the Near East represent the Neolithic parental populations, respectively. Using these parental populations for a large number of genetic markers, Belle and collaborators conclude that the Near-Eastern contribution to the European gene pool was between 46–66 percent (Belle et al. 2006). These estimates make sense in light of the above-mentioned archaeological data, which indicate that the Neolithic farmers moved along the seacoast, where they established settlements, and these eventually allowed farming to spread into the continent. In this manner the spread of agriculture is seen by most as a slow process, which allowed interaction and hybridization with the native Paleolithic peoples.

This example of gene flow in humans brings to our attention the fact that it is not appropriate to think of continental human groups as distinct, unchangeable genetic entities. Instead, the European gene pool is best understood as that of an admixed population, which descends from Paleolithic local groups who bred with advancing Neolithic farmers from the Middle East. This example also brings up the importance of considering environmental changes as catalysts for major evolutionary changes in our species – in this case, a massive movement of people from the Middle East into Europe, after climatic changes which forced them to move because of flooding and contributed to the adoption of agriculture. Lastly, this example points to the importance of multi-disciplinary research, including climatic studies, archaeology, and genetics.

The formation of the Indo-Costa-Rican population

Another massive migratory event in the history of our species was the enslavement and movement of people from Africa to the New World. Certainly, the forced movement of African peoples to the New World was a major evolutionary force in changing gene frequencies throughout North, Central and South America, as well as in the Caribbean (Madrigal 2006). A less well known migratory movement of people into the Caribbean is that of indentured servants from the Indian sub-continent, which peaked after the emancipation of the African slaves. Some regions of the Caribbean such as Trinidad, Guyana, and Suriname have large populations of descendants from these East-Indian migrants. In these three areas the Indo-Caribbean groups have maintained a strong sense of ethnic identity, which has allowed them to preserve various cultural practices in their religious and marital rules, and even in their language (Madrigal 1989; Madrigal 2006; Madrigal et al. 2001).

The reason why we are going to consider a Costa-Rican group in the context of the East-Indian migration to the Caribbean is that the Atlantic coast of the country has had strong historical ties with the Caribbean. After the invasion of Europeans, the native population of the Costa-Rican Atlantic coast was devastated, and it was pushed to high-altitude regions both by the spread of malaria and by pirate attacks. When the Costa-Rican government signed a contract with a US businessman to build a railroad from the central part of the country to the Atlantic coast and to develop banana production, massive numbers of descendants of African slaves from Jamaica migrated into the region. Although these migrants were not slaves, they lived in slave-like conditions under the watchful eye of Mr Minor C. Keith, who eventually founded the United Fruit Company; he inherited the contract from his uncle, Mr Henry Meiggs. It is said that almost 4,000 laborers died building the first twenty miles of rail – or, as the locals say, under every railroad tie there is a buried worker (Purcell 1993). The descendants of the Jamaican workers are a distinct ethic group in Costa Rica, one that has maintained its language and Afro-Caribbean culture (Madrigal 1989; Madrigal 2006; Madrigal et al. 2001; Purcell 1993).

When I, Lorena Madrigal, was completing my dissertation research among the descendants of the Jamaican workers, I was told one day by the nurse who was obtaining blood samples for me that we were coming upon the village where the *Culís* lived. No matter how much information I tried to get from her and other locals about who exactly these people were, I could not find out anything about their history. Many years passed, and I was able to go back to the field and try to solve the question of who the *Culís* were. When I arrived to the field with my team, which included a cultural anthropologist, we found a small community which wished to be studied: both the *Culís* themselves and their neighbors recognized them as ethnically distinct, but nobody else in Costa Rica knew about them. Indeed no anthropological study had been done on them. According to all of our informants, their ancestors had migrated from the Indian subcontinent, just as the ancestors of the large Indo-Guyanan, Trinidadian and Surinamese groups had done. In contrast with these groups, however, the Costa-Rican population lost its language and religious rituals. However, my colleague Flory Otárola wrote an ethnographic study on them, which details their distinct culture (Otárola-Durán 2007). In addition, we have discussed the marriage patterns of the population, which has maintained a staunch avoidance of consanguinity. Rather than marrying anyone with whom they are related, members of the group prefer to marry their neighbors, the descendants of the Jamaican workers (Madrigal et al. 2007). As a result, the community is fading as a separate and distinct group. They refer to themselves and are referred to by their neighbors by the term '*Culís*,' which is not a derogatory term in the region. We refer to them either in this manner or as Indo-Costa-Ricans.

For our genetic study of the Indo-Costa-Ricans (Castri et al. 2007), we looked both at maternally inherited markers (mitochondrial DNA or mtDNA) and at paternally inherited markers (the Y chromosome). We sampled each and every one of the group's families. For both types of markers we had to look for parental populations. As opposed to the Neolithic example, in which we only considered two parental groups (Basques and Middle-Easterners), here we had to consider four likely parental groups: Europeans, Amerindians, East Indians, and Africans. Our results surprised us: although for both mtDNA and Y chromosomal markers the *Culís* are of overwhelming East-Indian origin, the parental populations who contributed to the *Culí* maternal and paternal gene pools were different. Briefly, for the mitochondrial DNA the admixture estimates are 57 percent East-Indian, 32 percent African and 11 percent Amerindian. In contrast, for the Y chromosome the admixture estimates are 42 percent East-Indian, 37 percent African and 20 percent European. In other words, both paternal and maternal components indicate a predominance of East-Indian ancestry, but much more so for the females. What is fascinating is that, whereas the mitochondrial DNA shows evidence of an Amerindian component (11 percent), the Y-chromosomes do not. In contrast, whereas the Y-chromosomes show evidence of a European component (20 percent), the mtDNA does not.

The different maternal and paternal contributions to the Indo-Costa-Rican population can be understood in light of the history of gene flow in the entire Caribbean. It is well known that, in the early stages of the European invasion, the Europeans took 'as wives' Amerindian women, whereas the Amerindian males were summarily killed. In addition, it is well known that on the Caribbean plantations European women were rare and European males engaged in much gene flow with their African slaves. Most probably, both the Amerindian component in the mtDNA and the European component in the Y-chromosomal *Culís* gene pools arrived via marriage with the descendants of the African slaves, who themselves inherited European Y-chromosomal markers from the European slavers in Jamaica and Amerindian mtDNA markers from conquered Amerindian women. We have collected the entire genealogy of the Indo-Costa-Rican group, going back to the three original couples who first migrated to the region, and all marriages with non-*Culís* are marriages with people with English names, which is a strong indication that these spouses belong to the English-speaking neighboring group, descended from Jamaican workers (Madrigal et al. 2007). The absence of European mtDNA markers is explained through the absence of European women on the plantations, or through the impossibility for them to engage in gene flow with their slaves. The absence of any Amerindian Y-chromosomal markers is a loud reminder of the extinction of Amerindian males after the invasion of Europeans.

The history of the formation of the Indo-Costa-Rican gene pool is one which allows us to observe a very different effect of gene flow on the evolution of human populations from the ones we covered in the example of the formation of the European population. Whereas the Indo-Costa-Rican population is very small, the European population is very large. Whereas the parental contributions to the formation of the European gene pool involved both males and females, the parental contributions to the formation of the Indo-Costa-Rican group involved males and females of different populations.

GENETIC DRIFT

As you read in Chapter 2 of this volume, gene drift includes all the random factors which change gene frequencies in a population through time. Drift is particularly strong in small populations, and it eventually leads to the loss of variation. Genetic drift operates in three ways:

1 through the random sampling of gametes;
2 through the Founder's effect;
3 through the bottleneck effect.

We discuss these three ways briefly, and then we discuss examples of drift in human populations.

1 The random sampling of gametes: let us perform a genetic cross with a Punnet square, in which we cross two individuals who are heterozygote for blood type A – that is, both are AO and AO. What is the probability that they will produce a blood type O (OO) child? The probability is 25 percent. Let us assume that the same couple has another baby, for whom the probability of being OO remains the same. You can see that it is possible for such a couple to produce as many kids as they can, all of them of blood type O. In a single generation, a family lost the A allele, while the O allele became fixed. This happened only out of chance, due to random sampling of gametes. In the same manner, entire populations may loose alleles after a few generations.

2   The Founder's effect may act in one of two ways: either an individual leaves a very large genetic contribution to the next generation; or a small group of individuals starts a new population. In both of these cases, the genetic makeup of the population to which the extremely fertile person(s) contributed or the genetic makeup of the population which started from a few individuals will be different from that of the parental population.

3   The bottleneck effect occurs when a population is dramatically reduced in size and grows in size later, from the few descendants of the population. Most likely, the original and the descendant population will differ in their gene frequencies, and thus evolution has occurred.

We will illustrate genetic drift in human populations with two examples, which cover all its three forms. Instead of dividing our discussion by type of gene drift, we decided to divide it into two:

1   genetic drift which has lead to high frequencies of deleterious alleles;
2   genetic drift which has led to marked differences among groups that descend from African slaves in Central/South America and in an Atlantic archipelago.

1   Genetic drift which has lead to high frequencies of deleterious alleles

Do you know what Huntington's chorea, porphyria, and the Ellis van Creveld syndrome have in common? These diseases have high frequencies in circumscribed areas of the world despite the fact that they impair the fitness of the individuals who suffer from them, and seem to have achieved their high frequencies by genetic drift.

Huntington's chorea in Maracaibo, Venezuela   Huntington's chorea is a debilitating neurological condition of great social costs. It is usually expressed in middle age and leads to a slow neurological decline (including even an inability to eat) which ends in death. It was a Venezuelan researcher who first wondered why there were so many people affected by this condition in a circumscribed area of Venezuela, namely in Maracaibo. Negrette (1962) traced the genealogies of sufferers from the region, and he was able to show that all of them descended from a single woman. Simply put, the woman and her descendants had high fertility, and in a few generations, through Founder's effect, raised the frequency of the deleterious gene to its present high frequency. Currently there are at least 15,000 individuals who have been known to suffer from the disease and who descend from one single common ancestor (Project and Wexler 2004).

Variegate porphyria in South Africa   Those of you who are history buffs will remember porphyria as the disease which apparently afflicted King George III during the time of the American Revolution. The diagnosis of the king was undertaken by medical historians in the 1900s, on the basis of his symptoms of apparently 'losing his mind,' stomach problems, weakness, and bright red urine (Macalpine and Hunter 1969). More recently, hair was extracted from the remains of the king, and arsenic in high concentration was demonstrated to be in it. Cox and colleagues note that arsenic might have been given to the king as part of his therapy and that it could have contributed to his very severe symptoms (Cox et al. 2005).

There are at least seven mutations which may result in the disease porphyria, but all of them disrupt the normal 'construction' of the heme molecule, which carries the oxygen in the hemoglobin. The disease which is highly frequent in South Africa is variegate porphyria, which causes skin problems, lack of sensitivity in the fingers, and various neurological disorders, sometimes including severe mental retardation (Evans 1993; Hift et al. 1997). Most sufferers of the disease are heterozygotes, and those who are homozygote experience a more severe evolution of the disease. A detective-like work conducted by Dean (Dean 1953; Dean 1957; Dean 1963) showed that all sufferers of the disease descend from a specific marriage, namely between the Dutch Gerrit Janss and Ariaantje Adriaanse, one out of the eight female orphans who were sent as brides to Dutch settlers. We know that she arrived in 1688 and that the marriage occurred quickly. Because of the large fertility of this marriage and of those engaged in by their descendants, the gene that causes the disease became very frequent in the population.

The Ellis van Creveld syndrome in Pennsylvania   This disease, which produces a particular type of dwarfism, is characterized by cardiac malformation and a number of bone abnormalities, including polydactyly (extra digits). The syndrome has high frequencies among the Old Order Amish community of Lancaster County in Pennsylvania. All individuals who suffer from the disease have been traced back to a specific ancestral couple: Mr and Mrs King, who immigrated in 1744 and had no affected offspring. Apparently the recessive gene which causes the disease, became very frequent in the population because of Founder's effect, and eventually homozygote recessive individuals started to 'show up' in the gene pool (Volpe 1985).

2   Genetic drift which led to marked differences among groups that descend from African slaves in South/Central America and in an Atlantic island

In our discussion of gene flow, we mentioned the enforced migration of millions of people of African descent, who were brought to the American continent by European powers. Many of them ended up in a 'stop-over' island, close to the African coast and colonized by the Portuguese: Sao Tome. In South America many of the slaves were put to work on the plantations, just as their brothers and sisters were put to work in the Caribbean. Usually a European government or set of companies brought slaves from a specific region of Africa to the New World. When we look at the descendants of slaves from South America and in Sao Tome, we see that different communities are markedly different, genetically, not because they had ancestors from different areas of Africa but because of the process of genetic drift.

Rebellion and escape from slavers is not rare in slave societies – it never was. In South America runaway slaves succeeded in establishing viable small communities, frequently through intermarriage with Amerindians. The communities that ensued, originating from escaped slaves and Amerindians, were known as *Cimarrones* or 'Maroons.' In Brazil, it has been shown that there is remarkable heterogeneity among various populations which descend from African slaves. In some cases the diversity cannot be explained by geography; in other words, populations who are close geographically are remarkably different because they experienced a bottleneck: they remained genetically isolated, did not exchange genes, and differentiation was possible only through the action of genetic drift (Abe-Sandes et al. 2004; Bortolini et al. 1997a and b; Oliveira et al. 2002). In a similar fashion, the work of Michael Crawford (1983) among the Garifuna or 'Black Caribs' of Central America has demonstrated the enormous effect of gene drift in differentiating small groups which divide and colonize new areas.

Remarkably, we see the same process in the descendants of runaway slaves in Sao Tome, the Atlantic island close to Africa, which functioned as a 'stop-over' for Portuguese slavers on their way to the New World. According to Coelho and collaborators (2008), an ethnic group in this island, the so-called *Angolares*, had always claimed that it descended from a group of slaves who survived a shipwreck. Although there is no historical documentation of this story, the genetic data tend to confirm it: the *Angolares* are genetically distinct from their neighbors, which indicates that they descend from a small group of founders and became genetically distinct through a combination of random sampling of gametes and of the Founder's and the bottleneck effects. More remarkable still is the fact that the genetic difference between this group and its neighbors is particularly marked for the Y-chromosome, but not for the mtDNA. Coelho and colleagues suggest that the likely founders of the group were a patrilineal family which was homogeneous in its Y-chromosomes, but whose women came from other groups. Moreover, there are historical accounts of this group raiding neighbors for new wives – a situation which suggests that the group's mtDNA had a more heterogeneous origin than its Y-chromosomes, descended as these were from a few male founders. We should note that the differences between the *Angolares* and their neighbors cannot be explained in terms of natural selection, since they live in such close proximity in the same environment. Genetic drift is the only likely force that led to the differentiation of these groups.

In conclusion, genetic drift, the evolutionary force which includes purely random processes in the evolution of populations, has affected humans, and significantly so in some groups. It is easier to understand the action of genetic drift when we are discussing gene frequency differences between populations such as those who descend from runaway slaves in South America. But it is not so easy when we are discussing high frequencies of deleterious genes in a population such as that of Maracaibo, Venezuela. The best way in which we can explain this discrepancy is by using the analogy proposed by Steven J. Gould, between natural selection and a 'watch dog' (Gould 1989). Natural selection (the watch dog) can only 'see' (detect in the gene pool) that which is expressed phenotypically. If, for one or two generations, recessive genes rise in frequency because they are mostly in heterozygotes, natural selection cannot remove the genes because it (the 'watchdog') does not 'see' them. When those heterozygotes produce homozygote children, the 'watchdog' will probably remove them (if they promote a fatal disease), or at least will not allow them to be very fertile. However, by that time, the deleterious gene will be frequent. Thus, by genetic drift, we have populations with high frequencies of deleterious genes.

CONCLUSION

It is not uncommon to see reports in the popular press to the effect that 'humans are beyond evolution.' This is really a misconception. In this chapter we could have gone on and on, adducing more examples of evolution occurring before our eyes, even in populations such as those of the USA. Indeed some authors have actually proposed that there has been an acceleration in the rate of human adaptive evolution in recent times (Hawks et al. 2007).

It is certainly tempting to make predictions about what paths human evolution may take in the future. If global travel continues to increase and reproductive barriers among ethnic groups fall, few human populations will remain isolated, so that genetic drift is unlikely to be as important as it was in the past. Gene flow, on the contrary, is likely to exert a stronger unifying force than it did before. Natural selection is by no means likely to decrease, whether in the shape of major climatic changes affecting the entire world, or through enormous population pressure, as the human species continues to increase in size, through new pathogens, or through culturally induced changes such as sedentary lifestyles lived in the presence of nutrient-rich diets. As we are writing this chapter, we are at the beginning of what appears to be a major pandemic of an entirely new virus, which incorporates viral material from human, swine, and bird viruses. Clearly new viruses originate and evolve, and they have a great potential for affecting human evolution.

Humans, like any other living species, are and will continue to evolve. Whether such evolution occurs at the molecular and not at the phenotypic level, it is evolution nonetheless. Only extinct species do not evolve.

REFERENCES

Abbo, S, Gopher, A., Peleg, Z., Saranga, Y., Fahima, T., Salamini, F., and Lev-Yadun, S. (2006) The Ripples of 'the Big (Agricultural) Bang': The Spread of Early Wheat Cultivation. *Genome* 49: 861–863.

Abe-Sandes, K., Silva, W. A., and Zago, M. A. (2004) Heterogeneity of the Y Chromosome in Afro-Brazilian Populations. *Human Biology* 76: 77–86.

Armelagos, G. J., and Harper, K. N. (2005a) Genomics at the Origins of Agriculture, Part One. *Evolutionary Anthropology* 14: 68–77.

Armelagos, G. J., and Harper, K. N. (2005b) Genomics at the Origins of Agriculture, Part Two. *Evolutionary Anthropology* 14: 109–121.

Balaresque, P. L., Ballereau, S. J., and Jobling, M. A. (2007) Challenges in Human Genetic Diversity: Demographic History and Adaptation. *Human Molecular Genetics* 16 (Review Issue 2): R134–R139.

Beja-Pereira, A., Luikart G., England, P., Bradley, D., Jann, O., Bertorelle, G., Chamberlain, A., Nunes, T., Metodiev, S., Ferrand, N., and Erhardt, G. (2003) Gene-Culture Coevolution between Cattle Milk Protein Genes and Human Lactase Genes. *Nature Genetics* 35: 311–313.

Belle, E. M. S., Landry, P. A., and Barbujani, G. (2006) Origins and Evolution of the Europeans' Genome: Evidence from Multiple Microsatellite Loci. *Proceedings of the Royal Society, B – Biological Sciences* 273: 1595–1602.

Bersaglieri, T., Sabeti, P., Patterson, N., Vanderploeg, T., Schaffner, S., Drake, J., Rhodes, M., Reich, D., and Hirschhorn, J. (2004) Genetic Signatures of Strong Recent Positive Selection at the Lactase Gene. *American Journal of Human Genetics* 74: 1111–1120.

Bortolini, M. C., Salzano, F., Zago, M. A., DaSilva, W., and Weimer, T. (1997a) Genetic Variability in Two Brazilian Ethnic Groups: A Comparison of Mitochondrial and Protein Data. *American Journal of Physical Anthropology* 103: 147–156.

Bortolini, M. C., Zago, M. A., Salzano, F., SilvaJunior, W., Bonatto, S., DaSilva, M., and Weimer, T. (1997b) Evolutionary and Anthropological Implications of Mitochondrial DNA Variation in African Brazilian Populations. *Human Biology* 69: 141–159.

Castri, L., Otarola, F., Blell, M., Ruiz, E., Barrantes, R., Luiselli, D., Pettener, D., and Madrigal, L. (2007) Indentured Migration and Differential Gender Gene Flow: The Origin and Evolution of the East-Indian Community of Limon, Costa Rica. *American Journal of Physical Anthropology* 134: 175–189.

Cavalli-Sforza, L. L., and Piazza, A. (1993) Human Genomic Diversity in Europe: A Summary of Recent Research. *European Journal of Human Genetics* 1: 3–18.

Cavalli-Sforza, L. L., Menozzi, P., and Piazza, A. (1993) Demic Expansions and Human Evolution. *Science* 259: 639–646.

Coelho, M., Coia, C., Luiselli, D., Useli, A., Hagemeijer, T., Amorim, A., Destro-Bisol, G., and Rocha, J. (2008) Human Microevolution and the Atlantic Slave Trade: A Case Study from Sao Tome. *Current Anthropology* 49: 134–143.

Cox, T. M., Jack, N., Lofthouse, S., Watling, J., Haines, J., and Warren, M. (2005) King George III and Porphyria: An Elemental Hypothesis and Investigation. *The Lancet* 366: 332–335.

Crawford, M. H. (1983) The Anthropological Genetics of the Black Caribs (Garifuna) of Central America and the Caribbean. *Yearbook of Physical Anthropology* 26: 161–192.

Dean, G. (1953) Porphyria. *British Medical Journal* 2 (4849): 1291–1294.

Dean, G. (1957) Pursuit of a Disease. *Scientific American* 196: 133–142.

Dean, G. (1963) The Porphyrias: *A Story of Inheritance and Environment.* Philadelphia: J. B. Lippincott Company.

Duncan, C. J., and Scott, S. (2005) What Caused the Black Death? *Postgraduate Medical Journal* 81: 315–320.

Enattah, N. S., Jensen, T., Nielsen, M., Lewinski, R., Kuokkanen, M., Rasinpera, H., El-Shanti, H., Seo, J., Alifrangis, M., and Khalil, I. (2008) Independent Introduction of Two Lactase-Persistence Alleles into Human Populations Reflects Different History of Adaptation to Milk Culture. *American Journal of Human Genetics* 82: 57–72.

Evans, D. A. P. (1993) *Genetic Factors in Drug Therapy.* Cambridge: Cambridge University Press.

Faure, E., and Royer-Carenzi, M. (2008) Is the European Spatial Distribution of the HIV-1-Resistant CCR5-Delta 32 Allele Formed by a Breakdown of the Pathocenosis Due to the Historical Roman Expansion? *Infection Genetics and Evolution* 8: 864–874.

Gould, S. J. (1989) Through a Lens, Darkly… *Natural History* 9: 16–24.

Hawks, J., Wang, E., Cochran, G., Harpending, H., and Moyzis, R. (2007) Recent Acceleration of Human Adaptive Evoluton. *Proceedings of the National Academy of Sciences, USA* 104: 20753–20758.

Hedrick, P. W., and Verrelli, B. C. (2006) Ground Truth for Selection on CCR5-Delta 32. *Trends in Genetics* 22: 293–296.

Hift, R. J., Meissner, P., Corrigall, A., Ziman, M., Petersen L., Meissner, D., Davidson, B., Sutherland, J., Dailey, H., and Kirsch, R. (1997) Variegate Porphyria in South Africa, 1688–1996: New Developments in an Old Disease. *South African Medical Journal* 87: 722–731.

Hoff, C., Thorneycroft, I., Wilson, F., and Williams-Murphy, M. (2001) Protection Afforded by Sickle-Cell Trait (Hb AS): What Happens When Malarial Selection Pressures Are Alleviated? *Human Biology* 73: 583–586.

Jakobsson, M., Scholz, S. W., Scheet, P., Gibbs, J. R., VanLiere, J. M., Fung, H. C., Szpiech, Z. A., Degnan, J. H., Wang, K., Guerreiro, R., Bras, J. M., Schymick, J. C., Hernandez, D. G., Traynor, B. J., Simon-Sanchez, J., Matarin, M., Britton, A., van de Leemput, J., Rafferty, I., Bucan, M., Cann, H. M., Hardy, J. A., Rosenberg, N. A., and Singleton, A. B. (2008) Genotype, Haplotype and Copy-Number Variation in Worldwide Human Populations. *Nature* 451: 998–1003.

Lewontin, R. (1976) Adaptation. *Scientific American* 239 (3): 212–230.

Macalpine, I., and Hunter, R. (1969) Porphyria and King George III. *Scientific American* 221: 38–46.

Madrigal, L. (1989) Hemoglobin Genotype, Fertility and the Malaria Hypothesis. *Human Biology* 61: 311–325.

Madrigal, L. (2006) *Human Biology of Afro-Caribbean Populations.* Cambridge: Cambridge University Press.

Madrigal, L., and Barbujani, G. (2006) Partitioning of Genetic Variation in Human Populations and the Concept of Race. In M. Crawford (ed.), *Anthropological Genetics. Theory, Methods and Applications* (pp. 19–37). Cambridge: Cambridge University Press.

Madrigal, L., Ware, B., Hagen, E., Blell, M., and Otarola, F. (2007) The East Indian Diaspora in Costa Rica: Inbreeding Avoidance, Marriage Patterns, and Cultural Survival. *American Anthropologist* 109: 330–337.

Madrigal, L., Ware, B., Miller, E., Saenz, G., Chavez, M., and Dykes, D. (2001) Ethnicity, Gene Flow, and Population Subdivision in Limon, Costa Rica. *American Journal of Physical Anthropology* 14: 99–108.

Mielke, J. H., Konigsberg, L. W., and Relethford, J. H. (2006) *Human Biological Variation.* Oxford: Oxford University Press.

Negrette, A. (1962) *Corea de Huntington.* Maracaibo: Centro de investigacion Clinica, Facultad de Medicina, Universidad del Zulia.

Novembre, J., Galvani, A. P., and Slatkin, M. (2005) The Geographic Spread of the CCR5 Delta32 HIV-Resistance Allele. *PLoS Biology* 3: e339.

Oliveira, S. F., Pedrosa, M., Sousa, S., Mingroni-Netto, R., Abe-Sandes, K., Ferrari, I., Barbosa, A., Auricchio, M., and Klautau-Guimaraes, M. (2002) Heterogeneous Distribution of HbS and HbC Alleles in Afro-Derived Brazilian Populations. *International Journal of Human Genetics* 2: 153–160.

Otárola-Durán, F. (2007) Un Gajo de Limón: Los coolíes un grupo olvidado en la construcción de la Historia Nacional Costarricense. San Jose, Costa Rica: Universidad de Costa Rica.

Project, The US–Venezuela Collaborative Research, and Wexler, N. S. (2004) Venezuelan Kindreds Reveal that Genetic and Environmental Factors Modulate Huntington's Disease Age of Onset. *Proceedings of the National Academy of Sciences, USA* 101: 3498–3503.

Purcell, T. W. (1993) *Banana Fallout. Class, Color and Culture among West Indians in Costa Rica.* Los Angeles: University of California.

Sabeti, P. C., Walsh, E., Schaffner, S., Varilly, P., Fry, B., Hutcheson, H., Cullen, M., Mikkelsen, T., Roy, J., Patterson, N., Cooper, R., Reich, D., Altshuler, D., O'Brien, S., and Lander, E. S. (2005) The Case for Selection at CCR5-Delta 32. *PLoS Biology* 3: 1963–1969.

Tishkoff, S. A., Ibrahim, M., Omar, S. A., Lema, G., Nyambo, T. B., Ghori, J., Bumpstead, S., Pritchard, J. K., Wray, G. A., and Deloukas, P. (2006) Convergent Adaptation of Human Lactase Persistence in Africa and Europe. *Nature Genetics* 39: 31–40.

Turney, C. S. M., and Brown, H. (2007) Catastrophic Early Holocene Sea Level Rise, Human Migration and the Neolithic Transition in Europe. *Quarternary Science Reviews* 26: 2036–2041.

Twiss, K. C. (2007) The Neolithic of the Southern Levant. *Evolutionary Anthropology* 16: 24–35.

Volpe, E. P. (1985) *Understanding Evolution.* Dubuque: William C. Brown Publishers.

Weatherall, D. J. (2008) Genetic Variation and Susceptibility to Infection: The Red Cell and Malaria. *British Journal of Haematology* 141: 276–286.

Zeder, M. A. (2008) Domestication and Early Agriculture in the Mediterranean Basin: Origins, Diffusion, And Impact. *Proceedings of the National Academy of Sciences, USA* 105: 11597–11604.

Primates Defined

CHAPTER **13**

W. Scott McGraw

Unguiculate, claviculate placental mammals, with orbits encircled by bone; three kinds of teeth, at least one time of life; brain always with a posterior lobe and calcarine fissure; the innermost digit of at least one pair of extremities opposable; hallux with a flat nail or none; a well-developed caecum; penis pendulous; testes scrotal; always two pectoral mammae.

(Mivart 1873)

Although probably more intensely studied than any other mammalian order, the classification and nomenclature of the Primate has been, and to some extent still is, a matter for adverse comment, for strong differences of opinion, and in some respects even for despair.

(Hill 1953: 20)

In fact, it is not easy to give a clear-cut definition of the order as a whole ... and there is no single distinguishing feature which characterizes them all ... Further, while many other mammalian orders can be defined by conspicuous specializations of a positive kind which readily mark them off from one another, the Primates ... are to be mainly distinguished from other orders by a negative feature – their lack of specialization.

(Clark 1959: 42)

DEFINING ISSUES

Primates are among the most well known animals; however, compiling a list of their distinctive characters is challenging. The main obstacle is the fact that lemurs, lorises, tarsiers, monkeys and apes possess a modest number of specialized features, and the ones they have are often shared by other mammals. Most mammal groups have acquired sufficient unique modifications to make distinguishing one group from another straightforward. This is not the case with primates; viewed from a comparative mammalian perspective, humans and their relatives display few uniquely defining traits. However, while individual diagnostic traits are relatively few, specialized *combinations* of features readily distinguish primates from other mammals. Among the most important *feature complexes* are those pertaining to the visual–neural system, to the appendicular skeleton, and to life history; and it is the interaction of features within these complexes that sets primates apart from other mammalian groups (Ross and Martin 2007). In addition, primates display several dramatic trends in anatomy, physiology, and behavior which are less pronounced or absent in other mammalian groups. Understanding the direction, magnitude, and significance of these trends is vital to defining primates. This chapter reviews the most important characters, character complexes, and trends that define members of the primate order and provides some information on their adaptive context.

Modern and Archaic Primates

The class Mammalia contains approximately 5,400 living species, arranged into twenty-nine orders (Nowak 1991). Linnaeus was the initial architect of this ordering, and the first order he created – the Primates (meaning 'of the first rank') – began with four genera: *Homo* (containing humans, plus a form known as 'troglodytes'), *Simia* (containing monkeys and tarsiers), *Lemur* (containing lemurs and lorises) and *Vespertilio* (containing bats).[1] Bats have since been relegated to their own order – Chiroptera; however, the basic gradistic scheme recognized by Linnaeus – lemur–monkey–ape – remains. Linnaeus's original criteria for defining primates consisted of two characters: *Dentes primores superiors iv paralleli; mamammae pectorals ii* – that is, 'upper front teeth four in number, parallel; two pectoral mammary glands.' The suite of features used to distinguish primates from other mammals has grown in the last 250 years; however, the group bracketed by Linnaeus's definition has remained relatively stable throughout this time (Gregory 1910; Hill 1953).

The fossil record of primate evolution extends to at least 65 mya. Many authorities contend that the best candidate for the ancestor of modern primates lies within a group of early mammals known as 'plesiadapiforms.' The plesiadapiforms were a diverse and successful radiation that flourished throughout the Paleocene and early Eocene epochs. They are considered suitable candidates for being the ancestral primates, because their tooth cusp morphology was more similar to that of modern primates than the cusp morphology of other Paleocene mammals. But, although their dental anatomy makes them good potential ancestors, plesiadapiforms lack many features found in subsequent 'true primates.' For this reason most authorities do not place plesiadapiforms within the order Primates but refer to them as 'archaic' primates, in recognition of their role as precursors to true primates. The mammals who meet the minimum requirements for primate status are called 'euprimates,' or 'primates of modern aspect' in Simons's original phrase, to emphasize their possession of all features found in modern primates (Simons 1972). Several spectacular finds have fueled debate about the relationship between archaic primates and euprimates and which ones constitute the first members of the primate order. The stakes are high, because they bear directly on the priority given to features that bracket the order, as well as on the line where we draw the primate/non-primate boundary. Some authorities maintain that, because plesiadapiforms share derived features with modern primates, they should be included within the order (Bloch et al. 2007; Silcox 2007; Silcox et al. 2007). Others contend that, because these basal forms did not possess all features found in the modern forms (euprimates), they cannot be considered 'true' primates (Tavare et al. 2002; Kirk et al. 2003; Soligo and Martin 2006). Part of the problem derives from trying to apply a definition of modern primates to the fossil record, a point which Osman Hill made explicit nearly sixty years ago: "The level at which the distinguishing line is drawn between Primates and non-Primates depends on what definition is given to that order … the inclusion of such a fossil family as the Plesiadapidae involves the discarding of some classic Primate diagnostic features" (Hill 1953: 5). This chapter attempts to resolve none of these issues; it proceeds from the position that while the plesiadapiforms represent the most likely group from which modern primates arose, the definition of primates pertains to monophyletic euprimates and their descendants. Readers interested in a discussion of plesiadapiforms and primate origins should consult the Gunnell and Silcox's chapter in this volume.

PRIMITIVE EUTHERIAN MAMMALS: BASELINE FOR CHARACTERS, COMPLEXES, AND TRENDS

Descriptions of primates often begin with statements such as the following: primates are generalized mammals that have retained a primitive body plan with comparatively few modifications. Primates are obviously evolved animals. However, by and large, modern primates preserve a primitive anatomical configuration with many ancestral features and are not as specialized as other groups – for instance whales, ungulates, or bats. How do we know this? The answer comes from appreciating the anatomical diversity of living (extant) mammals and from comparing this diversity with that found in the extinct animals from which the modern forms evolved. The fossil record provides the referential baseline for highlighting which descendants have become most specialized and which ones are anatomically more conservative.

Mammals with placentas are known as 'eutherian mammals.' Eutherian mammals comprise most of the class Mammalia and are distinct from two other major mammalian groups: those that lay eggs – the monotremes (Prototheria) and those with pouches, the marsupials (Metatheria). Recent excavations in China have yielded several exquisitely preserved fossils that provide direct evidence of the structure of early mammals, including of the oldest and most primitive eutherians (Qiang et al. 1999; Ji et al. 2002). The discoveries reveal that early eutherians were tiny, agile, quadrupedal animals whose diets consisted largely of insects. These diminutive, shrew-sized animals had long tails, prognathic snouts, small brains, five digits on their hands and feet, and claws on the tips of their digits. Analyses of their limb structure suggest that these precursors of modern mammals were well adapted to climbing and could move with ease amid small branches of arboreal habitats.

Most descendants of this (or of some similarly configured) early mammal became specialized so as to move in environments other than trees. Primates did not. Primates are, and always have been, an arboreal radiation, and many features that distinguish them from other mammalian groups are adaptations for life in the canopy. Making a living in the trees can be difficult and dangerous, so selection should favor traits that decrease the risk of falling and increase the chances of finding food while avoiding predators. Although primates have solved the problems of moving in arboreal habitats in a variety of ways, a core of generalized features related to limb mobility and overall agility – features inherited from the primitive ancestor – is found in all primates and accounts for some of the most striking differences from other mammals, it should be emphasized that, while these limb adaptations facilitate an arboreal existence, the evolution of an arboreal lifestyle need not require them. There is a number of highly successful arboreal mammals, including squirrels and possums, who lack many of these features and are, obviously, not primates. In other words, arboreality alone cannot explain the evolution of primate features (Jones 1916; Cartmill 1972; Sussman 1991). Nevertheless, it is almost certainly the case that many characteristics of primates are associated in some fashion with the adaptive landscape of trees.

THE PRIMATE BAUPLAN

Postcranial features

Hands and feet Primitive eutherian mammals had five digits on their hands and feet, and primates retain five digits on their cheiridia.[2] Although pendactyly is an ancient mammalian feature retained in a number of extant mammal groups, primate hands and feet are distinguished by a major difference: an enhanced ability to grasp. This grasping or prehensile ability is brought about through a combination of features. First, the fingers and toes (or rays) of primates are characterized by increased mobility and by the ability to act independently of one another. Second, primate rays tend to be longer in relation to the rest of the hand and foot respectively; and this increased length, combined with an enhanced ability to flex or bend the fingers, promotes effective grasping. Third, the digits of most mammals with five digits tend to be oriented in a single plane. In primates, the first digits (toes and fingers) on the hand and feet are not in the same plane with the others. Instead, the fleshy surfaces at the tip of the hallux (big toe) and pollex (thumb) lie, to varying degrees, at right angles to the remaining digits. Because the hallux and the pollex are divergent and lie in different planes, they can more easily be brought into contact with, or be opposed to, the rest of the foot or hand. Since primates use their hands for so many activities, an opposable thumb combined with comparatively long and independently moving fingers is one of the most significant primate characteristics. For example, unlike most mammals, who bring their mouth to their food, primates tend to use their hands to bring food to their mouth (Napier 1993). Grasping feet with opposable big toes are useful for moving through the trees and are found in all primates except one: humans.[3] "Acquirement of prehensility of the hands and feet and of 'opposability' of the thumb and big toe are among the most striking and important evolutionary trends of the primates" (Napier and Napier 1967: 10).

Nails instead of claws The tips (apices) of the fingers and toes in primates differ in several important ways from those of other living mammals and from those of the eutherian ancestors. Early mammals had claws on their digits, but primates have replaced the claws with flattened nails.[4] Also, the apices of primate fingers and toes are characterized by soft-tissue expansions containing enriched nerve endings and capillary beds, which result in a widening of the cheiridial tip. These expanded apical tufts, in combination with the replacement of claws with nails, provide primates with an enhanced sense of touch and with the ability to grasp branches by using a friction grip rather than one involving clawed contact/penetration. The appearance of nails in the fossil record is central to indentifying the first primates; however, the adaptive significance of claw loss continues to be debated (Soligo and Muller 1999).

Forearm mobility The forearm is that portion of the forelimb which extends between the elbow and the wrist. In primitive eutherians, the two bones of the forearm – the radius and ulna – were unfused. These bones have become fused or greatly reduced in a number of mammalian groups, but in primates they remain unfused. Radio-ulnar fusion significantly limits the range of motion below the elbow; by retaining unfused forelimb bones, primates can easily rotate their forearms and hands toward the body (a process known as pronation or medial rotation) and away from the body (supination or lateral rotation). The capacity for flexible rotatory movement of the hands is important for grasping branches, for collecting, inspecting, and opening different foods, and for grooming conspecifics. In addition, the two bones of the leg (the portion of the hindlimb between knee and ankle) known as the tibia and fibula remain unfused in all living primates except the tarsier (*Tarsius*). In other mammals the bones are frequently fused, or the fibula is reduced.

Clavicle The clavicle or collar bone is an S-shaped bone that runs between the manubrium (top of the breast bone) and the scapula (shoulder blade), and to which several muscles that move the arm attach. The clavicle acts as a strut that helps to stabilize the shoulder area while it allows for a great range of motion. A clavicle was present in the primitive mammalian ancestor, but this bone has been lost in many descendant groups. Primates have retained a clavicle, and by doing so they gain great mobility at the shoulder, as well as in the entire forelimb. A high degree of forelimb flexibility is important to animals who move in environments with discontinuous supports like trees and who require enhanced manipulative abilities for obtaining food. The significance of clavicles (and claws) was so profound as to prompt Mivart (1873) to open his famous definition of primates with these features (see introductory quotation).

Quadrupedal idiosyncrasies Many mammals move on the ground or in the trees by placing weight on their four limbs, in a locomotor mode known as 'quadrupedalism.' Most primates move quadrupedally; however, the quadrupedal locomotion of primates is different from that of virtually all other mammalian quadrupeds in at least three ways. First, primates practice an uncommon kind of gait (which is the order or sequence in which the limbs contact the substrate). During walking they employ a diagonal-sequence gait, while the vast majority of non-primates use a lateral-sequence gait. Second, primates tend to protract or extend their arms more when the forelimbs contact the substrate. Finally, primates experience lower substrate reaction forces in the forelimbs than they do in their hindlimbs when they land. This combination of quadrupedal peculiarities is likely to be the product of the successful invasion of the small branch niche and was probably a key innovation in the radiation of primates (Schmitt and Lemelin 2002).

Truncal erectness Primates have evolved an array of locomotor adaptations that include quadrupedalism, forelimb suspension, knuckle-walking, vertical clinging and leaping, and bipedality. Despite this diversity in locomotor strategies, primates are all characterized by a common postural element: a tendency for the trunk to be oriented more upright, so that the long axis of the vertebral column tends more toward being perpendicular to the ground. In locomotor modes such as brachiation, vertical clinging and leaping, and bipedalism, the trunk is maintained in an erect or semi-erect position; but even primates that move quadrupedally usually adopt upright postures when they feed, rest, or socialize. The tendency for primates to adopt upright postures required the modification of several skeletal regions; however, one obvious benefit is that the upright posture liberated the hands from a purely supportive role to one involving more explorative and manipulative activities.

Features of the skull

Decreased reliance on olfaction In most mammalian groups, the sense of smell is the principal mechanism for obtaining information related to feeding, mating, predator avoidance and communication. Primates still are 'smelling animals'; however, compared to other mammals, they have decreased their reliance on olfaction in favor of an increased visual acuity. Animals with a highly developed sense of smell are characterized by features such as a prognathic face and an enlargement of those neural regions – the olfactory bulbs – which are responsible for processing chemical signals. Increased facial prognathism can be achieved through the forward projection of bones in the nasal region; expansion of the nasal cavity provides more surface area for nasal turbinates. Turbinates provide the platform for the tissues and neural cells (epithelium) involved in capturing chemical signals: the more surface area for turbinates, the better the ability to smell. The progressive shortening of the snout in primates almost certainly reflects a relaxed emphasis on the sense of smell. In addition to reducing the size of structures which capture smells, primates have reduced that part of the neural circuitry which transmits to the brain chemical signals from the olfactory cells in the nasal cavity. These switching stations for smell are known as olfactory bulbs, and there is a strong correlation across primates between the size of olfactory bulbs and their reliance on olfactory communication. Prosimians, particularly nocturnal forms who communicate through various scent glands, have relatively large olfactory bulbs, while monkeys, apes, and humans have rather diminuitive bulbs.

Orbital frontation and convergence The eyeballs sit within bony structures known as orbits. The orbits of primitive mammals, and those of many non-primate mammals today, are positioned on the sides of the skull; this results in expansive lateral visual fields – that is, in an enhanced peripheral vision. In primates, the orbits and their contents have undergone two significant changes: they have migrated toward the front of the skull, a process known as orbital convergence; and the margins have become more vertically oriented, a process known as orbital frontation (Noble et al. 2000). The forward and the vertical shifts in eye-socket orientation bring the visual fields from the sides of the skull forward, so that the fields overlap. Through this action both eyes are able to focus on the same object or area, a feature known as binocular vision. This results in 'stereopsis' – that is, the ability to see in three dimensions. Primates have the greatest orbital convergence and the largest binocular visual fields of all mammals (Heesy 2004, 2005). The ability to see in three dimensions and to judge distances is particularly important for animals who make their living within the structurally discontinuous environments of trees. Other mammals such as carnivores and bats have highly convergent orbits, but the combination of high orbital convergence, greatly enlarged brains, and a modified visual system is only seen in primates (Ross and Martin 2007).

Postorbital bars In many mammals, the bony socket housing the eyeball does not form a complete ring – that is, the lateral aspect of the orbital margin remains open.

A number of mammalian groups – including primates – have evolved a bar of bone on the orbit's lateral aspect so that the eyeball is surrounded by a complete ring. What purpose does this additional bar serve? As we have seen, the reorientation (frontation and convergence) of the orbits facilitates binocular vision, a trait that should have adaptive value for animals living in trees and requiring acute depth perception. A progressive shifting of the orbits from the sides to the front of the skull changes the way in which the chewing muscles act on the orbits when they are active. Recent comparative analyses suggest that the forward migration of the orbits makes them susceptible to deformation when a powerful chewing muscle (known as the *temporalis*) is used. These studies suggest that the postorbital bar functions as a strut to reinforce or stiffen the orbital cavity, preventing the orbital margin from being deformed. In other words, the post-orbital bar may prevent the disruption of normal visual functions in mammals with highly convergent orbits. Postorbital bars are found in a number of mammalian groups; however, because this is a derived feature of Euprimates (relative to archaic primates), an animal cannot be considered to be a primate if it lacks a postorbital bar.

Petrosal bulla   The middle ear of mammals contains three bones: the incus, the malleus and the stapes. These bones are housed in a bubble-like outgrowth of bone known as an 'auditory bulla,' which protects the base of the inner and middle ear. In most mammals, the auditory bulla is formed from the tympanic bone; however, in primates, it is derived from the petrous (petrosal) part of the temporal bone. A petrosal bulla is considered to be the only feature of the basicranium which is unique to primates (Rasmussen 2002), and its recognition in the fossil record has figured prominently in the classification of euprimates.

Dentition   Primate teeth are characterized by a combination of trends generally not found in other mammals. Most mammals have one or two types of teeth. Primate teeth are functionally differentiated into four types, known as incisors, canines, premolars, and molars. While most primates have at least one tooth of each *type*, primates have reduced the total *number* of teeth in their mouth – a process known as dental reduction. The primitive mammalian dental formula is 3.1.4.3, which means that each quadrant of the mouth contained three incisors, one canine, four premolars and three molars. Living primates have lost at least one incisor and one premolar in each of the four mouth quadrants. While the diversity of dental formulae yields a range of total tooth numbers, all primates have fewer teeth than their mammalian ancestor and generally fewer teeth than most non-primate mammals. Finally, primate teeth tend to be less specialized than those of other mammals. Primates are omnivores, being capable of eating a variety of food items which include fruit pulp, leaves, seeds, nuts, meat, insects, bark, and tree exudate. Primates have evolved adaptations to help facilitate the processing of specific food types, but no primate has evolved teeth so specialized as to be capable of processing a single food type only. On the contrary: primate teeth are comparatively generalized and designed for processing a diversity of foods.

Brain expansion   One of the most significant features distinguishing primates from other mammals is brain size: primates have very large brains for their body size. The average primate brain is approximately 2.3 times larger than that of non-primate mammals of similar body size. The portion of the brain which has expanded most is the outermost layer known as 'neocortex' (the Latin for 'new bark' or 'new shell'), and it is this region that is responsible for higher cognitive functions such as the coordination of sensory perception with motor commands, or spatial reasoning. All mammals possess a neocortex, but that of primates is both enlarged and characterized by many convolutions, wrinkles, and fissures, which provide additional surface areas. The neocortex of humans, for example, comprises nearly 80 percent of the total brain volume. Since the development and maintenance of brain tissue is metabolically costly (the brains of non-human primates consume approximately 8–9 percent of the total energy budget, while the human brain, even at rest, consumes 20–25 percent of that budget), the tremendous expansion in brain (neocortex) size must have provided a significant adaptive advantage for primates.

In addition to this great neocortical expansion, the primate brain is also characterized by other changes. Compared to other mammals, primates have decreased their reliance on smell and have reduced the size of those neural regions which process olfactory signals. As primates became more reliant on vision, those regions of the brain responsible for transmitting and interpreting visual signals and for integrating them with motor commands expanded and became more sophisticated. The regions in question are the primary visual cortex and the lateral geniculate nucleus. Recent comparative analyses have demonstrated a strong association between the size of these brain structures and the degree of binocularity or stereopsis across primates. This evidence suggests that the increase in brain size among primates is strongly associated with an enhanced visual specialization (Barton 2004; Ross and Martin 2007). In addition, primates are the only eutherian mammals capable of trichromatic vision (Bowmaker 1998; Leonhardt et al. 2008).

Life history and reproduction

Prolongation of prenatal and postnatal life Primates are distinguished from other mammals by a combination of trends related to reproduction and life history. First, their gestation period tends to be longer than that of other mammals of equivalent body size, and their fetal nourishment is more efficient. Many mammals give birth to multiple offspring, a practice not found in the majority of primates. Primates have reduced the number of offspring they produce, while increasing the amount of care given to each as an individual. This resulted in decreased levels of infant mortality among primates. Compared to most mammals, primates are born developmentally advanced, precocious, or 'precocial.' Nevertheless, they are completely dependent on parental (usually maternal) care for long periods of time. The extended period of infant dependence helps to establish strong bonds between mother and infant, and it is during this period that young primates acquire much of the knowledge they will need in order to survive. After infancy, primates typically are characterized by going through long periods of growth during the juvenile period. The length of this period is strongly associated with species longevity: those primates who live longer take longer to reach adulthood. The length of the adult period is also comparatively long in primates. The combination of extended infant, juvenile, and adult periods means that primates tend to live longer lives than other mammals of equivalent body size. For example, the average lifespan for a five-kilogram dog is twelve years, while that of a similarly sized primate is upwards to twenty-five years. Primates with comparatively short life spans tend to reach adulthood sooner. Large primates tend to reach maturity later and they live longer than smaller primates. Comparative analyses have revealed associations between the lengths of the pre-natal and post-natal periods and the patterns of brain growth (Leigh 2004).

Development of complex social systems   Like many other organisms, primates live in groups. What distinguishes group living among primates is the tendency to form relationships with individual group members. A large percentage of the daily, monthly, and lifetime activity budget of most primates is devoted to learning and cultivating relationships with other group members. One of the most fascinating aspects of primate sociality is the diversity of ways primates have ordered the rules governing individual relationships into different systems. Primates can be found living in:

1   single-male/multi-female groups
2   single-female/multi-male groups
3   multi-male/multi-female groups
4   monogamous pairs
5   bachelor troops
6   fission/fusion communities

– and so on. Individual relationships packaged into a variety of complex social systems are hallmarks of primate society.

Behavioral flexibility   Primates are characterized by big brains and high levels of intelligence. The high intelligence of primates is manifest in many ways: primates solve complex ecological problems, they readily distinguish relatives from non-relatives, they devise mechanisms for deception, they show capacities for symbolic thought (a prerequisite for language), they have a concept of self, they develop friendships, they make and use tool uses, and so on. Much of a primate's knowledge base, like that of other mammals, is hard wired or inherited genetically. What distinguishes primates from many other mammals is the level of information obtained through learning: many basic survival skills are acquired through active teaching from an infant's mother and through observation of other group members. The fact that so much critical information is *not* innate underscores the importance on the mother–infant bond for transmitting important social and ecological skills. One of the most intriguing developments in this arena concerns the extent to which learned behaviors vary in space and time. A large body of research suggests that behavioral variation among several primates is not the product of genetic differences or of responses to local ecological conditions. Comparative studies of chimpanzees, orangutans, gorillas, and several monkey species indicate that these primates show differences in learned behaviors. That is, groups of primates are now being distinguished on the basis of cultural differences. Recognition of this fact has forced anthropologists to re-think the features which are uniquely human.

CLASSIFICATION: GRADES VERSUS CLADES

The basic features presented above are characteristics that distinguish primates from non-primate mammals. Within the order, members can be grouped according to overall levels of complexity, shared features, and biogeography. The order Primates is divided into two suborders: Prosimii and Anthropoidea. The prosimian–anthropoid division is a *gradistic* one, which separates lower primates from higher primates on the basis of levels or grades of morphological complexity. The prosimian grade contains primates commonly referred to as lemurs, lorises, galagos, and tarsiers. Because these primates lack many of the specialized features found in higher primates, they are said to occupy a level of complexity most similar to that seen in the first true primates (euprimates). Prosimians, or lower primates, are therefore recognized by their retention of ancestral features combined with the *absence* of more specialized features found in higher primates. Prosimians are evolutionarily successful mammals characterized by a stage of morphological complexity similar to that seen in the first true primates approximately 50 mya. The other primate grade – Anthropoidea – contains monkeys, apes, and humans. These primates, like the prosimians, possess the minimum requirements for admission to the primate order, and they have also evolved a slew of additional features, which result in greater divergence from the first euprimates. Their suite of derived features not only unites the anthropoids, but also creates a different level of complexity. For this reason anthropoids are said to have achieved a stage of evolutionary development which goes beyond the prosimian grade.

The prosimian–anthropoid classification makes no attempt to establish ancestor–descendant relationships; it is a means of dividing primates on the basis of overall developmental stage (Fleagle 1999). An alternative scheme is to sort primates according to lines of descent. Descendants of a single common ancestor are said to comprise a monophyletic group. If primate classification were neat and tidy, members of the Anthropoidea and Prosimii would each be descended from a common ancestor. This appears to be the case for anthropoids, and recent fossil evidence suggests that the ancestor shared by all monkeys and apes arose in North Africa or India approximately 55 mya (Sige et al. 1990; Bajpai et al. 2008). The members within Prosimii, in contrast, are believed to have descended from two ancestors; that is, Prosimii is paraphyletic. The primate which prevents prosimian monophyly is the tarsier (genus *Tarsius*). Tarsiers are small, nocturnal primates found in the forests of southeast Asia (Wright et al. 2003). These enigmatic primates possess a number of features which ally them with the prosimians and which are absent in anthropoids. Such features are primitive (ancestral) for primates; they include an unfused mandibular symphysis, grooming claw on the second digit of the foot, multiple nipples, and a bicornuate uterus. A newly discovered feature concerns the pathway of a nerve known as the *chorda tympani*, which is involved in the sense of taste. In prosimians, this nerve passes over a muscle – the *tensor tympani* – that tightens the eardrum (or tympanic membrane), while in anthropoids the nerve passes below the muscle (Maier 2008).

In addition to sharing primitive features with other prosimians, tarsiers share several derived features with anthropoids, which suggests phyletic affinities between them. Features shared by tarsiers and anthropoids – but not by other non-tarsier prosimians – include a mobile upper lip, the lack of a *tapetum lucidum* (reflective layer of retinal cells facilitating night vision), a hemochorial placenta, a nose covered by skin (as opposed to a naked and wet rhinarium), reduced nasal turbinates, a reduced sphenoethmoid (or olfactory) recess, partial postorbital closure, blood supply to the brain via the promontory branch of the internal carotid artery, and similar dental proportions.[5]

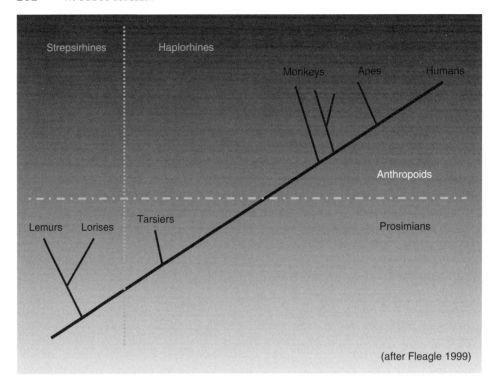

Fig. 13.1   Alternative schemes for dividing the primate order. The prosimian/anthropoid division emphasizes general stages – or grades – of evolution. The alternative classification emphasizes descent from common ancestors and divides primates into two monophyletic groups: Strepsirhines and Haplorhines

The fact that tarsiers possess shared derived features with anthropoids (while all other prosimians do not) implies that tarsiers are descended from a different ancestor from the one shared by lemurs, lorises, and galagos. Thus, despite shared organizational (gradistic) similarities, prosimians cannot be a monophyletic group, because one member has a different ancestor. In the alternative classificatory scheme, which emphasizes shared descent from a common ancestor, the non-tarsier prosimians (lemurs, lorises, and galagos) are placed in a clade known as Strepsirhini, while tarsiers are grouped with anthropoids in a clade known as Haplorhini. The pivotal taxon in the higher-order division of primates is the tarsier, and its evolutionary position continues to be a source of exploration and debate (Fleagle 1999). The key features associated with the strepsirhine and haplorhine clades are reviewed below (and see Figure 13.1).

Strepsirhine features and their distribution

Strepsirhines have the primitive primate features, for instance a simple postorbital bar, two mobile bones in forearm, five digits, and so on. They also retain a number of primitive mammalian features that have been lost in anthropoids. These include:

Prognathic face and reliance on olfaction   The sense of smell is still well developed in strepsirhines. Most of them have projecting nasal bones, which provide more surface area for the nasal turbinates, and specialized neural cells, which detect olfactory signals in the environment.

Rhinarium   The skin on the end of the nose of most mammals differs from normal skin by being wet and hairless and by containing specialized glands for the reception of chemical signals. This wet, naked region is called a 'rhinarium' and is involved in the collection of olfactory cues from the environment. The rhinarium communicates with the brain through an intimate connection with the vomeronasal (or Jacobson's organ), which is housed in the roof of the mouth (Hill 1972). This communication is facilitated by a cleft in an immobile upper lip anchored to the underlying gum. Most mammals, including the strepsirhines, possess a rhinarium, and an immobile clefted upper lip – features that have been lost in the haplorhines (including tarsiers).

Tapetum lucidum and nocturnality   Most strepsirhines are nocturnal (active at night). The night vision in strepsirhines is facilitated, apart from the enlarged orbits, by a specialized layer of retinal cells called *tapetum lucidum*, which allows enhanced vision even when light levels are quite low. A *tapetum* is found in many living mammal groups, and is likely to be a primitive mammalian character.

In addition to these primitive traits, the strepsirrhine clade is defined by several derived characteristics, which include:

Toothcomb   In strepsirhines, the incisors and canines of the mandible (lower jaw) are elongated and parallel and they project forward, much like the tines on a fork or a comb. This structure, called a 'toothcomb,' is used for grooming and feeding in several strepsirhine species.

Maxillary incisors   The front teeth (incisors) in the upper jaw (maxilla) of strepsirrhines are distinctive in that they are small, vertically oriented, and separated in the midline (median) by a gap.

Toilet claw   On the second digit of their feet, strepsirhines possess a claw that is used for grooming purposes.

The members of the strepsirhine clade are lemurs, lorises, and galagos (see Table 13.1). The ancestors of living stepsirhines ranged widely throughout the Old and New World, but today they are restricted to Asia, Africa and Madagascar. There are seven families of living stepsirrhines. The five families of lemurs are found only on the island of Madagascar and include some of the world's rarest and most endangered primates (Mittermeier et al. 2008). Each lemur family is characterized by a number of anatomical and behavioral idiosyncrasies (Tattersall 1982; Mittermeier et al. 1994). The galagids, or bush babies, are confined to Africa, whereas members of the lorisids are found both in Africa (potto, angwantibo) and in Asia (slender loris, slow loris).

Haplorhine features and their distribution
The haplorhines have the minimum primate characteristics described above, but they have lost several primitive mammalian features retained by the strepsirhines. Neither a nasal rhinarium nor a *tapetum lucidum* is present in tarsiers, monkeys, or apes.

Table 13.1 The diversity of living primates

	Order Primates	
	Suborder Strepsirhini	
Family Cheirogalidae		
Microcebus	Mouse lemur	Madagascar
Allocebus	Hairy-eared dwarf lemur	Madagascar
Mirza	Giant mouse lemur	Madagascar
Cheriogaleus	Greater dwarf lemur	Madagascar
Phaner	Fork-marked lemur	Madagascar
Family Lepilemuridae		
Lepilemur	Sportive lemur	Madagascar
Family Lemuridae		
Hapalemur	Bamboo lemur	Madagascar
Prolemur	Greater bamboo lemur	Madagascar
Lemur	Ring-tailed lemur	Madagascar
Eulemur	Brown lemur	Madagascar
Varecia	Ruffed lemur	Madagascar
Family Indriidae		
Avahi	Avahi	Madagascar
Propithecus	Sifaka	Madagascar
Indri	Indri	Madagascar
Family Daubentoniidae		
Daubentonia	aye-aye	Madagascar
Family Loridae		
Loris	Slender loris	Asia
Nycticebus	Slow loris	Asia
Arctocebus	Angwantibo	Africa
Perodicticus	Potto	Africa
Family Galagidae		
Galagoides	Dwarf galago	Africa
Galago	Lesser galago / bushbaby	Africa
Eoticus	Needle-clawed bushbaby	Africa
Sciurocheirus	Allen's galago	Africa
Otolemur	Greater galago	Africa
	Suborder Haplorhini	
	Infraorder Tarsiiformes	
Family Tarsiidae		
Tarsius	Tarsier	Asia
	Infraorder Platyrrhini	
Family Cebidae		
Cebus	Capuchins	Neotropics
Saimiri	Squirrel monkey	Neotropics
Subfamily Callitrichinae		
Callithrix	Marmoset	Neotropics
Leontopithecus	Golden lion tamarin	Neotropics
Saguinus	Tamarins	Neotropics

Table 13.1 (*cont'd*)

Infraorder Platyrrhini		
Callimico	Goeldi's marmoset	Neotropics
Cebuella	Pygmy marmoset	Neotropics
Family Pitheciidae		
Pithecia	Saki	Neotropics
Chiropotes	Bearded saki	Neotropics
Cacajao	Uakari	Neotropics
Subfamily Aotinae		
Aotus	Owl monkey	Neotropics
Subfamily Callicebinae		
Callicebus	Titi monkey	Neotropics
Family Atelidae		
Alouatta	Howler monkey	Neotropics
Ateles	Spider monkey	Neotropics
Brachyteles	Woolly spider monkey	Neotropics
Lagothrix	Woolly monkey	Neotropics
Oreonax	Yellow-tailed woolly monkey	Neotropics
Infraorder Catarrhini		
Superfamily Cercopithecoidea		
Subfamily Cercopithecinae		
Macaca	Macaque	Asia (Africa)
Lophocebus	Arboreal mangabey	Africa
Cercocebus	Terrestrial mangabey	Africa
Rungwecebus	Kipunji mangabey	Africa
Mandrillus	Mandrill and drill	Africa
Papio	Baboon	Africa
Theropithecus	Gelada	Africa
Allenopithecus	Swamp monkey	Africa
Miopithecus	Talapoin monkey	Africa
Erythrocebus	Patas monkey	Africa
Chlorocebus	Vervet/green monkey	Africa
Subfamily Colobinae		
Nasalis	Proboscis monkey	Asia
Presbytis	Surilis	Asia
Pygathrix	Douc langur	Asia
Rhinopithecus	Snub-nosed monkey	Asia
Semnopithecus	Indian or gray langur	Asia
Trachypithecus	Luntung	Asia
Procolobus	Olive colobus	Africa
Piliocolobus	Red colobus	Africa
Colobus	Black and white colobus	Africa
Superfamily Hominoidea (lower apes)		
Family Hylobatidae		
Bunopithecus	Hoolock gibbon	Asia
Hylobates	Lar or white-handed gibbon	Asia
Nomascus	Concolor or black-crested gibbon	Asia
Symphalangus	Siamang	Asia
Family Pongidae (great apes)		
Pongo	Orangutan	Asia
Pan	Chimpanzee, bonobo	Africa
Gorilla	Gorilla	Africa

Haplorhines have decreased their reliance on smell, show a reduced facial prognathism, have smaller olfactory bulbs, and possess fewer turbinates in their nasal cavity. An increased reliance on vision is reflected in more frontated and convergent orbits. Compared to strepsirhines, haplorhines are characterized by increased brain size, increased body size, and more conservative dentition. In addition to these trends and departures from the primitive condition, the haplorhines are distinguished by several derived features.

Fused mandible   In strepsirhines and in tarsiers, the right and left halves of the mandible are connected by cartilage and remain unfused. In haplorhines, the halves fuse at the midline, producing a rigid mandible.

Fused frontal bones   Among the strepsirhines and the tarsiers, the right and left halves of the frontal bone are connected by cartilage (metopic suture) and the bones usually remain unfused throughout adulthood. In haplorhines, this suture obliterates and the right and left halves become fused at the midline, forming a single frontal bone.

Postorbital closure   In addition to a postorbital bar, haplorhines have walled off the back of the orbital cavity with contributions from the frontal, zygomatic and sphenoid bones. This results in a condition known as postorbital closure. Tarsiers display partial postorbital closure.

Diurnality and color vision   With two exceptions (tarsiers and owl monkeys), haplorhine primates are active during daylight hours – in other words they are diurnal. Most haplorhines have three kinds of cones that permit trichromatic vision. Strepsirhines are generally able to see in varying shades of black and white.

Uterus   Haplorhines have a single-chambered uterus. The tarsier is exceptional in that it has a bicornate uterus, like the one found among strepsirhines.

Blood to the brain   The brain is supplied by branches of the internal carotid artery (ICA). One branch of the ICA passes through the stapes (stirrup) bone in the middle ear. A stapedial branch of the ICA is a primitive feature in mammals, and all strepsirhines retain one throughout adulthood. Among haplorhines a stapedial branch is present in the fetus; however, this artery becomes obliterated and lost during development. In tarsiers, monkeys, and apes, the major source of blood to the brain is another branch of the ICA, known as the promontory artery (Ankel-Simons 2000).

The haplorhine clade consists of the Tarsioidea (with *Tarsius* as the sole living member), Platyrrhini (New World monkeys) and Catarrhini (Old World monkeys and apes; see Table 13.1). The platyrrhine monkeys are found in the Neotropics, while living catarrhines are found in Africa and Asia. In addition to the basic biogeographic distinction, platyrrhines are distinguished from catarrhines by several features. The nostrils of New World monkeys are flat, widely spaced and point sideways ('platyrrhine' means 'broad-nosed'). In catarrhines, the nostrils are more closely approximated and converge toward the midline. Platyrrhines have one more premolar than catarrhines, and most New World monkeys have a dental formula of 2.1.3.3.[6] The bones in the temporal region of platyrrhines display a zygomatic–parietal articulation, while in catarrhines the frontal and sphenoid articulate together, thus preventing a zygomatic–parietal articulation. Platyrrhines do not possess the long, bony tube that exits the ear cavity of catarrhines; among platyrrhines, the corresponding feature is a simple ring. Platyrrhines range in body size from about 100 grams (pygmy marmosets) to over 11 kilograms (Mexican black howler monkey; Smith and Jungers 1997). All platyrrhines are predominantly arboreal, and some have evolved specialized adaptations for movement in the trees, including secondarily derived claws for clinging (the callitrichids) and prehensile tails (the atelines).

The catarrhines are divided into Cercopithecoidea (Old World monkeys) and Hominoidea (apes; see Table 13.1). It is not necessary to say 'Old World' apes, since apes have never existed anywhere but in the Old World. The superfamily Hominoidea is comprised of the lesser apes (gibbons and siamangs) and of the great apes (chimpanzees, gorillas, orangutans, humans). All hominoids are distinguished from cercopithecoids by features which include relatively larger brains, simple molars, lack of a tail, broader nose and face, and numerous postcranial adaptations for suspension and climbing such as short trunks, long forelimbs, mobile shoulder joints, and long fingers. The lesser apes are monkey-sized, and their weights range between 5.5 kg (the pileated gibbon) and 12 kg (the siamang). Great apes are much larger and include the largest living primate, the gorilla, which can weigh more than 200 kg (Smith and Jungers 1997).

All members of the family Cercopithecoidea are distinguished from apes by their possession of a tail, bilophodont molars, narrower faces, and longer trunks. The family is divided into two subfamilies: Cercopithecinae, commonly referred to as fruit-eating monkeys, and Colobinae, the leaf-eating monkeys of the Old World. Field studies have shown that the fruit-eating versus leaf-eating designation obscures significant dietary variations within both groups; nevertheless, several features that distinguish the two cercopithecoid subfamilies are related to the requirements of obtaining and processing fruits versus leaves. Colobine monkeys possess complex, multichambered (ruminant) stomachs, molars with high shearing crests, narrow incisors, deep jaws, reduced (or absent) thumbs, shortened nasal bones, and greater leaping capabilities. Cercopithecine monkeys have cheek pouches, wider incisors, shallow jaws, greater pollical opposability, and limbs tending to be of equal size (Strasser and Delson 1987, Fleagle 1999). The smallest cercopithecoids, namely the talapoin monkeys, weigh just over one kilogram, while the largest – the mandrills – weigh over thirty (Smith and Jungers 1997).

A Note on Conservation

Research into the boundaries and contents of the primate order is storied, but this remains an area of discovery (Mivart 1873; Clark 1959; Schultz 1969; Fleagle 1999). As the definition of primates evolves, the roster of extant primate species expands as well. Currently there are approximately 400 species of living primates, and the number is rising: thirty-nine lemur species have been described since 2000 (Mittermeier et al. 2008). Such increases might suggest that the world's population of primates is growing, but in fact primates are steadily decreasing. In general, the expansion of the primate roster has not come about as the result of newly discovered species populations

Table 13.2 Summary of primate taxa threatened within each major biogeographic region

Region	Genera	Species/ Subspecies	% Threatened[d]
Africa[a]	21	79	28%
Asia[b]	16	77	40%
Madagascar[c]	15	99	39%
Neotropics[d]	19	139	35%

[a] Data from Grubb et al. 2003.
[b] From Brandon-Jones et al. 2004.
[c] From Mittermeier et al. 2008.
[d] Website of IUCN/SSC Primate Specialist Group (http://www.primate-sg.org/diversity.htm).

in the wild, but is due rather to the recognition of 'cryptic,' specific or subspecific, diversity in existing populations. Arguments of 'taxonomic inflation' notwithstanding (e.g. Tattersall 2007; Meiri and Mace 2007), the number of non-human primates throughout the world is falling at an alarming rate. Because of their heritage as arboreal mammals, primates are especially vulnerable to deforestation and human hunting, two activities on the rise in many tropical regions. Approximately 90 percent of all living primates still rely on trees for food, safety, and shelter, and the percentage of threatened primates is a cause for great concern (see Table 13.2). We are now at a point where aggressive international efforts must be deployed in order to prevent the loss of our closest relatives. For example, the United Nations designated 2009 the *Year of the Gorilla*, in hopes that focusing the world's attention on this embattled ape might help to prevent its extinction. As we strive to understand the world's lemurs, lorises, monkeys, and apes, let's hope that 'last-ditch' measures will not be required to save them in the coming years.

SUMMARY

Living primates include forms commonly referred to as lemurs, lorises, galagos, tarsiers, monkeys, apes, and humans. Using the fossil record of early mammals and features of extant non-primate mammals as bases for comparisons, morphologists can identify the features that unite primates. Compared to many other mammalian groups, primates have not diverged significantly from the primitive mammalian condition and retain a generalized, unspecialized morphology. Many 'specializations' of primates are present in other mammalian groups. Although the list of distinctly primate features is not extensive, the group is distinguished via unique *suites of features*, combined with several important *trends* in anatomy and behavior that are less pronounced or absent in other mammalian groups. Many features are related to the demands of arboreal living and include an increased reliance upon vision (versus olfaction), enhanced brain power, and skeletal adaptations that facilitate movement through the trees.

The unique combination of primitive and derived features that are found in members of the primate order includes: decreased reliance on smell, reduced facial prognathism, reduction in the size of nasal turbinates and olfactory bulbs, increased reliance on vision, enhanced orbital frontation and orbital convergence, brain expansion (especially of the neocortex), generalized flexible limb structure, retention of clavicle, grasping hands and feet with enhanced manipulative abilities, replacement of claws by nails, tendency for upright posture, prolonged gestation period, longer periods of infant dependency, extended juvenile and adult periods, development of varied and complex social organizations emphasizing individual relationships, increased capacity for culture and learning.

The order Primates can be divided in several ways. A gradistic classification emphasizing overall level of organization places lemurs, lorises, galagos, and tarsiers in the suborder Prosimii. Higher primates, or anthropoids, include monkeys, apes, and humans. These forms have become more specialized by comparison with the first euprimates. Because tarsiers share several features with the anthropoids, prosimians cannot be considered monophyletic, since their members are not descended from a single common ancestor. A second means of classifying primates emphasizes shared descent from a common ancestor, and in this scheme primates are divided into two monophyletic clades: the Strepsirhini contains lemurs, lorises, and galagos, while the Haplorhini contains tarsiers, monkeys, apes, and humans. In addition to features primitive to all primates, the strepsirhines retain other primitive mammalian features, including a *tapetum lucidum*, a rhinarium, and a greater reliance on olfaction. Derived features of strepsirhines include a grooming claw on the second pedal digit and a toothcomb. The derived features and trends found in haplorhines include a fused mandible, fused frontal bones, postorbital closure, blood supply to the brain via the promontory branch of the internal carotid artery, single-chambered uterus, and an enlarged brain. Strepsirhines are found only in the Old World and include the lemurs of Madagascar, the galagos of Africa, and the lorises present in both Africa and Asia. Haplorhines are found in both the New World and the Old. Tarsiers are restricted to southeast Asia. Aside from humans, the only Haplorhines in the New World are monkeys: monkeys of the New World are referred to as platyrrhines. Old World haplorhines are known as catarrhines, and this group includes monkeys (Family Cercopithecoidea) and apes (Family Hominoidea).

ACKNOWLEDGMENTS

Many thanks to Walter Hartwig, Pierre Lemelin, John Fleagle, Randall Susman, Matt Cartmill, and Clark Larsen who provided valuable comments on this manuscript.

NOTES

1   Linneaus's ability to group closely related organisms was remarkable for its time. His *Lemur* genus contained prosimians as well as what we now refer to as *Cynocephalus volans*, a species of flying lemur. Flying lemurs are not lemurs (nor do they fly), and they are now placed in their own order: Dermoptera. However, recent molecular studies have shown that they are the closest living relatives of primates (Janecka et al. 2007).

2 A handful of primates, including spider monkeys, woolly monkeys, and colobus monkeys have greatly reduced or absent thumbs. The adaptive significance of pollical reduction is still not clear.
3 Humans have realigned their hallux with the other toes in order to facilitate their unique locomotor mode of bipedality.
4 Several primate groups have secondarily evolved claws. These include the callitrichids (marmosets and tamarins) of the Neotropics and the bizarre, yet spectacular, aye-aye from Madagascar.
5 Tarsiers are also unique in several respects. They have a unique dental formula (2.1.3.3/1.1.3.3), have claws on both the second and the third digit of their feet, and are the only totally animalivorous primates (in other words, their diet consisting entirely of insects or fauna).
6 The callitrichines, with the exception of *Callimico*, have lost a molar and have a dental formula of 2.1.3.2.

REFERENCES

Ankel-Simons, F. (2000) *Primate Anatomy*, 2nd edn. New York: Academic Press.
Bajpai, S., Kay, R. F., Williams, B. A., Das, D. P., Kapur, V. V., and Tiwari, B. N. (2008) The Oldest Asian Record of Anthropoidea. *Proceedings of the National Academy of Sciences, USA* 105: 11093–11098.
Barton, R. A. (2004) Binocularity and Brain Evolution in Primates. *Proceedings of the National Academy of Sciences, USA* 101: 10113–10115.
Bloch, J. I., Silcox, M. T., Boyer, D. M., and Sargis, E. J. (2007) New Paleocene Skeletons and the Relationship of Plesiadapiforms to Crown-Clade Primates. *Proceedings of the National Academy of Sciences, USA* 104: 1159–1164.
Bowmaker, J. K. (1998) Evolution of Colour Vision in Vertebrates. *Eye* 125: 541–547.
Brandon-Jones, D., Eudey, A. A., Geissman, T., Groves, C. P., Melnick, D. J., Morales, J. C., Shekelle, M., and Stewart, C.-B. (2004) Asian Primate Classification. *International Journal of Primatology* 25: 97–164.
Cartmill, M. (1972) Arboreal Adaptations and the Origin of the Primates. In R. H. Tuttle (ed.), *Functional and Evolutionary Biology of the Primates* (pp. 97–122). Chicago: Aldine-Atherton.
Clark, W. E. Le Gros (1959) *The Antecedents of Man*. Edinburgh: Edinburgh University Press.
Fleagle, J. G. (1999) *Primate Adaptation and Evolution*. New York: Academic Press.
Gregory, W. K. (1910) The Orders of Mammals. *Bulletin of the American Museum of Natural History* 27: 1–524.
Grubb, P., Butynski, T. M., Oates, J. F., Bearder, S. K., Disotell, T. R., Groves, C. P., and Struhsaker, T. T. (2003) Assessment of the Diversity of African Primates. *International Journal of Primatology* 24: 1301–1357.
Heesy, C. P. (2004) On the Relationship between Orbit Orientation and Binocular Visual Field Overlap in Mammals. *Anatomical Record Part A* 281A: 1104–1110.
Heesy, C. P. (2005) Function of the Mammalian Postorbital Bar. *Journal of Morphology* 264: 363–380.
Hill, W. C. (1953) *Primates. Comparative Anatomy and Taxonomy I – Strepsirhini*. Edinburgh: Edinburgh University Press.
Hill, W. C. (1972) *Evolutionary Biology of the Primates*. New York: Academic Press.
Janecka, J. E., Miller, W., Pringle, T. H., Wiens, F., Zitzmann, A., Helgen, K. M., Springer, M. S., and Murphy W. J. (2007) Molecular and Genomic Data Identify the Closest Living Relative of Primates. *Science* 318: 792–794.

Ji, Q., Luo, Z.-X., Yuan, C.-X., Wible, J. R., Zhang, J.-P., and Georgi, J. A. (2002) The Earliest Known Eutherian Mammal. *Nature* 416: 816–822.

Jones, F. W. (1916) *Arboreal Man*. London: E. Arnold.

Kirk, E. C., Cartmill, M., Kay, R. F., and Lemelin, P. (2003) Comment on 'Grasping Primate Origins.' *Science* 300: 741b.

Leigh, S. R. (2004) Brain Growth, Life History and Cognition in Primate and Human Evolution. *American Journal of Primatology* 62: 139–164.

Leonhardt, S. D., Tung, J., Camden, J. B., Neal, M., and Drea, C. M. (2008) Seeing Red: Behavioral Evidence of Trichromatic Color Vision in Strepsirrhine Primates. *Behavioral Ecology* 20: 1–12.

Maier, W. (2008) Epitensoric Position of the Chorda Tympani in Anthropoidea: A New Synamomorphic Character, with Remarks on the Fissure Glaseri in Primates. In E. J. Sargis and M. Dagosto (eds), *Mammalian Evolutionary Morphology: A Tribute to Frederick S. Szalay* (pp. 347–360). The Netherlands: Springer.

Meiri, S., and Mace, G. M. (2007) New Taxonomy and the Origin of Species. *PLoS Biology* 5 (7): 1385–1386.

Mittermeier, R. A., Tattersall, I., Konstant, B., Meyers, D., and Mast, R. B. (1994) *Lemurs of Madagascar*. Washington DC: Conservation International.

Mittermeier, R. A., Ganzhorn, J., Konstant, W., Glander, K., Tattersall, I., Groves, C., Rylands, A., Hapke, A., Ratsimbazafy, J., Mayor, M., Louis, E., Rumpler, Y., Schwitzer, C., and Rasoloarison, R. M., (2008) Lemur Diversity in Madagascar. *International Journal of Primatology* 29: 1607–1656.

Mivart, St G. J. (1873) On *Lepilemur* and *Cheirogaleus* and on the Zoological Rank of the Lemuroidea. *Proceedings of the Zoological Society* (London): 484–510.

Napier, J. R. (1993) *Hands*. Princeton: Princeton University Press.

Napier, J. R., and Napier, P. H. (1967) *A Handbook of Living Primates*. New York: Academic Press.

Noble, V. E., Kowalski, E. M., and Ravosa, M. J. (2000) Orbit Orientation and the Function of the Mammalian Postorbital Bar. *Journal of Zoology* (London) 250: 405–418.

Nowak, R. M. (1991) *Walker's Mammals of the World*. London: Johns Hopkins University Press.

Qiang, J., Zhexi, L., and Shu-an, J. (1999) A Chinese Triconodont Mammal and Mosaic Evolution of the Mammalian Skeleton. *Nature* 398: 326–330.

Rasmussen, D. T. (2002) The Origin of Primates. In W. C. Hartwig (ed.), *The Primate Fossil Record* (pp. 5–9). Cambridge: Cambridge University Press.

Ross, C. F., and Martin, R. D. (2007) The Role of Vision in the Origin and Evolution of Primates. In M. P. Todd and J. Kaas (eds), *Evolution of Nervous Systems*, Vol. 4: *The Evolution of Primate Nervous Systems* (pp. 59–78). Oxford: Elsevier.

Schmitt, D., and Lemelin, P. (2002) Origins of Primate Locomotion: Gait Mechanics of the Woolly Opossum. *American Journal of Physical Anthropology* 118: 231–238.

Schultz, A. H. (1969) *The Life of Primates*. New York: Universe Books.

Sige, B., Jaeger, J. J., Sudre, J., and Vianey-Liaud, M. (1990) *Altiatlasius kuolchii* n. gen. et sp. primate omomyide du Paléocène supérieur du Maroc, et les origins des euprimates. *Paleontographica* A 214: 31–56.

Silcox, M. T. (2007) Primate Taxonomy, Plesiadapiformes, and Approaches to Primate Origins. In M. J. Ravosa and M. Dagosto (ed.), *Primate Origins: Adaptations and Evolution* (pp. 143–178). New York: Springer.

Silcox, M. T., Boyer, D. M., Bloch, J. I., and Sargis, E. J. (2007) Revisiting the Adaptive Origins of Primates (again). *Journal of Human Evolution* 53: 321–324.

Simons, E. (1972) *Primate Evolution*. New York: Macmillan.

Smith, R. J., and Jungers, W. L. (1997) Body Mass in Comparative Primatology. *Journal of Human Evolution* 32: 523–559.

Soligo, C., and Martin, R. D. (2006) Adaptive Origins of Primate Revisited. *Journal of Human Evolution* 50: 414–430.

Soligo, C., and Muller, A. E. (1999) Nails and Claws in Primate Evolution *Journal of Human Evolution* 36: 97–114.

Strasser, E., and Delson, E. (1987) Cladistic Analysis of Cercopithecid Relationships. *Journal of Human Evolution* 16: 81–99.

Sussman, R. (1991) Primate Origins and the Evolution of Angiosperms. *American Journal of Primatology* 23: 209–233.

Tattersall, I. (1982) *The Primates of Madagascar*. New York: Columbia University Press.

Tattersall, I. (2007) Madagascar's Lemurs: Cryptic Diversity or Taxonomic Inflation? *Evolutionary Anthropology* 16: 12–23.

Tavare, S., Marshall, C. R., Will, O., Soligo, C., and Martin, R. D. (2002) Using the Fossil Record to Estimate the Age of the Last Common Ancestor of Extant Primates. *Nature* 416: 726–729.

Wright, P. C., Simon, E. L., and Gursky, S. (2003) *Tarsiers: Past, Present and Future*. New Brunswick: Rutgers University Press.

CHAPTER 14

Primate Behavior and Sociality

Karen B. Strier

INTRODUCTION

The behavior of non-human primates holds a special interest for biological anthropologists because of the comparative perspectives that our closest living relatives can
provide into the origins of human sociality. Pioneering field studies include those
conducted on the mantled howler monkey (*Alouatta palliata*) in Panama in the early
1930s (Carpenter 1934) and on the Japanese macaque (*Macaca fuscata*) at various
locations since the mid 1950s (Imanishi 1960). Subsequently, research focused more
explicitly on particular primates with either ecological or phylogenetic affinities with
hominids. The savannah-dwelling semi-terrestrial baboon (*Papio* spp.) was among the
first of these research subjects, because the ecological selection pressures that shape
the baboons' social adaptations were also thought to resemble those of hominids
occupying similar habitats (Washburn and DeVore 1961; see Figure 14.1). The great
apes, which include the chimpanzee (*Pan troglodytes*: Goodall 1971), the gorilla
(*Gorilla* spp.: Fossey 1983), and the orangutan (*Pongo* spp.: Galdikas 1995), were
also targeted early on because of the behavioral continuities that could be expected to
persist as a result of our shared common ancestry.

Baboons and great apes, which also include the bonobo (*Pan paniscus*), continue
to be among the most intensively studied primates, and long-term research on these
taxa from multiple study sites continues to provide invaluable insights that inform our
understanding of human behavioral evolution. Nowadays, however, most biological
anthropologists also appreciate the value of broader, more comprehensive comparisons, which take into account the diversity of social patterns exhibited across the order
Primates. Indeed, these broader comparative analyses have brought into focus the
effects of ecology and phylogeny on social behavior, and they are stimulating new
investigations into the ways in which other factors contribute to both inter and
intraspecific behavioral variation (Strier 2009). Now, when nearly half of the more
than 600 species and subspecies of primates are threatened with extinction, understanding their behavior is also regarded as critical to their effective conservation and
to management efforts on their behalf.

Figure 14.1   Yellow baboons (*Papio cynocephalus*) in Amboseli National Park, Kenya, a savanna woodland habitat. Photo by K. B. Strier

Methodological advances such as the use of field experiments to investigate cognitive capabilities for solving ecological and social problems (as in Cheney and Seyfarth 1990, 2007) and the development of non-invasive procedures for measuring hormones (as in Ziegler and Wittwer 2005) and genetic relationships (as in Di Fiore 2003) have provided essential tools for evaluating the mechanisms and the consequences of primate behavior (Setchell and Curtis 2003). Even earlier, however, observational studies were enhanced by the widespread adoption of systematic methods of behavioral sampling, which made it possible to control for potential observer biases and to compare the behavior of individuals within and between groups of the same and of different species (Altmann 1974). These methods have helped to transform the study of primate behavior from a largely descriptive endeavor into the more rigorous, quantitative science it is today.

Although many important discoveries about primates have come from captive studies (that is, research carried out on animals living in captivity rather than in their natural habitat), in this overview of primate social patterns I will emphasize findings from field studies because of the insights they provide into how ecological and demographic variables influence behavior. I begin by describing the basic characteristics of primate groups, which include their size and composition, and the degree to which group members maintain cohesive or fluid associations with one another. Much of the variation in group size and grouping patterns can be attributed to local ecological or demographic conditions, which differ between species as well as across populations of the same species and within populations over time. Other characteristics, such as whether groups are composed of extended networks of female or male kin or unrelated adults, tend to cluster differently within phylogenetic clades (Di Fiore and Rendall 1994) and coincide with other basic life history traits related to maturation and reproductive rates (Lee and Kappeler 2003). Distinguishing behavioral adaptations from traits that are shared among closely related species requires the use of phylogenetic controls, which are now widely employed in comparative analyses (Nunn and Barton 2001). Yet even phylogenetically conservative traits such as dispersal patterns can vary in response to local conditions (Moore 1984).

In the second section of this chapter, I consider the various social options that different types of groups provide and the extent to which observed social patterns are consistent with, or deviate from, predictions based on evolutionary and ecological theories. In principle, social behavior should be subject to the same kinds of selection pressures as other types of traits, and therefore behavior patterns that enhance fitness, or an individual's genetic contribution to future generations, should be favored over those that do not. Competition and cooperation over access to limited resources, such as food or mates, should dictate whether groups consist of biological kin or non-kin, as well as the types of relationships that these individuals maintain with one another. In practice, however, it is difficult to evaluate the fitness consequences of behavior without long-term demographic and genetic data. In addition, because primates adjust their behavior in response to local conditions and as a result of their individual experiences, many researchers now regard their social flexibility to be an adaptation that distinguishes primates from other animals with more restricted – and predictable – behavioral repertoires (Barrett and Henzi 2005).

It is not surprising that primates exhibit such high levels of phenotypic plasticity in their social lives when one considers the long length of their life spans in comparison with those of most other mammals of similar body size. Primate life spans generally scale with body size within phylogenetic clades, but most primates live long enough to experience a variety of social and ecological conditions over the course of their lives. The ability to respond to fluctuating conditions and unpredictable events has obvious advantages, but it also requires enhanced cognitive capacities, which have been associated with the correspondingly large size of primate brains. One hypothesis concerning the expansion of the neocortex, where most higher-level thought-processes occur, relates directly to the social flexibility required in order to keep track of multiple social relationships and social networks as the sizes of groups increase (Dunbar 2003). Enhanced cognitive abilities include the facility to learn, and long lives and group living provide the necessary time and contexts in which life-long social learning can occur.

In the final section of this chapter I turn to some of the greatest challenges to contemporary and future studies of primate behavior. These challenges begin and end with the precarious status of so many primates, which can be attributed to human activities that are threatening primate habitats and populations at an unprecedented pace. The urgency of conservation concerns has become a driving force behind the growth of primate field research and has influenced the directions that many of our research questions now take (Cowlishaw and Dunbar 2000). Ironically, however, the same human activities that are altering primate habitats and endangering their populations are also inadvertently creating unique opportunities to investigate how primates respond to different types of environmental change. Studies that are sensitive to the behavioral variation within and between populations can therefore provide insights into the adaptive potentials of primates and into the ways in which their social flexibility can contribute to their future survival in a rapidly changing world.

CHARACTERISTICS OF SOCIAL GROUPS

Most primates spend all or most of their lives in the company of other members of their species. Their groups vary in size and composition, which can range from small families, consisting of a single adult male and female with dependent offspring, to mixed sex and age classes of tens or even hundreds of individuals. Even when adults are most frequently encountered on their own or with dependent young, as is the case for orangutans, they are still members of larger communities composed of familiar individuals, who interact with one another differently than they interact with strangers (van Schaik 2004). Both the quality of social interactions and the amount of time individuals spend together distinguish social groups from aggregations, which form for the purpose of achieving mutual safety from predators or because the individuals are attracted to the same concentrated resources.

Predator pressures tend to favor larger groups over smaller ones because the chances of detecting and ultimately avoiding a predator are usually improved through the presence of extra ears and eyes. Some researchers regard the safety that group living provides as the basis of primate sociality in general (Hart and Sussman 2009). However, competition for access to food resources can exert an opposing force on group size if preferred foods such as energy-rich fruits are distributed in small patches that cannot feed as many individuals as protection from predators might favor. Often the ideal group size for many primates is a compromise between these safety and subsistence concerns (van Schaik 1983).

Primates cope with the problem of competition in small food patches either by living alone or in small cohesive groups in which members can feed together without conflict, or by living in large fluid communities, known as fission–fusion societies, in which party sizes shrink and swell according to the sizes of food patches available at any particular time. By contrast, the maintenance of large cohesive groups usually requires the capacity to switch to more abundant but less preferred foods, such as leaves, grasses, or herbaceous vegetation, when the large, preferred fruit patches are scarce. Although most primates consume a combination of fruit, which is prized for its readily digestible energy, and either insects or leaves, which are rich in protein, they vary in their morphological and physiological capabilities to process foods whose high fiber content make them more difficult to digest than fruit. Even when the necessary physical traits to process low quality foods are present, the nutritional costs of diet switching should only be tolerated when they are outweighed by the benefits of staying together instead of fissioning. Protection from predators represents one such benefit of remaining together; cooperating with one another as a group to defend high-quality food patches from other groups represents another (Wrangham 1980).

When cooperation over food is involved, females are usually found living in groups with their kin. To understand the power of food over females, it may help to step back a bit and consider the differences in male and female reproductive potential, or the number of offspring that each is physically capable of producing over the course of their lives. Obviously both males and females need to survive in order to reproduce, but only females bear the time and energetic burdens of gestation and lactation (Altmann 1980). The time and energy devoted to pregnancy and, with some notable exceptions, to nursing set biological limits on the maximum number of offspring that females can produce. These limits do not apply to males, whose reproductive potentials are limited only by their access to fertile females and by the number of fertilizations they achieve. In a small number of primates, such as marmosets (*Callithrix* spp.) and tamarins (*Saguinus* spp.), females can conceive again soon after giving birth, and can therefore be nursing one set of offspring while they are pregnant with the next. But these are unusual primates, because males and other group members do much of the infant carrying, providing some relief from the energetic burdens that other lactating mothers who carry their infants usually bear on their own.

There is little that female primates can do to reduce the time required by gestation and lactation without compromising their offsprings' survival, but they can offset the high energetic demands of these vital activities by satisfying their nutritional needs. Better fed females tend to have longer reproductive life spans, faster reproductive rates, and healthier offspring compared to poorly fed females, and the amount and quality of food that a female consumes affect her nutritional status. The energetic costs of female reproduction make food a limiting resource on female reproductive success, in much the same way in which fertilizable females are a limiting resource for males. And, if cooperation with group members provides access to more and better food in competitive confrontations against other groups, then females may fare better by cooperating with kin, with whom they also share some proportion of their genes.

These biological sex differences explain why the distribution of food is thought to influence whether females distribute themselves alone or in groups, and why the distribution of fertile females dictates the optimal distribution and behavior patterns of males (Emlen and Oring 1977; Wrangham 1979). When the distribution of food favors or permits females to live together, it may be possible for a single male to defend either a group of females or the foods that attract them, a situation which results in what is referred to as either female-defense or resource-defense polygyny, respectively. However, as the size of female groups or the number of groups in an area increase, pressure from unattached males in the neighborhood to join or take over a female group can make it difficult for a single male to repel intruders and retain his position for very long. One solution to this dilemma is to gain the females' support by proving one's superiority as an ally in defending food resources or in preventing other conspecifics from harassing females and their infants. Another solution is to join forces with one or more male allies. And, for the same genetic reasons why cooperation among females is more likely to involve close biological relatives, male kin are often one another's allies of choice.

Cooperating with male kin is also an alternative when females maintain fluid grouping patterns that result in their foraging on their own at least for some of the time. The amount of time females spend by themselves or with one another, and the density of females within an area, determine the feasibility of a male's associating with a single female, monitoring multiple independent females simultaneously, or cooperating with other males to monopolize a larger number of females than he could on his own.

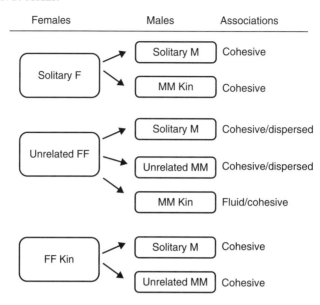

Figure 14.2   Primate group types. Based on the model in Foley and Lee (1989) of how groups shift from one type to another.

The effects of predators in general, and of food on females and of females on males can explain some of the variation in the number of adults of each sex that primate groups contain, whether or not groups with multiple adults of the same sex are biological kin, and the degree of cohesiveness or fluidity in their associations (Figure 14.2). However, the boundaries between these so-called group 'types' are often blurred in different ways. For example, a single species can have more than one type of group, such as in the case of the mountain gorilla (*Gorilla beringei*), where uni-male and multi-male groups live side by side in the same population. The composition of any group can change on account of specific demographic events such as deaths or the immigration or emigration of individuals, and as a result of more encompassing demographic conditions such as fluctuations in adult sex ratios within the local population. Because of these dynamics, a single individual can spend different times of his or her life in different types of groups (Robbins 2001).

Although some species are more likely, on average, to occur in certain types of groups, fluctuations in the distribution of food resources and in local demographic conditions can lead to differences in the normative grouping patterns. For example, when I first started studying the northern muriqui monkey (*Brachyteles hypoxanthus*) in 1982, the twenty-two members of my main study group traveled together as a cohesive, multi-male, multi-female unit. Within fifteen years, the group had grown to more than 2½ times its initial size, and grouping patterns had shifted to more fluid, fission–fusion associations, which have persisted as both the group and the population have continued to grow. Some of the same individuals who were present in 1982 are still alive and have participated in this behavioral change, but other, younger individuals have never experienced life in a cohesive group, and therefore have never had the opportunity to see and interact with all members of their group on a daily basis.

Social Options

The frequency with which group members associate and interact with one another varies within different groups as well as between groups of different types. To decipher the strength and quality of their relationships with one another, we rely on systematic observations, which can then be used to calculate the proportion of time individuals spend in close proximity and the rates and directionality of their affiliative and agonistic interactions. Primate spatial associations are rarely random, and, just like humans, most primates spend more of their time with close friends, family, or mates than with other individuals when they have the chance. Even when individuals pursue their own activities, higher rates of proximity imply a higher level of tolerance and generally lead to higher rates of affiliative interactions, such as grooming or embracing. When the pattern of initiating and maintaining spatial and affiliative interactions between pairs of individuals is symmetrical, we can infer that the relationship is mutually beneficial to both partners, whereas asymmetrical effort implies that one individual stands to benefit more from the relationship than the other. Variation in age, sex, physical and reproductive condition, and social rank contribute to the asymmetries in primate social relationships.

Maintaining close spatial and affiliative relationships is useful whenever having allies nearby increases the chances of gaining their support in aggressive interactions with other group members. In many cercopithecines, for example, females spend their lives in their natal groups, surrounded by their female relatives. Females can be individually ranked on the basis of whether they win or lose in agonistic interactions with other females in their matrilines, and matrilines can be ranked relative to one another. Cultivating allies who are likely to come to one's aid if the need should arise can be a good social investment, particularly in hierarchical societies where encounters with higher-ranking females, as well as with males, can pose risks. Not surprisingly, though, the importance of maintaining allies is proportional to the levels of competition within the group. In primates with more egalitarian societies such as those of the northern muriquis, the threat of being targeted for aggression by another group member is slim, and social relationships are less differentiated than they are in hierarchical societies (Figure 14.3).

Dispersal patterns determine the extent to which extended kin are available as potential social partners and allies (Strier 2008). Whether males, females, or both sexes disperse from their natal groups varies with phylogeny and with local ecological and demographic conditions. For example, although male-biased dispersal with female philopatry characterizes most cercopithecines, some colobines, white-faced capuchin monkeys (*Cebus capucinus*) and many lemurs, female-biased dispersal with male philopatry is found in chimpanzees and bonobos, as well as in the New World atelines, which include the spider monkey (*Ateles* spp.), the woolly monkey (*Lagothrix* spp.), and the muriqui. In other primates such as gorillas, howler monkeys, callitrichines, and several prosimians, bisexual dispersal is more common. However, many of these species also exhibit variation in their dispersal patterns that reflect local demographic conditions. For example, extended matrilines have been observed in the red howler monkey (*Alouatta seniculus*: Pope 2000) and in the buffy-headed marmoset (*Callithrix flaviceps*: Ferrari and Digby 1996) when demographic conditions result in the

Figure 14.3 Adult male northern muriquis (*Brachyteles hypoxanthus*) at the RPPN Feliciano Miguel Abdala, Minas Gerais, Brazil. Low rates of intra-group aggression among all group members and strong affiliative associations among philopatric males characterize social relationships in this egalitarian society. Photo by C. B. Possamai

retention of daughters in their natal groups. Similarly, although in the western gorilla (*Gorilla gorilla*) females typically disperse from their natal groups, genetic evidence indicates that many remain in their natal neighborhoods, where the potential for future interactions among them persist (Bradley et al. 2007).

Females who remain in their natal groups have the opportunity to bias their affiliative interactions and agonistic support in favor of their kin, but whether they do so depends on the relative fitness costs and benefits involved. Among female Japanese macaques, there appears to be a 'relatedness threshold,' and distantly related kin who fall below this threshold are generally not favored over unrelated females (Chapais 2001). However, we do not yet understand whether this threshold reflects a limit on the ability of primates to recognize distant kin or the minimal fitness gains that would accrue by helping more distant relatives. In both the rhesus macaque (*Macaca mulatta*) and yellow baboon (*Papio cynocephalus*), females favor close maternal kin over close paternal kin, which are themselves favored over non-kin (Widdig 2007). Familiarity is known to play an important role in kin recognition, but other mechanisms of phenotypic matching using chemical cues may also be involved.

Examples of kin-biased relationships among males in patrilocal societies are not as clear-cut as those among females in matrilocal societies, perhaps because fertilizations cannot be shared in the same way as food. In the patrilocal societies of chimpanzees, for example, males maintain hierarchical relationships with one another, and genetic studies have shown that higher-ranking males achieve more fertilizations than females. However, there is no evidence that paternally related male chimpanzees associate or affiliate preferentially with one another compared to other males within their communities, and therefore there is no parallel to the kin-biases exhibited by maternally related female macaques and baboons in their matrilocal societies (Langergraber et al. 2007).

Although the persistence of life-long associations and alliances with same-sexed kin requires co-residence in the same natal groups, both males and females can maintain some associations with kin if they transfer into the same groups with paternal kin in their age cohorts, or into the same groups that older maternal or paternal kin have previously joined. Related males who disperse together sometimes form cooperative alliances against other males, even if the fitness benefits of doing so are indirect. Coalitions between related male red howler monkeys are more successful in defending groups of females than single males or coalitions among unrelated males, even though genetic data have shown that often only one of the males sires the infants in their group (Pope 1990). Equally high levels of reproductive skew occur when pairs of related male moustached tamarins (*Saguinus mystax*) cooperate in defending a single breeding female and in caring for her offspring in their group (Huck et al. 2005).

The reproductive monopolies that the dominant male in multi-male groups of red howler monkeys and of moustached tamarins are known to achieve illustrate how misleading it can be to assume that mating systems are accurately reflected by the number of adults in a group. Both males and females in pair-bonded societies have been observed to engage in extra-pair copulations, and genetic studies of the fork-marked lemur (*Phaner furcifer*) have shown that not all of the infants are sired by their mother's so-called mate (Schülke et al. 2004). In multi-male groups of western lowland gorillas, paternity is biased heavily, but not entirely, in favor of alpha silverback males (Bradley et al. 2005). In the matrilineal, multi-male societies of the yellow baboons, paternity can be strongly skewed in favor of some, but not all, alpha males, depending on the length of time an alpha male can retain his status and on how stable or unstable male group membership is during these times (Altmann et al. 1996). Demographic conditions affect the number of male challengers, and male competitive abilities vary individually and as their physical and social skills change with age.

A male's physical condition and social skills affect not only his relationships with other males, but also his attractiveness to females as mates. A male olive baboon (*Papio anubis*) who invests time and energy in befriending females can improve his chances of being chosen as a preferred mating partner (Smuts 1985). In many other primates, a male's ability to provide protection extends beyond females, and can make the difference between saving and losing an infant to infanticide before it is weaned. The risks of infanticide are predicted to be high whenever a male without any genetic relationship to an infant can increase his chances of fertilizing the mother by interrupting lactation and its inhibitory effect on ovulation (Hrdy 1977). These conditions are ripe when a new, unrelated male takes over an established group with females who are nursing infants sired by his predecessor. In some species such as mountain gorillas, female groups may disintegrate when a silverback dies or is ousted by a marauding male, but in others, such as the Hanuman langur (*Semnopithecus entellus*), a female may mate and conceive her next infant with the same male whose aggression led to her previous infant's death, but who is more likely to protect than to harm his own progeny (Borries et al. 1999).

Females can reduce the risks of losing their infants to male aggression by confusing males about their potential paternity (Hrdy 1981). Mating with multiple males is not always an option if only one male is present, nor is it always advantageous, especially if male qualities vary and the costs of conceiving with a less preferred male are high. But, when multiple males are available and conception probabilities are low, then the protection that promiscuity can provide for the mother's infant should, theoretically, offset other risks. Although we do not yet know whether all male primates can recognize their own offspring, or what cues they rely on to do so, male yellow baboons have been found to support their juvenile offspring over non-offspring in agonistic interactions, and they appear to bias their support on the basis of the frequencies with which they mated with the infant's mother during her most fertile times (Buchan et al. 2003).

It is easier to assess the probabilities of conception in some primates than in others. In baboons and chimpanzees, for example, females have patches of skin on their rumps that visually inflate and deflate in response to hormonal fluctuations associated with their ovarian cycles. In most primates, however, males must rely on pheromonal or behavioral cues to assess a female's reproductive condition. Although females can't manipulate the pheromonal signals they emit any more than they can control their sexual swellings, they can – and do – alter their behavior to encourage or discourage the attentions of males. A number of field studies, conducted by measuring hormone levels in urine or fecal samples collected non-invasively from females in the wild, have shown that many female primates mate with different partners at times in their cycles when the chances of conception are low.

The decoupling of sex from reproduction *per se* was long thought to be one of the hallmarks of human relationships, yet we now know that sex can serve important social functions in other primates as well (Hrdy 1981). In bonobos, for example, relatedness among philopatric males should reduce the risks of male infanticide and therefore minimize the benefits of promiscuous mating selected to confuse paternity. Nonetheless, the high frequencies and diverse contexts in which female bonobos engage in sexual interactions both with males and with one another suggest that sex may also function to ease social tensions in their societies (de Waal 1995).

FUTURE CHALLENGES

The growth of primate field studies over the last half century has brought new insights into the diversity of primate social patterns from which our own sociality evolved. The initial emphases on ecological and phylogenetic determinants of behavior have been refined, as new empirical data have been incorporated into theories of behavioral evolution. Contemporary approaches to primate sociality are increasingly sensitive to the effects of local demographic conditions (Struhsaker 2008), and attentive to the underlying hormonal and physiological mechanisms and developmental processes that regulate behavior (Thierry 2008). Although the focus of most behavioral studies continues to be on individuals and their interactions within groups and communities, there is also greater recognition that primate groups and communities are situated within populations, whose dynamics and histories should not be ignored (Henzi and Barrett 2005; Strier 2009).

Expanding our comparative analyses so as to include populations represents a significant departure from past conventions, which focused on identifying normative, species-specific patterns. It is also an important next step in the process of interpreting intraspecific variation in relation to the interspecific variation upon which anthropological interest in primates was initially based. For example, comparisons among different populations of chimpanzees have revealed a combination of consistent social patterns, such as male philopatry, and differences, which include the associations between males and females and the levels of aggression exhibited between communities (Boesch et al. 2008). Our ability to distinguish phylogenetically conservative behavior patterns from more labile ones requires these types of comparisons within species as much as it requires comparisons between species.

Populations are also of critical importance in assessing the conservation status of endangered species. We know that large, continuous populations are less vulnerable to extinction because their size buffers them from demographic fluctuations, including the high mortality caused by unpredictable events such as epidemics, droughts, or devastating storms, and from the genetic risks that arise from the loss of alleles due to genetic drift and inbreeding depression in small, isolated populations. Human activities such as habitat fragmentation, hunting, logging, and other forms of disturbance can have negative impacts on the size of primate populations and can alter their demographic and genetic compositions. When these populations become too small and isolated from one another, their long-term viabilities are severely compromised. Even primates inhabiting the most remote, undisturbed areas are not immune from the effects of global climate change, which are predicted to alter vegetation such that the habitats may no longer be able to support viable populations.

Conservation efforts to protect primates and their habitats can produce promising results if they are implemented in time. Some of the most compelling success stories have involved primatologists, who have used their discoveries about the behavior of primates to attract attention to the conservation cause. Results have included the establishment of the Ranomafana National Park in Madagascar, which is now a sanctuary for at least twelve species of lemurs, in addition to other endangered wildlife (Wright 1992), and the reintroduction of the captive-bred golden lion tamarin (*Leontopithecus rosalia*) into what remains of the native habitat of this species in southeastern Brazil (Kleiman and Rylands 2002). In another protected fragment of Brazil's Atlantic Forest, one population of northern muriquis grew from fewer than fifty to nearly 300 individuals in less than thirty years. Although this population's remarkable recovery has been due to the commitment to conservation made by the owners of the forest that supports it, our knowledge of the demographic processes involved has been a product of ongoing behavioral research.

The muriquis' population recovery has been fascinating to follow because it has given us glimpses into which of their behavior patterns are most susceptible to change (Strier 1999). In addition to adopting fluid grouping patterns, they have also begun, unexpectedly, to spend increasing amounts of their time on the ground (Tabacow et al. 2009). This may be indicative of demographic pressures that are driving the muriquis to expand into new vertical niches, and it may reflect the establishment of a new behavioral tradition, which has spread along the male-biased social networks in their patrilocal society. Yet, perhaps because the muriquis still have ecological options, their unusual affiliative, egalitarian relationships with one another have not shown any signs of change. Whether their peacefulness will persist into the future is questionable, however, because recent birth cohorts have been strongly male-biased. When these males reach maturity, the number of males in the breeding population will exceed that of females, and levels of male competition for access both to mates and to social partners are expected to increase in response (Strier et al. 2006).

While such an extreme type of social transformation may seem implausible, this is exactly what happened, although in the opposite direction, in one troop of olive baboons at the Masai Mara Reserve in Kenya after all of the troop's most aggressive male members died from disease (Sapolsky and Share 2004). The surviving males in the troop were among the most pacifistic ones, and their interactions with one another and with females became measurably more affiliative once the composition of their group had changed.

The effects of local demographic and ecological events on social patterns may have even more significant consequences in small, isolated populations, because these lack access to immigrants who could import their own behavior along with their genes. For example, while the peaceful tradition that has become established in the baboon troop could potentially be reversed by the immigration of more aggressive males from other troops in their population, any future shift in the muriquis' breeding sex ratios will be entirely dependent on the number of males and females who are born and survive within the borders of the forest that supports their isolated population.

As populations of other primates become more fragmented and their habitats become increasingly altered, opportunities to identify the underlying causes of their behavioral differences will become even more numerous than they are today. Longitudinal studies can provide historical perspectives on the processes that lead to behavioral changes over time, and therefore contribute, along with comparative studies of multiple populations, to a better understanding of intraspecific variation in behavior. The integration of comparative knowledge of intraspecific and interspecific variation in primate social patterns is essential to evaluating conservation priorities and to developing informed management programs for the most threatened populations and species. Future generations of primatologists will be able to put into place the pieces of the puzzle of our own social evolution once the future of primates, and the clues they can offer, is secure.

ACKNOWLEDGMENTS

I am grateful to Clark Larsen for the invitation to contribute to this volume. I also thank Jon Marks for his comments and Carla Possamai for her muriqui photo.

REFERENCES

Altmann, J. (1974) Observational Study of Behavior: Sampling Methods. *Behaviour* 49: 227–267.
Altmann, J. (1980) *Baboon Mothers and Infants.* Cambridge MA: Harvard University Press.

Altmann, J., Alberts, S. C., Haines, S. A., Dubach, J., Muruthi, P., Coote, T., Geffen, E., Cheesman, D. J., Mututua, R. S., Saiyalele, S. N., Wayne, R. K., Lacy, R. C., and Bruford, M. W. (1996) Behavior Predicts Genetic Structure in a Wild Primate Group. *Proceedings of the National Academy of Sciences, USA* 93: 5797–5801.

Barrett, L., and Henzi, P. (2005) The Social Nature of Primate Cognition. *Proceedings of the Royal Society, B* 272: 1865–1875.

Boesch, C., Crockford, C., Herbinger, I., Wittig, R., Moebius, Y., and Normand, E. (2008) Intergroup Conflicts among Chimpanzees in Tai National Park: Lethal Violence and the Female Perspective. *American Journal of Primatology* 70: 519–532.

Borries, C., Launhardt, K., Epplen, C., Epplen, J. T., and Winkler, P. (1999) Males as Infant Protectors in Hanuman Langurs (*Presbytis entellus*) Living in Multimale Groups – Defence Pattern, Paternity and Sexual Behaviour. *Behavioral Ecology and Sociobiology* 46: 350–356.

Bradley, B. J., Doran-Sheehy, D. M., and Vigilant, L. (2007) Potential for Female Kin Associations in Wild Western Gorillas despite Female Dispersal. *Proceedings of the Royal Society, B* 274: 2179–2185.

Bradley, B. J., Robbins, M. M., Williamson, E. A., Steklis, H. D., Steklis, N. G., Eckhardt, N., Boesch, C., and Vigilant, L. (2005) Mountain Gorilla Tug-of-War: Silverbacks Have Limited Control over Reproduction in Multimale Groups. *Proceedings of the National Academy of Sciences, USA* 102: 9418–9423.

Buchan, J. C., Alberts, S. C., Silk, J. B., and Altmann, J. (2003) True Paternal Care in a Multi-Male Primate Society. *Nature* 425: 179–181.

Carpenter, C. R. (1934) A Field Study of the Behavior and Social Relations of Howling Monkeys. *Comparative Psychological Monographs* 48: 1–168.

Chapais, B. (2001) Primate Nepotism: What is the Explanatory Value of Kin Selection? *International Journal of Primatology* 22: 203–229.

Cheney, D., and Seyfarth, R. (1990) *How Monkeys See the World*. Chicago: University of Chicago Press.

Cheney, D., and Seyfarth, R. (2007) *Baboon Metaphysics: The Evolution of a Social Mind*. Chicago: University of Chicago Press.

Cowlishaw, G., and Dunbar, R. (2000) *Primate Conservation Biology*. Chicago: University of Chicago Press.

Di Fiore, A. (2003) Molecular Genetic Approaches to the Study of Primate Behavior, Social Organization, and Reproduction. *Yearbook of Physical Anthropology* 37: 62–99.

Di Fiore, A., and Rendall, D. (1994) Evolution of Social Organization: A Reappraisal for Primates by Using Phylogenetic Methods. *Proceedings of the National Academy of Sciences, USA* 91: 9941–9945.

Dunbar, R. I. M. (2003) The Social Brain: Mind, Language, and Society in Evolutionary Perspective. *Annual Review of Anthropology* 32: 163–181.

Emlen, S., and Oring, L. (1977) Ecology, Sexual Selection and the Evolution of Mating Systems. *Science* 197: 215–223.

Ferrari, S. F., and Digby, L. J. (1996) Wild *Callithrix* Groups: Stable Extended Families? *American Journal of Primatology* 38: 19–27.

Foley, R. A., and Lee, P. C. (1989) Finite Social Space, Evolutionary Pathways, and Reconstructing Hominid Behavior. *Science* 243: 901–906.

Fossey, D. (1983) *Gorillas in the Mist*. Boston: Houghton Mifflin Company.

Galdikas, B. M. F. (1995) *Reflections of Eden: My Years with the Orangutans of Borneo*. Boston: Little, Brown and Company.

Goodall, J. (1971) *In the Shadow of Man*. London: Collins.

Hart, D., and Sussman, R. W. (2009) *Man the Hunted: Primates, Predators, and Human Evolution*. New York: Westview Press.

Henzi, S. P., and Barrett, L. (2005) The Historical Socioecology of Savannah Baboons (*Papio hamadryas*). *Journal of Zoology* (London) 265: 215–226.

Hrdy, S. B. (1977) *The Langurs of Abu*. Cambridge MA: Harvard University Press.

Hrdy, S. B. (1981) *The Woman That Never Evolved*. Cambridge MA: Harvard University Press.

Huck, M., Lottker, P., Bohle, U. R., and Heymann, E. W. (2005) Paternity and Kinship Patterns in Polyandrous Moustached Tamarins (*Saguinus mystax*). *American Journal of Physical Anthropology* 127: 449–464.

Imanishi, K. (1960) Social Organization of Subhuman Primates in Their Natural Habitat. *Current Anthropology* 1: 393–407.

Kleiman, D. G., and Rylands, A. B. (eds) (2002) *Lion Tamarins: Biology and Conservation*. Washington DC: Smithsonian Institution Press.

Langergraber, K. E., Mitani, J. C., and Vigilant, L. (2007) The Limited Impact of Kinship on Cooperation in Wild Chimpanzees. *Proceedings of the National Academy of Sciences, USA* 104: 7786–7790.

Lee, P. C., and Kappeler, P. M. (2003) Socioecological Correlates of Phenotypic Plasticity of Primate Life Histories. In P. M. Kappeler and M. E. Pereira (eds), *Primate Life Histories and Socioecology* (pp. 41–65). Cambridge: Cambridge University Press.

Moore, J. (1984) Female Transfer in Primates. *International Journal of Primatology* 5: 537–589.

Nunn, C. L., and Barton, R. A. (2001) Comparative Methods for Studying Primate Adaptation and Allometry. *Evolutionary Anthropology* 10: 81–98.

Pope, T. R. (1990) The Reproductive Consequences of Male Cooperation in the Red Howler Monkey: Paternity Exclusion in Multi-Male and Single-Male Troops Using Genetic Markers. *Behavioral Ecology and Sociobiology* 27: 439–446.

Pope, T. R. (2000) Reproductive Success Increases with Degree of Kinship in Cooperative Coalitions of Female Red Howler Monkeys (*Alouatta seniculus*). *Behavioral Ecology and Sociobiology* 48: 253–267.

Robbins, M. M. (2001) Variation in the Social System of Mountain Gorillas: The Male Perspective. In M. M. Robbins, P. Sicotte, and K. J. Stewart (eds), *Mountain Gorillas* (pp. 29–58). Cambridge: Cambridge University Press.

Sapolsky, R. M., and Share, L. J. (2004) A Pacific Culture among Wild Baboons: Its Emergence and Transmission. *PLoS Biology* 2: 534–541.

Schülke, O., Kappeler, P. M., and Zischler, H. (2004) Small Testes Size despite High Extra-Pair Paternity in the Pair-Living Nocturnal Primate *Phaner furcifer*. *Behavioral Ecology and Sociobiology* 55: 293–301.

Setchell, J. M., and Curtis, D. J. (eds) (2003) *Field and Laboratory Methods in Primatology: A Practical Guide*. Cambridge: Cambridge University Press.

Smuts, B. B. (1985) *Sex and Friendship in Baboons*. New York: Aldine.

Strier, K. B. (1999) *Faces in the Forest: The Endangered Muriqui Monkeys of Brazil*. Cambridge MA: Harvard University Press.

Strier, K. B. (2007) *Primate Behavioral Ecology*, 3rd edn. Boston: Allyn and Bacon.

Strier, K. B. (2008) The Effects of Kin on Primate Life Histories. *Annual Review of Anthropology* 37: 21–36.

Strier, K. B. (2009) Seeing the Forest Through the Trees: Mechanisms of Primate Behavioral Diversity from Individuals to Populations and Beyond. *Current Anthropology* 50: 213–228.

Strier, K. B., Boubli, J. P., Possamai, C. B., and Mendes, S. L. (2006) Population Demography of Northern Muriquis (*Brachyteles hypoxanthus*) at the Estação Biológica de Caratinga/Reserva Particular do Patrimônio Natural-Feliciano Miguel Abdala, Minas Gerais, Brazil. *American Journal of Physical Anthropology* 130: 227–237.

Struhsaker, T. T. (2008) Demographic Variability in Monkeys: Implications for Theory and Conservation. *International Journal of Primatology* 29: 19–34.

Tabacow, F. P., Mendes, S. L., and Strier, K. B. (2009) Spread of a Terrestrial Tradition in an Arboreal Primate. *American Anthropologist* 111: 238–249.

Thierry, B. (2008) Primate Socioecology, the Lost Dream of Ecological Determinism. *Evolutionary Anthropology* 17: 93–96.

van Schaik, C. P. (1983) Why are Diurnal Primates Living in Groups? *Behaviour* 87: 120–144.

van Schaik, C. P. (2004) *Among Orangutans: Red Apes and the Rise of Human Culture.* Cambridge MA: Harvard University Press.

de Waal, F. B. (1995) Bonobo Sex and Society. *Scientific American* 272: 82–88.

Washburn, S. L., and DeVore, I. (1961) The Social Life of Baboons. *Scientific American* 204: 62–71.

Widdig, A. (2007) Paternal Kin Discrimination: The Evidence and Likely Mechanisms. *Biological Reviews* 82: 319–334.

Wrangham, R. W. (1979) On the Evolution of Ape Social Systems. *Social Science Information* 18: 335–368.

Wrangham, R. W. (1980) An Ecological Model of Female-Bonded Primate Groups. *Behaviour* 75: 262–299.

Wright, P. C. (1992) Primate Ecology, Rainforest Conservation, and Economic Development: Building a National Park in Madagascar. *Evolutionary Anthropology* 1: 25–33.

Ziegler, T. E., and Wittwer, D. J. (2005) Fecal Steroid Research in the Field and Laboratory: Improved Methods for Storage, Transport, Processing, and Analysis. *American Journal of Primatology* 67: 159–174.

Evolution of the Brain, Cognition, and Speech

CHAPTER **15**

Dean Falk

Ultimately, one would like to see the evidence for evolutionary modifications of the nervous system woven into a broader account of primate evolution, an account that relates changes in the nervous system to changes in other aspects of anatomy and, of course, to behavior.

Todd Preuss (2007a: 27)

Traditionally, most (but not all) neuroscientists have had little interest in evolutionary questions, while specialists in primate (including hominin) evolution often lacked detailed knowledge about the neurosciences. Consequently the literature about the evolution of the primate brain's neurological substrates and their associated cognitive functions is fragmented. This situation is addressed, in part, by a number of recent reviews of primate brain evolution, which summarize relevant comparative methods and quantitative techniques (for instance encephalization quotients), evidence from the fossil record of endocasts, and various hypotheses about the evolution of cognitive abilities, including language, musical abilities, and theory of mind (TOM), which set people apart from other primates – in degree, if not in kind (Barton 2006; Falk 2004a, 2007, in press; Roth and Dicke 2005; Tattersall 2008). Useful overviews are also now available that cover findings from comparative neuroanatomical studies of brains from living species, including higher primates (Kaas and Preuss 2008; Preuss 2007a, 2007b).

The disparity in approaches is also reflected, to some degree, in classical debates about the relative evolutionary importance of brain size versus cortical reorganization (reviewed in Falk et al. 2009). As just one example, one of the most exciting explorations of this dichotomy is related to the emerging field of evolutionary developmental biology (evo-devo; Carroll 2005; Goodman and Coughlin 2000). In 1995, Barbara Finlay and her colleagues demonstrated a conserved order in the way neurons are generated during neurodevelopment across 131 species of primates, bats, and insectivores that accounted for extremely robust (and predictable) allometric scaling of different parts of the brain (Finlay and Darlington 1995). Relatively larger structures such as the neocortex were generated late – that is, the number of their precursor neurons continued to divide for a longer duration, which prolonged the development of more neurons and thus the structure became larger, according to the principle "late equals large" (Finlay 2006: 77). Remarkably, 97 percent of the variance in the sizes of brain parts (excluding the limbic/olfactory components) was predicted by the size of the whole brain, which led to the conclusion that "the most likely brain alteration resulting from selection for any behavioral ability may be a coordinated enlargement of the entire nonolfactory brain" (Finlay and Darlington 1995: 1578). Nevertheless, the authors showed that the magnitude of variability (including the limbic factor) left room for species-specific brain adaptations – a fact which was lost on critics who suggested that brains evolved through selection operating on the sizes of specific but distributed neural systems (modular or mosaic evolution) rather than more globally (Barton 2006; Barton and Harvey 2000).

More recently, by using computer-simulated experiments on neural net architecture, Finlay and colleagues have explored the hypothesis that scaled-up cortical modules were significant drivers of brain evolution. They found little support for it or, for that matter, for the related suggestion that the relative size or number of cortical areas is related to niche-specific adaptations such as frugivory or folivary (Finlay 2006). In contrast to the modular hypothesis that cortical areas that implement high-level behaviors are the fundamental units of brain development and evolution, Finlay proposes that much smaller subnets (units of neural wiring that use modularity at a microscale to implement logical computations) may be the essential units (Finlay 2006). This hypothesis fits well with the observation that "functions may play more freely over the cortical matrix specified early in development than we have imagined" and the implication that "the neocortex is not a piecemeal collection of areas, each with its own discrete function, but is a generalized processing device" (Kaskan et al. 2005: 98). These observations, brought to us from the computational sciences, are also consistent with earlier ones about the conserved nature of neurogenesis (Finlay and Darlington 1995); with the fact that the major predictor of the sizes of various brain structures is the size of the whole brain (Finlay and Darlington 1995); with findings regarding the remarkable plasticity of the brain (Kaskan et al. 2005); and with information that is rapidly accumulating from functional imaging studies of the brain.

The dichotomous approaches of neuroscientists and evolutionary biologists have led, quite reasonably, to calls for greater integration of primate neuroscience with primate evolutionary biology (Preuss 2007a), and for more numerous comparative brain studies that identify multiple converging strands of evidence at different anatomical levels (Barton 2006). With respect to the extraordinary evolution of the human brain and cognition, it is also important to incorporate information from cultural and evolutionary anthropology, child development, and psycholinguistics (Falk 2009). An effort is made below to synthesize such data with recent findings from comparative neuroanatomy.

COMPARATIVE NEUROANATOMICAL EVIDENCE

Although casts of the braincase – called 'endocasts' – are useful for studying the evolution of the external morphology of primate brains, much more information has been gleaned by comparing neocortices from representatives of extant small-brained mammals

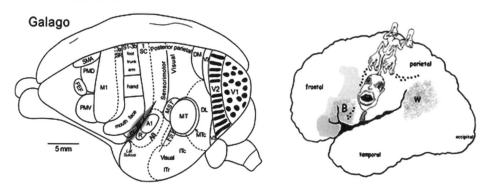

Figure 15.1   Left lateral views of a brain from a nocturnal prosimian (galago) and a human
Left: galago brain, which represents the fundamental brain organization of primates
Visual areas: primary (V1, with blobs), secondary (V2, with bands), third (V3), dorsomedial
(DM), middle temporal (MT, MTc), dorsolateral (DL), fundal-sulcal-temporal (FST), inferior
temporal with subdivisions (ITr, ITc);
Auditory cortex: primary (A1), rostral (R), belt (AB);
Somatosensory cortex: primary (S1–3b), parietal ventral (PV), secondary (S2), rostral belt
(3a, SR), caudal belt (1, SC);
Motor cortex: primary (M1), ventral premotor (PMV), dorsal premotor (PMD), supplementary
(SMA), frontal eye field (FEF). Provided courtesy of Jon Kaas (Kaas and Preuss 2008: p. 1031).
Right: human brain, with the lobes labeled. This image is not to scale, and is greatly simplified
(e.g. the legs and feet would normally extend over the middle of the brain and not be visible
from the side). Human brains have the same basic organization as the galago brain, but are much
larger and have more areas and subdivisions. The left hemisphere is dominant for language; W,
Wernicke's area for comprehension of language; B, Broca's speech area. All the hands and feet
of the homunculus are for the right side of the body. The hand and foot representations nearest
the occipital lobe belong to somatosensory cortex; the others to the motor cortex. Seeing tools
activates areas near the hand representations that would be involved in grasping them (top dots);
silently naming tools activates part of Broca's area (lower dots); the gray area in front of and
below B is activated during comprehension of sentences, while the gray region in front of and
above B is important for grammar. Image reproduced from Falk 2009.

(for example the North American opossum), prosimians, Old and New World monkeys,
apes, and humans. Using cladistic reasoning and information from the fossil record, such
data permit neuroscientists to tease out evolutionary changes that occurred in different
groups during primate evolution. Kaas and Preuss provide a detailed and technical overview of primate brain evolution on the basis of these techniques (Kaas and Preuss 2008),
the relevant highlights of which are summarized here.

Among living prosimians, brains from the small nocturnal galago from Africa
have been used most widely to represent ancestral primates. Like the brains of
anthropoid primates (monkeys, apes, and humans), galago brains have three visual
areas at the back (areas V1, V2, V3) and additional visual areas in the parietal and
temporal lobes, some of which appear to be distinctive to primates (see Figure 15.1;
also Kaas and Preuss 2008). The auditory system of galagos is comprised of several
areas in the temporal lobe that appear to be shared with other primates, some of
which may have been retained from non-primate ancestors. The somatosensory
cortex, however, differs from that of higher primates because of the connections

of some of its areas with the thalamus. Kaas and Preuss observe that the motor cortex of galagos is surprisingly advanced, having five or more premotor areas that also occur in anthropoids (Kaas and Preuss 2008).

Despite the fact that the galago's primary somatosensory cortex (S1–3b in Figure 15.1) appears to be relatively unchanged from non-primate ancestors, a variety of alterations in the sizes and number of its parts have evolved in different animals (Kaas and Preuss 2008). For example, much of S1 is devoted to tactile receptors for the highly sensitive bill of the duck-billed platypus; to receptors for the facial whiskers of rats; and to the long and fleshy nose appendages of the star-nosed mole (ibid.). Sometimes these expansions alter the grooves of the brain, or sulci, that separate the cerebral convolutions, or gyri. These grooves form what is called 'sulcal' patterns. Raccoons have greatly enlarged forepaw representations in their primary somatosensory cortices – in which, remarkably, the various digit and palm pad areas are demarcated from one another by sulci. This is a derived cortical morphology attributed to the fact that raccoons use their forepaws to an unusual degree to explore their environments (Welker and Campos 1963). Similarly, prehensile-tailed New World monkeys have enlarged tail representations that are demarcated by sulci (Felleman et al. 1983; Pubols and Pubols 1971), and gelada baboons have central sulci with unusual, hook-shaped lateral ends, which may be associated with the expanded face representations involved in producing lip-flips (Falk 1981). Harry Jerison has labeled such disproportionate allocations of somatosensory cortex the 'principle of proper mass' (Jerison 1973).

It is well known that bigger brains have more gyri (bulges) and sulci (valleys between the gyri) than smaller ones – which is true for primates as well as for other animals. Increased gyrification is due, at least in part, to mechanical effects in which surface areas of the brain buckle in order to keep pace with the volume, as brains enlarge (Jerison 1973). According to Van Essen, the pattern of connections within the brain influences the specific locations of gyri and sulci, tightly interconnected regions forming bulges, while poorly connected regions tend to be separated by sulci (Van Essen 1997, 2007). This makes sense in light of constraints on neurological 'wiring' related to distances between widely separated neurons – for instance the limits on the amount of myelinization (or development of myelin, the white matter that facilitates conduction between neurons) that can be accommodated within increasingly large brains (and their somewhat enlarged neurons), and the increased amount of time it takes to transmit impulses between more distant neurons (Hofman 2001).

Van Essen's hypothesis about the development of sulcal and gyral patterns is also intuitively satisfying, if one reflects on the raccoon digits mentioned above. But by what means did the entire paw's representation, and that of each digit within it, enlarge in the raccoon's somatosensory cortex? One suggestion is that, rather than simply being the result of an increase in the total number of neurons (Roth and Dicke 2005), which would substantially increase cortical thickness, such expansions are the result of an increase in the total number of vertically aligned minicolumns – that is, the ones that are perpendicular to the brain's surface – each one of which contains approximately the same number of neurons (Casanova and Tillquist 2008). Indeed it has been suggested, more generally, that the cortical expansion and the increased number of neurons entailed by the relatively enlarged (encephalized) brains of higher primates, as well as the emergence of higher cognition in humans, may be fundamentally related to increased numbers of the minicolumns and of their connections (ibid.).

Partly because of the longer distances between the increased number of neurons in larger brains, more of their masses are devoted to connections, which leads to the potential design problems mentioned above (Hofman 2001; Kaas and Preuss 2008). According to Kaas and Preuss, an evolutionary solution is for the total number of processing areas to be increased so that each is smaller; another is for functionally related areas to be grouped close together, thus reducing the need for long connections between them. Overall, this leads to an increased number of specialized areas in larger brains – a solution that also appears to have contributed to the increased functional differences between the two hemispheres in larger brains (Kaas and Preuss 2008). In keeping with these observations, Kaas and Preuss note that both New and Old World monkeys have all of the areas found in smaller galago brains (Figure 15.1), as well as additional ones over much of the brain's surface (Preuss 2007a). For example, certain areas of the somatosensory cortex have become more precisely differentiated from each other in monkeys compared to prosimians, while other areas in this part of the brain have become greatly expanded.

Unlike nocturnal galagos, Old World monkeys are all diurnal, and over thirty visual areas in various lobes of the brain have been proposed for them (Kaas and Preuss 2008). This is perhaps not so surprising, because it is well known that anthropoid primates, compared to their prosimian cousins, rely more on vision than on olfaction (Falk 2000). What may be less appreciated is that, in addition to being extremely visual animals, higher primates articulate with their environments largely by using their hands.

GRASPING HANDS AND 'GRASPING' BRAINS

Many animals use appendages of one kind or another to explore and manipulate their environments. As we have seen, highly specialized species may have disproportionately enlarged cortical representations for snouts (whiskers), bills, paws, trunks, and tails. For primates, it is hands; and, in higher primates especially, visually guided reaching is hypothesized to have been particularly important for ongoing brain evolution (Preuss 2007a). Reaching and grasping hands are also believed to have been among the suite of traits selected in basal primates near the beginning of the Cenozoic (approximately 65 mya) – presumably in conjunction with visually directed predation on insects in marginal growth and lower canopies of the tropical forest – in what some have dubbed the 'bug-snatching theory' (Cartmill 1974). Other traits included ocular convergence, stereoscopic vision, and developed visual areas; reduction of snout and decrease in the sense of olfaction; replacement of claws with nails; better hand–eye coordination; and a grasping hind foot for support and propulsion.

Over time, primate hands continued to evolve as modifications of the same basic plan (for example with lengthened or reduced digits, or with different degrees of muscular control) in different primate groups. In general, anthropoids gained better control over individual digits and mobility of the thumb improved in apes, and even more so in the relatively large, more muscular thumbs of humans (Schultz 1969). Receptors that mediate touch and cutaneous sensory ridges (dermatoglyphs) also developed, along with the changing gross anatomy of primate hands. As hands evolved in primates (including humans), so did areas of the brain that specialized in monitoring attention (looking) and in reaching and grasping movements ('vision for action') (Goodale and Milner 1992). These areas included parts of the posterior parietal lobe (PP) and the ventral premotor cortex (PMV; see Figure 15.1) of the frontal lobe (Preuss 2007a).

The PP 'vision for action' function in primates is associated with a main dorsal stream of visual processing that extends from the primary visual cortex (V1) to PP, which is concerned with the spatial location of objects (including moving ones) and has been called the 'where is it' system. Primates also have a second main visual processing stream, or ventral stream, which extends from V1 to the inferior temporal cortex (IT), contributes to the recognition of objects, and is known as the 'what is it' system (see Figure 15.1). With respect to these two systems, Preuss observes:

> Probably no one will be surprised to learn that structures related to vision were modified in stem primates, including systems specifically related to looking and visually guided reaching ... We might even regard the evolutionary parcellation of primate visual cortex into distinct dorsal and ventral processing systems as an elegant solution to the problem of how to accommodate the demands of both visually guided predation and plant foraging. (Preuss 2007b: 660)

Preuss cautions, however, that looking and reaching should not be regarded as a unitary thing, because in macaques and humans this deceptively simple-looking act is composed of an astonishing array of elements, each of which could have been modified during evolution. These elements include locating the target visually; determining its size and orientation; paying attention to the object; moving the head and the eyes so as to keep the target centrally focused; programming and initiating movement of the forelimb toward the object; adjusting movement of the forelimb as it progresses; preshaping the hand to grasp the object; and adjusting the final grip to the weight, compressibility, and texture of the target by using sensory feedback from the nervous system (Preuss 2007b).

Obviously, reaching and grasping under visual guidance is a major way in which primates 'grasp' their worlds. The reason why I have devoted so much of this brief overview to this topic is that current research from the neurosciences suggests that the neurological underpinnings for this not so simple act may have formed a major substrate from which higher cognition arose in anthropoids. In other words, evolution may have 'tinkered' or cobbled together the neurological substrates for the well known abilities of anthropoids to 'grasp' mentally their social and physical environments from areas of the brain that were initially involved in reaching and grasping objects (Jacob 1977). Such co-opted regions are sometimes referred to as 'exaptations,' or (less ponderously) as the result of 'cortical gerrymandering' (Finlay and Brodsky 2006: 87).

Take for example the PMV (see Figure 15.1) – which may be the clearest case for a new motor area in primates, and is distinctive because it represents "the face and forelimb virtually exclusively, and seems to play an important role in organizing grasping movements of the hands and mouth," which led Preuss to suggest that "this area evolved to organize the visually guided reaching and grasping behaviors of stem primates" (Preuss 2007a: 20). About twenty years ago, a new class of neurons was discovered in the anterior (rostral) portion of the PMV of macaques, called 'area F5' (Rizzolatti and Arbib 1998; Rizzolatti and Craighero 2004). Because these neurons had the remarkable property of firing not only when the monkeys grasped and manipulated an object, but also when the animals observed the experimenter doing the same thing, they were called 'mirror neurons.' In order to fire, mirror neurons require that a very specific action be executed or observed. Since their initial discovery in the inferior frontal lobe, mirror neurons have also been found in the inferior parietal cortex of monkeys, and others have been discovered that respond to sounds rather than to visual observations of specific actions.

According to their discoverers and others, mirror neurons function so as to 'represent' actions in the nervous system, and these representations can then be used to recognize, imitate, and understand the actions of others. Mirror neurons thus "represent the link between sender and receiver," and may therefore allow one monkey to understand the goals and intentions of another (Rizzolatti and Arbib 1998: 189). This gets very close to the concept called 'theory of mind' (TOM), which, in humans, refers to the cognitively advanced ability to infer the motivations and goals of another person from their behaviors – mind-reading, in other words. Although monkeys are not nearly as good at it as people, studies show that they (in this case, baboons) are capable of a certain amount of mind-reading (Cheney and Seyfarth 2007). In light of the above discussion, it is reasonable to hypothesize that the neurological substrates that allow baboons to 'grasp' what other baboons are thinking evolved from parts of the brain that were once dedicated to reaching and grasping, and involve mirror neurons.

Significantly, frontal and parietal areas in humans are now believed to have mirror systems that are homologous with the ones that contain mirror neurons in monkeys (Iacoboni et al. 1999; Rizzolatti and Arbib 1998). This is intriguing in light of research carried out by Andrew Meltzoff and his colleagues, who have shown that human babies have an inborn ability to imitate certain tongue, lip, mouth, and finger movements of adults and that this hypothetically facilitates their development of another ability, namely to infer mental states in others: "In ontogeny, infant imitation is the seed and the adult theory of mind is the fruit" (Meltzoff and Decety 2003: 491). Thus, when a newborn imitates an adult act such as tongue protrusion, the infant associates the visual observation of the adult with the subjective feeling of performing the gesture, and stores that association in memory. Because human infants are able to recognize the equivalence between acts they see and do, they are able to map the relationship between mental and motor experiences, which allows them to infer the experiences of others. "When infants see others acting 'like me,' they project that others have the same mental experience that is mapped to those behavioural states in the self" (Meltzoff and Decety 2003: 497). Meltzoff also speculates that the same kind of '*that*-looks-like-*this*-feels' process helps infants to develop a TOM that incorporates visual, tactile, and motor senses (Meltzoff 2007: 130).

The discoverers of mirror neurons and others believe that human language evolved from a fundamental mechanism that was originally related to the ability to recognize actions in others, and that manual gestures paved the way for the evolution of speech. This idea fits well with the hypothesis that evolution co-opted existing structures in our ancestors' brains to serve new functions. It also fits with the hypotheses that social factors were a main driver behind hominin brain evolution, and that an important result was a highly evolved and adaptive aptitude for detecting the emotional states, intentions, and motivations of others (TOM) (Byrne and Whiten 1988; Dunbar

1993; Herrmann et al. 2007). Interestingly, people who score relatively high on tests that quantify their empathy or degree of sensitivity to other people's perspectives appear to have the most active mirror neurons (Gazzola et al. 2006). It is fascinating to contemplate that mirror neurons that were initially involved in the reaching and grasping activities of our early ancestors may have formed a fundamental substrate for human brain evolution.

Language and the Evolution of the Human Brain

Human brains (and their neocortices) are greatly encephalized, being about three times the size expected in a non-human primate of similar body size (Passingham 1973, 1975; Stephan et al. 1970). Despite their size, however, human brains have the same fundamental organization shown in the diagram for the galago brain (Figure 15.1); but they have many more areas, specialized subdivisions of areas, and modified connections (pathways), due partly to the design features discussed above. The cartoon image of the left hemisphere of a human brain (known as a homunculus) in Figure 15.1 is greatly simplified and unscaled; nevertheless it shows that the representations of the different bodily parts in the sensory and motor cortices of people are arranged in the same order as in galagos: the representations of the mouth and face are lateral to those of the hands, and so on up to the foot areas, which are located near the midline on top. (This image is simplified because the legs and feet of the homunculus would normally extend over the middle of the brain and not be visible from the side.)

Like in galagos (and indeed as in many other animals), the sensory areas of humans are located caudally (that is, toward the back of the brain), while the motor representations course parallel to them in a rostral location (toward the front). For much of the homunculus, the left half of the brain represents the right half of the body and vice versa, because brain connections are mostly crossed (the face is an exception). This is why the homunculus in Figure 15.1 has only right hands and feet. Thus a pinched right thumb would be perceived in the thumb area toward the back of the left part of the brain, while the thumb region in front of that area would be involved in wiggling the right thumb. (Again, this is a simplification.) Notice also that the homunculus has relatively large representations for the hand, lips, and mouth (Kaas and Preuss 2008).

Preuss has argued eloquently that the parts of the brain that are involved in human language (and these are located mostly in the left hemisphere) were co-opted during evolution from regions that functioned for reaching and grasping in our ancestors (Preuss 2007b). This hypothesis is supported by functional imaging studies, as summarized in Figure 15.1's illustration of the left human hemisphere. The regions labeled W and B represent the classic sensory and motor (speech) areas for language: Wernicke's area and Broca's area respectively. Interestingly, the caudal portion of B – Brodmann's area (BA) 44 – has a greater volume in the left than in right hemisphere and has therefore been suggested as the "putative correlate of the functional lateralization of speech production" (Amunts et al. 1999: 319). BA 44 is also considered to be the homolog of F5 in macaques – that is, the area in which mirror neurons were first discovered (Rizzolatti and Arbib 1998). Merely seeing tools activates areas in the human brain near the hand representations that would be involved in grasping and using them (dots near the hands of the homunculus), while silently naming them activates neurons in part of BA 44 (dots near B; Grafton et al. 1997). Thus the parts of the brain involved in seeing, naming, and thinking about tools are next to, and in some cases partially overlap with, the sensory and motor areas that facilitate actually grasping and manipulating them (Chao and Martin 2000). No wonder that Preuss observed: "The intimate relationship between language, object representation, and grasping is a particularly dramatic illustration of how evolution co-opts and modifies existing structures to serve new functions" (Preuss 2007b: 664).

Grasping is not the only activity for which this generalization holds, because reading action-related words activates the motor homunculus and nearby areas that control a variety of voluntary movements. Thus an event-related functional magnetic resonance imaging (fMRI) study revealed that, in addition to activating left frontal and temporal cortices, passively reading the words 'lick,' 'pick,' and 'kick' activates areas in, or just rostral to, the parts of the motor homunculus that represent the tongue, hand, and foot, respectively (Hauk et al. 2004). This finding has far-reaching implications for how the brain processes word meaning, because it "rules out a unified 'meaning center' ... and supports a dynamic view according to which words are processed by distributed neuronal assemblies with cortical topographies that reflect word semantics" (ibid., p. 301).

Nevertheless, there appear to be areas in the human frontal lobe that process more subtle aspects of meaning that go beyond understanding isolated words. As the functional imaging and transcranial magnetic stimulation (TMS) studies of Kuniyoshi Sakai and others have shown, the lower gray area in front of and below B in the figure with the homunculus (Figure 15.1) is activated in the left hemisphere during the comprehension of sentences, both spoken and signed (Sakai 2005). However, comprehending sentences requires more than just understanding the meanings of individual words. As noted by Sakai, the sentence "John thinks that David praises his son" has a very different meaning from "John thinks that his son praises David," despite the fact that each sentence contains identical words. In order to understand the correct meaning of either sentence one must have a grasp of syntax, the part of grammar that specifies how words are arranged into phrases and sentences. The lower gray area in Figure 15.1 does not decode sentence meaning in isolation. Instead, it communicates with the larger gray region in front of the homunculus, which extends upward from B toward the hand representation. Sakai regards this latter region as a grammar center in the left hemispheres of humans, noting that its activation "is related to processes of analyzing syntactic structures ... The human left frontal cortex is thus uniquely specialized in the syntactic processes of sentence comprehension, without any counterparts in other animals" (Sakai 2005: 817).

The studies discussed above provide strong support for the hypothesis that the neurological substrates for human language were co-opted from regions of the brain that evolved in our early ancestors in order to facilitate reaching for and grasping insects and fruit (Preuss 2007b). Today, non-human primates explore and grasp their worlds largely with their hands; we 'grasp' ours primarily through language. In keeping with the opening quotation to this chapter, can this hypothesis be harmonized with aspects of anatomy and behavior that have been elucidated by evolutionary anthropology, psychology, and the hominin fossil record? More specifically, do these fields have anything to offer that might shed light on the relationship between grasping hands and the emergence of language?

MOTHERS, INFANTS, AND THE EMERGENCE OF LANGUAGE

What Darwinian natural selection depends on, of course, is differential reproduction through the successful transmission of favorable genes to future generations. Despite the fact that prehistoric women are now recognized for their contributions as food gatherers and grandmothers (Hawkes 2003; Zihlman 1985), there has been remarkably little discussion of the fact that, as with many mammals, the quality of early hominin mothering must have played an important role in the differential survival of infants, and thus it must have helped to shape the trajectory of hominin evolution at a fundamental level. Anatomical evidence from the hominin fossil record suggests that childbirth became increasingly difficult during hominin evolution because, given changes in the pelvis associated with the selection of bipedalism, the enlargement of brains (and of fetal heads) coincided with a narrowing of birth canals (Rosenberg and Trevathan 2001). The evolutionary solution to this obstetrical dilemma was for prehistoric mothers to give birth to smaller babies, less developed by comparison with their more apelike ancestors. This is why modern human infants are comparatively helpless.

I have hypothesized elsewhere that the shift toward bearing undeveloped infants was related to a decrease in the grasping abilities of prehistoric babies that, in turn, led to profoundly important changes in mother–infant interactions (Falk 2004b; Falk 2009). Except for humans, higher primate infants develop soon after birth the ability to cling autonomously to the chests and (later) to the backs of their traveling mothers. Such infant 'riding' means that monkey and ape mothers have their extremities free for other activities (Ross 2001). Although human babies retain a strong grasping reflex, they fail to develop an ape-like (or monkey-like) ability to cling independently onto their mothers (Halverson 1937). By the time prehistoric infants had lost the ability to grasp their mothers' fur effectively enough to 'ride' on them, mothers had little choice but to carry their offspring actively. Although this is accomplished in many parts of the world today through the use of baby slings, the latter had to be invented before this solution could be implemented, and there is nothing in the archaeological record to indicate that baby slings originated when bipedalism and big brains were beginning to cause obstetrical problems.

Primate infants, including humans, have a deeply engrained desire for close physical contact with care givers that goes beyond practical considerations such as the need to be nursed. This was famously demonstrated over half a century ago by Harry Harlow's experiments with newborn monkeys raised in isolation and with two surrogate 'mothers.' One was a wire-frame 'mother' with a nipple that provided nourishment; the other frame lacked a nipple, but was covered with soft terry cloth (Harlow 1958). Although the newborns fed from the frame with the nipple, they preferred to spend the rest of their time clinging to the terry-cloth 'mother.' Another example comes from the well known chimpanzee Joni, who was raised in the home of Nadia Ladygina-Kohts from 1913 to 1916 (Ladygina-Kohts et al. 2002). Joni was an infant when he arrived in the Kohts' household, and he readily adopted Nadia as his mother. However, he was locked every night in a cage where he obtained 'contact comfort' from rags, just as baby chimpanzees obtain comfort from their mothers. When the rags were removed in the mornings for airing, Joni became violent and "would not give up his rags for the world" (Ladygina-Kohts et al. 2002: 84). The psychological and developmental literature on human infants indicates that our babies also have an intense desire for physical contact with their care givers. It has been suggested, in fact, that in industrial societies the main reason why babies cry is to re-establish physical contact with care givers they are separated from (Small 1998). I also think that the 'blankies' our infants treasure may be stand-ins for the furry comfort once provided by the ancestral mothers' chests.

Comparative anatomical and fossil evidence shows that our ancestors' hands changed as they evolved, as detailed above (Schultz 1969; Susman 1994). We also know that there are functional correlates to the specialized anatomy of the human hand – for instance better precision grips, capable of more dexterous manipulations of objects. As noted, another change that occurred during the evolution of our hands is that human infants lost the ancestral ability to cling to their mothers for sustained periods of time. The examples discussed earlier, of raccoons and star-nosed moles, show that an enlarged or specialized peripheral structure (in this case, the human hand) is likely to be reflected in modifications of its representation in the brain. Additionally, representations for reaching and grasping in primates appear to have been tinkered, or co-opted, during the evolution of new neurological structures that were involved in understanding and communicating with others. This was also the case, I believe, during the emergence of proto-language in early hominins – an idea that I have dubbed the 'putting the baby down' (PTBD) hypothesis (Falk 2004b; Falk 2009).

A basic premise of the PTBD hypothesis is that foraging hominin mothers had to carry their nursing infants with them and, before the invention of baby slings, they did so in their arms (or on their hips). When mothers stopped to forage, naturally they would have set down their babies next to them, to free their own hands for digging tubers, for gathering other plant food, or simply to rest. (I hasten to add that successful mothers would have been unlikely to stash or park their babies away from them, because of predators.) For the first time in hominin prehistory, these physical separations would have stimulated the evolution of two-way vocal communications between mothers (shushing, soothing, melodic humming) and their nearby infants (crying, gurgling, cooing) to a degree not seen in living apes or monkeys. In other words, with the loss of constant physical contact between mothers and infants, the auditory/vocal channel would have flourished as a way of maintaining close contact.

I believe that certain vocalizations, which are universal in the world today – including lullabies, motherese (baby talk), and a derived form of crying in human babies – emerged from such beginnings (Falk 2009). The suggestion that motherese may not be universal is refuted elsewhere (ibid). In other words, voices began compensating for the loss of sustained grasping in infant hands and feet and for the decreased amount of cradling from their mothers' busy arms. It is, I further hypothesize, from such substrates that proto-language evolved. The matter goes beyond the scope of this brief overview, but elsewhere I detail, step by step, how such early communications between mothers and infants could have eventually led to the first words, to short sentences, to syntax, and to other aspects of grammar; how the latter could have become conventionalized across populations and transmitted vertically through generations; and ultimately how these developments (brought to us largely through the behaviors of prehistoric women and children) could have sparked the emergence of proto-language (Falk 2009).

Another point I want to make here is that evolutionary changes in the hominins' hands and feet must have been linked to changes in their representations of these parts in the brain. Evidence from comparative neuroanatomy suggests that these changes included the eventual modification (or co-option) of networks initially dedicated to manual exploration and manipulation through reaching and grasping – namely a modification toward serving new systems for 'grasping' the world linguistically. This meshes well with the PTBD hypothesis suggested by data from evolutionary anthropology, psychology, and the hominin fossil record – namely that it was the grasping hands and feet – or, rather, the lack thereof – that led to the development of motherese in the wake of extreme infant helplessness which, in turn, led eventually to the emergence of proto-language.

REFERENCES

Amunts, K., Schleicher, A., Bürgel, U., Mohlberg, H., Uylings, H. B., and Zilles, K. (1999) Broca's Region Revisited: Cytoarchitecture and Intersubject Variability. *Journal of Comparative Neurolology* 412 (2): 319–341.

Barton, R. A. (2006) Primate Brain Evolution: Integrating Comparative, Neurophysiological, and Ethological Data. *Evolutionary Anthropology* 15: 224–236.

Barton, R. A., and Harvey, P. H. (2000) Mosaic Evolution of Brain Structure in Mammals. *Nature* 405 (6790): 1055–1058.

Byrne, R. W., and Whiten, A. (1988) *Machiavellian Intelligence: Social Expertise and the Evolution of Intellect in Monkeys, Apes, and Humans.* Oxford: Oxford University Press.

Carroll, S. B. (2005) *Endless Forms Most Beautiful: The New Science of Evo Devo and the Making of the Animal Kingdom.* New York: Norton.

Cartmill, M. (1974) Rethinking Primate Origins. *Science* 184 (135): 436–443.

Casanova, M. F., and Tillquist, C. R. (2008) Encephalization, Emergent Properties, and Psychiatry: A Minicolumnar Perspective. *The Neuroscientist* 14 (1): 101–118.

Chao, L. L., and Martin, A. (2000) Representation of Manipulable Man-Made Objects in the Dorsal Stream. *Neuroimage* 12 (4): 478–484.

Cheney, D. L., and Seyfarth, R. M. (2007) *Baboon Metaphysics: The Evolution of a Social Mind.* Chicago: University of Chicago Press.

Dunbar, R. I. M. (1993) Coevolution of Neocortical Size, Group Size and Language in Humans. *Behavioral and Brain Sciences* 16: 681–735.

Falk, D. (1981) Sulcal Patterns of Fossil *Theropithecus* Baboons: Phylogenetic and Functional Implications. *International Journal of Primatology* 2: 57–69.

Falk, D. (2000) *Primate Diversity.* New York: W. W. Norton.

Falk, D. (2004a) Hominin Brain Evolution – New Century, New Directions. *Collegium Antropologicum* 28 (Suppl. 2): 59–64.

Falk, D. (2004b) Prelinguistic Evolution in Early Hominins: Whence Motherese? *Behavioral and Brain Sciences* 27 (4): 491–503 (discussion 503–583).

Falk, D. (2007) Evolution of the Primate Brain. In W. Henke, H. Rothe, and I. Tattersall (eds), *Handbook of Palaeoanthropology*, Vol. 2: *Primate Evolution and Human Origins* (pp. 1133–1162). Berlin: Springer-Verlag.

Falk, D. (2009) *Finding Our Tongues: Mothers, Infants and the Origins of Language.* New York: Pertheus (Basic Books).

Falk, D. (in press) Hominin Brain Evolution 1925–2007: An Emerging Overview. In S. C. Reynolds and A. Gallagher (eds), *African Genesis: Perspectives on Hominid Evolution.* Johannesburg: University of Witwatersrand.

Falk, D., Hildebolt, C., Smith, Morwood, K. M. J., Sutikna, T., Jatmiko, Saptomo, E. W., and Prior, F. (2009) LB1's Virtual Endocast, Microcephaly, and Hominin Brain Evolution. *Journal of Human Evolution*, doi:101016/jjhevol200810008.

Felleman, D. J., Nelson, R. J., Sur, M., and Kaas, J. H. (1983) Representations of the Body Surface in Areas 3b and 1 of Postcentral Parietal Cortex of *Cebus* Monkeys. *Brain Research* 268 (1): 15–26.

Finlay, B. L., and Brodsky, P. (2006) Cortical Evolution as the Expression of a Program for Disproportionate Growth and the Proliferation of Areas. In J. H. Kaas (ed.), *Evolution of Nervous Systems* (pp. 73–96). Oxford: Oxford University Press.

Finlay, B. L., and Darlington, R. B. (1995) Linked Regularities in the Development and Evolution of Mammalian Brains. *Science* 268 (5217): 1578–1584.

Gazzola, V., Aziz-Zadeh, L., and Keysers, C. (2006) Empathy and the Somatotopic Auditory Mirror System in Humans. *Current Biology* 16 (18): 1824–1829.

Goodale, M. A., and Milner, A. D. (1992) Separate Visual Pathways for Perception and Action. *Trends in Neuroscience* 15 (1): 20–25.

Goodman, C. S., and Coughlin, B. C. (2000) Introduction. The Evolution of Evo-Devo Biology. *Proceedings of the National Academy of Sciences, USA* 97 (9): 4424–4425.

Grafton, S. T., Fadiga, L., Arbib, M. A., and Rizzolatti, G. (1997) Premotor Cortex Activation during Observation and Naming of Familiar Tools. *Neuroimage* 6 (4): 231–236.

Halverson, H. M. (1937) Studies of the Grasping Responses of Early Infancy: *International Journal of Genetic Psychology* 51: 371–392.

Harlow, H. F. (1958) The Nature of Love. *American Psychologist* 13: 673–685.

Hauk, O., Johnsrude, I., and Pulvermuller, F. (2004) Somatotopic Representation of Action Words in Human Motor and Premotor Cortex. *Neuron* 41 (2): 301–307.

Hawkes, K. (2003) Grandmothers and the Evolution of Human Longevity. *American Journal of Human Biology* 15 (3): 380–400.

Herrmann, E., Call, J., Hernandez-Lloreda, M. V., Hare, B., and Tomasello, M. (2007) Humans Have Evolved Specialized Skills of Social Cognition: The Cultural Intelligence Hypothesis. *Science* 317 (5843): 1360–1366.

Hofman, M. A. (2001) Brain Evolution in Hominids: Are We at the End of the Road? In D. Falk and K. R. Gibson (eds), *Evolutionary Anatomy of the Primate Cerebral Cortex* (pp. 113–127). Cambridge: Cambridge University Press.

Iacoboni, M., Woods, R. P., Brass, M., Bekkering, H., Mazziotta, J. C., and Rizzolatti, G. (1999) Cortical Mechanisms of Human Imitation. *Science* 286 (5449): 2526–2528.

Jacob, F. (1977) Evolution and Tinkering. *Science* 196 (4295): 1161–1166.

Jerison, H. J. (1973) *Evolution of the Brain and Intelligence*. New York: Academic Press.

Kaas, J. H., and Preuss, T. M. (2008) Human Brain Evolution. In L. R. Squire (ed.), *Fundamental Neuroscience*, 3rd edn (pp. 1017–1038). San Diego: Academic Press.

Kaskan, P. M., Franco, E. C., Yamada, E. S., Silveira, L. C., Darlington, R. B., and Finlay, B. L. (2005) Peripheral Variability and Central Constancy in Mammalian Visual System Evolution. *Proceedings of the Royal Society B* 272 (1558): 91–100.

Ladygina-Kohts, N. N., de Waal, F. B. M., Vekker, B., and Yerkes Regional Primate Research Center. (2002) *Infant Chimpanzee and Human Child: A Classic 1935 Comparative Study of Ape Emotions and Intelligence*. Oxford–New York: Oxford University Press.

Meltzoff, A. N. (2007) 'Like Me': A Foundation for Social Cognition. *Developmental Science* 10 (1): 126–134.

Meltzoff, A. N., and Decety, J. (2003) What Imitation Tells Us about Social Cognition: A Rapprochement between Developmental Psychology and Cognitive Neuroscience. *Philosophical Transactions of the Royal Society B – Biological Sciences* 358 (1431): 491–500.

Passingham, R. E. (1973) Anatomical Differences between the Neocortex of Man and Other Primates. *Brain Behavior Evolution* 7 (5): 337–359.

Passingham, R. E. (1975) Changes in the Size and Organisation of the Brain in Man and His Ancestors. *Brain Behavior Evolution* 11 (2): 73–90.

Preuss, T. M. (2007a) Primate Brain Evolution in Phylogenetic Context. In J. H. Kaas and T. M. Preuss (eds), *Evolution of Nervous Systems*, Vol 4: *The Evolution of Primate Nervous Systems* (pp. 1–34). Oxford: Elsevier.

Preuss, T. M. (2007b) Evolutionary Specializations of Primate Brain Systems. In M. Ravosa and M. Dagasto (ed.), *Primate Origins: Adaptations and Evolution* (pp. 625–675). New York: Springer.

Pubols, B. H., Jr, and Pubols, L. M. (1971) Somatotopic Organization of Spider Monkey Somatic Sensory Cerebral Cortex. *Journal of Comparative Neurology* 141 (1): 63–75.

Rizzolatti, G., and Arbib, M. A. (1998) Language within Our Grasp. *Trends in Neuroscience* 21 (5): 188–194.

Rizzolatti, G., and Craighero, L. (2004) The Mirror-Neuron System. *Annual Review of Neuroscience* 27: 169–192.

Rosenberg, K. R., and Trevathan, W. R. (2001) The Evolution of Human Birth. *Scientific American* 285 (5): 72–77.

Ross, C. (2001) Park or Ride? Evolution of Infant Carrying in Primates. *International Journal of Primatology* 22: 749–771.

Roth, G., and Dicke, U. (2005) Evolution of the Brain and Intelligence. *Trends in Cognitive Sciences* 9 (5): 250–257.

Sakai, K. L. (2005) Language Acquisition and Brain Development. *Science* 310 (5749): 815–819.

Schultz, A. H. (1969) *The Life of Primates*. New York: Universe Books.

Small, M. F. (1998) *Our Babies, Ourselves: How Biology and Culture Shape the Way We Parent*. New York: Anchor Books.

Stephan, H., Bauchot, R., and Andy, O. J. (1970) Data on Size of the Brain and of Various Brain Parts in Insectivores and Primates. In C. R. Noback and W. Montagna (eds), *Advances in Primatology*, Vol 1: *The Primate Brain* (pp. 289–297). New York: Appleton–Century–Crofts.

Susman, R. L. (1994) Fossil Evidence for Early Hominid Tool Use. *Science* 265 (5178): 1570–1573.

Tattersall, I. (2008) An Evolutionary Framework for the Acquisition of Symbolic Cognition by *Homo sapiens*. *Comparative Cognition and Behavior Reviews* 3: 99–114.

Van Essen, D. C. (1997) A Tension-Based Theory of Morphogenesis and Compact Wiring in the Central Nervous System. *Nature* 385 (6614): 313–318.

Van Essen, D. C. (2007) Cerebral Cortical Folding Patterns in Primates: Why They Vary and What They Signify. In J. H. Kass and T. M. Preuss (eds), *Evolution of Nervous Systems*, Vol. 4 (pp. 267–289). London: Elsevier.

Welker, W. I., and Campos, G. B. (1963) Physiological Significance of Sulci in Somatic Sensory Cerebral Cortex in Mammals of the Family Procyonidae. *Journal of Comparative Neurology* 120: 19–36.

Zihlman, A. L. (1985) Gathering Stories for Hunting Human Nature. *Feminist Studies* 11: 365–377.

PART **III** The Past and
the Dead

CHAPTER 16 Primate Origins: The Early Cenozoic Fossil Record

Gregg F. Gunnell and
Mary T. Silcox

INTRODUCTION

Advances in the study both of molecules and of morphology over the last two decades have led to a growing consensus concerning the overall pattern of mammalian evolution (Springer et al. 2004). Within this context, most workers agree that the order Primates forms part of a clade, Euarchonta, which contains tree shrews (Scandentia) and flying lemurs (Dermoptera) and is part of a larger grouping, which in turn includes rodents (Rodentia) and rabbits (Lagomorpha). Although there are some areas of continuing dispute in terms of the branching order of these taxa (see for instance Olson et al. 2005; Janečka et al. 2007), the general position of primates within Mammalia seems to be broadly agreed upon. Many questions remain, however, about the details concerning the origin of primates, both in terms of where and when this event happened. The earliest potential primates known in the fossil record are from the latest Cretaceous or earliest Paleocene (approximately 65 mya) of North America, but molecular evidence suggests that primates may have existed as a distinct lineage before the Cretaceous/Tertiary boundary (Springer et al. 2003). This indicates either a substantial gap in the early fossil record or a problem with the molecular dates.

Disagreements also abound concerning the place of origin of primates. Both of the living groups closest to primates are restricted to southern Asia today, which some authors (for instance Beard 2004) cite as support for an Asian origin for the order. However, the most compelling case for the presence of Paleocene primates is found in North America, where a group of primate-like mammals, informally called 'plesiadapiforms,' was very diverse and abundant (Silcox and Gunnell 2008). Although 'plesiadapiforms' are also known from Europe, Asia, and possibly Africa, the oldest and most primitive members of the group all come from North America, providing support for a New World origin for the order Primates (Bloch et al. 2007; Silcox 2008).

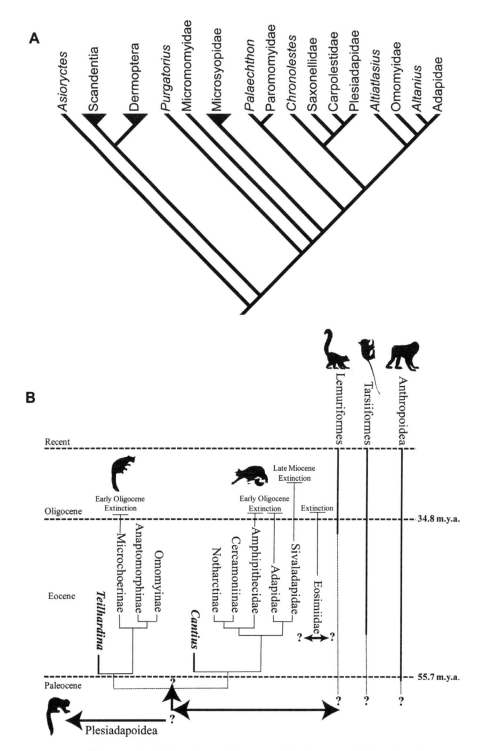

Figure 16.1 Phylogenetic relationships and temporal distributions of 'plesiadapiforms' and Euprimates. Outline figures adapted and modified from Fleagle 1999

A Hypothesis of relationships for 'plesiadapiforms' and extinct euprimates on the basis of a single most parsimonious tree from a cladistic analysis of 173 dental, cranial, and postcranial characters (Bloch et al. 2007). Dermoptera includes modern representatives of the order as well as members of the fossil family Plagiomenidae. Microsyopidae includes the European genus *Berruvius*

The first fossil evidence for more modern-looking primates (Euprimates) is found in the late Paleocene of Africa; this is followed closely by the appearance of the group in the earliest Eocene of Asia, North America, and Europe (Silcox 2008). As with primate origins, there are many questions about the origin of Euprimates. The earliest members of the group may trace their ancestry to some specific group of 'plesiadapiforms,' but this has yet to be conclusively demonstrated.

'PLESIADAPIFORMS,' THE FIRST RADIATION OF PRIMATES

The term 'plesiadapiforms' has come to be applied to a cluster of extinct mammals from the Paleocene and Eocene of North America, Europe, Asia, and possibly Africa (Figure 16.1, A). 'Plesiadapiforms' are generally similar in possessing enlarged upper and lower central incisors and lower molars with broad, well developed talonid basins. Features shared by many, but not all, 'plesiadapiforms' include small size, a reduction in the number of premolars and/or incisors, and an enlarged third or fourth lower premolar. The body size of 'plesiadapiforms' ranged between *Picromomys petersonorum*, which is smaller than a living mouse (10 grams: Silcox et al. 2002), to species about the size of a small cat (2–3 kg; Gingerich and Gunnell 2005; Silcox et al. 2009; Fleagle 1999). The group includes more than 120 named species, and the fossil record documents an impressive diversity of dental adaptations, ranging from *Purgatorius*, which is little removed in morphology from the most primitive eutherians, to some of the most specialized mammals known from the Paleocene. An expanding record of cranial and postcranial material (Figure 16.2, B–D) has begun to demonstrate that the group was morphologically diverse in other parts of the body as well, although all 'plesiadapiforms' known from below the head exhibit skeletal features for non-leaping arborealism (Bloch and Boyer 2007; Bloch et al. 2007).

The earliest representatives of this group are placed in the genus *Purgatorius*. When Van Valen and Sloan (1965) first described the genus, they attributed a fragment of a lower molar from the Hell Creek formation to the species *Purgatorius ceratops*, named in recognition of the apparent co-occurrence of this specimen with a *Triceratops* skeleton. They assigned the specimen to a latest Cretaceous age. It comes, however, from a mixed-age assemblage (Clemens 2004), and the specimen itself is not particularly diagnostic (in fact it may not even be a primate), so this represents only weak evidence for a Mesozoic record for Primates. A more diagnostic and firmly dated specimen of *Purgatorius* is known from the earliest Paleocene of Saskatchewan (Figure 16.2, A; Johnston and Fox 1984), at approximately 65 mya. At the other end of the temporal range, members of the 'plesiadapiform' families Paromomyidae and Microsyopidae persisted to the end of the middle Eocene in North America; but no 'plesiadapiforms' are known from the late Eocene, which implies that the group was extinct by around 37 mya (Silcox and Gunnell 2008).

In terms of geographic extent, much of the record comes from western North America (ibid.) and includes representatives of ten families (Purgatoriidae, 'Palaechthonidae,'

Figure 16.1
B   The Eocene record and possible relationships of Euprimates. Note that the Neogene (Miocene through Pliocene) and the Pleistocene are not shown in this figure. Also note that the Eocene–Oligocene boundary is shown, but only to indicate which lineages of euprimates go extinct after the boundary

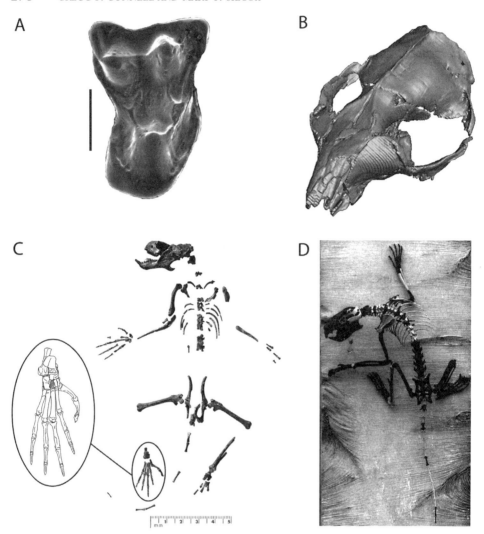

Figure 16.2 Specimens of 'plesiadapiforms' documenting some morphological features
A *Purgatorius*, RM2. The specimen is from the Ravenscrag Formation in Saskatchewan (about 65 mya; Johnston and Fox 1984) and represents some of the oldest evidence of the genus *Purgatorius* and of the order Primates. Scale bar = 1 mm. Modified from Silcox 2001
B Cranium of *Ignacius graybullianus* from the early Eocene of Wyoming. Image generated from an ultra-high resolution x-ray-computed tomography dataset (Silcox 2003) in Amira 3.1.1
C Skeleton of *Carpolestes simpsoni* from the late Paleocene of Wyoming, with a reconstruction of the anatomy of the foot showing the divergent, nail-bearing hallux. Modified from Bloch and Boyer (2002) and used by permission of the American Association for the Advancement of Science
D Mounted skeleton of *Plesiadapis cookei* from the late Paleocene of Wyoming. Image from Gingerich and Gunnell 2005

Paromomyidae, Micromomyidae, Microsyopidae, Picrodontidae, Picromomyidae, Plesiadapidae, Carpolestidae, Saxonellidae; see Figure 1A). There is, however, also extensive material of Microsyopidae (*Berruvius*), Plesiadapidae, Paromomyidae, Saxonellidae, and Toliapinidae known from Europe (Russell 1964; Godinot 1984; Hooker et al. 1999). There are eight potential species of Asian 'plesiadapiforms' (Beard and Wang

1995), which have been attributed to five families: Carpolestidae, Micromomyidae, Paromomyidae, Plesiadapidae, and 'Palaechthonidae.' However, questions remain about several of these attributions (Silcox 2008).

Although there are undoubted members of 'plesiadapiforms' from all three Laurasian continents, a potential African presence remains debatable. The latest Paleocene *Altiatlasius* from Morocco is sometimes included in the group (Hooker et al. 1999), but recent analyses have suggested that it is a euprimate (Bloch et al. 2007; Seiffert et al. in press). Tabuce et al. (2004) have argued that two Eocene species from Africa, which they place in the family Azibiidae, share a special relationship to carpolestids, but arguments can also be made for attribution to Euprimates or to an endemic African group of non-primates (Silcox 2008; Godinot in press).

Phylogeny

From the earliest discoveries of 'plesiadapiforms,' dental similarities to early Tertiary Euprimates have been noted – for instance broad talonid basins, an expanded m3 hypoconulid, and a crest extending from the protocone distolingually to the cingulum on P4 (and sometimes the upper molars), which has been referred to as the *Nannopithex* fold or postprotocingulum. The primate status of 'plesiadapiforms' began to be questioned in the late 1960s and early 1970s (Martin 1968; Cartmill 1972, 1974), on the basis of differences between members of the group known at the time and living primates, in features such as the absence of a postorbital bar and of nails (Figure 16.3). 'Plesiadapiforms' also lack the features for specialized leaping characteristic of most early Euprimates, such as elongate tarsal bones and deep distal femora (Figure 16.3).

A more substantive challenge to the primate status of 'plesiadapiforms' came from the suggestion that their closest affinities were to living dermopterans (flying lemurs, colugos) rather than to primates (Beard 1990; Kay et al. 1990). Beard (1993) argued that some 'plesiadapiforms' not only were phylogenetically related to dermopterans but also exhibited gliding behavior, in part on the basis of his interpretation that they exhibited elongate intermediate manual phalanges. Krause (1991) questioned Beard's attribution of isolated phalangeal elements to the hand rather than to the foot, and indeed subsequent specimens have demonstrated that micromomyids and paromomyids actually did not possess the manual phalangeal proportions of living dermopterans and lacked other characteristics common to living gliders (Bloch et al. 2007; Boyer and Bloch 2008). The cranial features argued to support a dermopteran relationship have also been found to either be primitive, or present in other euarchontans (Silcox 2003; Bloch and Silcox 2006).

Silcox (2001, 2008) conducted a comprehensive phylogenetic analysis that included dental, postcranial, and cranial characters and sampled all of the eleven 'plesiadapiform' families known at the time. Her work failed to uphold the dermopteran–'plesiadapiform' relationship, and suggested instead that 'plesiadapiforms' were stem primates. A subsequent analysis building on this work by incorporating material from several spectacular new finds of 'plesiadapiforms' (Bloch et al. 2007) has supported this basic conclusion and suggested that the sister taxon of Euprimates is the suprafamilial grouping of 'plesiadapiforms' called Plesiadapoidea, which includes *Chronolestes simul*, Plesiadapidae, Carpolestidae, and Saxonellidae (Figure 16.1, A–B). Although this result certainly has its detractors (for instance Soligo and Martin 2007), no authors have provided a similarly comprehensive analysis that has reached a

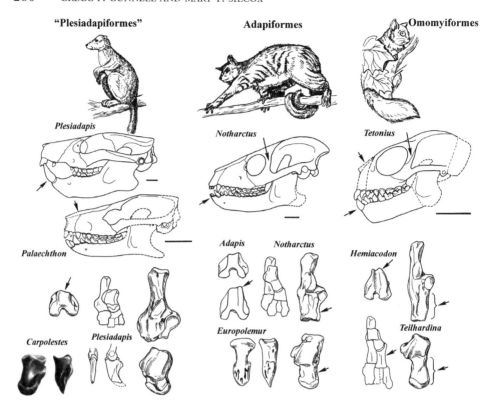

Figure 16.3 Morphological features of 'plesiadapiforms' and early Cenozoic Adapiformes and Omomyiformes. 'Plesiadapiforms' generally have longer snouts than early Cenozoic euprimates and lack the postorbital bar. Like omomyiforms, 'plesiadapiforms' possess larger upper and lower incisors, which contrast with the smaller incisors of adapiforms, while only adapiforms have enlarged and sexually dimorphic canines. Postcranially, most early Tertiary euprimates have features for leaping such as a deep distal femur and elongate tarsal bones; this contrasts with the flatter distal femur and shorter tarsals of 'plesiadapiforms' and of *Adapis*. (Modified from Rose 1995 and used by permission of John Wiley & Sons, Inc.) While most 'plesiadapiforms' contrast with euprimates in possessing claws on all of their digits, the hallux of *Carpolestes* bears a nail. (Modified from Bloch and Boyer 2002 and used by permission of the American Association for the Advancement of Science)

contradictory conclusion, and so this hypothesis currently stands as the best supported one for the relationships of 'plesiadapiforms' to living primates and to other euarchontans (tree shrews and colugos).

'Plesiadapiform' taxa of particular interest

Purgatorius   As the oldest and most primitive 'plesiadapiform' and primate genus, *Purgatorius* is important in documenting the earliest evolution of the group. The largest collection of *Purgatorius* specimens comes from early Paleocene deposits (64–65 mya) in Montana (Clemens 2004). Although much of this material remains unpublished, three specimens of particular note have been illustrated, including a maxilla with P4–M2

(Kielan-Jaworowska et al. 1979) and two fairly complete mandibles (Clemens 1974, 2004). The latter demonstrate that the lower dental formula of *Purgatorius* was 3.1.4.3 and that it had already evolved the enlarged i1 characteristic of other members of the group (Clemens 2004). This derived feature contrasts with the highly primitive nature of the rest of *Purgatorius*'s dentition and supports its alliance to 'plesiadapiforms.'

In light of its pivotal position as the oldest and most primitive primate known, surprisingly little has been published on the ecological characteristics of *Purgatorius*. Given its small size (smaller than 100 grams: Fleagle 1999) and pointed cusps, it seems likely that it included a substantial portion of insects in its diet. However, relative to contemporary specialized insectivorans, its teeth are lower crowned, with more bunodont (fat and rounded) cusps and broader talonid basins, suggesting the inclusion of fruit and other non-leafy plant materials in the diet. Indeed, a transition to a more omnivorous diet has long been considered a critical factor in the early evolution of the order Primates (see Szalay 1968). Cranial and postcranial material remains unknown (or unidentified) for *Purgatorius*, so other elements of its ecological profile continue to be elusive.

Plesiadapis tricuspidens and P. cookei   *Plesiadapis* is known from both sides of the Atlantic Ocean. The two best known species are late Paleocene *Plesiadapis tricuspidens* from Europe and *P. cookei* from western North America. The two species were probably similar in size (Boyer 2008); body mass estimates from the postcranium of *P. cookei* average approximately 2,200 grams (Gingerich and Gunnell 2005). Cranial material is known from multiple specimens of *P. tricuspidens* (Russell 1959, 1964; Gingerich 1976; Szalay et al. 1987). As in other 'plesiadapiforms,' its cranium is distinct from that of euprimates in having a relatively long snout and laterally oriented orbits and in lacking postorbital bars (Figure 16.3).

A cranium is also available for *Plesiadapis cookei*, as part of an associated skeleton (Figure 16.2, D; Bloch and Silcox 2001; Gingerich and Gunnell 2005; Silcox et al. 2009). A partial endocast has been prepared from the specimen (Gingerich and Gunnell 2005), showing that *Plesiadapis* possessed large olfactory bulbs and a short cerebrum, and suggesting that *Plesiadapis* was a 'nose first animal.'

Plesiadapis tricuspidens and *P. cookei* lack the specializations for granivory or folivory seen in some other members of the family (*Chiromyoides* and *Platychoerops* respectively: Gingerich 1976), and probably ate a broadly omnivorous diet, with the latter species perhaps being more folivorous (Boyer 2008).

Plesiadapis tricuspidens is known from very extensive postcranial material (Russell 1964; Bloch et al. 2007). Youlatos and Godinot (2004) compared *Plesiadapis tricuspidens* with *Ratufa*, the giant squirrel, suggesting that it may have been an arboreal quadruped capable of vertical claw-climbing.

Carpolestes simpsoni   A very well preserved skeleton (Figure 16.2, C; Bloch and Boyer 2002) and several crania (Bloch and Silcox 2006) of *Carpolestes simpsoni* have recently been discovered from the late Paleocene of Wyoming. *Carpolestes simpsoni* weighed about 100 grams and, like other carpolestids, had a specialized dental apparatus, with an enlarged, multicuspate, blade-like (plagiaulacoid) p4, and p3 and p4 that are enlarged with three rows of cusps (Bloch and Gingerich 1998). This configuration would have functioned to cut up foods such as fruit or insects, which combine a soft interior with a brittle or ductile exterior (Biknevicius 1986).

The postcranial skeleton of *Carpolestes simpsoni* exhibits a euprimate-like feature unknown in other 'plesiadapiform' – a nail on a divergent, grasping big toe (Figures 16.2, C and 16.3; Bloch and Boyer 2002) – which suggests that *C. simpsoni* may have been better adapted for moving in terminal branches than other members of the group (Bloch et al. 2007).

Cranially, *Carpolestes simpsoni* shares with *Plesiadapis* an apparently petrosal bulla, along with primitive features such as a relatively long snout, divergent orbits, and no postorbital bar (Bloch and Silcox 2006). The ear region is rather specialized, however, with a possible division between two chambers that is superficially similar to that seen in living tarsiers (ibid.). A phylogenetic analysis incorporating the *C. simpsoni* skeletal and cranial data placed carpolestids in a monophyletic Plesiadapoidea and concluded that this suprafamilial grouping is the euprimate sister taxon (Bloch et al. 2007; Figure 16.1, A).

Relevance of 'plesiadapiforms' to primate origins scenarios

Most 'plesiadapiforms' exhibit specializations which exclude them from direct ancestry to later euprimates. This is true, for example, of *Carpolestes simpsoni*: while its foot, with a nail-bearing divergent big toe, represents a morphology that might have given rise to the grasping foot of adapiforms and omomyiforms, its strange ear region and specialized dentition exclude it from direct euprimate ancestry. However, 'plesiadapiforms' continue to be the only fossil evidence available that may provide clues to the process of primate (and euprimate) origins.

Scenarios for primate origins   There are four main scenarios that have been proposed to explain primate origins. The first, dating back to the work of Elliot Smith and Wood Jones in the early twentieth century, is the 'arboreal hypothesis,' which explains the unique characteristics of primates as resulting from a life in the trees (Cartmill 1992). Szalay and Dagosto (1980) proposed a related scenario – the 'grasp-leaping' hypothesis, which emphasizes a particular mode of arboreal locomotion as being important: leaping, and then grasping onto a substrate to ensure a stable landing. Cartmill (1974) put forward the visual predation hypothesis, which suggests that a particular behavior, seeing and grasping insects, was central to the evolution of traits such as grasping extremities and convergent orbits. Sussman (1991) and Sussman and Raven (1978; see also Szalay 1968), on the other hand, emphasized fruit and nectar over insects in their primate origin scenario, suggesting that the key features of primates can be explained as adaptations to terminal branch feeding. Grasping traits would be critical in this fine branch milieu for offering stability, and primate dental traits would reflect this largely frugivorous diet. Finally, Rasmussen (1990) studied a living marsupial, *Caluromys*, which he felt could offer a good living model for early primates. This led him to suggest a 'combination hypothesis,' which united the terminal branch feeding and the visual predation scenarios. He suggested that, since insects are also attracted to the resources at the ends of branches, such as flowers, once primates were adept in this milieu there would be opportunities to broaden the diet so as to include insects caught through visual predation.

It seems clear now that primates evolved from an arboreal ancestor (Szalay and Drawhorn 1980; Silcox et al. 2007), which invalidates the arboreal scenario, since a move into the trees was not coincident with the evolution of primates' distinctive traits. All 'plesiadapiforms' except *Plesiadapis* had relatively elongate manual phalanges, which would have facilitated grasping, while *Carpolestes simpsoni* exhibits an additional specialization for this behavior in its divergent, nail-bearing big toe (Figures 16.2, C and 16.3; Bloch and Boyer 2002). No 'plesiadapiforms' show specialized euprimate visual features such as convergent orbits or a postorbital bar, or leaping specializations in the postcranium. The separation in time between the evolution of these features and the evolution of grasping traits in early primate evolution is problematic both for the grasp–leaping and for the visual predation hypotheses (Silcox et al. 2007). What's more, since the earliest euprimates were not particularly specialized for insectivory (Boyer 2007), it is not even clear that these taxa were visual predators. This also nullifies the combination hypothesis, which credited a central place for visual predation. This leaves the terminal branch feeding hypothesis as the best supported of the four scenarios. As discussed above for *Purgatorius*, there are indications, even in the earliest primates known, of some features for processing non-leafy plant products. Although postcranial material remains unknown for this genus, the most primitive primate skeleton available (which pertains to the micromomyid *Dryomomys szalayi*) already exhibits elongate manual phalanges (Bloch et al. 2007), supporting the possibility that terminal branch feeding evolved at the basal primate node. This suggests a central role in early primate evolution for traits associated with improved feeding on angiosperms.

EUPRIMATES: THE APPEARANCE OF PRIMATES OF MODERN ASPECT

While the Paleocene was dominated by 'plesiadapiforms,' the Eocene was the epoch when primates of modern aspect began to flourish (Figure 16.1, B). From relatively modest beginnings at the very end of the Paleocene and earliest moments of the Eocene (Sigé et al. 1990; Ni et al. 2004; Smith et al. 2006), euprimates rapidly radiated and diversified across the northern continents and Africa into a multitude of forms, often being present in great abundance (Rose 1995; Gunnell 1997; Gunnell and Rose 2002; Gunnell et al. 2008a).

All Eocene euprimates are advanced compared to 'plesiadapiforms' (Figure 16.3) in possessing derived characters such as postorbital bars, frontated orbits, and nails instead of claws on all digits. Additionally, many taxa possessed elongate hindlimbs and tarsal elements, which indicates that they were accomplished grasp-leapers, in the fashion of some living lemurs and galagids. Eocene euprimates ranged in size from tiny species, as small as ten grams (Gebo et al. 2000), to relatively large taxa like *Notharctus robustior* and *Pondaungia savagei* (each approximately seven kilograms: Fleagle 1999), which were similar in size to a modern macaque.

Phylogeny

Euprimates include two speciose extinct groups, Adapiforms and Omomyiforms. Adapiforms were generally larger than omomyiforms, they had smaller upper and lower central incisors, longer snouts, and smaller eyes which suggest diurnal habits, while omomyiforms were in all likelihood nocturnal (Rose 1995; Figure 16.3). The two groups have often been considered to be analogous to lemurs and galagos respectively, although the question remains open as to whether or not they shared a close relationship with these modern groups (see below). It seems fairly certain that adapiforms and omomyiforms shared a common ancestry, and that both groups probably originated in the late Paleocene (Rose 1995). However, where this common ancestor may have lived and what taxonomic group it may have represented are questions still open to debate. As discussed above, parsimony analysis supports a sister-group relationship between one group of 'plesiadapiforms' (Plesiadapoidea) and adapiforms and omomyiforms (Bloch et al. 2007; Figure 16.1, A). However, the most primitive and earliest known representatives of each of these Eocene groups – *Teilhardina* and *Cantius* – appear to be more primitive than any known plesiadapoid in some features (for instance the retention of four premolars: Figure 16.4, A–C) while in other features they seem to be derived (see list above). This indicates that there is still a gap in the fossil record to be filled at the base of Euprimates.

Even more questionable are the origins of the living groups of primates. Recent discoveries in Africa and Asia show that modern primate lineages can be traced far into the past, all three major groups originating by the Eocene. Lemuriforms are now know to have existed in Africa around 37 mya (Seiffert et al. 2003); tarsiiforms are present in Asia at least 50 mya (Beard 1998; Beard et al. 1994); and anthropoids are present in Africa at least by the early late Eocene, or earlier if late Paleocene *Altiatlasius* pertains to that group (Godinot 1994; in press; Seiffert et al. 2005; Sigé et al. 1990). If *Altiatlasius* is an anthropoid, then tarsiiforms and lemuriforms must have ancestries extending equally deeply in time and requiring ghost lineages of at least 6 and 19 million years, respectively. Given that adapiforms and omomyiforms are currently unknown from Paleocene aged deposits, phylogenetic hypotheses which link these extinct groups with explicit modern primate clades (for instance Ross et al. 1998) must be viewed with caution.

In addition to adapiforms, omomyiforms, and fairly clear members of modern groups of primates, there are a number of Eocene fossil groups whose affiliations are still in debate. These include two families that have been identified by some (Beard et al. 1994, 2007), but not by others (e.g. Miller et al. 2005), as anthropoids: the Eosimiidae and Amphipithecidae. Eosimiids, from the Eocene of Asia, were small primates who probably ate a diet of insects and fruit and were active in the daytime (Beard and Wang 2004; Bajpai et al. 2008). Amphipithecids were much larger, slow-moving arboreal quadrupeds from the Eocene of Asia, who probably ate a diet of fruit and seeds (Kay et al. 2004).

Biogeography

The earliest record of a euprimate is that of *Altiatlasius* (Figure 16.4, E) from the very latest Paleocene in North Africa (Sigé et al. 1990). Occurring only slightly later in time are the East Asian euprimates *Altanius*, *Baataromomys*, and *Teilhardina asiatica* (Dashzeveg and McKenna 1977; Ni et al. 2004, 2007). *Teilhardina* (Figure 16.4, C–D) migrated very quickly and was present across all of the northern continents in a very short time (in perhaps as little as 25 thousand years: Smith et al. 2006). *Teilhardina* represents the earliest known clear omomyiform, and it is joined in North America very shortly after its arrival by the earliest known adapiform, *Cantius* (Gingerich 1986; Figure 16.4, A).

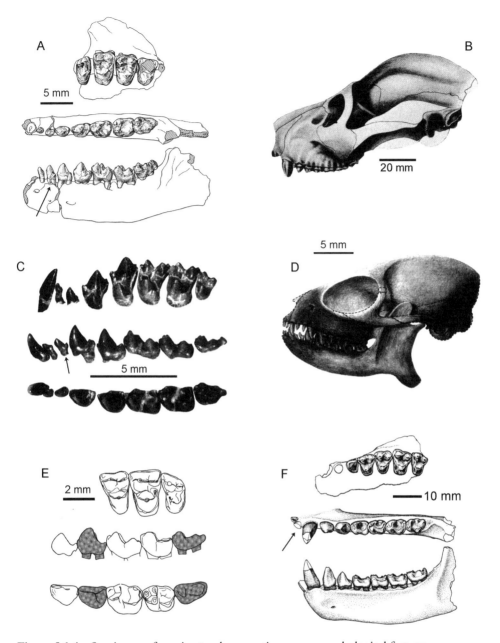

Figure 16.4 Specimens of euprimates documenting some morphological features

A Upper (top) and lower jaws of the adapiform *Cantius torresi* from the earliest Eocene of North America; arrow indicates double-rooted p2. Adapted from Gingerich 1995

B Lateral view of the skull of *Leptadapis magnus* from the middle Eocene of Europe, showing well developed sagittal crest. Adapted from Stehlin 1912

C–D Upper and lower dentition and reconstructed skull of *Teilhardina asiatica* from the earliest Eocene of Asia – arrow indicates single-rooted p2. Adapted from Ni et al. 2004 and used by permission of Nature Publishing Group

E Upper (top) and lower jaws of *Altiatlasius koulchii* from the latest Paleocene of North Africa. Adapted from Rose 1995 and used by permission of John Wiley & Sons, Inc.

F Upper (top) and lower jaws of *Sivaladapis nagrii* from the late Miocene of India; arrow points to spatulate incisors and projecting, dimorphic canines typical of adapiforms. Adapted from Gingerich and Sahni 1984

In terms of both diversity and abundance, the North American Eocene record of euprimates is unmatched elsewhere, especially in the early and middle Eocene (Gunnell et al. 2008a). North American Eocene euprimates include at least forty-three genera (thirty-six omomyiforms, seven adapiforms) and approximately 100 species (seventy-five omomyiforms, twenty-five adapiforms). Some species of the early Eocene adapiform *Cantius* are represented by literally thousands of specimens, suggesting that *Cantius* was a common primate in some ecological settings. North American Eocene euprimates are found as far south as Texas and Mississippi, as far west as California, and as far north as the plains of central Canada; but they are most common and abundant in what is now the Rocky Mountain West (especially in Wyoming, Utah, Montana, and Colorado: Gunnell et al. 2008a).

The Eocene euprimate record in Europe is, in some ways, the opposite of that of North America. While omomyiforms are very diverse in North America and adapiforms are abundant but less diverse, Europe is typified by a relatively low diversity of omomyiforms and a high diversity of adapiforms. Included among European Eocene euprimates are twenty-four genera (seven omomyiforms, seventeen adapiforms) and some sixty-eight species (twenty omomyiforms, forty-eight adapiforms: Gebo 2002; Gunnell and Rose 2002; Hooker 2007).

The Asian record of Eocene euprimates is unique in several ways. Much of the primate fauna seems to have been endemic and isolated into discrete Eastern and Central Asian provinces (Gunnell et al. 2008b). There was apparent interchange between Central Asia and Europe and between East Asia and North America at restricted intervals during the Eocene, but much of the Asian euprimate record is represented by groups not found elsewhere, including the adapiform family Sivaladapidae and the enigmatic Amphipithecidae and Eosimiidae. Also present in Asia is the endemic crown group family Tarsiidae. In total, the Asian Eocene record of euprimates includes some twenty-nine genera and approximately thirty-five species, representing a diversity of groups which included omomyiforms, adapiforms, tarsiiforms, amphipithecids and eosimiids (Gunnell et al. 2008b).

In nearly every way, the euprimate record from Africa is the most puzzling of all. It includes only a few apparent endemic forms, even though nearly all of the other African mammalian fauna of the Paleocene and Eocene appears to be made up of archaic endemic taxa (Afrotheria). African early Cenozoic euprimates include seventeen genera and nineteen species. Of these, two genera and species represent adapiforms, six genera and species represent lemuriforms (Godinot in press), and nine genera and eleven species represent archaic anthropoids (Seiffert et al. in press). As discussed above, the enigmatic Azibiidae may also represent euprimates (Silcox 2008).

Euprimate taxa of particular interest

Teilhardina   *Teilhardina* (Figure 16.4, C–D) is the earliest known and one of the most primitive representatives of Omomyiformes. It first appears in the very earliest Eocene in China (Ni et al. 2004; Bowen et al. 2002), where it is represented by a fairly complete skull and lower jaws. Like most other omomyiforms, *Teilhardina asiatica* was quite small (28 g: Ni et al. 2004); it possessed a relatively short rostrum, a complete postorbital bar, enlarged and forward facing orbits, and a globular and relatively large braincase; and it retained the primitive euprimate dental formula of 2.1.4.3, both p1 and p2 being single-rooted. It differed from the earliest known adapiforms in being smaller, in having a shorter rostrum and in lacking a second root on p2.

A parsimony analysis of euprimates including *T. asiatica* places this taxon at the base of the omomyiform clade, along with its sister taxon *T. belgica* from the earliest Eocene of Europe (Ni et al. 2004). As reconstructed by Ni and colleagues (2004), *T. asiatica* is interpreted to have had a diurnal activity pattern based on the relative size of the orbits, in which it would differ from the rest of the omomyiforms. However, this conclusion, and its relevance to the ancestral activity pattern of euprimates, has been questioned on a number of fronts (Bloch and Silcox 2006; Kirk 2006).

Notharctus   *Notharctus* is among the best known Eocene euprimates. It is represented by several nearly complete skeletons (Gregory 1920) and is a common element in the early middle Eocene of North America. It first appears in the latest early Eocene of North America (about 50 mya: Gunnell 2002) and disappears in the late middle Eocene (45 mya). Like most adapiforms, *Notharctus* was relatively large-bodied (4 to 7 kg: Fleagle 1999), had a long and low braincase, often with a sagittal crest present (Figure 16.4, B), a relatively long rostrum, complete postorbital bars, spatulate incisors, enlarged and sexually dimorphic canines, p2 double-rooted, and it retained the primitive euprimate dental formula of 2.1.4.3. Its small orbits suggest that it may have been diurnal. Probably *Notharctus* was folivorous but included relatively large amounts of fruit in its diet as well. Like all known adapiforms and omomyiforms, *Notharctus* had nails on all digits and an opposable hallux. It also had elongate hind limbs, deep distal femora, and modestly elongated tarsal elements – which suggest that it was an accomplished leaper, analogous to a modern indriid.

The Asian family Amphipithecidae appears to be closely related to the North American notharctines, which includes *Notharctus* (Figure 16.1B; Ciochon et al. 2001; Ciochon and Gunnell 2004; Gunnell et al. 2008b), but others have questioned this relationship and have suggested instead that amphipithecids are more closely related to African Oligocene anthropoids (Beard et al. 2007). Given the large and mostly endemic radiation of adapiforms present in the Eocene of Asia (Gunnell et al. 2008b), the inclusion of amphipithecids within Adapiformes is both geographically and taxonomically consistent with all known evidence.

Sivaladapis and Indraloris   The Sivaladapidae (Figure 16.4, F) is an endemic family of Asian adapiforms that first appeared in the late middle Eocene in China and Myanmar and persisted until the late Miocene in India (Gingerich and Sahni 1979, 1984; Gingerich et al. 1994; Beard et al. 2007). Sivaladapids are only known with certainty from dental evidence (but see Beard et al. 2007) and appear to have ranged in dietary adaptations from frugivory to folivory (Gingerich and Sahni 1984). The smallest sivaladapids are estimated to have had body weights of around 500 grams (Beard et al. 2007), while the larger forms may have exceeded 4.5 kilograms (Fleagle 1999).

Perhaps the most interesting aspects of the sivaladapid radiation concern their geographic distribution within Asia and the fact that sivaladapids persisted until nearly 8 mya, much later than any other group of adapiforms. Gunnell and colleagues (2008b) discuss the development of primate faunal provincialism in the Eocene of Asia. Except for the very earliest Eocene, when *Teilhardina* was able to move across all of the northern continents, the rest of the Asian Eocene is typified by the development of endemic faunas in East Asia (China, Mongolia, Myanmar, and Thailand) and Central Asia (Indo-Pakistan). During most of the Eocene there was little, if any, faunal interchange between East and Central Asia. Instead, each of the faunal provinces developed low-level and very intermittent faunal exchanges – East Asia with North America, and Central Asia with Europe. Sivaladapids fit this provincial pattern very well, all its taxa being restricted to the East Asian province until after the Eocene, when *Guangxilemur* appears in Pakistan (Marivaux et al. 2002). Sivaladapids then persist until the Miocene in both provinces, apparently dwindling and then finally going extinct in conjunction with the arrival of the first cercopithecoids from Africa in the Miocene (Ciochon and Gunnell 2004).

ORIGINS: CONCLUDING REMARKS

The origin of primates can be traced to an arboreal ancestry; but a move into the trees apparently was not, in and of itself, responsible for the beginnings of the order. On the basis of evidence now available from 'plesiadapiforms,' the terminal branch feeding hypothesis provides the best supported adaptive context for the advent of primates. All non-plesiadapid 'plesiadapiforms' have elongate hand digits, which suggests that many different groups were exploiting terminal branch habitats. Coupled with a move toward a more omnivorous diet, which included flowers, fruits, and insects, the exploitation of terminal branch habitats may have been the single-most important aspect leading to the divergence of primates.

As we have seen, aspects of the origin of euprimates remain elusive. 'Plesiadapiforms' are the best candidates for the ancestry of primates of modern aspect, but the earliest known euprimates seem to be both too primitive and too derived in different directions to have originated directly from any 'plesiadapiform' more specialized than *Purgatorius*. While all euprimates share a set of derived features that unite them, exactly how the extinct and extant taxa are related to one another is still ambiguous, and where and from whom euprimates evolved is problematic. It is possible that euprimates, as tropically adapted creatures, originated in a place where a fossil record will be difficult, if not impossible, to find. If such is the case, then perhaps we may never 'know' where and from what group euprimates ultimately came.

A similar situation appears to hold concerning the origin of anthropoid primates. In what seems to be an illogical turn of events, the earliest known euprimate, *Altiatlasius* from the late Paleocene of Africa, might well be an archaic anthropoid (Sigé et al. 1990; Godinot 1994; Seiffert et al. in press). If this is the case, then derivation of anthropoids from middle and late Eocene Asian taxa (eosimiids), some 12 to 15 million years later in time, seems incongruous, especially given the lack of apparent morphological overlap between *Altiatlasius* and any Asian taxon.

The Paleocene and Eocene fossil records of primates are rich, diverse, and abundant. The major patterns of evolution and diversification in 'plesiadapiforms,' omomyiforms, and adapiforms have been documented and are beginning to be established for the clades of living primates. Future discoveries will continue to add layers of information to the emerging story, but we may be a long way away from truly understanding the initial beginnings of primates, euprimates, and anthropoids.

Bajpai, S., Kay, R. F., Williams, B. A., Das, D. P., Kapur, V. V., and Tiwari, B. N. (2008) The Oldest Asian Record of Anthropoidea. *Proceedings of the National Academy of Sciences, USA* 105: 11093–11098.

Beard, K. C. (1990) Gliding Behavior and Palaeoecology of the Alleged Primate Family Paromomyidae (Mammalia, Dermoptera). *Nature* 345: 340–341.

Beard, K. C. (1993) Origin and Evolution of Gliding in Early Cenozoic Dermoptera (Mammalia, Primatomorpha). In R. D. E. MacPhee (ed.), *Primates and their Relatives in Phylogenetic Perspective* (pp. 63–90). New York: Plenum Press.

Beard, K. C. (1998) A New Genus of Tarsiidae (Mammalia: Primates) from the Middle Eocene of Shanxi Province, China, with Notes on the Historical Biogeography of Tarsiers. *Bulletin of the Carnegie Museum of Natural History* 34 (Theme Issue: Dawn of the Age of Mammals in Asia): 260–277.

Beard, K. C. (2004) *The Hunt for the Dawn Monkey: Unearthing the Origins of Monkeys, Apes, and Humans.* Los Angeles: University of California Press.

Beard, K. C. (2008) The Oldest North American Primate and Mammalian Biogeography during the Paleocene–Eocene Thermal Maximum. *Proceedings of the National Academy of Sciences, USA* 105: 3815–3818.

Beard, K. C., and Wang, J. (1995) The First Asian Plesiadapoids (Mammalia: Primatomorpha). *Annals of Carnegie Museum* 64: 1–33

Beard, K. C., and Wang, J. (2004) The Eosimiid Primates (Anthropoidea) of the Heti Formation, Yuanqu Basin, Shanxi and Henan Provinces, People's Republic of China. *Journal of Human Evolution* 46: 401–432.

Beard, K. C., Tao, Q., Dawson, M. R., Wang, B., and Li, C. (1994) A Diverse New Primate Fauna from Middle Eocene Fissure – Fillings in Southeastern China. *Nature* 368: 604–609.

Beard, K. C., Marivaux, L., Tun, S. T., Soe, A. N., Chaimanee, Y., Htoon, W., Marandat, B., Aung, H. H., and Jaeger, J.-J. (2007) New Sivaladapid Primates from the Eocene Pondaung Formation of Myanmar and the Anthropoid Status of Amphipithecidae. *Bulletin of the Carnegie Museum of Natural History* 39 (Theme Issue: Mammalian Paleontology on a Global Stage: Papers in Honor of Mary R. Dawson): 67–76.

Biknevicius, A. R. (1986) Dental Function and Diet in the Carpolestidae (Primates, Plesiadapiformes). *American Journal of Physical Anthropology* 71: 157–171.

Bloch, J. I., and Boyer, D. M. (2002) Grasping Primate Origins. *Science* 298: 1606–1610.

Bloch, J. I., and Boyer, D. M. (2007) New Skeletons of Paleocene–Eocene Plesiadapiformes: A Diversity of Arboreal Positional Behaviors in Early Primates. In M. J. Ravosa and M. Dagosto (eds), *Primate Origins: Adaptations and Evolution* (pp. 535–581). New York: Springer.

Bloch, J. I., and Gingerich, P. D. (1998) *Carpolestes simpsoni*, New Species (Mammalia, Proprimates) from the Late Paleocene of the Clarks Fork Basin, Wyoming. *Contributions from the Museum of Paleontology, University of Michigan* 30: 131–162.

Bloch, J. I., and Silcox, M. T. (2001) New Basicrania of Paleocene–Eocene *Ignacius*: Re-Evaluation of the Plesiadapiform–Dermopteran Link. *American Journal of Physical Anthropology* 116: 184–198.

Bloch, J. I., and Silcox, M. T. (2006) Cranial Anatomy of Paleocene 'Plesiadapiform' *Carpolestes simpsoni* (Mammalia, Primates) Using Ultra High-Resolution X-Ray Computed Tomography, and the Relationships of 'Plesiadapiforms' to Euprimates. *Journal of Human Evolution* 50: 1–35.

Bloch, J. I., Silcox, M. T., Boyer, D. M., and Sargis, E. J. (2007) New Paleocene Skeletons and the Relationship of 'Plesiadapiforms' to Crown-Clade Primates. *Proceedings of the National Academy of Sciences, USA* 104: 1159–1164.

Bowen, G. J., with Clyde, W. C., Koch, P. L., Ting, S., Alroy, J., Tsubamoto, T., Wang, Y., and Wang, Y. (2002) Mammalian Dispersal at the Paleocene/Eocene boundary. *Science* 295: 2062–2065.

Bown, T. M., and Rose, K. D. (1976) New Early Tertiary Primates and a Reappraisal of Some Plesiadapiformes. *Folia Primatologica* 26: 109–138.

Boyer, D. M. (2007) A Test of the Visual Predation Hypothesis of Euprimate Origins Using Diet-Correlated Measures of Tooth Shape. *Journal of Vertebrate Paleontology* 27: 51A.

Boyer, D. M. (2008) A Comparison of *Plesiadapis cookei* to *P. tricuspidens* (Mammalia, Plesiadapiformes): Evidence for Ecological Differences. *Journal of Vertebrate Paleontology* 28: 55A.

Boyer, D. M, and Bloch, J. I. (2008) Evaluating the Mitten-Gliding Hypothesis for Paromomyidae and Micromomyidae (Mammalia, 'Plesiadapiformes') Using Comparative Functional Morphology of New Paleogene Skeletons. In M. Dagosto and E. J. Sargis (eds), *Evolutionary Morphology: A Tribute to Frederick S. Szalay* (pp. 233–284). New York: Springer-Verlag.

Cartmill, M. (1972) Arboreal Adaptations and the Origin of the Order Primates. In Russell Tuttle (ed.), *The Functional and Evolutionary Biology of Primates* (pp. 97–122). Chicago: Aldine-Atherton.

Cartmill, M. (1974) Rethinking Primate Origins. *Science* 184: 436–443.

Cartmill, M. (1992) New Views on Primate Origins. *Evolutionary Anthropology* 1: 105–111.

Ciochon, R. L., and Gunnell, G. F. (2004) Eocene Large-Bodied Primates of Myanmar and Thailand: Morphological Considerations and Phylogenetic Affinities. In C. F. Ross and R. F. Kay (eds), *Anthropoid Origins: New Visions* (pp. 249–282). New York: Kluwer Academic/Plenum Publishers.

Ciochon, R. L., Gingerich, P. D., Gunnell, G. F., and Simons, E. L. (2001) Primate Postcrania from the Late Middle Eocene of Myanmar. *Proceedings of the National Academy of Sciences, USA* 98: 7672–7677.

Clemens, W. A. (1974) *Purgatorius*, an Early Paromomyid Primate (Mammalia). *Science* 184: 903–905.

Clemens, W. A. (2004) *Purgatorius* (Plesiadapiformes, Primates?, Mammalia), a Paleocene Immigrant into Northeastern Montana: Stratigraphic Occurrences and Incisor Proportions. *Bulletin of the Carnegie Museum of Natural History* 36 (Theme Issue: Fanfare for an Uncommon Paleontologist: Papers in Honor of Malcolm C. McKenna): 3–13.

Dashzeveg, D., and McKenna, M. C. (1977) Tarsioid Primate from the Early Tertiary of the Mongolian People's Republic. *Acta Palaeontologica Polonica* 22: 119–137.

Fleagle, J. G. (1999) *Primate Adaptation and Evolution*, 2nd edn. New York: Academic Press.

Gebo, D. L. (2002) Adapiformes: Phylogeny and Adaptation. In W. C. Hartwig (ed.), *The Primate Fossil Record* (pp. 21–43). Cambridge: Cambridge University Press.

Gebo, D. L., Dagosto, M., Beard, K. C., and Tao, Q. (2000) The Smallest Primates. *Journal of Human Evolution* 38: 585–594.

Gingerich, P. D. (1976) Cranial Anatomy and Evolution of Early Tertiary Plesiadapidae (Mammalia, Primates). *University of Michigan Papers on Paleontology* 15: 1–141.

Gingerich, P. D. (1986) Early Eocene *Cantius torresi* – Oldest Primate of Modern Aspect from North America. *Nature* 320: 319–321.

Gingerich, P. D. (1993) Early Eocene *Teilhardina brandti*: Oldest Omomyid Primate from North America. *Contributions from the Museum of Paleontology, University of Michigan* 28: 321–326.

Gingerich, P. D. (1995) Sexual Dimorphism in Earliest Eocene *Cantius torresi* (Mammalia, Primates, Adapoidea). *Contributions from the Museum of Paleontology, University of Michigan* 29: 185–199.

Gingerich, P. D., and Gunnell, G. F. (2005) Brain of *Plesiadapis cookei* (Mammalia, Proprimates): Surface Morphology and Encephalization Compared to Those of Primates and Dermoptera. *Contributions from the Museum of Paleontology, University of Michigan* 31: 185–195.

Gingerich, P. D., and Sahni, A. (1979) *Indraloris* and *Sivaladapis*: Miocene Adapid Primates from the Siwaliks of India and Pakistan. *Nature* 279: 415–416.

Gingerich, P. D., and Sahni, A. (1984) Dentition of *Sivaladapis nagrii* (Adapidae) from the Late Miocene of India. *International Journal of Primatology* 5: 63–79.

Gingerich, P. D., Holroyd, P. A., and Ciochon, R. L. (1994) *Rencunius zhoui*, New Primate from the Late Middle Eocene of Henan, China, and a Comparison with Some Early Anthropoidea. In John G. Fleagle and Richard F. Kay (eds), *Anthropoid Origins* (pp. 163–177). New York: Plenum Press.

Gingerich, P. D., Rose, K. D., and Smith, T. (2008) Oldest North American Primate. *Proceedings of the National Academy of Sciences, USA* 105: E30.

Godinot, M. (1984) Un nouveau genre de Paromomyidae (Primates) de l'éocène inférieur d'Europe. *Folia Primatologica* 43: 84–96.

Godinot, M. (1994) Early North African Primates and Their Significance for the Origin of Simiiformes (=Anthropoidea). In J. G. Fleagle and R. F. Kay (eds), *Anthropoid Origins* (pp. 235–295). New York: Plenum Press.

Godinot, M. (in press) Paleogene Prosimians. In L. Werdelin and W. J. Sanders (eds), *Cenozoic Mammals of Africa*. Berkeley: University of California Press.

Gregory, W. K. (1920) On the Structure and Relations of *Notharctus*, an American Eocene Primate. *Memoirs of the American Museum of Natural History* (New Series) 3: 49–243.

Gunnell, G. F. (1997) Wasatchian–Bridgerian (Eocene) Paleoecology of the Western Interior of North America: Changing Paleoenvironments and Taxonomic Composition of Omomyid (Tarsiiformes) Primates. *Journal of Human Evolution* 32: 105–132.

Gunnell, G. F. (2002) Notharctine Primates (Adapiformes) from the Early to Middle Eocene (Wasatchian–Bridgerian) of Wyoming: Transitional Species and the Origin of *Notharctus* and *Smilodectes*. *Journal of Human Evolution* 43: 353–380.

Gunnell, G. F., and Rose, K. D. (2002) Tarsiiformes: Evolutionary History and Adaptation. In W. C. Hartwig (ed.), *The Primate Fossil Record* (pp. 45–82). Cambridge: Cambridge University Press.

Gunnell, G. F., Rose, K. D., and Rasmussen, D. T. (2008a) Euprimates. In C. M. Janis, G. F. G. F. Gunnell, and M. D. Uhen (eds), *Evolution of Tertiary Mammals of North America*, Vol. 2: *Marine Mammals and Smaller Terrestrial Mammals* (pp. 239–261). Cambridge: Cambridge University Press.

Gunnell, G. F., Gingerich, P. D., Ul-Haq, M., Bloch, J. I., Khan, I. H., and Clyde, W. C. (2008b) New Primates (Mammalia) from the Early and Middle Eocene of Pakistan and Their Paleobiogeographic Implications. *Contributions from the Museum of Paleontology, University of Michigan* 32: 1–14.

Heesy, C. P., and Ross, C. (2001) Evolution of Activity Patterns and Chromatic Vision in Primates: Morphometrics, Genetics and Cladistics. *Journal of Human Evolution* 40: 111–149.

Hooker, J. J. (2007) A New Microchoerine Omomyid (Primates, Mammalia) from the English Early Eocene and Its Palaeobiogeographical Implications. *Palaeontology* 50: 739–756.

Hooker, J. J., Russell, D. E., and Phélizon, A. (1999) A New Family of Plesiadapiformes (Mammalia) from the Old World Lower Paleogene. *Palaeontology* 42: 377–407.

Janečka, J. E., Miller, W., Pringle, T. H., Wiens, F., Zitzmann, A., Helgen, K. M., Springer, M. S., and Murphy, W. J. (2007) Molecular and Genomic Data Identify the Closest Living Relative of Primates. *Science* 318: 792–794.

Jerison, H. J. (1973) *Evolution of the Brain and Intelligence*. New York: Academic Press.

Johnston, P. A., and Fox, R. C. (1984) Paleocene and Late Cretaceous Mammals from Saskatchewan, Canada. *Palaeontographica Abteilung A* 186: 163–222.

Kay, R. F., and Kirk, E. C. (2000) Osteological Evidence for the Evolution of Activity Pattern and Visual Acuity in Primates. *American Journal of Physical Anthropology* 113: 235–262.

Kay, R. F., Thorington, R. W., Jr, and Houde, P. (1990) Eocene 'Plesiadapiform' Shows Affinities with Flying Lemurs not Primates. *Nature* 345: 342–344.

Kay, R. F., Thewissen, J. G. M., and Yoder, A. D. (1992) Cranial Anatomy of *Ignacius graybullianus* and the Affinities of the Plesiadapiformes. *American Journal of Physical Anthropology* 89: 477–498.

Kay, R. F., Schmitt, D., Vinyard, C. J., Perry, J. M. G., Shigehara, N., Takai, M., and Egi, N. (2004) The Paleobiology of Amphipithecidae, South Asian Late Eocene Primates. *Journal of Human Evolution* 46: 3–25.

Kielan-Jaworowska, Z., Bown, T. M., and Lillegraven, J. A. (1979) Eutheria. In J. A. Lillegraven, Z. Kielan-Jaworowska, and W. A. Clemens (eds), *Mesozoic Mammals: The First Two-Thirds of Mammalian History* (pp. 221–258). Berkeley: University of California Press.

Kirk, E. C. (2006) Effects of Activity Pattern on Eye Size and Orbital Aperture Size in Primates. *Journal of Human Evolution* 51: 159–170.

Krause, D. W. (1991) Were Paromomyids Gliders? Maybe, Maybe not. *Journal of Human Evolution* 21: 177–188.

Lofgren, D. L. (1995) The Bug Creek Problem and the Cretaceous–Tertiary Boundary at McGuire Creek, Montana. *University of California Publications in Geological Sciences* 140: 1–185.

MacPhee, R. D. E., and Cartmill, M. (1986) Basicranial Structures and Primate Systematics. In D. R. Swisher and J. Erwin (eds), *Comparative Primate Biology*, Vol. 1: *Systematics, Evolution, and Anatomy* (pp. 219–275). New York: Alan R. Liss.

Marivaux, L., Welcomme, J.-L., Ducrocq, S., and Jaeger, J.-J. (2002) Oligocene Sivaladapid Primate from the Bugti Hills (Balochistan, Pakistan) Bridges the Gap between Eocene and Miocene Adapiform Communities in Southern Asia. *Journal of Human Evolution* 42: 379–388.

Martin, R. D. (1968) Towards a New Definition of Primates. *Man* 3: 377–401.

Miller, E. R., Gunnell, G. F., and Martin, R. D. (2005) Deep Time and the Search for Anthropoid Origins. *Yearbook of Physical Anthropology* 48: 60–95.

Ni, X., Wang, Y., Hu, Y., and Li, C. (2004) A Euprimate Skull from the Early Eocene of China. *Nature* 427: 65–68.

Ni, X., Beard, K. C., Meng, J., Wang, Y., and Gebo, D. L. (2007) Discovery of the First Cenozoic Euprimate (Mammalia) from Inner Mongolia. *American Museum Novitates* 3571: 1–11.

Olson, L. E., Sargis, E. J. and Martin, R. D. (2005) Intraordinal Phylogenetics of Treeshrews (Mammalia: Scandentia) Based on Evidence from the Mitochondrial 12S rRNA Gene. *Molecular Phylogenetics and Evolution* 35: 656–673.

Rasmussen, D. T. (1990) Primate Origins: Lessons from a Neotropical Marsupial. *American Journal of Primatology* 22: 263–277.

Rose, K. D. (1995) The Earliest Primates. *Evolutionary Anthropology* 3: 159–173.

Ross, C., Williams, B., and Kay, R. F. (1998) Phylogenetic Analysis of Anthropoid Relationships. *Journal of Human Evolution* 35: 221–306.

Russell, D. E. (1959) Le Crâne de *Plesiadapis*. *Bulletin de la Société Géologique de France* 4: 312–314.

Russell, D. E. (1964) Les Mammifères paléocènes d'Europe. *Mémoires du Muséum National d'Histoire Naturelle* (Nouvelle Série) 13: 1–324.

Seiffert, E. R., Simons, E. L., and Attia, Y. (2003) Fossil Evidence for an Ancient Divergence of Lorises and Galagos. *Nature* 422: 421–424.

Seiffert, E. R., Simons, E. L., Fleagle, J. G., and Godinot, M. (in press) Paleogene Anthropoids. In L. Werdelin and W. J. Sanders (eds), *Cenozoic Mammals of Africa*. Berkeley: University of California Press.

Seiffert, E. R., Simons, E. L., Clyde, W. C., Rossie, J. B., Attia, Y., Bown, T. M., Chatrath, P., and Mathison, M. E. (2005) Basal Anthropoids from Egypt and the Antiquity of Africa's Higher Primate Radiation. *Science* 310: 300–304.

Sigé, B., Jaeger, J.-J., Sudre, J., and Vianey-Liaud, M. (1990) *Altiatlasius koulchii* n. gen et sp., primate omomyidé du Paléocène supérieur du Maroc, et les origines des euprimates. *Palaeontographica Abteilung A* 214: 31–56.

Silcox, M. T. (2001) A Phylogenetic Analysis of Plesiadapiformes and Their Relationship to Euprimates and Other Archontans. PhD dissertation, Johns Hopkins University School of Medicine.

Silcox, M. T. (2003) New Discoveries on the Middle Ear Anatomy of *Ignacius Graybullianus* (Paromomyidae, Primates) from ultra High Resolution X-Ray Computed Tomography. *Journal of Human Evolution* 44: 73–86.

Silcox, M. T. (2008) The Biogeographic Origins of Primates and Euprimates: East, West, North, or South of Eden? In M. Dagosto and E. J. Sargis (eds), *Mammalian Evolutionary Morphology: A Tribute to Frederick S. Szalay* (pp. 199–213). New York: Springer-Verlag.

Silcox, M. T., and Gunnell, G. F. (2008) Plesiadapiformes. In C. M. Janis, G. F. Gunnell, and M. D. Uhen (eds), *Evolution of Tertiary Mammals of North America*, Vol 2: *Marine Mammals and Smaller Terrestrial Mammals* (pp. 207–238). Cambridge: Cambridge University Press.

Silcox, M. T., Rose, K. D., and Walsh, S. (2002) New Specimens of Picromomyids (Plesiadapiformes, ?Primates) with Description of a New Species of *Alveojunctus*. *Annals of Carnegie Museum* 71: 1–11.

Silcox, M. T., Sargis, E. J., Bloch, J. I., and Boyer, D. M. (2007) Primate Origins and Supraordinal Relationships: Morphological Evidence. In W. Henke and I. Tattersall (eds), *Handbook of Paleoanthropology*, Vol. 2: *Primate Evolution and Human Origins* (pp. 831–859). New York: Springer-Verlag.

Silcox, M. T., Bloch, J. I., Boyer, D. M., Godinot, M., Ryan, T. M., Spoor, F., and Walker, A. (2009) Semicircular Canal System in Early Primates. *Journal of Human Evolution* 56: 315–327.

Simpson, G. G. (1928) A New Mammalian Fauna from the Fort Union of Southern Montana. *American Museum Novitates* 297: 1–15.

Smith, T., Rose, K. D., and Gingerich, P. D. (2006) Rapid Asia–Europe–North America Geographic Dispersal of Earliest Eocene Primate *Teilhardina* during the Paleocene–Eocene Thermal Maximum. *Proceedings of the National Academy of Sciences, USA* 103: 11223–11227.

Soligo, C., and Martin, R. D. (2007) The First Primates: A Reply to Silcox et al. *Journal of Human Evolution* 53: 325–328.

Springer, M. S., W. J., Eizirik, E., and O'Brien, S. J. (2003) Placental Mammal Diversification and the Cretaceous–Tertiary Boundary. *Proceedings of the National Academy of Sciences, USA* 100: 1056–1061.

Springer, M. S., Stanhope, M. J., Madsen, O., and de Jong, W. W. (2004) Molecules Consolidate the Placental Mammal Tree. *Trends in Ecology and Evolution* 19: 430–438.

Stehlin, H. G. (1912) Die Säugetiere des schweizerischen Eocaens. Critischer Catalog der Materialien. 7ter Teil, erste Hälfte: Adapis. *Abhandlungen der Schweizerischen paläontologischen Gesellschaft* 38: 1165–1298.

Sussman, R. W. (1991) Primate Origins and the Evolution of Angiosperms. *American Journal of Primatology* 23: 209–223.

Sussman, R. W., and Raven, P. H. (1978) Pollination of Flowering Plants by Lemurs and Marsupials: A Surviving Archaic Coevolutionary System. *Science* 200: 731–736.

Szalay, F. S. (1968) The Beginnings of Primates. *Evolution* 22: 19–36.

Szalay, F. S., and Dagosto, M. (1980) Locomotor Adaptations as Reflected on the Humerus of Paleogene Primates. *Folia Primatologica* 34: 1–45.

Szalay, F. S., and Drawhorn, G. (1980) Evolution and Diversification of the Archonta in an Arboreal Milieu. In W. P. Luckett (ed.), *Comparative Biology and Evolutionary Relationships of Tree Shrews* (pp. 133–169). New York: Plenum Press.

Szalay, F. S., Rosenberger, A. L., and Dagosto, M. (1987) Diagnosis and Differentiation of the Order Primates. *Yearbook of Physical Anthropology* 30: 75–105.

Tabuce, R., Mahboubi, M., Tafforeau, P., and Sudre, J. (2004) Discovery of a Highly-Specialized 'Plesiadapiform' Primate in the Early-Middle Eocene of Northwestern Africa. *Journal of Human Evolution* 47: 305–321.

Van Valen, L. M., and Sloan, R. E. (1965) The Earliest Primates. *Science* 150: 743–745.

Youlatos, D., and Godinot, M. (2004) Locomotor Adaptations of *Plesiadapis tricuspidens* and *Plesiadapis* n. sp. (Mammalia, Plesiadapiformes) as Reflected on Selected Parts of the Postcranium. *Journal of Anthropological Science* 82: 103–118.

CHAPTER **17**

Catarrhine Cousins: The Origin and Evolution of Monkeys and Apes of the Old World

David R. Begun

INTRODUCTION

The history of paleoprimatology effectively begins with the discovery of a fossil from the gypsum quarries of Paris in the early nineteenth century. Georges Cuvier, whom many consider the father of vertebrate paleontology, described an odd-looking skull with cresty teeth and a long snout: *Adapis parisiensis*, which he considered to be a primitive artiodactyl (artiodactyls are even-toed ungulates such as cows, sheep and antelopes). It was actually the first fossil primate ever described. Cuvier was a brilliant comparative anatomist, and this error may seem curious. There are many reasons for his slip, which have to do with his religious convictions and with the political environment of post-revolutionary France. However, it can be said in his defense that the teeth of *Adapis* – which can be clearly classified as primate teeth, with the advantage of the copious fossil record available today – do look very similar to those of artiodactyls from the same time period – the Eocene. This is because Eocene primates and artiodactyls were not so far removed from their common ancestor; so, naturally, they resemble one another more closely than their modern descendants do. When Cuvier compared the teeth of *Adapis* to other fossils from the same quarries, it was reasonable and natural for him to conclude that this was a somewhat unusual early antelope.

Cuvier died in his prime, after a brief illness in 1832, before he could evaluate clearer evidence of fossil primates. In 1836 Edouard Lartet described a fossil that no one could deny was a primate: a primitive catarrhine from France, which was eventually dubbed *Pliopithecus* (Begun 2002b; catarrhines are Old World monkeys, apes, and humans). In the following years of the nineteenth century, fossils routinely linked to living Old World monkeys and apes were described from locations that were accessible to European researchers: India (now India and Pakistan), Egypt, and Europe itself (Begun 2002a; Begun 2002b; Kelley 2002; Rasmussen 2002). In the twentieth century, our knowledge of fossil catarrhines has greatly expanded so as to include specimens from much older sites in Africa and from numerous sites in Asia and Europe (Table 17.1). The diagram below lists the fossil catarrhines included in this review and their geological ages. The basic classification of living catarrhines adopted in this chapter is as follows (for the Cercopithecoidea only a few representative genera are listed):

Infraorder Catarrhini
  Superfamily Hominoidea
    Family Hominidae
      Subfamily Homininae
        Genus *Homo* (humans)
        Genus *Gorilla* (gorillas)
        Genus *Pan* (chimpanzees and bonobos)
      Subfamily Ponginae
        Genus *Pongo* (orangutans)
    Family Hylobatidae
      Genus *Hylobates* (gibbons and siamangs)
  Superfamily Cercopithecoidea
    Family Cercopithecidae
      Genera *Papio, Macaca, Cercocebus, Theropithecus* (baboons, macaques, mangabeys, geladas)
    Family Colobidae
      Genera *Colobus, Semnopithecus, Rhinopithecus* (colobus, langurs, odd nosed monkeys)

THE EARLIEST CATARRHINES

The best collection of early catarrhines comes from the Fayum deposits of Egypt, from which early primates have been described since the end of the nineteenth century (Rasmussen 2002). Max Schlosser described the first specimen from the Fayum in 1910; he was struck by its resemblance to Lartet's catarrhine and called his primate *Propliopithecus*, thereby implying that it was the ancestor of *Pliopithecus* (Schlosser 1910). In the years after the discovery of *Propliopithecus*, researchers working in the Fayum have unearthed the remains of a spectacular diversity of primates, including the fossil relatives of lemurs, tarsiers, primitive anthropoids, and catarrhines. *Propliopithecus* was the subject of much discussion during the first half of the twentieth century. It was widely viewed as a small ape, probably related to gibbons by way of *Pliopithecus*. More recent discoveries have shown, however, that the story is much more complicated. The Fayum catarrhines are distinguished from other Fayum primates in details of their dental anatomy, but mainly in having only two premolars on each side of each jaw (a dental quadrant). This is the most obvious difference between catarrhines and the other major group of anthropoids: the platyrrhines or New World monkeys, which have three premolars per quadrant.

Table 17.1 Fossil catarrhines and their geological ages and geographic distributions

Taxon	Age	Country/Region
Catopithecus	Late Eocene, 35.5–36 mya[a]	Egypt
Oligopithecus	Late Eocene, 34–35 mya	Egypt
Aegyptopithecus	Early Oligocene, 33–33.5 mya	Egypt
Propliopithecus	Early Oligocene, 33–34 mya	Egypt
Pliopithecus	Middle-late Miocene, 16–10 mya	Europe
Kamoyapithecus	Late Oligocene, 26 mya	Kenya
Proconsul	Early Miocene, 20–17 mya	Kenya
Afropithecus	Early Miocene, 17 mya	Kenya
Morotopithecus	Early or middle Miocene, 20–15 mya?	Uganda
Griphopithecus	Latest early Miocene, 16–16.5 mya	Germany, Slovakia, Turkey
Equatorius	Middle Miocene, 15 mya	Kenya
Kenyapithecus	Middle Miocene, 15–16 mya	Kenya, Turkey
Dryopithecus[b]	Middle/late Miocene, 12.5–9.5 mya	France, Spain, Germany, Hungary, Georgia
Sivapithecus[b]	Middle/late Miocene, 12.5–7 mya	India, Pakistan, Nepal
Ouranopithecus	Late Miocene, 9.5 mya	Greece
Lufengpithecus	Late Miocene, 9 mya	China
Gigantopithecus	Pleistocene, 1–0.5 mya	China,
Sahelanthropus	Late Miocene, 6–7 mya	Chad
Orrorin	Late Miocene, 6 mya	Kenya
Ardipithecus	Late Miocene, early Pliocene, 6–4 mya	Ethiopia
Victoriapithecus[c]	Early/middle Miocene, 19–12.5 mya	Kenya, Uganda
Mesopithecus	Late Miocene–Pliocene	Europe, Iran, Afghanistan

[a] mya = million of years ago.

[b] Simplified taxonomy. *Dryopithecus* is usually divided into several different genera. *Sivapithecus* also represents several related genera from Asia.

[c] Discussion of the huge number of fossil cercopithecoids is restricted to the earliest and best known species. See Jablonski (2002) for more details.

The best known of the Fayum catarrhines is *Aegyptopithecus*, first described by Elwyn Simons in 1965 (Simons 1965). *Aegyptopithecus* is known from several crania and mandibles as well as from a number of limb bones; it was the size of a small monkey or gibbon, about six kilograms (Ankel-Simons et al. 1998). *Aegyptopithecus* has a hominoid-like dentition, with two premolars (as in all catarrhines), upper molars with four cusps (as in many other primates), and lower molars with five cusps, which is unique to catarrhines (although many Old World monkeys have a modified pattern). The lower molar cusp pattern in *Aegyptopithecus* corresponds to the famous *Dryopithecus* Y-5 pattern, which has long been considered a hallmark of ape evolution (Figure 17.1). The fact that this feature is found in *Aegyptopithecus* indicates that Y-5 is not a shared derived character (that is, a feature indicating a close evolutionary relationship) of apes and humans, but is retained instead from a more primitive ancestor. This is a lesson demonstrating that not all the anatomical attributes which distinguish humans from monkeys are more advanced in humans. In a real evolutionary sense, our teeth are more primitive than those of living Old World monkeys.

Beyond the Y-5 lower molar morphology, there is not much else that links *Aegyptopithecus* to more advanced catarrhines. *Aegyptopithecus* is a great example of a missing link – a transitional form between prosimians, which still exist today, and living catarrhines. *Aegyptopithecus* is more like the prosimians in major attributes of the skull – for instance the size of the snout, which is large, and of the brain, which is small. This probably reflects behaviors more characteristic to living prosimians than to catarrhines, including a greater reliance on the sense of smell and a simpler social organization. Nevertheless, *Aegyptopithecus* was similar to all the living catarrhines and to many Malagasy prosimians in that it was active during the day (diurnal) and probably lived in social groups. Paleoprimatologists have deduced this from the size of its eye sockets, which are too small to accommodate the large eyes of nocturnal primates, and from the fact that males are larger than females and have large canine teeth, which project well beyond the level of the opposing teeth. In anthropoids, which tend to have more complex societies than prosimians, the males are often larger than the females, and they use their enlarged canines in displays among other males.

While the brain of *Aegyptopithecus*, which we know indirectly from casts of the interior of the brain case, is similar in size to that of prosimians of the same body size, in a few details it is more advanced. For example the frontal lobes – which are responsible for many higher-level cognitive functions, including the mediation of complex social interactions – are intermediate in size between those of prosimians and those of living catarrhines. The olfactory lobes, which are responsible for the sense of smell, are relatively small in *Aegyptopithecus*, which suggests that smell, although more important to *Aegyptopithecus* than to modern catarrhines, was perhaps less critical than in prosimians (Begun and Kordos 2004; Radinsky 1973, 1974).

Aegyptopithecus is known from a number of limb bones. These indicate that it was stoutly built and had relatively short limbs, unlike the specialized, elongated, and (usually) relatively slender limbs of catarrhines (Fleagle and Simons 1982). *Aegyptopithecus* may have been a cautious climber, spending most of its time in the trees. The Fayum deposits preserve abundant indications of an ancient forest – for instance fossilized trees, fruits, and other forest products – and of many of the animals found today in forests. One important feature in *Aegyptopithecus* is the entepicondylar foramen, a hole through the lower end of the humerus (upper arm bone) through which a large nerve and associated blood vessels pass. Catarrhines lack this hole, which causes the nerve to be more exposed on the surface of the bone and leads to an indescribable sensation you have upon hitting your 'funny bone.' There is no obvious adaptational explanation for this difference between catarrhines and other primates.

Other anthropoids from the deposits at the Fayum have a much less secure claim to catarrhine status. *Catopithecus* and *Oligopithecus* are, both, even more primitive than *Aegyptopithecus*. They are much smaller than *Aegyptopithecus* (or than any living catarrhine, for that matter), weighing about 500g, the size of the smallest living anthropoids (Rasmussen 2007). *Catopithecus*, the better known of the two, is sexually dimorphic in body mass and canine size, like *Aegyptopithecus*. Both have teeth that are difficult to distinguish from those of prosimians, though they do have only two premolars per quadrant. They also lack mandibular symphysis fusion, which means that each side of their lower jaw remains separate during life. In all other anthropoids, including of course catarrhines, the lower and upper jaw on each side fuse together before birth. So why do some researchers consider *Catopithecus* and *Oligopithecus* to be catarrhines? The two main arguments are that they have only two premolars per quadrant, as noted, and that they occur in the oldest levels of the Fayum deposits, so their very primitive morphology is expected, and represents morphological continuity over time from clearly prosimian to clearly catarrhine (Rasmussen 2002). However, the lack of mandibular symphyseal fusion and the very primitive look of the teeth require parallel evolution of the more modern-looking jaws and teeth in platyrrhines (New World monkeys) and catarrhines. Parallelism is common in evolution in general, and it is certainly common in primate evolution, but some researchers question the possibility that parallel evolution happened in anthropoids to such a great extent (Ross et al. 1998). Regardless of the outcome of this debate, the common ancestor of all living catarrhines probably resembled *Catopithecus* and *Oligopithecus.*

The Pliopithecoidea

There is a substantial gap in time and space between the propliopithecoids and the next most primitive catarrhine group, the pliopithecoids. Pliopithecoids are a very diverse and successful group of catarrhines that ranged from Spain to China between about 18 to 9 million years ago (mya) (Begun 2002b). They resemble living anthropoids much more closely in the overall anatomy of the skull, including the face and brain case, and their limbs are more elongated and slender, like in many anthropoids. Their claim to catarrhine status is, however, still more or less confined to their dental formula, which has two premolars in each quadrant. Their teeth are much more modern-looking than those of *Aegyptopithecus*. One big difference between the two is the development of *cingula* – ridges of enamel that run along the cheek side of lower molars and the tongue side of the upper molars. *Aegyptopithecus* has shelf-like *cingula* while *Pliopithecus* has thinner, ridge-like *cingula*, which closely resemble those of the earliest apes (hominoids) (Figure 17.1).

Pliopithecoids share another subtle feature with living catarrhines in the bony ear region. All living catarrhines and all fossil hominoids and Old World monkeys have a complete bony canal, called 'ectotympanic tube,' leading from the ear drum inside the ear to the outer ear hole (or external auditory meatus). Propliopithecoids, New World monkeys, and most prosimians lack this tube (tarsiers and some of their possible fossil relatives appear to have evolved this tube in parallel with catarrhines). Pliopithecoids are unlike living catarrhines in that their ectotympanic tubes are only partially formed by bone, or ossified: the remaining portion of their tube is composed of cartilage. Cartilage is not preserved in fossils. Nevertheless, it is reasonable to suggest that a partial tube would be a plausible intermediate condition between having no tube and having a complete bony tube.

According to a recent analysis, there are two large families of pliopithecoids, each having a large number of species (Begun 2002b). Given the limitations of space, I will confine my comments to the best known fossils: the pliopithecids of Europe known as *Pliopithecus* and *Epipliopithecus* (I will refer to them collectively as *Pliopithecus*). *Pliopithecus* is known from many jaws and teeth, a number of partial skulls and several partial skeletons. In the cranium, the face is shorter than that of *Aegyptopithecus*, and is without the elongated snout of the latter. The brain case is larger, and it enclosed a brain that was much more modern anthropoid-like than in *Aegyptopithecus* (Begun and Kordos 2004).

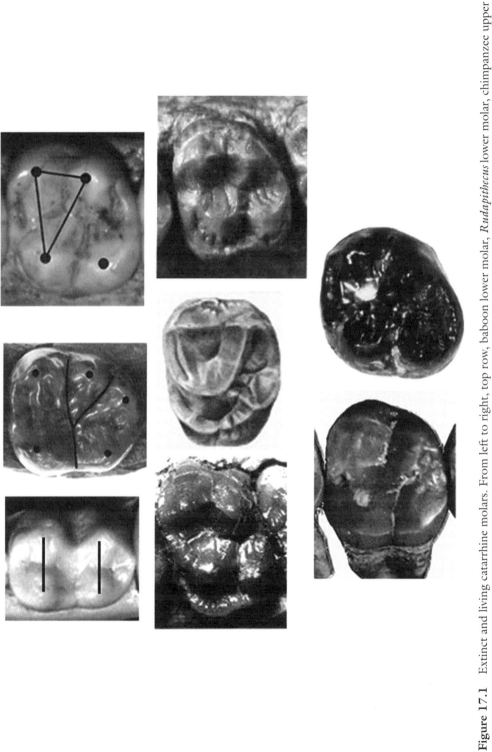

Figure 17.1 Extinct and living catarrhine molars. From left to right, top row, baboon lower molar, *Rudapithecus* lower molar, chimpanzee upper molar; middle row, *Aegyptopithecus*, *Epipliopithecus*, *Proconsul* upper molars; lower row, *Griphopithecus*, *Rudapithecus* upper molar. The bilophodont pattern of the baboon tooth is shown by the lines joining the cusps, and the Y-5 pattern is illustrated on the *Rudapithecus* lower molar. The trigon and hypocone are illustrated on the chimpanzee upper molar. Images are not to scale. *Aegyptopithecus* modified from Rasmussen 2002; *Epipliopithecus* modified from Zapfe 1960; *Proconsul* modified from Harrison 2002; *Griphopithecus* modified from Kelley 2002

The teeth of *Pliopithecus* are modern ape-like in their overall structure, with a well defined Y-5 pattern on the lower molars and a clear trigone and hypocone on the uppers (Figure 17.1). The teeth share features with living catarrhines that mainly consume soft fruits (gibbons, chimpanzees), and *Pliopithecus* is inferred to have preferred soft fruits as well. The canines are sexually dimorphic; but the degree of body mass dimorphism is not clear, though it seems to be lower than in *Aegyptopithecus*. What this means about their social behavior is not understood, but the fact that pliopithecoids are frequently found in large numbers in many sites suggests that they were quite social.

A number of partial skeletons of *Pliopithecus* are known from fissure fill deposits (that is, sink holes into which animal bones were washed) in Slovakia; these preserve very good evidence of the overall body shape. They are most similar to living New World monkeys in having relatively long and slender limbs, long and flexible backs, and strongly grasping hands and feet. They were clearly adapted to an arboreal life-style, and this is consistent with their inferred diet of fruits and with the evidence from other animals found with them in the sink holes.

Pliopithecoids represent another step in the evolution of modern catarrhines, but their place among the the latter is poorly understood. They are monkey-like in overall anatomy and superficially gibbon-like in their dentition, and hence they resemble living catarrhines much more than propliopithecoids. Pliopithecoids branched off from the common line that led to living Old World monkeys, apes, and humans, and they did so before Old World monkeys and hominoids branched off from one another. This is clear from the fact that the pliopithecoids retain such primitive characters as the entepicondylar foramen and an incompletely ossified ectotympanic tube. Currently it is thought that Old World monkeys and hominoids diverged by about 25 mya. So the pliopithecoids must have evolved before 25 mya, and there is therefore a gap of at least 7 million years between the most recent possible date of their origin and their first appearance in the fossil record – which is in China, about 18 mya. Since the probable ancestors of the pliopithecoids, the propliopithecids, are only known from Africa, the pliopithecoids probably came from Africa as well.

THE HOMINOIDEA

Hominoid origins (that is, the origins of apes and humans) are also difficult to pinpoint in the fossil record. The oldest fossils that most researchers attribute to the Hominoidea are assigned to the genus *Proconsul*, from 20-million-year-old (early Miocene) deposits in Kenya (Begun 2007; Harrison 2002). One site in Kenya called Lothidok, dated to 26 mya in late Oligocene – which means about half-way in age between the Fayum catarrhines and *Proconsul* – has yielded a jaw fragment of a genus called *Kamoyapithecus*. The teeth of *Kamoyapithecus* are similar to those of *Aegyptopithecus* in being broad and in having well developed *cingula*, but they are considerably larger. Not much else is known about *Kamoyapithecus*, but it does represent a link, in time and in size, between Oligocene primitive catarrhines and the first clear-cut hominoids.

Proconsul is the best known of a large number of fossil apes from the Miocene of East Africa. It was a very diverse and successful group, which lasted for about 10 million years, from about 20.5 to 10.5 mya (Begun 2007; Harrison 2002). There are three widely recognized species of *Proconsul*, ranging from the size of a female baboon (about 10 kg) to that of a female gorilla (about 80 kg). Many other fossil apes, perhaps related to *Proconsul*, lived at the same time in East Africa, but I will focus here only on *Proconsul*, as it is the best known and represents a very plausible candidate for the earliest known hominoid. *Proconsul* has the definitive catarrhine characters of two premolars, a complete ectotympanic tube, and a humerus without an entepicondylar foramen.

The best known *Proconsul* species are *P. heseloni* and *P. nyanzae*; they are known from Rusinga Island, just off the coast of Lake Victoria, in western Kenya. Well preserved crania, mandibles, and partial skeletons are known from both species (Begun 2007; Harrison 2002; Walker 1997; Walker and Teaford 1989; Walker et al. 1993; Ward 1993; Ward et al. 1993). *Proconsul* has a short face and a large brain by comparison with the previously discussed taxa. In relative size, the brain is similar to those of living baboons, which have some of the largest brains among Old World monkeys. It is also close in relative size to those of gibbons and siamangs (hylobatids, or so-called 'lesser apes'), but smaller than in great apes (Begun and Kordos 2004; Radinsky 1974). *Proconsul*'s brain may have been slightly more primitive than the brain in baboons today, but it was probably fairly similar and provided *Proconsul* with cognitive capacities that were probably comparable to those of the most intelligent living monkeys. Old World monkeys are highly intelligent, and they use their cognitive skills to negotiate their complex ecological and social worlds. Old World monkeys are generally highly social and form complexly organized social groups. They are very adaptable and able to exploit a wide range of resources, in large part as a result of their cleverness. *Proconsul* was probably similar, and had achieved a monkey-like grade or level of behavioral complexity.

The face and teeth of *Proconsul* are relatively unspecialized, which means that they do not have any features that appear to be adapted to a specialized diet. Instead, the molar teeth of *Proconsul* have fairly low, rounded cusps and small basins, suggesting a diet of soft fruits. The enamel was thicker than in most living apes, but the pattern of wear resembles more that of apes with thin enamel that eat soft fruits. *Proconsul* lacks the specialized front teeth, molar crests, or enlarged molars of later, more specialized hominoids. The jaws are also relatively slender and were incapable of generating the very powerful biting forces needed in order to consume hard or tough foods, as many later apes did.

More of the skeleton of *Proconsul* is known than is the case for nearly all other fossil apes. *Proconsul* has a narrow and deep thorax, like most quadrupeds, including monkeys, and its shoulders are positioned to the side of the body. This is the position of an animal that moves primarily with its arms below the body, like most mammals we are familiar with (dogs, cats, horses, cows, sheep, and the like). Modern apes and humans differ in that the arms are rotated toward the back, which creates shoulders facing away from the body. This shoulder position gives the apes a much more mobile shoulder and allows them to swing below branches with tremendous ease. Humans retain the ape-like anatomy despite their commitment to life on the ground. This is a strong indication of our close evolutionary relationship to apes. It has resulted in highly mobile shoulders, which are useful for carrying and throwing (among many other manipulative capacities). But *Proconsul* lacks these ape characters of the shoulder and surely moved much more like living monkeys, walking on the top of branches and on the palms of the hands on the ground. In keeping with this monkey-like lifestyle, *Proconsul* has arms and legs of roughly equal length, and a long and flexible lower back (Ward 2007).

There are some hints of more ape-like features in *Proconsul* that presage the specialized posture and locomotion of this group. The most obvious one is that *Proconsul* did not have a tail and, possibly as a consequence, it had a very powerful grip, both in the hands and in the feet (Begun et al. 1994; Kelley 1997; Ward et al. 1991). The hips and wrists of *Proconsul* show indications of somewhat higher levels of mobility than is typical of monkeys and closer to those encountered in apes, which tend to spread their limbs further away from the midline of their bodies as they negotiate a complex arboreal milieu.

The evolutionary position of *Proconsul* is relatively well established, though there is some debate on the topic. Most researchers accept that *Proconsul* is a primitive or stem ape, which means that it is more closely related to living apes and to humans than it is to Old World monkeys, but not specifically related to any single living ape lineage. It is at the stem of the radiation of apes but not in the crown – that is, not in those parts of the radiation that led to each living ape. In other words, *Proconsul* is an extinct side-branch of the early hominoids, but one that probably resembles closely the common ancestor all apes and humans actually share with each other.

As noted, beyond the catarrhine attributes of *Proconsul* there are a few subtle features that link it with hominoids. The body of *Proconsul* was monkey-like rather than ape-like (as noted earlier), but an important ape character is the presence of a likely coccyx or tail bone in place of an external tail. Among primates, only hominoids have a coccyx. Also as noted earlier, the wrists and hips of *Proconsul* give subtle hints of increased mobility, more like that seen in apes. But, overall, *Proconsul* is still quite primitive – which has prompted at least one prominent researcher to reject its hominoid status (Harrison 2002).

Other early fossil apes that lived around the same time as *Proconsul* and were broadly similar in anatomy include *Limnopithecus, Micropithecus, Rangwapithecus, Simiolus, Dendropithecus, Turkanapithecus* and *Kalepithecus*. Together they represent the first great radiation of fossil apes. We cannot be sure which, if any, of these fossil apes is directly related to later, more modern apes; but *Proconsul* currently seems to be the best candidate.

Morotopithecus is another distinctive contemporary of *Proconsul* that may provide us with additional clues about great ape origins. It is from Uganda and is dated to a period of either 15 or 20 mya. The age is unclear at this time. The most important specimens of *Morotopithecus* include a partial face and a lower back (lumbar) vertebra. The face and teeth are similar to those of *Afropithecus* (see below) and suggest a broadly similar diet. The lumbar vertebra is interpreted as unexpectedly ape-like in one subtle detail: the position of a bony spur called the transverse process, which is associated with the short stiff lower backs of living apes (MacLatchy et al. 2000; Ward 2007). However, this interpretation has not gone unchallenged (Nakatsukasa 2008). This debate has received a lot of attention in paleoanthropology, because *Morotopithecus* has been interpreted to be a 20 mya early great ape, which is about 5 million years older than previous estimates. This age would push back hominoid origins and the split between hominoids and Old World monkeys much further into the past than nearly all current estimates, requiring a considerable revision of our understanding of the fossil record. So, for these reasons and given the uncertainties mentioned earlier about the age and the anatomy of its vertebrae, *Morotopithecus* is best considered to be another early ape of unclear relationship to later apes. It may in fact be a close relative of the next fossil ape discussed here, *Afropithecus*.

Afropithecus is a large fossil ape, about the same size as the largest *Proconsul*, also known from 17 mya sites in Kenya. *Afropithecus* has distinctive large, thick or tusk-like canines, and strong thick incisors. It has molars with thick enamel, and powerfully built jaws. The attachment sites for the chewing muscles in *Afropithecus* are strongly developed, indicating that it had a very powerful bite and probably ate foods with tough or hard outer coverings – a dietary strategy known as 'hard-object feeding' (Leakey and Walker 1997). The internal anatomy of the teeth of *Afropithecus* has been investigated in order to determine how it grew, through the analysis of growth lines preserved in the enamel. It appears that *Afropithecus* grew more slowly than *Proconsul* and was in this way more similar to the great apes, which grow more slowly and take longer to reach maturity than do monkeys (Smith et al. 2003). This has profound implications concerning the biology of apes compared to that of monkeys (see below).

The face of *Afropithecus* is easily distinguished from that of *Proconsul*. The snout is long and narrow – but not because of a well developed sense of smell, as in *Aegyptopithecus*. Instead, the snout is large because of the large size of the roots of the canine teeth, which are massive. The lower jaw is large, and built so as to withstand powerful chewing forces. The zygomatic or cheek bones are reinforced and reflect a powerful chewing muscle, the masseter; and the frontal bone has strong ridges and a very deep postorbital constriction (a deep notch behind the eye sockets), indicating a large temporalis muscle. These are the principal chewing muscles, and they were much stronger in *Afropithecus* than in *Proconsul*. Unlike its jaws and teeth, the limbs of *Afropithecus* were very similar to those of *Proconsul*; overall they were more similar to those of monkeys than to those of apes.

The main differences between *Afropithecus* and *Proconsul* are in dietary strategy and growth, and these changes may have allowed *Afropithecus* or one of its descendants to expand their range into Eurasia (see below). In both cases, these changes may signal a great degree of adaptability. *Afropithecus*, with its powerful jaws and large teeth, was able to exploit a wider range of foods than *Proconsul*, including foods that were inaccessible to *Proconsul* because the outer coverings were too difficult for the teeth to penetrate. This may have allowed *Afropithecus* to range beyond the areas in which *Proconsul* could survive and may have given it an adaptive advantage in the more seasonal and more variable environments of Eurasia. In addition, the slower rate of growth in *Afropithecus* is associated in living apes with a larger brain and an extended period of infant dependence, which affords more time in which to learn about the social and ecological environment. We do not know to what extent *Afropithecus* resembled the great apes in behavior, but we can speculate that it may have been just different enough to exploit environments into which *Proconsul* could not expand.

Proconsul or *Proconsul*-like primitive apes were a very successful group, which continued to live in the forests of East Africa until about 10 mya, though it becomes rare after 17 mya. *Afropithecus* or a very similar form, *Heliopithecus*, expands into the northern part of the African continent, Saudi Arabia, where it is the first hominoid to leave Africa proper, around 17 mya. *Heliopithecus* is only known from a crushed upper jaw, but it closely resembled *Afropithecus*. Shortly afterwards a new type of hominoid appears in the eastern Mediterranean and Europe.

EXPANSION TO EURASIA

As noted, about 17 mya or so, early apes from Africa expanded their range into Eurasia. They first appear in Anatolia, the Asian part of Turkey, and in Germany, about 16.5 mya, just before the beginning of the middle Miocene (Heizmann and Begun 2001). These apes are known as *Griphopithecus*, and they differ from their African predecessors in a number of features. They have a more modern-looking dentition, with reduced cingula and with molars having broader, flatter cusps (Kelley 2002; see Figure 17.1). The enamel is thick, as in a number of early Miocene forms, but the wear pattern is different. *Griphopithecus* teeth tend to wear flatly, because the underlying dentine is flat rather than hilly as in *Proconsul* and *Afropithecus*. In the latter this results in wear featuring prominent pits of exposed dentine. The flat-wearing molars of *Griphopithecus* suggest a diet heavy in abrasives, whereby the exposed dentine, which is softer than enamel, would cause the tooth to wear out too quickly. A thick, more even layer of enamel may also be related to forceful crushing and grinding. We find similar-looking molars in later fossil apes, as well as in australopithecines and in early members of our own genus, *Homo*; these are generally interpreted as indicating a hard-object diet. Modern orangutans and some New World monkeys also have similar teeth. *Griphopithecus* may have eaten foods from the ground and inadvertently included grit; or it may have eaten foods with higher percentages of naturally occurring grit, which exists in many plants as a defense against predation. Either way, the teeth are more modern and suggest a change in diet.

Griphopithecus is known mostly from isolated teeth; but a few jaw fragments are also known, and they are consistent with the teeth in pointing to a diet that required heavy mastication. Very little is known of the postcranial skeleton of *Griphopithecus*. A number of phalanges (bones of the fingers and toes) and a few limb fragments indicate (as far as we can tell) a skeleton similar to that of *Proconsul* and *Afropithecus*: a generalized arboreal quadruped without any of the enhanced suspensory abilities we see in living hominoids (Begun 1992; Ersoy et al. 2008). *Griphopithecus* persists in Europe until about 14 mya. A very similar genus, *Equatorius*, is found in Kenya about 15 mya (Ward and Duren 2002). Another closely related form, *Kenyapithecus*, also appears – first in Turkey, at a site shared with *Griphopithecus*, and later, around 13.5 Ma, in Kenya. Finally, the last form we know from this group is *Nacholapithecus*, also from Kenya. It is similar to the others, except in the forelimbs, which are relatively large. This may be a sign of things to come, as all living hominoids except humans have much larger arms than legs. In *Nacholapithecus* the difference is less pronounced, but this probably means that *Nacholapithecus* used its forelimbs for climbing more than living monkeys do (Ishida et al. 2004).

This impressive diversity of middle Miocene taxa shows that the large area extending south, from Europe to East Africa, was inhabited by a successful second radiation of more modern-looking apes, endowed with powerful jaws and thickly enameled teeth. This region can be seen as a core from which the ancestors of the living great apes arose. We do not know whether the great apes came more directly from the

African members of this core group or from those in Europe, but around 12.5 mya we find the earliest member of each of the living groups of great apes: the pongines (orangutans and their fossil relatives) and the hominines (African apes, humans, and their fossil relatives). The earliest hominines and pongines are only known from Eurasia, and it is likely that they evolved on that continent.

Pongines

The oldest fossils usually attributed to the pongine subfamily are from India and Pakistan and belong to the genus *Sivapithecus* (Kelley 2002). *Sivapithecus* has been known to researchers since the nineteenth century, but until the 1980s its place in ape and human evolution was not well understood. *Sivapithecus* has large molars with broad, flat cusps and thick enamel. Its jaws are very powerfully built; overall, the jaws and the back teeth resemble those found in fossil humans such as *Australopithecus*. For years, smaller individuals of *Sivapithecus*, formerly called *Ramapithecus*, were considered likely candidates for direct human ancestry, given the australopithecine look of their back teeth and what was interpreted as human-like small canines. We now know that '*Ramapithecus*' has small canines because the specimens known are actually females of *Sivapithecus*; and, like in most anthropoids, females have smaller canines than males. We know now, through the discovery of a well preserved face, that *Sivapithecus* is closely related to living orangutans. Among the unique features shared between *Pongo* and *Sivapithecus* are tall, narrow eye sockets (orbits), separated by a narrow space between them, and a very elongated and concave face. The front part of the upper jaw, the premaxilla, which holds the incisor teeth, is greatly elongated, horizontal, and continuous with the floor of the nasal cavity. These are highly distinctive features, only seen in *Pongo* among the living apes; so, despite the australopithecine-like back teeth, *Sivapithecus* is nearly unanimously viewed as a fossil relative of the orangutan.

The oldest specimens considered to represent *Sivapithecus* are about 12.5 mya in age, and 13 to 16 mya is the figure often given as a maximum age for the *Pongo* lineage, assuming that the earliest members of the group have not yet been discovered. This is one of the most important divergence dates in paleoanthropology because it is used as a basis for calibrating divergence dates based on the analysis of DNA. Knowing the number of differences and the amount of time in which these changes have accumulated between the DNA sequences of African apes and of *Pongo*, researchers can estimate the rate of change in the DNA and can calculate divergence times between other lineages. It is on the basis of this type of analysis that it is possible to estimate the time of divergence between chimpanzees and humans to have been about 7–8 mya. Other important divergence dates are 9–10 mya for gorillas and 25 mya for Old World monkeys and apes.

Its jaws and teeth suggest that *Sivapithecus* was well adapted to feeding on a diversity of foods types. The pattern of tooth wear visible under the microscope, or the microwear, is similar to that seen in modern chimpanzees, which have a very broad diet. *Sivapithecus* was probably capable of generating in its jaws more power than modern chimpanzees – which may have allowed it to exploit foods with hard or tough outer coverings, perhaps in times of food scarcity. This dental adaptation was quite successful, and *Sivapithecus* and its relatives survived for more than 5 mya in Asia. An all-Asian radiation consisted of *Sivapithecus* and its relatives, which are found as far west as Turkey and as far south and east as China and Thailand (Kelley 2002). One relative of *Sivapithecus* that survived much longer is the incredible fossil ape *Gigantopithecus*, which is estimated to have been at least twice the size of living gorillas, and was by far the largest primate to ever have lived. *Gigantopithecus* survived to about 300,000 years ago and lived contemporaneously with fossil humans (*Homo erectus*) in China (Kelley 2002).

The limbs of *Sivapithecus* are less well known; for the most part, they are decidedly not orangutan-like (Madar et al. 2002). This is a classic example of mosaic evolution, where different features of a lineage evolved at different rates and times. *Sivapithecus* probably had a body type broadly like that of apes, with a broad chest and arms hanging from the side rather than supporting the body from below; but it was not a highly suspensory ape, like the living orangutans. *Sivapithecus* probably spent more more time on the ground, though it was surely an excellent climber. Finally, its teeth have been analyzed for growth studies. Researchers have concluded that *Sivapithecus* grew just like the modern great apes. This involves a lengthy period of maturation, dependence on parents, and a large and slowly growing brain (Kelley 2004).

Hominines

At the same time when the pongines were evolving in Asia, the hominines were evolving in Europe. The oldest hominine, not surprisingly, is about the same age as the oldest pongine. *Dryopithecus*, mentioned earlier, is the oldest hominine currently known. It is known from sites in France and Spain that are dated to about 12.5 mya (Begun 2002a). The small sample first described by Lartet in 1856 consists of a lower jaw and the shaft of an upper arm bone (humerus). Although fragmentary specimens accumulated for the next 100 years, like *Sivapithecus*, the role of *Dryopithecus* in ape and human evolution was not clear until better specimens were discovered, since the 1970s on. In 2004 a partial skeleton of *Dryopithecus* (or *Pierolapithecus*) was found in Spain. This skeleton includes parts of the vertebral column, ribs, wrists, and hands, as well as much of a face (Moyà-Solà et al. 2004). The vertebrae and ribs indicate an ape-like body form, and the wrists and hands show that this animal was a strong climber – with flexible limbs, probably somewhat suspensory, as in living apes. The humerus from the Lartet collection is long and slender, like in living apes, and was probably longer than the hindlimbs. Another partial skeleton of a closely related species preserves portions of the arms and legs, and clearly shows ape-like limb proportions (long arms and short legs). This is the first solid evidence of an ape body plan in the fossil record.

The jaws and teeth of *Dryopithecus* and of its close relatives have been much studied. They closely resemble those of chimpanzees, as Lartet remarked long ago. The structure of the teeth, with their thin enamel and widely spaced cusps, was adapted to a diet of soft fruits, as in living chimpanzees. This is also suggested by microwear. The jaws are more slender than in *Sivapithecus*, and so are all the muscle attachment sites. The front teeth of *Dryopithecus* may have been adapted to tearing through tough outer coverings, opening up more feeding options, but *Dryopithecus* was not a hard-object feeder.

Another very important site in Europe is in Hungary, where another close relative of *Dryopithecus*, called *Rudapithecus*, is known. The *Rudapithecus* sample is the only one from Eurasia with well preserved skulls and includes two brain cases (Kordos and Begun 2001, 2002). In fact there are only two Miocene hominoid specimens that include remains of the face, braincase, and mandible of a single individual, well preserved together, out of the thousands of recovered specimens. The other specimen is a *Proconsul* skull. The skull of *Rudapithecus* shows us that it had a brain the size of that of a chimpanzee. This is the first direct evidence of modern hominid brain size in the fossil record (Begun and Kordos 2004). The face of *Rudapithecus* is quite similar to that of African apes, in the same ways that the face of *Sivapithecus* resembles that of orangutans. The premaxilla is shorter, more vertical, and separated from the rest of the palate by a gap, just like in African apes, especially gorillas. The face is also tilted downward relative to the braincase, as in African apes and humans. In *Sivapithecus* and orangutans the face is tilted upward.

As in other Miocene apes, researchers have studied the internal structure of the teeth of *Dryopithecus*; and, as in *Sivapithecus*, the teeth grew at great ape rates. This is consistent with the direct evidence from a large brain in *Rudapithecus* and probably means that *Dryopithecus* and relatives behaved in a way much closer to that of modern great apes in terms of their relationship to the environment and in the complexity of their social groups. Along with *Sivapithecus*, these are really the first modern great apes, and their adaptations form the basis for subsequent developments, which lead to the origin of the human lineage.

The skeleton of *Dryopithecus* and relatives is better known than that of *Sivapithecus*. As mentioned, these animals had a body similar to that of the modern great ape, but probably more similar to that of modern orangutans than to that of modern African apes. *Dryopithecus* spent nearly all of its time in the trees and was highly suspensory, while modern African apes are more terrestrial and engage in an unusual mode of locomotion, known as 'knuckle-walking.' This behavior evolved in the common ancestor of African apes and humans after the lineage of *Dryopithecus* had branched off.

THE CERCOPITHECOIDEA

Although it has been estimated on the basis of genetic evidence that hominoids and cercopithecoids diverged from one another by about 25 mya, the oldest known Old World monkey fossils date to about 19 mya. *Victoriapithecus* is known from a number of sites in Kenya and Uganda, and a closely related form, *Prohylobates*, is known from Libya, Egypt and Kenya (Benefit and McCrossin 2002). *Victoriapithecus* is a stem cercopithecoid, which means that it is not specifically related to either of the main groups of living cercopithecoids, the colobines and the cercopithecines. The most important diagnostic feature of Old World monkeys is bilophodonty. Bilophodont molars have four principal cusps, arranged into two transverse sets connected by a ridge or loph (Figure 17.1). These teeth permit Old World monkeys to efficiently slice fibrous foods such as leaves. They are much more specialized than the molars of hominoids. Although all Old World monkeys have bilophodont molars, in *Victoriapithecus* the lophs are less completely formed (Benefit and McCrossin 2002). In modern colobines, or leaf-eating monkeys, the lophs tend to be higher and sharper than in cercopithecines, but all Old World monkeys have enhanced slicing teeth compared to those of the apes.

Victoriapithecus is also primitive compared to living cercopithecoids: it has a relatively large snout and small brain, and in this way it resembles *Aegyptopithecus*, though it is not so primitive. *Victoriapithecus* is about the size of a small living monkey weighing about 6kg. Its body plan is essentially like that of monkeys today, and is most similar to monkeys that spend a greater percentage of their time on the ground. Its arms and legs are of equal length, and its back is positioned parallel to the ground or to branches. This animal was unlike apes, which, as noted, have longer arms, more erect or vertical posture, and lack tails.

Victoriapithecus was a relatively rare component of the fauna in the early Miocene, but it became more common in the middle Miocene. In the late Miocene, another fossil Old World monkey evolves that would become highly successful for millions of years in Eurasia: *Mesopithecus* is the first modern monkey, a member of the colobines or leaf-eating monkeys (Jablonski 2002). Rare before a date of around 10 mya, *Mesopithecus* became widespread in Europe and western Asia after that, as the climate became drier and more seasonal (with more pronounced differences between the winter and summer months). At one time researchers believed that *Mesopithecus* may have outcompeted and actively replaced apes in Europe, contributing to their extinction in Eurasia. However, most researchers suggest today that *Mesopithecus* was simply better equipped to survive the climate changes occurring during the Miocene. *Mesopithecus* and Miocene apes are never found in the same localities at the same time, and they seem to have been very different in their ecological preferences. They were probably never in direct competition.

Mesopithecus is a colobine in terms of its classification, which means that it is more closely related to living leaf-eating monkeys such as colobus monkeys or langurs than to cercopithecines like macaques or baboons. However, *Mesopithecus* appears to have had a preference for dryer climates than those inhabited by living colobines, all of which live in dense forests, and in that way it was ecologically more similar to cercopithecines. *Mesopithecus* was a typical-looking monkey in terms of limb proportions and overall body plan, but it probably spent more time on the ground than most monkeys, especially colobines, do today.

A number of other extinct Miocene Old World monkeys are known, which differ from *Mesopithecus* in size or in fairly subtle anatomical features. Other extinct Plio-Pleistocene Old World monkeys greatly extend the range of variation in size and anatomy known from living species, and include such forms as baboons the size of small gorillas (Delson et al. 2000). Many species develop impressive specializations to exploit a wide range of resources, especially in open country settings in East Africa, where a great number of Old World monkeys are known in association with early human sites. Most of the genera of living Old World monkeys that are known in the fossil record appeared in the Pliocene or Pleistocene. The radiation of Old World monkeys is among the most impressive such phenomena among primates or any other mammal family, and it attests to the flexibility and adaptability of these creatures. Old World monkeys were noticeably more terrestrial in the beginning, and the largely arboreal nature of the group today is a relatively recent development. As Jablonski (2002) suggests, a few relatively generalized, more terrestrial Old World monkeys are able to survive in proximity to humans. Most living Old World monkeys may either

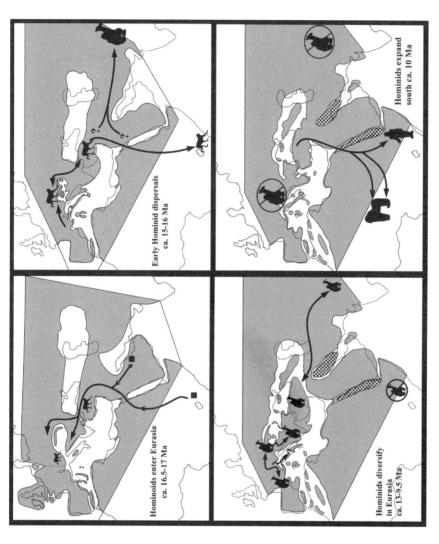

Figure 17.2 Maps illustrating hominoid dispersals during the Miocene. Between 16.5 and 17 mya, a hominoid expands its range out of Africa for the first time. Around 15 mya, thickly enameled hominoids are fairly widespread north and south of the Mediterranean. By 13 mya, descendants from this group split into two lineages: the pongines in Asia and the hominines in Europe. Hominoids become very rare in Africa after this time. Some time around 10–11 mya, hominines from Europe disperse back into Africa, while pongines disperse into southeast Asia (not shown). Hominoids go extinct in most of Eurasia after about 9 mya . Modified from Begun 2005

Within the figure:

Early Hominid dispersals
ca. 15-16 Ma

Hominoids enter Eurasia
ca. 16.5-17 Ma

Hominoids expand
south ca. 10 Ma

Hominoids diversify
in Eurasia
ca. 13-9.5 Ma

have moved into more forested settings, or descend from populations that lived already in those settings, where the impact from human activities was historically less than elsewhere. Today, of course, many Old World monkeys, apes, and nearly every other non-human primate are in danger of extinction as a result of our impact upon the environment.

SUMMARY

The fossil record of catarrhines reveals many events in the evolutionary transformation leading from prosimians to apes (Figure 17.2). *Aegyptopithecus* is a transitional form, barely recognizable as a catarrhine, with a snout and a brain more prosimian than anthropoid. The earliest apes, represented by *Proconsul*, had clearly made the transition to a catarrhine grade of organization, but they were more monkey-like than ape-like in most attributes. One member of the early Miocene hominoid radiation evolved a more modern dentition and pattern of growth and development, which may have allowed it to expand its range into Eurasia. Once in Eurasia, the descendants of this pioneering early great ape experienced a series of adaptive radiations: first a centralized core group of apes with powerful jaws and thickly enameled teeth; and then two branches, one in Asia, the pongines, and one in Europe, the hominines. During the course of these evolutionary events, the basic attributes of the living great apes and of the ancestors of humans were developing in the context of the ecological conditions of Europe and Asia. The more seasonal and variable ecology of Eurasia provided the selection for a hominid pattern of behavior, large brains, complex social relations, and elaborate strategies of foraging and of reproductive biology. As the environment of Eurasia became increasingly seasonal and drier, apes were replaced by monkeys. The apes that survived moved south, tracking the milder conditions, and became relict populations in Southeast Asia (*Pongo*) and Africa (hominines). Most hominoids remain confined to tropical forests today. One lineage, however, moved beyond the trends set in the Miocene, developing a more terrestrial lifestyle, perhaps with the ability to range across a wider range of environments. This is of course our own lineage. Aside from humans, the most successful descendants of the fossil catarrhines are the Old World monkeys, whose diversity today rivals that of Miocene apes.

REFERENCES

Ankel-Simons, F. J., Fleagle, G., and Chatrath, P. S. (1998) Femoral Anatomy of *Aegyptopithecus zeuxis*, an Early Oligocene Anthropoid. *American Journal of Physical Anthropology* 106: 413–424.

Begun, D. R. (1992) Phyletic Diversity and Locomotion in Primitive European Hominids. *American Journal of Physical Anthropology* 87: 311–340.

Begun, D. R. (2002a) European Hominoids. In W. C. Hartwig (ed.), *The Primate Fossil Record* (pp. 339–368). Cambridge: Cambridge University Press.

Begun, D. R. (2002b) The Pliopithecoidea. In W. C. Hartwig (ed.), *The Primate Fossil Record* (pp. 221–240). Cambridge: Cambridge University Press.

Begun, D. R. (2005) *Sivapithecus* Is East and *Dryopithecus* Is West, and Never the Twain Shall Meet. *Anthropological Science* 113: 53–64.

Begun, D. R. (2007) Fossil Record of Miocene Hominoids. In W. Henke and I. Tattersall (eds), *Handbook of Palaeoanthropology*, Vol. 2: *Primate Evolution and Human Origins* (pp. 921–977). Berlin: Springer.

Begun, D. R., and Kordos, L. (2004) Cranial Evidence of the Evolution of Intelligence in Fossil Apes. In A. E. Russon and D. R. Begun (eds), *The Evolution of Thought: Evolutionary Origins of Great Ape Intelligence* (pp. 260–279). Cambridge: Cambridge University Press.

Begun, D. R., Teaford, M. F., and Walker, A. (1994) Comparative and Functional Anatomy of *Proconsul* Phalanges from the Kaswanga Primate Site, Rusinga Island, Kenya. *Journal of Human Evolution* 26: 89–165.

Benefit, B. R., and McCrossin, M. L. (2002) The Victoriapithecidae, Cercopithecoidea. In W. C. Hartwig (ed.), *The Primate Fossil Record* (pp. 241–253). Cambridge: Cambridge University Press.

Delson, E., Terranova, C. J., Jungers, W. L., Sargis, E. J., Jablonski, N. G., and Dechow, P. C. (2000) Body Mass in Cercopithecidae (Primates, Mammalia): Estimation and Scaling in Extinct and Extant Taxa. *American Museum of Natural History, Anthropological Papers* 83: 1–159.

Ersoy, A., Kelley, J., Andrews, P., and Alpagut, B. (2008) Hominoid Phalanges from the Middle Miocene Site of Paşalar, Turkey. *Journal of Human Evolution* 54 (4): 518–529.

Fleagle, J. G., and Simons, E. L. (1982) The Humerus of *Aegyptopithecus zeuxis:* A Primitive Anthropoid. *American Journal of Physical Anthropology* 59: 175–193.

Harrison, T. (2002) Late Oligocene to Middle Miocene Catarrhines from Afro-Arabia. In W. C. Hartwig (ed.), *The Primate Fossil Record* (pp. 311–338). Cambridge: Cambridge University Press.

Heizmann, E., and Begun, D. R. (2001) The Oldest European Hominoid. *Journal of Human Evolution* 41: 465–481.

Ishida, H., Kunimatsu, Y., Takano, T., Nakano, Y., and Nakatsukasa, M. (2004) *Nacholapithecus* Skeleton from the Middle Miocene of Kenya. *Journal of Human Evolution* 46: 1–35.

Jablonski, N. G. (2002) Fossil Old World Monkeys: The Late Neogene. In W. C. Hartwig (ed.), *The Primate Fossil Record* (pp. 255–299). Cambridge: Cambridge University Press.

Kelley, J. (1997) Paleobiological and Phylogenetic Significance of Life History in Miocene Hominoids. In D. R. Begun, C. V. Ward, and M. D. Rose (eds), *Function, Phylogeny and Fossils: Miocene Hominoid Evolution and Adaptations* (pp. 173–208). New York: Plenum Publishing Co.

Kelley, J. (2002) The Hominoid Radiation in Asia. In W. C. Hartwig (ed.), *The Primate Fossil Record* (pp. 369–384). Cambridge: Cambridge University Press.

Kelley, J. (2004) Life History and Cognitive Evolution in the Apes. In A. E. Russon and D. R. Begun (eds), *The Evolution of Thought: Evolutionary Origins of Great Ape Intelligence* (pp. 280–297). Cambridge: Cambridge University Press.

Kordos, L., and Begun, D. R. (2001) A New Cranium of *Dryopithecus* from Rudabánya, Hungary. *Journal of Human Evolution* 41: 689–700.

Kordos, L., and Begun, D. R. (2002) Rudabánya: A Late Miocene Subtropical Swamp Deposit with Evidence of the Origin of the African Apes and Humans. *Evolutionary Anthropology* 11: 45–57.

Leakey, M., and Walker, A. (1997) *Afropithecus:* Function and Phylogeny. In D. R. Begun, C. V. Ward, and M. D. Rose (eds), *Function, Phylogeny and Fossils: Miocene Hominoid Evolution and Adaptations* (pp. 225–239). New York: Plenum Publishing Co.

MacLatchy, L., Gebo, D., Kityo, R., and Pilbeam, D. (2000) Postcranial Functional Morphology of *Morotopithecus bishopi*, with Implications for the Evolution of Modern Ape Locomotion. *Journal of Human Evolution* 39: 159–183.

Madar, S. I., Rose, M. D., Kelley, J., MacLatchy, L., and Pilbeam, D. (2002) New Sivapithecus Postcranial Specimens from the Siwaliks of Pakistan. *Journal of Human Evolution* 42: 705–752.

Moyà-Solà, S., Köhler, M., Alba, D. M., Casanovas-Vilar, I., and Galindo, J. (2004) *Pierolapithecus catalaunicus*, a New Middle Miocene Great Ape from Spain. *Science* 306: 1339–1344.

Nakatsukasa, M. (2008) Comparative Study of Moroto Vertebral Specimens. *Journal of Human Evolution* 55 (4): 581–588.

Radinsky, L. (1973) *Aegyptopithecus* Endocasts: Oldest Record of a Pongid Brain. *American Journal of Physical Anthropology* 39: 239–248.

Radinsky, L. (1974) The Fossil Evidence of Anthropoid Brain Evolution. *American Journal of Physical Anthropology* 41: 15–28.

Rasmussen, D. T. (2002) Early Catarrhines of the African Eocene and Oligocene. In W. C. Hartwig (ed.), *The Primate Fossil Record* (pp. 203–220). Cambridge: Cambridge University Press.

Rasmussen, D. T. (2007) Fossil Record of the Primates from the Paleocene to the Oligocene. In W. H. Henke and I. Tattersall (eds), *Handbook of Palaeoanthropology*, Vol. 2: *Primate Evolution and Human Origins* (pp. 889–920). Berlin: Springer.

Ross, C. F., Williams, B., and Kay, R. F. (1998) Phylogenetic Analysis of Anthropoid Relationships. *Journal of Human Evolution* 35: 221–306.

Schlosser, M. (1910) Über einige fossile Säugetiere aus dem Oligocän von Ägypten. *Zoologischer Anzeiger* 35: 500–508.

Simons, E. L. (1965) New Fossil Apes from Egypt and the Initial Differentiation of Hominoidea. *Nature* 205: 135–139.

Smith, T. M., Martin, L. B., and Leakey, M. G. (2003) Enamel Thickness, Microstructure and Development in *Afropithecus turkanensis*. *Journal of Human Evolution* 44 (3): 283–306.

Walker, A. (1997) *Proconsul*: Function and phylogeny. In D. R. Begun, C. V. Ward, and M. D. Rose (eds), *Function, Phylogeny and Fossils: Miocene Hominoid Evolution and Adaptations* (pp. 209–224). New York: Plenum Publishing Co.

Walker, A., and Teaford, M. F. (1989) The Hunt for *Proconsul*. *Scientific American* 260: 76–82.

Walker, A., Teaford, M. F., Martin, L. B., and Andrews, P. (1993) A New Species of *Proconsul* from the Early Miocene of Rusinga/Mfango Island, Kenya. *Journal of Human Evolution* 25: 43–56.

Ward, C. V. (1993) Torso Morphology and Locomotion in Proconsul Nyanzae. *American Journal of Physical Anthropology* 92 (3): 291–328.

Ward, C. V. (2007) Postcranial and Locomotor Adaptations of Hominoids. In W. Henke and I. Tattersall (eds), *Handbook of Palaeoanthropology*, Vol. 2: *Primate Evolution and Human Origins* (pp. 1011–1030). Berlin: Springer.

Ward, C. V., Walker, A., and Teaford, M. F. (1991) *Proconsul* Did not Have a Tail. *Journal of Human Evolution* 21: 215–220.

Ward, C. V., Walker, A., Teaford, M.F., and Odhiambo, I. (1993) A Partial Skeleton of *Proconsul nyanzae* from Mfango Island, Kenya. *American Journal of Physical Anthropology* 90: 77–111.

Ward, S. C., and Duren, D. L. (2002) Middle and Late Miocene African Hominoids. In W. C. Hartwig (ed.), *The Primate Fossil Record* (pp. 385–397). Cambridge: Cambridge University Press.

Zapfe, H. (1960) Die Primatenfunde aus der Miozänen Spaltenfüllung von Neudorf an der March (Dévínská Nová Ves), Tschechoslovakei. Mit anhang: Der Primtenfund aus dem Miozän von Klein Haderdorf in Niederosterreich. *Schweizerische Paleontologische Abhandlungen* 78: 1–293.

18 The Earliest Hominins

Scott W. Simpson

The last twenty years have been among the richest and most productive periods in the history of human evolutionary studies. The most visible evidence for this wealth is the large number of high-quality hominin fossils recovered throughout the Old World, which have extended our knowledge of human origins well beyond 4 million years ago. This, in tandem with the great diversity of new analytic and contextual studies – for instance the sequencing of mitochondrial and nuclear DNA, isotopic geochemistry, computed tomography (CT) and micro-CT imaging, three-dimensional shape analyses, and geospatial analyses – has contributed immensely to our understanding of the paleobiology of our ancestors. Rather than finally resolving many of the phyletic and adaptive issues of hominin evolution, this wealth of new fossil data has revealed a more complex – and interesting – picture of the history of our lineage. As additional fossil, anatomical, and biomolecular knowledge accrues, we are developing a better understanding of the hominins long and complex evolutionary path. The aim of this review is to summarize the currently recognized diversity of hominins, who span a time frame between approximately 7 and 1.2 million years ago (mya), divided into three periods: the period before the australopithecines, which goes back beyond 4.2 mya; the period of the early australopithecines, which lasted from 4.2 to 2.9 mya; and the period of the late australopithecines, which extended between 2.6 and 1.2 mya.

WHAT IS A HOMININ?

A hominin (that is, a member of the subtribe Hominina)[1] is a direct or collateral human ancestor, who separated phyletically from our closest living relative, the chimpanzee (genus *Pan*). Analyses of genetic distance between the African great apes suggest that the human–chimpanzee split occurred between 5 and 8 mya or earlier (see the review by Bradley 2008; Suwa et al. 2007a), and the gorilla–chimpanzee/human split, between 9 and 12 mya (Suwa et al. 2007a). The genetic evidence can provide some insight into the timing of these cladistic events. However, the sequence and context of anatomical and behavioral adaptations that characterize our lineage can only be revealed by the fossil evidence. Although it is the history of descent that defines our membership in the hominin lineage, in the fossil record we must identify those uniquely hominin anatomical traits necessary to assign a fossil to our lineage. Modern humans, who posses large brains, symbolically based language, and a commitment to technology, are a very specialized type of hominin, who adopted these traits only recently (within the last 2.6 million years). Prior to that time, our ancestors were identified by bipedalism (walking on two legs) and through specializations in their dentition, especially a change in the canine function. Our ancestry is not one of a single unbroken lineage over the last seven million years. There existed multiple other lineages of hominins – our phylogenetic cousins – who coexisted with our forebears, had very different anatomies and behaviors, and are now extinct. To understand more fully our evolutionary history, we must study both the paleobiology of our own ancestors and that of our now extinct near relatives.

The separation of the last common ancestor (LCA) of the chimpanzee–human population into hominin and chimpanzee lineages (and perhaps also into other now extinct taxa) was probably a consequence of the allopatric division of the LCA gene pool, due perhaps, in turn, to some unique ecological changes that occurred across the late Miocene African landscape. Although the earliest hominins were phyletic hominins, they were probably not morphological hominins, as they would have lacked the derived anatomical traits – such as bipedalism, or the absence of a canine honing complex – that were acquired after the speciation event. The first uniquely hominin adaptations were undoubtedly behavioral, with the anatomical responses to these novel behaviors subsequently refined by intraspecific microevolution. For example, hominins were behaviorally bipedal – an adaptation that improved their reproductive fitness – prior to being anatomically bipedal. Only when these behavioral differences are identifiable in the anatomy can we document the origins of the hominin lineage in the fossil record.

Two significant changes distinguish modern and ancient hominins from all other primates: bipedal locomotion and the loss of the sectorial canine complex. The former reflects anatomical adaptations to substrate usage (arboreality or terrestriality), and the latter reflects a different means of mediating male–male confrontations or intersexual choice. The transition from quadrupedality to striding bipedality is unique among mammals and required a significant reorganization of the entire musculoskeletal system, from the basicranium to the foot.

The canines in the living large-bodied apes are dimorphic: males have substantially longer and more robust canines than females. The primate upper canine has a unique occlusal relationship with the mandibular P3. As the jaws open and close, the long upper canine rubs against the lower P3 and sharpens the distal edge of the canine without reducing its height, and this is known as the sectorial wear complex. This wear on the maxillary canine's disto-lingual surface characterizes nearly all monkeys and apes and results in a 'knife-like' upper canine, which is essential in displays or aggressive interactions that occur between conspecific males during reproductive and territorial competitions.

BEFORE THE AUSTRALOPITHECINES: THE HOMININ FOSSIL RECORD BETWEEN 7 AND 4.2 MYA

Although this section will focus on the named taxa, other hominin fossils are known from this period (see for example the maxillary M3 and mandibular I1 from the less than 6.54 (+/– 0.07)-million-year-old Upper Nawata Formation in Lothagam,

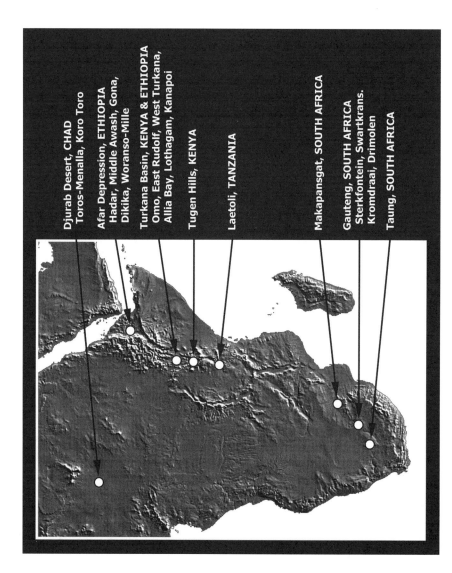

Djurab Desert, CHAD
Toros-Menalla, Koro Toro

Afar Depression, ETHIOPIA
Hadar, Middle Awash, Gona,
Dikika, Woranso-Mille

Turkana Basin, KENYA & ETHIOPIA
Omo, East Rudolf, West Turkana,
Allia Bay, Lothagam, Kanapoi

Tugen Hills, KENYA

Laetoli, TANZANIA

Makapansgat, SOUTH AFRICA

Gauteng, SOUTH AFRICA
Sterkfontein, Swartkrans.
Kromdraai, Drimolen

Taung, SOUTH AFRICA

Figure 18.1 The major hominin fossil localities. Topographic map produced by the United States National Geophysical Data Center.

Kenya: Leakey and Walker 2003; see Figure 18.1 for this and other localities discussed in this chapter). Specific taxonomic and functional assessments await the recovery of additional, similarly aged fossils from those deposits.

Sahelanthropus tchadensis (Brunet et al. 2002)

Sahelanthropus tchadensis is currently the oldest identified hominin, known from a collection of dentognathic fossils from the now hyper-arid Toros-Menalla area in the Djurab Desert of northern Chad. Preliminary biochronological analyses suggested an age of 6–7 mya. The application of a new radiometric dating approach (^{10}Be/^{9}Be; Lebatard et al. 2008) has indicated an age of the deposits between 6.8 and 7.2 mya. The type specimen (TM266-01-060-1) – a deformed but nearly complete cranium (see digital reconstruction in Zollikofer et al. 2005) – has a brain volume of 360–370 milliliters (ml), which is about the same size as modern chimpanzees. Characters that identify these fossils as hominin and ally it with later hominins include: reduced size and apical wear of the canine teeth; inferiorly oriented and anteriorly positioned *foramen magnum*; intermediate enamel thickness; and reduced subnasal prognathism (Brunet et al. 2002, 2005; Zollikofer et al. 2005; Guy et al. 2005). Curiously, the supraorbital tori are very thick – more so than in extant apes, or in any other early hominin – and the midface is supero-inferiorly short.

The canine's apical wear indicate that this species lacked sectorial wear. The evidence for bipedalism is inferred from the orientation of the *foramen magnum* and basicranial anatomy. Like in later bipedal hominins and unlike in apes, the plane of the *foramen magnum* opening is nearly perpendicular to a vertical plane defined by the margins of the orbits. This is thought to reflect the head's position as sitting atop the vertebral column rather than somewhat anteriorly to it, as it does in quadrupeds (including the great apes).

Ecologically, the habitats sampled at Toros-Menalla are dominated by grassland and wooded grassland perilacustrine zones (that is, zones adjacent to lakes) occupied by numerous grazing herbivores, although both gallery forests and more desertic zones were nearby (Vignaud et al. 2002).

Orrorin tugenensis (Senut et al. 2001)

The recovery in 2001 of a series of 5.7–6.0-million-year-old (Sawada et al. 2002) dentognathic and postcranial fossils led to the naming of a new hominin species, *Orrorin tugenensis* (Senut et al. 2001). The generic name translates roughly as 'original man' in the local Tugen language, and the Latin 'tugenensis' indicates its discovery from the Tugen Hills of Kenya. Significant anatomical features demonstrated by these fossils include a large triangular maxillary canine, with a disto-lingually facing wear facet described as 'almost sectorial' (ibid., p. 140). Although the molar crown enamel was initially described as thick, a reassessment of the specimen (Pickford and Senut 2005) demonstrated an intermediate thickness, similar to that of the ardipithecines and *Sahelanthropus*.

Perhaps the most significant fossils known from *Orrorin* are three proximal femora (Galik et al. 2004; Pickford et al. 2002; see also White 2006). One of them (BAR 1002'00), although lacking the greater trochanter, retains a complete femoral head and neck – anatomy necessary to reconstruct locomotor behavior. As observed in other bipedal hominins, the femur has a somewhat elongated femoral neck, a shallow trochanteric fossa, and an *m. obturator externus* groove on the posterior surface of the femoral neck. Computed tomography images of the femoral neck suggest that the cortical bone on the superior surface of the neck is thin – a condition uniquely found in striding bipeds (Lovejoy 1988; Ohman et al. 1997). Thus, the two defining apomorphic criteria of hominins – bipedal locomotion and absence of a fully sectorial canine – are present in this taxon. Pickford and colleagues (2002) suggest that this proximal femur morphology is more similar to that of modern *Homo* than it is to any of the Plio-Pleistocene australopithecines – a hypothesis which effectively excludes any australopithecine from the ancestry of the genus *Homo*. In contrast, Richmond and Jungers (2008) document similarity of the *Orrorin* femora with the early australopithecine femora.

Orrorin apparently occupied a more open habitat, populated by mixed-habitat fauna such as impalas. The presence of multiple species of leaf-eating *Colobus* monkeys indicate a more wooded habitat in association with the nearby rivers and lake (Pickford and Senut 2001).

Ardipithecus kadabba (Haile-Selassie et al. 2004)

Ardipithecus kadabba was originally identified as a late Miocene subspecies of *Ar. ramidus* (namely *Ardipithecus ramidus kadabba*: Haile-Selassie 2001). These 5.2–5.8-million-year-old fossils from the Afar Depression of Ethiopia are phenetically similar (which suggests phylogenetic relatedness) to the 4.4-million-year-old *Ar. ramidus*. This critical collection of Middle Awash Late Miocene fossils (MALM) includes dentognathic remains (mandible with associated teeth and isolated teeth) and post-cranial remains (clavicle, humerus, ulna, and manual and pedal phalanges fragments). For the most part, the postcrania are frustratingly uninformative about locomotion. An exception is a pedal proximal phalanx: while being curved and long in length, it has a dorsally facing proximal articular facet – an orientation seen in hominins, who experience hyperdorsiflexion at the metatarsophalangeal joint during bipedal walking.

The recovery of additional fossil remains from the Middle Awash study area (Haile-Selassie et al. 2004) included functionally and behaviorally significant portions of anatomy, and especially of the morphology and functional wear of the C/P3 complex. Importantly, the recovery of a slightly worn large, triangular maxillary canine (ASK-VP-3/400), which exhibits a very primitive morphology, necessitated a revised functional assessment of the *Ar. r. kadabba* dentition. In tandem with the mandibular third premolar (coming from a different individual), it was suggested that, in addition to the apical wear present on the canine, the presence of a small wear facet on the mesio-buccal face of the P3 indicated some retention of the primitive, albeit derived, occlusal relationship between the upper canine and the lower P3. This occlusal pattern is unique in hominins and, despite many other morphological similarities with *Ar. ramidus*, indicated that MALM fossils should be elevated to species status known as *Ar. kadabba*.

More recently, a series of late Miocene teeth attributed to either *Ar. kadabba* or *Ardipithecus* have been recovered at another location in the Afar Region of Ethiopia by the Gona Paleoanthropological Research Project (Simpson et al. 2006). These seven isolated teeth are found in deposits from two time periods: approximately 5.5 mya and 6.2–6.4 mya (Kleinsasser et al. 2008). Unfortunately the combination of a heavily worn maxillary canine and an unworn mandibular P3 makes it difficult to determine whether a sectorial wear pattern was present.

Both the Middle Awash Late Miocene and the Gona project collections were derived primarily from habitats ranging from well watered woodland to grassy woodland.

Ardipithecus ramidus (White et al. 1994, 1995)

Beginning in 1992, the recovery of 4.4-million-year-old fossils, primarily from the Aramis drainage in the Middle Awash project area, provided the first substantial evidence for a hominin taxon older than 4 mya. The original announcement of these fossils (White et al. 1994) recognized the uniqueness of the collection, but took a taxonomically conservative stance and attributed the fossils to a new species within the already existing genus *Australopithecus*, naming it '*ramidus*' (from the word 'root' in the Afar language of Ethiopia). The discovery of additional fossils, most notably of the partial skeleton ARA-VP-6/500 during the 1994 field season (Figure 8.2) required a reassessment of the taxon; and a new genus, '*Ardipithecus*' (a name which combines the Afar word for 'ground' and the ancient Greek word for 'ape,' *pithekos*) was proposed in order to account for the novel anatomy represented by the new fossils. *Ar. ramidus* fossils are also known from the 4.3–4.7-million-year-old Sagantole Formation in the Gona project area (Semaw et al. 2005). A 4.41–4.48-million-year-old mandibular fragment known as the Tabarin mandible (KNM-TH 13150: Hill 1985; Deino et al. 2002) from the Tugen Hills of Kenya is also reasonably assignable to *Ar. ramidus*.

The completeness of the ARA-VP-6/500 skeleton (nicknamed 'Ardi') – which includes near-complete hands and feet, tibia, ulna, radius, and a crushed but reconstructable skull and pelvis – allowed the locomotor skeleton to be reconstructed with a great degree of accuracy. These analyses required a reassessment of the paleobiology of the earliest hominins (White et al. 2009). Most remarkable is the foot, which has a functionally grasping great toe, yet also demonstrates adaptations to habitual bipedality in the lateral side of the foot (Lovejoy et al. 2009a). The hand shows a significantly greater degree of mobility at the wrist and midcarpal joints than is present in extant apes (Lovejoy et al. 2009b). Like the foot, the pelvis shows an unusual mix of derived bipedal characters (low ilium with a laterally facing gluteal surface, prominent anterior inferior iliac spine) and ape-like anatomies (ilium, pubis, transversely narrow true pelvis; Lovejoy et al. 2009c). Thus *Ar. ramidus* is an unusual and unpredicted mix of adaptations to terrestrial bipedalism and to arboreal quadrupedalism. There is no evidence of African ape-like locomotor adaptations (long metacarpals, a less mobile wrist, reduced thumb, stiff lower spine, mobile midtarsus) in *Ardipithecus*. This indicates that those adaptations arose independently in the chimpanzees and gorillas once they became separate lineages and that knuckle-walking and vertical climbing were never part of the hominin locomotor repertoire or present in the LCA (Lovejoy et al. 2009d).

Examination of the canine teeth in *Ar. ramidus* shows clearly that they were not involved in a sectorial wear pattern and that dental sexual dimorphism was minor, with little difference in size or morphology between the largest and smallest teeth (Suwa et al. 2009). The canine tooth crowns also formed over a shorter duration than is observed in modern apes, and the emergence of the tooth does not seem to

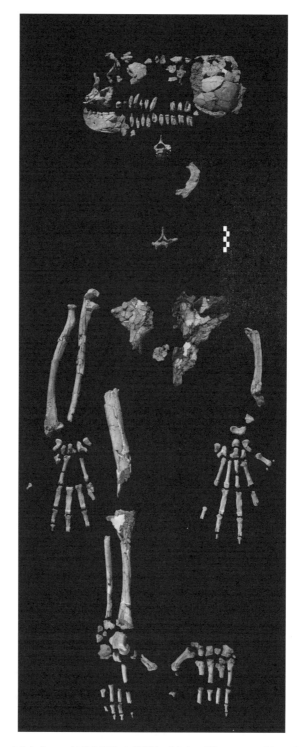

Figure 18.2 Partial skeleton (ARA-VP-6/500) of 4.4-million-year-old *Ardipithecus ramidus*, discovered in the Middle Awash Research Project area, Afar, Ethiopia. This adult female stood about 1.2 meters tall. © T. D. White

be linked with sexual maturity, as in primates. Males and females appear to have had about the same body size. The absence of sexual dimorphism has implications for the social behavior in *Ardipithecus* and indicates that male–male competition was mediated in fundamentally different ways than those observed in extant apes (Lovejoy 2009).

Ecological reconstructions from the three areas span from forests in the Tugen Hills (Pickford et al. 2004), humid woodland with a grassy substrate at Aramis (WoldeGabriel et al. 1994, 2009), and areas of woodland and grassy woodland at Gona (Semaw et al. 2005; Levin et al. 2008).

LATE MIOCENE AND EARLY PLIOCENE HOMININ EVOLUTION OVERVIEW

Prior to 1992, the hominin fossil record predating the earliest reliable appearance of *Australopithecus afarensis* (see review by Hill and Ward 1988) of 3.6 mya in Laetoli, Tanzania (Leakey et al. 1976) was quite sparse. With the discovery of *Ar. ramidus* fossils, which are about 4.4 million years old (White et al. 1994), and with the naming of the late Miocene taxa *Ar. kadabba*, *O. tugenensis*, and *S. tchadensis*, the pre-*afarensis* period is becoming increasingly well known.

The three late Miocene taxa span up to 1.7 million years and thousands of kilometers across Africa. They are demonstrably hominin through the presence of a canine that is reduced in size, apically worn and non-sectorial, and through evidence of bipedality. It is important to note that these taxa are found in three separate depo-basins with distinct faunal composition. *Sahelanthropus* and most of the *Orrorin* fossils were found in perilacustrine environments with significantly open (wooded grassland) habitats, whereas *Ar. kadabba* was more commonly found in wooded or forested habitats. This indicates that, soon after diverging from the chimpanzee–human last common ancestor, the hominins were widely dispersed in space and capable of exploiting a diversity of habitats.

If the geologic age of 6.8–7.2 mya for *Sahelanthropus* is reliable, then the biomolecular estimates of the timing of the chimpanzee–human divergence (5–7 mya: Kumar et al. 2005; Suwa et al. 2007a) must be reassessed. The adoption of some form of bipedalism and loss of the sectorial C/P3 complex (which reflects a change in social behavior) must have occurred very early in the hominin lineage. These breakthrough adaptations allowed an exploitation of novel habitats not open to the other great ape species existing at the time – notably the ancestors of the modern chimpanzee and gorilla who, for the most part, inhabit relict Miocene forests.

The phyletic relatedness of the three late Miocene taxa remains unclear. Aside from issues of biological variation due to broad spatial and temporal distribution, there is the unfortunate fact that the three samples tend to document different and generally non-overlapping portions of the anatomy. For example, although bipedalism is proposed for all three groups, each species' locomotion is inferred from a different part of the skeleton, which renders difficult our understanding of the degree of adaptation to bipedality, as well as of the nature of bipedalism. Where the anatomy does overlap (for example in the maxillary canine), only preliminary descriptions have been published to date, a situation that precludes formal comparisons between samples. Haile-Selassie and colleagues (2004) raised the possibility that all three taxa are part of a single lineage. Given our current knowledge about these fossil samples, this hypothesis cannot be rejected; but in practice it is reasonable and useful to retain the separate names. However, we must remember that the retention of these names, while scientifically practical, may provide artificial support for a late Miocene hominin radiation. At this time and until thorough direct comparisons of the fossils are made, caution is urged about relying on such limited data for making definitive phylogenetic assessments.

The hominins' anatomical and behavioral transition to bipedality is unique among mammals in that it required a significant reorganization of the musculo-skeletal system. These changes resulted in a reduced ability for arboreal climbing – the historical adaptive home of the great apes. This, in turn, led to a change in diet and a decreased reliance on the protection offered by trees from terrestrial predators. As observed in *Ar. ramidus*, this change in locomotion included a phase where elements of both arboreal and terrestrial adaptations were present. Clearly, careful climbing was central to the adaptive niche of *Ar. ramidus*. However, the reproductive fitness of *Ar. ramidus* must have been improved by behaviors requiring terrestrial bipedality even though the musculo-skeletal anatomy shows an incomplete transition which precluded such behaviors as long-distance walking or running. This transition also had unintended health consequences: becoming bipedal leads to an increased risk of degenerative changes in the foot, knee, hip, and spine, as well as a decrease in size of the bony birth canal that resulted in increased difficulty of parturition. Therefore the challenges imposed by this anatomical reorganization must have been overcome by the resulting increase in fitness and survivorship in those ancient hominins who adopted the new behaviors.

A number of models attempting to explain this unique adaptation have been proposed. Darwin (1871) suggested that it was the adoption of tools that drove this change. The use and manufacture of tools requires significant manual ability; thus it was thought that making, using, and carrying tools changed the requirements for the upper limb from locomotion to manipulation. In addition, the regular reliance on tools was considered to render the large canines less effective for protection, competition, or dietary specializations, and this would have led to their reduction in size. This intuitively compelling model (see Washburn 1960) lacks a strong causal link between increased fitness and tool use, bipedalism, and canine size (Holloway 1967) – especially given the significant reliance on tools displayed by other animals, including chimpanzees, who are not bipedal and retain large canine teeth in males.

More recently, suggestions that bipeds are more energetically efficient than quadrupeds (Rodman and McHenry 1980; Bramble and Lieberman 2004), better adapted to minimize tropical sun exposure (Wheeler 1984), and have superior foraging effectiveness (Jolly 1970; Hunt 1994) have been proposed to explain bipedality. Unfortunately these unicausal models either are empirically inaccurate (for instance the energetic costs of locomotion are similar in quadrupeds and bipeds, yet bipedality can entail greater risks: Lovejoy 1988) or do not explain increases in fitness in bipedalism adopters. For example, the attempts to explain striding bipedalism as a result of foraging activities – a model usually based on feeding behaviors in extant primates, such as gelada baboons (Jolly 1970) or chimpanzees (Hunt 1994) – have not borne fruit, as these behaviors are highly stylized in the non-human primates, lack any anatomical similarity to striding bipedality, and have an uncertain relationship with fitness.

One model that attempts explicitly to link fitness, anatomy, and behavior is that proposed by Lovejoy (1981, 1993, 2009). The model focuses on the male provisioning for females. This behavior – best pursued bipedally – builds strong bonds between mating pairs (which are common in pair-bonded mammals and birds). This phenomenon has the benefit of ensuring paternity, and thus confers a direct reproductive return on these behaviors. In addition, a shortening of interbirth interval, which results in higher fecundity and greater offspring survivorship, can follow as a consequence of the additional paternal investment. The female choice of mates is central to this model, and competition among males for reproductive access to females with hidden signs of ovulation is perhaps best pursued by emphasizing intersexual social bonds rather than through intrasexual physical competition. This new behavioral pattern could then have led to the loss of the large sectorial canine (Holloway 1967).

Any model of the origins of bipedalism must be subject to thorough examination and regular evaluation in light of new behavioral, anatomical, and fossil data. The difficulty in modeling the origins of bipedality is that it occurred only once among mammals, and the adoption of a simple referential model is unfortunately unavailable (Sayers and Lovejoy 2008).

THE EARLY AUSTRALOPITHECINES: THE HOMININ FOSSIL RECORD BETWEEN 4.2 AND 2.9 MYA

Australopithecus anamensis (Leakey et al. 1995)
Australopithecus anamensis is now known from Kenya (Kanapoi, 4.17–4.07 mya, and Allia Bay, about 3.9 mya; Leakey et al. 1995, 1998) and Ethiopia (Asa Issie and Aramis, about 4.2–4.1 mya; White et al. 2006). This species is clearly a primitive australopithecine: it has a large non-sectorial canine, enlarged molar and premolar tooth crowns with thickened enamel, parallel post-canine tooth rows, a shallow palate, prognathic face, small brain, and canine and body size dimorphism. Although diagnostic locomotor anatomy is poorly known for this species, the elements that are known (proximal and distal tibia, radius, capitate, femoral shaft) are very similar in form to those of the 3.4–3.0-million-year-old *Au. afarensis* (Ward et al. 2001; White et al. 2006), which indicates a significant commitment to terrestrial bipedality.

On the basis of associated fauna, isotopic analyses of the soil carbonates, and sedimentology, the reconstructed habitats for the Asa Issie fossils were a "narrow range of habitats varying from closed to grassy woodlands" (White et al. 2006: 885). The Kanapoi site appears to have been somewhat more open, with areas of woodland or bushland habitats in close proximity to a gallery forest (Leakey et al. 1995).

Australopithecus afarensis (Johanson et al. 1978)
The significance of the 2.95–3.6-million-year-old *Au. afarensis* is perhaps due to the history of human evolutionary studies as much as it is the quality and quantity of the fossils. When it was described in the 1970s, *Au. afarensis* was the oldest and most primitive ancient hominin known, and it returned the focus of studies of early (over 2.5-million-year-old) hominids to the East African Rift. Until that time, the earliest known species was the approximately 2.6-million-year-old *Au. africanus*, from the

poorly dated cave infills from South Africa. Fossils attributed to *Au. afarensis* include a significant and well preserved collection, which features the iconic 'Lucy' (A.L. 288–1), a partial skeleton from the Hadar area in the Afar Depression of Ethiopia, and the 3.6-million-year-old fossils from Laetoli, Tanzania, with additional fossils from the Turkana Basin deposits in Kenya and Ethiopia. The A. L. 333 site at Hadar site contains fossils from at least seventeen individuals, including juveniles, small-sized adults (most likely females), and large adults (males; see Johanson 2004 for a review). More recently recovered specimens – like the significantly complete 2.95-million-year-old A.L. 444–1 male skull (Kimbel et al. 2004); the Maka, Ethiopia specimens (White et al. 2000; Lovejoy et al. 2002); and the extraordinary infant skeleton, DIK-1-1 ('Selam'), from Dikika, Ethiopia (Alemseged et al. 2006) – provide an increasingly complete representation of anatomical variation in this taxon. The most extraordinary *Au. afarensis* remnant is the series of hominin footprints impressed into a 3.6-million-year-old volcanic tuff from Laetoli, Tanzania (Leakey and Hay 1979), which dramatically and unambiguously demonstrate a true bipedal gait. Despite differences in anatomical detail and age between the Hadar and Laetoli samples, they were combined into a single taxon, with the majority of specimens derived from Ethiopia and the type specimen (LH4 mandible) from Tanzania (Johanson et al. 1978). Like *Au. anamensis*, *Au. afarensis* demonstrates post-canine tooth crown enlargement with thick enamel and retention of enlarged anterior teeth (although it shows additional canine reduction). Brain size in *Au. afarensis* is small (387–550 ml; Holloway et al. 2004).

With the recovery of this large, well preserved and well dated sample from Hadar, issues such as locomotion, populational and ontogenetic variation, magnitude and nature of sexual dimorphism, possibility of intraspecific anagenesis, and limb proportions and body shape could be addressed for the first time. The extensive fossil collection, especially the postcrania, in tandem with the Laetoli footprints, allowed a reliable reconstruction of bipedal locomotion. Phenetic differences from modern humans – such as long, curved pedal phalanges, more mobile midtarsus, and relatively short hindlimbs, perhaps reflecting a kinematically different bipedal gait – may suggest a capacity to exploit a broader range of substrates, including arboreality (Stern and Susman 1983). However, the absence of arboreal specializations (such as metacarpal elongation and short lumbar column) and the widespread and systemic modification of the musculo-skeletal system in *Au. afarensis* (for instance a short, laterally flaring ilium, with a laterally facing attachment for the *m. gluteus minimus* and *m. gluteus medius*; long femoral neck, lumbar lordosis, broad sacrum, valgus knee, trabecularized calcaneus, longitudinal plantar arch, adducted great toe, and so on) indicates a strong commitment to terrestrial striding bipedality. Thus the primitive aspects of the *Au. afarensis* skeleton most likely reflect primitive retentions rather than specific adaptations to an arboreal substrate.

Australopithecus afarensis at Hadar occupied riverine and lake-margin areas that included "bushland, open woodland, and shrubland with varying regions of wetlands or edaphic grasslands" (Reed 2008: 763). Laetoli paleoecology is reconstructed as ranging from grasslands and shrublands dominated by grazing herbivores to gallery forests along the seasonal rivers (Su and Harrison 2007). Thus *Au. afarensis* was not limited to a single habitat type and was capable of participating in a variety of mammalian guild structures throughout the East African Rift zone.

Kenyanthropus platyops (Leakey et al. 2001)

The 3.3–3.5-million-year-old fossils attributed to *Kenyanthropus platyops* ('flat-faced man from Kenya') were discovered on the west side of Lake Turkana in Kenya, by a team led by Meave Leakey. The type specimen is a highly fragmented and heavily distorted, but fundamentally complete, cranium (KNM-WT 40000). The cranium, although similar in size both to *Au. afarensis* and to *Au. africanus*, exhibits a number of traits (such as flattened midface, less facial prognathism – including a transversely and sagittally flattened subnasal clivus and a small external auditory meatus – and small molar crowns) that distinguish it from either species to the extent that the recognition both of a new species and of a new genus is required. However, the post-fossilization deformation of the type cranium obscures anatomical details of the face and vault to such a degree that reservations about its taxonomic distinctiveness have been raised (White 2003). Ecologically, *K. platyops* seems to overlap with the Ethiopian *Au. afarensis* habitat types, although perhaps it lived in somewhat wetter and more vegetated zones.

Australopithecus bahrelghazali (Brunet et al. 1996)

The *Au. bahrelghazali* of about 3.5 mya is notable for expanding the distribution of early hominins into the paleo-Lake Chad basin in North–Central Africa – well beyond the East African Rift deposits or South African karstic caves from which all early hominins were previously known. Recent analyses using the ^{10}Be/^{9}Be approach (Lebatard et al. 2008) suggest an age close to 3.6 mya for the now hyper-arid Koro Toro area of the Bahr-el-ghazal region in the Djurab Desert of Chad. Unfortunately this taxon has few known specimens (an anterior mandible fragment nicknamed 'Abel' (KT 12/H1) and the associated maxillary P3 (KT 12/H2)); however, it can be distinguished from the other early australopithecines by displaying a distinctive mandibular symphysis (Guy et al. 2008) and differences in mandibular premolar root number.

The habitats sampled at Koro Toro were quite open and dominated by C_4 tropical grasses and grazing herbivores (alcelaphine and antilopine bovids, notochoerine suids, equids, and so on; Zazzo et al. 2000).

EARLY AUSTRALOPITHECINES: OVERVIEW

The period between 4.2 and 4.4 mya documents the apparently rapid transition to a new type of small-brained, bipedal hominin: the australopithecines. These hominids are known from East and North–Central Africa prior to 3 mya, and they ranged into South Africa after that time. They are distinguishable from the ardipithecines by an increase in the size and enamel thickness of the post-canine teeth, a change of form in the maxillary canine, body size, magnitude of dimorphism, and locomotion.

Currently *Au. anamensis* is the only species recognized between 4.2 and 3.9 mya. It appears to be intermediate in form between the earlier *Ar. ramidus* and the subsequent *Au. afarensis*, especially in canine size and shape and in mandibular deciduous P3 form. The Middle Awash project recovered *Ar. ramidus* and *Au. anamensis* fossils in close spatial and stratigraphic proximity (White et al. 2006). The two species shared a very similar ecological context, which may suggest an *in situ* transition between the species, with a rapid replacement of the ardipithecines by *Australopithecus* between 4.4 and 4.2 mya. However, the possibility of an allopatric origin of *Au. Anamensis*, with a subsequent invasion of the Afar region, cannot be ruled out at this time.

Four hominin species are currently identified in the span between 4.2 and 2.9 mya: *Au. anamensis*, *Au. afarensis*, *Au. bahrelghazali*, and *K. platyops*. Anatomical differences between *Au. anamensis* and *Au. afarensis* are readily apparent, allowing a reliable sorting of the two species. However, the distinctiveness is primarily a matter of degree rather than of fundamental differences in form and adaptation. If one arranges in chronological succession the four major samples of *Au. anamensis* and *Au. afarensis* – Kanapoi→Allia Bay→Laetoli→Hadar – the morphology strongly suggests phyletic relatedness and evolutionary anagenesis (Kimbel et al. 2006). In such circumstances the species boundary may be a product of the sequence of discovery and sample composition. The discovery of additional, chronologically intermediate, fossils may blur the species differences even further (Haile-Selassie 2008).

Although the *K. platyops* holotype cranium was crushed and distorted, it was considered by its describers to retain enough distinctive anatomy to allow for a reliable differential diagnosis. This led to two phyletic proposals about *K. platyops*: first, that it was phyletically distinct from the contemporary and near-sympatric *Au. afarensis*; and, second, that it was uniquely ancestral to *Homo rudolfensis* – a taxon which includes the larger-brained, flatter-faced, approximately 1.9-million-year-old KNM-ER 1470 cranium. However, other researchers (for example White 2003) concluded that the magnitude of distortion of the cranium introduced by the significant amount of fragmentation rendered the original shape of the cranium difficult to assess. It is estimated that over 1,100 small fragments comprise the face alone. Thus the morphological features that used to diagnose this taxon, especially the 'flat face,' may be a byproduct of the taphonomic history of the type cranium. Hence allocation to a new genus and species would not be justified. Additional, better preserved fossils from this period are necessary in order to resolve this issue.

If *Kenyanthropus* is a distinct lineage, then it has significant implications for our understanding of hominin diversity in the Turkana Basin. It also raises the question of phyletic origins – where and when did it originate, and what was its ancestor? – as well as ecological issues related to resource use and competition with the sympatric *Au. afarensis*. The approximately 3.5 mya *Au. bahrelghazali* collection from Chad significantly expands the known range of early australopithecines 2,500 km beyond the East African Rift, along the periphery of the Miocene relict tropical forests. If the 3.5-million-year-old *Au. bahrelghazali* is a separate species too, that – together with the recognition of *Kenyanthropus* – would document a significant radiation of early australopithecine lineages across Africa. However, given the few remains currently known for those taxa, some have suggested that a separate name is unwarranted, either for *Au. bahrelghazali* (White et al. 2000) or for *Kenyanthropus* (White 2003), as both can be comfortably included in the known range of variation of *Au. afarensis*. This single taxon was a spatially extensive and genetically coherent population, spread across widely separated depo-basins (paleo-Lake Chad, Afar Depression, Omo/Turkana Basin, Laetoli) and ecological zones throughout eastern and northern Africa.

THE LATER AUSTRALOPITHECINES: THE HOMININ FOSSIL RECORD BETWEEN 2.6 AND 1.2 MYA

Australopithecus garhi (Asfaw et al. 1999)

This enigmatic 2.5-million-year-old cranium (BOU-VP-12/130) from the Hata Member in sediments located on the Bouri Peninsula in the Middle Awash (Ethiopia) project area defies simple phyletic allocation and functional assessment. Although additional hominid fossils, including a partial skeleton, were found at the same horizon, they are not allocated formally to *Au. garhi*, although they could be members of that taxon. This cranium is clearly an *Australopithecus* on account of its small brain size (about 450 ml) and thick-enamelled, very large crowned molars and premolars; yet it also contains some characters found in later *Homo*, such as similar canine/postcanine tooth proportions and a rounded anterior alveolar margin. In addition, the type specimen is unique by possessing a canine with a large occlusal area and unusual morphology. A major contributing factor to the lack of understanding of this species is the paucity of fossils from this period in East Africa. Therefore a complete sense of the degree of anatomical variation is unknown, and the representativeness of the type cranium requires additional fossil examples. These fossils were recovered in a perilacustrine zone with edaphic grasslands, occupied by a diversity of grazing bovids (de Heinzelin et al. 1999).

Australopithecus africanus (Dart 1925)

Australopithecus africanus ('the southern ape of Africa') was the first truly ancient hominid discovered. At a time when the large-brained, primitive-jawed 'Piltdown'-based model of human evolution was dominant, Dart's announcement of a small-brained juvenile fossil skull from the Transvaal (specifically, from the site of Taung) of South Africa ran counter to expectations, both because of its anatomy (small brain and less 'ape-like' teeth) and because of the place where it was found; for at that time Asia – and not southern Africa – was widely considered to be the home of the earliest hominins. Since the 1920s, hundreds of fossils assigned to *Au. africanus* have been recovered from karstic caves in South Africa, most notably from the sites of Sterkfontein (Members 2 and 4), Makapansgat, and Gladysvale. These caves were produced through ground water percolation and dissolution of the limestone deposits, and most of the caverns were accessible via vertical 'chimneys,' which were perhaps surrounded with trees and shrubs at their openings on the otherwise grassy landscape. Thus the accumulations of bones in the caves represented the individuals who, and the elements which, fell into these openings – a phenomenon reflecting perhaps the collecting behaviors of terrestrial (Brain 1981) or even avian (Berger and Clarke 1995) predators. Fortunately these remains are numerous and sometimes articulated; they include for instance the near-complete StW 573 skeleton (Clarke 2008). On the other hand, these fossils tend to be distorted and poorly dated. In addition, some of them were found in the debris left over from the mining of these caves, and this created difficulties in their stratigraphic association. In the absence of nearby volcanic activity, the dating of the sites is based primarily on biochronology, and the sites are generally dated to between 2.3 and 2.8 mya. Although older dates are possible, younger ages cannot be ruled out.

The *Au. africanus* collections are extensive and include multiple male, female, and juvenile crania and mandibles; hundreds of teeth; and postcrania – notably the small-bodied partial skeleton Sts 14, with a pelvis, lumbar and thoracic vertebrae, ribs, and a partial femur; and the larger-bodied Stw 431 partial skeleton. The crania are small-brained (435–560 ml) globular vaults with larger molar and premolar teeth and smaller canines, and they still retain prognathic faces. The chewing muscles can be large, but they are not hypertrophied to the extent of those found in the 'robust' australopithecines (e.g. *Au. robustus, Au. aethiopicus, Au. boisei*). These individuals are fully adapted to bipedalism: they have pelvic and vertebral specializations, a valgus knee, and a permanently adducted great toe. In many anatomical details, their postcrania are quite similar to those of the more northern and somewhat older *Au. afarensis*, although *Au. africanus* exhibits larger post-canine teeth and smaller canines.

Their preferred habitats are generally reconstructed as more open locales, with a terrestrial fauna adapted to grazing.

Australopithecus robustus (Broom 1938)

The discovery of ancient hominins prompted others – notably Robert Broom – to look for hominin fossils in South Africa. Broom's discoveries at the cave site known as Kromdraai led to the naming of a new species, *Paranthropus robustus*, in 1938. Subsequently the name of the genus *Paranthropus* was considered to be a junior synonym to *Australopithecus*, and the taxon is now commonly referred to as *Au. robustus*. The fossils from the cave sites of Kromdraai, Swartkrans (both very close to Sterkfontein), and, more recently, Drimolen (Keyser 2000, Keyser et al. 2000) have depositional histories similar to those of the *Au. africanus* fossils.

Significant fossil collections are known, especially from Swartkrans, but these consist primarily of dentognathic remains. *Australopithecus robustus* is readily distinguishable from the slightly older *Au. africanus* through the enlargement of its post-canine teeth; the reduction of its canines and incisors, which results in a flatter, less prognathic face; and the hypertrophied chewing musculature, notably the *temporalis* muscles, which occupy the lateral side of the small-brained cranial vault (less than 550 ml) and often meet at the midline, forming a bony sagittal crest. The thick-enamelled teeth generally wear flat, losing the cuspal topography. Unfortunately few undistorted postcrania are known, but what little is available suggests a similar bodily form to that of *Au. africanus*.

The dating of these sites suffers from the same limitations as the other South African cave sites; they are dated, through biochronological analyses of the fauna, to between 1.5 and 2.0 mya.

Australopithecus aethiopicus (Arambourg and Coppens 1968)

This species was named on the basis of an edentulous mandible from the Shungura Formation sediments that outcrop along the Omo River in southern Ethiopia. These deposits are part of the Lake Turkana basin in Kenya and Ethiopia, which is supplied in large part by the south-flowing Omo River. This approximately 2.3-million-year-old mandible has a very thick corpus and a buttressed symphysis, with large post-canine tooth roots and small anterior tooth alveoli. Poorly known and often overlooked, the species languished until the recovery in 1985 of the KNM-WT 17000 cranium

(Walker et al. 1986). This small-brained cranium (410 ml), nicknamed 'the black skull,' is distinctive for its large post-canine dentition, unflexed cranial base, prognathic lower midface, and large sagittal crest. Unfortunately the species is still poorly represented by fossils (primarily dental remains) and is known only from the 2.3–2.6-million-year-old Turkana basin deposits.

Australopithecus boisei (Leakey 1959)

After surveying the deposits in Olduvai Gorge, Tanzania for over twenty years, Mary Leakey discovered a well preserved 1.8-million-year-old cranium, the Olduvai Hominid 5 (OH 5), in 1959. This iconic specimen was the first major discovery of a hominin in East Africa and it had the resulting effect of stimulating hominin paleontological research in the area. Initially the cranium was assigned to the newly created genus *Zinjanthropus*; it is now allocated to *Australopithecus*. The OH 5 cranium (Tobias 1967) has among the largest hominin post-canine teeth known; very small, vertically implanted canines and incisors; a tall but not prognathic lower midface; anteriorly positioned and laterally flaring zygomatic arches; prominent sagittal and nuchal crests; and a small brain size. Additional *Au. boisei* fossils have been recovered from Olduvai Gorge; the Turkana basin deposits in Ethiopia and Kenya; the southern Ethiopia site of Konso (Suwa et al. 1997); and from Malawi in the southern portion of the East African Rift (Kullmer et al. 1999). Unfortunately the postcrania of this species are very poorly known, so details of its the species' stature, bodily form, and body size dimorphism remain unknown.

These fossils commonly are found in very well dated deposits, now known to span between 1.2 and 2.3 mya old. Ecologically, it appears that *Au. boisei* occupied more open habitats, in association with grazing bovids and suids (Reed 1997; Suwa et al. 1997).

THE LATER AUSTRALOPITHECINES: OVERVIEW

Between 2.6 and 2.9 mya, a hominin radiation occurred (Suwa et al. 1996). Although the region in Africa where this speciation event orginated is currently unknown, the event itself resulted in at least two (and probably more) lineages, which exhibited fundamental differences in adaptation and which rapidly spread throughout Africa. These two adaptive roles are characterized by the elaboration and enlargement of the dentognathic structures – namely in the 'robust' australopithecines (or paranthropines) – and by a lineage (the genus *Homo*) that ultimately reduced its tooth crown dimensions and enlarged its brain.

From what is known, *Au. afarensis* seems to be a reasonable stem hominin from which the East African 'robust' lineage (*Au. aethiopicus*→*Au. boisei*), *Au. garhi*, and the early *Homo* lineage arose. Resolving the phyletic position of the South African australopithecines (*Au. africanus* and *Au. robustus*) has been especially intractable, despite extensive collections. *Au. africanus* has been identified variously as the LCA of the 'robust' and *Homo* lineages, replacing *Au. afarensis* in this role (Skelton et al. 1986), or as uniquely ancestral to the 'robust' lineage (Johanson and White 1979).

One of the proposed phyletic possibilities of *Au. garhi* is that it was a transitional taxon between *Australopithecus afarensis* and early *Homo*. Evidence for this would be the proposed apomorphic crown proportions. Similarly aged deposits from the Middle Awash study area (for instance Gamedah) have yielded additional, more gracile hominid fossils, which are not assignable to *Au. garhi* as the latter is currently defined – a fact which raises the possibility that multiple taxa were present about 2.5 mya in the Afar Depression.

The 'robust' australopithecines include *Au. robustus*, *Au. aethiopicus*, and *Au. boisei*. An alternative taxonomy assigns these taxa to the genus *Paranthropus*, a name that recognizes a common and distinct phyletic relatedness for the 'robust' species. All three share a common dentognathic adaptation (large, thick-enamelled molars and premolars, large and robust mandibular corpora with tall rami, reduced incisors and canines, 'dished' faces, laterally projecting and anteriorly positioned zygomatic arches, sagittal crests, and small brains). This anatomical complex, supported by additional evidence such as that of enamel microwear, isotopic composition of the enamel, and flat-wearing teeth, indicates a highly abrasive, lower-quality herbivorous diet, which requires intense masticatory preparation. This is probably an adaptation to open terrestrial habitats, which were expanding in Africa throughout the latter half of the Pliocene and early Pleistocene, and it placed a dietary emphasis on seeds and hard fruits. Unfortunately the paucity of reliably allocated or anatomically complete postcrania for any 'robust' australopithecine precludes a detailed discussion of their locomotor adaptations, limb proportions, or body form.

At approximately 2.3 mya, anatomical differences in dental morphology and facial architecture appear which distinguish *Au. aethiopicus* from *Au. boisei* (Suwa et al. 1996). Phyletically, it appears that these East African 'robust' australopithecines are part of a single, continuous lineage, which arose from *Au. afarensis*. The origins of the South African *Au. robustus* are more obscure. The South African fossils defy the standard contention that more and better preserved fossils will resolve these issues, as many fossils of this species are known, yet there is no consensus on phyletic origins or taxonomic diversity. A clarification of the stratigraphy and dating of all of these cave sites should help to resolve these issues. *Au. robustus* has been variously identified as part of a monophyletic robust australopithecine radiation assigned to the genus *Paranthropus* that includes the East African *Au. (P.) aethiopicus* and *Au. (P.) boisei*; or as a separate and independently derived robust australopithecine species. Similarity with the East African forms suggests a common phyletic origin (*Paranthropus*) and adaptation. However, differences in anatomical detail, such as tooth morphology and craniofacial anatomy, may indicate that these are evolutionary parallelisms rather than shared specializations which occurred in two places (southern Africa and the East African Rift).

The genus *Homo*, too, arose at about that time. The oldest known specimens are a temporal bone (KNM-BC-1) from Chemeron in Kenya (around 2.4 mya: Hill et al. 1992) and a maxilla (A.L. 666-1) from Hadar, Ethiopia (2.33 mya: Kimbel et al. 1996). This adaptation is widely connected with the origins of stone tool use and manufacture, which is first evident about 2.6 mya (Semaw et al. 1997, 2003; de Heinzelin et al. 1999). In association with these stone tools there is direct evidence of butchery or carcass harvesting (de Heinzelin et al. 1999), which indicates for the first time in hominins a regular exploitation of animal resources. Some early members of

Homo – for example AL 666-1, 2.33 mya (Kimbel et al. 1996); OH 62, 1.78 mya (Johanson et al. 1987); KNM-ER 1470, 1.88 mya – exhibit larger post-canine tooth crowns, which suggests that early *Homo* retained this primitive condition to some degree in a polymorphic species, or that multiple 'early *Homo*' taxa coexisted.

Homo and 'robust' australopithecine fossils are known from sites in South Africa (such as Swartkrans, Drimolen (Keyser et al. 2000)) and in East Africa (Olduvai Gorge, Turkana Basin, and Konso) which indicate that these hominins had the potential for encounters in their shared home ranges across a span that lasted at least 0.5 million years. It is tempting to think that the dentognathic specializations of the 'robust' australopithecines is a response to reducing competition for dietary resources by niche partitioning with the sympatric members of *Homo*. The robust australopithecines, unlike *Homo*, did not expand out of Africa despite the absence of insurmountable physical barriers. This biogeographical history suggests strong differences in adaptive ability and perhaps dietary preferences between *Homo* and the 'robust' australopithecines: the latter had less capacity to invade and exploit novel habitats.

The extinction of the 'robust' australopithecines occurred sometime about 1.1–1.2 mya, in both South and East Africa. There is little evidence to indicate a widespread turnover in open-adapted fauna at this time, which suggests that the extinction of the 'robust' australopithecines was not the consequence of environmental changes. Was their demise a result of competition with *Homo erectus*? Their protracted sympatry suggests that this may not be the case. However, as the technical sophistication of *Homo erectus* improved, its members may have been able to adapt behaviorally to an increasing diversity of environments, whereas the 'robust' australopithecines' capacity to modify their behavior and anatomy may have been insufficient in the face of the pervasive adaptive abilities of *Homo*.

DISCUSSION

With the recovery of increasingly ancient hominin fossils, it is apparent that bipedalism was one of the earliest adaptations adopted by hominins as there is reasonable evidence for this stretching back 6 million years. Bipedalism is widely regarded as the anatomical result of an extraordinary and unparalleled shift in behavior, uniquely expressed in the hominin lineage. Although a simple change in environment requiring a shift of optimal habitats exploited by the early hominins from forested to more open woodland makes an intuitively compelling argument, no other species has adopted bipedalism, even though multiple Miocene-age ape species have been exposed to similar environmental changes. In addition, these models where the environment plays a determining role do not adequately explain how fitness is improved by bipedality or how the tremendous inertia of anatomic, demographic, and social structures correlated to locomotor changes was overcome. Natural selection favors those adaptations that directly impact on reproductive success, survivorship, or access to food – the "fundamental selective triad" (Lovejoy 1993) and bipedalism directly improved the fitness of those who adopted it.

Another unique trait in the hominin lineage is the absence of the sectorial canine complex. No other primate has reduced the size and changed the function of the canines to the extent that hominins have. In most monkeys and in all extant apes, the male maxillary canine is a very large, projecting tooth, which occludes against the mesio-buccal face of the lower third premolar (P3) – a process that results in producing a sharp, knife-like distal edge of the canine. Even with advanced wear, the apes can retain a tall, projecting canine that shows this disto-lingual honing wear. Hominin maxillary canines have wear on both their apical and distal surfaces. Apical wear is present in the earliest stages of attrition in the hominin canine, resulting in a reduction of the crown height even at young ages. The wear on the distal margin is a flat linear facet that does not result in the sharpening of the distal margin. The non-hominin canine is often sexually dimorphic in size and shape, and this reflects the social function of the tooth (male–male competition). Exceptions to this rule of canine dimorphism in non-human primates are instructive. For example, in the mon-omorphic gibbons, the females have enlarged their canines, as the pair-bonded males and females share the role of territorial defense. In *Brachyteles* (a New World platyr-rhine monkey), males have reduced their canines while retaining the honing func-tion, perhaps as an adaptation to reduced male–male competition and territorial control (Plavcan and van Schaik 1997). Male primates must retain unique access to two necessary and interrelated resources: territory and reproductive access to females. Many of the intrasexual conflicts that occur in the males include visual displays of the canine teeth and biting. Thus the canines are important anatomical structures that act as behavioral signals necessary to determine social rank and reproductive success. Reduction in canine size and the loss of the honing function in hominins is unique among the apes and indicates that the early hominins adopted a novel means of resolving male intrasexual conflicts, or that females were preferentially choosing small-canined males as mates (this would be perhaps the developmental correlate of some other preferred behavioral character – for example reduced aggression, greater cooperation, and so on).

To date, both of these characters reliably identify the earliest known hominins, although it must be recognized that they (and other hominin traits) arose – or became fixed in the hominin lineage – only after separation from the chimpanzee–human last common ancestor and after the adoption of the unique behaviors that characterize the hominins. Therefore paleontologists will be able to identify ancient hominins once their morphology has adapted to these novel behaviors, but not all the phyletic hom-inins. This fact may perhaps lead to the misidentification of the earliest phyletic hominins as apes – which should be indistinguishable (or poorly distinguishable) from the LCA. Therefore the origin of the hominin lineage will predate the identification of the earliest morphological hominin.

The transition to the australopithecine pattern appears to occur abruptly between 4.4–4.2 mya and is readily identifiable through changes in canine form and through larger and thicker enameled post-canine teeth. The adaptive motivation for this transition is unclear, although changes in the dentition appear to be linked with diet: thickened enamel and enlarged post-canine teeth seem to be associated with tougher consistency or with harder, more brittle foodstuffs (Teaford and Ungar 2000; Ungar 2004). Although the fine details in locomotion and substrate preference are not well known for *Au. ana-mensis*, it appears that a greater behavioral and anatomical commitment to bipedality occurred at this time. This australopithecine dental morphotype continues, with minor changes (Kimbel et al. 2006), until about 2.9 mya. This was then followed by a phyletic radiation, which resulted in multiple taxa elaborating upon this adaptive complex with even larger and thicker enameled molars and premolars teeth (*Au. africanus*, *Au. robustus*, *Au. garhi*, *Au. aethiopicus*, and *Au. boisei*). In addition, at some time between 2.6 and 2.9 mya, a new lineage (or lineages) of *Homo* arose that increased the size of its brain, adopted stone tool use and manufacture, and lacked extreme post-canine megadontia. It is unclear what factors led to, or induced, this radiation.

FUTURE RESEARCH

Even with the numerous recent advances in this area, substantial and substantive questions about the early stages of human evolution remain. Biomolecular estimates of the divergence dates of the African ape lineages (gorilla–chimpanzee/human: about 7–9 mya; chimpanzee–human: 5–7 mya) still require support from the fossil record as there are very few fossil apes from a period of 5–10 mya in Africa and Europe: Chorora, Ethiopia (Suwa et al. 2007a); *Samburupithecus* (Ishida and Pickford 1997); Hominoidea *gen. et sp. indet.* (Pickford et al. 2008); *Ouranopithecus* (Koufos and de Bonis 2005). Thus the timing, location, context, and anatomy of the various ape–human last common ancestors are poorly known. In addition, the earliest identified hominins, such as *Sahelanthropus*, may predate the estimated origins of our lineage – which indicates that further work is necessary in order to reconcile the paleontological and biomolecular dating of hominin origins (Suwa et al. 2007a). It is also unclear how many hominin taxa existed throughout Africa and whether speciation of the LCA resulted in a singular hominin basal population, or whether the living hominins are part of a late Miocene radiation. In addition, the near-complete absence of chimpanzee (McBrearty and Jablonski 2005) and gorilla (or gorriloid: Suwa et al. 2007a) fossils is a major gap in our understanding of when, where, and in what habitats our closest relatives evolved to their current state. The biogeography of the early hominins remains poorly known and requires paleontological prospecting in new areas throughout Africa – work which is best identified through the use of new tools of remote imaging and geospatial analysis of data (Conroy et al. 2008).

The paleobiology of these early ancestors is now better understood through more sophisticated and rigorous studies of the fossils themselves. For example, ancient diets are being better characterized through analyses of enamel microwear (Scott et al. 2006; Solounias and Semprebon 2002), more sophisticated studies of cusp topography (Ungar 2004) and enamel thickness (Kono 2004), and analyses of enamel stable isotope chemistry (Sponheimer and Lee-Thorp 2007; Levin et al. 2008). Locomotor patterns and substrate preferences have benefited by the combination of anatomical and engineering studies (Crompton et al. 2008).

Fossils still form the foundation of all of these studies. Our generation may be experiencing a 'golden age' of field discoveries; however, this may not last long, due to the depletion of the most easily accessible fossils (White 2004). Even extensive and well preserved fossil collections like those of *Au. afarensis* from Hadar are insufficient to address fully issues of growth and populational variation. Thus, to further our understanding of our ancestors, we must be more intensive in our surveys for additional fossils and more ambitious in the development of novel means of assessing their biology.

NOTE

1 The use of the term 'hominin' (referring to the subtribe designation Hominina) rather than 'hominid' to describe members of the human radiation since our cladogenic split from the chimpanzee lineage is a recognition of the history of relatedness among living large-bodied apes as defined by degree of DNA, other biochemical, and anatomical similarity. Formerly, 'hominid' (family: Hominidae) was the preferred – and still commonly used – nomen for the human lineage until it was recognized that the great apes (chimpanzees, gorillas, and orangutans or 'pongids' [family 'Pongidae']) do not share a common origin and have a separate evolutionary history distinct from humans. Humans are now known to be part of the great ape (humans, chimpanzees, gorillas, and orangutans [Family: Hominidae]) radiation. The large-bodied Asian apes (orangutans [Subfamily: Ponginae]) then split from the African apes (Subfamily: Homininae) with gorillas (Tribe Gorillini) branching off from the Hominini (chimpanzees and humans) about 9–12 Ma. The Hominini split into the chimpanzee (subtribe Panina) and humans and relatives (Subtribe: Hominina or 'hominin') about 7–9 Ma. This realignment of terms now makes the evolutionary history and taxonomic nomenclature more consistent.

REFERENCES

Alemseged, Z., Spoor, F., Kimbel, W. H., Bone, R., Geraads, D., Reed, D., and Wynn, J. (2006) A Juvenile Early Hominin Skeleton from Dikika, Ethiopia. *Nature* 443: 296–301.
Arambourg, C., and Coppens, Y. (1968) Découverte d'un australopithécien nouveau dans les gisements de l'Omo (Éthiopie). *South African Journal of Science* 64: 58–59.
Asfaw, B., White, T., Lovejoy, O., Latimer, B., Simpson, S., and Suwa, G. (1999) *Australopithecus garhi*: A New Species of Early Hominid from Ethiopia. *Science* 284: 629–635.
Berger, L. R., and Clarke, R. J. (1995) Eagle Involvement in Accumulation of the Taung Child Fauna. *Journal of Human Evolution* 29: 275–299.
Bradley, B. J. (2008) Reconstructing Phylogenies and Phenotypes: A Molecular View of Human Evolution. *Journal of Anatomy* 212: 337–353.
Brain, C. K. (1981) *The Hunters or the Hunted? An Introduction to African Cave Taphonomy.* Chicago IL: University of Chicago Press.
Bramble, D. M., and Lieberman, D. E. (2004) Endurance Running and the Evolution of *Homo. Nature* 432: 345–352.
Broom, R. (1938) The Pleistocene Anthropoid apes of South Africa. *Nature* 142: 377–379.
Brunet, M., Beauvilain, A., Coppens, Y., Heintz, E., Moutaye, A. H. E., and Pilbeam, D. (1996) *Australopithecus bahrelghazali*, une nouvelle espèce d'hominidé ancien de la région de Koro Toro (Tchad). *Comptes Rendus de l'Académie des Sciences – Series IIA – Earth and Planetary Science* 322: 907–913.
Brunet, M., Boisserie, J.-R., Ahounta, D., Blondel, C., de Bonis, L., Coppens, Y., Denys, C., Duringer, P., Eisenmann, V., Fronty, P., Geraads, D., Fanoné, G., Guy, F., Lehman, T., Lihoreau, F., Likius, A., Louchart, A., Mackaye, H. T., Otero, O., Campomanes, P. P., Pilbeam, D., Ponce de Leon, M., Rage, J.-C., Schuster, M., Tassey, P., Valentin, X., Vignaud, P., Viriot, L., and Zollikofer, C. (2005) *Sahelanthropus tchadensis*: The facts. *South African Journal of Science* 100: 443–445.
Brunet, M., Guy, F., Pilbeam, D., Mackaye, H. T., Likius, A., Ahounta, D., Beauvilain, A., Blondel, C., Bocherens, H., Boisserie, J.-R., de Bonis, L., Coppens, Y., Dejax, J., Denys, C., Duringer, P., Eisenmann, V., Fanoné, G., Fronty, P., Geraads, D., Lehmann, T., Lihoreau, F., Louchart, A., Mahamat, A., Merceron, G., Mouchelin, G., Otero, O., Campomanes, P. P.,

Ponce de Léon, M., Rage, J.-C., Sapanet, M., Schuster, M., Sudre, J., Tassey, P., Valentin, X., Vignaud, P., Ciriot, L., Zazzo, A., and Zollikofer, C. (2002) A New Hominid from the Upper Miocene of Chad, Central Africa. *Nature* 418: 145–151.

Clarke, R. J. (2008) Latest Information on Sterkfontein's *Australopithecus* Skeleton and a New Look at *Australopithecus*. *South African Journal of Science* 104: 443–449.

Conroy, G. C., Anemone, R. L., van Regenmorter, J., and Addison, A. (2009) Google Earth, GIS, and the Great Divide: A New and Simple Method for Sharing Paleontological Data. *Journal of Human Evolution* 55: 751–755.

Crompton, R. H., Vereecke, E. E., and Thorpe, S. K. S. (2008) Locomotion and Posture from the Common Hominoid Ancestor to Fully Modern Hominins, with Special Reference to the Last Common Panin/Hominin Ancestor. *Journal of Anatomy* 212: 501–543.

Dart, R. A. (1925) *Australopithecus africanus*: The Man–Ape of South Africa. *Nature* 115: 195–199.

Darwin, C. R. (1871) *The Descent of Man*. London: John Murray.

de Heinzelin, J., Clark, J. D., White, T. D., Hart, W., Renne, P., WoldeGabriel, G., Beyene, Y., and Vrba, E. (1999) Environment and Behavior of 2.5-Million-Year-Old Bouri Hominids. *Science* 284: 625–629.

Deino, A. L., Tauxe, L., Monaghan, M., and Hill, A. (2002) ^{40}Ar/^{39}Ar Geochronology and Paleomagnetic Stratigraphy of the Lukeino and Lower Chemeron Formations at Tabarin and Kapcheberek, Tugen Hills, Kenya. *Journal of Human Evolution* 42: 117–140.

Galik, K., Senut, B., Pickford, M., Gommery, D., Kuperavage, A. J., and Eckardt, R. B. (2004) External and Internal Morphology of the BAR 1002'00 *Orrorin tugenensis* Femur. *Science* 305: 1450–1453.

Guy, F., Mackaye, H.-T., Likius, A., Vignaud, P., Schmittbuhl, M., and Brunet, M. (2008) Symphyseal Shape Variation in Extant and Fossil Hominoids and the Symphysis of *Australopithecus bahrelghazali*. *Journal of Human Evolution* 55: 37–47.

Guy, F., Lieberman, D. E., Pilbeam, D., Ponce de Leon, M., Likius, A., Mackaye, H. T., Vignaud, P., Zollikofer, C., and Brunet, M. (2005) Morphological Affinities of the *Sahelanthropus tchadensis* (Late Miocene Hominid from Chad) Cranium. *Proceedings of the National Academy of Sciences* 102: 18836–18841.

Haile-Selassie, Y. (2001) Late Miocene Hominids from the Middle Awash, Ethiopia. *Nature* 412: 178–181.

Haile-Selassie, Y. (2008) New Early Pliocene Hominid Fossils from the Woranso-Mille (Central Afar, Ethiopia) and the Question of Phyletic Evolution in Early *Australopithecus*. *Journal of Vertebrate Paleontology* 28 (Suppl. 3): 87A.

Haile-Selassie, Y., Suwa, G., and White, T. D. (2004) Late Miocene Teeth from Middle Awash, Ethiopia, and Early Hominid Dental Evolution. *Science* 303: 1503–1505.

Hill, A. (1985) Early Hominid from Baringo, Kenya. *Nature* 315: 222–224.

Hill, A., and Ward, S. C. (1988) Origin of the Hominidae: The Record of African Large Hominoid Evolution between 14 My and 4 My. *Yearbook of Physical Anthropology* 31: 49–83.

Hill, A., Ward, S., Deino, A., Curtis, G., and Drake, R. (1992) Earliest *Homo*. *Nature* 355: 719–722.

Holloway, R. L. (1967) Tools and Teeth: Some Speculations regarding Canine Reduction. *American Anthropologist* 69: 63–67.

Holloway, R. L., Broadfield, D. C., and Yuan, M. S. 2004 *The Human Fossil Record. Volume 3: Brain Endocasts*. Hoboken NJ: Wiley-Liss.

Hunt, K. (1994) The Evolution of Human Bipedality: Ecology and Functional Morphology. *Journal of Human Evolution* 26: 183–202.

Ishida, H., and Pickford, M. (1997) A New Late Miocene Hominoid from Kenya: *Samburupithecus kiptalami* gen. et sp. nov. *Comptes Rendus Earth and Planetary Sciences* 325: 823–829.

Jolly, C. J. (1970) The Seed-Eaters: A New Model of Hominid Differentiation Based on a Baboon Analogy. *Man* 5: 5–26.

Johanson, D. C. (2004) Lucy, Thirty Years Later: An Expanded View of *Australopithecus afarensis*. *Journal of Anthropological Research* 60: 465–486.

Johanson, D. C., and White, T. D. (1979) A Systematic Assessment of Early African Hominids. *Science* 203: 321–329.

Johanson, D. C., White, T. D., and Coppens, Y. (1978) A New Species of the Genus *Australopithecus* (Primates: Hominidae) from the Pliocene of Eastern Africa. *Kirtlandia* 28: 1–11.

Johanson, D. C., Masao, F. T., Eck, G. G., White, T. D., Walter, R. C., Kimbel, W. H., Asfaw, B., Manega, P., Ndessokia, P., and Suwa, G. (1987) New Partial Skeleton of *Homo habilis* from Olduvai Gorge, Tanzania. *Nature* 327: 205–209.

Keyser, A. (2000) The Drimolen Skull: The Most Complete Australopithecine Cranium and Mandible to Date. *South African Journal of Science* 96: 189–193.

Keyser, A. W., Menter, C. G., Moggi-Cecchi, J., Pickering, T. R., and Berger, L. (2000) Drimolen: A New Hominid-Bearing Site in Gauteng, South Africa. *South African Journal of Science* 96: 193–197.

Kimbel, W. H., Rak, Y., and Johanson, D. C. (2004) *The Skull of* Australopithecus afarensis. Oxford University Press: Oxford.

Kimbel, W. H., Lockwood, C. A., Ward, C. V., Leakey, M. G., Rak, Y., and Johanson, D. C. (2006) Was *Australopithecus anamensis* Ancestral to *A. afarensis*? A Case of Anagenesis in the Hominin Fossil Record. *Journal of Human Evolution* 51: 134–152.

Kimbel, W. H., Walter, R. C., Johanson, D. C., Reed, K. E., Aronson, J. L., Assefa, Z., Marean, C. W., Eck, G. G., Bobe, R., Hovers, E., Rak, Y., Vondra, C., Yemane, T., York, D., Chen, Y., Evensen, N. M., and Smith, P. E. (1996) Late Pliocene *Homo* and Oldowan Tools from the Hadar Formation (Kada Hadar Member), Ethiopia. *Journal of Human Evolution* 31: 549–561.

Kleinsasser, L., Quade, J., Levin, N. E., Simpson, S. W., MacIntosh, W., and Semaw, S. (2008) Geochronology of the Adu-Asa Formation at Gona, Ethiopia. In J. Quade and J. Wynn (eds), *The Geology of Early Humans in the Horn of Africa* (pp. 33–65). Boulder, CO: Geological Society of America Special Paper 446.

Kono, R. T. (2004) Molar Enamel Thickness and Distribution Patterns in Extant Apes and Humans: New Insights Based on a 3-Dimensional Whole Crown Perspective. *Anthropological Science* 112: 121–146.

Koufos, G. D., and de Bonis, L. (2005) The Late Miocene Hominoids *Ouranopithecus* and *Graecopithecus*. Implications about Their Relationships and Taxonomy. *Annales de Paléontolgie* 91: 227–240.

Kullmer, O., Sandrock, O., Abel, R., Schrenk, F., Bromage, T. G., and Juwayeyi, M. (1999) The first *Paranthropus* from the Malawi Rift. *Journal of Human Evolution* 37: 121–127.

Kumar, S., Filipski, A., Swarna, V., Walker, A., and Hedges, B. (2005) Placing Confidence Limits on the Molecular Age of the Human-Chimpanzee Divergence. *Proceedings of the National Academy of Sciences, USA* 102: 18842–18847.

Latimer, B. (1991) Locomotor Adaptations in *Australopithecus afarensis*: The Issue of Arboreality. In Y. Coppens and B. Senut (eds), *Origine(s) de la bipédie chez les hominids* (pp. 169–176). CNRS: Paris.

Leakey, L. S. B. (1959) A New Fossil Skull from Olduvai. *Nature* 184: 491–493.

Leakey, M. D., and Hay, R. L. (1979) Pliocene Footprints in the Laetolil Beds at Laetoli, Northern Tanzania. *Nature* 278: 317–323.

Leakey, M. G., and Walker, A. C. (2003) The Lothagam Hominids. In M. G. Leakey and J. M. Harris (eds), *Lothagam: The Dawn of Humanity in Eastern Africa* (pp. 249–260). New York: Columbia University Press.

Leakey, M. G., Feibel, C. S., McDougall, I., and Walker, A. C. (1995) New Four-Million-Year-Old Hominid Species from Kanapoi and Allia Bay, Kenya. *Nature* 376: 565–571.

Leakey, M. G., Feibel, C. S., McDougall, I., Ward, C., and Walker, A. C. (1998) New Specimens and Conformation of an Early Age for *Australopithecus anamensis. Nature* 393: 62–66.

Leakey, M. D., Hay, R. L., Curtis, G. H., Drake, R. E., Jackes, M. K., and White, T. (1976) Fossil Hominids from the Laetolil Beds. *Nature* 262: 460–466.

Leakey, M. G., Spoor, F., Brown, F. H., Gathogo, P. N., Kiarie, C., Leakey, L. N., and McDougall, I. (2001) New Hominin Genus from Eastern Africa Shows Diverse Middle Pliocene Lineages. *Nature* 410: 433–440.

Lebatard, A.-E., Bourlès, D. L., Duringer, P., Jolivet, M., Braucher, R., Carcaillet, J., Schuster, M., Arnaud, N., Monié, P., Lihoreau, F., Likius, A., Mackaye, H. T., Vignaud, P., and Brunet, M. (2008) Cosmogenic Nuclide Dating of *Sahelanthropus tchadensis* and *Australopithecus bahrelghazali*: Mio-Pliocene Hominids from Chad. *Proceedings of the National Academy of Sciences* 105: 3226–3231.

Levin, N. E., Simpson, S. W., Quade, J., Cerling, T. E., and Frost, S. R. (2008) Herbivore Enamel and Soil Carbon Isotopic Composition and the Environmental Context of *Ardipithecus* at Gona, Ethiopia. In J. Quade and J. Wynn (eds), *The Geology of Early Humans in the Horn of Africa* (pp. 215–234). Boulder, CO: Geological Society of America Special Paper 446.

Lovejoy, C. O. (1981) The Origin of Man. *Science* 211: 341–350.

Lovejoy, C. O. (1988) Evolution of Human Walking. *Scientific American* 256: 118–125.

Lovejoy, C. O. (1993) Modeling Human Origins: Are We Sexy because We're Smart, or Smart because We're Sexy? In D. T. Rasmussen (ed.), *The Origin and Evolution of Humans and Humanness* (pp. 1–28). Sudbury, MA: Jones and Bartlett.

Lovejoy, C. O. (2009) Reexamining Human Origins in Light of *Ardipithecus ramidus. Science* 326: 74e1–74e8.

Lovejoy, C. O., Latimer, B., Suwa, G., Asfaw, B., and White, T. D. (2009a) Combining Prehension and Propulsion: The Foot of *Ardipithecus ramidus. Science* 326: 72e1–72e8.

Lovejoy, C. O., Meindl, R. S., Ohman, J. C., Heiple, K. G., and White, T. D. (2002) The Maka Femur and Its Bearing on the Antiquity of Human Walking: Applying Contemporary Concepts to Morphogenesis to the Human Fossil Record. *American Journal of Physical Anthropology* 119: 97–133.

Lovejoy, C. O., Simpson, S. W., White, T. D., Asfaw, B., and Suwa, G. (2009b) Careful Climbing in the Miocene: The Forelimbs of *Ardipithecus ramidus* and Humans are Primitive. *Science* 326: 70e1–70e8.

Lovejoy, C. O., Suwa, G., Simpson, S. W., Matternes, J. H., and White, T. D. (2009d) The Great Divide: *Ardipithecus ramidus* Reveals the Postcrania of Our Last Common Ancestors with the African Apes. *Science* 326: 100–106.

Lovejoy, C. O., Suwa, G., Spurlock, L., Asfaw, B., and White, T. D. (2009c) The Pelvis and Femur of *Ardipithecus ramidus*: The Emergence of Upright Walking. *Science* 326: 71e1–71e6.

McBrearty, S., and Jablonski, N. G. (2005) First Fossil Chimpanzee. *Nature* 437: 105–108.

Ohman, J. C., Krochta, T. J., Lovejoy, C. O., Mensforth, R. P., and Latimer, B. (1997) Cortical Bone Distribution in the Femoral Neck of Hominids: Implications for Locomotion of *Australopithecus afarensis. American Journal of Physical Anthropology* 104: 117–131.

Pickford, M., and Senut, B. (2001) The Geological and Faunal Context of Late Miocene Hominid Remains from Lukeino, Kenya. *Comptes Rendus de l'Académie des Sciences – Series IIA – Earth and Planetary Science* 332: 145–152.

Pickford, M., and Senut, B. (2005) Hominoid Teeth with Chimpanzee- and Gorilla-Like Features from the Miocene of Kenya: Implications for the Chronology of Ape-Human Divergence and Biogeography of Miocene Hominoids. *Anthropological Science* 113: 95–102.

Pickford, M., Senut, B., and Mourer-Chauviré, C. (2004) Early Pliocene Tragulidae and Peafowls in the Rift Valley, Kenya: Evidence for Rainforest in East Africa. *Comptes Rendus Paleovol* 3: 179–189.

Pickford, M., Senut, B., Gommery, D., and Treil, J. (2002) Bipedalism in *Orrorin tugenensis* Revealed by Its Femora. *Comptes Rendus Palevol* 1: 1–13.

Pickford, M., Senut, B., Morales, J., and Braga, J. (2008) First Hominoid from the Late Miocene of Niger. *South African Journal of Science* 104: 337–340.

Plavcan, J. M., and van Schaik, C. P. (1997) Interpreting Hominid Behavior on the Basis of Sexual Dimorphism. *Journal of Human Evolution* 32: 345–374.

Reed, K. E. (1997) Early Hominid Evolution and Ecological Change through the African Plio-Pleistocene. *Journal of Human Evolution* 32: 289–322.

Reed, K. E. (2008) Paleoecological Patterns at the Hadar Hominin Site, Afar Regional State, Ethiopia. *Journal of Human Evolution* 54: 743–768.

Richmond, B. G., and Jungers, W. L. (2008) *Orrorin tugenensis* Femoral Morphology and the Evolution of Hominin Bipedalism. *Science* 319: 1662–1665.

Rodman, P. S., and McHenry, H. M. (1980) Bioenergetics and the Origin of Hominid Bipedalism. *American Journal of Physical Anthropology* 52: 103–106.

Sawada, Y., Pickford, M., Senut, B., Itaya, T., Hyodo, M., Miura, T., Kashine, C., Chujo, T., and Fujii, H. (2002) The Age of *Orrorin tugenensis*, an Early Hominid from the Tugen Hills, Kenya. *Comptes Rendus Palevol* 1: 293–303.

Sayers, K., and Lovejoy, C.O. (2008) The Chimpanzee Has No Clothes: A Critical Examination of *Pan troglodytes* in Models of Human Evolution (with Comments). *Current Anthropology* 49: 87–114.

Scott, R. S., Ungar, P. S., Bergstrom, T. S., Brown, C. A., Childs, B. E., Teaford, M. F., and Walker, A. (2006) Dental Microwear Texture Analysis: Technical Considerations. *Journal of Human Evolution* 51: 339–349.

Semaw, S., Renne, P., Harris, J. W. K., Feibel, C. S., Bernor, R. L., Fesseha, N., and Mowbray, K. (1997) 2.5-Million-Year-Old Stone Tools from Gona, Ethiopia. *Nature* 385: 333–336.

Semaw, S., Rogers, M. J., Quade, J., Renne, P. R., Butler, R. F., Dominguez-Rodrigo, M., Stout, D., Hart, W. S., Pickering, T., and Simpson, S. W. (2003) 2.6-Million-Year-Old Stone Tools and Associated Bones from OGS-6 and OGS-7, Gona, Afar, Ethiopia. *Journal of Human Evolution* 45: 169–177.

Semaw, S., Simpson, S. W., Quade, J., Levin, N. E., Renne, P., MacIntosh, R., Butler, R., Dominguez-Rodrigo, M., and Rogers, M. (2005) Early Pliocene Hominids and Their Environments from Gona, Ethiopia. *Nature* 433: 301–305.

Senut, B., Pickford, M., Gommery, D., Mein, P., Cheboi, K., and Coppens, Y. (2001) First Hominid from the Miocene (Lukeino Formation, Kenya). *Comptes Rendus de l'Académie des Sciences – Series IIA – Earth and Planetary Science* 332: 137–144.

Simpson, S. W., Quade, J., Kleinsasser, L., Levin, N., Macintosh, W., Dunbar, N., and Semaw, S. (2006) Late Miocene Hominid Teeth from Gona Project Area, Ethiopia. *American Journal of Physical Anthropology* 132 (S44): 219.

Skelton, R. R., McHenry, H. M., and Drawhorn, G. M. (1986) Phylogenetic Analysis of Early Hominids. *Current Anthropology* 27: 21–43.

Solounias, N., and Semprebon, G. (2002) Advances in the Reconstruction of Ungulate Ecomorphology with Application to Early Fossil Equids. *American Museum Novitates* 3366: 1–49.

Sponheimer, M., and Lee-Thorp, J. (2007) Hominin Paleodiets: The Contribution of Stable Isotopes. In W. Henke and I. Tattersall (eds), *Handbook of Paleoanthropology* (pp. 555–585). Berlin: Springer.

Stern, J. T., and Sussman, R. L. (1983) The Locomotor Anatomy of *Australopithecus afarensis*. *American Journal of Physical Anthropology* 60: 279–317.

Su, D., and Harrison, T. (2007) The Paleoecology of the Upper Laetolil Beds at Laetoli: A Reconsideration of the Large Mammal Evidence. In R. Bobé, A. Alemseged, and A. K. Behrensmeyer (eds), *Hominin Environments in the East African Pliocene: An Assessment of the Faunal Evidence* (pp. 279–313). Dordrecht: Springer.

Suwa, G., White, T. D., and Howell, F. C. (1996) Mandibular Postcanine Dentition from the Shungura Formation, Ethiopia: Crown Morphology, Taxonomic Allocations, and Plio-Pleistocene Hominid Evolution. *American Journal of Physical Anthropology* 101: 247–282.

Suwa, G., Kono, R. T., Katoh, S., Asfaw, B., and Beyene, Y. (2007a) A New Species of Great Ape from the Late Miocene Epoch in Ethiopia. *Nature* 448: 921–924.

Suwa, G., Kono, R. T., Simpson, S. W., Asfaw, B., Lovejoy, C. O., and White, T. D. (2009) Paleobiological Implications of the *Ardipithecus ramidus* Dentition. *Science* 326: 94–99.

Suwa, G., Nakaya H., Asfaw B., Saegusa H., Amzaye A., Kono R. T., and Beyene Y. (2003) Plio-Pleistocene Terrestrial Mammal Assemblage from Konso, Southern Ethiopia. *Journal of Vertebrate Paleontology* 23: 901–916.

Suwa, G., Asfaw, B., Haile-Selassie, Y., White, T. D., Katoh, S., WoldeGabriel, G., Hart, W. K., Nakaya, H., and Beyene, Y. (2007b) Early Pleistocene *Homo erectus* Fossils from Konso, Southern Ethiopia. *Anthropological Science* 115: 133–151.

Suwa, G., Asfaw, B., Beyene, Y., White, T. D., Katoh, S., Nagaoka, S., Nakaya, H., Uzawa, K., Renne, P., and WoldeGabriel, G. (1997) The First Skull of *Australopithecus boisei*. *Nature* 389: 489–492.

Teaford, M. F., and Ungar, P. (2000) Diet and the Evolution of the Earliest Human Ancestors. *Proceedings of the National Academy of Science* 97: 13506–13511.

Tobias, P. V. (1967) *Olduvai Gorge*, Vol. 2: *The Cranium and Maxillary Dentition of* Australopithecus (Zinjanthropus) boisei. Cambridge: Cambridge University Press.

Ungar, P. (2004) Dental Topography and Diets of *Australopithecus afarensis* and Early *Homo*. *Journal of Human Evolution* 46: 605–622.

Vignaud, P., Duringer, P., Mackaye, H. T., Likius, A., Blondel, C., Boisserie, J.-R., de Bonis, L., Eisenmann, V., Etienne, M.E., Geraads, D., Guy, F., Lehman, T., Lihoreau, F., Lopez-Martinez, N., Mourer-Chauviré, C., Otero, O., Rage, J. C., Schuster, M., Viriot, L., Zazzo, A., and Brunet, M. (2002) Geology and Palaeontology of the Upper Miocene Toros-Menalla Hominid Locality, Chad. *Nature* 418: 152–155.

Vrba, E. S. (1995) On the Connections between Paleoclimate and Evolution. In E. S. Vrba, G. H. Denton, T. C. Partridge, and L. H. Burckle (eds), *Paleoclimate and Evolution with Emphasis on Human Origins* (pp. 24–45). New Haven: Yale University Press.

Walker, A., Leakey, R. E., Harris, J. M., and Brown, F. H. (1986) 2.5-Myr *Australopithecus boisei* from West of Lake Turkana, Kenya. *Nature* 322: 517–522.

Ward, C., Leakey, M. G., and Walker, A. (2001) Morphology of *Australopithecus anamensis* from Kanapoi and Allia Bay, Kenya. *Journal of Human Evolution* 41: 255–368.

Washburn, S. L. (1960) Tools and Human Evolution. *Scientific American* 253: 62–75.

Wheeler, P. E. (1984) The Evolution of Bipedality and Loss of Functional Body Hair in Humans. *Journal of Human Evolution* 13: 91–98.

White, T. D. (1995) African Omnivores: Global Climatic Change and Plio-Pleistocene Hominids and Suids. In E. S. Vrba, G. H. Denton, T. C. Partridge, and L. H. Burckle (eds), *Paleoclimate and Evolution with Emphasis on Human Origins* (pp. 369–385). New Haven: Yale University Press.

White, T. D. (2003) Early Hominids – Diversity or Distortion. *Science* 299: 1994–1997.

White, T. D. (2004) Managing Paleoanthropology's Nonrenewable Resources: A View from Afar. *Comptes Rendus Paleovol* 3: 339–349.

White, T. D. (2006) Early Hominid Femora: The Inside Story. *Comptes Rendus Paleovol* 5: 99–108.

White, T. D., Suwa, G., and Asfaw, B. (1994) *Australopithecus ramidus*, a New Species of Early Hominid from Aramis, Ethiopia. *Nature* 371: 306–312.

White, T. D., Suwa, G., and Asfaw, B. (1995) Corrigendum: *Australopithecus ramidus*, a New Species of Early Hominid from Aramis, Ethiopia. *Nature* 375: 88.

White, T. D., Suwa, G., Simpson, S. W., and Asfaw, B. (2000) Jaws and Teeth of *Australopithecus afarensis* from Maka, Middle Awash, Ethiopia. *American Journal of Physical Anthropology* 111: 45–68.

White, T. D., Asfaw, B., Beyene, Y., Haile-Selassie, Y., Lovejoy, C. O., Suwa, G., and Wolde-Gabriel, G. (2009) *Ardipithecus ramidus* and the Paleobiology of Early Hominids. *Science* 326: 75–86.

White, T.D., WoldeGabriel, G., Asfaw, B., Ambrose, S., Beyene, Y., Bernor, R. L., Boisserie, J.-R., Currie, B., Gilbert, H., Haile-Selassie, Y., Hart, W. K., Hlisko, L. J., Howell, F. C., Kono, R. T., Lehmann, T., Louchart, A., Lovejoy, C. O., Renne, P. R., Saegusa, H., Vrba, E. S., Wesselman, H., and Suwa, G. (2006) Asa Issie, Aramis and the Origin of *Australopithecus*. *Nature* 440: 883–889.

WoldeGabriel, G., White, T. D., Suwa, G., Renne, P., de Heinzelin, J., Hart, W. K., and Heiken, G. (1994) Ecological and Temporal Placement of Early Pliocene Hominids at Aramis, Ethiopia. *Nature* 371: 330–333.

WoldeGabriel, G., Haile-Selassie, Y., Renne, P. R., Hart, W. K., Ambrose, S. H., Asfaw, B., Heiken, G., and White, T. (2001) Geology and Palaeontology of the Late Miocene Middle Awash Valley, Afar Rift, Ethiopia. *Nature* 412: 175–178.

WoldeGabriel, G., Ambrose, S. A., Barboni, D., Bonnefille, R., Bremond, L., Currie, B., DeGusta, D., Hart, W. K., Murray, A. M., Renne, P. R., Jolly-Saad, M. C., Stewart, K. M., and White, T. D. (2009) The Geological, Isotopic, Botanical, Invertebrate, and Lower Vertebrate Surroundings of *Ardipithecus ramidus*. *Science* 326: 65e1–65e5.

Zazzo, A., Bocherens, H., Brunet, M., Beauvilain, A., Billiou, D., Taisso Mackaye, H., Vignaud, P., and Mariotti, A. (2000) Herbivore Paleodiet and Paleoenvironmental Changes in Chad during the Pliocene Using Stable Isotope Ratios of Tooth Enamel Carbonate. *Paleobiology* 26 (2): 294–309.

Zollikofer, C. P. E., Ponce de Leon, M. S., Lieberman, D. E., Guy, F., Pilbeam, D., Likius, A., Mackaye, H. T., Vignaud, P., and Brunet, M. (2005) Virtual Cranial Reconstruction of *Sahelanthropus tchadensis*. *Nature* 434: 755–759.

19 Origins, Evolution, and Dispersal of Early Members of the Genus *Homo*

G. Philip Rightmire

INTRODUCTION

Numerous discoveries have established that genus *Homo* has deep roots in Africa. Some of the earliest fossils differing from the australopiths appear in the Turkana Basin (northern Kenya) and in the Hadar region (Ethiopia) about 2.3 mya. On the basis of apparent brain expansion, rounding of the cranial vault, reduction of the masticatory complex, and narrowing of the premolar and molar teeth, a number of later specimens, both from Olduvai Gorge in Tanzania and from the Turkana localities, have been attributed to *Homo habilis*. Also, it has been argued that a second, larger-brained taxon is present in the record. Since the early 1990s, a subset of the East African remains has been set apart as *Homo rudolfensis*. An obvious problem is the scarcity of fossils that are reasonably complete and/or possess useful morphology. Especially in the case of *Homo rudolfensis*, for which there is a famous cranium (KNM-ER 1470) but no reliably associated postcranial bones, the sample size is small. Indeed it has been difficult to devise a solid basis for diagnosing one early species in relation to another. Whether one or two groups should be recognized, and whether they are sufficiently like later humans to merit placement within *Homo*, are questions on which there is no firm consensus.

   A third hominin is known from eastern and northwestern Africa, and probably from South Africa as well. Much information bearing on the origin and evolution of *Homo erectus* has been recovered at Olduvai Gorge and Koobi Fora in East Turkana. Also, a nearly complete subadult skeleton (KNM-WT 15000) from Nariokotome in West Turkana has provided insight into the growth and bodily form of one early member of this species. Recently there have been intriguing new finds from Ileret and Olorgesailie in Kenya and from Bouri (Daka) in Ethiopia. These crania confirm that some *Homo erectus* individuals are quite small (Potts et al. 2004; Spoor et al. 2007), and it is apparent that size variation within the African populations is substantial. The larger calvaria (that is, vault of the skull) from Daka shares numerous morphological features with that of *Homo erectus* from Java and China, supporting the view that the African and Far Eastern hominins belong to a single, widely dispersed paleospecies (Rightmire 1990; Asfaw et al. 2002; Antón 2003).

Additional fossils that can be grouped with *Homo erectus* come from the Georgian Caucasus. Since 1991, excavations at Dmanisi have produced crania, lower jaws with teeth, postcranial bones, and numerous crude stone artefacts. Studies of the sedimentary context in which the bones and the artefacts occur indicate that the material was sealed in the deposits over a brief interval about 1.77 mya (Lordkipanidze et al. 2007). Thus, in paleontological terms, the Dmanisi assemblage documents a single paleodeme (Howell 1999). It is important to point out that this situation is very rare. At Plio-Pleistocene sites such as Koobi Fora in Kenya or Sangiran in Java, the fossils are scattered through sediments accumulated over hundreds of thousands of years, and variation due to sampling from different time periods cannot be ignored. At Dmanisi, however, morphological differences among individuals can be attributed more confidently to intragroup variation.

Much has been said about the origins, diversification, and phyletic history of species within the *Homo* clade. The goal of this chapter is to highlight some of the main themes which have emerged and to note that key questions remain unresolved. It is helpful to reassess our understanding of earlier *Homo* in Africa in the light of recent finds from western Asia and the Far East. This exercise demonstrates that we know very little about sex dimorphism and other sources of variation in the most ancient populations. It is hardly surprising that experienced workers have not been able to agree on just where species boundaries lie. The extent to which the named taxa document distinct evolutionary lineages remains unclear. Also, there is doubt as to which of the early hominins may have evolved toward *Homo erectus*. The fossils from Dmanisi offer a fresh perspective in this regard.

EARLY *HOMO* IN AFRICA

The oldest fossils representative of *Homo* include a maxilla with teeth from Hadar, an isolated lower molar from West Turkana, and probably a mandible from Uraha in Malawi. While the well preserved Hadar specimen shares a number of derived traits with later hominins from Olduvai Gorge and Koobi Fora (Kimbel et al. 1997), the isolated molar and the damaged mandible are less informative. Because the evidence from morphology is sparse, it has been difficult to determine whether these fossils should be attributed to *Homo habilis* or whether they constitute early traces of *Homo rudolfensis*. Other specimens are not quite so ancient but are more complete. Several partial crania (OH 7, OH 13, OH 16, OH 24), lower jaws, limb, hand and foot

---

B   KNM-ER 3733, an early African *Homo erectus* from Koobi Fora. Cranial capacity is 848 cm³. The vault is relatively long and low, with projecting supraorbital tori and an angled occiput, while the nasal saddle is prominent

C   Sangiran 17 from Java. This large (male?) *Homo erectus* from southeast Asia has a brain volume of 1004 cm³, a thickened supraorbital region, an elongated cranium with an expanded nuchal plane, and massive facial bones

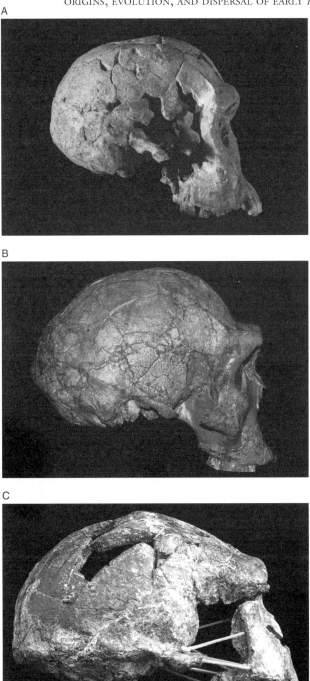

Figure 19.1   Lateral views of three of the most complete crania referred to *Homo habilis* and *Homo erectus*

A   KNM-ER 1813 from Koobi Fora. This gracile representative of *Homo habilis* has a brain volume of only 510 cm³, but it differs from australopiths in its rounded vault, less massive face, square upper molars, and generally smaller cheek teeth

bones, and portions of a small skeleton (OH 62) have been collected at Olduvai
Gorge, and there is a comparable assemblage from Koobi Fora. The latter includes
three rather complete crania (KNM-ER 1470, KNM-ER 1805, KNM-ER 1813),
several mandibles, and a highly fragmented skeleton (KNM-ER 3735). In the more
than four decades since *Homo habilis* was introduced by Leakey and colleagues (1964),
this material has been sorted in several different ways. A case can be made for lumping
all of the early *Homo* fossils together as a single, highly dimorphic species (Tobias
1991). However, there is substantial agreement that the resulting hypodigm displays
so much variation that partitioning is warranted. The fossils have been assigned to two
or more groups by a number of workers (Wood 1991; 1992; Rightmire 1993;
Blumenschine et al. 2003). The composition of these hypodigms has shifted, partly as
a consequence of the varying emphasis placed on characters such as brain size, facial
prognathism, and dental root morphology. Interestingly, it is OH 7 (the type specimen of *Homo habilis*) that has several times been transferred between a group composed of relatively small crania and a larger-brained hypodigm, best documented by
KNM-ER 1470. As a result of this uncertainty regarding OH 7, the name *Homo
habilis* has in the past been associated with rather different sets of fossils. Following
Wood (1992), OH 7 is here placed with the other Olduvai fossils (now including the
OH 65 maxilla), along with gracile individuals (such as KNM-ER 1813) from Koobi
Fora (Figure 19.1).

In this restricted sense, *Homo habilis* can be characterized as having a mean endocranial capacity of about 610 cm³, thin vault bones, a forwardly placed *foramen magnum*,
nasal bones that widen inferiorly, a relatively narrow midface with a near-vertical
infraorbital (malar) region, and overall reduction of tooth size in comparison to australopiths (Wood 1991). Postcranial bones thought to belong with this hypodigm
show adaptations for bipedal locomotion. The OH 8 foot has a human-like metatarsal
robusticity pattern, and there is convincing evidence that the first metatarsal was
adducted, even if the foot retained a degree of grasping ability (Aiello and Dean
1990). However, the presence of a longitudinal arch cannot be confirmed, and the
OH 8 talus differs in key features from the human pattern (Lewis 1989). The argument for bipedalism is strengthened if the OH 8 fossils are paired with the OH 35
tibia and fibula, as proposed by Susman and Stern (1982). This association is supported by taphonomic evidence, although there are indications that the distal articular surface of the tibia may not conform to the talar trochlea (Aiello et al. 1998).
There is also a question as to whether OH 8 and OH 35 are sampled from stratigraphic levels of the same age (Susman 2008). Comparison with the limb bones shows
the foot to be relatively short, as in modern humans, rather than elongated, as in apes.
Unfortunately the more complete but damaged skeleton of OH 62 is of only limited
utility. A preliminary estimate for the humero-femoral index suggests primitive proportions and a robust arm (Johanson et al. 1987), but later studies of OH 62 and
KNM-ER 3735 conclude that *Homo habilis* probably possessed a hindlimb which was
long relative to that of australopiths (Haeusler and McHenry 2004).

Homo rudolfensis is documented principally by fossils from Koobi Fora. Because it
is the most complete cranium in the hypodigm, KNM-ER 1470 has routinely been
emphasized in published descriptions of the species. This practice has perhaps exaggerated the impression that *Homo rudolfensis* is big-brained in relation to *Homo
habilis*. In fact KNM-ER 1470 is the sole individual for which brain volume (750 cm³)

can be measured reliably. The KNM-ER 3732 cranium retains facial parts along with the frontal and parietal bones, and a partial endocast. This material provides only a general indication of brain size. Both of the Koobi Fora specimens show that the facial skeleton is markedly orthognathic, with a massive, anteriorly inclined infraorbital surface (Wood 1991). KNM-ER 1470 also exhibits a flattening of the maxillary clivus below the nose. Here the facial morphology contrasts with that found in *Homo habilis*, where there is greater subnasal projection. This difference is unlikely to reflect sex dimorphism, as it is just the reverse of the condition observed in living hominoid primates, where (smaller) females tend to have flatter lower faces than the (larger) more prognathic males.

No tooth crowns are preserved for KNM-ER 1470. The anterior and posterior permanent teeth associated with a damaged juvenile cranium (KNM-ER 1590), presumed to belong to the same species, are very large; but there is otherwise little information relating to the upper dentition of *Homo rudolfensis*. Mandibles are somewhat more plentiful, as there are five specimens from Koobi Fora. Several are fragmentary, but KNM-ER 1802 is reasonably complete, showing marked relief on the external corpus and eversion of the base. A robust mandible (UR 501) from Uraha does not display either of these traits, and it carries premolars and molars with large crown areas. Thus it is mainly on the evidence of premolar crown shape (relatively broad) and premolar root morphology (plate-like) that UR 501 has been assigned to *Homo rudolfensis* (Bromage et al. 1995; Schrenk et al. 2007).

Postcranial specimens that have frequently been linked with *Homo rudolfensis* include a pelvic bone, femora, and several other limb elements. The fossils are indeed *Homo*-like in their anatomy, rather than similar to known australopiths. However, they were not found with skulls or with diagnostic dental remains. It is not certain that any of this postcranial material belongs with *Homo rudolfensis*, and the pelvis and/or the femora may actually be drawn from populations of *Homo erectus*. Given this lack of associated limbs, there are no solid estimates for body size or proportions, and only few clues concerning the locomotor capabilities of *Homo rudolfensis*.

When all of the early African specimens are considered, it is apparent that there are important differences from the australopiths. At the same time, *Homo habilis* and *Homo rudolfensis* do not possess many derived characters of the skull and postcranial skeleton that are known to have evolved in *Homo erectus* and later humans. This raises a question concerning the classification of these hominins within our genus, as this was advocated by Leakey and colleagues (1964) and accepted by most subsequent workers. Wood and Collard (1999) have noted that neither *Homo habilis* nor *Homo rudolfensis* seems to meet the criteria for membership in *Homo*, when the genus is defined as a monophyletic group whose members (species) share a single adaptive zone. In support of their view, Wood and Collard argue that the two species are not demonstrably more similar to humans than to australopiths in traits such as body mass and limb proportions, relative size of the teeth and jaws, diet, and life history. Controversy over definitions of the genus category will probably continue. Also, the evidence bearing on several of the functional and behavioral attributes (locomotion, developmental schedules, and life history) discussed by Wood and Collard is sparse and simply not adequate at present. Under these circumstances, many paleoanthropologists will be reluctant to remove the Olduvai and Koobi Fora fossils from the hypodigm of *Homo*.

If caveats of this nature are set aside, it is possible to compile a list of features that characterize emerging *Homo*. Such definitions of our genus have been formulated before, by Le Gros Clark (1964), Leakey and colleagues (1964), Howell (1978), and others, including Wood and Collard (1999). Here anatomical observations that can be made directly on the fossils are emphasized, without inferences as to diet, behavior, or life history. The list is relatively brief, as it omits features (a bony chin, reduced canine size) included in some earlier definitions that have proved to be uninformative.

One character that distinguishes *Homo* from the australopiths is brain size. Several of the Olduvai and Koobi Fora crania have capacities in the $600 \, cm^3$ to $700 \, cm^3$ range. Coupled with the (limited) postcranial evidence suggesting that individuals referred to the species *Homo habilis* are small and lightly built, this information makes it likely that encephalization (brain size relative to body mass) was increased in comparison to that of other ancient hominins. The cranium displays reduced parietal curvature and a large occipital angle, which reflects greater rounding of the posterior vault. The facial skeleton, and particularly its masticatory components (the zygomaxillary region and the mandible), are smaller than in species of *Australopithecus*. In anterior view, the maxillary walls appear to be vertical and do not taper superomedially. This gives the maxilla a 'squared off' appearance, different from the triangular outline seen in *Australopithecus afarensis* or in *Australopithecus africanus* (Kimbel et al. 1997). The floor of the nose (nasal sill) is platform-like, and there may be transverse (lateral or spinal) crests. The sill is set at a nearly acute angle to the subnasal part of the maxilla. Below the nasal aperture, the facial contour is flattened from side to side, and there is less projection than in other groups. The palate is relatively broad. Other distinguishing characters appear in the dentition. The M^1 crown is square in shape (length/width index of about 1.0) rather than buccolingually broad, as in *Australopithecus* (where the length/width index is reduced). In M^2 the mesial (anterior) cusps dominate the distal (posterior) cusps, and the paracone bulges buccally relative to the metacone, giving the tooth an asymmetric (rhomboidal) outline (Brown and Walker 1993; Kimbel et al. 1996). M_1 is buccolingually narrow in relation to its length (Tobias 1991). Given the obvious problems encountered in interpreting the significance of the few postcranial remains associated (more or less securely) with early *Homo* at Olduvai and Koobi Fora, anatomy of the limbs, hand, and foot cannot be emphasized in any definition. However, it is evident that *Homo habilis* was capable of bipedal locomotion, even if this creature continued to engage in some climbing in the trees.

HOMO ERECTUS IN AFRICA AND THE FAR EAST

Homo erectus is well represented in Africa, but the first fossils attributable to this species were found in Java. The discoverer was the young Dutch anatomist Eugene Dubois, who sailed to the East Indies to search for the missing link. Just a few months after starting to excavate at Trinil in 1891, Dubois's workers came across a skullcap, and later across a complete femur. These fossils established *Pithecanthropus* (now *Homo*) *erectus* as a rather small-brained but erect biped whoseemed to be intermediate between apes and humans. Over the last century, many more fossils have been added to this inventory. Along with the original skullcap from Trinil, there are numerous partially complete crania and mandibles from the Sangiran region (see Table 19.1).

Table 19.1 Localities yielding more complete and/or well preserved fossils attributed to *Homo erectus*[a]

	Crania	*Mandibles*	*Postcranial bones*
Southeast Asia			
Trinil	Trinil 2		Femur, femoral fragments
Sangiran	Sangiran 2, 4, 10, 12, 17, 27, Skull IX	Sangiran 1b, 5, 6, 8, 9, 22	Femora
Ngandong	Ngandong 1, 3, 6, 7, 10, 11, 12		Tibia A, tibia B
Sambungmacan	Sambungmacan 1, 3, 4		Tibia
Ngawi	Ngawi 1		
Mojokerto	Perning 1		
China			
Zhoukoudian	Skulls II, III, V, X, XI, XII	A II, B I, G I, H I, H IV, K I, M II, PA 86	Clavicle, humeri, femora, and a tibia
Gongwangling	PA 1051–6		
Chenjiawo		PA 102	
Hexian	PA 830		
Tangshan	Nanjing 1, 2		
Western Asia			
Dmanisi	D2280, D2282, D2700, D3444	D211, D2600, D2735, D3900	Vertebrae, ribs, clavicles, a scapula, humeri, femora, a tibia, and foot bones of several individuals
North Africa			
Ternifine		Ternifine 1, 2, 3	
Eastern Africa			
Koobi Fora and Ileret	KNM-ER 3733, 3883, 42700	KNM-ER 730, 820, 992	Femora, tibia, talus, partial skeletons (2)
Nariokotome	KNM-WT 15000A	KNM-WT 15000B	Skeleton
Olorgesailie	KNM-OL 45500		
Olduvai Gorge	OH 9, OH 12	OH 22, OH 23, OH 51	Pelvic bone, femur
Konso		KGA10–1	
Bouri	BOU-VP-2/66		
Gona			Vertebra, pelvis
Buia	UA-31		Pelvic bone
South Africa			
Swartkrans		SK 15	

[a] Table compiled by author. Listing is incomplete, in that many fragmentary specimens are omitted, as are isolated teeth. Fossils of uncertain taxonomic status (e.g. the SK 847 partial cranium) are not included.

Other important localities include Ngawi, Ngandong, Sambungmacan, and Mojokerto (Perning) in Java. As is well known, excavations conducted in the 1920s and 1930s at Zhoukoudian in China yielded an assemblage of well preserved fossils, nearly all of which were subsequently lost. Fortunately, Franz Weidenreich's monographs, photographs, and carefully made casts provide a very complete record of these important relics. Additional *Homo erectus* skull parts are known from Gongwangling, Chenjiawo, Hexian, and Tangshan (Nanjing) in China. In Africa, this species has been unearthed at Ternifine (Tighenif) near the Mediterranean coast of Algeria, at Swartkrans in South Africa, and at Olduvai Gorge. Specimens from Koobi Fora include a fine cranium (KNM-ER 3733), several incomplete vaults, mandibles, isolated post-cranial bones, and two partial skeletons. At Nariokotome, most of a young male skeleton (KNM-WT 15000) was excavated in the 1980s. More recently, fossils have been collected at Olorgesailie, Konso (southern Ethiopia), and Bouri (Daka).

Compared to that of earlier hominins, the braincase of *Homo erectus* is enlarged (Figure 19.1). Cranial capacities range from 600 cm³ to over 1200 cm³, and the average is about 970 cm³. The skull is relatively long and low in contour, with pronounced postorbital narrowing, a short parietal arc, and an angled (flexed) occipital. The supraorbital torus is projecting and thickened, a midline keel is often present, and crests in the mastoid region are well developed. The nuchal plane tends to be expanded in relation to the occipital upper scale. An occipital transverse torus is variably expressed, but it is usually prominent in larger individuals. The cranial base and mandibular fossa exhibit a number of (primitive?) features shared with *Homo habilis*, along with some aspects of tympanic plate and petrous temporal morphology that appear to be specialized. The facial skeleton is relatively massive, broad in its upper portion, and set forward from the anterior cranial fossa. The *Homo erectus* nasal and alveolar regions exhibit significant prognathism. The nasal aperture is wider than in *Homo habilis*, and the nasal saddle tends to be more prominent. Mandibles are similar in proportions to those of some *Homo habilis* specimens (for instance OH 13), but the corpus is less thickened than in KNM-ER 1802 or UR 501. The symphyseal profile is receding, and there is never much indication of a bony chin. Whether measured in absolute terms (crown surface area) or in relation to estimated body mass (megadontia), postcanine tooth size is reduced in *Homo erectus* (McHenry and Coffing 2000).

Estimates for stature, weight, and various limb indices are available for KNM-WT 15000; this individual is quite tall and linear, with a relatively small bi-iliac (hip) diameter and long legs. Overall, the boy is built like modern humans adapted to tropical environments (Ruff and Walker 1993). Given its probable age of just eight or nine years at death, the Nariokotome skeleton is surprisingly large in comparison to most other conspecific individuals from Koobi Fora and Olduvai. Nevertheless, it is apparent that average body mass for *Homo erectus* is greater than that of *Homo habilis* or of the australopiths. It has been argued that this increase reflects a change in diet. Apart from foraging for plants and fruit, *Homo erectus* probably consumed more meat and bone marrow. Such high protein foods and fat would have facilitated the production of a larger, and hence energetically more 'expensive,' brain (Aiello and Wheeler 1995). Also, bodily proportions and other musculo-skeletal specializations can be interpreted to show that *Homo erectus* was capable of endurance running. The ability to run over long distances at a moderate pace and without tiring is a human trait, and such endurance would have been advantageous to earlier hominins. For example, *Homo erectus* might have been able to reach animal carcasses (fresh kills) and to obtain meat by scavenging in advance of other predators (Bramble and Lieberman 2004).

Another discovery bearing on the bodily form of *Homo erectus* has been reported recently from Ethiopia. Pieces of a pelvis have been collected from deposits at Gona that are probably close to 1.0 million years in age (Simpson et al. 2008). The new specimen is attributed to *Homo erectus* on the basis of morphology, and also because no other hominin species have been found at Gona in this time period. However, the postcranial material is not associated with a skull or with dental remains, and there remains a possibility that it documents another taxon. The pelvis is remarkably complete, and it differs in anatomically important ways from that of KNM-WT 15000. Apparently female, the pelvis is relatively small but broad transversely, with a large bi-iliac diameter. The iliac blades flare outward, as is true for australopiths. The acetabulum is smaller than in other early Pleistocene specimens, indicating that stature must be much reduced in comparison to that of the Nariokotome boy, who was about 1.57 m tall when he died (Ruff 2007). However, the birth canal is spacious and probably capable of passing an infant with a neonatal brain of a size intermediate between that of chimpanzees and that of recent humans. If the new pelvis is indeed that of a *Homo erectus* female, then the marked contrasts with KNM-WT 15000 indicate a high level of sex dimorphism in this species.

The fossils from Gona and Nariokotome, along with skulls and teeth of juvenile individuals from Asia, provide clues as to development and reproductive strategies of *Homo erectus*. This species almost certainly differs from modern humans by having a somewhat accelerated life history profile (Smith 1993; Dean et al. 2001; Dean 2006). This implies alterations in the growth process. For example, the *Homo erectus* brain may have matured over a relatively short time period, as is true of apes (Coqueugniot et al. 2004; Hublin and Coqueugniot 2006; but see also Leigh 2006; DeSilva and Lesnik 2006). Supraorbital tori, which are so prominent in this species, must have begun to enlarge early in ontogeny, before the cessation of brain growth. Even in the infant cranium from Mojokerto (Java), a small but clearly defined browridge is developed. Also, the *Homo erectus* vault must have expanded posteriorly to a degree not seen in recent humans. This extra growth would help to produce the low neurocranial profile and elongated occiput that are characteristic of the species.

Although *Homo erectus* may have grown up rapidly in comparison to recent humans, this species was probably already slowing its life history relative to earlier *Homo* and the australopiths. The Gona pelvis suggests that the *Homo erectus* fetal brain grew at a rate approaching that of modern babies, while children matured at a rate intermediate between that of apes and humans (Simpson et al. 2008). If childhood were extended by comparison to the australopith condition, then it would be possible to build a larger and metabolically more expensive brain. The high costs of brain growth may thus have led to a lengthening of the interval prior to a mother's first reproduction. In general, it can be stated that the evolution of a prolonged life history is tied to increased encephalization (Barrickman et al. 2008). Adjustments foreshadowing the modern pattern seem to have begun with *Homo erectus*, but these changes were not completed until later, perhaps with the advent of *Homo sapiens* about 200,000 years ago.

DISCOVERIES AT DMANISI

Outside of Africa and of the Far East, ancient *Homo* is increasingly well documented at Dmanisi, in the Georgian Caucasus. Radiometric and biochronological evidence shows that the West Asian population is broadly coeval with both *Homo habilis* and

Homo erectus in East Africa. The very complete crania, entire mandibles, and teeth from Dmanisi are clearly representative of genus *Homo*. Five individuals can be identified. One skull (D2700/D2735) is subadult, while another (D3444/D3900), displaying severe resorption of the alveolar processes and retaining only a single (lower) tooth at death, is probably an older adult. There is considerable variation in morphology within the Dmanisi assemblage. Indeed differences among the specimens have led some workers to claim that multiple species may be documented (Schwartz and Tattersall 2003), or that size variation exceeds the level expected for populations belonging to genus *Homo* (Skinner et al. 2006).

Capacities obtained for four of the Dmanisi crania range from 600 cm³ to 775 cm³. In order to draw comparisons with other samples, it is appropriate to employ a measure of relative variation. A size-independent statistic that has been demonstrated to be useful in paleontological situations is the coefficient of variation (CV). Where the number of individuals is small, the CV may be modified as $(1 + 1/4\,N) \times (100s/\overline{X})$, following Sokal and Braumann (1980). The resulting unbiased statistic is V*. For endocranial volume, V* is 12.3 at Dmanisi, 13.0 for a sample of six *Homo habilis* and *Homo rudolfensis* individuals (Tobias 1991), and 14.1 for 32 *Homo erectus* specimens (Rightmire 2004). The CV is about 12 to 15 for modern humans. Here there is no indication that variation within the Dmanisi paleodeme is excessive in relation to that found in other hominins. The same conclusion has been reached in a resampling study, which shows sex dimorphism to be a sufficient explanation for brain size differences in the Caucasus population (Lee 2005).

Certain linear dimensions of the braincase do appear to be more variable at Dmanisi than in other groups. V*s for cranial length, for maximum frontal breadth, and for the parietal arc approach values calculated for a much larger sample of African and Asian *Homo erectus* and are greater than in recent *Homo sapiens*. Facial traits exhibiting substantial variation are supraorbital torus thickness and cheek height. Both of these measurements also show high intragroup variability in other ancient *Homo* taxa. This is predictable, given the finding that facial structures subject to high magnitudes of mechanical strain tend to be more variable than the neurocranium and the skull base (Wood and Lieberman 2001). Indeed, cheek height is particularly variable in recent humans.

Several complete mandibles have been recovered at Dmanisi, and one of them (D2600) is quite large. This individual has been described as possessing a novel combination of features, not observed in *Homo rudolfensis*, *Homo habilis*, or *Homo erectus* (Gabunia et al. 2002). However, D2600 presents obvious signs of periodontal disease, and this has affected the original morphology. Corpus size alone does not preclude placing D2600 with the other Dmanisi jaws. Bootstrap analyses of mandibular measurements indicate that size differences at Dmanisi may be large by modern human and chimpanzee standards, but not significantly greater than in other ape reference groups (Rightmire et al. 2008).

Information accumulating to date does not support a hypothesis to the effect that two species are present in the Dmanisi deposits. Neither the cranial volume nor the dimensions of the face exceed the amount of intraspecies variation expected on the basis of appropriate comparisons. Indeed, anatomical studies suggest that the Dmanisi skulls share a common bauplan and can be accommodated in one taxon (Lordkipanidze et al. 2006; Rightmire et al. 2006). In some respects, this assemblage resembles *Homo habilis*.

The supraorbital tori are well defined but not greatly thickened, and there is very marked postorbital constriction. The mastoid region is inflated and laterally projecting. There may be little or no expression of a transverse torus on the occiput. Also, D2700 displays orbital proportions, nasal bone shape, a midfacial profile, and a forward sloping maxillary clivus, similar to the condition found in KNM-ER 1813. However, many of the resemblances to *Homo habilis* appear to be either related to size, or primitive in the sense that they are common not only to earlier *Homo* but also to species of *Australopithecus* and/or extant apes. By themselves, these characters do not support (or rule out) a close link to the hypodigm containing KNM-ER 1813 and OH 13.

The Dmanisi skulls share many traits with *Homo erectus*. These include low cranial profile, flattened frontal, sagittal keeling, reduced width of the parietal vault in relation to the cranial base, cresting in the mastoid region, shape of the low temporal squama, angled occiput (D2280, D3444), depth and architecture of the mandibular fossa, and orientation of the petrous axis. In the elevation of the nasal saddle and lack of surface relief on the nasal sill, the facial skeleton is also like that of *Homo erectus*. Additional similarities include the shape of the mandibular corpus and the occurrence of multiple mental foramina (in D211 and D2600). Most measurements of tooth size place the Dmanisi hominins within the range observed for *Homo erectus*. While some of these characters are distributed widely in other taxa and thus have descriptive value only, other traits are more clearly diagnostic for African or Asian *Homo erectus*. When this evidence from skulls and teeth is weighed carefully, it is reasonable to place the Dmanisi population with *Homo erectus*.

Along with craniodental remains, the site at Dmanisi has produced a number of postcranial bones. Two broken humeri are subadult and most probably belong with the D2700/D2735 skull. Additional specimens are fully adult and probably associated with (at least two of) the other crania. One set of remains includes a femur, a patella, and a tibia, along with a talus. The lower limb is thus remarkably complete. On the basis of femoral head diameter and tibial length, it can be estimated that this Dmanisi individual would have had a body mass of slightly more than 50 kg and a stature close to 1.40 m (Lordkipanidze et al. 2007). Here there is a marked contrast to the Nariokotome individual, who was considerably taller even as a boy. Despite small body size, the Dmanisi hominins must have been habitual bipeds. Leg length relative to body mass is closer to that of KNM-WT 15000 (and *Homo sapiens*) than to australopiths. Also, the morphology of several adult and subadult metatarsals is consistent with a fully adducted great toe and with the presence of transverse and longitudinal arches in the foot (Pontzer, personal communication). These structural features suggest efficient striding on the ground.

QUESTIONS CONCERNING THE ORIGINS OF *HOMO ERECTUS*

There remains the question of how the Dmanisi paleodeme is related to African and Asian populations of *Homo erectus*. Certainly there is an overall resemblance to the skulls from Koobi Fora, but there are also differences. The latter are partly related to size, but they include aspects of vault shape and facial morphology. Similarities to fossils from Sangiran are less numerous. Also, the Caucasus population presents a few characters that appear to be unique (Rightmire et al. 2006). These findings are in accord with the view that *Homo erectus* is a geographically dispersed, polytypic species. One hypothesis that has been widely favored holds this species to have originated in eastern Africa. According to this thinking, a population of *Homo habilis* or *Homo rudolfensis* individuals gave rise to *Homo erectus*, as suggested by the time-stratigraphic sequences at Olduvai Gorge and in the Turkana Basin. Groups of *Homo erectus* individuals then ventured out of Africa, leaving abundant traces of their passing in the Jordan Valley, and to the north, in the Georgian Caucasus. From sites such as Dmanisi, the hominins could have spread westward into Europe, and also across southern Asia, to the Far East. This scenario implies that differences between African *Homo erectus* and the Dmanisi fossils reflect geographic distance, adaptation to new environments in western Asia, or drift within small isolated populations.

Problems with such an 'African origins' hypothesis have been noted, and it is increasingly clear that alternatives must be explored (Dennell and Roebroeks 2005). As has been emphasized, the Georgian crania are small and lack strong crests or tori. There are numerous resemblances to *Homo habilis* from East Africa. Skulls presently included within this latter hypodigm constitute plausible structural antecedents to *Homo erectus* (Lieberman et al. 1996; Strait et al. 1997; Kimbel et al. 2004). Therefore it can be argued that a population composed of such small-brained and lightly built individuals is ancestral to the Dmanisi hominins. On this view, early (pre-*erectus*) *Homo* dispersed from Africa into western Asia, sometime prior to 1.8 mya. There is at present little hard evidence to support such a claim, as fossils and stone artefacts of the requisite age have not yet been documented unequivocally in the Levant or in Arabia. Nevertheless, a *habilis*-like founding population could later have evolved the anatomical bauplan seen at Dmanisi.

This 'Asian origins' hypothesis fits comfortably within the constraints imposed by geochronology. Dates for Koobi Fora (Feibel et al. 1989; Gathogo and Brown 2006) allow the possibility that *Homo erectus*, having evolved in western Eurasia, returned to Africa, where the species is sampled in the Turkana Basin, at Olduvai Gorge, Konso, and Bouri (Daka). It is reasonable to suppose that the Dmanisi paleodeme is also related to populations of the Far East. Dates emerging from fieldwork at Sangiran and in the Nihewan Basin of northern China show that these areas were inhabited from 1.7 to 1.6 mya, by hominins who must have moved through the southern parts of Asia (Swisher et al. 1998; Larick et al. 2001; Zhu et al. 2004). Here caution is appropriate, however. While there is clear evidence for human presence at Dmanisi about 1.8 mya, there is no certainty that people managed to colonize this region on a long-term basis. Indeed it seems likely that many of the earliest dispersals eastward into Asia resulted in occupations that were ephemeral, and the early Pleistocene record does not document any continuity of populations through southern Asia to the Far East (Dennell 2003).

SPECIATION IN THE MIDDLE PLEISTOCENE?

After dispersing across much of the Old World, *Homo erectus* persisted longer in some geographic areas than in others. At Zhoukoudian, and perhaps in other localities in China, the species seems to have survived until about 300,000 years ago. Dates from Ngandong and Sambungmacan in Java are considerably more recent (Yokoyama et al.

2008). The pattern documented for the Far East contrasts with that found in Africa, where *Homo erectus* disappears from the record at a relatively early date. This suggests that a western branch of the species may have given rise to later people, and it is in Europe and Africa that more advanced hominins make their first appearance. Crania from Middle Pleistocene sites such as Bodo in Ethiopia, Broken Hill (Kabwe) in Zambia, Petralona in Greece, Arago Cave in France, and Sima de los Huesos in Spain have capacities of 1,100 cm³ or greater. Changes in the form of the braincase, and some facial traits, provide a basis for recognizing these middle Pleistocene assemblages as representative of species which are distinct from *Homo erectus*.

On one reading of this evidence, at least two lineages are identified. A European branch including the Neandertals can be traced back to Sima de los Huesos, and thus nearly to the base of the middle Pleistocene. A second lineage is deeply rooted in Africa. Some members of this group exhibit morphology that is archaic, but nevertheless suggestive of a link with anatomically modern humans. There is also an alternative perspective, holding that morphological differences among the most ancient European and African specimens are minor and can be attributed to geography and intragroup variation. The very complete Petralona cranium, for example, is demonstrably similar to the Broken Hill one, both in overall form and in a number of discrete traits. Here it is argued that many of the fossils should be placed together in one geographically dispersed taxon, named *H. heidelbergensis*. This species is considered to be ancestral both to the Neandertals in Europe and to the earliest populations of *Homo sapiens* in Africa. Questions concerning the evolution of our own species are explored further in Fred Smith's chapter in the present volume.

ACKNOWLEDGMENTS

Colleagues at numerous museums and universities have allowed me access to *Homo* fossils in their care, and I am very grateful for this help. The students and professionals who have joined in the excavations and worked in the laboratory at Dmanisi also deserve thanks. I am indebted particularly to David Lordkipanidze for his support at the Georgian National Museum. The Leakey Foundation, the American Philosophical Society, and the National Science Foundation have funded much of the research on which this chapter is based.

REFERENCES

Aiello, L. C., and Dean, M. C. (1990) *An Introduction to Human Evolutionary Anatomy*. London: Academic Press.

Aiello, L.C., and Wheeler, P. (1995) The Expensive Tissue Hypothesis: The Brain and Digestive System in Human and Primate Evolution. *Current Anthropology* 36: 199–221.

Aiello, L. C., Wood, B., Key, C., and Wood, C. (1998) Laser Scanning and Paleoanthropology: An Example from Olduvai Gorge, Tanzania. In E. Strasser, J. Fleagle, A. Rosenberger, and H. McHenry (eds), *Primate Locomotion: Recent Advances* (pp. 223–236). New York: Plenum Press.

Antón, S. (2003) Natural History of *Homo erectus*. *Yearbook of Physical Anthropology* 46: 126–170.

Asfaw, B., Gilbert, W. H., Beyene, Y., Hart, W. K., Renne, P. R., WoldeGabriel, G., Vrba, E., and White, T. D. (2002) Remains of *Homo erectus* from Bouri, Middle Awash, Ethiopia. *Nature* 416: 317–320.

Barrickman, N. L., Bastian, M. L., Isler, K., and van Schaik, C. P. (2008) Life History Costs and Benefits of Encephalization: A Comparative Test Using Data from Long-Term Studies of Primates in the Wild. *Journal of Human Evolution* 54: 568–590.

Blumenschine, R. J., Peters, C. R., Masao, F. T., Clarke, R. J., Deino, A. L., Hay, R. L., Swisher, C. C., Stanistreet, I. G., Ashley, G. M., McHenry, L. J., Sikes, N. E., van der Merwe, N. J., Tactikos, J. C., Cushing, A. E., Deocampo, D. M., Njau, J. K., and Ebert, J. I. (2003) Late Pliocene *Homo* and Hominid Land Use from Western Olduvai Gorge, Tanzania. *Science* 299: 1217–1221.

Bramble, D. M., and Lieberman, D. E. (2004) Endurance Running and the Evolution of *Homo*. *Nature* 432: 345–352.

Bromage, T. G., Schrenk, F., and Zonnefeld, F. W. (1995) Paleoanthropology of the Malawi Rift: An Early Hominid Mandible from the Chiwondo Beds, Northern Malawi. *Journal of Human Evolution* 28: 71–108.

Brown, B., and Walker, A. (1993) The Dentition. In A. Walker and R. Leakey (eds), *The Nariokotome* Homo erectus *Skeleton* (pp. 161–192). Cambridge: Harvard University Press.

Coqueugniot, H., Hublin, J. J., Veillon, F., Houët, F., and Jacob, T. (2004) Early Brain Growth in *Homo erectus* and Implications for Cognitive Ability. *Nature* 431: 299–302.

Dean, M. C. (2006) Tooth Microstructure Tracks the Pace of Human Life-History Evolution. *Proceedings of the Royal Society* B 273: 2799–2808.

Dean, M. C., Leakey, M. G., Reid, D. J., Schrenk, F., Schwartz, G. T., Stringer, C., and Walker, A. (2001) Growth Processes in Teeth Distinguish Modern Humans from *Homo erectus* and Earlier Hominins. *Nature* 414: 628–631.

Dennell, R. (2003) Dispersal and Colonization, Long and Short Chronologies: How Continuous is the Early Pleistocene Record for Hominids Outside East Africa? *Journal of Human Evolution* 45: 421–440.

Dennell, R., and Roebroeks, W. (2005) An Asian Perspective on Early Human Dispersal from Africa. *Nature* 438: 1099–1104.

DeSilva, J., and Lesnik, J. (2006) Chimpanzee Neonatal Brain Size: Implications for Brain Growth in *Homo erectus*. *Journal of Human Evolution* 51: 207–212.

Feibel, C. S., Brown, F. H., and McDougall, I. (1989) Stratigraphic Context of Fossil Hominids from the Omo Group Deposits, Northern Turkana Basin, Kenya and Ethiopia. *American Journal of Physical Anthropology* 78: 595–622.

Gabunia, L., de Lumley, M. A., Vekua, A., Lordkipanidze, D., and de Lumley, H. (2002) Découverte d'un nouvel hominidé a Dmanissi (Transcaucasie, Géorgie). *Comptes Rendus Palevol* 1: 243–253.

Gathogo, P. N., and Brown, F. H. (2006) Revised Stratigraphy of Area 123, Koobi Fora, Kenya, and New Age Estimates of its Fossil Mammals, Including Hominins. *Journal of Human Evolution* 51: 472–479.

Haeusler, M., and McHenry, H. M. (2004) Body Proportions of *Homo habilis* Reviewed. *Journal of Human Evolution* 46: 433–465.

Howell, F. C. (1978) Hominidae. In V. J. Maglio and H. B. S. Cooke (eds), *Evolution of African Mammals* (pp. 154–248). Cambridge MA: Harvard University Press.

Howell, F. C. (1999) Paleo-Demes, Species Clades, and Extinctions in the Pleistocene Hominin Record. *Journal of Anthropological Research* 55: 191–243.

Hublin, J. J., and Coqueugniot, H. (2006) Absolute or Proportional Brain Size: That Is the Question. A Reply to Leigh's (2006) Comments. *Journal of Human Evolution* 50: 109–113.

Johanson, D. C., Masao, F. T., Eck, G. G., White, T. D., Walter, R. C., Kimbel, W. H., Asfaw, B., Manega, P., Ndessokia, P., and Suwa, G. (1987) New Partial Skeleton of *Homo habilis* from Olduvai Gorge, Tanzania. *Nature* 327: 205–209.

Kimbel, W. H., Johanson, D. C., and Rak, Y. (1997) Systematic Assessment of a Maxilla of *Homo* from Hadar, Ethiopia. *American Journal of Physical Anthropology* 103: 235–262.

Kimbel, W. H., Rak, Y., and Johanson, D. C. (2004) *The Skull of* Australopithecus afarensis. Oxford: Oxford University Press.

Kimbel, W. H., Walter, R. C., Johanson, D. C., Reed, K. E., Aronson, J. L., Assefa, Z., Marean, C. W., Eck, G. G., Bobe, R., Hovers, E., Rak, Y., Vondra, C., Yemane, T., York, D., Chen, Y., Evensen, N. M., and Smith, P. E. (1996) Late Pliocene *Homo* and Oldowan Tools from the Hadar Formation (Kada Hadar Member), Ethiopia. *Journal of Human Evolution* 31: 549–561.

Larick, R., Ciochon, R. L., Zaim, Y., Sudijono, Suminto, Rizal, Y., Aziz, F., Reagan, M., and Heizler, M. (2001) Early Pleistocene ^{40}Ar/^{39}Ar Ages for Bapang Formation Hominins, Central Jawa, Indonesia. *Proceedings of the National Academy of Sciences, USA* 98: 4866–4871.

Leakey, L. S. B., Tobias, P. V., and Napier, J. R. (1964) A New Species of the Genus *Homo* from Olduvai Gorge. *Nature* 202: 7–9.

Lee, S. H. (2005) Is Variation in the Cranial Capacity of the Dmanisi Sample Too High to Be from a Single Species? *American Journal of Physical Anthropology* 127: 263–266.

Le Gros Clark, W. E. (1964) *The Fossil Evidence for Human Evolution*. Chicago: University of Chicago Press.

Leigh, S. R. (2006) Brain Ontogeny and Life History in *Homo erectus*. *Journal of Human Evolution* 50: 104–108.

Lewis, O. J. (1989) *Functional Morphology of the Evolving Hand and Foot*. Oxford: Oxford University Press.

Lieberman, D. E., Wood, B. A., and Pilbeam, D. R. (1996) Homoplasy and Early *Homo*: An Analysis of the Evolutionary Relationships of *Homo habilis sensu stricto* and *H. rudolfensis*. *Journal of Human Evolution* 30: 97–120.

Lordkipanidze, D., Jashashvili, T., Vekua, A., Ponce de Leon, M. S., Zollikofer, C. P. E., Rightmire, G. P., Pontzer, H., Ferring, R., Oms, O., Tappen, M., Bukhsianidze, M., Agusti, J., Kahlke, R., Kiladze, G., Martinez-Navarro, B., Mouskhelishvili, A., Nioradze, M., and Rook, L. (2007) Postcranial Evidence from Early *Homo* from Dmanisi, Georgia. *Nature* 449: 305–310.

Lordkipanidze, D., Vekua, A., Ferring, R., Rightmire, G. P., Agusti, J., Kiladze, G., Mouskhelishvili, A., Nioradze, M., Ponce de Leon, M. S., Tappen, M., and Zollikofer, C. (2006) A Fourth Hominin Skull from Dmanisi, Georgia. *The Anatomical Record* 288A: 1146–1157.

McHenry, H. M., and Coffing, K. (2000) *Australopithecus* to *Homo*: Transformations in Body and Mind. *Annual Review of Anthropology* 29: 125–146.

Potts, R., Behrensmeyer, A. K., Deino, A., Ditchfield, P., and Clark, J. (2004) Small Mid-Pleistocene Hominin Associated with East African Acheulean Technology. *Science* 305: 75–78.

Rightmire, G. P. (1990) *The Evolution of* Homo erectus. *Comparative Anatomical Studies of an Extinct Human Species*. Cambridge: Cambridge University Press.

Rightmire, G. P. (1993) Variation among Early *Homo* Crania from Olduvai Gorge and the Koobi Fora Region. *American Journal of Physical Anthropology* 90: 1–33.

Rightmire, G. P. (2004) Brain Size and Encephalization in Early to Mid-Pleistocene *Homo*. *American Journal of Physical Anthropology* 106: 61–85.

Rightmire, G. P., Lordkipanidze, D., and Vekua, A. (2006) Anatomical Descriptions, Comparative Studies and Evolutionary Significance of the Hominin Skulls from Dmanisi, Republic of Georgia. *Journal of Human Evolution* 50: 115–141.

Rightmire, G. P., Van Arsdale, A.P., and Lordkipanidze, D. (2008) Variation in the Mandibles from Dmanisi, Georgia. *Journal of Human Evolution* 54: 904–908.

Ruff, C. B. (2007) Body Size Prediction from Juvenile Skeletal Remains. *American Journal of Physical Anthropology* 133: 698–716.

Ruff, C. B., and Walker, A. (1993) Body Size and Body Shape. In A. Walker and R. Leakey (eds), *The Nariokotome* Homo erectus *Skeleton* (pp. 234–265). Cambridge MA: Harvard University Press.

Schrenk, F., Kullmer, O., and Bromage, T. (2007) The Earliest Putative *Homo* Fossils. In W. Henke and I. Tattersall (eds), *Handbook of Paleoanthropology*, Vol. 3: *Phylogeny of Hominids* (pp. 1611–1631). Berlin: Springer.

Schwartz, J. H., and Tattersall, I. (2003) *The Human Fossil Record*, Vol. 1: *Terminology and Craniodental Morphology of Genus* Homo *(Europe)*. New York: Wiley–Liss.

Simpson, S. W., Quade, J., Levin, N. E., Butler, R., Dupont-Nivet, G., Everett, M., and Semaw, S. (2008) A Female *Homo erectus* Pelvis from Gona, Ethiopia. *Science* 322: 1089–1092.

Skinner, M. M., Gordon, A. D., and Collard, N. J. (2006) Mandibular Size and Shape Variation in the Hominins at Dmanisi, Republic of Georgia. *Journal of Human Evolution* 51: 36–49.

Smith, B. H. (1993) The Physiological Age of KNM-WT 15000. In A. Walker and R. Leakey (eds), *The Nariokotome* Homo erectus *Skeleton* (pp. 195–220). Cambridge MA: Harvard University Press.

Sokal, R. R., and Braumann, C. A. (1980) Significance Tests for Coefficients of Variation and Variability Profiles. *Systematic Zoology* 29: 50–66.

Spoor, F., Leakey, M. G., Gathogo, P. N., Brown, F. H., Antón, S. C., McDougall, I., Kairie, C., Manthi, F.K., and Leakey, L. N. (2007) Implications of New Early *Homo* Fossils from Ileret, East of Lake Turkana, Kenya. *Nature* 448: 688–891.

Strait, D. S., Grine, F. E., and Moniz, M. A. (1997) A Reappraisal of Early Hominid Phylogeny. *Journal of Human Evolution* 32: 17–82.

Susman, R. L. (2008) Brief Communication: Evidence Bearing on the Status of *Homo habilis* at Olduvai Gorge. *American Journal of Physical Anthropology* 137: 356–361.

Susman, R. L., and Stern, J. T. (1982) Functional Morphology of *Homo habilis*. *Science* 217: 931–934.

Swisher, C. C., Scott, G. R., Curtis, G. H., Butterworth, J., Antón, S. C., Jacob, T., Suprijo, A., Widiasmoro, S., and Koeshardjono (1998) The Antiquity of *Homo erectus* in Java: ^{40}Ar/^{39}Ar Dating and Paleomagnetic Study of the Sangiran Area. Sun City: Dual Congress 1998 (abstract).

Tobias, P. V. (1991) *Olduvai Gorge*, Vol. 4: *The Skulls, Endocasts and Teeth of* Homo habilis. Cambridge: Cambridge University Press.

Wood, B. (1991) *Koobi Fora Research Project*, Vol. 4: *Hominid Cranial Remains*. Oxford: Clarendon Press.

Wood, B. (1992) Origin and Evolution of the Genus *Homo*. *Nature* 355: 783–790.

Wood, B., and Collard, M. (1999) The Human Genus. *Science* 284: 65–71.

Wood, B., and Lieberman, D. E. (2001) Craniodental Variation in *Paranthropus boisei*: A Developmental and Functional Perspective. *American Journal of Physical Anthropology* 116: 13–25.

Yokoyama, Y., Falgueres, C., Semah, F., Jacob, T., and Grün, R. (2008) Gamma-Ray Spectrometric Dating of Late *Homo erectus* Skulls from Ngandong and Sambungmacan, Central Java, Indonesia. *Journal of Human Evolution* 55: 274–277.

Zhu, R., Potts, R., Xie, F., Hoffman, K. A., Deng, C. L., Shi, C. D., Pan, Y. X., Wang, H.Q., Shi, R. P., Wang, Y. C., Shi, G. H., and Wu, N. Q. (2004) New Evidence on the Earliest Human Presence at High Northern Latitudes in Northeast China. *Nature* 431: 559–562.

20 Species, Populations, and Assimilation in Later Human Evolution

Fred H. Smith

The late part of the middle and late Pleistocene witnessed the continued spread of the genus *Homo* throughout most of Africa, Europe, Asia, Australasia, and finally into the Americas. An earlier form of *Homo*, probably *Homo erectus*, first migrated out of Africa in excess of 1.5 mya and established a human presence in southern Eurasia. During the final 600,000 years (600 ky) of the Pleistocene, regional human populations became increasingly differentiated from each other. Over this span, there is at least one additional major episode of migration 'out of Africa.' This post-erectine out of Africa migration period reflects the spread of modern human anatomical form from an African homeland. Both the genetic and the morphological data point to migrations beginning probably from East Africa sometime between about 150,000 and 100,000 years ago. These movements extended throughout other parts of Africa, and ultimately throughout the remainder of the earth (Bräuer 2008; Trinkaus 2005; Pearson 2008; Cartmill and Smith 2009). However, whether this phenomenon represented the spread of a new species of human, which essentially replaced aboriginal groups throughout Eurasia, or a novel population of a polytypic single species is still a matter of intense debate. In either case, a complex pattern of interaction between migrant and indigenous populations must have characterized this part of the human evolutionary record, much as it has in more recent human history.

By 400,000 years ago (400 kya), humans in Europe, Africa, and Asia were beginning to exhibit regional morphological differences. Certainly these humans were still quite similar across the continents in having expanded brains and braincases compared to those of *Homo erectus* (Figure 20.1). They also retained a number of primitive (ancestral) features: prognathic faces and prominent supraorbital tori, receding mandibular symphyses with no 'chin,' large anterior teeth, and muscular postcranial skeletons. But there are also differences in body shape and in the details of craniofacial anatomy from region to region. About 100,000 years ago regional differentiation was

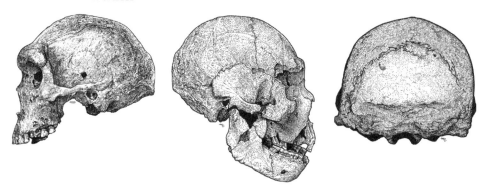

Figure 20.1   Heidelberg specimens from Kabwe (Kabwe 1), Zambia (left); Sima de los Huesos (skull 5), Spain (center); and Petralona, Greece (right). © Matt Cartmill

clearly established. This included the appearance of the distinctive Neandertals in Europe and central Asia; of early modern people in Africa and the Levant; possibly the survival of late *Homo erectus* in Australasia; the existence of some form of archaic *Homo* in eastern Asia; and perhaps the existence of predecessors to the pint-sized people living on the Indonesian island of Flores. For many paleoanthropologists, these hominin samples could represent as many as five separate species coexisting as separate entities in the later Pleistocene.

THE BASIS FOR SPLITTING, THE NATURE OF SPECIES, AND SOME THEORETICAL ISSUES

In a 1986 essay, Tattersall decried the classification of all post-*Homo erectus* hominins as members of *Homo sapiens*, and particularly the designation of all pre-modern forms of *Homo* as members of 'archaic' *H. sapiens* (Tattersall 1986). The concept of an archaic *H. sapiens* stage or grade was declared to be out of touch with modern evolutionary biology and a case of 'special pleading' applied to human evolution. Tattersall based these criticisms on patterns observed in other organisms, particularly in cercopithecine primates, which suggested that the morphological variation observed in the post-*H. erectus* sample must represent multiple species. This argument for increased species diversity in later human biological history is intimately tied to the 'punctuated equilibrium' perspective on macroevolution. Essentially, this perspective emphasized that speciation was always a branching process (cladogenesis), and thus reflected the axiom that evolution was a 'bush, not a ladder.' The use of a 'grade' concept reflected in the concept of archaic *H. sapiens* was labeled as outmoded 'ladder thinking' (Eldredge and Tattersall 1982). Although punctuated equilibrium is rarely mentioned any more, its principles still underlie the quest for 'bushiness' in the later human fossil record.

Cladogenesis is essentially allopatric speciation, a form of speciation that normally occurs when peripheral populations of a species become physically isolated from the main body of that species. This isolation derives most commonly from the formation of some natural barrier to gene flow. In these relatively small marginal populations, environmental stresses are likely to be greater and genetic changes are more likely to become established during isolation. Thus the biology of these populations may develop significant differences by comparison with those displayed by the main body of the species.

However, in Mayr's 'biological species' concept (BSC), another step must occur to mark true speciation (Mayr 1963). It does not matter how distinctive, from a morphological point of view, two populations may become in relation to each other; they remain the same species until a reproductive barrier is established. Sometimes such a barrier occurs despite the presence of relatively little morphological divergence (as happened in the case of Old World monkeys of the genus *Cercopithecus*). In other cases, significant degrees of morphological differences exist without the establishment of reproductive isolation. An excellent example is that of feral and domesticated suids in the mountains and valleys of East Tennessee, which differ markedly in anatomy but are interfertile (Smith 1994).

In the fossil record, reproductive isolation is difficult, if not impossible, to identify. Thus most paleontologists do not recognize species on the basis of the BSC. Paleontological species are based on assessments of morphology which include both the patterns of similarities among groups and the gaps between groups. Many different approaches to such assessments have been developed, and some of them have attempted to relate morphology to implications of reproductive separation among groups of fossils (Foley 1991; Holliday 2003; Cartmill and Smith 2009). Notable among these are Patterson's (1992) 'specific mate recognition' concept and Simpson's (1961) 'evolutionary species' concept. The former asserts that species should be recognized only on the basis of features related to mate recognition and actual reproduction, and the latter implies that species maintained their morphological identity through reproductive exclusivity. The reality is that these species concepts are essentially variants of morphospecies. They can be defined as various approaches to the assessment of morphological patterning. Currently the emphasis is on finding patterns of shared derived (synapomorphic) features in order to define alpha taxonomic groupings, and the search for such features has dominated modern paleoanthropology for many years. However, a quarter of a century ago, Gingerich (1984) pointed out that the judicious use of other types of features should not be excluded uncritically from taxonomic decisions.

How much splitting of lineages, and thus formation of separate species, is to be expected in the evolution of a specific mammal depends particularly on three factors: geographic range, adaptive pattern, and body size. Mammals with large ranges, which cover multiple ecological zones, are more likely to speciate, as are those living at the tropics compared to those living at higher latitudes (Foley 1991). Foley also suggests that speciation rates increase in taxonomic groups with ranges which extend to islands, where the possibility of isolation is increased. While these characteristics apply to hominins in general, they particularly explain the species diversity of pre-Pleistocene hominins; and the latter observation may be particularly pertinent to the case of the tiny late Pleistocene Flores hominins. However, Foley also notes that lineages with broad dietary and overall adaptive strategies show reduced speciation rates. He argues that, compared to earlier hominins, *H. erectus* and latter members of *Homo* probably exploited a much wider range of dietary resources, including significant amounts of meat. On the basis of a northern canid analogy, another study demonstrates the probable high habitat tolerance of middle and late Pleistocene hominins, considering it a significant factor in limiting the opportunities for hominin speciation (Arcadi 2006). Add to this *Homo*'s markedly more complex technological capabilities (Klein 1999), and middle and late Pleistocene members of *Homo* emerge as consummate generalists. Compared to specialized species, generalized species tend to exploit wider geographic and ecological ranges, show greater intraspecific variation, and exhibit less of a tendency to split (Vrba 1984; Arcadi 2006).

The cultural capabilities of middle and late Pleistocene *Homo* bear special mentioning in this context. Viewed in the modern world, culture is seen more as a specializing agent, promoting separation between groups on the basis of differences in behavior and other cultural accoutrements (Klein 1999; Premo and Hublin 2009). But, as White emphasized sixty years ago, culture is also a means of adaptation (White 1949), defining a very unique and all-encompassing resource exploitation strategy for humans. Culture as an adaptive mechanism further defines humans as the consummate generalist species; and it is reasonable to expect that the impact of this generalist adaptive strategy would have severely limited the ability of the middle and late Pleistocene hominin lineage to speciate.

Body size also must be considered in comparative assessments of mammalian speciation. Species diversity in mammals is generally tied to overall body mass, as larger forms exhibit less taxonomic diversity. Conroy (2002) compared speciosity in Pleistocene *Homo* with that of all the available mammals that fall within *Homo*'s body size range of 30–65 kg. He found that mammals of early *Homo* body size generally do not exhibit large numbers of species. In fact, he argued that recognition of more than two synchronic species in early *Homo* would put the human lineage at odds with the pattern for similar-sized mammals.

A final critical issue concerns how long it takes for reproductive isolation, complete or partial (according to Haldane's rule: sterility of one sex), to be established in medium-size mammals. Using estimates from the fossil record and data on documented extant species hybridization, Holliday (2006) determined that the most rapid attainment of partial reproductive isolation was between the genera *Bos* and *Bison*, in 1 million years, and the most rapid attainment of complete isolation was between horses and zebras/donkeys (genus *Equus*), in approximately 2 million years. Employing molecular clock data, partial isolation is established most quickly between lions and tigers (genus *Panthera*), in 1.55 million years, and complete isolation is most rapidly established between red-fronted and Thompson's gazelles (genus *Gazella*), in 1.4 million years. These time spans are all longer that the entire late middle and upper Pleistocene.

The combined results of these studies do not necessarily demonstrate that multiple species of *Homo* could not have existed during the middle and late Pleistocene, but they do suggest that the insistence on relatively high species diversity in this span of hominin biological history may not necessarily reflect biological reality. Put another way, the recent proliferation of Pleistocene *Homo* species appears questionable, not unequivocally supported on theoretical grounds. At the very least, the burden should be on those who defend multiple species to demonstrate the biological validity of each species.

HEIDELBERGS AND THE ORIGIN OF REGIONAL HUMAN DIVERSITY

In Africa, post-*erectine* humans are represented by remains from a geographically diverse series of sites widely spread in Africa, Europe, and possibly Asia. Currently many paleoanthropologists place these remains in *Homo heidelbergensis*, but of course not all agree (see below). To avoid the taxonomic quagmire, these hominins will be referred to as 'Heidelbergs.'

The dating of the African Heidelberg sites is difficult. The oldest is probably Bodo, at around 600,000 years ago (Clark et al. 1994). Recent faunal assessments suggest a comparable age for Saldanha, but possibly that age might even approach 1 million years (Klein et al. 2006). Most other specimens generally are estimated at 300,000–600,000 years ago, but these dates are generally based on fauna and thus are approximate. Probably the most informative site is Kabwe, or Broken Hill, in Zambia, which has yielded a complete cranium (Kabwe 1), a second maxilla, and a series of postcranial remains. Despite the relatively strong chemical homogeneity of these remains, the association among the cranial and postcranial ones is not certain (see Cartmill and Smith 2009). The Kabwe 1 cranium (Figure 20.1) is the best known specimen among the African Heidelbergs. Like others in this group, it shows the combination of primitive and advanced cranial features described previously, except that here there is no mandible. The face exhibits total facial prognathism similar to that of erectines: the lateral face (zygomatic region) is placed forward, along with the midface. Other features are more advanced. The cranial capacity measures 1325 cm³, which is relatively large for this time period. Compared to many erectines, African Heidelbergs exhibit a 30 percent increase in brain size, which is likely to reflect a significant shift in human brain-to-body size patterning during this time span (Ruff et al. 1997), and changes in the nose and palate, which are shared with other later members of *Homo* (Rightmire 2008). The postcranial elements have distinctly primitive features (Pearson 2000); but the most significant characteristic of the most complete specimen, a tibia, is that its length suggests body proportions reflecting a relatively warm environment. This indicates that a relatively 'tropical' body form continues to characterize the Pleistocene African Heidelbergs.

In Europe, the Heidelbergs range from Greece (Petralona) to Germany (Steinheim, Reilingen, and Mauer), to England (Swanscombe and Boxgrove), and to Spain (Sima de los Huesos). Dating estimates range from about 600,000 to as recently as 200,000 years ago (Cartmill and Smith 2009), but many of the specimens are not directly dated. Similarities between European and African representatives have been observed for some time (Rightmire 1998, 2008). The general similarity is based on their shared advanced features by comparison with erectines (increased cranial capacity and expanded neurocrania; see Figure 20.1), as well as on shared primitive retentions (prominent supraorbital tori, total facial prognathism, absence of chins). However, the two regional samples differ in some details. For example, European forms often exhibit incipient suprainiac fossae and occipital bunning, features generally associated with Neandertals (Santa Luca 1978). In addition, the infraorbital area in specimens like the Petralona cranium and skull 5 from Sima de los Huesos closely approach the Neandertal pattern. Also, aspects of the postcrania from Boxgrove (England) and from Sima de los Huesos suggest that body forms were more adapted to cold than the African body forms (Trinkaus et al. 1999; Arsuaga et al. 1999). On the basis of the presumably shared derived features, there is a consensus that the European Heidelbergs represent a clear ancestral line to the Neandertals (Wolpoff 1999; Rightmire 1990, 1998; Arsuaga at al 1997; Dean et al. 1998).

Certain Asian specimens are best considered Heidelbergs as well (Cartmill and Smith 2009). These include Zuttiyeh and the Tabuˉn pre-level C remains (Israel),

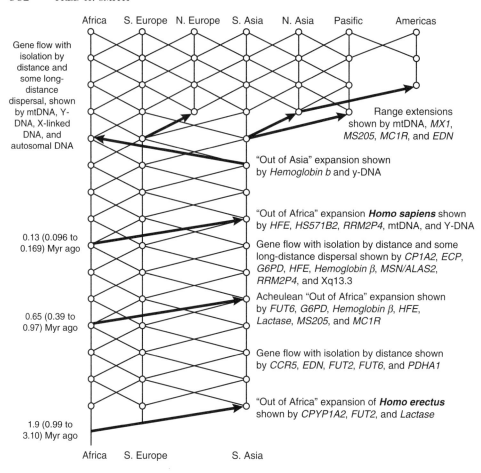

Africa   S. Europe N. Europe   S. Asia   N. Asia   Pasific   Americas

Gene flow with
isolation by
distance and
some long-
distance
dispersal, shown
by mtDNA, Y-
DNA, X-linked
DNA, and
autosomal DNA

Range extensions
shown by mtDNA, *MX1,*
MS205, MC1R, and *EDN*

"Out of Asia" expansion shown
by *Hemoglobin b* and y-DNA

"Out of Africa" expansion **Homo sapiens** shown
by *HFE, HS571B2, RRM2P4,* mtDNA, and Y-DNA

0.13 (0.096 to
0.169) Myr ago

Gene flow with isolation by distance and some
long-distance dispersal shown by *CP1A2, ECP,
G6PD, HFE, Hemoglobin β, MSN/ALAS2,
RRM2P4,* and Xq13.3

Acheulean "Out of Africa" expansion shown
by *FUT6, G6PD, Hemoglobin β, HFE,
Lactase, MS205,* and *MC1R*

0.65 (0.39 to
0.97) Myr ago

Gene flow with isolation by distance shown
by *CCR5, EDN, FUT2, FUT6,* and *PDHA1*

"Out of Africa" expansion of **Homo erectus**
shown by *CPYP1A2, FUT2,* and *Lactase*

1.9 (0.99 to
3.10) Myr ago

Africa   S. Europe   S. Asia

Figure 20.2 Schematic drawing showing Templeton's interpretation of three 'out of Africa' migration phenomena, as well as evidence of some genetic contributions from Asia. © Matt Cartmill

Kocabas, (Turkey), Narmada (India), Yuxian and possibly Dali (China), and Sambungmacan and Ngandong (Indonesia). Many consider the Indonesian sample to represent late surviving *Homo erectus*, as the two do share some strong similarities (Santa Luca 1980; Rightmire 1990). All of these sites appear to fall within the appropriate time frame for Heidelbergs – except possibly Ngandong, which has been dated to as recently as 53,000–27,000 years ago (Swisher et al. 1996). As detailed elsewhere, these dates are questionable and may be 200,000 years older; and the Ngandong people exhibit the same pattern of neurocranial and brain size expansion (28 percent, compared to that of Indonesian erectines) as other Heidelbergs (Cartmill and Smith 2009).

It is not easy to determine the ultimate origin of the Heidelbergs. Some assert that Heidelbergs evolved out of erectines in different regions of the Old World (Wolpoff 1999). These would not be independent origins, but rather the result of gene flow among regional lineages of humans – in other words, multiregional evolution. However, a recent suggestion, based on genetic data (Figure 20.2), asserts that Heidelbergs spread out of Africa around 650,000 years ago (Templeton 2005). This is an intriguing idea, but the fossil record to date can neither support nor refute it. Interestingly, the recently discovered Kocabaş specimen (Kappelman et al. 2008) might provide a 500,000-year old indication of a connection between Africa and Europe; but more fossil evidence is needed to address this issue adequately.

Finally, there is the question of taxonomy. Do Heidelbergs form a cohesive species, separate from other members of *Homo*? Can the African and European Heidelbergs be accommodated in one species? Some have argued that the African forms should be placed in a separate species from the European Heidelbergs: that the latter (*H. heidelbergensis*) would be ancestral to Neandertals, and the former (*H. rhodesiensis*) would be ancestral ultimately to modern humans in Africa (Bermúdez de Castro et al. 1997). However, the morphometric similarities among the African and European Heidelbergs argue against this dual species model (Rightmire 2008). While the emerging consensus is that *H. heidelbergensis* is the valid taxon for these humans, it has not been defined on the basis of specific, uniquely derived features. Rightmire (1990, 1998, 2008) has marshaled the characteristic features for *H. heidelbergensis*; but, as he accurately notes, these features are a mosaic of traits shared either with more primitive or with more derived forms of *Homo*. There are no unique and defining features that unite the Heidelbergs (Smith and Cartmill 2009). While the concept of *H. heidelbergensis* plays an important role in the quest for 'bushiness' in the later human evolutionary record, the fact is that the species' existence as a distinctly defined unit is contentious. Certainly the Heidelberg sample is broadly intermediate between erectines and later humans, but that, in itself, is weak justification for a formal taxonomic distinction.

NEANDERTALS AND THEIR 'CONTEMPORARIES'

Neandertals, a distinct form of *Homo sapiens* in the later Pleistocene, are by far the best known and most intensely studied fossil human sample. First recognized at the original Neandertal site in Germany in 1856, Neandertals are found in all but the northern-most reaches in Europe and in western and Central Asia. In addition to their entire skeletal anatomy, an impressive amount is also known about their behavior, adaptive pattern, and genome. There is a consensus that in Europe Neandertals gradually emerged from European Heidelbergs, but there is disagreement as to whether they emerged by accretion of Neandertal features over time, in isolation (Dean et al. 1998), or simply as the European lineage in the interconnected web of regional lineages that form the basis of the multiregional evolution perspective (Wolpoff 1999). Both viewpoints agree that the boundary between Heidelberg and Neandertal in Europe is rather arbitrary. In fact some would include European Heidelbergs in the presumptive Neandertal species *Homo neanderthalensis*.

A case can be made that the hominins from the 210,000-year-old site of Ehringsdorf in Germany represent the earliest sample which can be unequivocally considered Neandertals in the strict sense, and a series of sites dating from between 200,000 and 100,000 years ago exclusively yield Neandertals. These sites include Biache-St Vraast (France), Krapina (Croatia), and Saccopastore (Italy). The 'classic Neandertal' sites – including La Chapelle-aux-Saints and La Ferrassie (France), Guattari (Italy), and the Neander Valley – span a period from approximately 75,000

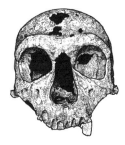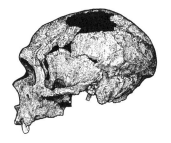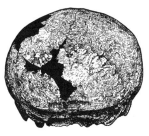

Figure 20.3   The Neandertal cranium from La Chapelle-aux-Saints (France) in front (left), side (middle), and rear (right) views. © Matt Cartmill

to 40,000 years ago. The latest Neandertal fossil sites include Zafarraya (Spain: 33,200 years ago), St Cesaire (France: 36,000 years ago), Hyena Cave at Arcy-sur-Cure (France: 33,800 years ago), and Vindija (Croatia: 32,000 yeas ago) (Hublin et al. 1995, 1996; Higham et al. 2006; Lévêque and Vandermeersch 1981), but archaeological sites without remains suggest that Neandertals may have survived on the Iberian Peninsula for some 8,000 more years (Zilhão 2006; Finlayson 2004).

Like in the case of Heidelbergs, much of the distinctive morphology of Neandertals is based on the retention of primitive features: their large, prognathic faces – accompanied by chinless mandibles, pronounced supraorbital tori, low cranial vaults, and large anterior teeth derive from Neandertal ancestry (Figure 20.3). In other ways, Neandertals are clearly derived compared to earlier forms. Neandertals exhibit expanded brains, with the average Würm European Neandertal cranial capacity at 1423 cm³. Consequently the cranial vault is also expanded relative to the cranial base, the width of the braincase being now markedly larger than that of the cranial base (Figure 20.3). Some other features appear to be distinctive, or apomorphic, for Neandertals, although earlier stages in the development of many of these features can be seen in European Heidelbergs. For example, due to the expanded width of the brain case, Neandertals have a characteristic oval shape when viewed from the rear. Other distinctive features include the form of the temporal bone, the inferior projection of the occipitomastoid region of the cranial base, the presence of suprainiac fossae on the occipital, the formation of occipital bunning on the rear of the cranium, and a series of mandibular details. However, perhaps the most distinctive proposed apomorphy of Neandertals is their facial prognathism. Neandertals exhibit prognathism along the midline of the face, but the lateral face (the lateral part of the zygomatic bone) is relatively less forwardly projecting. One view holds that the facial midline area is moved forward relative to the lateral face, which would constitute an apomorphic condition (Rak 1986). Another view is that the lateral face retreats in relation to the midline of the face, which would reflect an intermediate stage between the total facial prognathism of earlier humans and the relative lack of prognathism (or orthognathism) of modern humans (Trinkaus 2006; Smith and Paquette 1989).

Neandertals also have distinctive features in their postcranial skeleton. Many of these are primitive retentions. For example, the thick cortical bone of Neandertal long bones reflects a pattern of heavy loading of the limbs, particularly the lower limb, relating to locomotor and other activities. This, along with other indications of powerful muscularity, characterizes the Neandertals.

Probably the most significant features concern their overall body form. Neandertals had a barrel-shaped thorax and relatively short distal limb segments in both arm and leg (Holliday 1997a, 1997b; Ruff et al. 2002). These features are generally considered to indicate a body form adapted to cold, evolved so as to enhance heat conservation. In fact, the Neandertal body form has been called 'hyper-arctic,' because it appears to be even more cold-adapted than that of living people such as the Inuit and Lapps. It has even been suggested that climate adaptation and the resulting thorax shape might explain certain unusual features in the Neandertal pelvis, including the long, thin superior pubic rami at the front of the pelvic girdle (Rosenberg 1988; Cartmill and Smith 2009).

Neandertals in western Asia are known from a range extending from the Levant of Israel into Iraq and the Caucasus region of Russia. Near-Eastern Neandertals exhibit the distinctive features noted for European Neandertals, except that they have relatively higher cranial vaults, lack occipital bunning, and do not show as extreme a pattern of distal element shortening in the arm. Purported Neandertal remains from Central Asia also show differences from the European representatives. Teshik Tash in Uzbekistan has yielded a burial of an 8 or 9-year-old, with Mousterian tools and a Pleistocene fauna. Despite its young age at death, the Teshik Tash skull already manifests a Neandertal-like cranial vault with a suprainiac fossa, the characteristic Neandertal morphology of the mastoid and occipitomastoid eminence, an oval shape from the rear, and a continuous supraorbital torus. The facial skeleton also appears to be Neandertal-like. Analysis of mitochondrial DNA from the Teshik Tash left femur, as well as from subadult limb bones from Okladnikov Cave, also in central Asia, reveal the presence of uniquely Neandertal sequences (Krause et al. 2007). The record strongly suggests that Teshik Tash exhibits Neandertal biological affinities (contra Glantz et al. 2009) and indicates that Neandertal influences reached further east than has traditionally been accepted.

Even further east, the sparse human fossil record yields archaic folk who are apparently not so closely related to Neandertals. These fossils include the Dali cranium (see above), the partial skeleton from Jinniushan (about 200,000 years), the fragmentary Maba cranium (about 135,000 years), and a series of other less complete specimens, all from China (Wu and Poirier 1995). These remains are relatively primitive, but they are certainly not Neandertals. While they share features with late Chinese erectines, it is unclear if they primarily evolve from erectines in China (Wolpoff 1999) or derive from a Heidelberg expansion into East Asia. The Jinniushan skull is more gracile than Dali's, with a higher, rounder cranial vault, thinner vault bones, and a much thinner supraorbital torus. The cranial capacity is $1390\,cm^3$, comparable to that of other late archaic peoples. The face is also gracile, but generally similar to Dali's in that it appears to be relatively flat (total facial prognathism), with a broad nose and interorbital area. A detailed analysis of body form for the Jinniushan skull shows that the specimen had a wide trunk, large body mass and short limbs (Rosenberg et al. 2006). On the basis of its location relatively far north in China, Jinniushan represents a cold-adapted population, with an overall body form much like that of the similarly adapted European Neandertals, but with a different cranial anatomy.

ARCHAIC HUMAN ADAPTATION AT HIGHER LATITUDES

Regardless of whether the anatomy results from genetics or from other factors (Serrat et al. 2008), European Neandertals and higher-latitude Asians are adapted for life in the cold. The same seems also true for archaic humans further east. But, all other things being equal, body form alone has limited impact on adaptation to cold (Aiello and Wheeler 2003). However, all other things were probably not equal. On the basis of analogy with modern circumpolar populations, it is likely that Neandertals had significantly higher basal metabolism rates (BMR) than more equatorial populations, due in part to the effects of temperature and day lengths on thyroid function (Leonard 2002; Leonard et al. 2002). The combination of a stocky, beefy body build with the generation of more internal heat would seem to be key to the survival of high-latitude Neandertals under periglacial conditions, and possibly to that of north-latitude archaic humans in general. Some form of body covering and other cultural factors provided additional buffering.

A large body and an elevated BMR are energetically expensive features to maintain. One model calculates that an adult Neandertal would have required 3,500–5,000 kilocalories a day to survive in cold conditions (Churchill 2006). There is evidence from stable-isotope studies and from archaeology that Neandertals obtained those calories primarily from meat – from a diet rich in fat and high in calories (Richards et al. 2000; Kuhn and Steiner 2006).

The total energy budget of an organism is expended on normal maintenance or survival activities (moving and various physiological functions), growth and development, and reproduction (Leonard 2002; Sorensen and Leonard 2001). Given the pattern of adaptation, maintenance or survival demands would have literally required almost all of the energy which the Neandertal diet could provide, leaving precious little energy for reproduction. In this context, it is likely that Neandertals had lower long-term fertility rates than modern humans. Also, archaeologically based calculations of overall population size indicate that middle Paleolithic people were slightly more than 1 million and that population density was 0.03 persons per square kilometer (Hassan 1981). While such estimates are far from secure, they are about three times smaller than the equivalent estimates for early modern people. These studies strongly suggest that Neandertals and other archaic folk were very rare on the landscape, particularly in the north.

AFRICA AND THE ORIGIN OF MODERN HUMANS

While European Heidelbergs gave rise to Neandertals, the descendants of African Heidelbergs did not continue to exhibit large, prognathic faces. They were characterized instead by reduced faces, which appear to approach orthognathism, and by such modern-like features as canine fossae. However, braincases are still primitive, showing relatively low cranial vaults and pronounced supraorbital tori. Cranial capacity averages 1367 cm³, which is virtually identical to the overall European Neandertal mean (Cartmill and Smith 2009). These African Heidelberg descendants are found at a smattering of sites extending throughout Africa. The sites themselves date from approximately 270,000 years ago to some time between 190,000 and 130,000 years ago (Bräuer 2008; Cartmill and Smith 2009). Unfortunately there are no surviving adult mandibles,

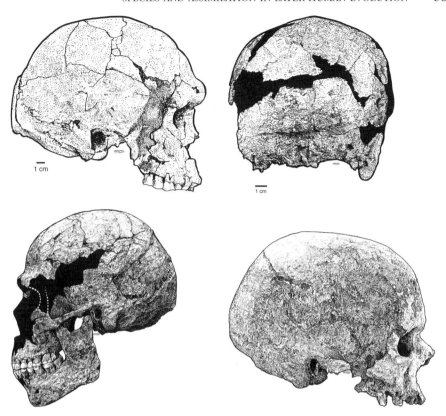

Figure 20.4   Early modern human crania from Herto (Herto 1), Ethiopia (top left); Omo Kibish 1 (top right); Skhūl (Skhūl 5), Israel (bottom left); Cro-Magnon (Cro-Magnon 1) from France (bottom right). © Matt Cartmill

only one postcranial element, and virtually no teeth. Still, the cranial mosaic clearly indicates a lineage evolving toward the modern human morphological pattern. Taxonomically, this sample has been assigned to the species *Homo helmei* (see Stringer 1994), but it is more informally known as the African Transitional Group (ATG).

Whereas the ATG is widely spread in Africa, the earliest evidence of modern humans is more restricted. Three sites in East Africa yield evidence of very early modern anatomy. Herto (Ethiopia) yields two adult crania, a child's cranium, and other fragments that date between 154,000 and 160,000 years ago (Clark et al. 2003). The most complete adult (Herto 1) exhibits a high and relatively rounded cranial vault, a modern face, and a rear vault contour that shows a maximum breadth high on the parietals, just like in recent humans (Figure 20.4). The face is modern and orthognathic, but still has a well developed supraorbital torus. The 6/7-year-old Herto 5 cranium also exhibits a modern form (White et al. 2003). Over forty years ago, the Omo Kibish site KHS yielded a partial skeleton referred to as Omo 1 (Day 1969). The skull of this specimen is fragmentary but clearly shows a modern cranial form, a chin, and a modern face. However, like Herto 1, the Omo Kibish skull maintains a supraorbital torus. The even more fragmentary postcranial skeleton has been recently described in detail as fully modern and relatively tall (Pearson et al. 2008). The latter suggests a likely tropical body form, but there is simply not enough data to be certain of this. The Omo 1 skeleton was excavated just above the

Nakaa'kire tuff, dated to 196,000 +/− 2,000 years in member 1 of the Kibish Formation (Brown and Fuller 2008). While the skeleton may come close to this age, the fact is that is could be somewhat younger. Finally, the Singa cranium (Sudan) exhibits a modern overall form (Stringer et al. 1985) and apparently dates between 133,000 and 160,000 years ago (see discussion in Cartmill and Smith 2009).

   The first comprehensive case for an early transition to modern humans in Africa on the basis of the fossil record was made by Bräuer (1984). Stringer and Andrews (1988) supplemented the fossil argument with genetic data, particularly the mitochondrial DNA study by Cann and colleagues (1987), to establish the 'recent African origin' model of modern human origins. This perspective generally views the origin of modern people as the result of a cladogenetic speciation that resulted in the species *Homo sapiens*. Recent statements of this perspective can be found in several sources (Stringer 1994; Bräuer 2006, 2008; Mellars 2006; Pearson 2008; Hublin and Bailey 2006; Tattersall and Schwartz 2008), although Bräuer does not place Neandertals in a separate species. Following Cann and colleagues' influential study, many researchers have used genetic data to argue for separate species status for modern humans from Neandertals, and presumably other archaic humans as well. These data have been derived from studies of modern human genetic variation and extrapolations from these, as well as from results of ancient DNA analysis conducted on Neandertals and early modern humans (Weaver and Roseman 2008, Serre et al. 2004, Green et al. 2006, Noonan et al. 2006).

THE RADIATION OF MODERN HUMANS

From East Africa, modern humans spread throughout Africa and ultimately into Eurasia. The first evidence of modern human morphology outside of Africa is from the sites of Skhūl and Qafzeh in the Levant of southwest Asia. These sites yield a very informative sample of skeletal remains of both adults and subadults, which are associated with Mousterian tools very similar to those associated with European and Asian Neandertals. A good 'summary estimate' for the dates of the Skhūl/Qafzeh sample is 80,000 to 100,000 years ago, although some Skhūl specimens might be younger (Grün 2006). The total morphology of the specimens, both young and adult, is essentially modern. The crania have a vault shape very similar to that described for early modern Africans, even in the maintenance of a supraorbital torus in most adults (Figure 20.4; Vandermeersch 1981). There are also several relatively complete mandibles, which show the development of chins and other modern human features (Rak et al. 2002). The postcranial anatomy is modern and the body form is linear, with relatively long distal limb segments. This body shape comes closest to that of recent African populations, who are adapted to a more tropical climate, and contrasts markedly with that of the Neandertals (Holliday 2000). However, one individual (Skhūl 5) is somewhat more like Neandertals in body form; and this along with other features could mean that the biological boundary between Neandertals and early moderns in western Asia may be more porous that the promoters of multiple species claim it to be. Another study uses morphometric analysis of crania to indicate the likelihood of a small degree of interbreeding between early moderns and Neandertals in the Near East (Thackeray et al. 2005).

The earliest well dated modern specimen from mainland East Asia is the approximately 34,000-year-old Tianyuan 1 skeleton near Zhoukoudian, which preserves a partial mandible and some thirty postcranial elements (Shang et al. 2007). The mandible exhibits modern features, and the postcrania are also modern. On the basis of partially reconstructed elements, Tianyuan 1 also appears to have high crural indices, which indicates a relatively tropical ancestry. H. Shang and colleagues (2007) conclude that substantial gene flow from early modern populations to the south and west probably explains the origin of modern populations in this region; but they also note that the Tianyuan 1 specimen also preserves a few features which reflect some local archaic contributions to the early modern population of China. Other modern specimens may be older, for instance the Liujiang cranium in southern China; but the association of the specimen with dates higher than 68,000 years ago is not reliable (Wu and Poirier 1995). Thus it is not certain that moderns reached eastern mainland Asia earlier than 34,000 years ago – but it is possible.

In Australasia, controversial dates on the Willandra Lakes (Lake Mungo) 3 skeleton indicate that people could have reached Greater Australia (Sahulland) about 62,000 years ago (Thorne et al. 1999), but others argue that a more reasonable time frame is 35,000–40,000 years (Bowler et al. 2003). The earliest Australians are all modern people morphologically, and the Willandra Lakes 3 skeleton suggests a relatively linear body build. Early Australians exhibit considerable variability. The oldest known modern specimen from Sundaland is a Niah Cave (Borneo) juvenile recently dated to at least 35,000 years ago (Barker et al. 2007). Niah is also modern, and there is no evidence of any potential post-erectine specimens here, except possibly the Ngandong people.

EARLY MODERN EUROPEANS AND THE PATTERN OF MODERN HUMAN ORIGINS

Current evidence points to an age of about 35,000 years for modern humans in Europe, although some archaeological evidence may suggest an initial date of 40,000 years ago (Bar-Yosef 2006; Mellars 2006; Churchill and Smith 2000; Trinkaus 2005). In either case, Europe is probably a late frontier for early modern people. The earliest fossil remains are from Oase (Romania) and Mladeč (Czech Republic), dating to 35,000 and 32,000 years ago respectively (Trinkaus 2005); followed by a series of other remains, including the Cro-Magnon (France) specimens, that falls between 26,000 and 32,000 years ago (Churchill and Smith 2000, Trinkaus 2005, Cartmill and Smith 2009). Early modern Europeans (EME) are fundamentally modern in skull form and are, overall, more similar to early modern West Asians and Africans than to the indigenous Neandertals (Figure 20.4). EME also lack supraorbital tori, which are present in earlier moderns from Asia and Africa. Additionally, the EME body form also differs from that of Neandertals in being more linear and having longer distal limb segments – which suggests an origin for EME in warmer environs (Holliday 1997a, 2000). The extent of cortical bone in the long bones is reduced, but there is no striking reduction of muscularity. These morphological differences have long been interpreted by many researchers as reflecting a migration into Europe of modern people who ultimately replaced the Neandertals. The European replacement is viewed as the archetypical case supporting a cladogenetic speciation explanation for modern humans (*H. sapiens*) and the placement of Neandertals in a different species (*H. neanderthalensis*) (Gould 1987, 1988).

Supporters of the 'recent African origins' model (RAO) generally hold that early modern humans replaced archaic folk throughout the Old World. In this view, the replacement by the *Homo sapiens* lineage-species is essentially complete, with no negligible contributions of archaic people to regional modern populations. In addition to morphological discontinuity, the proponents of RAO also point to genetic evidence as demonstrating a recent African origin for the modern human gene pool. This genetic evidence involves extrapolations from patterns of diversity among living human genetic diversity, as well as apparently distinctive differences between Neandertal DNA and recent human DNA (see reviews in Relethford 2001, Weaver and Roseman 2008). The strength of this evidence makes RAO a very robust and widely accepted explanation for the beginning of people like us worldwide.

The best-known competing perspective is the 'multiregional evolution' model (MRE; Wolpoff 1999). MRE argues that there is no specific geographic region where the total modern human morphological complex developed. Rather, it argues that specific features develop in different regions and then spread through gene flow. These features coalesce at different times in different regions, depending mainly on the pattern of gene flow, on the local selective environment, and on genetic drift. This is a complex process and, theoretically, a sound model. The major issue concerns whether MRE fits the available evidence from the fossil and molecular biological records.

In general MRE argues that in various regions of Eurasia local continuity could be as important as gene flow, or even more so (with or without migrating populations). The extent of continuity would, of course, be variable; but it seems that MRE sees more continuity in Australasia and East Asia than in Europe (Wolpoff 1999). However, even in Europe MRE studies have suggested that a Neandertal contribution of as much as 50 percent cannot be excluded (Wolpoff et al. 2004). Opponents of MRE have argued that the traits used to support continuity actually represent shared primitive retentions, characteristics of limited or questionable genetic background or are not unique enough to specific regions to be used as regional indicators – or some combination of the above (Pearson 2004; Hublin and Bailey 2006; Bräuer et al. 2006).

MRE supporters have argued that the genetic data are open to other interpretations than replacement and the recognition of multiple species. For example, the evolutionary neutrality of the mitochondrial genome has been questioned (Hawks 2006), which would call into doubt the projected timing of the modern human appearance in Africa and of the migrations out of that continent. Differences in relative population size during the Pleistocene may also be responsible for genetic patterns that mimic replacement (Relethford 2001). A final example involves the analysis of ten human genetic systems (mtDNA, six nuclear DNA sequences, a Y chromosome and two X-linked sequences), which showed that these data were not commensurate with the thesis of a single, recent migration out of Africa, but rather suggested three major events of 'out of Africa' migrations (Figure 20.2). The two earlier migrations established lines of alleles in various areas of Eurasia – lines that were not derived from the recent migration defined by RAO (Templeton 2005). These ancient alleles are also found in recent Eurasian populations, which means that not all alleles originated from the most recent migrations out of Africa, recognized by RAO as the modern human lineage-species.

Table 20.1   Presence of selected discrete and metric traits in the skulls of late Pleistocene humans from Europe and western Asia. Data are from Frayer (1992), except where otherwise specified. Incidences of discrete traits are expressed as percentages; nasion-projection data are in mm. Numbers in parentheses indicate sample sizes. Definitions for the features are given in Frayer (1992)

Sample	Suprainiac fossa	Anterior mastoid tubercle	Horizontal-oval mandibular foramen projection[a]	Nasion
European Neandertals	100 (23)[b]	34.8 (23)	52.6 (19)	29.3 (11)
EUP	38.5 (26)	20.0 (25)	18.2 (22)	21.9 (16)
Late UP	23.7 (37)	0 (19)	6.7 (30)	19.3 (23)
Skhūl/Qafzeh	14.2 (7)[c]	40.0 (5)	0 (2)	12.4 (3)
European Mesolithic	19.3 (161)	0 (179)	1.9 (161)	19.4 (114)

[a] Projection of nasion anterior to the bi-fmt plane. This is the plane that extends between the two frontomalare temproale (see Appendix).

[b] Frayer (1992) considers one Neandertal from Krapina (Kr 11.5) to lack a fossa. However, FS believes that this specimen does not preserve the area necessary to make a judgment on presence or absence of the fossa.

[c] Frayer (1992) identifies suprainiac fossae in both Qafzeh 6 and Skhūl 9; FS identifies a fossa only in the later specimen.

THE ASSIMILATION ALTERNATIVE

In 1989, an alternative model for modern human origins was proposed – the 'assimilation' model (AM; Smith et al. 1989). The AM agrees with RAO that the preponderance of available evidence, both morphological and genetic, indicates an initial origin of modern human morphology in Africa around 160,000 years ago. However, the AM sees evidence for introgression between expanding modern populations and the archaic aborigines they encountered in various regions of Eurasia. The AM differs from MRE by positing that the archaic contribution to modern populations was always relatively small, and thus continuity would only be found in limited details of anatomy.

As an example, Table 20.1 presents data for four features, three of which show a closer connection between EME and Neandertals than between EME and their presumptive ancestors from the Near East. These data can be potentially explained in three ways. First, these features – as well as others, like occipital bunning (also highly frequent in Neandertals and EME, but not in Skhūl/Qafzeh) and the cold-adapted limb proportions of the 24,500-year-old Lagar Velho child from Portugal (Trinkaus and Zilhão 2002) – may represent Neandertal contributions to EME populations. Second, these same features may not be homologous in Neandertals and EMEs and thus they may reflect no biological connection between them. Third, the features could be basically homologues that have evolved independently in moderns and Neandertals and just happen to be present in higher frequencies in EME than in other modern populations. The last explanation seems unlikely, but the other two are distinct possibilities. Supporters of RAO strongly uphold the second alternative and do not accept any morphological evidence of regional continuity anywhere in Eurasia.

Specifically, they argue that features claimed to demonstrate such continuity are homoplasies. Supporters of continuity try to counter such arguments. A detailed assessment of these arguments is beyond the scope of the present review, but one may wish to ask ask if other data might shed light on this question.

Although most of the genetic evidence probably indicates an African origin for the vast majority of modern human genes, that is not true for all genes. The evidence in question is reviewed by Templeton (2005), who demonstrates that some nuclear genes are likely to have an Asian origin (Figure 20.2). Also, Evans and colleagues (2006) identify a specific group of closely related variants of the microcephalin (MCPH1) gene: the haplotype D group, which arose from a common ancestor about 37,000 years ago. According to this research, the mutation arose from a lineage that diverged from the modern human one significantly earlier; entered the modern human gene pools through admixture with the representatives of this lineage; and rose quickly to a frequency of about 70 percent, through positive selection. The positive selection stems from the fact that, although the exact function of MCPH1 is unclear, it is critical to normal brain development and function. Evans and colleagues note that finding a gene that reflects relatively low levels of admixture is generally difficult because weakly selected or neutral alleles from such a source would tend to be lost by drift or other factors. MCPH1 is an exception, because of the strong positive selection acting on it. They conclude that their work on microcephalin supports the possibility of low levels of admixture between modern and archaic humans around 37,000 years ago.

The 'mostly out of Africa' genetic model reflected by the above examples (see Relethford 2001) fits nicely with the AM and with the assertion that what probably happened to Neandertals and other archaic folk was demographic and genetic swamping by numerically superior populations of modern humans over a few millennia (Smith et al. 2005; Cartmill and Smith 2009). Such a model is commensurate with the previously stated argument that archaic people, especially Neandertals, were relatively rare on the landscape compared with early moderns (Hassan 1981; Premo and Hublin 2009); it is also commensurate with indications of ecological niche (and of resulting geographic) expansion by early moderns (Banks et al. 2008). Thus relatively little archaic Eurasian biological contribution would be expected in early moderns; and, as the data in Table 20.1 also reflect, this contribution would generally decrease over time, with the increased impacts of swamping. The only exception could be certain genetic features with strong positive selection; but it may be that no such features exist in the skeletal morphology.

Perhaps evidence of archaic contributions could be found in the ancient DNA of early modern people. In Europe, the available mtDNA sequences in European upper Paleolithic skeletons (of 32,000 to 24,000 years ago) reveal no Neandertal contribution (Caramelli et al. 2003; Serre et al. 2004); but it is noted by Serre and colleagues that the available data can only exclude a Neandertal contribution of more than 25 percent. Twenty-five percent is far above what the AM would predict. A single mtDNA sequence from an early modern Australian, Willandra Lakes (Mungo) 3, represents a haplotype not found in modern Australians or in other recent humans (Adcock et al. 2001). If this lineage could go extinct in less than 30,000 years, so too could any mitochondrial lineages potentially contributed by Neandertals or other archaic Eurasians to the earliest modern populations.

A final issue concerns the amount of time, or generations, necessary for speciation in medium-sized mammals (Holliday 2006). Even if one adopts the maximum suggestion of 700,000–800,000 years for the divergence of Neandertal and modern human lineages, there is still not sufficient time, presumably, for the establishment of reproductive isolation between these lineages, even if the morphology appears to be very different (Cartmill and Smith 2009). This is especially true in view of the larger body size (Conroy 2002) and the very broad, generalist adaptation of the genus *Homo*.

'RACES,' NOT SPECIES

Based on these factors, the argument that post-erectine humans represent a single lineage (species) is much more robust than many supporters of RAO imply. Neandertals (and other archaic populations) are regional human groups with distinctive sets of anatomical and genetic features, but they are not unequivocally different species. Rather, they conform to the textbook definition of subspecies (or races) as given by Mayr (1963). Many anthropologists have argued for some time that living humans do not conform to the biological concept of race (for an overview, see Larsen 2008), and genetic studies show that living humans have truncated genetic diversity compared to other wide-ranging mammalian species. In fact it has been shown that, if one combines Neandertal and living human mitochondrial DNA, the variation is similar to that seen in the living subspecies (races) of chimpanzees (Morin et al. 1994). The fact is that all living humans are evolved from what was the late Pleistocene African 'race' of humans which became *Homo sapiens sapiens*. To see true 'racial' variation in humans, one has to go to the fossil record. It is the Neandertals, the Ngandong people, the archaic East Asians, and possibly others that reflect the original regional Eurasian adaptations of humans. Thus a good case can be made that these groups should be taxonomically designated as subspecies, and not as species. These earlier subspecies are extinct, but not in the classic sense of the concept. Rather they have been assimilated into a larger human subspecies – us. This 'extinction' through assimilation (cf. Levin 2002) has been, and continues to be, a common theme in recent human history. The evidence suggests that it probably explains the evolutionary history of middle and late Pleistocene humans as well.

REFERENCES

Adcock, G., Dennis, E., Easteal, S., Huttley, G., Jerimn, L., Peacock, W., and Thorne, A. (2001) Mitochondrial DNA Sequences in Ancient Australians: Implications for Modern Human Origin. *Proceedings of the National Academy of Sciences, USA* 98: 537–542.

Aiello, L., and Wheeler, P. (2003) Neanderthal Thermoregulation and the Glacial Climate. In T. van Andel and W. Davies (eds), *Neanderthals and Modern Humans in the European Landscape during the Last Glaciation* (pp. 147–166). Cambridge: McDonald Institute for Archaeological Research.

Arcadi, A. (2006) Species Resilience in Pleistocene Hominids That Traveled Far and Ate Widely: An Analogy to the Wolf-Like Canids. *Journal of Human Evolution* 51: 383–394.

Arsuaga, J., Martínez, I., Gracia, A., and Lorenzo, C. (1997) The Sima de los Huesos Crania (Sierra de Atapuerca, Spain). A Comparative Study. *Journal of Human Evolution* 33: 219–281.

Arsuaga, J., Lorenzo, C., Carretero, J., Gracia, A., Martínez, I., García, N., Bermúdez de Castro, J., and Carbonell, E. (1999). A Complete Human Pelvis from the Middle Pleistocene of Spain. *Nature* 399: 255–258.

Banks, W., d'Errico, F., Peterson, A. T., Kageyama, M., Sima, A., and Sánchez-Goñi, M.-F. (2008) Neanderthal Extinction by Competitive Exclusion. *PLoS One* 3: e3972 (www.plosone.org).

Barker, G., Barton, H., Bird, M., et al. (2007) The 'Human Revolution' in Lowland Tropical Southeast Asia: The Antiquity and Behavior of Anatomically Modern Humans at Niah Cave (Sarawak, Borneo). *Journal of Human Evolution* 52: 243–261.

Bar-Yosef, O. (2006) Neanderthals and Modern Humans: A Different Interpretation. In N. Conard (ed.), *When Neanderthals and Modern Humans Met* (pp. 467–482). Tübingen: Kerns-Verlag.

Bermúdez de Castro, J., Arsuaga, J, Carbonell, E., Rosas, A., Martínez, I., and Mosquera, M. (1997) A Hominid from the Lower Pleistocene of Atapuerca, Spain: Possible Ancestor to Neandertals and Modern Humans. *Science* 276: 1392–1395.

Bowler, J., Johnson, H., Olley, J., Prescott, J., Roberts, R., Shawcross, W., and Spooner, N. (2003) New Ages for Human Occupation and Climatic Change at Lake Mungo, Australia. *Nature* 421: 837–840.

Bräuer, G. (1984) A Craniological Approach to the Origin of Anatomically Modern *Homo sapiens* in Africa and Implications for the Appearance of Modern Europeans. In F. H. Smith and F. Spencer (eds), *The Origins of Modern Humans. A World Survey of the Fossil Evidence* (pp. 327–410). New York: Liss.

Bräuer, G. (2006) The African Origin of Modern Humans and the Replacement of the Neanderthals. In R. Schmitz (ed.), *Neanderthal 1856–2006* (pp. 337–372). Mainz: Verlag Philipp von Zabern.

Bräuer, G. (2008) The Origin of Modern Human Anatomy: By Speciation or Intraspecific Evolution? *Evolutionary Anthropology* 17: 22–37.

Bräuer, G., Broeg, H., and Stringer, C. (2006) Earliest Upper Paleolithic Crania from Mladeč, Czech Republic and the Question of Neanderthal–Modern Continuity: Metrical Evidence from the Fronto-Facial Region. In K. Harvati and T. Harrison (eds), *Neanderthals Revisited: New Approaches and Perspectives* (pp. 269–279). Dordrecht: Springer.

Bräuer, G., Collard, M., and Stringer, C. (2004) On the Reliability of Recent Tests of the Out of Africa Hypothesis for Modern Human Origins. *Anatomical Record* 279A: 701–707.

Brown, F., and Fuller, C. (2008) Stratigraphy and Tephra of the Kibish Hominin Sites KHS and PHS, Lower Omo Valley, Ethiopia. *Journal of Human Evolution* 55: 366–403.

Cann, R., Stoneking, M., and Wilson, A. (1987) Mitochondrial DNA and Human Evolution. *Nature* 325: 31–36.

Caramelli, D., Lalueza-Fox, C., Vernesi, C., Lari, M., Casoli, A., Mallegni, F., Chiarelli, B., Dupanloup, I., Bertranpetit, J., Barbujani, G., and Bertorelli, G. (2003) Evidence for a Genetic Discontinuity between Neandertals and 24,000-year-old Anatomically Modern Europeans. *Proceedings of the National Academy of Sciences, USA* 100: 6593–6597.

Cartmill, M., and Smith, F. H. (2009) *The Human Lineage*. Hoboken: Wiley–Blackwell.

Churchill, S. (2006) Bioenergetic Perspectives on Neanderthal Thermoregulatory and Activity Budgets. In K. Harvati and T. Harrison (eds), *Neanderthals Revisited: New Approaches and Perspectives* (pp. 113–133). Dordrecht: Springer.

Churchill, S., and Smith, F. H. (2000) Makers of the Earliest Aurignacian of Europe. *Yearbook of Physical Anthropology* 43: 61–115.

Clark, J. D., Beyenne, Y., WoldeGabriel, G., Hart, W., Renne, P., Gilbert, H., Aefluer, A., Suwa, G., Katoh, S., Ludwig, K., Boisserie, J., Asfaw, B., and White, T. (2003) Stratigraphic, Chronological and Behavioural Context of Pleistocene *Homo sapiens* from Middle Awash, Ethiopia. *Nature* 423: 747–752.

Clark, J. D., de Heinzelin, J., Schick, K., Hart, W., White, T., WoldeGabriel, G., Walter, R., Suwa, G., Asfaw, B., Vrba, E., and Haile-Selassie, Y. (1994) African *Homo erectus*: Old Radiometric Ages and Young Oldowan Assemblages in the Middle Awash Valley, Ethiopia. *Nature* 264: 1907–1910.

Conroy, G. (2002) Speciosity in the Early *Homo* Lineage: Too Many, Too Few, or Just About Right? *Journal of Human Evolution* 43: 759–766.

Day, M. (1969) Omo Human Skeletal Remains. *Nature* 222: 1135–1138.

Dean, D., Hublin, J., Holloway, R., and Ziegler, R. (1998) On the Phylogenetic Position of the Pre-Neandertal Specimen from Reilingen, Germany. *Journal of Human Evolution* 34: 485–508.

Eldredge, N., and Tattersall, I. (1982) *The Myths of Human Evolution*. New York: Columbia University Press.

Evans, P., Mekel-Bobrov, N., Vallender, E., Hudson, R., and Lahn, B. (2006) Evidence that the Adaptive Allele of the Brain Size Gene Microcephalin Introgressed into *Homo sapiens* from an Archaic *Homo* Lineage. *Proceedings of the National Academy of Sciences, USA* 103: 18178–18183.

Finlayson, C. (2004) *Neanderthals and Modern Humans. An Ecological and Evolutionary Perspective*. Cambridge: University of Cambridge Press.

Foley, R. (1991) How Many Species of Hominid Should Their Be? *Journal of Human Evolution* 20: 413–427.

Frayer, D. (1992) Evolution at the European Edge: Neanderthal and Upper Paleolithic Relationships. *Préhistoire européenne* 2: 9–69.

Gingerich, P. (1984) Primate Evolution: Evidence from the Fossil Record, Comparative Morphology, and Molecular Biology. *Yearbook of Physical Anthropology* 27: 57–72.

Glantz, M., Athreya, S., and Ritzman, T. (2009) Is Central Asia the Eastern Outpost of the Neandertal Range? A Reassessment of the Teshik Task Child. *American Journal of Physical Anthropology* 138: 45–61.

Gould, S. (1987) Bushes All the Way Down. *Natural History* 96: 12–19.

Gould, S. (1988) A Novel Notion of Neanderthal. *Natural History* 97: 16–21.

Green, R., Krause, J., Ptak, S., Briggs, A., Ronan, M., Du, L., Egholm, M., Rothberg, J., Paunović, M., and Pääbo, S. (2006) Analysis of One Million Base Pairs of Neanderthal DNA. *Nature* 444: 330–336.

Grün, R. (2006) Direct Dating of Human Fossils. *Yearbook of Physical Anthropology* 49: 2–48.

Hassan, F. (1981) *Demographic Archaeology*. New York: Academic Press.

Hawks, J. (2006) Selection on Mitochondrial DNA and the Neanderthal Problem. In K. Harvati and T. Harrison (eds), *Neanderthals Revisited: New Approaches and Perspectives* (pp. 221–238). Dordrecht: Springer.

Higham, T., Bronk-Ramsey, C., Karavanić, I., Smith, F., and Trinkaus, E. (2006) Revised Direct Radiocarbon Dating of the Vindija G$_1$ Upper Paleolithic Neandertals. *Proceedings of the National Academy of Sciences, USA* 103: 553–557.

Holliday, T. (1997a) Body Proportions in Late Pleistocene Europe and Modern Human Origins. *Journal of Human Evolution* 32: 423–447.

Holliday, T. (1997b) Postcranial Evidence of Cold Adaptation in European Neandertals. *American Journal of Physical Anthropology* 104: 245–258.

Holliday, T. (2000) Evolution at the Crossroads: Modern Human Emergence in Western Asia. *American Anthropologist* 102: 54–68.

Holliday, T. (2003) Species Concepts, Reticulation, and Human Evolution. *Current Anthropology* 44: 653–673.

Holliday, T. (2006) Neanderthals and Modern Humans: An Example of a Mammalian Syngameon? In K. Harvati and T. Harrison (eds), *Neanderthals Revisited: New Approaches and Perspectives* (pp. 281–297). Dordrecht: Springer.

Hublin, J.-J., and Bailey, S. (2006) Revisiting the Last Neanderthals. In N. Conard (ed.), *When Neanderthals and Modern Humans Met* (pp. 105–128). Tübingen: Kerns-Verlag.

Hublin, J.-J., Ruiz, C., Lara, P., Fontugne, M., and Reyss, J. (1995) The Mousterian Site of Zafarraya (Andalucia, Spain): Dating and Implications on the Paleolithic Peopling Process of Western Europe. *Comptes Rendus de l'Académie des Sciences de Paris* 312 (Série II a): 931–937.

Hublin, J.-J., Spoor, F., Braun, M., Zonneveld, F., and Condemi, S. (1996) A Late Neanderthal Associated with Upper Paleolithic Artifacts. *Nature* 381: 224–226.

Kappelman, J., Alçiçek, M., Kazanci, N., Schultz, M., Özkul, M., and Şen, Ş (2008) Brief Communication: First *Homo erectus* from Turkey and Implications for Migrations into Temperate Eurasia. *American Journal of Physical Anthropology* 135: 110–116.

Klein, R. (1999) *The Human Career. Human Biological and Cultural Origins*, 2nd edn. Chicago: University of Chicago Press.

Klein, R., Avery, G., Cruz-Uribe, K., and Steele, Y. (2006) The Mammalian Fauna Associated with an Archaic Hominin Skullcap and Later Acheulean Artifacts at Elandsfontein, Western Cape Province, South Africa. *Journal of Human Evolution* 52: 164–186.

Krause, J., Orlando, L., Serre, D., Viola, B., Prüfer, K., Richards, M., Hublin, J.-J., Hänni, C., Derevienko, A., and Pääbo, S. (2007) Neandertals in Central Asia and Siberia. *Nature* 442: 902–904.

Kuhn, S., and Steiner, M. (2006) What's a Mother to Do? The Division of Labor among Neandertals and Modern Humans in Eurasia. *Current Anthropology* 47: 953–980.

Larsen, C. S. (2008) *Our Origins. Discovering Physical Anthropology*. New York: Norton.

Leonard, W. (2002) Food for Thought. *Scientific American* 287: 106–115.

Leonard, W., Sorensen, M., Galloway, V., Spencer, G., Mosher, M., Osipova, L., and Spitsyn, V. (2002) Climatic Influences on Basal Metabolic Rates among Circumpolar Populations. *American Journal of Human Biology* 14: 609–620.

Levin, D. (2002) Hybridization and Extinction. *American Scientist* 90: 254–261.

Lévêque, F., and Vandermeersch, B. (1981) Le Néanderthalien de Saint-Césaire. *La Recherche* 12: 242–244.

Mayr, E. (1963) *Animal Species and Evolution*. Cambridge: Harvard University Press.

Mellars, P. (2006) A New Radiocarbon Revolution and the Dispersal of Modern Humans in Eurasia. *Nature* 438: 931–935.

Morin, P., Moore, J., Chakraborty, R., Jin, L., Goodall, J., and Woodruff, D. (1994) Kin Selection, Social Structure, Gene Flow, and the Evolution of Chimpanzees. *Science* 265: 1193–1201.

Noonan, J., Coop, G., Kudaravalli, S., Smith, D., Krause, J., Alessi, J., Chen, F., Platt, D., Pääbo, S., Pritchard, J., and Rubin, E. (2006) Sequencing and Analysis of Neanderthal Genomic DNA. *Science* 314: 1113–1118.

O'Connell, J. (2006) How Did Modern Humans Displace Neanderthals? Insights from Hunter–Gatherer Ethnography and Archaeology. In N. Conard (ed.), *When Neanderthals and Modern Humans Met* (pp. 43–64). Tübingen: Kerns-Verlag.

Patterson, H. (1992) The Recognition Concept of Species. In M. Ereshefsky (ed.), *The Units of Evolution: Essays on the Nature of Species* (pp. 139–158). Cambridge MA: MIT Press.

Pearson, O. (2000) Postcranial Remains and the Origin of Modern Humans. *Evolutionary Anthropology* 9: 229–247.

Pearson, O. (2004) Has the Combination of Genetic and Fossil Evidence Solved the Riddle of Modern Human Origins? *Evolutionary Anthropology* 13: 145–159.

Pearson, O. (2008) Statistical and Biological Definitions of 'Anatomically Modern' Humans: Suggestions for a Unified Approach to Modern Morphology. *Evolutionary Anthropology* 17: 38–48.

Pearson, O., Royer, D., Grine, F., and Fleagle, J. (2008) A Description of the Omo 1 Postcranial Skeleton, Including Newly Discovered Fossils. *Journal of Human Evolution* 55: 421–437.

Premo, L. S., and Hublin, J.-J. (2009) Culture, Population Structure, and Low Genetic Diversity in Pleistocene Hominins. *Proceedings of the National Academy of Sciences, USA* 106: 33–37.

Rak, Y. (1986) The Neanderthal: A New Look at an Old Face. *Journal of Human Evolution* 15: 151–164.

Rak, Y., Ginzburg, A., and Geffen, E (2002) Does *Homo neanderthalensis* Play a Role in Modern Human Ancestry? The Mandibular Evidence. *American Journal of Physical Anthropology* 119: 199–204.

Relethford, J. (2001) *Genetics and the Search for Modern Human Origins*. New York: Wiley–Liss.

Richards, M., Pettitt, P., Trinkaus, E., Smith, F., Paunović, M., and Karavanić, I. (2000) Neanderthal Diet and Vindija and Neanderthal Predation: The Evidence from Stable Isotopes. *Proceedings of the National Academy of Sciences, USA* 97: 7663–7666.

Rightmire, G. P. (1990) *The Evolution of Homo Erectus*. Cambridge: Cambridge University Press.

Rightmire, G. P. (1998) Human Evolution in the Middle Pleistocene: The Role of *Homo heidelbergensis*. *Evolutionary Anthropology* 6: 218–227.

Rightmire, G. P. (2008) *Homo* in the Middle Pleistocene: Hypodigms, Variation, and Species Recognition. *Evolutionary Anthropology* 17: 8–21.

Rosenberg, K. (1988) The Functional Significance of Neandertal Pubic Length. *Current Anthropology* 29: 595–617.

Rosenberg, K., Ziné, L., and Ruff, C. (2006) Body Size, Body Form and Encephalization in a Middle Pleistocene Archaic Human from Northern China. *Proceedings of the National Academy of Sciences, USA* 103: 3352–3556.

Ruff, C., Trinkaus, E., and Holliday, T. (1997) Body Mass and Encephalization in Pleistocene *Homo*. *Nature* 387: 173–176.

Ruff, C., Trinkaus, E., and Holliday, T. (2002) Body Proportions and Size. In J. Zilhão and E. Trinkaus (eds), *Portrait of the Artist as a Young Child. The Gravettian Human Skeleton from the Abrigo do Lagar Velho and its Archaeological Context* (pp. 365–391). Lisbon: *Trabalhos de Arqueologia* Number 22.

Santa Luca, A. (1978) A Re-Examination of Presumed Neanderthal Fossils. *Journal of Human Evolution* 7: 619–636.

Santa Luca, A. (1980) The Ngandong Fossil Hominids. *Yale University Publications in Anthropology* (New Haven) 78: 1–175.

Serrat, M., King, D., and Lovejoy, C. O. (2008) Temperature Regulates Limb Length in Homeotherms by Directly Modulating Cartilage Growth. *Proceedings of the National Academy of Sciences, USA* 105: 19348–19353.

Serre, D., Langaney, A., Chech, M., Teschler-Nikola, M., Paunović, M., Mennecier, P., Hofreiter, P., Possnert, G., and Pääbo, S. (2004) No Evidence of Neandertal mtDNA Contribution to Early Modern Humans. *PLoS* (*Public Library of Science*) *Biology* 2: 313–317.

Shang, H., Tong, H., Zhang, F., Chen, F., and Trinkaus, E. (2007) An Early Modern Human from Tianyuan Cave, Zhoukoudian, China. *Proceedings of the National Academy of Sciences USA* 104: 6573–6578.

Simpson, G. G. (1961) *Principles of Animal Taxonomy*. New York: Columbia University Press.

Smith, F. (1994) Samples, Species and Speculations in the Study of Modern Human Origins. In M. Nitecki and D. Nitecki (eds), *Origins of Anatomically Modern Humans* (pp. 227–249). New York: Plenum.

Smith, F. (2002) Migrations, Radiations, and Continuity: Patterns in he Evolution of Middle and Late Pleistocene Humans. In W. Hartwig (ed.), *The Primate Fossil Record* (pp. 437–456). Cambridge: University of Cambridge Press.

Smith, F., Falsetti, A., and Donnelly, S. (1989) Modern Human Origins. *Yearbook of Physical Anthropology* 32: 35–68.

Smith, F., and Paquette, S. (1989) The Adaptive Basis of Neandertal Facial Form, with Some Thoughts on the Nature of Modern Human Origins. In E. Trinkaus (ed.), *The Emergence of Modern Humans. Biolcultural Adaptations in the Later Pleistocene* (pp. 181–210). Cambridge: University of Cambridge Press.

Smith, F., Janković, I., and Karavanić, I. (2005) The Assimilation Model, Modern Human Origins in Europe, and the Extinction of the Neandertals. *Quaternary International* 137: 7–19.

Sorensen, M., and Leonard, W., (2001) Neandertal Energetics and Foraging Efficiency. *Journal of Human Evolution* 40: 483–495.

Stringer, C. (1994) Out of Africa: A Personal History. In M. Nitecki and D. Nitecki (eds), *Origins of Anatomically Modern Humans* (pp. 149–174). New York: Plenum.

Stringer, C., and Andrews, P. (1988) Genetic and Fossil Evidence for the Origin of Modern Humans. *Science* 239: 1263–1268.

Stringer, C., Cornish, L., and Stuart-Macadam, P. (1985) Preparation and Further Study of the Singa Skull from the Sudan. *Bulletin of the British Museum of Natural History (Geology)* 38: 347–358.

Swisher, C., Rink, W., Antón, S., Schwarcz, H., Curtis, G., Suprijo, A., and Widiasmoro, S. (1996) Latest *Homo erectus* of Java: Potential Contemporaneity with *Homo sapiens* in Southeast Asia. *Science* 274: 1870–1874.

Tattersall, I. (1986) Species Recognition in Human Paleontology. *Journal of Human Evolution* 15: 165–175.

Tattersall, I., and Schwartz, J. (2008) The Morphological Distinctiveness of *Homo sapiens* and Its Recognition in the Fossil Record: Clarifying the Problem. *Evolutionary Anthropology* 17: 49–54.

Templeton, A. (2005) Haplotype Trees and Modern Human Origins. *Yearbook of Physical Anthropology* 48: 33–59.

Thackeray, F., Maureille, B., Vandermeersch, B., Braga, J., and Chaix, R. (2005) Morphometric Comparasions between Neanderthals and 'Anatomically Modern' *Homo sapiens* from Europe and the Near East. *Annals of the Transvaal Museum* 42: 47–51.

Thorne, A., Grün, R., Mortimer, G., Spooner, N., Simpson, J., McCulloch, M., Taylor, A., and Curnoe, D. (1999) Australia's Oldest Human Remains: Age of the Lake Mungo 3 Skeleton. *Journal of Human Evolution* 36: 591–612.

Trinkaus, E. (2005) Early Modern Humans. *Annual Review of Anthropology* 34: 207–230.

Trinkaus, E. (2006) Modern Human versus Neandertal Evolutionary Distinctiveness. *Current Anthropology* 47: 597–620.

Trinkaus, E., and Zilhão, J. (2002) Phylogenetic Implications. In J. Zilhão and E. Trinkaus (eds), *Portrait of the Artist as a Young Child. The Gravettian Human Skeleton from the Abrigo do Lagar Velho and its Archaeological Context* (pp. 497–518). Lisbon: *Trabalhos de Arqueologia* Number 22.

Trinkaus, E., Stringer, C., Ruff, C., Hennessy, R., Roberts, M., and Parfitt, S. (1999) Diaphyseal Cross-Sectional Geometry of the Boxgrove 1 Middle Pleistocene Human Tibia. *Journal of Human Evolution* 37: 1–25.

Vandermeersch, B. (1981) *Les Hommes fossiles de Qafzeh (Israël)*. Paris: CNRS.

Vrba, E. (1984) Evolutionary Pattern and Process in the Sister-Group Alcelaphini–Aepycerotini (Mammalia: Bovidae). In N. Eldredge and S. Stanley (eds), *Living Fossils* (pp. 62–79). New York: Springer.

Weaver, T., and Roseman, C. (2008) New Developments in the Genetic Evidence for Modern Human Origins. *Evolutionary Anthropology* 17: 69–80.

White, L. A. (1949) *The Science of Culture: A Study of Man and Civilization*. New York: Farrar, Straus and Cudahy.

White, T., Asfaw, B., DeGusta, D., Gilbert, H., Richards, G., Suwa, G., and Howell, F. C. (2003) Pleistocene *Homo sapiens* from Middle Awash, Ehiopia. *Nature* 423: 742–747.

Wolpoff, M. (1999) *Paleoanthropology*, 2nd edn. New York: McGraw-Hill.

Wolpoff, M., Mannheim, B., Mann, A., Hawks, J., Caspari, R., Rosenberg, K., Frayer, D., Gill, G., and Clark, G. (2004) Why not the Neandertals? *World Archaeology* 36: 527–546.

Wu, X., and Poirier, F. (1995) *Human Evolution in China*. Oxford: Oxford University Press.

Zilhão, J. (2006) Neandertals and Moderns Mixed, and It Matters. *Evolutionary Anthropology* 15: 183–195.

CHAPTER 21 Bioarchaeology: Health, Lifestyle, and Society in Recent Human Evolution

Clark Spencer Larsen and Phillip L. Walker

The study of human remains from archaeological contexts has a long history. Indeed, it is the study of remains of past humans that begins the history of biological anthropology. Much of this record – even into recent times – was dominated by a focus on cranial typology and classification (for discussion, see Cook 2006 and Little and Sussman's chapter in the present volume). In the twentieth century, as biological anthropologists began to explore in further detail variations within and between populations, temporal trends in cranial morphology, the influence of extrinsic factors on skeletal growth and development, and modern statistical analysis, it became clear that the typological–racial paradigm, so entrenched in anthropological method and theory, was inappropriate for interpreting biological variation. Rather, variation – in present and past populations – is best understood as the result of dynamic processes involving the interaction between biology and culture. This *biocultural* approach came into play in the late 1960s and 1970s, especially with the influence of George Armelagos, Jane Buikstra and their students on the study of archaeological human remains from diverse settings in Africa and North America (Armelagos 1969; Carlson and Van Gerven 1977, 1979; Buikstra 1977, 1988). Their work set the course of modern bioarchaeology and established its central role in understanding recent human adaptation and evolution.

The current usage of the term 'bioarchaeology' was first introduced by Jane Buikstra (1977) in reference to multidisciplinary research on human remains in the lower Illinois River Valley, especially in relation to mortuary behavior and social organization, health, demography, population history, and activity. Her approach to the study of archaeological human remains was grounded in the scientific method and it presented a strong case for the view that these remains have much to tell us about the human condition in regional perspective. In the next ten years, two papers defined in broader terms the issues addressed today in the field. One was largely devoted to diet and to nutrition in particular (Huss-Ashmore et al. 1982), the other to bioarchaeology in general (Larsen 1987). This later paper was expanded to a book-length treatment of the topic (Larsen 1997). More recently, a new treatment of the field provides an historical overview of different areas dealing with the study of ancient remains (Buikstra and Beck 2006).

Contrary to Goldstein's (2006) assertion that the study of human remains has largely involved a disengagement of the archaeologist from the concerns of physical anthropologist, whereby the latter "does not necessarily need the archaeologist once the archaeologist has excavated bones" (2006: 376–377), there has been a growing movement linking archaeology and biological anthropology in the development of research programs. This melding of two branches of anthropology has proved to be of critical importance to the understanding of health, disease, lifestyle, social history, and other areas. The field has grown from a methodologically driven tool to a theoretically informed discipline, generating a new understanding both of the biological and of social past of humans (Knudson and Stojanowski 2009; Gowland and Knüsel 2006).

Bioarchaeology is the study of human remains from archaeological contexts, especially during the last 10,000 years of human evolution. (Paleoanthropologists, generally speaking, study fossilized remains dating from the Pleistocene or earlier periods.) 'Contexts' involve here more than just what is found in a burial or cemetery. Rather, contexts refer to the skeletons together with all the circumstances that shaped the lives of the person or persons represented by these skeletons. Specifically, bioarchaeology strives to understand human biology within a broad cultural context, by linking biology to culture. This biocultural paradigm is now well established in this and other areas of biological anthropology, especially in so far as it pertains to understanding human variability.

THE ELEMENTS OF BIOARCHAEOLOGY

The skeleton is a rich record of a person's life history, from the stage prior to birth, when bones and teeth are beginning to form, through infancy to childhood, adolescence, and adulthood. This is because the living skeleton is dynamic: over the course of life, bone tissue forms and remodels, teeth develop and wear, and growth and development continue even after the skeleton and the dentition have reached adulthood. Moreover, these processes are influenced by all circumstances of life and living, for instance access to nutrients, exposure to infectious pathogens, and physical activity – to name just a few (and see below). The two dominant areas of bioarchaeological inquiry are health and lifestyle (the latter is narrowly defined, for our purposes here, as activity and workload). The broad perspective – dealing with all times and all places – is possible because of the samples, in many circumstances very large, of individuals represented in cemeteries worldwide. There is a long history in biological anthropology of studying skeletons from cemeteries; but only within the last three or four decades has much of the attention shifted to regarding these skeletons as members of once living populations, *as though they were alive today*. That is, bioarchaeology is not just the biological study of death and the dead. Rather, its focus is on reconstructing and interpreting living worlds.

Measuring and interpreting health and lifestyle

Central to health and wellbeing is nutritional adequacy. For normal growth and development from conception through adulthood, humans require adequate protein and energy (see Dufour's chapter in the present volume). While it is difficult to measure nutritional quality in past populations, much can be inferred via dietary reconstruction. Until the later twentieth century, dietary reconstruction in archaeological settings was accomplished mostly through the study of animal and plant remains recovered from habitation contexts. While this approach provides a record of the presence and consumption of specific foods, it gives only limited insight into nutrition, since we can never know the quantity of foods consumed solely on on the basis of plant and animal remains.

With respect to maize consumption and nutritional inference, a wonderful breakthrough began with the pioneering research undertaken by Vogel and van der Merwe (1977) on prehistoric maize consumers in New York State. Their investigation of bone chemistry proved to be a powerful tool for dietary reconstruction and nutritional inference at individual and populational level. This approach focuses mostly on dietary reconstruction through the analysis of carbon stable isotopes, and specifically on the ratios of $^{13}C/^{12}C$ (Katzenberg 2008; Schoeninger's chapter in the present volume) and on how diet is revealed in the tissues of animal (including human) consumers. Stable isotope values reflect variation in the way plants 'fix' carbon in photosynthesis. For example maize, a plant with a C_4 photosynthetic pathway, has more ^{13}C in relation to ^{12}C than other plants from temperate regions have. In addition, ratios of $^{13}C/^{12}C$ are useful for identifying the amount of marine foods vs terrestrial foods consumed by humans (Katzenberg 2008). Later research on stable nitrogen isotopes revealed that the higher the trophic level, the greater the enrichment in ^{15}N relatively to ^{14}N (Katzenberg 2008). Thus humans who consume a high amount of meat should have a higher $^{15}N/^{14}N$ ratio. In addition to carbon and nitrogen stable isotope ratios, oxygen and strontium isotopes have been used to identify diet and foodways.

These approaches to paleodiet provide details on the importance of different kinds of foods, thus allowing inferences to be made about nutrition. Stable isotope analysis revealed that native North American populations probably consumed maize for centuries, but maize did not become a central component of diet until after about AD 800 in eastern North America (Ambrose 1987; Schwarcz 2006). The adoption of a maize-based diet indicates the likelihood of a decline in nutritional health. That is, maize is deficient in key aminoacids essential for growth and development; it has phytic acid, which lowers the bioavailability of iron; and it is a starch. Indeed the study of many thousands of human skeletons by bioarchaeologists reveals the consequences of an increasingly compromised nutritional status, namely reduction in growth rates in juveniles, reduction in adult terminal height (stature), evidence of iron deficiency anemia, and tooth decay (Larsen 1995).

Dental caries, or tooth decay, is a key marker of the kinds of foods eaten in recent human evolution. With some exceptions, populations living exclusively on wild, non-domesticated plants and animals have relatively few carious lesions. As soon as agriculture was adopted, many of these same populations had a higher prevalence of dental caries. Dental caries, a disease process, is caused by the production of lactic acid by normal oral flora (for instance by *Streptococcus mutans*). Lactic acid is a byproduct of the metabolism of carbohydrates, especially sugars and starches (Hillson 2008).

Other infectious diseases documented in past populations include treponematosis (venereal syphilis, nonvenereal/endemic syphilis, and yaws), tuberculosis, and leprosy (Ortner 2008). In some areas of the world these diseases were highly prevalent – for instance endemic (nonvenereal) syphilis in eastern North America, tuberculosis in both New World and Old World settings, and leprosy in northern Europe. These diseases are very clearly associated with population sedentism, crowding, poor sanitation, and reduced nutrition. Many infections documented in past populations cannot be linked to a particular pathogen. In recent years, however, the increased ability to extract and amplify the DNA of the disease-causing organisms has added to our diagnostic precision and knowledge of the history of specific infectious diseases (Stone 2008).

Stress – physiological disruption resulting from impoverished environmental circumstances – is experienced by all populations and all societies. Stress deriving from poor health due to poor nutrition, disease, or the synergistic interaction between nutrition and disease can be so severe that the cells responsible for the development of teeth and bones can be disrupted. Disruption of dental growth results in enamel deficiencies, called enamel hypoplasia (see Guatelli-Steinberg's chapter in the present volume). Typically, these deficiencies are expressed as lines, or bands, of enamel deficiency. Hypoplasias are especially prevalent in populations exposed to forms of stress caused by overcrowding, reduced nutrition, or increased exposure to infectious disease.

Lifestyle and adaptation: Above and below the neck

Beginning with pioneering work by David Carlson and Dennis Van Gerven (1977), there has been an increased interest in human cranial morphology, not for typology and classification, but rather as a source of information on the craniofacial function and for inferences about dietary adaptation. Their study of craniofacial changes in the Nile River Valley of Sudan (Nubia) revealed a reduction in robustness, decrease in tooth and jaw size, and a broadening and shortening of the skull. In relation to the increased focus on domesticated plants, food technology change, and other factors, they linked these changes in skeletal morphology to a diminished masticatory demand. Since their study, similar changes have been documented in other regions of the globe, where transitions took places from foraging to farming and to intensifed farming (Larsen 1997).

The inferred reduction in masticatory stress has also been documented via the analysis of both macroscopic and microscopic tooth wear in a range of Holocene human populations. For example the teeth of foragers tend to be flat, whereas farmers' teeth tend to be cupped (Smith 1984). In addition, with some exceptions, the severity of wear tends to be greater in foraging societies than in farming societies, reflecting the combination between changes in subsistence technology and food preparation (for instance the use of ceramic vessels to boil food) and the kinds of foods eaten (Larsen 1995).

New insights into dental function and dietary adaptation have come from the study of microscopic damage on the occlusal surfaces of teeth. In particular, the application of scanning electron microscopy reveals that humans who eat soft or otherwise relatively non-abrasive foods display fewer microwear features like scratches and pits (Teaford 1991; Ungar et al. 2008). Basically, the larger picture of recent human evolution – that is, evolution over the last five to six thousand years – reveals a decline in the texture, toughness, and consistency of food, which results in less tooth wear and in a reduced demand on the masticatory muscles and supporting bone. Simply put, reduced masticatory demands have produced alteration in the form and distribution of bone. The outcome for modern human evolution consits in the aforementioned changes in craniofacial morphology. In addition, the decrease in jaw size which followed upon these masticatory changes has caused a reduction of space for the dentition. As a result, recent human evolution has known a dramatic increase in malocclusion and tooth crowding – byproducts of the reduction in the texture and toughness of food.

The postcranial skeleton provides a record for understanding behavior and lifestyle as it relates to bodily movement, workload, and lifestyle. The articular ends of bones – such as in the legs and arms – are well adapted to mechanical loading. That is, when you walk or run, the knee joint is subjected to considerable mechanical forces deriving from body weight, muscles, and gravity. With repeated loading over the course of a person's lifetime, and depending on the amount and frequency of the load, the cartilage lining the surface of the articular joint begins to break down, erode, and, in extreme circumstances, it disappears altogether. In addition, the edges of the joint develop spicules of bony projections, called 'marginal lipping.' Pathologists, physicians, and anthropologists have long observed the presence of these degenerative changes, called 'osteoarthritis' or 'degenerative joint disease.' These pathological changes have been identified in a wide range of past populations and have been interpreted to reflect a variety of circumstances involving climate, health, genetics, and lifestyle. Radin and co-workers (1991), for instance, show that the mechanical environment figures most prominently in understanding the presence and severity of the condition. The study of osteoarthritis in past settings reveals a tendency for decline to set in preferentially in association with the shift to farming in various context (Bridges 1992). However, there is a high degree of variation (Larsen 1997). Nonetheless, the patterns of an increased prevalence of the degenerative joint disease in high workload environments, for instance among native laborers employed in Spanish colonial settings (Klaus et al. 2009), provides insight into the mechanical function and biological costs of labor, with its excessive mechanical demands placed on articular joints.

Bone form such as the midshafts of long bones is controlled both by genetic and by environmental factors. While the overall form of bones is genetically determined, the finer details of shape are often influenced by the mechanical environment. In this respect, skeletons record past behavior and are amenable to behavioral interpretations, especially at a general level (Katzenberg and Saunders 2008; Ruff 2008). This perspective is grounded in 'Wolff's law,' which states that bone adapts to its mechanical environment during life: bone tissue is placed in the direction of mechanical demand.

While the external dimensions (for instance diaphyseal diameters and circumferences) traditionally collected by biological anthropologists provide some perspective on activity – larger diaphyses generally indicate greater strength and a higher level of activity than smaller diaphyses – it is the distribution of bone in cross-section that proves to be of the greatest value for inferring activity. In particular, biological anthropologists have applied engineering beam theory to the study of skeletal morphology (Ruff 2008): when viewed in cross-section, the further the material is placed from a central axis, the stronger the section and its ability to resist breakage are; and this is due to bending or twisting during loading. For example, as you walk or run, your femora are subject to bending and twisting, which is due in large part just to body weight. Comparison between the foragers' and the farmers' cross-sectional geometric properties – that is, measures of the bone's resistance to mechanical forces – shows a general reduction in bone strength which, anthropologists believe, reflects a decline in mechanical loading in the shift from foraging to farming in this subsistence change (Ruff et al. 1984; Ruff and Larsen 2001).

In addition to change in activity associated with the shift from foraging to farming, terrain has a strong influence on mechanical loading. Comparisons between populations living in diverse settings – mountains, great plains, and the coast – in North America show a clear terrain-related adaptation. The more rugged the terrain is, the greater the bone strength (Ruff 1999, 2008). This finding is consistent with the notion that habitual travel in rugged terrain places greater mechanical demands on the skeleton.

Recent criticisms of the application of Wolff's law in reconstructing behavior and activity focus on experimental research (see Ruff et al. 2006). A number of experimental studies reveal no clear relationship between strain (deformation due to loading) and cross-sectional geometry, which suggests that cross-sectional geometry cannot be used to reconstruct a history of mechanical loading (Lieberman et al. 2004). Ruff and collaborators (2006) make, however, the strong case that strain and load are two different factors. Moreover, recent research which measures physical activity in boys over a sixteen-month period reveals that bending strength is greater in boys who are physically active than in boys who are not (Macdonald et al. 2009).

Relatedness, biological distance, and population history

Study of skeletal morphology reveals the high degree of plasticity of skeletal tissue and the way it responds to its mechanical–environmental circumstances. Skeletal morphology is also, in part, genetically determined, and a long history of the study of polygenic skeletal and dental traits has proved fundamental to intragroup and intergroup population history. Biological distance (biodistance) analysis focuses on patterns of biological variation, usually followed through the simultaneous consideration of multiple skeletal and dental traits, by using multivariate statistics (Harris 2008; Scott and Turner 1997). Two classes of traits are used in biodistance analysis: metric and non-metric traits. The former consist in dimensions – such as tooth lengths and breadths – and various craniofacial and postcranial measurements. Dental dimensions are under greater genetic control than skeletal measurements, and thus they provide closer approximations of heritability. Non-metric traits are represented by a long list of dental and skeletal variants (Scott 2008; Turner et al. 1991; Saunders and Rainey 2008). Some non-metric traits are recorded in dichotomous fashion, as being present or absent. But in reality most 'discrete' traits are gradations on a continuum of morphology. For example, the classic shovel-shaped incisors, first studied in detail by Hrdlička (1920) and now well known as a trait linking Native Americans to a common northern Asian ancestor, are present in one out of seven ordinal grades, ranging from slight to highly pronounced (Turner et al. 1991). The application of methods for biodistance analysis has helped to clarify biological relationships within populations (Jacobi 2000), to identify patterns of post-marital residence (Schillaci and Stojanowski 2003; Tomczak and Powell 2003), to document regional patterns of interactions (Griffin et al. 2001; Stojanowski 2005), and to address the question of population origins on a continental scale (Powell 2005).

The genetic code provides details on biological relationships in remarkable detail (see O'Rourke's chapter in this volume). With the development of a technology that makes possible the identification of DNA in ancient tissues, a new window is starting to open in biodistance analysis; the results include the identification of the sex of individuals, the discovery of population origins, and disease diagnosis (Stone 2008). The development of this area has provided exciting new opportunities to address long-standing issues that are simply not resolvable through traditional biodistance analysis, which depends on non-metric and metric trait analysis. For example, in prehistoric populations from the American Great Basin, Kaestle and collaborators (1999) and O'Rourke and collaborators (1999) have successfully documented biological history in western North America, linking earlier ancient populations from California to later populations in western Nevada and Utah and to Puebloan groups.

Bone chemistry is also providing profound new insights into understanding the movement of people, sometimes over great distances during the course of a person's lifetime. Variation in the geochemical landscape is reflected in the dental and skeletal tissues. For example, strontium isotope ratios ($^{87}Sr/^{86}Sr$) and oxygen isotope ratios ($^{18}O/^{16}O$) vary predictably in local geology, and hence in the water and food consumed by humans. If a person lives in the same place during the development of the enamel and bone, or during earlier periods in life when the teeth are forming (as opposed to later periods, when the skeleton is maturing), then the stable isotope ratios should remain unchanged. However, if the person's residence changes, the stable isotope ratios should be different (Bentley 2006). Moreover, someone with an isotope ratio different from that of other members of a population is as an immigrant. This approach has identified immigrants in a range of settings and circumstances (see Knudson et al. 2005; Tiesler and Cucina 2006; Grupe et al. 1997; Bentley et al. 2005). These chemical signatures are enormously informative about key development in the past, including insight into human migration during the Neolithic (Bentley et al. 2002).

CURRENT DEVELOPMENTS IN A RAPIDLY CHANGING FIELD

Someone writing an overview of bioarchaeology twenty-five years ago would be amazed at the remarkable developments in the field and at the great expansion in research and publication of scientific results from all corners of the world. We believe that this growing interest in bioarchaeology reflects the recognition that human remains from archaeological settings, especially when viewed in their full cultural, social, and environmental contexts, provide an extraordinarily rich record for addressing hypotheses and questions about our recent hominid past. In addition to close collaboration with archaeologists and the wealth of contextual information derived from their research, our own sense of the field is that bioarchaeology has enjoyed its greatest successes when it involved collaboration with disciplines which have developed methods and insights that help to address common interests – for instance ecology, evolutionary biology, engineering, physics, chemistry, geology, climatology, demography, and epidemiology.

In our view, some of the most productive and compelling bioarchaeological research has been on larger studies, involving key topics and analysis at the regional scale. Few would argue against the notion that a pivotal development in recent hominin evolution was the shift from a way of life based exclusively on hunting, gathering, and collecting wild plants and animals to one based exclusively (or nearly so) on domesticated plants and animals – all of which occurred just within the last 10,000 years. When placed in the context of the fact that humans and human-like ancestors have been around for perhaps as long as seven million years, this transition was a remarkably fast one. Bioarchaeologists have developed enormous records of research that tell us a great deal about the outcome of the transition to this new lifestyle and its consequences for humanity. Their material affords glimpses into the state of health and lifestyle of living societies around the globe (Cohen 1989; Cohen and Armelagos 1984; Cohen and Crane-Kramer 2007; Larsen 1995, 2006; Steckel et al. 2002; Steckel and Rose 2002).

What does this record specifically show? In the broad sweep, the studies of hundreds of thousands of human skeletons derived from archaeological settings spanning the last 10,000 years reveal a record of generally, although certainly not exclusively, compromised health. More precisely, bioarchaeologists use a number of indicators which, by themselves, are not very specific in point of causation but, collectively, present a compelling picture of major shifts in health – general physiological disruption, specific and non-specific pathologies, deterioration of growth and development from birth through senescence – which permits inferences about the quality of life. Virtually any place where a substantial record of skeletal remains has been studied reveals an increase in morbidity which reflects poor health. The record of the foraging-to-farming transitions is most detailed for North America (see Larsen 2000, and many individual local and regional studies).

There is some evidence to suggest that different kinds of crops have led to economic and living circumstances which resulted either in no decline in health or in a moderate decline only. For example, in some regions of Asia, rice agriculture may not have produced the kinds of health damage documented by bioarchaeologists in the Americas (Tayles et al. 2000; but see Temple and Larsen 2007). In eastern North America, populations who cultivated a number of other crops long before maize show no clear evidence of a decline in health. Moreover, many of the health changes are related indirectly to the adoption of particular kinds of crops. The direct health consequences are obvious: the adoption of domesticated plant carbohydrates – for example maize in the New World and wheat in the Old World – resulted in an increase in dental caries. The indirect health consequences of higher physiological stress, poor growth, and elevated prevalence of bone infection may have also involved specific new foods as contributing factors; but another important factor, which must be reckoned with in interpreting these phenomena of health degradation, was the increase in the size and concentration of populations – a factor that promotes the spread of infectious disease. Indeed the population explosion caused by higher fertility and birthrates in the Neolithic and afterwards is now well documented in the skeletal record (Buikstra et al. 1986; Bocquet-Appel and Naji 2006; Bocquet-Appel et al. 2008) and shows a strong concurrence with changes in morbidity.

Scholars – especially historians and sociologists – have long been interested in the history of violence. But, despite the importance of violence and of its causes, anthropologists have only rarely focused on this fundamental topic, some arguing that it is recent in human history, not experienced in some societies, and rare in others (see Keeley 1996; Fry 2005). Human remains are a compelling source of information for addressing anthropological and historical issues related to the history of violence. When viewed in the broader context of reconstructions of climate, diet, and society, bioarchaeology provides a unique and arguably more robust record, both for the history and for the causes of interpersonal violence (Walker 2001). Analysis of human remains from well back into the Pleistocene reveals the presence of traumatic injuries – cutmarks, fractures, cranial trauma, and other clear markers of violent encounters – and their patterning is highly informative about the presence and the degree of interpersonal aggression in a range of contexts (Lambert 1997, 2002; Walker 2001; Martin and Frayer 1997). This record emphasizes the existence of a link between environmental deterioration, population size, and competition for resources. Under threat of diminished availability of resources, humans sometimes resort to violence. The bioarchaeological record provides us with a deep historical record of the causes and consequences of violence.

Some of the best materials in this type of record consist in detailed studies of the presence, type, and prevalence of traumatic injuries in prehistoric societies in North America. In Santa Barbara, in the Channel Island region of southern California, Walker and Lambert show significant temporal variation in violence, mostly documented as non-lethal depressed fractures and lethal projectile wounds (Walker 1989; Walker and Lambert 1989; Lambert 1997). Over time, the prevalence of violence increased, coinciding with a growth in population and with increased drought. Walker and colleagues make a strong case for the thesis that the combination between population increase and competition for resources was likely to be at the root of the intensification in stress and violent encounters, as groups competed for food (and see Milner et al. 1991; Bridges 1996; Mensforth 2007; Jacobi 2007). Some violence is extreme, involving the consumption of victims (see White 1992; Turner and Turner 1999; Billman et al. 2000) and widespread mutilation (e.g. Willey 1990).

The study of violence as documented through human remains makes it clear that these remains are both a biological and a *social* record of the human past. Viewed in larger perspective, human remains provide an important perspective on changing patterns of individual and group identity over time (Stojanowski 2005, 2009; Griffin et al. 2001; Klaus and Tam 2009). Comparisons between dental biodistance markers in temporal series of native populations of the colonial era in Spanish Florida reveal a high degree of genetic distance in the first half of the sixteenth century; this reflects limited gene flow over long distances and isolation of the population (Stojanowski 2009; Griffin et al. 2001). After the mid-century, though, genetic distance decreased dramatically, indicating long-distance migration and heightened gene flow during the Spanish period, whiuch was characterized by extensive population collapse. This has important implications for group identity: the later period saw the biological and social amalgamation of groups with separate identities into a single biological population and the formation of a single group identity across the region.

Study of gender has a strong record in bioarchaeology, especially in connection to health and lifestyle. Although gender has a complex relation with biological sex, bioarchaeology can clarify aspects pertaining both to sex and to the social construction of gender. Variation in paleopathological indicators reveals some key trends, which speak to universal behaviors that affect health – but with some interesting exceptions. In this regard, nearly universally, female skeletons display less degenerative joint disease and other markers of physical activity than male skeletons (Bridges 1992; Larsen 1997). On the other hand, Peterson's (2002) impressive study of musculo-skeletal stress markers (MSMs) in early agricultural populations of the southern Levant expresses frequencies of similar height in both sexes, which she interprets to represent equally high levels of demand during the transition from foraging to farming. The conflation of levels of degenerative joint disease in native populations from the Spanish mission in the Georgia Bight reveals a growing similarity of high workload, especially in comparison with prehistoric populations (Larsen and Ruff 1994). In agricultural societies, women often display a higher degree of prevalence of dental caries than men. Larsen (1983, 1998) suggests that a higher rate of tooth decay in women than men represents a health outcome related to the division of labor: women are responsible for the preparation of food and have greater access than men to plant carbohydrates on a regular basis (although see alternative explanation by Lukacs et al. 2008).

Conclusions and Future Directions

There has been a remarkable rise of scientific and scholarly profile in bioarchaeology in the last several decades: from a field that, in the mid-twentieth century, was represented mostly through appendices to archaeological reports, bioarchaeology has become a discipline addressing central issues in biological anthropology. We believe that this is due to the growing recognition that human remains provide a record of biology which informs our understanding of the past as well as opening a window into social behavior. On the basis of the increasing body of research completed by biological anthropologists and others, we see a continuing growth – which is made possible by new and exciting theoretical advances and fueled by the increasing interdisciplinarity of the field. Bioarchaeologists have always been adept at borrowing ideas from other disciplines; right now they are collaborating with a variety of scientists and scholars in order to foster greater appreciation for humans as a biological and as a social organism. Bioarchaeology has responded to a range of criticisms adduced in the last several decades. For example, Wood and co-workers (1992) pointed out that health profiles developed from ancient skeletons may present a very biased picture: skeletal series with lots of pathology may be healthier than others, with minimal pathology. After all, longer-living individuals would simply be around for longer (they are the survivors) than shorter-lived individuals (the non-survivors or the less healthy), and hence they would accumulate a higher record of pathology. It is unlikely that Wood and co-workers intended bioarchaeologists to draw this conclusion from *all* the skeletal samples. On the contrary, their critique calls upon bioarchaeologists to evaluate not just the skeletons, but the broader context in which the population lived.

Moreover, the criticism raises the important point that linking community health and skeletal indicators of morbidity should not be an intuitive exercise. Rather, the entire context of subsistence, settlement pattern, population size and growth, environment and social–cultural context, and population structure must be taken into account (Goodman 1993). These criticisms have helped to transform the field, from one of description (see Armelagos et al. 1982) to one based on hypothesis testing (Armelagos and Van Gerven 2003; Stojanowski and Buikstra 2005; Larsen 2010). The increased rigor of method and theory displayed in bioarchaeology has served to promote hypothesis-driven research, from the individual level to a global scale. Moreover, it has inspired the development of new and ambitious research programs in the United States, Britain, and elsewhere, which are generating a new and informed understanding of the history of the human condition over the last 10,000 years of human evolution.

REFERENCES

Ambrose, S. H. (1987) Chemical and Isotopic Techniques of Diet Reconstruction in Eastern North America. In W. F. Keegan (ed.), *Emergent Horticultural Economies of the Eastern Woodlands* (pp. 78–107). Southern Illinois University at Carbondale, Center for Archaeological Investigations, Occasional Paper, 7.

Armelagos, G. J. (1969) Disease in Ancient Nubia. *Science* 163: 255–259.

Armelagos, G. J., and Van Gerven, D. P. (2003) A Century of Skeletal Biology and Paleopathology: Contrasts, Contradictions, and Conflicts. *American Anthropologist* 105: 53–64.

Armelagos, G. J., Carlson, D. S., and Van Gerven, D. P. (1982) The Theoretical Foundations and Development of Skeletal Biology. In F. Spencer (ed.), *A History of American Physical Anthropology: 1930–1980* (pp. 305–328). New York: Academic Press.

Bentley, R. A. (2006) Strontium Isotopes from the Earth to the Archaeological Skeleton: A Review. *Journal of Archaeological Method and Theory* 13: 135–187.

Bentley, R. A., Pietrusewsky, M., Douglas, M. T., and Atkinson, T. C. (2005) Matrilocality during the Prehistoric Transition to Agriculture in Thailand? *Antiquity* 79: 865–881.

Bentley, R. A., Price, T. D., Luning, J., Gronenborn, D., Wahl, J., and Fullager, P. D. (2002) Human Migration in Early Neolithic Europe. *Current Anthropology* 43: 799–804.

Billman, B. R., Lambert, P. M., and Leonard, B. L. (2000) Cannibalism, Warfare, and Drought in the Mesa Verde Region during the Twelfth Century AD. *American Antiquity* 65: 145–178.

Bocquet-Appel, J.-P., and Naji, S. (2006) Testing the Hypothesis of a Worldwide Neolithic Demographic Transition: Corroboration from American Cemeteries. *Current Anthropology* 47: 341–365.

Bocquet-Appel, J.-P., Naji, S., and Bandy, M. (2008) Demographic and Health Changes during the Transition to Agriculture in North America. In J.-P. Bocquet-Appel (ed.), *Recent Advances in Paleodemography: Data, Techniques, Patterns* (pp. 277–292). Dordrecht: Springer.

Bridges, P. S. (1992) Prehistoric Arthritis in the Americas. *Annual Review of Anthropology* 21: 67–91.

Bridges, P. S. (1996) Warfare and Mortality at Koger's Island, Alabama. *International Journal of Osteoarchaeology* 6: 66–75.

Buikstra, J. E. (1977) Biocultural Dimensions of Archeological Study: A Regional Perspective. In R. L. Blakely (ed.), *Biocultural Adaptation in Prehistoric America* (pp. 67–84). Athens: Univerity of Georgia Press.

Buikstra, J. E., (1988) *The Mound-Builders of Eastern North America: A Regional Perspective.* Amsterdam: Elfde Kroon-Voordracht.

Buikstra, J. E., and Beck, L. A. (eds) (2006) *Bioarchaeology: The Contextual Analysis of Human Remains.* Burlington MA: Academic Press.

Buikstra, J. E., Konigsberg, L. W., and Bullington, J. (1986) Fertility and the Development of Agriculture in the Prehistoric Midwest. *American Antiquity* 51: 528–546.

Carlson, D. S., and Van Gerven, D. P. (1977) Masticatory Function and Post-Pleistocene Evolution in Nubia. *American Journal of Physical Anthropology* 46: 495–506.

Carlson, D. S., and Van Gerven, D. P. (1979) Diffusion, Biological Determinism, and Biocultural Adaptation in the Nubian Corridor. *American Anthropologist* 81: 561–580.

Cohen, M. N. (1989) *Health and the Rise of Civilization.* New Haven CT: Yale University Press.

Cohen, M. N., and Armelagos, G. J. (eds) (1984) *Paleopathology at the Origins of Agriculture.* Orlando FL: Academic Press.

Cohen, M. N., and Crane-Kramer, G. M. M. (eds) (2007) *Ancient Health: Skeletal Indicators of Agricultural and Economic Intensification.* Gainesville FL: University Press of Florida.

Cook, D. C. (2006) The Old Physical Anthropology and the New World: A Look at the Accomplishments of an Antiquated Paradigm. In J. E. Buikstra and L. A. Beck (eds), *Bioarchaeology: The Contextual Analysis of Human Remains* (pp. 27–71). Burlington MA: Academic Press.

Fry, D. P. (2005) *The Human Potential for Peace: An Anthropological Challenge to Assumptions about War and Violence.* New York: Oxford Unversity Press.

Goldstein, L. (2006) Mortuary Analysis and Bioarchaeology. In J. E. Buikstra, and L. A. Beck (eds), *Bioarchaeology: The Contextual Analysis of Human Remains* (pp. 375–387). Burlington MA: Academic Press.

Goodman, A. H. (1993) On the Interpretation of Health from Skeletal Remains. *Current Anthropology* 34: 281–288.

Gowland, R., and Knüsel, C. (eds) (2006) *Social Archaeology of Funerary Remains.* Oxford: Oxbow.

Griffin, M. C., Lambert, P. M., and Driscoll, E. M. (2001) Biological Relationships and Population History of Native Peoples in Spanish Florida and the American Southeast. In C. S. Larsen (ed.), Bioarchaeology of Spanish Florida: The Impact of Colonialism. (pp. 226–273). Gainesville FL: University Press of Florida.

Grupe, G., Price, T. D., Schröter, P., Söllner, F., Johnson, C. M., and Beard, B. L. (1997) Mobility of Bell Beaker Oeople Revealed by Strontium Isotope Ratios of Tooth and Bone: A Study of Southern Bavarian Skeletal Remains. *Applied Geochemistry* 12: 517–525.

Harris, E. F. (2008) Statistical Application in Dental Anthropology. In J. D. Irish, and G. C. Nelson (eds), *Technique and Application in Dental Anthropology* (pp. 35–67). Cambridge: Cambridge University Press.

Hillson, S. W. (2008) The Current State of Dental Decay. In J. D. Irish, and G. C. Nelson (eds), *Technique and Application in Dental Anthropology* (pp. 111–135). Cambridge: Cambridge University Press.

Hrdlička, A. (1920) Shovel-Shaped Teeth. *American Journal of Physical Anthropology* 3: 429–465.

Huss-Ashmore, R., Goodman, A. H., and Armelagos, G. J. (1982) Nutritional Inference from Paleopathology. In M. B. Schiffer (ed.), *Advances in Archaeological Method and Theory*, Vol. 5 (pp. 395–474). New York: Academic Press.

Jacobi, K. P. (2000) *Last Rites for the Tipu Maya: Genetic Structuring in a Colonial Cemetery.* Tuscaloosa: University of Alabama Press.

Jacobi, K. P. (2007) Disabling the Dead: Human Trophy Taking in the Prehistoric Southeast. In R. J. Chacon, and D. H. Dye (eds), *The Taking and Displaying of Human Body*

Parts as Trophies by Amerindians (pp. 299–338). New York: Springer Science and Business Media LLC.

Kaestle, F. A., Lorenz, J. G., and Smith, D. G. (1999) Molecular Genetics and the Numic Expansion: A Molecular Investigation of the Prehistoric Inhabitants of Stillwater Marsh. In B. E. Hemphill and C. S. Larsen (eds), *Prehistoric Lifeways in the Great Basin Wetlands: Bioarchaeological Reconstruction and Interpretation* (pp. 167–183). Salt Lake City: University of Utah Press.

Katzenberg, M. A. (2008) Stable Isotope Analysis: A Tool for Studying Past Diet, Demography, and Life History. In M. A. Katzenberg, and S. R. Saunders (eds), *Biological Anthropology of the Human Skeleton*, 2nd edn (pp. 413–442). Hoboken NJ: Wiley–Liss.

Katzenberg, M. A., and Saunders, S. R. (eds) (2008) *Biological Anthropology of the Human Skeleton*, 2nd edn. Hoboken NJ: Wiley–Liss.

Keeley, L. H. (1996) *War before Civilization: The Myth of the Peaceful Savage*. New York: Oxford University Press.

Klaus, H. D., and M. E. Tam (2009) Surviving Contact: Biological Transformation, Burial, and Ethnogenesis in the Colonial Lambayeque Valley, North Coast of Peru. In K. J. Knudson and C. M. Stojanowski (eds), *Bioarchaeology and Identity in the Americas* (pp. 126–154). Gainesville FL: University Press of Florida.

Klaus, H. D., Larsen, C. S., and Tam, M. E. (2009) Economic Intensification and Degenerative Joint Disease: Life and Labor on the Postcontact North Coast of Peru. *American Journal of Physical Anthropology* 139: 204–221.

Knudson, K. J., and Stojanowski, C. M. (eds) (2009) *Bioarchaeology and Identity in the Americas*. Gainesville FL: University Press of Florida.

Knudson, K. J., Tung, T., Nystrom, K. C., Price, T. D., and Fullagar, P. D. (2005) The Origin of the Juch'uypampa Cave Mummies: Strontium Isotope Analysis of Archaeological Human Remains from Bolivia. *Journal of Archaeological Science* 32: 903–913.

Lambert, P. M. (1997) Patterns of Violence in Prehistoric Hunter–Gatherer Societies of Coastal Southern California. In D. L. Martin and D. W. Frayer (eds), *Troubled Times: Violence and Warfare in the Past* (pp. 77–109). Amsterdam: Gordon and Breach Publishers.

Lambert, P. M. (2002) The Archaeology of War: A North American Perspective. *Journal of Archaeological Research* 10: 207–241.

Larsen, C. S. (1983) Behavioural Implications of Temporal Change in Cariogenesis. *Journal of Archaeological Science* 10: 1–8.

Larsen, C. S. (1987) Bioarchaeological Interpretations of Subsistence Economy and Behavior from Human Skeletal Remains. In M. B. Schiffer (ed.), *Advances in Archaeological Method and Theory*, Vol. 10 (pp. 339–445). San Diego CA: Academic Press.

Larsen, C. S. (1995) Biological Changes in Human Populations with Agriculture. *Annual Review of Anthropology* 24: 185–213.

Larsen, C. S. (1997) *Bioarchaeology: Interpreting Behavior from the Human Skeleton*. Cambridge: Cambridge University Press.

Larsen, C. S. (1998) Gender, Health, and Activity in Foragers and Farmers in the American Southeast: Implications for Social Organization in the Georgia Bight. In A. L. Grauer and P. Stuart-Macadam (eds), *Sex and Gender in Paleopathological Perspective* (pp. 165–187). Cambridge: Cambridge University Press.

Larsen, C. S. (2000) *Skeletons in Our Closet: Revealing Our Past through Bioarchaeology*. Princeton NJ: Princeton University Press.

Larsen, C. S. (2003) Animal Source Foods and Human Health During Evolution. *Journal of Nutrition* 133: 1S–5S.

Larsen, C. S. (2006) The Agricultural Revolution as Environmental Catastrophe: Implications for Health and Lifestyle in the Holocene. *Quaternary International* 150: 12–20.

Larsen, C. S. (2010) Description, Hypothesis Testing, and Conceptual Advances in Physical Anthropology: Have We Moved On? In M. A. Little and K. A. R. Kennedy (eds),

Histories of American Physical Anthropology in the Twentieth Century (pp. 233–241) Lanham MD: Lexington Books.

Larsen, C. S., and Ruff, C. B. (1994) The Stresses of Conquest in Spanish Florida: Structural Adaptation and Change before and after Contact. In C. S. Larsen and G. R. Milner (eds), *In the Wake of Contact: Biological Responses to Conquest* (pp. 21–34). New York: Wiley–Liss.

Larsen, C. S., Ruff, C. B., Schoeninger, M. J., and Hutchinson, D. L. (1992) Population Decline and Extinction in La Florida. In J. W. Verano and D. H. Ubelaker (eds), *Disease and Demography in the Americas* (pp. 25–39). Washington: Smithsonian Institution Press.

Lieberman, D. E., Polk, J. D., and Demes, B. (2004) Predicting Long Bone Loading from Cross-Sectional Geometry. *American Journal of Physical Anthropology* 123: 156–171.

Lukacs, J. R. (2008) Fertility and Agriculture Accentuate Sex Differences in Dental Caries Rates. *Current Anthropology* 49: 901–914.

Macdonald, H. M., Cooper, D. M. L., and McKay, H. A. (2009) Anterior–Posterior Bending Strength at the Tibial Shaft Increases with Physical Activity in Boys: Evidence for Non-Uniform Geometric Adaptation. *Osteoporosis International* 20: 61–70.

Martin, D. L., and Frayer, D. W. (eds) (1997) *Troubled Times: Violence and Warfare in the Past.* Amsterdam: Gordon and Breach.

Mensforth, R. P. (2007) Human Trophy Taking in Eastern North America during the Archaic Period: The Relationship to Warfare and Social Complexity. In R. J. Chacon and D. H. Dye (eds), *The Taking and Displaying of Human Body Parts as Trophies by Amerindians* (pp. 222–277). New York: Springer.

Milner, G. R., Anderson, E., and Smith, V. G. (1991) Warfare in Late Prehistoric West–Central Illinois. *American Antiquity* 56: 581–603.

O'Rourke, D. H., Parr, R. L., and Carlyle, S. W. (1999) Molecular Genetic Variation in Prehistoric Inhabitants of the Eastern Great Basin. In B. E. Hemphill and C. S. Larsen (eds), *Prehistoric Lifeways in the Great Basin Wetlands: Bioarchaeological Reconstruction and Interpretation* (pp. 84–102). Salt Lake City: University of Utah Press.

Ortner, D. J. (2008) Differential Diagnosis of Skeletal Lesions in Infectious Disease. In R. Pinhasi and S. Mays (eds), *Advances in Human Palaeopathology* (pp. 191–214). Chichester: John Wiley and Sons.

Peterson, J. (2002) *Sexual Revolutions: Gender and Labor at the Dawn of Agriculture.* Walnut Creek CA: Altamira.

Powell, J. F. (2005) *The First Americans: Race, Evolution, and the Origin of Native Americans.* Cambridge: Cambridge University Press.

Radin, E. L., Burr, D. B., Caterson, B., Fyhrie, D., Brown, T. D., and Boyd, R. D. (1991) Mechanical Determinants of Osteoarthrosis. *Seminars in Arthritis and Rheumatism* 21 (3 Suppl. 2): 12–21.

Robbins, L. M., and Neumann, G. K. (1972) *The Prehistoric People of the Fort Ancient Culture of the Central Ohio Valley.* Museum of Anthropology, University of Michigan, Anthropological Papers No. 47.

Ruff, C. B. (1999) Skeletal Structure and Behavioral Patterns of Prehistoric Great Basin Populations. In B. E. Hemphill and C. S. Larsen (eds), *Understanding Prehistoric Lifeways in the Great Basin Wetlands: Bioarchaeological Reconstruction and Interpretation* (pp. 290–320). Salt Lake City: University of Utah Press.

Ruff, C. B. (2008) Biomechanical Analyses of Archaeological Human Skeletons. In M. A. Katzenberg and S. R. Saunders (eds), *Biological Anthropology of the Human Skeleton*, 2nd edn (pp. 183–206). Hoboken NJ: Wiley–Liss.

Ruff, C. B., Holt, B. H., and Trinkaus, E. (2006) Who's Afraid of the Big Bad Wolff? 'Wolff's Law' and Bone Functional Adaptation. *American Journal of Physical Anthropology* 129: 484–498.

Ruff, C. B., and Larsen, C. S. (2001) Reconstructing Behavior in Spanish Florida: The Biomechanical Evidence. In C. S. Larsen (ed.), *Bioarchaeology of Spanish Florida: The Impact of Colonialism* (pp. 113–145). Gainesville FL: University Press of Florida.

Ruff, C. B., Larsen, C. S., and Hayes, W. C. (1984) Structural Changes in the Femur with the Transition to Agriculture on the Georgia Coast. *American Journal of Physical Anthropology* 64: 125–136.

Saunders, S. R., and Rainey, D. L. (2008) Nonmetric Trait Variation in the Skeleton: Abnormalities, Anomalies, and Atavisms. In M. A. Katzenberg and S. R. Saunders (eds), *Biological Anthropology of the Human Skeleton* (pp. 533–559). Hoboken NJ: Wiley–Liss.

Schillaci, J., and Stojanowski, C. (2003) Postmarital Residence and Biological Variation at Pueblo Bonito. *American Journal of Physical Anthropology* 120: 1–15.

Schwarcz, H. P. (2006) Stable Carbon Isotope Analysis and Human Diet: A Synthesis. In J. Staller, R. Tykot, and B. Benz (eds), *Histories of Maize* (pp. 315–321). Burlington MA: Academic Press.

Scott, G. R. (2008) Dental Morphology. In M. A. Katzenberg and S. R. Saunders (eds), *Biological Anthropology of the Human Skeleton* (pp. 265–298). Hoboken NJ: Wiley–Liss.

Scott, G. R., and Turner II, C. G. (1997) *The Anthropology of Modern Human Teeth: Dental Morphology and Its Variation in Recent Human Populations.* Cambridge: Cambridge University Press.

Scott, G. R., Halffman, C. M., and Pedersen, P. O. (1991) Dental Conditions of Medieval Norsemen in the North Atlantic. *Acta Archaeologica* 62: 183–207.

Smith, B. D. (1995) *The Emergence of Agriculture.* New York: Scientific American Library.

Smith, B. H. (1984) Patterns of Molar Wear in Hunter–Gatherers and Agriculturalists. *American Journal of Physical Anthropology* 63: 39–56.

Steckel, R. H., and Rose, J. C. (eds) (2002) *The Backbone of History: Long-Term Trends in Health and Nutrition in the Americas.* New York: Cambridge University Press.

Steckel, R. H., Rose, J. C., Larsen, C. S., and Walker, P. L. (2002) Skeletal Health in the Western Hemisphere from 4000 BC to the present. *Evolutionary Anthropology* 11: 142–155.

Stojanowski, C. M. (2005) *Biocultural Histories in La Florida: A Bioarchaeological Perspective.* Tuscaloosa: University of Alabama Press.

Stojanowski, C. M. (2009) Bridging Histories: The Bioarchaeology of Identity in Postcontact Florida. In K. J. Knudson and C. M. Stojanowski (eds), *Bioarchaeology and Identity in the Americas* (pp. 59–81). Gainesville FL: University Press of Florida.

Stojanowski, C. M., and Buikstra, J. E. (2005) Research Trends in Human Osteology: A Content Analysis of Papers Published in the *American Journal of Physical Anthropology. American Journal of Physical Anthropology* 128: 98–109.

Stone, A. C. (2008) DNA Analysis of Archaeological Remains. In M. A. Katzenberg and S. R. Saunders (eds), *Biological Anthropology of the Human Skeleton*, 2nd edn (pp. 461–483). Hoboken NJ: Wiley–Liss.

Tayles, N., Domett, K., and Nelsen, K. (2000) Agriculture and Dental Caries? The Case of Rice in Prehistoric Southeast Asia. *World Archaeology* 32: 68–83.

Teaford, M. F. (1991) Dental Microwear: What Can It Tell Us about Diet and Dental Function? In M. A. Kelley and C. S. Larsen (eds), *Advances in Dental Anthropology* (pp. 341–356). New York: Wiley–Liss.

Temple, D. H., and Larsen, C. S. (2007) Dental Caries Prevalence as Evidence for Agriculture and Subsistence Variation among the Prehistoric Yayoi of Japan: Biocultural Interpretations of an Economy in Transition. *American Journal of Physical Anthropology* 134: 501–512.

Tiesler, V., and Cucina, A. (eds) (2006) *Janaab' Pakal of Palenque: Reconstructing the Life and Death of a Maya Ruler.* Tucson: University of Arizona Press.

Tomczak, P., and Powell, J. (2003) Postmarital Residence Practices in the Windover Population: Sex-Based Dental Variation as an Indicator of Patrilocality. *American Antiquity* 68: 93–108.

Turner II, C. G., Nichol, C. R., and Scott, G. R. (1991) Scoring Procedures for Key Morphological Traits of the Permanent Dentition: The Arizona State University Dental Anthropology System. In M. A. Kelley and C. S. Larsen (eds), *Advances in Dental Anthropology* (pp. 13–31). New York: Wiley–Liss.

Turner II, C. G., and Turner, J. A. (1999) *Man Corn: Cannibalism and Violence in the Prehistoric American Southwest.* Salt Lake City: University of Utah Press.

Ungar, P. S., Scott, R. S., Scott, J. R., and Teaford, M. (2008) Dental Microwear Analysis: Historical Perspectives and New Approaches. In J. D. Irish and G. C. Nelson (eds), *Technique and Application in Dental Anthropology* (pp. 389–425). Cambridge: Cambridge University Press.

Vogel, J. C., and van der Merwe, N. J. (1977) Isotopic Evidence for Early Maize Cultivation in New York State. *American Antiquity* 42: 238–242.

Walker, P. L. (1989) Cranial Injuries as Evidence of Violence in Prehistoric Southern California. *American Journal of Physical Anthropology* 80: 313–323.

Walker, P. L. (2001) A Bioarchaeological Perspective on the History of Violence. *Annual Review of Anthropology* 30: 573–596.

Walker, P. L., and Lambert, P. (1989) Skeletal Evidence for Stress during a Period of Cultural Change in Prehistoric California. In L. Capasso (ed.), *Advances in Paleopathology* (pp. 207–212). *Journal of Paleopathology*, Monographic Publications.

White, T. D. (1992) *Prehistoric Cannibalism at Mancos 5MTUMR-2346.* Princeton: Princeton University Press.

Willey, P. (1990) *Prehistoric Warfare on the Great Plains: Skeletal Analysis of the Crow Creek Massacre Victims.* New York: Garland Publishing.

Wood, J. W., Milner, G. R., Harpending, H. C., and Weiss, K. M. (1992) The Osteological Paradox: Problems in Inferring Prehistoric Health from Skeletal Samples. *Current Anthropology* 33: 343–358.

CHAPTER 22 Paleopathology: A Contemporary Perspective

Jane E. Buikstra

INTRODUCTION

In the study of ancient disease, physical anthropologists focus on two lines of evidence – primary and secondary (Roberts 2002: 3). The former includes skeletal remains, mummified tissues, and clinical studies of pathological conditions. Secondary sources encompass iconographic representations, documents, archaeologically recovered non-primary materials, and ethnographic information from traditional living groups. This chapter will emphasize primary sources, while also including products of human alimentary processes (coprolites/colon contents) and ancient organisms associated with remains (microorganisms/parasites).

While frequently attributed to the French physician and Egyptologist Sir Marc Armand Ruffer, the term 'paleopathology' was actually coined by the American physician Robert Wilson Schufeldt in an 1892 article published in *Popular Science Monthly*. Schufeldt emphasized a broad-based paleopathology: the study of pathological conditions in any extinct or fossil organism (Cook and Powell 2006). Over time, however, the subject and its practitioners have increasingly focused upon the human condition – although, as will be noted later in this chapter, animal paleopathology has seen renewed interest.

'Paleopathology' is frequently glossed as 'the study of ancient disease,' a seemingly elegant and straightforward characterization, which nonetheless requires clarification of the terms 'disease' and 'ancient.' 'Disease' is generally defined as "an impairment of health or a condition of abnormal functioning" (wordnet. princeton.edu/perl/webwn). Thus paleopathologists study not only infectious diseases, but also myriads of other conditions that affect health – for example arthropathies (diseases of joints); congenital anomalies; circulatory, endocrine, growth (dysplasias), hematological and metabolic disorders; oral pathologies; neoplastic conditions; and trauma. Length constraints necessarily limit discussion here to recent advances in studying ancient disease; the interested reader can be referred to excellent comprehensive texts by Aufderheide and Rodríguez-Martín (1998), Ortner (2003), and Roberts and Manchester (2005).

The term 'ancient' might imply that paleopathology focuses exclusively upon archaeological and historical contexts. This is not the case. As the Paleopathology Association motto states, *Mortui viventes docent* ('The dead teach the living') – which symbolizes the growing number of examples wherein the deep time perspective offered by paleopathology meaningfully informs contemporary medical science. The following examples of transdisciplinary research illustrate this point.

Bone loss in nineteenth-century and more ancient materials has been studied to assess whether or not abnormal bone loss (osteopenia) and bone loss leading to increased risk of fractures (osteoporosis) are very recent phenomena, attributable to contemporary lifestyles, or if today's pattern has extensions into deep time (Brickley and Ives 2008). Bioarchaeological and historical evidence for nineteenth-century London, for example, identifies patterns of age-related bone loss and osteoporosis which are similar to those of today (Brickley 2002). By contrast, medieval remains (eleventh- to sixteenth-century) from North Yorkshire, United Kingdom, present age-related bone loss which is distinctly different from more recent historical and contemporary models (Agarwal et al. 2004). These and other comparative studies thus help to inform our contemporary perspective on osteopenia and osteoporosis.

Similarly, evaluating the nature of past neoplastic processes, especially for malignant conditions (cancers), holds some potential for assessing the degree to which cancer is a recent phenomenon. Such knowledge will help us to appreciate how today's lifestyle choices, environmental conditions, and industrialization have fostered an increasingly carcinogenic world, although paleopathologists are presently divided about the manner is which cancer rates in the past should be estimated (see Roberts and Manchester 2005, Ortner 2003, Aufderheide and Rodríguez-Martín 1998). Thus, while contemporary medical science would gain by being informed on the problem of cancer risks in the past, the issue is still a subject of debate.

American Indian tribes such as the Omaha are interested in how recent dietary changes have affected their risk of disease. The Omaha Tribe and the physical anthropologist Karl Reinhard have collaborated in research centered upon ancestral Omaha human remains. The Omaha have been particularly interested in the reconstructions of diet and activity performed by Reinhard and colleagues, which indicate that the current, and high, diabetes rates among the Omaha result from recent changes in lifestyle (Reinhard et al. 1994; Reinhard 2000; Reinhard et al. in press).

Tuberculosis has recently re-emerged as a pandemic, in fact as a global health burden. While certain risk factors such as HIV are also recent, it is clear that the bacillus that causes tuberculosis, *Mycobacterium tuberculosis*, has an ancient history (see below, 'Infectious Disease and Human Host–Pathogen Relationships') and appears to have had epidemic cycles, which are poorly understood and can be studied only by combining clinical knowledge with knowledge derived from historical and archaeological sources (Roberts and Buikstra 2003).

Twentieth-century archival tissues samples and frozen remains from the 1918–1919 'Spanish' flu' pandemic, which killed an estimated 40 million people, have served to anchor ancient DNA (aDNA) studies of the deadly causative virus. Results indicate that this influenza strain is intermediate between mammals and birds, having been transmitted to mammals only shortly before 1918. Such pioneering work has led to complete sequencing and has facilitated the development of antiviral drugs and vaccines (Drancourt and Rauolt 2005; Reid et al. 1999).

These are but a few examples that illustrate why studying disease in deep time has relevance for contemporary global health. The remainder of this chapter focuses upon recent developments in the study of *ancient* diseases, and it begins by briefly embedding today's research in historical contexts, then it goes on to consider both the invasive and the non-invasive methods for observing disease in human remains, including standardized gross descriptions, computerization, imaging, histology (on this topic, see also Stout's chapter in the present volume), and molecular approaches (on this topic, see also Kaestle's chapter in the present volume). After a discussion of three specific, bone-seeking infectious diseases placed in co-evolutionary perspective, an example of recent changes in disease diagnosis is considered, then followed by global comparative evaluations of population health; the latter are based primarily upon markers of non-specific stress. The chapter then addresses the rapidly developing field of mummy science and the related topic of paleoparasitology. Other subjects of salience – including animal disease, disability and identity, and violence – are also considered. I then briefly look at the manner in which interdisciplinary communication and collaboration are encouraged through professional associations, workshops, and congresses, and I close by exploring possible future directions for paleopathology.

HISTORY

Although eighteenth-century Renaissance scholars identified diseases in the excavated bones of animals such as elephants, amphibians, cave bears, hyenas and humans, the first systematic studies of ancient disease date to the nineteenth century (Aufderheide and Rodríguez-Martín 1998; Cook and Powell 2006); they were due for the most part to initiatives taken by medical doctors and anatomists who were primarily concerned with documenting human morphological variation. Nevertheless, trauma, cranial deformation, arthropathies, infectious disease, congenital anomalies, and tumors were reported by the end of the nineteenth century (Buikstra 2006).

Among the first systematic studies that focused specifically upon disease in ancient communities were those of Joseph Jones, who explored evidence for syphilis in pre-Columbian American remains (Cook and Powell 2006). At the turn of the twentieth century, Sir Marc Armand Ruffer (1859–1917) commenced pioneering studies of Egyptian materials, including mummified remains, which set a high standard for future researchers.

For much of the subsequent half-century, however, there were but few high points in the study of ancient disease. Medical historian Saul Jarcho (1966) criticized paleopathologists for failing to: (1) develop deep syntheses; (2) generate truly significant contributions; (3) promote communication between medical scientists and anthropologists; (4) advance the scientific study of mummies; and (5) create systematic data retrieval systems, registries, or topical indices. The profession has responded to such concerns, as is demonstrated in the contemporary conduct of paleopathology, which will be discussed in the remainder of this chapter. As we shall also see, a few of Jarcho's concerns remain germane today.

STRIKING A BALANCE: CASE STUDIES, DISEASE DIAGNOSIS, AND POPULATION HEALTH IN COMPARATIVE PERSPECTIVE

Studies of ancient disease fall into four categories according to topic. These are:

1   methodological and technological advances;
2   case studies, which are detailed descriptions of individual or small groups of remains undertaken with the goal of providing either new information toward facilitating differential diagnoses, or new evidence concerning temporal or geographic distributions in the past;
3   specific diseases, including their identification, comparisons across time and space, and host–parasite co-evolution;
4   population health, which consists of characterizations and comparisons.

We will look at each of these four subjects in turn; but first we would like to consider their relative value, in response to recent critiques.

Armelagos and Van Gerven (2003) and Armelagos (2003) have argued for a problem-oriented paleopathology, explicitly contrasting this approach with a field driven by biomedical or clinical interests in disease diagnoses and in distributions in time and space. They argue, in the same spirit, that technical advances have encouraged method-driven approaches and that description is all too common (items 1–3 above). They favor biocultural studies of population health (item 4 above). In this chapter I argue for balance, noting the remarkable impact of methodological advances in imaging, histology, and especially molecular approaches. As Mays (2009) argues, case studies have an important role in paleopathology if they extend our knowledge of a condition in time or space, contribute substantially to ongoing debate in the field, hold some particular significance, local historical or cultural, or provide key information concerning a condition not well described in current texts. An exemplary study, by Lagia and colleagues (2007), of a documented case of thalassemia from Greece fulfills most of Mays's criteria.

ASSUMPTIONS AND METHODOLOGIES

In interpreting ancient disease, certain assumptions about the relationship between ancient and modern conditions are necessary; in particular, one needs to postulate that the two are sufficiently similar for a contemporary label to be used. In certain examples such as healed fractures and benign tumors, this is easily justified. In the case of less obvious examples, a rigorous protocol for the observation and interpretation of abnormal tissue changes must be applied.

Studies of ancient disease necessarily begin with distinguishing the evidence of pathology from post-mortem (taphonomic) changes. Next, using standard terminology, paleopathologists generate descriptions of abnormal changes observed grossly, through imaging techniques, and through invasive methods such as histology and molecular biology. Comprehensive protocols applying standardized terminology to gross observations have been advanced by Buikstra and Ubelaker (1994) and modified by Brickley and McKinley (2004). Standards for recording the non-specific indicators of stress have emerged within the 'history of health in Europe' project, developed by Richard Steckel, Phillip Walker, Clark Larsen, and Kimberly Williams (to be found at http://global.sbs.ohio-state.edu/).

Databases that facilitate data recording and analysis have developed from such protocols. For example, the Repatriation Office of the National Museum of Natural History has developed a comprehensive data entry system based on the results of Buikstra and Ubelaker (1994). This relational database (*Osteoware*), available free of charge, will be released in 2009 and will include a module on pathology (S. Ousley and C. Dudar, personal communication, 2009). In the UK, the more than 17,000 skeletons held by the Museum of London are being entered into an Oracle relational database (Wellcome Osteological Research Database, or WORD) that was launched in 2007. Pathology is a part of this comprehensive database, which emphasizes both the description and the subsequent classification into congenital, infectious, joint disease, trauma, metabolic, endocrine, neoplastic, or circulatory (White 2008).

In developing differential diagnoses, paleopathologists commonly follow either a clinical, case-based approach or an epidemiological strategy. The former is illustrated in paleopathology texts, while the latter takes several forms. One epidemiological perspective involves explicitly adding demographic and contextual lines of evidence to the differential diagnosis. These additions include pattern fit and key diagram models. The former is suitable for conditions with high population prevalence, for instance the treponemal disease in ancient North America (Powell and Cook 2005a); the latter is appropriate for relatively rare conditions, such as ancient tuberculosis (Buikstra 1976). In addition, researchers have explicitly adapted epidemiological models to the discussion of disease prevalence (Waldron 2007; Pinhasi and Turner 2008).

Available non-invasive methods used to enhance diagnostic specificity include sophisticated imaging strategies drawn from the biomedical sciences – a tradition which started with the study of human and animal mummies in 1896, the year after Röntgen's development of the X-ray (Aufderheide 2003). X-ray radiography (flat screen) JE continue to be used to investigate disease in ancient bones and mummified materials, having been joined by a number of other methods, including computerized tomography (CT). Micro-CT is also appropriate in the study of materials which are less than 14 cm in diameter, since it provides pixel images in the micrometer range (Saab et al. 2008). For example, brain tissue from the mummy Nakht has been explored through both CT and micro-CT scans (Chhem 2008), while sixteenth-century rheumatoid arthritis has been identified in a mummy from Italy through CT (Ciranni et al. 2002).

All radiographic methods require the use of ionizing radiation, and this may alter the target material, including the aDNA of hosts and pathogens alike. Therefore these techniques may be considered invasive rather than non-invasive. For this reason, current experimentation with magnetic resonance imaging (MRI) is a welcome advancement. Thus far results have been mixed, as basic MRI techniques require re-hydration of desiccated tissues and are inappropriate for dry bone. Recently, however, MRI studies of dry brain tissue (Karlik et al. 2007) and of full mummies (Rühli et al. 2007), which have been carried out through the use of ultra-short-echo-time (UTE-MRI), suggest that MRI may be adapted to studies in paleopathology.

The challenge in applying such high-tech approaches, however, is to move past the exploratory phase to the generation of new knowledge of past disease in a rigorous, scientific manner, addressing issues related to health in past societies. As O'Brien and colleagues (2009) discovered in their survey of CT studies, 65 percent of them were driven by curiosity rather than by clearly articulated research questions or hypotheses. Disappointingly, a third of the authors failed to describe their protocols in sufficient detail for the results to be reproduced by other workers. Thus the need for scientific rigor and problem-oriented research remains largely unmet even when such advanced technologies are applied to ancient remains.

Another non-invasive method for studying mummies is endoscopy, whereby a flexible fiberglass tube with a lens at the distal end is inserted through a small aperture (about 2 cm in diameter) into the body. Images are transmitted both to the operator and to a video screen. Endoscopic methods have been used to identify various conditions, including true disease remnants such as hydatid cysts and pneumoconiosis, along with artefacts of the embalming process. Although this method is considered non-invasive, it may require creating a small incision into the skin, through which the tube is inserted. In addition, there is the risk of damaging brittle tissues as the endoscope traverses the body (Aufderheide 2003; Lynnerup 2007).

Two invasive methods, paleohistology and aDNA analysis, also enhance current studies in paleopathology. Histological methods were first applied to the study of early disease during in the nineteenth century, the term 'paleohistology' being coined by Moodie (1923a). While these early methods favored decalcification and the embedding of bone in paraffin, contemporary techniques for hard tissues utilize different embedding agents, for instance epoxy resins, and light microscopy. Schultz (2003) recommends grinding sections to translucency (15–100 µm (micrometer)) and using transmitted light visualizations, preferably with polarized light – although thicker sections may be used for reflected light microscopy. This approach has been employed in case studies of tumors, scurvy, rickets, treponematosis, leprosy, tuberculosis, and Paget's disease, as well as for population-based inferences (Grupe and Garland 1993; Schultz 2003).

Histological studies of desiccated soft tissues complement osteological investigations. As summarized by Aufderheide (2003: 373–374), diagnoses of various conditions, unapproachable in skeletonized remains, have been strengthened through the paleohistological study of mummified soft tissues; these conditions include anthracosis, cirrhosis, colon adenocarconima, pneumonia, and silicate pneumoconiosis.

Molecular methods have produced significant results in the study of ancient pathogen DNA (see also Kaestle's chapter in the present volume). Researchers have reported aDNA for the pathogens that caused Chagas' disease, influenza, leprosy, malaria, plague, bilharzia, syphilis, trench fever, tuberculosis, and typhoid fever, and for various endoparasites and ecto-parasites (Drancourt and Rauolt 2005; Papagrigorakis et al. 2006).

Of special concern in these molecular approaches is rigor at every stage of analysis. A number of researchers have criticized the manner in which pathogen aDNA research is conducted and reported (Cooper and Poinar 2000; Drancourt and Rauolt 2005; Roberts and Ingham 2008).

INFECTIOUS DISEASE AND HUMAN HOST–PATHOGEN RELATIONSHIPS

Did Columbus discover venereal syphilis along with the riches of the New World, returning with it to Europe at the wane of the fifteenth century? When this question – a seeming preoccupation of paleopathologists and the public alike – was posed to the eminent paleopathologist Donald Ortner (2005: xix–xx), he opined that he would rather focus upon how the treponematoses inform our understanding of human host–pathogen co-evolution, emphasizing that ancient human remains provide a 'powerful source of information.'

Thus host–pathogen co-evolution has emerged center-stage in the study of infectious diseases. With the 'molecular revolution,' a new appreciation has come for the intricate balance struck by pathogens and for the way they may develop new adaptive mechanisms over time. Here we concentrate upon three of the infectious diseases that affect bone and have long co-evolved with our species: treponematosis, tuberculosis, and leprosy. Rather than describing bony changes (already described thoroughly in paleopathology texts), this discussion will emphasize current knowledge concerning the history of these diseases in relationship to the human condition.

The natural history of treponematosis continues to be controversial. As Ortner (2003) emphasizes, a great deal hinges upon the degree to which the four clinically recognized expressions of the disease (pinta, yaws, endemic syphilis or bejel, and venereal syphilis) reflect either context-specific expressions of a single pathogen, or different species. If the first is indeed the case, then scholars are challenged to establish the factors that influence the expression of the syndromes. If the latter, then the evolutionary forces that led to the differentiation of the pathogens must be explained. Molecular biology has yet to clarify the issue fully (Ortner 2003; Powell and Cook 2005a; Roberts and Manchester 2005).

Turning to the skeletal record for treponemal disease, a recent North American synthesis (Powell and Cook 2005b) provides compelling evidence against Columbian origins – that is, against the argument that Columbus and his crew brought to Europe a venereal pathogen taken from the New World. This perspective is not, however, shared by Harper and colleagues (2008), who argue for a New World origin on the basis of a phylogeny inferred from contemporary molecular variation in treponematoses. Most agree, however, that treponematosis existed in the New World prior to the era of exploration, and its prevalence and age-specific predilections point to non-venereal transmission. What about Old World examples?

The number of Old World examples of syphilis is slowly growing, yet small (Brothwell 2005; Roberts and Manchester 2005). There are some convincing (rare) cases collected from throughout western Europe, and even from sub-Saharan Africa. Clinical experience indicates that, while the prevalence of bony lesions among those suffering from tertiary syphilis is relatively high (about 20 percent), the overall expected prevalence for a community at risk is low (Powell and Cook 2005a). Rare cases are to be anticipated, a situation which thus illustrates the fact that isolated case studies can be quite important in the study of host–pathogen evolution.

Until the contemporary molecular evidence concerning the treponemal species question is sorted out and further phylogenies are estimated, the issue of New World/Old World origins is likely to remain inconclusive and definitive statements about host–pathogen relationships for the treponematoses cannot be made. Because DNA from ancient suspected treponemal remains is notoriously difficult to extract and amplify (compare Kolman et al. 1999 with Bouwman and Brown 2005), testing these phylogenies currently requires that we focus upon the record of diagnostic skeletal lesions, viewed in temporal and spatial contexts.

By contrast, molecular evidence both for contemporary and for ancient variation in mycobacterial pathogens has led to remarkable advances in identifying ancient disease and in modeling co-evolutionary histories. The models for tuberculosis are more advanced than those for leprosy (Stone et al. in press).

A spectacular recent development has been the generation of phylogenetic models that push the origins of *M. tuberculosis* into deep time, perhaps 35,000 years to 2.5–3 million years, the human pathogen being older than *M. bovis*. Prevailing wisdom had established that the zoonotic, bovine form adapted to humans in the course of intensified animal husbandry in the Eastern Mediterranean approximately 10,000 years ago – an assertion supported by considerable archaeological evidence (Roberts and Buikstra 2003). Similarly startling is the evidence that relationships developed in Africa between the human *M. tuberculosis* (or a progenitor strain) and some archaic species; then the former moved to South and southeast Asia. At some time during this process, the selection of a virulent form led to the formation of the European strain, which moved from Europe and spread across the globe during the age of exploration, swamping the indigenous American *M. tuberculosis*, which had entered the hemisphere through early migrants from Asia (Stone et al. in press).

Recent research (Wilbur et al. 2008) has addressed the problem of the enigmatic absence of skeletal tuberculosis in situations where there is a reasonable expectation for its presence. Cemeteries at institutions for the nineteenth and early twentieth-century disadvantaged have been excavated, for example, as have myriad ancient Maya remains; and yet there little evidence of diagnostic spinal deformities (Pott's disease) or other indications of skeletal tuberculosis. Wilbur and colleagues (2008) address this issue by considering the complex interplay between immune competency and nutrition and by thus developing a nuanced appreciation for the myriad factors that influence disease expression.

There remain many unsolved puzzles in modeling the global history of the mycobacterial diseases. For example, while an African origin for tuberculosis and perhaps leprosy is accepted on the basis of molecular evidence (Roberts and Manchester 2005; Stone et al. in press), the course taken by their endemic and pandemic histories remains unclear. Did leprosy originate in Africa or in South Asia? Is its origin to be placed in the Pleistocene or in the Holocene? Why did leprosy peak in Europe during the late Middle Ages? Is there any cross-immunity between leprosy and tuberculosis, and does the rise of tuberculosis in Europe help to explain leprosy's diminished frequency in southern and then northern Europe? Why do the first pieces of evidence from historical documents for lepromatous (severe) leprosy come from South (600 BC) and East Asia (300 BC), when the only skeletal confirmation is a single case in Thailand? (Roberts and Manchester 2005; Stone et al. in press). Evolutionary molecular models for ancient and contemporary *M. leprae*, as yet undeveloped, should resolve co-evolutionary relationships between humans and leprosy, as well as between humans and the two mycobacterial diseases considered here.

IRON DEFICIENCY ANEMIA RECONSIDERED

Porosity on the superior aspect of the orbits (cribra orbitalia) and across the cranial vault (porotic hyperostosis) has been considered, especially in the western hemisphere, to be evidence of iron deficiency anemia (see for instance El-Najjar et al. 1975). Recently, however, this association has been called into question, as Ortner (2003) has argued compellingly that cribra orbitalia is frequently associated with scurvy. On the basis of clinical information, Phillip Walker and colleagues (2009) have asserted that porotic hyperostosis is linked to a nutritional megaloblastic anemia and frequently to vitamin B_{12} deficiency rather than to iron deficiency anemia. This example illustrates the importance of contemporary knowledge derived from biomedical sources and the value of a constant critical review of received wisdom in paleopathology, as it underscores the dynamic nature of the field.

GLOBAL HEALTH

The 1984 landmark publication *Paleopathology at the Origins of Agriculture* (Cohen and Armelagos 1984) wedded archaeological interest in exploring the mechanisms that stimulated agricultural intensification with the study of 'non-specific indicators of stress' in temporally sequential, regionally derived skeletal series that represented the requisite time periods. Such indicators include developmental enamel defects, stunting, cortical thickness of long bones, cribra orbitalia, porotic hyperostosis, periosteal reactions on long bones, trauma, osteoarthritis, and oral pathology.

This comparative study concluded that in many parts of the globe health was compromised through this significant shift in subsistence strategy, and the editors asserted that agricultural intensification had been stimulated by stress and need rather than through choice and invention. Subsequent research (Cohen and Crane-Kramer 2007) reaffirmed the landmark conclusions reached in 1984 and expanded the earlier database so as to include further samples from Africa and southeast Asia, in addition to the primarily European and western hemisphere sequences. Thus data drawn from paleopathology were used in global tests of the theoretical models of the intensification of food production.

A second significant effort at global comparisons, influenced by the Cohen and Armelagos study, has been the 'backbone of history' project, which is focused on the western hemisphere (Steckel and Rose 2002). In this case, an economic historian and numerous bioarchaeologists joined forces in order to evaluate the quality of human life through the study of skeletal attributes similar to those recorded by Cohen's bioarchaeological colleagues. This study is currently being extended to European contexts (http://global.sbs.ohio-state.edu/).

The 'history of health in the western hemisphere' project focused upon collecting extensive data sets that measured qualitative factors like climate, political complexity, location, and subsistence, along with skeletal data reflecting non-specific stress. The 'health index,' a quantitative measure based upon rating each skeletal variable on a scale of 0 to 100, was also developed, and groups were thus compared across the hemisphere. The results of this study also indicate that, throughout the history of the human condition, health has declined. In the closing chapter, the authors conclude that life became 'nasty, brutish and short' for the typical person with the rise of agriculture, government, and urbanization (Steckel and Rose 2002: 573).

The approaches taken by both projects have excited critique, both methodologically and theoretically. Wood and colleagues (2002), for example, suggest that there may be a positive correlation between observed skeletal pathology and good health, given that one must live sufficiently long to register a bony insult rather than dying precipitously and thus providing a seemingly 'healthy' skeleton for bioarchaeologists.

From an epidemiological perspective, Pinhasi and Turner (2008) criticize the statistical approach taken in constructing the 'health index.' Cook (2007) expresses concern over the use of stature as a proxy for health, also noting discrepancies between historical accounts and inferences made by using stature data to characterize health.

A further significant issue involves basic differences between the two approaches. The 'western hemisphere' and the 'European health' projects have emphasized geographic and temporal coverage along with data quantity. The approach taken by Cohen and colleagues has focused first on defining relatively nuanced, regional patterns. The productive tension between these two contrastive research strategies will doubtless continue, adding to our knowledge of ancient health – broadly defined.

At present, both in the global and in the regional-to-global examples, researchers have focused upon finding universal or nearly universal patterns. In future studies, it may become important to focus upon the explanatory power gained by exploring those cases where expectations fail to be met.

PALEOPATHOLOGY, MUMMY STUDIES, AND MUMMY SCIENCE

Mummies – either human or of other animals – have excited the interest of the lay public and scientists alike since Napoleon invaded Egypt in 1798. For the paleopathologist, this has meant an opportunity to examine tissues other than bones and teeth, with the hope of obtaining information about disease and health beyond that afforded by hard tissues. There are attendant challenges, however, because desiccation, in the case of dry environments, alters tissue form such that even the most skilled of anatomists are challenged to recognize internal organs. Deposition in acid bogs produces tanned corpses or 'bog bodies,' whose apparent external integrity belies the demineralized osseous tissues within. Artificial mummies inevitably present evidence of tissue destruction that occurred during preparation procedures, while the viscera of naturally mummified corpses may be destroyed from within, due to bacterial action. Even so, as noted above, there are diseases that have been identified in desiccated soft tissues but are unknowable from skeletonized remains (Aufderheide 2003; Cockburn et al. 1998, Lynnerup 2007).

PALEOPARASITOLOGY

Matter recovered from mummies (hair, tissues, and alimentary tracks), coprolites, and archaeological deposits such as privies, the remains of parasites, their eggs, nits, and tracks provide key evidence of disease, community health, host diet, and migration history, as well as cultural and climatic change. Disease prevalence may be inferred through studies of egg frequencies in coprolites (Dittmar 2009).

Begun with Ruffer's 1910 recovery of blood fluke eggs in Egypt, methodological advances have increased the potential for recovery and identification of diseases; for example, recent aDNA applications have revealed the presence of parasitic pathogens from 9,000-year-old mummified tissues without other overt evidence. Similarly, coprolites may serve as a source of parasite aDNA. The diseases that have been identified through aDNA study include Chagas' disease, leishmaniasis, and helminthic infections by whipworms, roundworms and pinworms, along with human fleas and head lice (Dittmar 2009).

Until the 1990s there was little theory in the study of ancient parasites. Since that time, theoretical developments have led to a proliferation of terms applied to the study, with nuanced differences in emphasis: 'Paleoparasitology' typically emphasizes the biological aspect of the study, while 'archaeoparasitology' links it to the social sciences, especially archaeology and bioarchaeology. 'Pathoecology' expressly focuses upon the environmental determinants of disease, and its name also symbolizes the explicitly interdisciplinary and collaborative nature of the study of ancient parasites (Reinhard and Bryant 2008).

ANIMAL PALEOPATHOLOGY

The paleopathology envisioned by Schufeldt studied the disease of any fossil or extinct organism (Powell and Cook 2006). Moodie's (1923a, 1923b) paleopathology was also broad and comparative, while emphasizing animal disease. Although a few scholars such as Brothwell have steadfastly championed animal paleopathology during the twentieth century (see Baker and Brothwell 1980), the field has become focused upon human disease. This appears to be changing, however, with the formation of a working group on 'veterinary paleopathology' (now 'animal palaeopathology') within the International Council for Archaeozoology (ICAZ) in 1999 (Thomas n.d.).

With the establishment of the ICAZ working group (APWG), the field has moved toward explicitly addressing theoretical and methodological concerns not unfamiliar to those who study human paleopathology:

1   the lack of integration with archaeological data and contexts;
2   the lack of consistent, standard scoring procedures;
3   the limited understanding of fundamental biomedical processes that underlie pathological lesions.

Within the past ten years, the field of animal paleopathology has expanded markedly, due to a number of factors, including APWG, but also under the influence of a growing awareness of the field's obvious potential in regions other than the Old World. Future goals include gaining greater methodological sophistication, understanding the nature of diseases for which there are currently no clinical models, developing standardized recording systems, and appreciating greater biological and epidemiological sensitivity to contexts (Thomas n.d.).

DISABILITY AND IDENTITY

The study of disability and identity as a form of paleopathology is in a nascent phase. Early attempts to consider compassion and caring for infirm individuals have been effectively critiqued by medical anthropologist Katherine Dettwyler (1991) as being anthropologically naïve and insensitive.

In this context there are two related but distinctive concepts that require definition. For example, Cross (1999) contrasts impairment, which we can interpret archaeologically, and disability, which depends upon the reaction of the affected individual and his/her social group to impairments such as cleft palates, dwarfism, or the life-long effects of a bout of polio. Contemporary definitions of disability are socially mediated and thus vary from culture to culture, or even among social classes (Buikstra and Scott 2009). In studies of disease or disability in relation to identity, reactions from *both* the individual and society to a pathological condition are of central significance.

The study of disability requires careful consideration of individual lives, evidence of impairment, and archaeological contexts. For example, Knüsel (1999) contrasts three medieval English burials: all adult males with deforming pathologies that would have affected mobility. One had suffered traumatic injury to the right knee. Another had a displaced proximal right femur epiphysis, probably reflecting onset in adolescence. Finally, an elderly male with leprosy also presented a series of healed fractures that yielded limb asymmetries. The first two had been interred in privileged situations; the second, in fact, was interred beneath the altar of St Giles Church, with a mortuary chalice and paten. Knüsel suggests that the deformity may have advantaged this priest, linking him to his patron, St Giles, who had also suffered a deforming injury. The leper, by contrast, was segregated and placed, together with similarly afflicted individuals, in the cemetery of a *leprosarium*. In this example, the infectious disease assumed primary significance for the socially constructed disability persona. Thus descriptions of impairment and inferences about disability may be advanced through the study of remains within their funerary contexts, which include location in the grave as a significant dimension of variability.

INTERPERSONAL VIOLENCE, WARFARE, AND CANNIBALISM

During the past quarter century, paleopathologists have contributed significantly to issues surrounding violence in the past. While many earlier researchers had accepted prevailing wisdom concerning the lack of violent behaviors among earlier Native Americans, a view perhaps introduced, or at least encouraged, by Europeans, recent years have witnessed convincing evidence for warfare and other forms of interpersonal violence well before the fifteenth century (Walker 2001). Bioarchaeological evidence has, for example, been used to support cannibalism in the American southwest (Billman et al. 2000; Turner and Turner 1999; White 1992), although archaeologists and bioarchaeologists have proposed alternative interpretations (Darling 1999; Walker 1998).

Other recent studies have focused upon gender-specific violence. Martin and Akins (2001), for example, infer the presence of a female underclass for the period AD 1,000–1,300 in southwest Colorado, while extreme peri-mortem violence has been conjectured as evidence of political intimidation within the same region (Lekson 2002). In fact a recent review has concluded that there is bioarchaeological evidence for violence throughout the whole human history; in North America, it extends from the existence of the dart or spear point in the Kennewick Man throughout the pre-contact period and beyond (Walker 2001).

PALEOPATHOLOGY AS PROFESSION: ORGANIZATIONS, CONGRESSES, AND SHORT COURSES

The cornerstone – the international professional organization for paleopathologists – is the Paleopathology Association (PPA), begun in 1973 with an autopsy (PUM II) and a symposium attended by medical scientists and anthropologists. This was soon followed by a newsletter designed to maintain the stimulating communication flow initiated by the conference, and a fledging learned society was born. Nurtured by the heroic efforts of Eve and Aidan Cockburn, the PPA has held annual meetings since 1976, in conjunction with the American Association of Physical Anthropologists. To maintain international communication, from the same year on the PPA has also sponsored biennial meetings in a variety of European settings and, since 2005, biennial Paleopathology Association Meetings in South America (PAMinSA; see Powell n.d.).

The subject matter and collaborative spirit of the PPA has inspired other developments, including international congresses on the epidemiology and pathology of infectious disease. The first one of these focused upon syphilis (1993), and it was followed by subsequent congresses on tuberculosis, leprosy, and plague. These have stimulated considerable productive communication and collaborations across the many specialties that relate to each disease, and a symposium volume has emerged from each (summarized in Pálfi et al. n.d.).

Folks with special interests in mummified remains and bog bodies have also organized a series of six world congresses on mummy studies, with the inaugural meeting held in 1992. Each mummy congress has been well attended by medical and anthropological scientists and practitioners, and a series of proceedings volumes have been published (summarized in Lynnerup n.d.).

RECENT ADVANCES AND FUTURE DIRECTIONS

The field of paleopathology has obviously responded effectively to Jarcho's (1966) critique. There are numerous deep syntheses, either focused upon mummy science and specific diseases or in the form of general paleopathology texts. The recovery of ancient pathogen DNA should fulfill Jarcho's 'truly significant' category, especially that of the 1918 influenza virus. International organizations and congresses now regularly promote communication between medical scientists and anthropologists, and such communication includes mummy studies. The twenty-first century has also witnessed the development of databases grounded in standard terminology for skeletal gross anatomy.

What challenges remain to be addressed? One of the key challenges, as emphasized above, is to integrate effectively state-of-the-art biomedical technology with the study of ancient disease, both in individual perspective and in population perspective. This is being most effectively accomplished in molecular and histological studies, although in the former issues of protocols and reporting remain. Non-invasive state-of-the-art imaging technological applications largely remain at the case level, frequently without explicit goals. Another concern is that the proliferating congresses should not dichotomize the field between representatives of the medical sciences, who would naturally attend the mummy congresses, and the anthropologists attending the meetings sponsored by the PPA. In sum, it appears nonetheless that the field is much healthier and vital than it was half a century ago. What the future holds depends upon continued collaborations between biomedical and anthropological scholars.

REFERENCES

Agarwal, S. C., Dumitriv, M., Tomlinson, G. A., and Grynpas, M. D. (2004) Medieval Trabecular Bone Architecture: The Influence of Age, Sex, and Lifestyle. *American Journal of Physical Anthropology* 124: 33–44.

Armelagos, G. J. (2003) Bioarchaeology as Anthropology. *Archaeological Papers of the American Anthropological Association* 13 (1): 27–40.

Armelagos, G. J., and Van Gerven, D. P. (2003) A Century of Skeletal Biology and Paleopathology: Contrasts, Contradictions, and Conflicts. *American Anthropologist* 105 (1): 53–64.

Aufderheide, A. C. (2003) *The Scientific Study of Mummies.* Cambridge: Cambridge University Press.

Aufderheide, A. C., and Rodríguez-Martín, C. (1998) *The Cambridge Encyclopedia of Human Paleopathology.* Cambridge: Cambridge University Press.

Baker, J. R., and Brothwell, D. R. (1980) *Animal Diseases in Archaeology.* London and New York: Academic Press.

Billman, B. R., Lambert, P. M., and Leonard, B. L. (2000) Cannibalism, Warfare, and Drought in the Mesa Verde Region during the Twelfth Century AD. *American Antiquity* 65 (1): 145–178.

Bouwman, A. S., and Brown, T. A. (2005) The Limits of Biomolecular Palaeopathology: Ancient DNA Cannot Be Used to Study Venereal Syphilis. *Journal of Archaeological Science* 32: 703–713.

Brickley, M. (2002) An Investigation of Historical and Archaeological Evidence for Age-Related Bone loss and Osteoporosis. *International Journal of Osteoarchaeology* 12: 364–371.

Brickley, M., and Ives, R. (2008) *The Bioarchaeology of Metabolic Bone Disease.* Oxford: Elsevier.

Brickley, M., and McKinley, J. I. (eds) (2004) *Guidelines to the Standards for Recording Human Remains.* Reading: BABAO, Department of Archaeology, University of Southampton, and the Institute of Field Archaeologists.

Brothwell, D. R. (2005) North American Treponematosis against the Bigger World Picture. In M. L. Powell and D. C. Cook (eds), *The Myth of Syphilis* (pp. 480–496). Gainesville FL: University Press of Florida.

Buikstra, J. E. (1976) The Caribou Eskimo: General and Specific Disease. *American Journal of Physical Anthropology* 43: 350–368.

Buikstra, J. E. (2006) A Historical Introduction. In J. E. Buikstra and L. E. Beck (eds), *Bioarchaeology: The Contextual Analysis of Human Remains* (pp. 7–25). New York: Academic Press.

Buikstra, J. E., and Scott, R. E. (2009) Identity Formation: Communities and Individuals. In K. Knudson and C. Stojanowski (eds), *Bioarchaeology and Identity* (pp. 24–55). Gainesville FL: University Press of Florida.

Buikstra, J. E., and Ubelaker, D. (1994) *Standards for Data Collection from Human Skeletal Remains: Proceedings of a Seminar at the Field Museum of Natural History.* Fayetteville AR: Arkansas Archaeological Survey Press.

Chhem, R. K. (2008) Paleoradiology: History and New Developments. In R. K. Chhem and D. R. Brothwell (eds), *PaleoRadiology: Imaging Mummies and Fossils* (pp. 2–14). Berlin, Heidelberg and New York: Springer-Verlag.

Ciranni, R., Garbini, F., Neri, E., Melai, L., Giusti, L., and Fornaciari, G. (2002) The 'Braids Lady' of Arezzo: A Case of Rheumatoid Arthritis in a Sixteenth-Century Mummy. *Clinical and Experimental Rheumatology* 20: 745–752.

Cockburn, A., Cockburn, E., and Reyman, T. A. (eds) (1998) *Mummies, Disease, and Ancient Cultures.* 2nd edn. New York: Cambridge University Press.

Cohen, M. N., and Armelagos, G. J. (eds) (1984) *Paleopathology at the Origins of Agriculture.* New York: Academic Press.

Cohen, M. N., and Crane-Kramer, G. (2007) *Ancient Health: Skeletal Indication of Agricultural and Economic Interpretations of the Human Past: Local, Regional, and Global Perspectives.* Gainesville FL: University Press of Florida.

Cook, D. C. (2007) Maize and Mississippians in the American Midwest: Twenty Years Later. In M. N. Cohen and G. M. Crane-Cramer (eds), *Ancient Health: Skeletal Indication of Agricultural and Economic Interpretations of the Human Past: Local, Regional, and Global Perspectives* (pp. 1–9). Gainesville FL: University Press of Florida.

Cook, D. C., and Powell, M. L. (2006) The Evolution of American Paleopathology. In J. E. Buikstra and L. E. Beck (eds), *Bioarchaeology: The Contextual Analysis of Human Remains* (pp. 281–322). New York: Academic Press.

Cooper, A., and Poinar, H. N. (2000) Ancient DNA: Do It Right or Not At All. *Science* 289: 1139.

Cross, M. (1999) Accessing the Inaccessible: Disability and Archaeology. *Archaeological Review from Cambridge: Archaeology and Disability* 15: 7–30.

Darling, J. A. (1999) From Hobbes to Rousseau and Back Again. *Science* 285: 537.

Dettwyler, K. A. (1991) Does Paleopathology Provide Evidence for 'Compassion'? *American Journal of Physical Anthropology* 84: 375–384.

Dittmar, K. (2009) Old Parasites for a New World: The Future of Paleoparasitological Research. A Review. *Journal of Parasitology* 95: 365–371.

Drancourt, M., and Raoult, D. (2005) Palaeomicrobiology: Current Issues and Perspectives. *Nature Reviews Microbiology* 3: 23–35.

El-Najjar, M. Y., Lozoff, B., and Ryan, D. (1975) The Paleoepidemiology of Porotic Hyperostosis in the American Southwest: Radiological and Ecological Considerations. *American Journal of Roentgenology, Radium Therapy, and Nuclear Medicine* 125: 918–924.

Grupe, G., and Garland, A. (eds) (1993) *Histology of Ancient Human Bone: Methods and Diagnosis.* Berlin: Springer-Verlag.

Harper, K. N., Ocampo, P. S., Steiner, B. M., George, R. W., and Silverman, M. S. (2008) On the Origin of the Treponematoses: A Phylogenetic Approach. *PLoS Neglected Tropical Diseases* 2 (1): e148. doi: 10.1371/journal.pntd.0000148.

Jarcho, S. (1966) The Development and Present Condition of Human Palaeopathology in the United States. In S. Jarcho (ed.), *Human Palaeopathology* (pp. 3–30). New Haven CT: Yale University Press.

Karlik, S. J., Bartha, R., Kennedy, K., and Chhem, R. (2007) MRI and Multinuclear MR Spectroscopy of 3,200-year-old Egyptian Mummy Brain. *American Journal of Roentgenology* 189 (2): W105–110.

Knüsel, C. (1999) Orthopaedic Disability: Some Hard Evidence. *Archaeological Review from Cambridge: Disability and Archaeology* 15: 31–53.

Kolman, C. J., Centurion-Lara, A., Lukehart, S.A., Owsley, D. A., and Tuross, N. (1999) Identification of *Treponema pallidum* Subspecies *pallidum* in a 200-year-old Skeletal Specimen. *Journal of Infectious Diseases* 180: 2060–2063.

Lagia, A., Eliopoulos, C., and Manolis, S. (2007) Thalassemia: Macroscopic and Radiological Study of a Case. *International Journal of Osteoarchaeology* 17: 269–285.

Lekson, S. H. (2002) War in the Southwest, War in the World. *American Antiquity* 67 (4): 607–624.

Lynnerup, N. (2007) Mummies. *Yearbook of Physical Anthropology* 50: 162–190.

Lynnerup, N. (n.d.) The Mummy Congresses. In J. E. Buikstra and C. R. Roberts (eds), *A History of Paleopathology.* Manuscript submitted for publication.

Martin, D. L., and Akins, N. J. (2001) Unequal Treatment in Life as in Death: Trauma and Mortuary Behavior at La Plata (AD 1000–13000). In D. R. Mitchell and J. L. Brunson-Hadley (eds),

Ancient Burial Practices in the American Southwest: Archaeology, Physical Anthropology, and Native American Perspectives (pp. 223–248). Albuquerque: University of New Mexico Press.

Mays, S. A. (2009) Human Osteoarchaeology in the UK 2001–2007: A Bibliometric Perspective. *International Journal of Osteoarchaeology*: DOI: 10.1002/oa.1021.

Moodie, R. L. (1923a) *Paleopathology: An Introduction to the Study of Ancient Evidences of Disease*. Urbana: University of Illinois Press.

Moodie, R. L. (1923b) *The Antiquity of Disease*. Chicago: University of Chicago Press.

O'Brien, J. J., Battista, J. J., Romagnoli, C., and Chhem, R. K. (2009) CT Imaging of Human Mummies: A Critical Review of the Literature (1979–2005). *International Journal of Osteoarchaeology* 19: 90–98.

Ortner, D. J. (2003) *Identification of Pathological Conditions in Human Skeletal Remains*. 2nd edn. San Diego CA: Elsevier.

Ortner, D. J. (2005) Foreword. In M. L. Powell and D. C. Cook (eds), *The Myth of Syphilis* (pp. ix–xx). Gainesville FL: University Press of Florida.

Pálfi, G., Dutour, O. J., and Roberts, C. A. (n.d.) The International Congresses on Infectious and Epidemic Diseases. In J. E. Buikstra and C. R. Roberts (eds), *A History of Paleopathology*. Manuscript submitted for publication.

Papagrigorakis, M. J., Yapifakis, C., Synodinos, P. N., and Baziotopoulou-Valavani, E. (2006) DNA Examination of Ancient Dental Pulp Incriminates Typhoid Fever as a Probable Cause of the Plague of Athens. *International Journal of Infectious Diseases* 10 (3): 206–214.

Pinhasi, R., and Turner, K. (2008) Epidemiological Approaches in Palaeopathology. In R. Pinhasi and S. Mays (eds), *Advances in Human Palaeopathology* (pp. 177–188). Chichester: Wiley.

Powell, M. L. (n.d.) The History of the Paleopathology Association. In J. E. Buikstra and C. R. Roberts (eds), *A History of Paleopathology*. Manuscript submitted for publication.

Powell, M. L, and Cook, D. C. (2005a) Treponematosis: Inquiries into the Nature of a Protean Disease. In M. L. Powell and D. C. Cook (eds), *The Myth of Syphilis* (pp. 9–62). Gainesville FL: University Press of Florida.

Powell, M. L, and Cook, D. C. (eds) (2005b) *The Myth of Syphilis*. Gainesville FL: University Press of Florida.

Reid, A. H., Fanning, T. G., Hultin, J. V., and Taubenberger, J. K. (1999) Origin and Evolution of the 1918 'Spanish' Influenza Virus Hemagglutinin Gene. *Proceedings of the National Academy of Science, USA* 96: 1651–1656.

Reinhard, K. J. (2000) Reburial, International Perspectives. In L. Ellis (ed.), *Archaeological Method and Theory: An Encyclopedia* (pp. 512–518). New York and London: Garland Publishing, Inc.

Reinhard, K. J., and Bryant, V. M. (2008) Pathoecology and the Future of Coprolite Studies in Bioarchaeology. In A. W. M. Stodder (ed.), *Reanalysis and Reinterpretation in Southwestern Bioarchaeology* (pp. 199–216). Arizona State University Anthropological Research Papers No. 59.

Reinhard, K. J., Johnson, K., LeRoy-Toren, S., Wieseman, K., Teixeira-Santos, I., and Vieira, M. (in press) Understanding the Relationship between Ancient Diet and Modern Diabetes through Coprolite Analysis: A Case Example from Antelope Cave, Mojave County, Arizona. In K. D. Sobolik (ed.), *Innovations in Paleoethnobotany*. Texas A&M Press, College Station.

Reinhard, K. J., Tieszen, L. L., Sandness, K. L., Beiningen, L. M., Miller, E., Ghazi, A. M., Miewald, C. E., and Barnum, S. V. (1994) Trade, Contact, and Female Health in Northeast Nebraska. In C. S. Larsen and G. R. Milner (eds), *In the Wake of Contact: Biological Responses to Conquest* (pp. 63–74). New York: Wiley–Liss.

Roberts, C. A. (2002) Palaeopathology and Archaeology: The Current State of Play. In R. Arnott (ed), *The Archaeology of Medicine*. British Archaeological Reports. International Series 1046 (pp. 1–20). Oxford: Archaeopress.

Roberts, C. A., and Buikstra, J. E. (2003) *The Bioarchaeology of Tuberculosis: A Global View on a Reemerging Disease*. Gainesville FL: University Press of Florida.

Roberts, C. A., and Ingham, S. (2008) Using Ancient DNA Analysis in Palaeopathology: A Critical Analysis of Published Papers, With Recommendations for Future Work. *International Journal of Osteoarchaeology* 18: 600–613.

Roberts, C. A., and Manchester, K. (2005) *The Archaeology of Disease*. 3rd edn. Stroud, UK/Ithaca NY: Sutton Publishing/Cornell University Press.

Rühli, F. J., von Waldburg, H., Nielles-Vallespin, S., Böni, T., and Speier, P. (2007) Clinical MR-Imaging of Ancient Dry Mummies without Rehydration. *Journal of the American Medical Association* 298: 2618–2620.

Saab, Ge., Chhem, R. K., and Bohay, R. N. (2008) Paleoradiographic Techniques. In R. K. Chhem and D. R. Brothwell (eds), *PaleoRadiology: Imaging Mummies and Fossils* (pp. 15–54). Berlin: Heidelberg, and New York: Springer-Verlag.

Schultz, M. (2003) Light Microscopic Analysis in Skeletal Paleopathology. In D. J. Ortner (ed.), *Identification of Pathological Conditions in Human Skeletal Remains*, 2nd edn (pp. 73–108). San Diego CA: Elsevier.

Steckel, R. H. (2003) Research Project: A History of Health in Europe from the Late Paleolithic Era to the Present. *Economics and Human Biology* 1: 139–142.

Steckel, R. H., and Rose, J. C. (eds) (2002) *The Backbone of History: Health and Nutrition in the Western Hemisphere*. New York and Cambridge: Cambridge University Press.

Stone, A. C., Wilbur, A., Buikstra, J. E., and Roberts, C. A. (in press) Mycobacterial Disease in Perspective. *Yearbook of Physical Anthropology*.

Thomas, R. (n.d.) Non-Human Paleopathology. In J. E. Buikstra and C. R. Roberts (eds), *A History of Paleopathology*. Manuscript submitted for publication.

Turner II, C. G., and Turner, J. A. (1999) *Man Corn: Cannibalism and Violence in the Prehistoric American Southwest*. Salt Lake City: University of Utah Press.

Waldron, T. (2007) *Palaeoepidemiology*. Walnut Creek CA: Left Coast Press.

Walker, P. L. (2001) Bioarchaeological Perspective on the History of violence. *Annual Review of Anthropology* 30: 573–596.

Walker, P. L., Bathurst, R. R., Richman, R., Gjerdrum, T., and Andrushko, V. A. (2009) The Causes of Porotic Hyperostosis and Cribra Orbitalia: A Reappraisal of the Iron-Deficiency-Anemia Hypothesis. *American Journal of Physical Anthropology* 139: 109–125.

Walker, W. H. (1998) Where are the Witches of Prehistory? *Journal of Archaeological Method and Theory* 5: 245–308.

White, T. D. (1992) *Prehistoric Cannibalism at Mancos 5MTUMR-2346*. Princeton: Princeton University Press.

White, W. (2008) Databases. In R. Pinhasi and S. Mays (eds), *Advances in Human Palaeopathology* (pp. 177–188). Chichester: Wiley.

Wilbur, A. K., Farnbach, A. W., Knudson, K. J., and Buikstra, J. E. (2008) Diet, Tuberculosis, and the Paleopathological Literature. *Current Anthropology* 49: 963–991.

Wood, J. W., Holman, D. J., O'Connor, K. A., and Ferrell, R. J. (2002) Mortality Models of Paleodemography. In R. D. Hoppa and F. W. Vaupel (eds), *Paleodemography: Age Distributions from Skeletal Samples* (pp. 129–168). Cambridge: Cambridge University Press.

CHAPTER 23 Issues in Forensic Anthropology

Douglas H. Ubelaker

With increasing frequency, physical anthropologists apply their knowledge and methodology to issues directed toward their laboratories by the legal community. Collectively, such applications, and the method and theory supporting them, represent the rapidly expanding field of forensic anthropology. Most of this effort is directed toward the identification and interpretation of recovered skeletal remains. On occasion, forensic anthropologists also contribute to the evaluation of fleshed remains (especially those in an advanced state of decomposition or showing other forms of soft tissue alteration); to various issues relating to living persons; and to a variety of other problems.

The applications of forensic anthropology are largely defined by the circumstances of the cases and the nature of the material presented. Each case presents unique challenges. To meet these challenges, the forensic anthropologist must consult the supportive published literature, available analytical methodology and his or her experience in choosing the most relevant approaches. Such applications in the last few decades have defined the evolving scientific needs of the field and stimulated considerable research. The result is a vigorous subdiscipline of physical anthropology and forensic science that utilizes the scientific methodology of the parent academic disciplines and includes substantial approaches and databases special to the field.

A BRIEF HISTORY

Historical developments in forensic anthropology generally can be traced to European initiatives in comparative anatomy and in growth and development. The early history of forensic anthropology is closely linked to that of physical anthropology. Aspects that are particular to forensic anthropology include the work of Alphonse Bertillon, who attempted to use a detailed system of anthropometry to facilitate medico-legal identification (Spencer 1997).

In the United States, growth of forensic anthropology was initially stimulated through the involvement of physicians and anatomists in local forensic cases. Well known examples of such involvement include the analysis of remains and testimony by

Oliver Wendell Holmes (1809–94) and Jeffries Wyman (1814–74) in the John W. Webster trial for the murder of Dr George Parkman at Harvard University, as well as George Dorsey's (1868–1931) contributions to the Adolph Luetgert trial in Chicago (Stewart 1979).

This period also witnessed the beginnings of a new phenomenon: scholars in physical anthropology were extending their research interests into forensic anthropology. Stewart (1979) bestowed the title of 'father of forensic anthropology in the United States' upon Thomas Dwight (1843–1911) for his early contributions to the field (Dwight 1878, 1881, 1890a, 1890b, 1894a, 1894b, 1905). Other noteworthy contributors of this early era include Harris Hawthorne Wilder (1864–1928), Paul Stevenson (1890–1971), and T. Wingate Todd (1885–1938), as well as case involvement from Earnest A. Hooton (1887–1954) and Aleš Hrdlička (1869–1943). Hrdlička initiated casework by the Smithsonian Institution for the FBI Headquarters in Washington DC and published on forensic topics (Ubelaker 1999a).

The modern era of forensic anthropology is usually credited to the work of Wilton Krogman (1903–87), T. D. Stewart (1901–97), and Mildred Trotter (1899–1991), who published key works, securing the field recognition (see Krogman 1939, 1962; McKern and Stewart 1957; Stewart 1948, 1951, 1970, 1979; Stewart and Trotter 1954, 1955; Trotter and Gleser 1952).

Key historical developments include organizational advancements as well. In 1972, fourteen founding members created a section of physical anthropology within the American Academy of Forensic Sciences. This new section, with its annual meeting, provided a forum for research presentation and case discussion, focusing specifically on forensic issues.

Through the leadership of Ellis R. Kerley (1924–98) and others, the American Board of Forensic Anthropology (ABFA) was formed in 1977. This board offers certification for forensic anthropologists, who qualify by having the necessary credentials and by passing an examination.

Another significant development is the 2003 formation of the Forensic Anthropology Society of Europe. This organization, affiliated to the International Academy of Legal Medicine, offers the European community training and scholarly interaction in forensic anthropology (Baccino 2005).

In 2009 the field of forensic anthropology has grown dramatically, so as to include many educational initiatives, broad research addressing many issues specific to the field, and active involvement of forensic anthropologists in diverse applications. Noteworthy among these initiatives are contributions to investigations of human rights abuses, of natural disasters, and of other events leading to mass human fatalities.

CERTIFICATION

As discussed above, the American Board of Forensic Anthropology, Inc. represents a key certification body. The ABFA seeks to improve the practice of forensic anthropology and to grant certificates to worthy individuals. Diplomate status is limited to those who:

1 are permanent residents of the United States, Canada, or their territories;
2 possess a PhD with an emphasis in physical anthropology and training in those areas relevant for forensic applications;

3   have three years of relevant post-doctorate experience;
4   pass an examination administered by the ABFA.

By January 2009, seventy-seven anthropologists had been granted diplomate status.

Diplomate status with the American Board of Forensic Anthropology offers foren-sic anthropologists a key credential, which documents to the legal system and to those in need of forensic anthropological services that the holder is qualified. Ultimately, however, the legal system is the gatekeeper by determining who is qualified to render opinions on forensic anthropology matters. How are qualified anthropologists recog-nized among those who are not ABFA certified, especially those who are not residents of North America and are not eligible to become ABFA certified?

Although other organizations promote forensic anthropology in other regions of the world, they do not offer certification. For example, the Forensic Anthropology Society of Europe offers training and enhances communication among those who work on anthropological issues, but membership is available to all those who express an interest (Baccino 2005).

The Latin American Forensic Anthropology Association (ALAF) represents another important organizational development within forensic anthropology, but it does not yet offer certification. Formed in 2003, this organization states that one of its goals is to form an "independent accreditation board that will certify qualified practitioners of forensic anthropology" (Argentine Forensic Anthropology Team 2008). Discussion of the standards to be employed in accreditation emphasizes professional experience, noting the paucity in Latin America of advanced degree programs with a focus on forensic anthropology.

Debate continues on this issue. Should certification be limited to those residents of North America who are qualified and make the effort to meet the standards of the ABFA? Clearly, many anthropologists who are not ABFA diplomates are active in the field and make valuable contributions, including court testimony.

The value of ABFA diplomate status should be emphasized, especially to the legal system. Maintenance of this system requires a great deal of effort for all involved, especially the officers of the ABFA Board of Directors. This effort should be rewarded with broad recognition of the importance of diplomate status.

At the same time new measures are needed, especially for those residing outside of North America, in order to clarify the qualifications of those involved. Mechanisms need to be established to recognize experience, training, formal education, and other forms of preparation. Such recognition, coupled with rigorous testing, should aid the process of determining who is qualified to participate in forensic anthropological investigations.

LEGAL ACCEPTANCE OF METHODOLOGY

In recent years, issues have emerged regarding the use of forensic science expert tes-timony in legal procedures. These issues cluster within two general categories:

1   heightened scrutiny and criticism of some aspects of forensic science from the general scientific community;

2   court decisions that have attempted to define the use of experts and expert meth-
    odology in the courtroom.

In 2003, the editor of *Science* wrote an editorial titled "Forensic Science: Oxymoron?"
calling attention to the growing scientific criticism which targeted some areas of
forensic science (Kennedy 2003). Reactions have been strong on all sides of the issues
raised, but these developments have stimulated a review by the National Academies of
Science, as well as research and discussion within the forensic community. The basic
question is whether some aspects of forensic science are soundly rooted in good science or have evolved over the years within the forensic framework in a manner that
lacks scientific rigor.

In the legal arena prior to 1993, most people recognized that the 1923 court decision in the case of *Frye* v. *United States* (293 F. 1013 (D.C. Cir. 1923)) offered guidelines regarding expert testimony. If an expert was subject to a 'Frye Hearing,' the
court examined if the methodology utilized was generally accepted within the scientific community.

In 1993, a Supreme Court decision in the case of *Daubert* v. *Merrell Dow
Pharmaceuticals, Inc.* (509 US 579 (1993)) produced guidelines that superseded
those of the Frye decision. The Daubert decision shifted onto the presiding judge the
responsibility for determining acceptance, which in the Frye ruling resided with the
scientific community. Acting as the scientific gatekeeper, the judge must evaluate scientific testimony on the basis of five primary criteria. These criteria are designed to
establish whether the scientific methodology

1   is testable and was tested through the scientific method;
2   was subject to peer-review;
3   is based on established standards;
4   has a known error rate;
5   is widely accepted by the scientific community.

An additional key legal development occurred in 1999, with the Supreme Court decision in the case of *Kumho Tire Co.* v. *Carmichael* (526 US 137 (1999)). In this decision, the Court concluded that

1   forensic experts can develop theories based on observation and experience and
    apply those to a case;
2   diverse aspects of forensic testimony should be evaluated with the same degree of
    rigor;
3   the Daubert guidelines should be regarded as being flexible and not necessarily
    applicable universally to scientific testimony.

While these developments have not targeted forensic anthropology directly, they have
stimulated considerable discussion and research within the field (Bohan and Heels
1995; Cheng and Yoon 2005; Faigman et al. 1994; Grivas and Komar 2008; Kaiser
1998; Risinger et al. 2002; Saks 2000; Sanders 2001). The general reactive tendency
has been to re-examine techniques in order to make them more quantifiable and less
subjective (Christensen 2004, 2005), as well as to examine accuracy and interobserver
and intraobserver error. While these developments are positive and have improved the

quality of methodology in forensic anthropology, many aspects of anthropological analysis remain interpretive. Experience continues to play a dominant role in case interpretation, and most research indicates that holistic approaches produce more accurate results than the use of single techniques. Reducing complex anthropological interpretation to simplified techniques, which can easily be tested for error rates and similar factors, risks to loose much of the scholarly punch of analysis. As supported by the Kumho decision, much of diverse anthropological analysis and interpretation must call upon experience and broad observation if it is indeed to maximize the information retrieved.

THE FORENSIC ANTHROPOLOGY LABORATORY

Physical anthropologists who choose to enter the world of forensic anthropology learn quickly (hopefully) that major adjustments need to be made in the quality control of the materials examined. Due to the legal context of forensic work, strict controls need to be maintained on equipment, on evidence, and on the environment of the analysis. Procedures should document the prevention of contamination and the inadvertent loss of evidence, which could impact a case interpretation negatively. These concerns call for thoughtful organization and protocols for the forensic anthropology laboratory (Warren et al. 2008).

The bottom line in forensic laboratory management is that procedures need to be in place which secure the evidence and document the chain of custody. Gone are the days when cases could be left unattended on the laboratory table, along with other collections of human remains, for extended periods of time, being fully accessible to students, volunteers, and those involved in unrelated activities. Chain of custody must be maintained to document the location and the access of personnel to the remains at all times. Security systems must be capable of ensuring and documenting the safety and integrity of the evidence (Warren et al. 2008).

To anthropologists used to a more casual approach to the use of materials in their labs, the forensic context requires some adjustment. If an extra metatarsal from a younger individual is found in the forensic analysis of a complete human skeleton, does this finding document the fact that a second victim is involved, or does it mean merely that someone used the skeleton for teaching purposes in the laboratory and accidentally mixed in another bone from the teaching collection? If the forensic examiner finds a cut on a bone, does this finding point to a victim of stabbing, or does it merely suggest that a student tried to clean the bone in the laboratory and left the mark behind? These are the kinds of questions that emerge unless the laboratory has strict controls, which clarify the possibilities throughout the analysis process.

AGE ESTIMATION

The accurate estimation of age at death represents an important component of forensic anthropological analysis. Such estimates can greatly aid the investigation and may lead to the identification of a recovered skeleton. They can also be useful in the process of excluding missing persons mistakenly thought to be perhaps represented by remains. For these reasons, it is essential for the estimates advanced in forensic reports to be both accurate and realistic, given the nature of the evidence presented. The age range reported must be appropriate to the methodology utilized, as well as to the skeletal attributes presented by the available evidence.

In regards to the skeletal attributes relied upon to estimate chronological age of an individual, research has generally documented increased variation with advancing age (Ubelaker 1999b). Thus, whereas it may be possible to estimate reliably the age of fetal remains at death within weeks (Fazekas and Kósa 1978), the age range of older adults may encompass decades. Throughout the aging process, regional variation, life style, diet, and various environmental factors influence the rate and nature of age changes (Stinson 2000). Thus age estimation is a relatively complex process, which is benefited by the experience of the examiner.

Coupled with the call for quantification, for the establishment of error rates, and for standardization – a call which emanates largely from the legal community – various innovative statistical approaches have been advanced. Notable among these are the tests of interobserver error (Bouvier and Ubelaker 1977), the testing of different techniques on the same samples (ibid.; Galera et al. 1995; Martrille et al. 2007); the testing of methods on different samples (Megyesi et al. 2006; Prince and Ubelaker 2002; Ubelaker and Parra 2008); and Bayesian statistics and transition analysis (Boldsen et al. 2002; Milner et al. 2008). Many of these developments are driven by the fact that individual methods reflect the nature of the samples they are derived from and tested upon. Problems arise when the underlying samples are not representative of the cases the methods are applied to. Fortunately, this concern has stimulated considerable research that has advanced the accuracy of age estimation significantly.

Another key issue involves the selection of just which methods to utilize, especially in the estimation of the age of adults. Should the most accurate single method be employed (Saunders et al. 1992), or are the results obtained by using multiple age indicators more accurate (Acśadi and Nemeskéri 1970; Bedford et al. 1993)? Selection and use of aging methodology is complex and should be guided by the nature of the skeletal remains available, as well as by judgments regarding method effectiveness. For example, in the analysis of the skeleton of a young child, long bone length and dental eruption provide some useful age information, but the final estimate should be heavily influenced by the extent of dental formation, since research demonstrates that, in that age group, dental formation has the highest correlation with chronological age and the least population variation (Scheuer and Black 2000; Ubelaker 1987).

Although research indicates that different adult age indicators are of varying accuracy and are most applicable at different periods in the adult aging process, all offer some useful information. Baccino and Zerilli (1997) suggested a procedure in which pubic symphysis morphology is consulted first. If the initial phases of symphyseal development are found, they should be extensively relied upon for age determination, since research has demonstrated that the assessment of pubic symphysis morphology is an effective technique in applications to younger adults. If later phases are found, Baccino and Zerilli recommend relying more on the Lamendin dental technique (Lamendin et al. 1992), which offers greater reliability in older adults.

In a blind testing of the results yielded by four aging methods (pubic symphysis, sternal rib ends, bone histology and the Lamendin dental technique) performed on a

French autopsy sample of known age at death, two independent observers documented that experience plays a significant role in the accuracy of application, especially with such complex histological techniques (Baccino et al. 1999). This research also documented the fact that, for each observer, various methods of using multiple techniques produced more accurate results than any one individual technique.

Research also suggests that some consideration needs to be devoted to variation in the nature and timing of a population's aging. For example the Kerley method of histological age determination is based on a modern military sample from the United States, and its application to a demographically very different sample from the Dominican Republic produced significant variance in the estimated ages (Ubelaker 1981). Schaffer and Black (2005) documented that age progression in epiphyseal union in a Bosnian sample differed from that suggested by studies of samples from different populations.

CONCEPTS OF RACE

Most missing persons are described through reference to some sort of racial category; thus 'race' becomes an issue in forensic anthropological analysis. In attempting to be useful on this issue, anthropologists need to recognize the social dimensions of public perceptions of race and to communicate opinions appropriately. Analysis may reveal a pattern of attributes which suggest that, during life, the individual represented by the remains related to a particular social category of race. The pattern may support opinions about that individual's ancestry.

Since discussions of 'race' stir passions within the scholarly community, word choice is important. It can be argued that the term 'race' is no longer useful, since it seems to mean different things to different people and has a certain historical baggage. Nevertheless, forensic anthropologists continue to make significant contributions on this topic, both in casework and in research.

The term 'Hispanic' is particularly problematic because it encompasses individuals of Spanish heritage regardless of their ancestry, genotype, or phenotype. This and other related issues can be dealt with through adequate description and careful wording in reports. The challenge is to provide useful information, which may aid an investigation without putting forward misleading categories. It also is important not to force an opinion when the data do not permit an assessment. Skeletons (especially the fragmentary ones) of many individuals present such a mixture of traits and measurements that it is not possible to suggest affinity with a particular group.

Although thoughtful analysis of ancestry may utilize both observations and measurements, the measurement-based software FORDISC is particularly useful (Ousley and Jantz 2005). This system offers customized discriminant function equations, which utilize whatever measurements can be taken and deliver a classification complete with the relevant statistics needed for interpretation. Although FORDISC represents a valuable tool, it is limited by the nature of the database it draws from. If a skeleton originates from an individual/population not well represented within the database, the quality of the classification is affected (Ubelaker et al. 2002). Fortunately the associated statistics can give hints when such situations occur.

Regional Variation and Secular Change

Nearly all areas of forensic anthropology applications are impacted by the human variation manifest in regional variation and secular change. As documented collections and worldwide research in this area increase, they illuminate the importance of these factors. In the course of history, new methods developed from well documented collections have been seen to show great promise, only to find their utility diminished later, when they were applied to more diverse samples. A major new frontier that emerges in forensic anthropology represents the development of such collections and research.

The good news is that this challenge is being met. As interest and activity in forensic anthropology grow worldwide, new collections, both of data and of skeletons, are being assembled. As existing methods are tested by these new resources, knowledge grows regarding the extent of variation involved. In scholarly areas in which variation is strong (for instance in sexual dimorphism, ancestry assessment, stature calculation), a population-specific methodology can be developed. This development has prompted the journal *Forensic Science International* to create a section specifically designed for new datasets emerging in forensic anthropology.

In regard to many of our techniques, decades have passed since their initial formulation. Are these methods, and the data they are based upon, still relevant to modern applications? To what extent has secular change occurred impacting the attributes examined?

Within the United States this question can be examined, to a limited extent, through comparisons of modern samples with the data obtained from the older ones. Of particular value is the modern database which contributes to the development of FORDISC discussed above. This database was constructed by using information collected from modern forensic cases that have been identified. Comparison with the samples assembled in the past decades reveals aspects of secular change and documents the need to maintain currency in methodology (Jantz and Jantz 1999; Meadows and Jantz 1995).

Identification Issues

Much of the effort in forensic anthropological analysis is geared toward identification. Interpretations of age at death, sex, ancestry, living stature, time since death, medical history, and other attributes help to narrow the search for the person represented by the recovered remains. A positive identification results when unique characteristics are found both on the recovered remains and on the ante-mortem records of a once living person. Such identifications in forensic anthropology usually originate from radiographic comparisons, since X-rays of the living person can reveal bony details that can in turn be examined on the recovered remains.

The process of positive identification involves several stages of interpretation. First, matching attributes must be found in the ante-mortem and post-mortem materials. Differences must be explained by such factors as the quality of the images available, post-mortem alterations in the recovered remains, or ante-mortem changes in the living person that occurred between death and the time when the ante-mortem radiographs were taken. Once this process is completed, an assessment must be made regarding the uniqueness of the matching features. If the assemblage of matching features is unique, then a positive identification results. If they are judged not to be unique, then a determination follows, to the effect that the remains could belong to the suggested individual, but that the association cannot be proven through the comparison. Thus a 'match' does not automatically yield a positive identification: the uniqueness of the attributes under comparison must be established first.

In many cases matching attributes are found, but these fall somewhat short of the evidence needed for a positive identification. This problem is especially acute in areas of the world and in socio-economic contexts in which radiographs and other medical/dental records are not available. The ante-mortem evidence available frequently involves memories of family and friends, and it results in possible or putative identifications. Material culture can also contribute (Birkby et al. 2008; Komar and Lathrop 2008). Judgments are required in order to decide at what point the evidence is sufficient to justify identification. Inadequate evidence can lead to errors of identification.

INTELLECTUAL BORDERS

Although forensic anthropology has a specific methodology and a subject matter not shared with other disciplines, it also involves some intellectual overlap with other areas of forensic science. Many anthropologists work with fleshed remains – even remains that are subject to conventional autopsy. Although this is usually a cooperative venture involving forensic pathologists, it can produce overlapping areas of opinion, especially relating to the interpretation of trauma. Forensic pathologists are charged with making the determination of the cause and manner of death. However, particularly in skeletal cases, forensic anthropologists may glean the evidence which supports an opinion.

Some intellectual overlap is also apparent in the study of teeth. Forensic odontologists have the unique expertise of assessing products of dental practice, but their knowledge of dental anatomy and their dental age estimation techniques are shared with forensic anthropologists.

Anthropologists frequently work closely with, and to some extent their expertise overlaps with that of, forensic entomologists, forensic botanists, DNA specialists, and tool mark examiners. In analysis, questions such as this one arise: Who is best qualified to interpret and report on tool marks in bone – the forensic anthropologist, who has experience in appreciating the nature of bone modification, or the tool mark examiner, who specializes in correlations between tool markings and the tools that produced them?

FACIAL IMAGERY

Facial approximation (estimating what the facial image of a person was from the evidence of a recovered skull) and photographic superimposition (usually comparing an ante-mortem photograph with a skull) represent two common areas of facial imagery that frequently involve anthropologists. Facial approximation (also termed 'facial reproduction' and 'facial reconstruction') involves a combination of art and science, and is employed only as a last resort, in order to reach out to the public for leads in an investigation. The technique is not used directly for identification purposes. A variety of approaches are available involving clay modeling, sketches and computer-generated images. The effort is challenging in that it can involve artists who utilize the data produced by anthropologists concerning the characteristics of the individual, or anthropologists who happen to have artist skills, or it can adopt a team approach, involving collaboration between the artist and anthropologist.

Interpretations regarding photographic superimposition involve all of the concerns, requirements and caveats of all identification techniques. In the case of skull/photograph comparisons, the technique is normally used for exclusion, or in order to indicate the possibility that the skull and the image are of the same person. Methodology has improved dramatically with new technology, but the underlying concerns remain the same.

RECENT ADVANCES AND EMERGING TECHNOLOGY

Major advances in forensic anthropology stem from new databases, new technology, new applications of the existing technology, and sustained experimental research. As discussed above, growing collections and databases throughout the world have enabled research and conclusions which only a decade ago were not possible to reach. The new knowledge on the impact of human variation on methodology greatly augments the field and strengthens interpretation.

A recent database of analyses of many samples of bone, tooth, and other materials, generated by using scanning electron microscopy/energy dispersive spectroscopy, allows examiners to differentiate small fragments of bone and tooth from other materials of similar appearance (Ubelaker et al. 2002). Comparison of the forensic specimen can be made with the spectral database of known materials, which focuses primarily on the proportions of calcium and phosphorus. This technique will differentiate bone and tooth from most other materials; but it cannot distinguish between what is human and what is non-human.

New applications of the technique of protein radio immunoassay (pRIA) allow species identification of small bone and tooth fragments (Ubelaker et al. 2004). This procedure will not only differentiate human from non-human fragments, but will allow the determination of the species of the non-human material present. Using small samples (200 milligrams or less), the technique involves protein extraction, followed by a solid-phase double-antibody radioimmunoassay – a technique which employs controls of antisera produced in rabbits and of radioactively marked antibody of rabbit gamma globulin produced in donkeys.

Studies of cementum formation and racemization in teeth offer great promise for a more precise age estimation, if taphonomic and other methodological issues can be worked out. The microscopic study of the alternating bands of opaque and translucent dental cementum shows potential in quantifying the age at death (Wittwer-Backofen et al. 2004) and in clarifying the season of death (Wedel 2007). Another promising area of research involves racemization methodology, which assesses changes of L-form amino acids to D-form in human proteins (Ohtani et al. 2005; Ohtani and Yamamoto 2005).

Analysis of radiocarbon, especially in regard to the modern bomb curve, enables determinations of time since death more accurately than was previously possible (Ubelaker 2001). The atmospheric testing of nuclear weapons in the 1950s and early 1960s produced high levels of artificial radiocarbon, which were incorporated by humans through the food chain. Although levels have been steadily reducing since the peak in 1963, they remain above the pre-1950 values. If radiocarbon analysis of recovered human samples reveals the higher levels, the investigator knows that the individual must have been alive after 1950. Tissue-specific analysis can in principle generate information regarding both the birth date and the death date (Lynnerup et al. 2008; Spalding et al. 2005; Ubelaker et al. 2006; Ubelaker and Buchholz 2006).

New three-dimensional approaches to cranial morphology allow greater precision in assessments of population affinities and ancestry (Ross et al. 2002, 2004). Moving beyond caliper-generated measurements, these computer-assisted approaches involve more sophisticated shape analysis, offering greater insight into potential population relationships.

Chemical approaches offer great promise in estimating the geographical origins of individuals. The value of isotopic analysis has long been recognized in dietary reconstruction (Ambrose and Norr 1993; Katzenberg 1992; Schwarcz and Schoeninger 1991). Recently, researchers have focused attention on the isotopic analysis of human materials in order to assess geographical origins in forensic contexts. The following two studies represent a case in point.

Beard and Johnson (2000) recognize that the quantities of strontium isotopes vary considerably geologically and geographically. Due to dietary factors, strontium isotopes also vary considerably in human bones and teeth, reflecting the geographical origins of the food and water ingested. Thus the strontium isotope analysis of human tissues produces data providing information about geographical origins. The authors note that the analysis of bone samples produces average values which reflect the materials ingested during the last years of life, since bone remodels and continuously incorporates new dietary strontium during the period of bone formation. In contrast, the strontium isotope analysis of dental enamel reveals information about the geographic origins of dietary materials during the childhood of the individual, since dental enamel does not remodel.

Ehleringer and colleagues (2008) address the issue of the geographic origins of human remains through the analysis of hydrogen and oxygen isotope ratios in human hair. As with the strontium isotopes discussed above, hydrogen and oxygen isotope concentrations also vary geographically and become incorporated in human hair through the diet, especially through the drinking of local tap water. In a forensic context, the analysis of hair, and specifically of keratin, might reveal whether the person represented displayed values consistent with a local origin or is likely to have originated elsewhere. Analysis of different aspects of the hair might reflect the geographical history of the individual in the relatively short periods of time before death represented by hair growth patterns.

The future remains particularly bright for forensic anthropology – not only because of these technological developments, but also, and primarily, because of the growing student and other scholarly interest in the field. This interest translates into new cohorts of emerging forensics anthropologists, who will continue to transform the field through research and casework.

REFERENCES

Acśadi, G., and Nemeskéri, J. (1970) *History of Human Life Span and Mortality*. Budapest: Akadémiai Kiadó.

Ambrose, S. H., and Norr, L. (1993) Experimental Evidence for the Relationship of the Carbon Isotope Ratios of Whole Diet and Dietary Protein to Those of Bone Collagen and Carbonate. In J. B. Lambert and G. Grupe (eds), *Prehistoric Human Bone: Archaeology at the Molecular Level* (pp. 1–38). Berlin: Springer-Verlag.

Argentine Forensic Anthropology Team (2008) Latin American Forensic Anthropology Association (ALAF). Electronic document. http://eaaf.typepad.com/alaf/.

Baccino, E. (2005) Forensic Anthropology Society of Europe (FASE), a Subsection of the IALM, is 1 Year Old. *International Journal of Legal Medicine* 119: N1.

Baccino, E., and Zerilli, A. (1997) The Two Step Strategy (TSS) or the Right Way to Combine a Dental (LAMENDIN) and an Anthropological (SUCHEY-BROOKS System) Method for Age Determination (Abstract). *Proceedings of the American Academy of Forensic Sciences* 3: 150.

Baccino, E., Ubelaker, D. H., Hayek, L.-A. C., and Zerilli, A. (1999) Evaluation of Seven Methods of Estimating Age at Death from Mature Human Skeletal Remains. *Journal of Forensic Sciences* 44: 931–936.

Beard, B. L., and Johnson, C. M. (2000) Strontium Isotope Composition of Skeletal Material Can Determine the Birth Place and Geographic Mobility of Humans and Animals. *Journal of Forensic Sciences* 45: 1049–1061.

Bedford, M. E., Russell, K. F., Lovejoy, C. O., Meindl, R. S., Simpson, S. W., and Stuart-Macadam, P. L. (1993) Test of the Multifactorial Aging Method Using Skeletons with Known Ages-at-Death from the Grant Collection. *American Journal of Physical Anthropology* 91: 287–297.

Birkby, W. H., Fenton, T. W., and Anderson, B. E. (2008) Identifying Southwest Hispanics Using Nonmetric Traits and the Cultural Profile. *Journal of Forensic Sciences* 53: 29–33.

Bohan, T. L., and Heels, E. J. (1995) The Case Against *Daubert*: The New Scientific Evidence 'Standard' and the Standards of the Several States. *Journal of Forensic Sciences* 40: 1030–1044.

Boldsen, J. L., Milner, G. R., Konigsberg, L. W., and Wood, J. W. (2002) Transition Analysis: A New Method for Estimating Age from Skeletons. In R. D. Hoppa and J. W. Vaupel (eds), *Paleodemography: Age Distribution From Skeletal Samples* (pp. 73–106). Cambridge: Cambridge University Press.

Bouvier, M., and Ubelaker, D. H. (1977) A Comparison of Two Methods for the Microscopic Determination of Age at Death. *American Journal of Physical Anthropology* 46: 391–394.

Cheng, E. K., and Yoon, A. H. (2005) Does *Frye* or *Daubert* Matter? A Study of Scientific Admissibility Standards. *Virginia Law Review* 91: 471–513.

Christensen, A. M. (2004) The Impact of *Daubert*: Implications for Testimony and Research in Forensic Anthropology (and the Use of Frontal Sinuses in Personal Identification). *Journal of Forensic Sciences* 49: 427–430.

Christensen, A. M. (2005) Testing the Reliability of Frontal Sinuses in Positive Identification. *Journal of Forensic Sciences* 50: 18–22.

Dwight, T. (1878) *The Identification of the Human Skeleton. A Medico-Legal Study*. Boston: David Clapp and Son.

Dwight, T. (1881) The Sternum as an Index of Sex and Age. *Journal of Anatomy and Physiology* 15: 327–330.

Dwight, T. (1890a) The Sternum as an Index of Sex, Height and Age. *Journal of Anatomy and Physiology* 24: 527–535.

Dwight, T. (1890b) The Closure of the Cranial Sutures as a Sign of Age. *Boston Medical and Surgical Journal* 122: 389–392.

Dwight, T. (1894a) Methods of Estimating the Height from Parts of the Skeleton. *Medical Record* 46: 293–296.

Dwight, T. (1894b) The Range and Significance of Variations in the Human Skeleton. *Boston Medical and Surgical Journal* 13: 361–389.

Dwight, T. (1905) The Size of the Articular Surfaces of the Long Bones as Characteristic of Sex. An Anthropological Study. *American Journal of Anatomy* 4: 19–32.

Ehleringer, J. R., Bowen, G. J., Chesson, L. A., West, A. G., Podlesak, D. W., and Cerling, T. E. (2008) Hydrogen and Oxygen Isotope Ratios in Human Hair Are Related to Geography. *Proceedings of the National Academy of Sciences, USA* 105: 2788–2793.

Faigman, D. L., Porter, E., and Saks, M. J. (1994) Check Your Crystal Ball at the Courthouse Door, Please: Exploring the Past, Understanding the Present, and Worrying about the Future of Scientific Evidence. *Cardozo Law Review* 15: 1799–1835.

Fazekas, I. G., and Kósa, F. (1978) *Forensic Fetal Osteology*. Budapest: Akadémiai Kiadó.

Galera, V., Ubelaker, D. H., and Hayek, L. C. (1995) Interobserver Error in Macroscopic Methods of Estimating Age at Death from the Human Skeleton. *International Journal of Anthropology* 10 (4): 229–239.

Grivas, C. R., and Komar, D. A. (2008) *Kumho, Daubert*, and the Nature of Scientific Inquiry: Implications for Forensic Anthropology. *Journal of Forensic Sciences* 53: 771–776.

Jantz, L. M., and Jantz, R. L. (1999) Secular Change in Long Bone Length and Proportion in the United States, 1800–1970. *American Journal of Physical Anthropology* 110: 57–67.

Kaiser, J. (1998) Should Engineer Witnesses Meet Same Standards as Scientists? *Science* 281: 1578.

Katzenberg, M. A. (1992) Advances in Stable Isotope Analysis of Prehistoric Bones. In S. R. Saunders and M. A. Katzenberg (eds), *The Skeletal Biology of Past Peoples: Research Methods* (pp. 105–120). New York: John Wiley and Sons.

Kennedy, D. (2003) Forensic Science: Oxymoron? *Science* 302: 1625.

Komar, D. A., and Lathrop, S. (2008) The Use of Material Culture to Establish the Ethnic Identity of Victims in Genocide Investigations: A Validation Study from the American Southwest. *Journal of Forensic Sciences* 53: 1035–1039.

Krogman, W. M. (1939) A Guide to the Identification of Human Skeletal Material. *FBI Law Enforcement Bulletin* 8: 3–31.

Krogman, W. M. (1962) *The Human Skeleton in Forensic Medicine*. Springfield IL: Charles C. Thomas.

Lamendin, H., Baccino, E., Humbert, J. F., Tavernier, J. C., Nossintchouk, R. M., and Zerilli, A. (1992) A Simple Technique for Age Estimation in Adult Corpses: The Two Criteria Dental Method. *Journal of Forensic Sciences* 37: 1373–1379.

Lynnerup, N., Kjeldsen, H., Heegaard, S., Jacobsen, C., and Heinemeier, J. (2008) Radiocarbon Dating of the Human Eye Lens Crystallines Reveal Proteins without Carbon Turnover throughout Life. *PLoS One* 3 (1). Electronic document available at: http://dx.doi.org/10.1371%2Fjournal.pone.0001529.

Martrille, L., Ubelaker, D. H., Cattaneo, C., Seguret, F., Tremblay, M., and Baccino, E. (2007) Comparison of Four Skeletal Methods for the Estimation of Age at Death on White and Black Adults. *Journal of Forensic Sciences* 52: 302–307.

McKern, T. W., and Stewart, T. D. (1957) *Skeletal Age Changes in Young American Males. Technical Report EP-45*. Natick MA: Quartermaster Research and Development Center, Environmental Protection Research Division.

Meadows, L., and Jantz, R. L. (1995) Allometric Secular Change in the Long Bones from the 1800s to the Present. *Journal of Forensic Sciences* 40: 762–767.

Megyesi, M. S., Ubelaker, D. H., and Sauer, N. J. (2006) Test of the Lamendin Aging Method on Two Historic Skeletal Samples. *American Journal of Physical Anthropology* 131: 363–367.

Milner, G. R., Wood, J. W., and Boldsen, J. L. (2008) Advances in Paleodemography. In M. A. Katzenberg and S. R. Saunders (eds), *Biological Anthropology of the Human Skeleton*, 2nd edn (pp. 561–600). New York: John Wiley and Sons, Inc.

Ohtani, S., and Yamamoto, T. (2005) Strategy for the Estimation of Chronological Age Using the Aspartic Acid Racemization Method with Special Reference to Coefficient of Correlation Between D/L Ratios and Ages. *Journal of Forensic Sciences* 50: 1020–1027.

Ohtani, S., Abe, I., and Yamamoto, T. (2005) An Application of D- and L-aspartic Acid Mixtures as Standard Specimens for the Chronological Age Estimation. *Journal of Forensic Sciences* 50: 1298–1302.

Ousley, S. D., and Jantz, R. L. (2005) *FORDISC 3.0: Personal Computer Forensic Discriminant Functions.* Knoxville: The University of Tennessee.

Prince, D. A., and Ubelaker, D. H. (2002) Application of Lamendin's Adult Dental Aging Technique to a Diverse Skeletal Sample. *Journal of Forensic Sciences* 47: 107–116.

Risinger, D. M., Saks, M. J., Thompson, W. C., and Rosenthal, R. (2002) The *Daubert/Kumho* Implications of Observer Effects in Forensic Science: Hidden Problems of Expectation and Suggestion. *California Law Review* 90: 3–56.

Ross, A. H., Ubelaker, D. H., and Falsetti, A. B. (2002) Craniometric Variation in the Americas. *Human Biology* 74: 807–818.

Ross, A. H., Slice, D. E., Ubelaker, D. H., and Falsetti, A. B. (2004) Population Affinities of 19th Century Cuban Crania: Implications for Identification Criteria in South Florida Cuban Americans. *Journal of Forensic Sciences* 49: 11–16.

Saks, M. J. (2000) The Aftermath of *Daubert*: An Evolving Jurisprudence of Expert Evidence. *Jurimetrics* 40: 229–241.

Sanders, J. (2001) *Kumho* and How We Know. *Law and Contemporary Problems* 64: 373–415.

Saunders, S. R., Fitzgerald, C., Rogers, T., Dudar, C., and McKillop, H. (1992) A Test of Several Methods of Skeletal Age Estimation Using a Documented Archaeological Sample. *Canadian Society of Forensic Science Journal* 25: 97–118.

Schaefer, M. C., and Black, S. M. (2005) Comparison of Ages of Epiphyseal Union in North American and Bosnian Skeletal Material. *Journal of Forensic Sciences* 50: 777–784.

Scheuer, L., and Black, S. (2000) *Developmental Juvenile Osteology.* San Diego: Academic Press.

Schwarcz, H. P., and Schoeninger, M. J. (1991) Stable Isotope Analyses in Human Nutritional Ecology. *Yearbook of Physical Anthropology* 34: 283–321.

Spalding, K. L., Buchholz, B. A., Bergman, L. E., Druid, H., and Frisén, J. (2005) Age Written in Teeth by Nuclear Tests. *Nature* 437 (7057): 333–334.

Spencer, F., (1997) Bertillon, Alphonse (1853–1914). In F. Spencer (ed.), *History of Physical Anthropology*, Vol. 1. (pp. 170–171). New York: Garland Publishing, Inc.

Stewart, T. D. (1948) Medico-Legal Aspects of the Skeleton. I. Sex, Age, Race and Stature. *American Journal of Physical Anthropology* 6: 315–321.

Stewart, T. D. (1951) What the Bones Tell. *FBI Law Enforcement Bulletin* 20: 1–5.

Stewart, T. D. (1979) *Essentials of Forensic Anthropology: Especially as Developed in the United States.* Springfield IL: Charles C. Thomas.

Stewart, T. D. (ed.) (1970) *Personal Identification in Mass Disasters.* Washington DC: Smithsonian Institution.

Stewart, T. D., and Trotter, M. (eds) (1954) *Basic Readings on the Identification of Human Skeletons: Estimation of Age.* New York: Wenner-Gren Foundation for Anthropological Research, Inc.

Stewart, T. D., and Trotter, M. (1955) Role of Physical Anthropology in the Field of Human Identification. *Science* 122: 883–884.

Stinson, S. (2000) Growth Variation: Biological and Cultural Factors. In S. Stinson, B. Bogin, R. Huss-Ashmore, and D. O'Rourke (eds), *Human Biology: An Evolutionary and Biocultural Perspective* (pp. 425–464). New York: Wiley–Liss, Inc.

Trotter, M., and Gleser, G. C. (1952) Estimation of Stature from Long Bones of American Whites and Negroes. *American Journal of Physical Anthropology* 10: 463–514.

Ubelaker, D. H. (1981) Approaches to Demographic Problems in the Northeast. In D. R. Snow (ed.), *Foundations of Northeast Archaeology* (pp. 175–194). New York: Academic Press.

Ubelaker, D. H. (1987) Estimating Age at Death from Immature Human Skeletons: An Overview. *Journal of Forensic Sciences* 32: 1254–1263.

Ubelaker, D. H. (1999a) Aleš Hrdlička's Role in the History of Forensic Anthropology. *Journal of Forensic Sciences* 44: 724–730.

Ubelaker, D. H. (1999b) *Human Skeletal Remains, Excavation, Analysis, Interpretation*, 3rd edn. Washington DC: Taraxacum.

Ubelaker, D. H. (2001) Artificial Radiocarbon as an Indicator of Recent Origin of Organic Remains in Forensic Cases. *Journal of Forensic Sciences* 46: 1285–1287.

Ubelaker, D. H., and Buchholz, B. A. (2006) Complexities in the Use of Bomb-Curve Radiocarbon to Determine Time since Death of Human Skeletal Remains. *Forensic Science Communications* 8 (1). Electronic document. http://www.fbi.gov/hq/lab/fsc/backissu/jan2006/research/2006_01_research01.htm.

Ubelaker, D. H., and Parra, R. C. (2008) Application of Three Dental Methods of Adult Age Estimation from Intact Single Rooted Teeth to a Peruvian Sample. *Journal of Forensic Sciences* 53: 608–611.

Ubelaker, D. H., Buchholz, B. A., and Stewart, J. E. B. (2006) Analysis of Artificial Radiocarbon in Different Skeletal and Dental Tissue Types to Evaluate Date of Death. *Journal of Forensic Sciences* 51: 484–488.

Ubelaker, D. H., Lowenstein, J. M., and Hood, D. G. (2004) Use of Solid-Phase Double-Antibody Radioimmunoassay to Identify Species from Small Skeletal Fragments. *Journals of Forensic Sciences* 49: 924–929.

Ubelaker, D. H., Ross, A. H., and Graver, S. M. (2002) Application of Forensic Discriminant Functions to a Spanish Cranial Sample. *Forensic Science Communications* 4 (3). Electronic document. http://www.fbi.gov/hq/lab/fsc/backissu/july2002/ubelaker1.htm.

Ubelaker, D. H., Ward, D. C., Braz, V. S., and Stewart, J. (2002) The Use of SEM/EDS Analysis to Distinguish Dental and Osseus Tissue from Other Materials. *Journal of Forensic Sciences* 47: 940–943.

Warren, M. W., Walsh-Haney, H. A., and Freas, L. E. (eds) (2008) *The Forensic Anthropology Laboratory*. Boca Raton: CRC Press.

Wedel, V. L. (2007) Determination of Season at Death Using Dental Cementum Increment Analysis. *Journal of Forensic Sciences* 52: 1334–1337.

Wittwer-Backofen, U., Gampe, J., and Vaupel, J. W. (2004) Tooth Cementum Annulation for Age Estimation: Results From a Large Known-Age Validation Study. *American Journal of Physical Anthropology* 123: 119–129.

24 Paleogenetics: Ancient DNA in Anthropology

Frederika A. Kaestle

INTRODUCTION

Physical anthropologists have used molecular characters of modern populations to explore human variability and human prehistory for decades (see Relethford's and O'Rourke's contributions in the present volume). But, because DNA degrades over time after death – mostly due to the damaging effects of water and oxygen, which cause hydrolysis and oxidation – the majority of molecular genetic techniques were unsuited to the very low concentration and extremely short fragments of DNA that remain from ancient sources. But the development of the Polymerase Chain Reaction (PCR) techniques on ancient DNA (aDNA) in the late 1980s allowed for the first time a reliable way to access this genetic information, which resulted in the direct incorporation of data from past populations in molecular analyses (see O'Rourke's discussion of PCR in this volume). Anthropologists were quick to apply these techniques to ancient samples for the production of previously unobtainable data (Pääbo 1993). New molecular genetics methods which have been developed in the last few years, such as pyrosequencing, are opening even more doors for the exploration of past genetic variation.

Early results suggested that aDNA could be recovered from remains which were tens of millions of years old; but these initial findings have now been shown to be the result of contamination from modern sources. Current work suggests that DNA cannot survive longer than a few hundred thousand years, and even that is possible only under the best preservation circumstances (Willerslev et al. 2003). Nevertheless, studies of aDNA from remains within this time frame have the potential to add greatly to our understanding of human evolution and history.

The application of aDNA techniques in anthropology permits analyses of patterns of molecular variability in both human and non-human organisms – analyses designed to test hypotheses about human origins and behavior. Genetic data from ancient individuals can be used to reconstruct the origin of populations and to inform our understanding of their migrations. Hypotheses of population replacement or admixture can be tested by comparing aDNA from ancient populations dating from periods before and after the inferred population movement. Additionally, such data can be used to reconstruct ancestor–descendant relationships between populations, and to discern patterns of inter-relatedness between ancient groups. Further, these data can elucidate aspects of social structure and mortuary practices. Such analyses allow the determination of the sex of human remains (which is particularly useful with fragmentary or subadult remains, which cannot be reliably sexed by using standard bioarchaeology methods: see Larsen and Walker's chapter in this volume), as well as the development of an understanding of the spatial patterning of maternal and paternal lineages across burials. From such data, hypotheses concerning social status, marriage patterns, burial customs, and differential patterns of disease and mortality by sex or family can be tested. As we gain a better understanding of the human genome through the identification of specific genes and their phenotypic consequences, aDNA approaches are increasingly used to reconstruct the phenotypes of these ancient individuals. Non-human remains can also be subjected to aDNA analysis, so as to illuminate several aspects of human prehistory. The patterns of molecular diversity in non-human species can assist in the understanding of hunting and of dietary behavior, tracing the domestication of animal and plant species, reconstructing past environments and movements of people, and reconstructing the histories of ancient diseases.

BACKGROUND

Within the context of aDNA studies, there are two main sources of DNA: the cellular nucleus and the organelles. Although the vast majority of genomic DNA is present in the nucleus of a cell, each cell only contains two copies of nuclear DNA (one paternal and one maternal). On the other hand, although the mitochondrial and chloroplast organelles only contain a small amount of the total genomic DNA per cell, there are often thousands of copies of mitochondrial or chloroplast genome per cell, because there are hundreds of each organelle within the cell, each one containing multiple copies of organellar DNA. This higher copy number per cell results in a higher likelihood of recovery of intact segments of DNA from these organelles by comparison with nuclear DNA, and most aDNA studies have concentrated on this organellar DNA. However, with improved extraction and amplification techniques, as well as with new developments in sequencing and genotyping technologies, nuclear DNA is increasingly a target of aDNA studies. This broadens significantly the horizon of potential hypotheses that can be tested by using aDNA, although such studies involve substantially higher failure rates.

Examining mitochondrial DNA (mtDNA) allows us to trace maternal lineages through time and maternal relationships between individuals, as mtDNA is passed only from mother to child. A number of mitochondrial markers are also geographically specific, and in some cases they are limited in distribution to a single population. Autosomal nuclear markers (found on the non-sex chromosomes) can be utilized for paternity and maternity testing (especially using microsatellite markers), and for detecting the presence/absence of particular genetic diseases or of other phenotypically informative or geographically specific genetic variation. Nuclear markers on the sex chromosomes have most often been used to sex ancient individuals genetically (especially juveniles or partial remains), and can also be used to identify Y chromosome paternal lineages that trace paternal relationships and show geographic specificity. Although many studies concentrate on a single genetic system, such as the mitochondrial genome or the Y chromosome lineage, it is preferable to test hypotheses using multiple genetic markers.

When analyzing non-human animal species, mitochondrial and nuclear DNA can be used in the same ways described above, as well as for species identification. Chloroplasts, found in plants, have varied inheritance patterns. In some cases chloroplast DNA could be used to trace maternal or paternal lineages of plants, but in general it is, anthropologically, more useful in the identification of plant genera and, in some cases, species, which can be achieved by typing regions of the genome that contain genus/species-specific DNA sequences. DNA from infectious organisms such as bacteria and viruses can also be detected in ancient remains, and can be used to identify infected individuals, to determine the specific cause of paleopathologies, and to explore the co-evolution of humans and their diseases.

When one analyzes multiple samples from a population, one can apply the methods of population genetics – including the construction of phylogenetic trees or networks, and various estimates of genetic diversity, of genetic distance between populations, and of gene flow between populations (for further discussion, see Relethford's and O'Rourke's contributions in the present volume). The possible applications of aDNA techniques in anthropology are limited only by the imagination. The most common applications to date will be discussed below.

METHODS

What follows is a brief summary of important methodological considerations involved in aDNA analysis (for further details, see Kaestle and Horsburgh 2002). Ancient DNA has now been successfully extracted from a wide variety of organic remains including teeth, bone, and preserved soft tissues like hair, skin, muscle and brain, as well as from plant remains such as seeds. Less obvious sources of aDNA have included coprolites (preserved feces), blood residue on stone tools, and permafrost soil. Although most of the successful aDNA studies focus on samples that are less than 10,000 years old, DNA quality in ancient samples is more dependent on the conditions of the archaeological site from which they were excavated than on the absolute age of the sample. The best conditions for DNA preservation are depositional environments that are cold, dry, anaerobic and of a neutral to slightly basic pH (a quantification of the concentration of hydrogen atoms). In addition, the DNA extraction process can co-extract compounds that inhibit the PCR and/or interfere with the DNA detection methods, such that the preserved aDNA cannot be analyzed and high levels of such inhibitors can prove an insurmountable problem. Further, it is possible that X-raying or Computerized Tomography (CT) scanning samples will increase the fragmentation of the endogenous DNA (Götherström et al. 1995, Grieshaber et al. 2008), so the post-excavation history of the samples is also important.

In addition to DNA degradation levels, the contamination of aDNA samples with modern DNA is of great concern. Because contaminating DNA originates from a modern source, it is of higher quality than the targeted aDNA sample; therefore it will be detected preferentially, and often it will overwhelm any ancient signal. Such contamination can derive from a variety of sources, including the DNA of workers who have handled the samples before they reach the laboratory, for instance archaeologists and museum staff. Additionally, some relatively standard procedures for dealing with skeletal remains, such as washing or coating them with stabilizers, can worsen the contamination problems. DNA can also be introduced into samples from lab sources such as personnel, modern DNA extracted for other purposes, the aDNA that has been PCR-amplified for analysis, and the labware and reagents used in DNA extraction and amplification.

Consequently, the laboratories in which aDNA analyses are performed must be physically separated from other laboratories conducting molecular analyses, and must be dedicated solely to the extraction of DNA from ancient samples. Additionally, lab personnel should not move from laboratories in which modern and post-PCR work is conducted directly into the aDNA labs, because of the high probability of their transporting DNA on their clothing, hair and shoes. To protect samples from the transfer of modern DNA from skin, hair, respiration, and other sources, lab workers should utilize a combination of disposable lab coats or coveralls, hairnets, shoe covers, gloves, and facemasks. The lab should be at positive pressure, with HEPA-filtered air, to avoid the introduction of contaminating DNA through airflow. All reagents and labware should be guaranteed by the manufacturer to be DNA-free when possible, or otherwise to be of molecular grade or of similar quality. Additionally, reagents should be purchased or dispensed into small volumes that will be used quickly, to avoid the introduction of DNA into stock solutions. Finally, lab surfaces need to be regularly wiped with bleach and subjected to periods of UV-irradiation, in order to prevent the accumulation of DNA.

Despite all of these precautions, it is inevitable that instances of contamination will occur. Thus, it is imperative to utilize negative controls in all aDNA extractions and amplifications, so as to detect any contamination. In addition, extractions must be made from at least two independent samples per individual, and results must be confirmed from multiple tests of each extract. Many studies also include the independent replication of results in separate aDNA labs, and/or the cloning of PCR products for confirmatory sequencing.

Before aDNA extraction can begin, the surface of the sample must be treated to remove contaminating (exogenous) DNA that was deposited prior to the sample's arrival in the laboratory. Decontamination can be achieved by physically removing the surface of the sample, by treating it with bleach, by irradiating it with UV light, or most often by a combination thereof. From that point on various relatively standard DNA extraction procedures can be used, for instance phenol-chloroform isolation or silica binding. Note that these extraction processes will isolate all the DNA present in a sample, including the intended target DNA, as well as any other DNA – fungal, bacterial, from plants, or from other sources – that has accumulated from the depositional context.

Depending on the goal of the study, particular genetic loci within the mitochondrial, nuclear, or chloroplast genome will be targeted for analysis. The DNA fragment of interest is usually copied (amplified) by using PCR, although some newer approaches such as pyrosequencing detect sequence variation in other ways. The section of DNA most frequently targeted is the control region of the mitochondrial genome, which contains three segments of hypervariable sequence; most aDNA studies focus on the first segment. Once amplified, the DNA of interest can be examined by direct sequencing, by using restriction enzymes that cleave the DNA at specific sequences, or by other standard methods, for the purpose of discerning sequence differences between individuals. The resulting DNA data can by analyzed in a myriad of ways, but they all seek to recognize meaningful patterns in the variability between individuals and groups. These methods include genetic distance statistics, phylogenetic trees and networks, cluster analyses, and simulation analyses (see the chapters by Relethford and O'Rourke in this volume).

Although aDNA methods are derived from standard modern DNA protocols, the proper extraction and analysis of aDNA is quite demanding, and methods continue to evolve. Ancient DNA studies routinely report failure rates of over 50 percent, and often discard weeks or months worth of data because of contamination problems. Therefore, this is not a task either for the impatient or for the ill trained. However, there is sufficient evidence today to make one confident that aDNA can be recovered from a multitude of sources, dating as far back as tens of millennia in the past.

On the other hand, aDNA analyses are generally destructive. Thus, it is important to bear in mind our commitment to the proper stewardship of anthropological material – an irreplaceable resource. In many cases, aDNA analysis may not be the most productive approach to hypothesis testing – for example in the identification of individual 'immigrants' into a population, which may be more profitably approached through stable isotope analyses (see Larsen and Walker's contribution in this volume); or in establishing 'cultural affiliation' between a single very ancient individual and a living population (see Kaestle and Smith 2005). A much more complex set of issues surrounds the idea of accountability (Watkins et al. 2000), including the responsibility of the researcher to consult with groups who may be affected by the research, and the idea of beneficence (NCPHS 1979), which is central to studies involving human subjects. There is a large body of literature discussing these issues as applied to archaeology and physical anthropology in general (see Vitelli 1996, or Cantwell et al. 2000), as well as concerns specific to aDNA (see Kaestle and Horsburgh 2002 for an extensive discussion). Although it is impossible to obtain informed consent from deceased individuals, aDNA researchers should bear in mind the rights and interests of direct descendants and of other living people who consider themselves to be culturally affiliated to the people being studied. This process can be extremely complicated, involving difficulties in delineating the community, in identifying the legitimate political institutions or leaders of these groups, and in reaching community-wide consensus.

APPLICATIONS

Ancient DNA methods have been applied widely in anthropology. These studies have involved both human and non-human sources of DNA, and have ranged from hypotheses concerning whole species to hypotheses that focus on single individuals. This discussion is not meant to offer a complete review; additional examples and applications can be found in the literature and they are reviewed by Kaestle and Horsburgh (2002), by Schlumbaum and colleagues (2008), and by Stone (2008).

Human sources

Much of aDNA research in anthropology has utilized human sources for DNA. These studies have focused primarily on testing bioarchaeological hypotheses, although some attention has also been given to phylogenetic questions.

Species The clarification of relationships between modern humans and other hominids has been approached through aDNA techniques. The position of Neandertals in our evolutionary history has been debated ever since they were recognized as similar, but not identical, to modern humans. Although it has been argued that anatomically modern humans interbred with Neandertals (see Smith's chapter in this volume), analyses of their mitochondrial and nuclear genomes do not support a history of significant admixture (for further discussion, see Relethford's chapter in this volume).

Large population movements Human populations have made several significant expansions, including the initial movement out of Africa, the peopling of continents – Australia and the Americas – the expansion of Bantu speakers throughout Africa, and the spread into the Pacific Islands. All of these have been the focus of study that uses DNA from living populations (for examples, see the chapters by Relethford and O'Rourke in the present volume); but aDNA methods offer a temporal component to hypothesis testing which is unavailable by other means.

For example, it has been shown that the crania of the first inhabitants of the Americas, the Paleoindians, are morphologically distinct from those of living Native Americans, which suggests that living Native Americans are not direct descendants of the initial colonizers of the Americas (Steele and Powell 1992; Munford et al. 1995; Morell 1998). However, analyses of the mtDNA from these ancient individuals has confirmed the presence of lineages found among living Native Americans, and this supports some measure of continuity between the two (Kaestle and Smith 2005; Smith et al. 2006). In fact, mitochondrial analyses of one of these Paleoindians from the On Your Knees Cave site in Alaska's Prince of Wales Island, dating to 10,300 years ago, have been used to demonstrate that the initial peopling of the Americas was more diverse than previously thought: they suggest a higher rate of evolution for mtDNA than many previous phylogenetic studies – which means that the age of events calculated on the basis of the slower mutation rates are likely to be too old (Kemp et al. 2007). This would resolve the conflict between the archaeological evidence of a peopling of the Americas about 15,000 years ago and the previous estimates, from molecular genetics, of a period longer than 20,000 years.

Local population movements and continuity In addition to larger population movements, evidence from archaeology, linguistics, historical documents and modern genetic variation has supported hypotheses of smaller-scale population movements or connections between groups through time. Cases include contact between Old World populations, for instance along the Silk Road or during the Viking conquests, as well as contacts in the New World, for instance the population replacement in the Great Basin and the movement of the Athapaskan speakers into the Southwest. These hypotheses can be directly addressed by using aDNA from sites that predate and postdate the hypothesized movement or span the temporal range of proposed continuity.

For example, there has been a decades-long debate over the cause of significant changes in material culture, subsistence strategy, and settlement patterns that occurred about one thousand years ago in the US Great Basin. Some anthropologists have argued that these changes were the result of local cultural adaptation to a changing environment, while others suggest that they must be due to a major population replacement in the area (Madsen and Rhode 1994). In order to test the hypothesis of a significant population replacement, mitochondrial sequences from forty ancient individuals from two sites in the western Great Basin that predate the supposed population movement were compared to sequences from hundreds of living Native Americans from the region (Kaestle and Smith 2001). These analyses provide evidence of a genetic discontinuity, which signals both a population movement into the area – a movement which accompanied the above-mentioned cultural changes – and some gene flow between the ancient and the more recent groups – a phenomenon which indicates that the movement into the region was accompanied by admixture between the two populations. In order to explore this question further, a computer model was developed to simulate microevolutionary processes such as genetic drift and local gene flow; this model allowed for varying population sizes, population growth, levels of gene flow, and number of generations, in order to determine under what conditions local processes could account for the observed differences between the ancient and modern Great Basin groups (Cabana et al. 2008). This study showed that simple *in situ* processes could account for the differences between the ancient and the modern Great Basin groups if gene flow was very low between local 'districts' within the Great Basin; but, on the basis of archaeological, ethnographic and theoretical literature, this low level of gene flow is unlikely. At the higher levels of gene flow between local 'districts,' which is more probable, *in situ* microevolutionary forces can be rejected as the cause of the observed differences if the temporal gap between the ancient and the modern groups is of about 1200–1500 years or shorter (the median date for these samples). This suggests that gene flow from an external source is required to account for the differences observed, consistent with the earlier aDNA analyses (Kaestle and Smith 2001).

Mortuary practices and sociocultural reconstruction   In general, it is believed that kinship and sex (which has a complicated relationship with gender) were the primary structural elements upon which ancient social organization, intercommunity and intracommunity relationships, status and position within the socio-political hierarchy, and inheritance of social prerogatives were based. Kinship and sex have been assessed through archaeological context and conventional physical anthropological analysis (see Larsen and Walker's chapter in the present volume). However, these methods are limited by factors such as the degree of preservation of the remains, ambiguities in physical markers, particularly in children, and the inability to detect specific biological relationships like parentage or sibship. Ancient DNA analysis provides a means to mitigate some of these limitations by enabling a genetic discrimination of kinship and a precise determination of sex. Assessment of the level and pattern of genetic variation among males and females at a site can also be used to test hypotheses of patrilocal or matrilocal marriage patterns.

For example, kinship has been suggested to explain burial patterns in several instances within historical Mississippian sites (of about 1,000 years ago) in the Eastern Woodlands. Co-burials of women and children are common at Mississippian cemeteries, and it has been suggested that these are parent–offspring co-burials; but the only way to confirm this relationship is through aDNA. Because mothers and their offspring will possess identical mtDNA, mitochondrial sequences were compared for seven co-burials from the Schild Mississippian site in west and central Illinois (Raff 2008, Raff et al. n.d.c). In three cases a single child was co-buried with an adult woman, while in four cases two children were co-buried with an adult woman, which gives a total of eighteen individuals. MtDNA was not recovered from four children, but all the remaining individuals were successfully assigned to mitochondrial lineages. In no case did the mitochondrial sequence of the child match that of the woman with whom they were buried. Thus, none of these co-burials includes mothers and their biological offspring, and we must re-evaluate our interpretation of Mississippian woman–child co-burials.

More generally, patterns of burials within rows or mounds at Mississippian sites are often ascribed to kinship. It has been proposed that the characteristics common to many historical eastern Woodlands tribes (unilateral matrilineal descent, matrilocal clans) derive from the ancient southeastern Mississippian pattern (Hudson 1976; Hall 1997), and it is often assumed that matrilineal relationships shaped burial practices for the ancient Mississippians. At Schild, Goldstein (1980) identified the arrangement of burials into rows oriented east–west throughout the Mississippian site, and hypothesized that these rows were related to kinship. However, a study of the mtDNA from twenty-three individuals buried in five hypothesized rows demonstrated that they did not contain individuals related matrilineally. This situation suggests either that matrilineal descent did not shape the mortuary practices of the Schild Mississippians, or that we have not correctly identified the patterns of association within the cemetery (Raff 2008; Raff et al. n.d.c).

Genetic sexing can also help to make sense of the mortuary practices and behaviors of ancient peoples. For example, thirty-seven children representing a sacrificial offering were recovered from Temple R at the Aztec city of Tlatelolco – a city dated to AD 1428–67, and now located in modern Mexico City. This temple is dedicated to Ehecatl–Quetzalcoatl, the Aztec male god of wind and rain, to whom, according to early Spanish accounts, children were sacrificed. It has been proposed that the Aztecs believed sacrificial victims to be incarnations or personifications of the gods to whom they were sacrificed, and hence that these children must have been male. By detecting differences between the sequence of the amelogenin gene on the X and Y chromosomes, it was possible to identify the sex of twenty-six of the Tlatelolco children as male, and none as female, which lends strong support to the interpretation that these children were personifying Ehecatl–Quetzalcoatl (De La Cruz et al. 2008).

Identifying phenotype Analyses of genetic variation at known genes may inform us on the phenotype of an individual. The phenotype may be suggested by analyses of the skeleton or of other remains – for example when paleopathological attributes indicate that an individual suffered from a genetic disease. In other cases the phenotype may be undetectable through other means, such as in the case of the ABO blood type. As our knowledge of the genetic causes of a phenotype increases with ongoing research on skin, hair and eye color, height, and other physical attributes, aDNA research has the potential to draw for us a more detailed picture of the appearance of ancient people. Many hypotheses about the evolution of these phenotypes can also be tested by using aDNA evidence.

It has been suggested for instance that the mutations associated with lactase persistence (LP), which allows individuals to drink milk after weaning, evolved because they provided a selective advantage in dairying populations, who had regular access to raw milk. The increase in frequency of the mutation associated with LP in Europe is usually attributed to the hypothesis that selection favored this trait after the spread of cattle breeds into Europe (see O'Rourke in this volume); but the estimates concerning a time of origin for these mutations among European populations have provided a wide bracket, between about 2,000 and 20,000 years ago (Bersaglieri et al. 2004). On the other hand, one can say, on the basis of archaeological evidence, that dairying began in Europe between about 8,000 and 5,000 years ago (Burger et al. 2007). Thus, the DNA-based dates for the origin of the LP mutation open up the possibility of a competing hypothesis, namely that "human populations were already differentiated with regard to LP frequency before the development of dairying, and the presence of LP determined the adoption of milk production and consumption practices" (Burger et al. 2007: 3736). To test the two competing hypotheses, fifty-one samples from early Holocene sites in Europe were examined for the presence of the mutation in intron 13 of the *MCM6* gene – located upstream from the *LCT* gene and the most common cause of LP in European populations – as well as for the G to A transition at intron 9 – which is less strongly associated with LP in Europeans (Burger et al. 2007). Ten individuals were successfully typed, eight dating from between 7,000 and 8,000 years ago, one from 4,300 years ago, and one from 1,500 years ago. Only the 1,500-year-old individual possessed LP-associated mutations. The absence of LP-associated mutations in the more ancient individuals is most consistent with the hypothesis that these mutations were at low frequency until dairying spread into the region, when selection favored an increase in their frequency, consistent with the first hypothesis.

Non-human sources

Non-human sources of aDNA can be preferable to human sources due to three factors. First, there is often less reluctance to perform destructive analyses on non-human remains. Second, it is often easier to avoid and detect laboratory contamination of non-human samples, especially when working with uncommon species. Third, some questions can be more easily and appropriately explored using non-human samples.

Population movement and contact When people move, they bring their animals, plants, and infections along with them. Sometimes simply detecting the presence of a particular species is enough to prove population contact; in other cases tracing patterns of relationships within the species can also inform us as to how humans themselves moved.

For example, understanding the spread of animals throughout the Pacific Islands has improved our appreciation of the patterns of human settlement and contact in the region (for a review of the modern human genetic data regarding this question, see Relethford's contribution in this volume). In particular, Matisoo-Smith and her colleagues (1998, 2004) have studied the Pacific rat, transported to the east across the Pacific Ocean by the first colonizers of the region. By examining the ancient patterns of molecular diversity in this species across the islands of the Pacific, these researchers have been able to clarify some of the paths of colonization and patterns of interaction between prehistoric Polynesians. Their results suggest that the popular models of Pacific colonization are too simplistic, and they support instead a more complex pattern of *in situ* development, combined with (possibly multiple) intrusion from external sources. At the eastern edge of the Pacific, aDNA analysis has also provided evidence for contact between ancient Polynesians and Native Americans, by demonstrating the presence of pre-Columbian chickens from Polynesia at the El Arenal site in Chile and by suggesting that these ancient Polynesian chickens are the ancestors of the modern Aruacana chicken (Storey et al. 2007, 2008).

Dietary and environmental reconstruction and domestication   While the proximate goal of many aDNA studies is the identification of archaeological species, especially those present in small or undiagnostic fragments, often the ultimate goal is elucidating dietary patterns, reconstructing past environments, or increasing our understanding of the process and pattern of the domestication of a plant or animal.

For example, the analysis of aDNA from coprolites has been used to study the diets of prehistoric peoples. By amplifying sections of mitochondrial and chloroplast genomes from three coprolites found at Hinds Cave, Texas, and dating from more than 2,000 years ago, Poinar and his colleagues (2001) have identified several species of plants and animals – including antelope, rabbit, packrat, squirrel, hackberry, oak, and legumes – which in all probability made up the diet of the Native Americans who inhabited the region. Pyrosequencing approaches have also been applied to two coprolites from the Cueva de los Muertos Chiquitos in Durango, Mexico dating from approximately 1,300 years ago; these analyses were designed to identify the microbial taxa present in the gut (the 'microbiome') of these individuals, as well as dietary components (Tito et al. 2008). In addition to identifying microbial taxa typical of the human gastrointestinal track, they found DNA from maize, an important component of the regional diet.

Our understanding of the domestication of the dog has also been informed by aDNA studies. Although genetic studies of modern dogs and wolves have demonstrated that dogs were domesticated from the Old World grey wolf, there remains disagreement about the time and number of domestication events (Degoilloux et al. 2009). While most archaeological evidence suggests a period of domestication approximately 15,000 years ago or later, genetic evidence has supported the hypothesis that domestication took place any time between then and 130,000 years ago. Similarly, genetic evidence has been interpreted as supporting either multiple origins or a single origin from East Asian wolves. But the modification of the gene pool of both wolf and dog populations introduced through human agency – through hunting, habitat destruction, and artificial selection – makes it difficult to extrapolate from modern samples the ancient pattern of genetic variation in the ancestral gene pool of these animals, and thus aDNA provides an important window into the process of this earliest domestication. Ancient mtDNA analyses of European canids have revealed significant differences between genetic variation in these populations and in modern canids, including the widespread distribution of variants that are today more limited geographically (Degoilloux et al. 2009; Germonpré et al. 2009; Malmström et al. 2008; Verginelli et al. 2005). While these data support the idea of a single origin for the domesticated dog, they also recommend caution in assigning a geographic origin to this process until ancient Asian canid sequences are obtained. Ancient mtDNA analyses of pre-Columbian dogs from the New World also indicate that they are descended from Old World ancestors and are not the product of a second domestication of wolves in the Americas. Hence, it is plausible to infer that they accompanied the first human migrants across the Bering land bridge (Leonard et al. 2002).

Infectious disease   Anthropologists are very interested in understanding the evolution of human diseases and the way they affected our ancestors, as changes in the patterns and influence of infectious organisms are likely to have played an important role in shaping human evolution, demography, and culture (see the chapters by Sattenspiel and Herring and by Buikstra in the present volume). Unfortunately, it is very difficult to identify infected individuals in the archaeological record, as most infectious diseases leave little or no sign on the skeleton, and those that do affect the skeleton can manifest their presence through patterns indistinguishable from those of each other, of inherited diseases, or of trauma. Thus, understanding ancient infectious diseases is increasingly accomplished through aDNA methods.

One major object of focus in aDNA approaches to infectious disease is tuberculosis (TB). TB is caused by several closely related species of bacteria, united in the *Mycobacterium tuberculosis* complex (MTC). Some of them primarily infect humans, while others prefer non-human mammalian hosts. Although it was thought that humans initially acquired TB from domesticated animals such as cattle, genetic evidence now supports the hypothesis that humans passed the infection to other animals, leaving the problem of the original source of human TB open to question. TB was also among the diseases that devastated Native American populations following European contact, and it was consequently thought to have been newly introduced to the continent. However, paleopathology studies have now confirmed the presence of infection in pre-Columbian populations (see for instance Roberts and Buikstra 2003). Little is known about how TB came to infect American populations prior to European contact, which strain(s) may have been present, or how contact with Old World strain(s) changed the epidemiological arena. Exploration of these questions had been limited to a paleopathological approach dependent on the diagnosis of bone lesions, which are quite rare in infected individuals. But the application of aDNA methods has increased our understanding of the patterns of TB infection in prehistory. For example, the hypothesis that MTC was introduced to Africa from eighteenth-century Europe has been refuted by studies detecting MTC DNA in African populations before European contact (Lev et al. 2001; Spigelman et al. 2002). Several aDNA studies have also detected MTC in prehistoric American populations, a fact which confirms the view that the disease was not introduced to the New World during the colonial period, and also suggests ways to improve the paleopathological diagnosis of infection (Arriaza et al. 1995; Raff et al. 2006). New MTC sequence data from the Schild site (mentioned above) suggest that the pre-Columbian New World strain may be distinct from modern TB as well (Raff 2008; Raff et al. n.d.a), and further exploration of this ancient genome should help us to understand the evolution of this disease.

CONCLUSIONS

Ancient DNA research has helped to answer many pressing questions in anthropology, and the potential for future success has increased dramatically with the development of new high through-put and massively parallel techniques, which make possible large-scale projects such as the sequencing of whole ancient genomes (Millar et al. 2008). These technologies also make it easier to access ancient nuclear DNA, allowing an examination of ancient phenotypic variation, especially as our knowledge of the human genome grows. As the costs of these new technologies come down, aDNA analyses will be applied to a wider range of projects. And, as more labs are equipped for aDNA research, an increasing number of ancient individuals will be studied through the use of molecular genetic methods, a process which will expand our database of ancient sequences. With information from large numbers of individuals recovered from many ancient sites, the potential for understanding population interaction both locally and globally increases. For example, we now have data from almost a dozen pre-Columbian midwestern U.S. sites, and more is on the way (see Bolnick and Smith 2007; Raff 2008; Raff et al. n.d.b; Shook and Smith 2008; Stone and Stoneking 1998). As long as high standards with regard to contamination control and detection are maintained, the future is bright for ancient DNA research.

REFERENCES

Arriaza B. T., Salo, W., Aufderheide, A. C., and Holcomb, T. A. (1995) Pre-Columbian Tuberculosis in Northern Chile: Molecular and Skeletal Evidence. *American Journal of Physical Anthropology* 98: 37–45.

Bersaglieri, T., Sabeti, P. C., Patterson, N., Vanderploeg, T., Schaffner, S. F., Drake, J. A., Rhodes, M., Reich, D. E., and Hirschhorn, J. N. (2004) Genetic Signatures of Strong Recent Positive Selection at the Lactase Gene. *American Journal of Human Genetics* 74: 1111–1120.

Bolnick, D. W., and Smith, D. G. (2007) Migration and Social Structure among the Hopewell: Evidence from Ancient DNA. *American Antiquity* 72 (4): 627–664.

Burger, J., Kirchner, M., Bramanti, B., Haak, W., and Thomas, M. G. (2007) Absence of the Lactase-Persistence-Associated Allele in Early Neolithic Europeans. *Proceedings of the National Academy of Sciences, USA* 104 (10): 3736–3741.

Cabana, G., Hunley, K., and Kaestle, F. A. (2008) Population Continuity or Replacement? A Novel Computer Simulation Approach and Its Application to the Numic Expansion (Western Great Basin, USA). *American Journal of Physical Anthropology* 135 (4): 438–447.

Cantwell, A.-M., Friedlander, R., and Tramm, M. L. (2000) *Ethics and Anthropology: Facing Future Issues in Human Biology, Globalism, and Cultural Property*. New York: New York Academy of Sciences.

De La Cruz, I., González-Oliver, A., Kemp, B. M., Román, J. A., Smith, D. G., and Torre-Blanco, A. (2008) Sex Identification of Children Sacrificed to the Ancient Aztec Rain Gods in Tlatelolco. *Current Anthropology* 49 (3): 519–526.

Deguilloux, M. F., Moquel, J., Pemonge, M. H., and Colombeau, G. (2009) Ancient DNA Supports Lineage Replacement in European Dog Gene Pool: Insights into Neolithic Southeast France. *Journal of Archaeological Science* 36: 513–519.

Germonpré, M., Sablin, M. V., Stevens, R. E., Hedges, R. E. M., Hofreiter, M., Stiller, M., and Després, V. R. (2009) Fossil Dogs and Wolves from Paleolithic Sites in Belgium, the Ukraine and Russia: Osteometry, Ancient DNA and Stable Isotopes. *Journal of Archaeological Science* 36: 473–490.

Gobalet K. W. (2001) A Critique of Faunal Analysis: Inconsistency among Experts in Blind Tests. *Journal of Archaeological Science* 28: 377–386.

Goldstein, L. G. (1980) *Mississippian Mortuary Practices: A Case Study of Two Cemeteries in the Lower Illinois Valley*. Evanston: Northwestern University Archaeological Program.

Götherström A., Fischer, C., Lindén, K., and Lidén, K. (1995) X-raying Ancient Bone: A Destructive Method in Connection with DNA Analysis. *Laborativ Arkeologi* 8: 26–28.

Grieshaber, B. M., Osbourne, D. L., Doubleday, A. F., and Kaestle, F. A. (2008) A Pilot Study into the Effects of X-ray and Computed Tomography Exposure on the Amplification of DNA from Bone. *Journal of Archaeological Sciences* 35 (3): 681–687.

Hall, R. L. (1997) *An Archaeology of the Soul: North American Indian Belief and Ritual*. Urbana: University of Illinois Press.

Higuchi, R., Bowman, B., Freiberger, M., Ryder, A. O., and Wilson, A. C. (1984) DNA Sequence from the Quagga, an Extinct Member of the Horse Family. *Nature* 312: 282–284.

Hudson, C. (1976) *The Southeastern Indians*. Knoxville: University of Tennessee Press.

Kaestle, F. A., and Horsburgh, K. A. (2002) Ancient DNA in Anthropology: Methods, Applications and Ethics. *Yearbook of Physical Anthropology* 45: 92–130.

Kaestle, F. A., and Smith, D. G. (2001) Ancient Native American DNA from Western Nevada: Implications for the Numic Expansion Hypothesis. *American Journal of Physical Anthropology* 115: 1–12.

Kaestle, F. A., and Smith, D. G. (2005) Working with Ancient DNA: NAGPRA, Kennewick Man and Other Ancient Peoples. In T. R. Turner (ed.), *Biological Anthropology and Ethics* (pp. 241–262). Albany NY: State University of New York Press.

Kemp, B. M., Malhi, R. S., McDonough, J., Bolnick, D. A., Eshleman, J. A., Rickards, O., Martinez-Labarga, C., Johnson, J. R., Lorenz, J. G., Dixon, E. J., Fifield, T. E., Heaton, T. H., Worl, R., and Smith, D. G. (2007) Genetic Analysis of Early Holocene Skeletal Remains from Alaska and Its Implications for the Settlement of the Americas. *American Journal of Physical Anthropology* 132: 605–621.

Leonard, J., A., Wayne, R. K., Wheeler, J., Valadez, R., Guillén, S., and Vilá, C. (2002) Ancient DNA Evidence for Old World Origin of New World Dogs. *Science* 298: 1613–1616.

Lev, G., Bercovier, H., Brittain, D., and Greenblatt, C. (2001) Spoligotyping of Ancient Tubercle Bacilli. *Ancient Biomolecules* 3: 306.

Madsen, D. B., and Rhode, D. (1994) *Across the West: Human Population Movement and the Expansion of the Numa*. Salt Lake City: University of Utah Press.

Malmström, H., Vilá, C., Gilbert, M. T. P., Stora, J., Willerslev, E., Holmlund, G., and Götherström, A. (2008) Barking Up the Wrong Tree: Modern Northern European Dogs Fail to Explain Their Origin. *BMC Evolutionary Biology* 8: 71.

Matisoo-Smith, E., Roberts, R. M., Irwin, G. J., Allen, J. S., Penny, D., and Lambert, D. M. (1998) Patterns of Prehistoric Human Mobility in Polynesia Indicated by mtDNA from the Pacific Rat. *Proceedings of the National Academy of Sciences, USA* 95: 15145–15150.

Matisoo-Smith, E., and Robins, J. H. (2004) Origins and Dispersal of Pacific Peoples: Evidence from mtDNA Phylogenies of the Pacific Rate. *Proceedings of the National Academy of Sciences, USA* 101: 9167–9172.

Millar, C. D., Huynen, L., Subramanian, S., Mohandesan, E., and Lambert, D. M. (2008) New Developments in Ancient Genomics. *Trends in Ecology and Evolution* 23 (7): 386–393.

Morell, V. (1998) Kennewick Man's Trials Continue. *Science* 280: 190–192.

Munford, D., Zanini, M. C., and Neves, W. A. (1995) Human Cranial Variation in South America: Implications for the Settlement of the New World. *Brazilian Journal of Genetics* 18: 673–688.

NCPHS [National Commission for the Protection of Human Subjects of Biomedical and Behavioral Research] (1979) The Belmont Report: Ethical Principles and Guidelines for the Protection of Human Subjects of Research. *OPRR Reports* (April) 18: 1–8.

Pääbo, S. (1993) Ancient DNA. *Scientific American* (Nov.) 269 (5): 86–92.

Poinar H. N., Kuch, M., Sobolik, K. D., Barnes, I., Stankiewicz, A. B., Kuder, T., Spaulding, W. G., Bryant, V. M., Cooper, A., and Pääbo, S. (2001) A Molecular Analysis of Dietary Diversity for Three Archaic Native Americans. *Proceedings of the National Academy of Sciences, USA* 98 (8): 4317–4322.

Raff, J. A. (2008) An Ancient DNA Perspective on the Prehistory of the Lower Illinois Valley. PhD dissertation, Indiana University, Bloomington.

Raff, J. A., Cook, D. C., Bolnick, D., and Kaestle, F. A. (n.d.a) Prehistoric Tuberculosis in the Midwest. Department of Anthropology, Indiana University, Bloomington (unpublished MS).

Raff, J., Cook, D., and Kaestle, F. (2006) Tuberculosis in the New World: A Study of Ribs from the Schild Mississippian Population, West-Central Illinois. *Memórias do Instituto Oswaldo Cruz* 101 (Suppl. 2): 25–27.

Raff, J., Cook, D., and Kaestle, F. (n.d.b) Testing the Madonna and Child Trope. Department of Anthropology, Indiana University, Bloomington (unpublished MS).

Raff, J. A., Cook, D. C., Spencer, S. D., and Kaestle, F. A. (n.d.c) Mortuary Practices at Schild: Ancient DNA Evidence. Department of Anthropology, Indiana University, Bloomington (unpublished MS).

Roberts, C. A., and Buikstra, J. E. (2003) *The Bioarchaeology of Tuberculosis: A Global View on a Reemerging Disease*. Gainesville: University Press of Florida.

Schlumbaum A., Tensen, M., and Jaenicke-Després, V. (2008) Ancient Plant DNA in Archaeobotany. *Vegetation History and Archaeobotany* 17 (2): 233–244.

Shook, B. A. S., and Smith, D. G. (2008) Using Ancient mtDNA to Reconstruct the Population History of Northeastern North America. *American Journal of Physical Anthropology* 137: 14–29.

Smith, D. G., Malhi, R. S., Eshleman, J. A., and Kaestle. F. A. (2006) Mitochondrial DNA Haplogroups of Paleoamericans in North America. In R. Bonnichsen, B. Lepper, D. G. Steele, D. Stanford, C. N. Warren, and R. Gruhn (eds), *PaleoAmerican Origins: Moving Beyond Clovis* (pp. 243–254). College Station TX: Texas A&M University Press.

Spigelman, M., Matheson, C., Lev, G., Greenblatt, C., and Donoghue, H. D. (2002) Confirmation of the Presence of Mycobacterium Tuberculosis Complex-Specific DNA in Three Archaeological Specimens. *International Journal of Osteoarchaeology* 12: 393–401.

Steele, D. G., and Powell, J. F. (1992) Peopling of the Americas: Paleobiological Evidence. *Human Biology* 64 (3): 303–336.

Stone, A. C. (2008) DNA Analysis of Archaeological Remains. In M. A. Katzenberg and S. R. Saunders (eds), *Biological Anthropology of the Human Skeleton*, 2nd edn (pp. 461–483). Hoboken: John Wiley and Sons, Inc.

Stone, A. C., and Stoneking, M. (1998) MtDNA Analysis of a Prehistoric Oneota Population: Implications for the Peopling of the New World. *American Journal of Human Genetics* 62: 1153–1170.

Storey, A. A., Quiroz, D., Ramírez, J. M., Beavan-Athfield, N., Addison, D. J., Walter, R., Hunt, T., Athens, J. S., Huynen, L., and Matisoo-Smith, E. A. (2008) Pre-Columbian Chickens, Dates, Isotopes and mtDNA. *Proceedings of the National Academy of Sciences, USA* 105 (48): E99.

Storey, A. A., Ramírez, J. M., Guiroz, D., Burley, D. V., Addison, D. J., Walter, R., Anderson, A. J., Hunt, T. L., Athens, J. S., Huynen, L., and Matisoo-Smith, E. A. (2007) Radiocarbon and DNA Evidence for a Pre-Columbian Introduction of Polynesian Chickens to Chile. *Proceedings of the National Academy of Sciences, USA* 104 (25): 10335–10339.

Tito, R. Y., Macmil, S., Wiley, G., Najar, F., Cleeland, L., Qu, C., Wang, P., Romagne, F., Leonard, S., Ruiz, A. J., Reinhard, K., Roe, B. A., and Lewis, C. M. (2008) Phylotyping and Functional Analysis of Two Ancient Human Microbiomes. *PLoS One* 3 (11): e3703.

Verginelli, F., Capelli, C., Coia, V., Musiani, M., Falchetti, M., Ottini, L., Palmirotta, R., Tagliacozzo, A., De Rossi Mazzorin, I., and Mariani-Costantini, R. (2005) Mitochondrial DNA from Prehistoric Canids Highlights Relationships between Dogs and South-East European Wolves. *Molecular Biology and Evolution* 22 (12): 2541–2551.

Vitelli, K. D. (1996) *Archaeological Ethics.* Walnut Creek CA: Altamira Press.

Watkins J., Goldstein, L., Vitelli, K. D., and Jenkins, L. (2000) Accountability: Responsibilities of Archaeologists to Other Interest Groups. In M. J. Lynott and A. Wylie (eds), *Ethics in American Archaeology*, 2nd edn (pp. 40–44). Kansas: Allen Press.

Willerslev, E., Hansen, A. J., Binladen, J., Brand, T. B., Gilbert, M. T. P., Shapiro, B., Bunce, M., Wiuf, C., Gilichinsky, D. C., and Cooper, A. (2003) Diverse Plant and Animal Genetic Records from Holocene and Pleistocene Sediments. *Science* 300 (5620): 791–795.

PART IV The Living and the Dead

CHAPTER 25 Diet Reconstruction and Ecology Using Stable Isotope Ratios

Margaret J. Schoeninger

INTRODUCTION

Over thirty years ago, an archaeologist collaborated with a geochemist (Vogel and van der Merwe 1977; van der Merwe and Vogel 1978) to revolutionize our understanding of the introduction of maize agriculture in North, Central, and South America. Since then, the use of light element stable isotope (carbon, nitrogen, oxygen, and, most recently, hydrogen) data for addressing questions of anthropological significance has exploded within multiple fields. Van der Merwe and Vogel's deceptively simple and elegant approach used the stable isotope composition of carbon ($^{13}C/^{12}C$) in human bone collagen. Within a couple of years their approach was verified through experiments showing a correlation between the ratio in bone collagen and in bone apatite on the one hand, and the carbon isotope ratio in diet on the other, and between nitrogen isotope ratio in bone collagen and the ratio in diet (DeNiro and Epstein 1978; DeNiro and Epstein 1981b). Now, in addition to basic diet reconstruction, anthropologists use stable isotope data for questions relating to forensics (Ehleringer et al. 2008), residential mobility (Knudson and Price 2007), management of domestic animals (Balasse et al. 2003), reconstructing paleoenvironmental conditions (Wynn 2000), diet-related status differentials and gender differences in diet (Kellner and Schoeninger 2008), changes in diet throughout human evolution (Lee-Thorp and Sponheimer 2006), and ecological differences across non-human primate populations (Schoeninger et al. 1999).

Stable isotope analysis melds aspects of an historical science (geology) and aspects of an experimental science (chemistry) with elements from a more theoretical science (physics). This chapter introduces the basics of this approach, so that the reader can evaluate the papers they can read in journals spanning ecology, physical anthropology, archaeology, geosciences, paleontology, food science, and medical science. In addition, my purpose is to introduce the reader to those areas within biological anthropology that have made use of stable isotope analysis. For greater detail on the material presented here, the reader is directed to the classic geochemistry text (Hoefs 1997) and to review books on isotopes in ecology (Rundel et al. 1989; Fry 2006; Michener and Lajtha 2007).

Background

Many elements occur in more than one form and are called isotopes; for instance, ^{12}C and ^{13}C are stable carbon isotopes of the element carbon, whereas ^{14}C is an unstable, or radioactive, carbon isotope. All isotopes of a single element have the same number of electrons and protons, but they differ in the number of neutrons in their nuclei. Some elements, for example carbon (C) and Sr (strontium), have both stable isotopes and radioactive isotopes; but this chapter deals only with the stable forms. The isotopes of an element share the same chemical properties, because chemical reactions are determined largely by electron configurations; but these isotopes differ in mass (numbers of neutrons), and hence molecules containing different isotopes (for instance $^{13}CO_2$ versus $^{12}CO_2$) react at different rates and the strengths of the bonds they form differ. The effects are most apparent among the light elements (hydrogen (H), carbon (C), nitrogen (N), oxygen (O)), because the differential between the isotopes is large compared with the average mass of the element. Among the light elements, molecules with the 'lighter' isotope (^{12}C) react faster than those molecules containing the 'heavier' isotope (^{13}C), and their bonds break more easily. In other words, $^{12}C-^{14}N$ bonds form and break more rapidly than do bonds consisting of $^{12}C-^{15}N$, $^{13}C-^{14}N$, or $^{13}C-^{15}N$.

As the isotopes within an element circulate in the biosphere, these differences among reaction rates result in products which contain relative amounts of each stable isotope that are different from those found in the starting components (that is, the substrate) of a reaction. For example, bone collagen is a protein made up of individual amino acids, each of which is a product resulting from reactions on starting components from food and the breakdown products from an animal's own tissues. The $^{13}C/^{12}C$ ratio of the carbon in each amino acid and in bone collagen (product) differs from the $^{13}C/^{12}C$ ratio of the carbon in the animal's diet and in the breakdown products (substrate). Normally bone collagen has relatively more ^{13}C than the diet has, because bonds with ^{12}C break more readily and more ^{12}C is excreted. Hence we say that bone collagen is enriched in ^{13}C relative to its substrate (diet and breakdown products), and that excreted materials are depleted in ^{13}C relative to the substrate. Similarly, the $^{18}O/^{16}O$ ratio in bone mineral (product) differs from the $^{18}O/^{16}O$ ratio in the animal's body water, which is the substrate for the oxygen in bone mineral.

The difference in isotope ratio between product and substrate is called fractionation. For collagen synthesis, enzymatic control determines the magnitude of the fractionation; this is a case of kinetic isotope fractionation. For bone mineral synthesis, the temperature of the reaction determines the magnitude of fractionation; this is an equilibrium isotope fractionation.

Among heavier elements like strontium (mass of 87.62), the mass difference between the isotopes is trivial by comparison to the overall mass of the element. Within strontium, metabolic reactions such as photosynthesis, bone mineral synthesis, or amino acid synthesis do not change the $^{87}Sr/^{86}Sr$ ratio of the product (plant tissue or bone mineral) relative to the ratio within the substrate. Instead, the ratio of $^{87}Sr/^{86}Sr$ in biological tissues directly reflects the substrate, which for strontium is a rock or soil, or the water in which soil or rocks have dissolved.

With the exception of strontium, the transfer of elements from the geosphere to the biosphere and the transfer between different compartments of each sphere are associated with predictable, sequential changes from the natural abundance isotope ratios through kinetic and equilibrium isotope fractionation (see Figures 3.1 and 3.2 in Fry 2006). Examples include the transfer of carbon from the ocean to the atmosphere and the transfer from plant tissue to animal tissue. The changes involved in these transfers are, however, small, so that the direct reporting of isotope ratios (such as $^{13}C/^{12}C$) is impractical. For this reason, isotope ratios are represented as δ values ($\delta^{13}C$) – that is, as the difference between the isotope ratio within the sample of interest and that within an internationally recognized standard (for instance PDB, a marine limestone, for carbon, AIR, atmospheric nitrogen, for nitrogen, SMOW, standard mean ocean water, or PDB for oxygen, and SMOW for hydrogen). The numeric value of the difference between the sample and the standard is multiplied by 1,000, to give per mil (per thousand) notation (‰). Normal δ values for each of the elements are presented in the sections that follow.

The applications of the isotope approach are universal, and any presentation of short length will necessarily be unable to cover all of them. For the present introduction, I can only regret all the marvelous papers that could not be included.

CARBON ISOTOPE RATIOS: $^{13}C/^{12}C$ REPRESENTED AS $\delta^{13}C$

Most of the world's active cycling carbon is sequestered in the ocean as dissolved carbonate. During the exchange between oceanic carbon and atmospheric carbon dioxide (CO_2), atmospheric CO_2 (product) is depleted in ^{13}C relative to oceanic carbon (substrate) by equilibrium isotope fractionation. Today's atmospheric CO_2 has a $\delta^{13}C$ value around –8‰ (Wahlen 1994), while surface ocean CO_2 has a value around 1‰. Plant $\delta^{13}C$ values are determined by kinetic isotope fractionation during the photosynthetic fixation of atmospheric CO_2. The average value for plants that follow the dominant terrestrial C_3 pathway (herbaceous plants and trees) is around –26 to –28‰; plants that utilize the C_4 pathway (tropical and salt grasses) average around –12‰; and plants that utilize the CAM pathway (succulents) commonly have values near those of C_4 plants (O'Leary 1988; see Figure 25.1). There is, however, a large range around each of the average values; this is due in part to the actual source of the CO_2 available to the plant (well mixed atmosphere versus closed canopy forest understory) and to the rate of photosynthesis, which is affected by the amount of sunlight (among other things, discussed further below).

The $\delta^{13}C$ value of plants and animals dating to more than 100 years ago is approximately 1.5‰ higher than that of today's plants and animals. Large-scale forest burning (that is, combustion of C_3 plants) and use of fossil fuels (mostly C_3 plants) have dumped huge amounts of ^{12}C-enriched CO_2 (approximately –26‰) into our atmosphere. The result is atmospheric CO_2 levels that are higher than any in the last 5 million years and over, and an atmosphere with $\delta^{13}C$ values, which are around –8‰ rather than around –6.5‰, as in the nineteenth century (Friedli et al. 1986).

The $\delta^{13}C$ values of animals are positively correlated to those of their diets (DeNiro and Epstein 1978). Animals feeding on C_3 plants have $\delta^{13}C$ values that are lower (see the camelids from highland Peru and the antelopes from the SW USA in Figure 25.1) than those of animals feeding on C_4 plants (see turkeys and bison in Figure 25.1). Shortly after DeNiro and Epstein demonstrated experimentally in 1978 that the $\delta^{13}C$

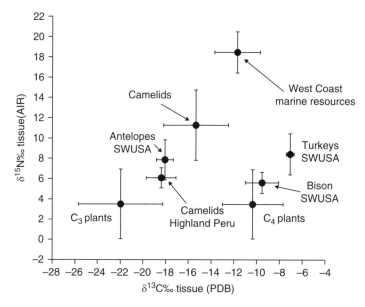

Figure 25.1 Typical carbon and nitrogen stable isotope ratios, expressed in δ notation, for the range of C_3 and C_4 plants and animals feeding on them. The camelids from highland Peru and the antelopes from the southwestern (SW) USA show $\delta^{13}C$ values consistent with feeding on C_3 plants, whereas the bison and turkeys from the southwestern USA ate C_4 plants. Both groups of animals have $\delta^{15}N$ values reflecting a trophic level increase over that of the plants they ate. In both carbon and nitrogen, the camelids from the coast of Peru (Camelids Coastal) show values indicative of feeding on marine plants like seaweeds. The marine resources from the west coast (both California and Peru) are highly elevated in $\delta^{15}N$ values; this is due to the length of the trophic pyramid in the marine system along that coast, which includes toothed whales and other secondary carnivores. Redrawn from Kellner and Schoeninger 2008

values in chitin, muscle, bone collagen, and bone apatite of animals – in a range extending from insects to mice – varied positively with the $\delta^{13}C$ of their diets, Krueger and Sullivan (1984) proposed a model describing these relationships. On the basis of published data from wild fauna and from archaeological humans, they reasoned that the $\delta^{13}C$ values in bone collagen ($\delta^{13}C_{collagen}$) reflect the $\delta^{13}C$ in dietary protein ($\delta^{13}C_{diet\ protein}$), whereas the $\delta^{13}C$ values in bone apatite and tooth enamel ($\delta^{13}C_{apatite}$) reflect the $\delta^{13}C$ in total energy (carbohydrate, lipid, and protein not used in the animal's own protein synthesis). This conclusion became known as the 'routing model' (Krueger and Sullivan 1984). A recent meta-analysis (Kellner and Schoeninger 2007) compared experimental data from rats, mice, and pigs designed to test the model (Ambrose and Norr 1993; Howland et al. 2003; Jim et al. 2004; Tieszen and Fagre 1993). That meta-analysis confirmed the conclusions of the experimental studies that $\delta^{13}C_{diet}$ could be estimated accurately on the basis of $\delta^{13}C_{apatite}$. The meta-analysis also showed that $\delta^{13}C_{collagen}$ correlated more tightly with $\delta^{13}C_{diet}$ than with $\delta^{13}C_{diet\ protein}$, which means that a significant amount of the carbon in bone collagen is coming from the carbohydrate and lipid fraction of diet (that is, from diet energy), and not from the diet protein. Thus, although still widely cited, the 'routing model' is not supported in the form originally proposed.

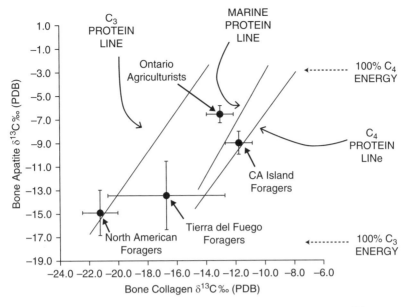

Figure 25.2 The δ^{13}C values in bone mineral (apatite), plotted against the δ^{13}C values in bone collagen. The lines are regression lines derived from experimental animals fed controlled diets with known δ^{13}C values both in diet protein and in the energy fraction of the diet (carbohydrate plus lipid plus excess protein). The leftmost line represents animals fed C_3 protein only, whereas the one to the right represents animals fed C_4 protein only. The middle line represents animals fed marine protein. At the top of each line animals ate only C_4 sources of energy, and at the bottom they ate only C_3 sources of energy. Those fed a mixture of the two sources plot along the middle of each line. Thus animals fed only C_3 protein and C_3 sources of energy plot at the bottom end of the leftmost line and those fed only C_4 protein and C_4 sources of energy plot at the top end of the line to the right. Data from several human groups with well characterized diets are plotted and compared with the regression lines (see text for explanation). Most human groups plotted as expected, on the basis of published floral and faunal data supporting the use of this model for reconstructing diets in human groups where floral and faunal data are absent. Redrawn from Kellner and Schoeninger 2007

In addition, the meta-analysis demonstrated that a plot of $\delta^{13}C_{collagen}$ against $\delta^{13}C_{apatite}$ of all experimental fauna revealed two parallel regression lines: individuals eating only C_3 protein fell in the more negative zone, about 6‰ to the left of individuals eating only C_4 protein (Figure 25.2). Those eating only C_3 energy plotted at the more negative lower end of the graph, while those eating only C_4 energy plotted at the top; those with mixed sources of energy plotted midway along their respective regression lines. Animals fed on marine protein plotted along a third line, which converged on the C_4 protein line – probably because the amount of marine protein in the experimental diets was quite low. Archaeological populations, which were selected for extensive floral and fauna information on human diet, largely adhered to the model described by the experimental fauna. North American foraging populations from Georgia (Tucker 2002) and Ontario (Harrison and Katzenberg 2003) plotted on the C_3 protein line at the C_3 energy portion of the line (Figure 25.2), and maize agriculturists from Ontario (ibid.) plotted midway between the C_3 protein and C_4 protein lines, in a position congruent with the fact that a major portion of their energy came from maize. For the most part, the model showed for the first time a simple means of identifying the source of dietary protein within diets containing both C_3 and C_4 foods.

The plots of archaeological populations with significant reliance on marine foods did not, however, fall as expected. Samples from various sites within Tierra del Fuego (Yesner et al. 2003) show a huge range of variation within both $\delta^{13}C_{collagen}$ and $\delta^{13}C_{apatite}$, while samples from one of the California Channel Islands (San Nicolas: Harrison and Katzenberg 2003) overlap the C_4 protein lines, even though few C_4 foods occur in the region (Figure 25.2). Subsequent analyses, including some of nitrogen isotope data (Froehle et al. 2009), clarified the situation, which is discussed further below.

Much of the variation mentioned above within C_3 plants is associated with the level of canopy cover, which affects both the $\delta^{13}C$ value in the carbon dioxide available to growing plants and the rate of photosynthesis (van der Merwe and Medina 1989; Broadmeadow et al. 1992; Heaton 1999). The $\delta^{13}C$ value of CO_2 within semi-evergreen tropical forests (that is, more closed canopies) has been reported at over 2‰ below well mixed atmospheric CO_2 (Broadmeadow et al. 1992); this is partially due to the addition of ^{12}C-enriched CO_2 respired from microbial activity, which varies dramatically both temporally and spatially (Pataki et al. 2003). Plant tissues, however, integrate this variation (Bowling et al. 2003); and, in turn, the $\delta^{13}C$ values of both proteins and minerals found in large herbivores from across continents and species integrate plant variation (Cerling et al. 2003; Krigbaum 2003; Bump et al. 2007).

A series of studies across several species of extant primates feeding on a wide range of C_3 foods (including prosimians, monkeys, and apes) demonstrate that their hair $\delta^{13}C$ values correlate with canopy cover irrespective of their specific diets, phyletic assignment, or gross metabolic differences (Schoeninger et al. 1999). Two species of Central American monkeys, spider monkey (*Ateles geoffroyi*) and the capuchin monkey (*Cebus capucinus*) (Schoeninger et al. 1997), a single chimpanzee (*Pan troglodytes*) from west Africa (M. J. Schoeninger and J. J. Moore, unpublished data), and two prosimian populations of ring-tailed lemurs (*Lemur catta*) from Madagascar (Loudon et al. 2007) all have $\delta^{13}C$ values in hair of around –25‰, although diets differ markedly across these species.

In contrast, all primate species from deciduous woodlands had their $\delta^{13}C$ values in hair around –24‰ to –23‰. The samples include two New World monkey species – the mantled howler monkey (*Alouatta palliata*) from Costa Rica, and the muriqui (*Brachyteles arachnoides*) from Brazil (Schoeninger et al. 1997); two galago species (*Galago zanzibaricus* and *Otolemur garnettii*) from Kenya (Schoeninger et al. 1998); a population of chimpanzees from the Democratic Republic of Congo (Schoeninger et al. 1999); and three populations of sifakas (*Propithecus diadema*) from Madagascar (McGee and Vaughn 2003). Primate species from open canopy woodlands, which were significantly drier and more open than the two previous types of habitats, had hair values between –22‰ and –21‰. These included two prosimian species from Madagascar, lepilemur (*Lepilemur leucopus*) (Schoeninger et al. 1998) and ring-tailed lemur (*Lemur catta*) (Loudon et al. 2007), and two populations of chimpanzees, one from Tanzania and another from Senegal (Schoeninger et al. 1999; Sponheimer et al. 2006). The data from different studies are not identical, however, and larger samples should be taken from a wider range of habitats for comparison with extant vegetation and canopy cover, in order to refine the relationship between primate hair $\delta^{13}C$ values and canopy cover. If a primate 'isoscape' (that is, a clinal distribution of primate hair $\delta^{13}C$ values see Schoeninger 2009b) could be developed, it could expand our understanding of the original expanse of various primate populations before the decimation of so many species, which is currently going on.

Other studies have used the $\delta^{13}C$ values in various materials in order to reconstruct general aspects of the ecology of past environments and the diets of our early hominin relatives. Some estimated the presence of C_3 and C_4 plant types by analyzing the $\delta^{13}C$ values in the bone mineral of various ungulate species (Cerling 1979; Cerling et al. 1988; Kingston et al. 1994); others used paleosols and carbonate nodules, although these are not always available or well preserved (Wynn 2000; Cerling et al. 1988; Kingston 2007). Among European Neandertals, the $\delta^{13}C$ values in collagen (Boucherens 2009) demonstrate that they foraged in open country habitats. Neandertals may have inhabited forested regions; but open country herd animals are easier to locate and appear to have been their primary hunting targets. Among earlier members of the human lineage, only tooth enamel is available, and it is necessary to consider diagenesis (the post-mortem alteration of the carbonate fraction) – which can be a significant problem (Koch et al. 1997). Unfortunately, there is no generally accepted method of assessing diagenesis in fossil tooth enamel (although see Shemesh 1990). In East Africa some 3.9-million-year-old tooth enamels were extensively altered mineralogically, whereas others, from the same excavation site, were not (Kohn et al. 1999). Altered enamels have values more similar to sediment values than do unaltered enamels; and, because the sediments have high $\delta^{13}C$ values, the result of diagenesis is to inflate the apparent dietary dependence of hominins on foods (animal or plant) that have C_4 values (Schoeninger et al. 2003). In South Africa diagenetic alteration of 1‰ to 2‰ occurs (Lee-Thorp 2000), which would overemphasize the dietary dependence on foods like grasses, sedges, and open-country fauna (insect and vertebrate). Both the East African *Homo habilis* and *Paranthropus boisei* (van der Merwe et al. 2008) and the South African *Australopithecus africanus* and *Paranthropus robustus* (Sponheimer et al. 2005) foraged in open country or in drought-type habitats rather than in closed canopy situations and some individuals (especially *Paranthropus*) apparently ate foods with a C_4 signal. The identity of these foods and the level of dependence on foods with C_4 values are still the subject of much deliberation and discussion.

NITROGEN ISOTOPE RATIOS: $^{15}N/^{14}N$ REPRESENTED AS $\delta^{15}N$

The major nitrogen reservoir is the atmosphere, and the $\delta^{15}N$ of well mixed atmosphere is defined at 0.0‰. The transfer of inorganic nitrogen (N_2 gas) into the biological realm depends on specialized organisms such that those found in nodules on the roots of leguminous plants (called nitrogen-fixing plants), which can have values close to zero (Spielmann et al. 1990; Coltrain and Stafford 2002), although this is not always the case (Schoeninger 1995). Most plants, however, take up soil nitrogen, which is more positive than atmospheric nitrogen; thus most plants have values higher than 0‰ (Virginia and Delwiche 1982 and see Figure 25.1). Marine organisms tend to have more positive $\delta^{15}N$ values than do terrestrial organisms, except in regions like coral reefs, where nitrogen-fixing blue–green algae comprise the base of the food chain (Schoeninger and DeNiro 1984). The higher marine values result from bacterial activity and from the greater length of trophic chains in the ocean than in terrestrial environments (Figure 25.1).

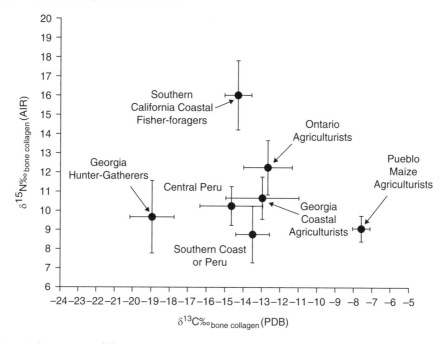

Figure 25.3 Typical $\delta^{13}C$ values and $\delta^{15}N$ values in bone collagen from several archaeological human groups from North and South America. The Georgia hunter–gatherers ate only plants and animals from their woodland (C_3) environment, whereas the Pueblo maize agriculturists ate only maize (C_4) and animals who fed on C_4 plants. Their $\delta^{15}N$ values are virtually identical, indicating similar intakes of animal foods. The Central and southern coastal Peruvian populations included maize; but apparently they ate little marine foods. In contrast, the higher $\delta^{15}N$ values in the Ontario agriculturists show the influence of eating anadromous fish (fish dwelling in the ocean for a part of their lives). The Georgia coastal agriculturists grew some maize and ate marine foods of lower trophic position (mollusks and near-shore fish). In contrast, the southern California fisher–foragers show a strong marine signal, both in $\delta^{15}N$ and in $\delta^{13}C$ values. These people ate marine foods from high trophic levels such as dolphins, seals, and tuna. In the coastal populations, where maize was part of the diet, the $\delta^{15}N$ values identify the level of dependence on marine foods, as well as the types of marine foods eaten. Redrawn from Kellner and Schoeninger 2008

The $\delta^{15}N$ values in the tissues of animals are positively correlated with the values in their diets (DeNiro and Epstein 1981b; Hare et al. 1991). The source of the nitrogen in bone collagen is largely ingested, a minimal amount being recycled from one's own body (Ambrose 2000). There is a consistent increase of 3.5‰ in $\delta^{15}N$ values between trophic levels (Schoeninger and DeNiro 1984; Minagawa and Wada 1984; Ambrose 2000); and human omnivory has been estimated in broad relative terms in some regions (Ambrose et al. 2003) and in more specific terms in other regions, where plants are unavailable for much of the year (Richards et al. 2000). Humans who eat marine foods show higher $\delta^{15}N$ than those who do not, when the populations sampled are from similar regions (Sealy and van der Merwe 1986; see Figure 25.3). Exceptions to this general rule occur in desert areas, where water or caloric stress affects metabolism (Ambrose and DeNiro 1986; Heaton et al. 1986; Sealy et al. 1987), and in warm-water reefs or other areas with shallow coastal margins, where blue–green algae fix atmospheric nitrogen directly (Keegan and DeNiro 1988; Wallace et al. 2006; compare coastal Georgia with coastal southern California in Figure 25.3).

The combination of $\delta^{13}C_{collagen}$ and $\delta^{15}N_{collagen}$ has proven especially productive for investigating agricultural origins and spread in the southeastern US, where the consumption of marine foods can confound interpretations of $\delta^{13}C_{collagen}$ or $\delta^{13}C_{apatite}$ (Schoeninger et al. 1990). Prior to the introduction of maize, people in this region depended on local C_3 plants and fauna (Tucker 2002), and on marine foods available along the coast (Schoeninger et al. 1990). Around AD 1000, maize horticulture became available across a wide portion of the southeast, although the actual dependence on maize varied significantly from region to region (Hutchinson 2004; Larsen et al. 2007). This situation contrasts with the Neolithic transition in coastal areas of Europe, where populations apparently abandoned fishing when they undertook an agricultural way of life (Richards et al. 2003). The stable isotope data from Georgia indicate that maize became a major item of diet only after contact with Spanish colonizers in the late sixteenth century (Schoeninger 2009a).

Adding $\delta^{15}N_{collagen}$ values to the comparison of $\delta^{13}C_{collagen}$ and $\delta^{13}C_{apatite}$ values shown in Figure 25.2 clarifies specific aspects of several populations' diet (Froehle et al. 2009). Among C_3-based foragers, those from Ontario had an average $\delta^{15}N_{collagen}$ value of 12.2 +/– 1.0‰ compared to 9.5 +/– 2.1‰ in those from Georgia, demonstrating the importance of fish in the former group (Katzenberg 1989). Among coastal foragers, those from Tierra del Fuego (14.8 +/– 3.2‰, range = 10.6–18.8‰) had lower values than the California islanders (17.8 +/– 1.4‰, range = 14.9–20.8‰); and the former showed a bi-model distribution that is non-overlapping (10.6–13.2‰ vs 15.1–18.8‰) when plotted by region. Clearly some populations in Tierra del Fuego ate less marine foods than others – and they ate marine foods of lower trophic levels (such as mollusks or herbivorous fish) than did the California islanders.

HYDROGEN ISOTOPE RATIOS: D/H REPRESENTED AS δ^2H OR δD

Hydrogen is ubiquitous in the geosphere, and the huge relative mass difference between its two stable isotopes (^2H or D and ^1H) means that hydrogen exhibits the largest fractionations among the light stable isotopes. Equilibrium isotope fractionations during the transfer of water from the ocean to the atmosphere and during precipitation produce patterned differences between the δ^2H values in rainwater and in surface water, versus the values in the plants and animals that rely on rainwater and surface water (White 1989; Ziegler 1989). Over twenty years ago, δ^2H was suggested as a tracer in food web studies (Estep and Dabrowski 1980); but this method was seldom used (although see Cormie et al. 1994b), because of difficulties in controlling for the exchangeable hydrogen atoms within organic material (Bowen et al. 2005) and accounting for the multiple sources of hydrogen in tissues (DeNiro and Epstein 1981a). Recently, however, several laboratories demonstrated the effectiveness of δ^2H values in various tissues for identifying trophic position in food web studies (Birchall et al. 2005), animal migration patterns (Hobson and Wassenaar 1997; Hobson et al. 2004), paleoclimate (Leyden et al. 2006), and human paleodiet (Reynard and Hedges 2008). While still somewhat experimental (Wassenaar and Hobson 2002), δ^2H values show great promise in forensic cases (Bowen et al. 2009) as well as in other applications. For instance CAM plants show diagnostic δ^2H values compared to other plants, which might prove useful in identifying CAM plants as a dietary item in regions where eating maize would confound interpretation of the $\delta^{13}C$ values (Sternberg 1989; Ziegler 1989).

OXYGEN ISOTOPE RATIOS: $^{18}O/^{16}O$ REPRESENTED AS $\delta^{18}O$

Oxygen has three stable isotopes (^{18}O, ^{17}O, and ^{16}O); but $^{18}O/^{16}O$ is usually measured because it affords the greater relative mass difference. The water cycle of evaporation and condensation produces the general global patterns of $\delta^{18}O$ in waters (Craig 1961; Gat 1980; Gat and Gonfiantini 1981) and in animal tissues (Longinelli 1984). Nevertheless, variables such as the temperature of precipitation (summer versus winter, altitudinal and latitudinal variation), the rainfall amount (El Niño vs La Niña), air-circulation patterns, distance from the ocean, and others also affect the $\delta^{18}O$ in waters and must be considered in local situations.

The $\delta^{18}O$ values of phosphate and carbonate in animal bone and tooth enamel show a general correlation with local precipitation (Koch et al. 1989, 1996), although physiological parameters vary across animal species in ways that can differentially affect animal $\delta^{18}O$ values (Bryant and Froelich 1995; Fricke and O'Neil 1996). Animals who obtain most of their body water by drinking surface water have $\delta^{18}O$ values in their bone mineral and tooth enamel that correlate with rainfall $\delta^{18}O$ values (Huertas et al. 1995). In contrast, those who obtain most of their body water from their diets vary in association with local relative humidity (Ayliffe and Chivas 1990; Cormie et al. 1994a). Seasonal variation in rainfall is recorded by intratooth variation in $\delta^{18}O$ values (Fricke et al. 1998; Balasse 2002), proving useful in the reconstruction of aspects of behavior within pastoral populations (Balasse et al. 2003) or of paleoclimatic variables such as temperature, rainfall, and humidity (Bryant et al. 1994; Fricke et al. 1995 – and see Bryant 1996; Schoeninger et al. 2000). More recently, the $\delta^{18}O$ values of tooth enamel have been compared with the value found in bone mineral in order to determine migration patterns in prehistoric human populations, particularly in Mesoamerica and South America (White et al. 2004; Knudson and Buikstra 2007; Knudson and Price 2007). Since tooth enamel is formed in infancy and early childhood, while bone in the adult body records the last several years of life, differences between the two should indicate migration from the place of birth to a new region.

STRONTIUM ISOTOPE RATIOS: $^{87}Sr/^{86}Sr$

The distribution of stable isotope ratios of strontium differs from that of the familiar strontium concentration in biological systems. Elemental concentration functions as a trophic level indicator (Schoeninger 1989; Sillen and Lee-Thorp 1994); but, because there is no measurable fractionation during transfer between the geosphere and the biosphere, the $^{87}Sr/^{86}Sr$ ratio in animal bones and teeth reflects an averaging of the $^{87}Sr/^{86}Sr$ ratios in the animal's diet and drinking water (Faure and Powell 1972; Ericson 1985, 1989). Very old rocks contain significantly more ^{87}Sr than rocks of recent origin, because ^{87}Sr is a long-term decay product of the radioactive isotope ^{87}Rb. This means that, in regions where there are distinctive ^{87}Sr/^{86}Sr ratios, it is possible to identify the area of origin. When there is no diagenetic alteration of the original bio-logical level of strontium (Nelson et al. 1986; Hoppe et al. 2003), intra-tooth varia-tion in ^{87}Sr/^{86}Sr ratios or the difference between tooth enamel and bone ^{87}Sr/^{86}Sr ratios can identify migratory behavior in animals (Hoppe et al. 1999), including humans.

The application of ^{87}Sr/^{86}Sr ratios for understanding human behavior has been used across a large number of regions. The approach clarified the origin of a highly ranked individual from Tikal in Mesoamerica (Wright 2005); suggested migratory behavior in archaeological and fossil populations in South Africa (Sealy et al. 1991; Sillen et al. 1998), central Europe (Price et al. 1994a), Briton areas (Montgomery et al. 2003), and southwestern US (Price et al. 1994b); and revealed possible marriage patterns in South America (Ericson 1985). The most detailed study, however, concerns South America, where Knudson and colleagues have addressed patterns of population and individual movements across the Peruvian highlands (Knudson et al. 2004; Knudson et al. 2005; Knudson and Buikstra 2007; Knudson and Price 2007).

CONCLUSIONS

Thirty years ago no one could have predicted the astounding range of applications of stable isotope data within anthropology; and it is not possible at this point to predict all of its possible applications in the future. A few areas seem particularly promising. First, the development of new technical methods is astounding; such methods include residue analyses (Mukherjee et al. 2008), specific amino acid anal-yses (Corr et al. 2009), and continued development of δ^2H (δD) in climate studies (Kirsanow et al. 2008).

In addition, there are several large, overarching projects which investigate human biological and social change through time and where stable isotope analysis plays one of several interrelated parts. For example, the 'global history of health' project (co-directed by Clark Larsen, Paul Steckel, and Paul Sciulli) compares estimates of ancient human health with human diet (see Steckel et al. 2002 for a preliminary report), in order to provide the first rigorous evaluation of the impact of human subsistence strategies on health. In the Andean highland and lowland regions of South America, several projects are beginning to clarify how the emergence of two powerful states (Wari and Tiwanaku) combined with environmental change to impact on specific local communities. Stable isotope analyses are central to delineating the climate change (Magilligan et al. 2008), to identifying migrants (Buzon et al. 2007; Knudson and Torres-Rouff 2009), and to elucidating the effect of imperial powers on subsist-ence strategies, health, and social structure in peripheral communities (Kellner and Schoeninger 2008). The interactions between colonial powers and their associated communities clearly differed across the Andean region, and also between it as a whole and North America (Larsen 2001; Hutchinson 2004).

Climate reconstruction, both on the archaeological and on the paleontological scale, is another exciting area in its own right, given the practical importance of understanding climate change for today's world. Archaeological samples hold the promise of understanding the specifics of climate change and its impact on actual human populations in the past, which should be useful in our present-day preparations and expectations. Physical and paleo-oceanographers, atmospheric chemists and geochemists might clarify the variables and processes that cause climate change; but they lack the human scale that bioarchaeology and paleoanthropology provide. The Andean projects mentioned above are one example (Magilligan et al. 2008). Another (among many) comprises paleoecology and paleoclimate reconstruction across Africa and Eurasia during the time when the human lineage separated from ape-like ancestors, radiated, and then resulted in the single lineage we see today. In Africa, the painstaking work of John Kingston and colleagues (Kingston 2007; Kingston and Harrison 2007; Kingston et al. 2007) includes carbonate nodule and tooth enamel analyses, mapping of modern environmental signatures, and consideration of orbital parameters to provide a background for understanding Plio-Pleistocene hominin evolution in East Africa. Expanding these kinds of study to other geographical regions, or placing fossils from multiple time periods in a context was not anticipated before the present developments within stable isotope analysis (for examples, see Lee-Thorp and Sponheimer 2006; Hartman 2008; Hallin et al. n.d.).

Finally, primate behavioral ecology is also benefiting from stable isotope studies. Stable isotope data in various samples, including feces (Codron et al. 2006) and hair, as discussed earlier, combined with observations on diet and behavioral data from long-term field projects (for instance Phillips-Conroy in the Awash National Park in Ethiopia), will establish the accuracy with which diet can be predicted from the samples. Once the predictive power is established, stable isotope analysis of fossils (for which see Codron et al. 2005, 2006), of museum collections, and of primate populations which cannot be observed directly (for instance because they are nocturnal or unabituated to humans) will expand our knowledge of diet and ecology in all these groups.

The list could go on and on; but, with apologies to those projects that space prevented my mentioning, this chapter must end. The work, however, will not. Stable isotope data are such powerful proxy measures of multiple variables that it is now almost impossible for a single person to keep up with the literature on this subject. Perhaps that is the highest complement that one can give to the two authors who started us all on this fascinating path with their presentation to the Annual Meeting of the Society for American Archaeology those many years ago: Vogel and van der Merwe (1976). I hope they both find satisfaction in observing the vast literature that now exists.

ACKNOWLEDGMENTS

I greatly appreciate the invitation, made to me by Clark Larsen, to contribute this chapter. I am especially grateful to my collaborators over the years, most notably to Matt Kohn (Boise State) and to John Valley (U. WI); to Corina Kellner (NAU), Clark Larsen (OSU), Jim Moore (UCSD), Christopher Peebles (IU), and Katherine Spielmann (ASU), who provided me with opportunities to delve into the prehistory of several geographic regions and periods of time. Finally, I wish to thank the National Science Foundation, Wenner Gren, Sigma Xi, and the Leakey Foundation, which supported much of the research reported here.

REFERENCES

Ambrose, S. H. (2000) Controlled Diet and Climate Experiments on Nitrogen Isotope Ratios of Rats. In S. H. Ambrose and M. A. Katzenberg (eds), *Biogeochemical Approaches to Paleodietary Analysis* (pp. 243–259). New York: Kluwer Academic/Plenum Publishers.

Ambrose S. H., and DeNiro, M. J. (1986) The Isotopic Ecology of East African Mammals. *Oecologia* 69: 395–406.

Ambrose S. H., and Norr, L. (1993) Experimental Evidence for the Relationship of the Carbon Stable Isotope Ratios of Whole Diet and Dietary Protein to Those of Bone Collagen and Carbonate. In J. B. Lambert and G. Grupe (eds), *Prehistoric Human Bone: Archaeology at the Molecular Level* (pp. 1–38). Berlin: Springer-Verlag.

Ambrose, S. H., Buikstra, J. E., and Krueger, H. W. (2003) Gender and Status Differences in Diet at Mound 72, Cahokia, Revealed by Isotopic Analysis of Bone. *Journal of Anthropological Archaeology* 22 (3): 217–226.

Ayliffe, L. K., and Chivas, A. R. (1990) Oxygen Isotope Composition of the Bone Phosphate of Australian Kangaroos: Potential as a Palaeoenvironmental Recorder. *Geochimica et Cosmochimica Acta* 54: 2603–2609.

Balasse, M. (2002) Reconstructing Dietary and Environmental History from Enamel Isotopic Analysis: Time Resolution of Intra-Tooth Sequential Sampling. *International Journal of Osteoarchaeology* 12: 155–165.

Balasse, M., Smith, A., Ambrose, S. H., and Leigh, S. R. (2003) Determining Sheep Birth Seasonality by Analysis of Tooth Enamel Oxygen Isotope Ratios: The Late Stone Age Site of Kasteelberg (South Africa). *Journal of Archaeological Science* 30: 205–215.

Birchall J., O'Connell, T. C., Heaton, T. H. E., and Hedges, R. E. M. (2005) Hydrogen Isotope Ratios in Animal Body Protein Reflect Trophic Level. *Journal of Animal Ecology* 74: 877–881.

Boucherens, H. (2009) Neanderthal Dietary Habits: Review of the Isotopic Evidence. In J.-J. Hublin and M. P. Richards (eds), *The Evolution of Hominin Diets: Integrating Approaches to the Study of Palaeolithic Subsistence*. Vertebrate Paleobiology and Paleoanthropology Series (pp. 241–251). New York: Springer.

Bowen, G. J., Chesson, L., Nielson, K., Cerling, T. E., and Ehleringer, J. R. (2005) Treatment Methods for the Determination of δ^2H and $\delta^{18}O$ of Hair Keratin by Continuous-Flow Isotope-Ratio Mass Spectrometry. *Rapid Communications in Mass Spectrometry* 19: 2371–2378.

Bowen, G. J., Ehleringer, J. R., Chesson, L., Thompson, A. H., Podlesak, D. W., and Cerling, T. E. (2009) Dietary and Physiological Controls on the Hydrogen and Oxygen Isotope Ratios of Hair from Mid-20th Century Indigenous Populations. *American Journal of Physical Anthropology* 139: 494–504.

Bowling, D. R., Pataki, D. E., and Ehleringer, J. R. (2003) Ecosystem Isotope Exchange and Whole-Canopy Discrimination in *Medicago Sativa*. *Agricultural and Forest Meteorology* 116: 159–179.

Broadmeadow, M. S. J., Griffiths, H., Maxwell, C., and Borland, A. M. (1992) The Carbon Isotope Ratio of Plant Organic Material Reflects Temporal and Spatial Variations in CO_2 within Tropical Forest Formations in Trinidad. *Oecologia* 89: 435–441.

Bryant, D. J. (1996) Oxygen Isotope Composition of Human Tooth Enamel from Medieval Greenland: Linking Climate and Society: Comment and Reply. *Geology*: 477–479.

Bryant, J. D., and Froelich, P. N. (1995) A Model of Oxygen Isotope Fractionation in Body Water of Large Mammals. *Geochimica et Cosmochimica Acta* 59: 4523–4537.

Bryant, J. D., Luz, B., and Froelich, P. N. (1994) Oxygen Isotopic Composition of Fossil Horse Tooth Phosphate as a Record of Continental Paleoclimate. *Palaeogeography, Palaeoclimatology, Palaeoecology* 107: 210–212.

Bump, J. K., Fox-Dobbs, K., Bada, J. L., Koch, P. L., Peterson, R. O., and Vucetich, J.A. (2007) Stable Isotopes, Ecological Integration and Environmental Change: Wolves Record Atmostpheric Carbon Isotope Trend Better Than Tree Rings. *Proceedings of the Royal Society B* 274 (1624): 2471–2480.

Buzon, M. R., Conlee, C. A., Simonetti, A., and Creaser, R. A. (2007) $^{87}Sr/^{86}Sr$ Isotope Analysis of Human Remains from the Site of La Tiza, Peru. *Abstracts of the Annual Meetings of the Society for American Archaeology.* 10.

Cerling, T. E. (1979) Paleochemistry of Plio-Pleistocene Lake Turkana, Kenya. *Palaeogeography, Palaeoclimatology, Palaeoecology* 27: 247–285.

Cerling, T. E., Bowman, J. R., and O'Neil, J. R. (1988) An Isotopic Study of a Fluvial–Lacustrine Sequence: The Plio-Pleistocene Koobi-Fora Sequence, East Africa. *Palaeogeography, Palaeoclimatology, Palaeoecology* 63: 335–356.

Cerling, T. E., Harris, J., and Passey, B. (2003) Diets of East African Bovidae Based on Stable Isotope Analyses. *Journal of Mammalogy* 84 (2): 456–470.

Codron, D., Lee-Thorp, J. A., Sponheimer, M., de Ruiter, D., and Codron, J. (2006) Inter- and Intrahabitat Dietary Variability of Chacma Baboons (*Papio ursinus*) in South African Savannas Based on Fecal δ13C, δ15N, and %N. *American Journal of Physical Anthropology* 129 (2): 204–214.

Codron, D., Lee-Thorp, J. A., Sponheimer, M., de Ruiter, D., and Codron, J. (2008) What Insights Can Baboon Feeding Ecology Provide for Early Hominin Niche Differentiation? *International Journal of Primatology* 29 (3): 757–772.

Codron, D., Luyt, J., Lee-Thorp, J., Sponheimer, M., de Ruiter, D., and Codron, J. (2005) Utilization of Savanna-Based Resources By Plio-Pleistocene Baboons. *South African Journal of Science* 101: 245–248.

Coltrain, J. B., and Stafford, T. W. J. (2002) Climate and Diet in Fremont Prehistory: Economic Variability and Abandonment of Maize Agriculture in the Great Salt Lake Basin. *American Antiquity* 67 (3): 453–485.

Cormie, A. B., Luz, B., and Schwarcz, H. P. (1994a) Relationship between the Hydrogen and Oxygen Isotopes of Deer Bone and Their Use in the Estimation of Relative Humidity. *Geochimica et Cosmochimica Acta* 58 (16): 3439–3449.

Cormie, A. B., Schwarcz, H. P., and Gray, J. (1994b) Relation between Hydrogen Isotopic Ratios of Bone Collagen and Rain. *Geochimica et Cosmochimica Acta* 58 (1): 377–391.

Corr, L. T., Richards, M. R., Grier, C., Mackie, A., Beattie, O., and Evershed, R. P. (2009) Probing Dietary Change of the Kwäday Dän Ts'ìnchi Individual, an Ancient Glacier Body from British Columbia: II. Deconvoluting Whole Skin and Bone Collagen $\Delta^{13}c$ Values via Carbon Isotope Analysis of Individual Amino Acids. *Journal of Archaeological Science* 36 (1): 12–18.

Craig, H., (1961) Isotopic Variations in Meteoric Waters. *Science* 133: 1702–1703.

DeNiro, M. J., and Epstein, S. (1978) Influence of Diet on Distribution of Carbon Isotopes in Animals. *Geochimica et Cosmochimica Acta* 42 (5): 495–506.

DeNiro, M. J., and Epstein, S. (1981a) Hydrogen Isotope Ratios of Mouse Tissues Are Influenced by a Variety of Factors Other Than Diet. *Science* 214: 1374–1375.

DeNiro, M. J., and Epstein, S. (1981b) Influence of Diet on the Distribution of Nitrogen Isotopes in Animals. *Geochimica et Cosmochimica Acta* 45: 341–351.

Ehleringer, J. R., Bowen, G. J., Chesson, L.. A., West, J. G., Podlesak, D. W., and Cerling, T. E. (2008) Hydrogen and Oxygen Isotope Ratios in Human Hair Are Related to Geography. *Proceedings of the National Academy of Sciences, USA* 105 (8): 2788–2793.

Ericson, J. E. (1985) Strontium Isotope Characterization in the Study of Prehistoric Human Ecology. *Journal of Human Evolution* 14: 503–514.

Ericson, J. E. (1989) Some Problems and Potentials of Strontium Isotope Analysis for Human and Animal Ecology. In P. W. Rundel, J. R. Ehleringer, and K. A. Nagy (eds), *Stable Isotopes in Ecological Research* (pp. 251–259). New York: Springer-Verlag.

Estep, M. F., and Dabrowski, H. (1980) Tracing Food Webs with Stable Hydrogen Isotopes. *Science* 209: 1537–1538.

Faure, G., and Powell, J. L. 1972. *Strontium Isotope Geology*. New York: Springer-Verlag.

Fricke, H. C., and O'Neil, J. R. (1996) Inter- and Intra-Tooth Variation in the Oxygen Isotope Composition of Mammalian Tooth Enamel: Some Implications for Paleoclimatological and Paleobiological Research. *Palaeogeography, Palaeoclimatology, Palaeoecology* 126: 91–99.

Fricke, H. C., Clyde, W. C., and O'Neal, J. R. (1998) Intra-Tooth Variations in Δ^{18}o (PO_4) of Mammalian Tooth Enamel as a Record of Seasonal Variations in Continental Climate Variables. *Geochimica et Cosmochimica Acta* 62 (11): 1839–1850.

Fricke, H. C., O'Neil, J. R., and Lynnerup, N. (1995) Oxygen Isotope Composition of Human Tooth Enamel from Medieval Greenland: Linking Climate and Society. *Geology* 23 (10): 869–872.

Friedli, H., Lotscher, H., Oeschger, H., Siegenthaler, U., and Stauffer, B. (1986) Ice Core Record of the 13C/12C Ratio of Atmospheric CO2 in the Past Two Centuries. *Nature* 324: 237–238.

Froehle, A. W., Kellner, C. M., and Schoeninger, M. J. (2009) A Three-Variable Analysis of Carbon and Nitrogen Isotope Values Discriminates between Dietary Energy and Protein Sources in Prehistoric Humans. *American Journal of Physical Anthropology* 138 (S48): 130.

Fry, B. (2006) *Stable Isotope Ecology*. New York: Springer.

Gat, J. R. (1980) The Isotopes of Hydrogen and Oxygen in Precipitation. In P. Fritz and J. Fontes (eds), *Handbook of Environmental Isotope Geochemistry* (pp. 21–47). Amsterdam: Elseview.

Gat, J. R., and Gonfiantini, R. (eds) (1981) Stable Isotope Hydrology: Deuterium and Oxygen-18 in the Water Cycle. International Atomic Energy Agency, Vienna Technical Reports.

Hallin, K. A., Schoeninger, M. J., and Schwarcz, H. P. (n.d.) Paleoclimate during Neandertal and Early Modern Human Occupation at Amud and Qafzeh, Israel: The Stable Isotope Data. *Journal of Human Evolution*, in review.

Hare, P. E., Fogel, M. L., Stafford, T. W., Jr, Mitchell, A. D., and Hoering, T. C. (1991) The Isotopic Composition of Carbon and Nitrogen in Individual Amino Acids Isolated from Modern and Fossil Proteins. *Journal of Archaeological Science* 18 (3): 277–292.

Harrison, R. G., and Katzenberg, M. A. (2003) Paleodiet Studies Using Stable Carbon Isotopes from Bone Apatite and Collagen: Examples from Southern Ontario and San Nicolas Island, California. *Journal of Anthropological Archaeology* 22: 227–244.

Hartman, G. (2008) *The Environmental Origins of Plants and Herbivores in the Southern Levant: An Isotopic Approach*. Cambridge MA: Harvard University.

Heaton, T. H. E. (1999) Spatial, Species, and Temporal Variations in the 13C/12C Ratios of C3 Plants: Implications for Palaeodiet Studies. *Journal of Archaeological Science* 26: 637–649.

Heaton, T. H. E., Vogel, J. C., von la Chevallerie, G., and Gollett, G. (1986) Climatic Influence on the Isotopic Composition of Bone Nitrogen. *Nature* 322: 822–823.

Hobson, K. A., and Wassenaar, L. I. (1997) Linking breeding and Wintering Grounds of Neotropical Migrant Songbirds Using Stable Hydrogen Isotopic Analysis of Feathers. *Oecologia* 109: 142–148.

Hobson, K. A., Bowen, G. J., Wassenaar, L. I., Ferrand, Y., and Lormee, H. (2004) Using Stable Hydrogen and Oxygen Isotope Measurements of Feathers to Infer Geographical Origins of Migrating European Birds. *Oecologia* 141: 477–488.

Hoefs, J. (1997) *Stable Isotope Geochemistry*. New York: Springer-Verlag.

Hoppe, K. A, Koch, P. L., and Furutani, T. T. (2003) Assessing the Preservation of Biogenic Strontium in Fossil Bones and Tooth Enamel. *International Journal of Osteoarchaeology* 13: 20–28.

Hoppe, K. A., Koch, P. L., Carlson, R. W., and Webb, S. D. (1999) Tracking Mammoths and Mastodons: Reconstruction of Migratory Behavior Using Strontium Isotope Ratios. *Geology* 27 (5): 439–442.

Howland, M. R., Corr, L. T., Young, S. M., Jones, V., Jim, S., van der Merwe, N. J., Mitchell, A. D., and Evershed, R. P. (2003) Expression of the Dietary Isotope Signal in the Compound-Specific Δ¹³C Values of Pig Bone Lipids and Amino Acids. *International Journal of Osteoarchaeology* 13 (1–2): 54–65.

Huertas, A. D., Iacumin, P., Stenni, B., Chillon, B. S., and Longinell, A. (1995) Oxygen Isotope Variations of Phosphate in Mammalian Bone and Tooth Enamel. *Geochimica et Cosmochimica Acta* 59 (20): 4299–4305.

Hutchinson, D. L. (2004) *Bioarchaeology of the Florida Gulf Coast: Adaptation, Conflict, and Change*. Gainesville: University Press of Florida.

Jim, S., Ambrose, S. H., and Evershed, R. P. (2004) Stable Carbon Isotopic Evidence for Differences in the Dietary Origin of Bone Cholesterol, Collagen, and Apatite: Implications for Their Use in Paleodietary Reconstruction. *Geochimica et Cosmochimica Acta* 68 (1): 61–72.

Katzenberg, M. A. (1989) Stable Isotope Analysis of Archaeological Faunal Remains from Southern Ontario. *Journal of Archaeological Science* 16: 319–329.

Keegan, W. F., and DeNiro, M. J. (1988) Stable Carbon- and Nitrogen-Isotope Ratios of Bone Collagen Used to Study Coral-Reef and Terrestrial Components of Prehistoric Bahamian Diet. *American Antiquity* 53 (2): 320–336.

Kellner, C. M., and Schoeninger, M. J. (2007) A Simple Carbon Isotope Model for Reconstructing Human Diet. *American Journal of Physical Anthropology* 133 (4): 1112–1127.

Kellner, C. M., and Schoeninger, M. J. (2008) Wari's Imperial Influence on Local Nasca Diet: The Stable Isotope Evidence. *Journal of Anthropological Archaeology* 27: 226–243.

Kingston, J. D. (2007) Shifting Adaptive Landscapes: Progress and Challenges in Reconstructing Early Hominid Enviornments. *American Journal of Physical Anthropology* 134 (S45): 20–58.

Kingston, J. D., and Harrison, T. (2007) Isotopic Dietary Reconstructions of Pliocene Herbivores at Laetoli: Implications for Early Hominin Evolution. *Palaeogeography, Palaeoclimatology, Palaeoecology* 243: 272–306.

Kingston, J. D., Marino, B. D., and Hill, A. (1994) Isotopic Evidence for Neogene Hominid Paleoenvironments in the Kenya Rift Valley. *Science* 264: 955–959.

Kingston, J. D., Deino, A., Hill, A., and Edgar, R. (2007) Astronomically Forced Climate Change in the Kenyan Rift Valley 2.7–2.55 Ma: Implications for the Evolution of Early Hominin Ecosystems. *Journal of Human Evolution* 53 (5): 487–503.

Kirsanow, K., Makarewicz, C., and Tuross, N. (2008) Stable Oxygen (δ¹⁸O) and Hydrogen (δD) Isotopes in Ovicaprid Dentinal Collagen Record Seasonal Variation. *Journal of Archaeological Science* 35: 3159–3167.

Knudson, K. J., and Buikstra, J. (2007) Residential Mobility and Resource Use in the Chiribaya Polity of Southern Peru: Strontium Isotope Analysis of Archaeological Tooth Enamel and Bone. *International Journal of Osteoarchaeology* 17: 563–580.

Knudson, K. J., and Price, T. D. (2007) Utility of Multiple Chemical Techniques in Archaeological Residential Mobility Studies: Case Studies from Tiwanaku- and Chiribaya-Afficiated Sites in the Andes. *American Journal of Physical Anthropology* 132: 25–39.

Knudson, K. J., and Torres-Rouff, C. (2009) Investigating Cultural Heterogeneity and Multiethnicity in San Pedro de Atacama, Northern Chile through Biogeochemistry and Bioarchaeology. *American Journal of Physical Anthropology* 138: 473–485.

Knudson, K. J., Price, T. D., Buikstra, J., and Blom, D. E. (2004) The Use of Strontium Isotope Analysis to Investigate Tiwanaku Migration and Mortuary Ritual in Bolivia and Peru. *Archaeometry* 46: 5–18.

Knudson, K. J., Tung, T., Nystrom K. C., Price, T. D., and Fullagar, P. D. (2005) The Origin of the Juch'uypampa Cave Mummies: Strontium Isotope Analysis of Archaeological Human Remains from Bolivia. *Journal of Archaeological Science* 32: 903–913.

Koch, P. L., Fisher, D. C., and Dettman, D. (1989) Oxygen Isotope Variation in the Tusks of Extinct Proboscideans: A Measure of Season of Death. *Geology* 17: 515–519.

Koch, P. L., Tuross, N., and Fogel, M. L. (1997) The Effects of Sample Treatment and Diagenesis on the Isotopic Integrity of Carbonate in Biogenic Hydroxylapatite. *Journal of Archaeological Science* 24: 417–429.

Kohn, M. J., Schoeninger, M. J., and Barker, W. W. (1999) Altered States: Effects of Diagenesis on Fossil Tooth Chemistry. *Geochimica et Cosmochimica Acta* 63 (18): 2737–2747.

Kohn, M. J., Schoeninger, M. J., and Valley, J. W. (1996) Herbivore Tooth Oxygen Isotope Compositions: Effects of Diet and Physiology. *Geochemica et Cosmochemica Acta* 60 (20): 3889–3896.

Krigbaum, J. (2003) Neolithic Subsistence Patterns in Northern Borneo Reconstructed with Stable Carbon Isotopes of Enamel. *Journal of Anthropolgical Archaeology* 22: 292–304.

Krueger, H. W., and Sullivan, C. H. (1984) Models for Carbon Isotope Fractionation between Diet and Bone. In J. R. Turnlund and P. E. Johnson (eds), *Stable Isotopes in Nutrition* (pp. 205–220). Washington DC: American Chemical Society Symposium Series.

Larsen, C. S. (ed.) (2001) *Bioarchaeology of Spanish Florida: The Impact of Colonialism*. Gainesville: University Press of Florida.

Larsen, C. S., Hutchinson, D. L., Stojanowski, C. M., Williamson, M. A., Griffin, M. C., Simpson, S. W., Ruff, C. B., Schoeninger, M. J., Norr, L., Teaford, M., Driscoll, E. L., Schmidt, C. W., and Tung, T. A. (2007) Heath and Lifestyle in Georgia and Florida: Agricultural Origins and Intensification in Regional Perspective. In M. N. Cohen and G. M. M. Crane-Kramer (eds), *Ancient Health: Skeletal Indicators of Agricultural and Economic Intensitifaction* (pp. 14–27). Gainesville: University Press of Florida.

Lee-Thorp, J. A. (2000) Preservation of Biogenic Carbon Isotopic Signals in Plio-Pleistocene Bone and Tooth Mineral. In S. H. Ambrose and M. A. Katzenberg (eds), *Biogeochemical Approaches to Paleodietary Analysis* (pp. 89–115). New York: Kluwer Academic/Plenum Publishers.

Lee-Thorp, J. A., and Sponheimer, M. (2006) Contributions of Biogeochemistry to Understanding Homin Dietary Ecology. *Yearbook of Physical Anthropology* 13 (S43): 131–148.

Leyden, J. J., Wassenaar, L. I., Hobson, K. A., and Walker, E. G. (2006) Stable Hydrogen Isotopes of Bison Bone Collagen as a Proxy for Holocene Climate on the Northern Great Plains. *Palaeogeography, Palaeoclimatology, Palaeoecology* 239 (1): 87–89.

Longinelli, A. (1984) Oxygen Isotopes in Mammal Bone Phosphate: A New Tool for Paleohydrological and Paleoclimatological Research? *Geochimica et Cosmochimica Acta* 48: 385–390.

Loudon, J. E., Sponheimer, M., Sauther, M. L., and Cuozzo, F. P. (2007) Intraspecific Variation In Hair Delta C-13 and Delta N-15 Values of Ring-Tailed Lemurs (*Lemur Catta*) with Known Individual Histories, Behavior, and Feeding Ecology. *American Journal of Physical Anthropology* 133 (3): 978–985.

Magilligan, F. J., Goldstein, P. S., Fisher, G. B., Bostick, B. C., and Manners, R. B. (2008) Late Quaternary Hydroclimatology of a Hyper-Arid Andean Watershed: Climate Change, Floods, and Hydrologic Responses to the El Niño-Southern Oscillation in the Atacama Desert. *Geomorphology* 101: 14–32.

McGee, E. M., and Vaughn, S. E. (2003) Variations in Stable Isotope Composition of *Propithecus Diadema Edwardsi* from Disturbed and Undisturbed Rainforest Habitats in Ranomafana National Park, Madagascar. *American Journal of Physical Anthropology* 120 (S36): 149.

Michener, R., and Lajtha, K. (eds) (2007) *Stable Isotopes in Ecology and Environmental Science*, 2nd edn. Oxford: Blackwell Publishing.

Minagawa, M., and Wada, E. (1984) Stepwise Enrichment of ^{15}N along Food Chains: Further Evidence and the Relation between d^{15}N and Animal Age. *Geochimica Cosmochimica Acta* 48 (5): 1135–1140.

Montgomery, J., Budd, P., and Neighbour, T. (2003) Sr Isotope Evidence for Population Movement within the Hebridean Norse Community of NW Scotland. *Journal of the Geological Society* 160: 649–653.

Mukherjee, A. J., Gibson, A. M., and Evershed, R. P. (2008) Trends in Pig Product Processing at British Neolithic Grooved Ware Sites Traced through Organic Residues in Potsherds. *Journal of Archaeological Science* 35 (7): 2059–2073.

Nelson, B. K., DeNiro, M. J., Schoeninger, M. J., and DePaolo, D. J. (1986) Effects of Diagenesis on Strontium, Carbon, Nitrogen, and Oxygen Concentration and Isotopic Composition of Bone. *Geochimica et Cosmochimica Acta* 50: 1941–1949.

O'Leary, M. H. (1988) Carbon Isotopes in Photosynthesis. *BioScience* 38 (5): 328–336.

Pataki, D. E., Ehleringer, J. R., Flanagan, L. B., Yakir, D., Bowling, D. R., Still, C. J., Buchmann, N., Kaplan, J. O., and Berry, J. A. (2003) The Application and Interpretation of Keeling Plots in Terrestrial Carbon Cycle Research. *Global Biogeochemical Cycles* 17 (1): 1021–1015.

Price, T. D., Grupe, G., and Schröter, P. (1994a) Reconstruction of Migration Patterns in the Bell Beaker Period by Stable Strontium Isotope Analysis. *Applied Geochemistry* 9: 413–417.

Price, T. D., Johnson, C. M., Ezzo, J. A., Ericson, J., and Burton, J. H. (1994b) Residential Mobility in the Prehistoric Southwest United States: A Preliminary Study Using Strontium Isotope Analysis. *Journal of Archaeological Science* 21 (3): 315–330.

Reynard, L. M., and Hedges, R. E. M. (2008) Stable Hydrogen Isotopes of Bone Collagen in Palaeodietary and Palaeoenvironmental Reconstruction. *Journal of Archaeological Science* 35: 13934–11942.

Richards, M. P., Schulting, R. J., and Hedges, R. E. M. (2003) Sharp Shift in Diet at Onset of Neolithic. *Nature* 425: 366.

Richards, M. P., Pettitt, P. B., Trinkaus, E., Smith, F. H., Saunovic, M., and Karavanic, I. (2000) Neanderthal Diet at Vindija and Neanderthal Predation: The Evidence from Stable Isotopes. *Proceedings of the National Academy of Sciences, USA* 97: 7663–7666.

Rundel, P. W., Ehleringer, J. R., and Nagy, K. A. (eds) (1989) *Stable Isotopes in Ecological Research*. New York: Springer-Verlag.

Schoeninger, M. J. (1989) Prehistoric Human Diet. In T. D. Price (ed.), *Chemistry of Prehistoric Human Bone* (pp. 38–67). Cambridge: Cambridge University Press.

Schoeninger, M. J. (1995) Dietary Reconstruction in the Prehistoric Carson Desert: Stable Carbon and Nitrogen Isotopic Analysis. In C. S. Larsen and R. L. Kelly (eds), *Bioarchaeology of the Stillwater Marsh: Prehistoric Human Adaptation in the Western Great Basin* (pp. 96–106.). New York: American Museum of Natural History, Anthropological Papers 77.

Schoeninger, M. J. (2009a) Stable Isotope Evidence for the Adoption of Maize Agriculture. In Mark Cohen (ed.), *Conversation of the Origin of Agriculture. Current Anthropology* (Special Volume) 50: 633–640.

Schoeninger, M. J. (2009b) Toward a Primate Isoscape: δ13C and Canopy Cover. In J. West, G. Bowen, T. Dawson, and K. Tu (eds), *Isoscapes: Understanding Movement, Pattern, and Process on Earth Through Isotope Mapping* (pp. 1–17). New York: Springer Environmental Sciences. Available at: DOI 10.1007/978-90-481-3354-3_15.

Schoeninger, M. J., and DeNiro, M. J. (1984) Nitrogen and Carbon Isotopic Composition of Bone Collagen from Marine and Terrestrial Animals. *Geochimica et Cosmochimica Acta* 48: 625–639.

Schoeninger, M. J., Iwaniec, U. T., and Glander, K. E. (1997) Stable Isotope Ratios Monitor Diet and Habitat Use in New World Monkeys. *American Journal of Physical Anthropology* 103: 69–83.

Schoeninger, M. J., Iwaniec, U. T., and Nash, L. T. (1998) Ecological Attributes Recorded in Stable Isotope Ratios of Arboreal Prosimian Hair. *Oecologia* 113: 222–230.

Schoeninger, M. J., Kohn, M. J., and Valley, J. W. (2000) Tooth Oxygen Isotope Ratios as Paleoclimate Monitors in Arid Ecosystems. In S. H. Ambrose and M. A. Katzenberg (eds), *Biogeochemical Approaches to Paleodietary Analysis in Archaeology* (pp. 117–140). New York: Plenum Press.

Schoeninger, M. J., Moore, J., and Sept, J. M. (1999) Subsistence Strategies of Two 'Savanna' Chimpanzee Populations: The Stable Isotope Evidence. *American Journal of Primatology* 47: 297–314.

Schoeninger, M. J., Reeser, H., and Hallin, K. (2003) Paleoenvironment of Australopithecus Anamensis at Allia Bay, East Turkana, Kenya: Evidence from Mammalian Herbivore Enamel Stable Isotopes. *Journal of Anthropolgical Archaeology* 22: 200–207.

Schoeninger, M. J., van der Merwe, N. J., Moore, K., Lee-Thorp, J., and Larsen, C. S. (1990) Decrease in Diet Quality between the Prehistoric and the Contact Periods. In C. S. Larsen (ed.), *The Archaeology of Mission Santa Catalina De Guale*, Vol. 2: *Biocultural Interpretations of a Population in Transition* (pp. 78–93). New York: American Museum of Natural History.

Sealy, J. C., and van der Merwe, N. J. (1986) Isotope Assessment and the Seasonal-Mobility Hypothesis in the Southwestern Cape of South Africa. *Current Anthropology* 27 (2): 135–150.

Sealy, J. C., van der Merwe, N. J., Lee-Thorp, J. A., and Lanham, J. L. (1987) Nitrogen Isotopic Ecology in Southern Africa: Implications for Environmental and Dietary Tracing. *Geochimica et Cosmochimica Acta* 51: 2707–2717.

Sealy, J. C., van der Merwe, N. J., Sillen, A., Krueger, F. J., and Krueger, H. W. (1991) [87]Sr/[86]Sr as a Dietary Indicator in Modern and Archaeological Bone. *Journal of Archaeological Science* 18 (3): 399–416.

Shemesh, A. (1990) Crystallinity and Diagenesis of Sedimentary Apatites. *Geochimica et Cosmochimica Acta* 54: 2433–2438.

Sillen, A., Hall, G., Richardson, S., and Armstrong, R. (1998) [87]Sr/[86]Sr Ratios in Modern and Fossil Food-Webs of the Sterkfontein Valley: Implications for Early Hominid Habitat Preference. *Geochimica et Cosmochimica Acta* 62 (14): 2463–2473.

Sillen, A., and Lee-Thorp, J. A. (1994) Trace Element and Isotopic Aspects of Predator–Prey Relationships in Terrestrial Foodwebs. *Palaeogeography, Palaeoclimatology, Palaeoecology* 107: 243–255.

Spielmann, K. A., Schoeninger, M. J., and Moore, K. (1990) Plains-Pueblo Interdependence and Human Diet at Pecos Pueblo, New Mexico. *American Antiquity* 55 (4): 745–765.

Sponheimer, M., Lee-Thorp, J., de Ruiter, D., Codron, D., Codron, J., Baugh, A. T., and Thackeray, F. (2005) Hominins, Hedges, and Termites: New Carbon Isotope Data from Sterkfontein Valley and Kruger National Park. *Journal of Human Evolution* 48: 301–312.

Sponheimer, M., Loudon, J. E., Codron, D., Howells, M. E., Pruetz, J. D., Codron, J., de Ruiter, D. J., and Lee-Thorp, J. A. (2006) Do 'Savanna' Chimpanzees Consume C_4 Resources? *Journal of Human Evolution* 51: 128–133.

Steckel, R. H., Rose, J. C., Larsen, C. S., and Walker, P. L. (2002) Skeletal Health in the Western Hemisphere from 4000 BC to the present. *Evolutionary Anthropology* 11: 142–155.

Sternberg, L. S. L. (1989) Oxygen and Hydrogen Isotope Ratios in Plant Cellulose: Mechanisms and Applications. In P. W. Rundel, J. R. Ehleringer and K. A. Nagy (eds), *Stable Isotopes in Ecological Research* (pp 124–141). New York: Springer-Verlag..

Tieszen, L. L., and Fagre, T. (1993) Effect of Diet Quality and Composition on the Isotopic Composition of Respiratory CO2, Bone Collagen, Bioapatite, and Soft Tissues. In J. B. Lambert and G. Grupe (eds), *Prehistoric Human Bone: Archaeology at the Molecular Level* (pp. 121–156). Berlin: Springer-Verlag.

Tucker, B. D. (2002) Culinary Confusion: Using Osteological and Stable Isotopic Evidence to Reconstruct Paleodiet for the Ocmulgee/Blackshear Cordmarked People of the South Central Georgia. MA Thesis, Georgia State University.

van der Merwe, N. J., and Medina, E. (1989) Photosynthesis and $^{13}C/^{12}C$ Ratios in Amazonian Rain Forests. *Geochimica et Cosmochimica Acta* 53: 1091–1094.

van der Merwe, N. J, and Vogel, J. C. (1978) ^{13}C Content of Human Collagen as a Measure of Prehistoric Diet in Woodland North America. *Nature* 276: 815–816.

van der Merwe, N., Masao, F., and Bamford, M. K. (2008) Isotopic Evidence for Contrasting Siets of Early Hominins *Homo habilis* and *Australopithecus boisei* of Tanzania. *South African Journal of Science* 104: 153–156.

Virginia, R. A., and Delwiche, C. C. (1982) Natural ^{15}N Abundance of Presumed N_2-Fixing and Non-N_2-Fixing Plants from Selected Ecosystems. *Oecologia* 54: 317–325.

Vogel, J. C., and van der Merwe, N. J. (1976) Isotopic Evidence for Early Maize Cultivation in New York State. Abstracts for the Annual Meeting of the Society for American Arcaheology: 11.

Vogel, J. C., and van der Merwe, N. J. (1977) Isotopic Evidence for Early Maize Cultivation in New York State. *American Antiquity* 42: 238–242.

Wahlen, M. (1994) Carbon Dioxide, Carbon Monoxide and Methane in the Atmosphere: Abundance and Isotopic Composition. In K. Lajtha and R. H. Mitchener (eds), *Stable Isotopes in Ecology and Environmental Science* (pp. 93–113). Oxford: Blackwell Scientific Publications.

Wallace, B. P., Seminoff, J. A., Kilham, S. S., Spotila, J. R., and Dutton, P. H. (2006) Leatherback Turtles as Oceanographic Indicators: Stable Isotope Analyses Reveal a Trophic Dichotomy between Ocean Basins. *Marine Biology* 149: 953–960.

Wassenaar, L. I., and Hobson, K. A. (2002) Comparative Equilibration and Online Technique for Determination of Non-Exchangeable Hydrogen of Keratins for Use in Animal Migration Studies. *Isotopes in Environmental Health* S39: 1–7.

White, C. D., Storey, R., Longstaffe, F., and Spence, M. W. (2004) Immigration, Assimilation, and Status in the Ancient City of Teotihuacan: Stable Isotope Evidence from Tlajinga 33. *Latin American Antiquity* 15: 176–197.

White, J. W. C. (1989) Stable Hydrogen Isotope Ratios in Plants: A Review of Current Theory and Some Potential Applications. In P. W. Rundel, J. R. Ehleringer and K. A. Nagy (eds), *Stable Isotopes in Ecological Research* (pp. 142–162). New York: Springer-Verlag.

Wright, L. E. (2005) In Search of Yax Nuun Ayiin I: Revisiting the Tikal Project's Burial 10. *Ancient Mesoamerica* 16: 89–100.

Wynn, J. G. (2000) Paleosols, Stable Carbon Isotopes, and Paleoenvironmental Interpretation of Kanapoi, Northern Kenya. *Journal of Human Evolution* 39: 411–432.

Yesner, D., Figuerero Torres, M. J., Guichon, R. A., and Borrero, L. A. (2003) Stable Isotope Analysis of Human Bone and Ethnohistoric Subsistence Patterns in Tierra del Fuego. *Journal of Anthropological Archaeology* 22: 279–291.

Ziegler, H. (1989) Hydrogen Isotope Fractionation in Plant Tissues. In P. W. Rundel, J. R. Ehleringer and K. A. Nagy (eds), *Stable Isotopes in Ecological Research* (pp. 105–123). New York: Springer-Verlag.

CHAPTER 26 Current Concepts in Bone Biology

James H. Gosman
and Samuel D. Stout

INTRODUCTION

Because physical anthropology seeks to understand biological aspects of human and non-human primates, past and present, its research often involves the analysis of skeletal remains. Bioarchaeologists, paleontologists, forensic anthropologists, and paleopathologists investigate skeletal remains in order to draw inferences about the corresponding people's lives. Such inferences extend over the realm of diseases, levels of physiological stress and trauma suffered by the individuals in question, physical activity, and aspects of behavior. Essential to all these endeavors is an understanding of the biology underlying skeletal growth and development, diseases, and skeletal adaptation. Toward this end, we shall review in this chapter some current concepts in bone biology.

The skeleton grows, adapts, and maintains itself through the activity of tissue-forming and tissue-resorbing cells. In bone, these cells include the bone-forming cells – osteoblasts – and related cells such as osteocytes and bone lining-cells, as well as the bone-resorbing cells – osteoclasts. At tissue level, these cells function primarily through two major processes: bone remodeling, whereby temporally and focally coordinated groups of these cells, called basic multicellular units of remodeling (BMUs), resorb and replace defined packets of bone; and bone modeling, in which the same cells work independently to sculpt and repair bone. The latter process, modeling, normally occurs primarily in the growing skeleton and to a lesser degree in adulthood and in fracture repair. This chapter will summarize current mechanobiological concepts related to key skeletal cellular and metabolic processes formatted within the four-envelope bone structure: periosteal, haversian, endosteal, and trabecular.

MECHANOBIOLOGY

Although bone plays an important role in mineral homeostasis, its primary function is mechanical. The interrelationship between biology and mechanical environment is the foundation of mechanobiology and the reason for coining this word in order to name it: 'mechanobiology' is intended to designate the influence of the loading environment on bone structure and biology (Jacobs 2000). Understanding the influence of mechanical loads on cancellous bone structure began in mid-nineteenth century, with the Swiss anatomist von Meyer's drawings of the internal structure of the proximal femur (Roesler 1987). Wolff's outspoken advocacy of the relationship between skeletal form and function, which he termed the 'trajectorial theory' of trabecular alignment, has lead to widespread acceptance of this general concept into the present and continuing (Wolff 1986). Foreshadowing current research, Wolff proposed that cancellous bone architecture was based on a "law according to which alterations in the internal architecture clearly observed and followed mathematical rule" (Roesler 1987). Wolff's statement about the form and the function of bone referred to a static mathematical relationship between trabecular architecture and stress trajectories. Wolff casts a long shadow onto research approaches which attempt to find appropriate parameters "by which structural and geometrical properties can be described under a more-or-less general principle" (Huiskes 2000: 146; Ruff et al. 2006).

There is another paradigm passed down from the nineteenth century. Wilhelm Roux focused on the relationship of biological processes to trabecular architecture and external load. He suggested that functional adaptation of trabecular bone is self-regulated and organized by bone cells responding to locally derived mechanical (and other) stimuli (Roux 1881). This is the modern equivalent of a biological regulatory system, which produces a structure adapted to mechanical demands on the basis of its own characteristics (Huiskes 2000). Huiskes argues that any further understanding of the nature of bone architecture and adaptation will develop from the study of bone 'production technology' (versus design; ibid.).

Recent research in cortical and cancellous bone analyses includes computational, imaging, experimental, and cellular/molecular studies designed to determine the structural and material consequences and the biological processes of various loading regimes (Lanyon 1996; Robling et al. 2006) on the basis of advances in theoretical modeling of mechanobiology (Cadet et al. 2003; Jacobs 2000; Tanck et al. 2006). It is these advances (micro-CT imaging, quantitative three-dimensional analysis, molecular and systems biology, and large-scale finite element method of computer-based simulation) that have, in part, stimulated the increasing interest in bone functional adaptation as a robust portal for understanding skeletal adaptation and behavior in extant and in past human populations.

Carter and Beaupré (2001) have described a comprehensive equilibrium model, the 'mechanobiological hypothesis' (Pearson and Lieberman 2004), which is based on a "simple mathematical rule relating cyclic tissue stress to bone apposition and resorption" (Carter et al. 1996: 5S). The *apparent level* approach is taken. The best way of understanding this approach is by saying that it considers the *net effect* of cellular or mechanical behavior, without needing to account for each cell, osteon, trabecula, or action individually (Jacobs 2000). The apparent level of skeletal modeling takes a complex microarchitectural structure and homogenizes the various structures and mechanical forces. This type of analysis belongs in the engineering field of continuum mechanics. The general equilibrium model assumes that bone acts so as to maintain a mechanically stable stress–strain range in response to mechanical loads. Bone requires, for its maintenance, a certain level of daily mechanical stimulation from various activities of living (for instance walking, running, or climbing). The appropriate level of mechanical stimulation for bone apposition versus resorption is site-specific and based on biologically interdependent influences between genetic components, systemic factors, and local tissue interactions (for the mathematical model, see Carter and Beaupré 2001).

The mechanobiological hypothesis considers bone growth as having two components, one biological and the other mechanobiological. The biological component is controlled by genes and hormones, thus following the normal trajectory and velocity of growth: decreasing to mid-childhood, increasing during the adolescent spurt, and decreasing to near zero at maturity. The mechanobiological component models an optimal strain level in bone in response to load (Bertram and Biewener 1988). The mechanical influences become increasingly dominant, and the systemic biological influences decrease in influence, during growth and development. After the age of 10, mechanobiology predominates, maintaining daily stress stimulus (strain magnitude x loading cycles) within a 'lazy zone,' in which little bone apposition or resorption occurs (Carter et al. 1996).

Biological factors – genetic, hormonal, nutritional, and local tissue interactions – interrelate with, and change, the mechanobiological response (Carter and Beaupré 2001). These local tissue interactions may involve physiochemical influences between adjacent cells and tissues, involving the local expression of growth factors, cytokines, and bone induction factors (for example bone morphogenetic proteins (BMPs). There may be a cellular response involving the recruitment and activity of osteoblasts and osteoclasts, which results in the alteration of the mechanobiologically mediated rate of bone apposition and resorption. In addition, there may be an interaction and change in the mechanobiological sensitivity, responsiveness, and/or regulatory signaling (ibid.).

During ontogeny, increased loads above the lazy zone result in bone apposition; decreased loads result in bone resorption. Mature bone is predicted to respond to similar load changes by periosteal deposition and endosteal resorption. This model accounts for site-specific and age-specific variability on the basis of cellular factors such as the availability of osteoblast precursor cells and/or osteoclasts (ibid.). Multiple simulation studies demonstrate that this model "successfully predicts the appositional bone growth and modeling observed in the diaphyseal cross section" beginning from the fetal femoral anlagen to maturity (Carter et al. 1996: 5S). The same mechanobiological hypothesis predicts the observed macro and microarchitecture of proximal (or distal) cancellous bone, formed by endochondral ossification (Carter and Beaupré 2001). Furthermore, the changes in geometry, microarchitecture, and density, which occur in mature cortical and cancellous bone as a result of skeletal adaptation to physical activities, can be accurately simulated. Changes in bone mass (thickness and density) occur with increases or decreases in load magnitude or cycle. Changes in architectural patterns (distribution and anisotropy) occur with alterations in the direction of load (ibid.).

The strength of the mechanobiological hypothesis exists in its ability to predict accurately the observed skeletal changes. It is, clearly, an oversimplification of the complex hierarchical biological system of bone growth, development, (re)modeling, and repair. A recent advance is in the domain of tissue level of analysis, which accounts for individual trabeculae and osteons. This domain is called 'direct microstructural modeling' (DMM; Jacobs 2000). The micromechanical environment of individual trabeculae of cancellous bone can be studied *in vivo* in small animals and *in vitro* in whole human bones. Detailed microstructural cellular response behaviors and mechanobiological consequences can be modeled – for example by supporting the hypothesis advanced by Huiskes and colleagues (1998), that "the stress concentration surrounding osteoclast resorption cavities is responsible for localizing osteoblastic bone formation during infilling of the cavity" (Jacobs 2000). This developing technology specifically avoids some of the simplifying assumptions made in apparent level modeling and holds the promise for a more precise determination of quantitative mechanical loading on an individual trabecula/osteon scale. This method has been made possible by advances in ultra-high-resolution CT scanners and in finite element solutions for very large dataset models (100 million to 1 billion elements).

Carpenter and Carter (2008) have proposed a novel mechanobiological model, based upon experimental evidence in which tension and pressure influence bone formation and resorption. In their model, pressure on the periosteal surface can impede bone formation and induce resorption, and periosteal tension strains running perpendicular to bone surfaces can impede bone resorption and stimulate formation. Results from computer simulations which apply the model to tibiae of rats suggest that periosteal pressures, in concert with intracortical stresses and other mechanobiological factors, play an important role in determining cross-sectional shapes in bone. The results of this work are directly relevant to the ongoing discourse in physical anthropology concerning the validity of cross-sectional cortical geometry and its usefulness in informing us on human behavior. The authors indicate that bone cross-sectional *size* may be related to the more distant mechanical environment, whereas bone cross-sectional *shape* is influenced by local periosteal loads (ibid.).

Sample and colleagues (2008) add to the complexity of the mechanisms involved in skeletal responses to mechanical loading. They present evidence in support of a controversial idea – although not a new one: namely that the innervation of bone has a functional role in skeletal adaptation to mechanical signals. In experiments using a laboratory rat model, they demonstrate that loading in one region of a long bone may induce corresponding bone formation at distant sites on the same bone and in distant bones, where strain was not altered by loading. Rubin and Rubin (2008) assert that Sample and colleagues (2008) provide intriguing new evidence that the innervation may play an important role in the adaptive response of bone to mechanical signals. They also advise that bone loss (resorption) after extended periods of bed rest and in response to conditions of hypogravity underscore the importance of mechanical loading.

Advances in understanding skeletal mechanobiology, structure, and adaptation will probably develop along the lines of microstructural (possibly nanostructural) and cellular models, ultimately providing the capability of evaluating temporospatial changes in the bone envelopes. Some basic considerations on the cellular 'actors' and on their regulatory interactions are essential to understanding the proposed models, as well as the empirical data from recent skeletal research and the implications for physical anthropology.

CELLULAR ACTORS

Osteoblasts

Bone strain (or the lack of it) is mediated through the cellular responses of the osteoblast and osteoclast lineages. The osteoblast lineage is comprised of mesenchymally derived cells, including osteoblasts, osteocytes, and bone-lining cells. In general terms, osteoblasts form bone by synthesizing the collagen matrix and by secreting calcium phosphate mineral; osteocytes and bone-lining cells may regulate metabolic and sensory functions (Pearson and Lieberman 2004). Each cell type is phenotypically unique and endowed with particular identifying biochemical markers (Massaro and Rogers 2004). Differentiation along a specific lineage is triggered by a genetic regulatory cascade, which for osteoblasts includes genes coding for core binding factor alpha 1, collagen 1, bone sialoprotein, osteopontin, and osteocalcin (St-Arnaud 2003).

Osteoblasts are genetically sophisticated fibroblasts (Ducy et al. 2000b) originating in a variety of tissues, including the periosteum and endosteum. The only morphological feature specific to osteoblasts versus fibroblasts is the presence of a specific extracellular matrix. Differentiated osteoblasts produce a mucoprotein matrix, called osteoid, in which collagen fibrils are enmeshed. This is followed by the mineralization of the osteoid through the deposition of inorganic crystals of calcium phosphate on the collagen fibers. The search for osteoblastic differentiation factors has lead to the identification of *Cbfa1* (core-binding factor-α1; also known as Runx2) as a dominant osteoblast-specific transcription factor (Harada and Rodan 2003; Karsenty 2001). Other transcription factors involved in osteoblast differentiation include the Indian hedgehog growth factor (Ihh; Ducy et al. 2000b) and the Wnt (a group of proteins important to skeletal morphogenesis and maintenance, named after the 'wingless' gene in *Drosophila melanogaster*) signaling pathway by way of the cell surface receptor LRP5 (low-density lipoprotein receptor-related protein 5; see Hu et al. 2005; Williams and Insogna 2009). Presently the regulatory genetic architecture and mechanisms are poorly understood, but they are topics of intense research interest.

Bone formation through differentiated osteoblasts is controlled by complex, hierarchical, homeostatic, biological systems. Modulators of bone mass include a polygenic regulatory system, calcium availability, sex steroids, nutrition, and mechanical usage. The central regulation of the osteoblast function involves the endocrine system, comprising as it does parathyroid hormone (PTH); 1, 25(OH)$_2$ vitamin D; calcitonin; and the sex steroids. These hormones have various roles in different contexts. Estrogen is particularly important in bone formation and resorption, up-regulating osteoblast activity. Estrogen receptors (ERα and ERβ) in osteocytes and osteoblasts have critical roles in mechanotransduction and in the osteogenic response to strain (Pearson and Lieberman 2004). PTH and vitamin D are mineral-sensitive hormones, which stimulate osteoclasts and inhibit osteoblasts. Calcitonin is a mineral-building hormone secreted by the thyroid which up-regulates osteoblasts and down-regulates osteoclasts. Recent research has demonstrated a possible central 'master-regulator' of bone formation in the hormone Leptin (Ducy et al. 2000a), which is produced in adipose tissue and inhibits the osteoblast function through hypothalamic and sympathetic nervous system signaling pathways (Harada and Rodan 2003).

The transcriptional and growth factor regulation of the osteoblastic function is controlled, with temporal and spatial specificity, by a system of autocrine and paracrine signaling. *Cbfa1* is currently the key player, bridging the gap between osteoblast differentiation and osteoblast function. *Cbfa1* is regulated by several families of growth factors – including BMPs, fibroblast growth factors, insulin-like growth factors, transforming growth factors, and platelet-derived growth factors (Jee 2001).

Research on the effects of aging on osteoblast and osteoprogenitor cells has demonstrated the possible effects of senescence on these cells in relation to diminished synthetic capacity – that is, a decline in the number of progenitor cells which can be recruited to differentiate into osteoblasts (Nashida and Endo 1999) – and in relation to a reduced sensitivity to mechanical signals (Donahue et al. 2003). In addition to changes in hormone levels, these are important factors in the age-related imbalance of bone deposition and resorption – especially notable in trabecular bone.

Osteocytes

Osteocytes are differentiated osteoblasts that have become embedded in the mineralized matrix they have created as osteoblasts. These abundant cells (Mullender et al. 1996) reside within cavities termed 'lacunae' and make physical contact – with each other, with osteoblasts, with bone lining cells, and possibly with osteoclasts by way of cellular processes passing through tunnels called 'canaliculi' (Donahue et al. 2003; Martin et al. 1998). Gap junctions allow osteocytes to form a functional syncytium linking all the cells within bone; this is the basis of their possible role as mechanosensory cells. Mechanosensitivity has been demonstrated in osteocytes by *in vitro* and *in vivo* studies of pulsating, steady, and oscillating fluid flow, as well as by changing the levels of substrate strain – which has resulted in increased mRNA expression, gene up-regulation, and the metabolic synthesis of various active compounds (Donahue et al. 2003). Interestingly, osteocytic cells contribute little to bone formation or resorption directly. Their role is thought to involve the communication of load-induced signals to the affector cells: osteoblasts and osteoclasts.

Recent research has demonstrated functionally coupled gap junctions between osteocytes, themselves, and osteoblasts (Yellowley et al. 2000). This discovery supports the hypothesis that osteocytes appraise mechanical signals and regulate bone adaptation (Mullender and Huiskes 1997). The aging effects on osteocytes include a reduction in the density of lacunae and in the number of osteocytes, and the decreased ability of the surviving cells to respond to biochemical and mechanical stimuli (Pearson and Lieberman 2004). Concurrent with these aging changes is the accumulation of microcracks/damage in bone, a phenomenon which renders the bone prone to fracture.

Bone-lining cells

Bone-lining cells (BLC) are quiescent osteoblasts that "escaped being buried by newly formed bone and remained on the surface when bone formation ceased" (Martin et al. 1998: 48). These cells flatten against the bone surface, maintaining communication with osteocytes and with each other through gap-junctioned processes, while they also maintain receptors for parathyroid hormone, estrogen, and paracrine signaling. The BLCs are thought to be part of a system which is responsive to chemical and mechanical stimuli, is responsible for mineral transfer (Martin et al. 1998), and may activate bone (re)modeling, making it deposit or resorb bone according to strain levels (Martin 2003). Mullender and Huiskes (1997: 527) examined regulatory computer models to find out whether BLCs could potentially regulate bone remodeling in cancellous bone by themselves, without input from osteocytes. They concluded "that mechanical information at the bone surface may not be sufficient to adequately regulate functional bone adaptation."

Osteoclasts

Osteoclasts are derived from a fusion of many (ten to twenty) hematopoietic precursor cells: mononuclear phagocytes which originate in the bone marrow (Boyle et al. 2003). As part of the macrophage lineage, these cells become differentiated at, or near, the bone surface, and have the function of resorbing bone. Pettit and colleagues (2008) have shown that the endosteum and periosteum contain a population of resident tissue macrophages, which they term 'OsteoMacs' and which play an important role in bone modeling and remodeling.

The activated osteoclasts, the end products of osteoclastogenesis, adhere to the bone by a ruffled surface which creates a seal (Teitelbaum 2000), allowing bone resorption to occur from the effects of decreasing the local pH (a measure of increase acidity in a substance or solution) and from the secretion of various anti-collagen proteolytic enzymes. Osteoclast differentiation and function is regulated by at least twenty-four known genes, including those encoding tartrate-resistant acid phosphatase (TRAP), cathepsin K (CATK), calcitonin receptor, and the β_3-integrin (Boyle et al. 2003). Two hematopoietic factors are necessary and sufficient for osteoclastgenesis and maturation: TNF-related cytokine RANKL and the polypeptide growth factor CSF-1 (colony-stimulating factor-1).

The regulation of osteoclast transcription includes important molecules synthesized by osteoblasts (and by other cells). Three important molecules are RANK, RANKL, and osteoprotegerin (OPG). Osteoclastogenesis and bone resorption are coordinated by the RANKL/RANK/OPG regulatory axis (Boyle et al. 2003; Robling et al. 2006). RANKL (cytokine) and RANK (transmembrane signaling receptor) are required for osteoclast differentiation, activation, and bone resorption. OPG (soluble protein) blocks osteoclast formation and bone resorption and induces apoptosis by acting as a decoy receptor: it blocks RANKL by binding to its cellular receptor RANK. An overexpression of OPG reduces the production of osteoclasts, causing osteopetrosis; a deletion of OPG results in enhanced bone resorption and osteoporosis. "Expression of RANKL and OPG is therefore coordinated to regulate bone resorption and density positively and negatively by controlling the activation state of RANK on osteoclasts" (Boyle et al. 2003: 338). Additional stimulators of the osteoclastic function are PTH; 1, 25 (OH)$_2$ vitamin D; the thyroid hormone; glucocorticoids; IGF-1; and BMP-2 and -4. Additional inhibitors of the osteoclastic function are calcitonin, nitric oxide, gonadal steroids, and interleukin-1 and -6 (ibid.).

The effect of aging on osteoclasts is usually framed in terms of adult skeletal disease (osteoporosis, periodontal disease, rheumatoid arthritis, multiple myeloma, and metastatic cancers): here there is evidence of excessive osteoclastic activity which leads to an imbalance in bone remodeling in favor of resorption (Duong and Rodan 2001). Specific age-related metabolic changes in these cells have not been identified (Boyle et al. 2003).

The strain stimulus responsible for osteoclastic activity and, ultimately, for bone adaptation is likely to work through a regulatory system of soluble signals which are released by osteoblasts (bone-lining cells) and integrate these two cellular functions – the osteoblastic and the osteoclastic. Research is progressing rapidly in the direction of reconstructing the osteoclast-signaling network and its role in bone (re)modeling, density, maintenance, and adaptation (see Martin et al. 1998; Martin 2003; Mullender and Huiskes 1997).

(RE-)MODELING

Bone is composed of four skeletal envelopes on which modeling and remodeling occur: the trabecular, endosteal, periosteal, and Haversian surfaces (Martin et al. 1998). Although the effects of the modeling and remodeling processes differ at each surface, a general description of (re)modeling and of the instrument of remodeling, the basic multicellular unit (BMU) is given below. Modeling is "the principal mode of bone cell coordination in the growing skeleton" (Parfitt 2003: 4). During ontogeny, bone is formed in one location and resorbed in another, to accommodate the changes of bone size and shape. This is orchestrated through the combination of genetic, systemic biological, and local mechanical factors. As bones grow in length and width, which is the result of endochondral ossification and periosteal intramembranous bone apposition, they are sculpted by periosteal and endosteal resorption and formation at different locations (Martin et al. 1998). The modeling process involves independent actions from the osteoblasts and the osteoclasts. The periosteal envelope is especially active in the modeling process during ontogeny, and to a much lesser extent during adult life. It is responsible for increasing bone diameter. This redistribution of bone is a relatively continuous process, which results in a net gain in bone mass (Parfitt 2003) in relation to the increase in body mass during growth and development. The rate and extent of modeling is greatly reduced after skeletal maturity. The end result of the modeling process is the acquisition of skeletal shape, architecture, and mass appropriate to biological and mechanical requirements. Examples include tibial metaphyseal 'cut-back,' diaphyseal enlargement or drift, and cranial re-shaping so as to accommodate the increase in brain size. The mechanical control of this process of growth and adaptation is thought to be accounted for by the osteoblast/osteocyte bone-lining cell signal transduction syncytium, which responds to increased strain in the local matrix and triggers bone formation or resorption until the strains are normalized (Huiskes et al. 2000; Sommerfeldt and Rubin 2001).

Bone remodeling (bone maintenance) is the "mechanism of bone replacement in the vertebrate skeleton" (Parfitt 2002: 5). This process is characterized by the sequentially synchronized 'coupled' actions of osteoclasts and osteoblasts (activation–resorption–formation), which occur on the same surface. Remodeling, which continues throughout life, generally does not affect the size and shape of the bone; but a net bone loss may result. Remodeling is a process occurring on the Haversian, trabecular, and endosteal envelopes. Bone replacement is initiated by osteoclastic resorption, followed soon after by osteoblastic formation. The temporary, cyclic, anatomic structure responsible for this process has been named by Frost 'the basic multicellular unit' (BMU: Frost 1969; see also Parfitt 2002). This structure will be discussed in the following section.

Bone remodeling has three apparent purposes:

1   Its metabolic function provides a mechanism for the maintenance of calcium homeostasis by promoting the exchange of calcium ions at the bone surface (Martin et al. 1998).
2   Its structural function provides a mechanism for skeletal adaptation to the mechanical environment.

3 Its maintenance function provides a mechanism for the repair of fatigue damage created in bone by repetitive cycles of mechanical loading (Burr 2002).

It is argued that the "main purpose of remodeling is to prevent degradation of function (microdamage) as bone becomes older" (Parfitt 2002). The load-bearing function of bone is threatened by the accumulation of fatigue microdamage, which is targeted for remodeling (Burr 2002).

Basic multicellular unit (BMU)

Remodeling is carried out by a cyclic and temporary anatomic structure: the BMU. These anatomical units are most readily identified in the cortical (osteonal) bone. They have also been described in the cancellous (hemi-osteonal) bone (Parfitt 1994). Parfitt argues that BMUs in cancellous bone "travel across the surface digging a trench rather than a tunnel, but maintaining its [the bone's] size, shape and individual identity by the continuous recruitment of new cells, just as in cortical bone" (Parfitt 1994: 273). Hauge and colleagues (2001) describe a specialized structure referred to as 'the bone remodeling compartment' (BRC), which is associated with bone remodeling in cancellous bone. The compartment is described as resembling a roof of flattened cells, which persist as a canopy over the BMU during bone remodeling.

A fully developed BMU consists of a team of osteoclasts forming the cutting (hemi-) cone, a team of osteoblasts behind forming the closing cone, some form of vascular supply, and associated connective tissue (ibid.). The capillary in cortical bone or the specialized sinusoid (BRC) in cancellous bone (Melsen et al. 1995) are at the heart of the BMU, being ideally situated so as to coordinate the coupled functions activation, resorption, and formation (Parfitt 2000). Preosteoclasts, originating in the bone marrow, arrive at the resorption site through blood circulation. The individually differentiated osteoclasts turning over at a rate of 8 percent per day are short-lived (twelve days). Osteoblasts from precursors in the local connective tissue refill the resorbed bone at each successive cross-sectional location, maintaining three-dimensional organization. Some of the cells in the osteoblastic team become buried as osteocytes, some die (average life span is measured in weeks), and some become relatively quiescent bone-lining cells. The BMU exists and travels in three dimensions, excavating and refilling a trench in cancellous bone of $200\,\mu m$ (micrometer) at about $10\,\mu m$ per day for 100 days, while maintaining the proper spatial and temporal relationships among the bone's cellular elements (Parfitt 1994).

The life span of the BMU has a beginning (origination), a middle (progression), and an end (termination). Its duration in cancellous bone is approximately three months. The origination is described as beginning on a small area of quiescent bone surface, and it involves the digestion of the endosteal membrane by enzymes released from lining cells. These changes in lining cell morphology expose the mineralized bone surface. The process of neoangiogenesis provides the capability for the egress of circulating mononuclear osteoclast precursors at precisely the correct location. Their attraction to the region of the exposed mineral and their subsequent fusion into osteoclasts allow the assembly of a number of osteoclasts sufficient to form the cutting (hemi-)cone (Parfitt 2002). Progression is travel in a particular direction for a particular time. Constant re-supply of osteoclast precursors is necessary. The steering of BMUs is guided in two directions: in the direction of the principal stress (Burger et al. 2003) and towards microdamage (Martin 2007). On the basis of the results of finite element analysis, Van Oers and colleagues (2008) proposed a model in which strain-induced osteocyte signals inhibit osteoclast activity and stimulate osteoblast activity. The model can explain several characteristics of the BMUs: osteonal and trabecular load alignment, resorption of dead osteocytes, smaller osteons diameters in high strain regions, and double-ended and drifting osteons (Van Oers et al. 2008). At termination, the BMU stops moving forward, the supply of osteoclast precursors is turned off, and refilling by osteoblasts is completed. BMU remodeling can function in two modes:

1   the conservation mode, in which the completed BMU has resorbed and formed equal amounts of bone; and
2   the disuse mode, in which the completed BMU forms less bone than has been resorbed (Frost 2003).

Activation frequency is a two-dimensional concept expressing the overall intensity of bone remodeling. Seven years ago it was redefined as the conversion of a region of bone surface from quiescence to remodeling activity (Parfitt 2002). When applied to cancellous bone, it refers to the probability that a new cycle of remodeling will be initiated at any point on the surface (Parfitt et al. 1987). This index incorporates both the birthrate of new BMUs and the average distance along which each one moves. Martin (1994) offers a discussion of the importance which both these factors – the birthrate of new BMUs and the distances traveled by them – have for histological definitions of activation rate.

   The BMU remodeling process is thought to have targeted and non-targeted components (Burr 2002). Parfitt (2002) and Burr (2002) have recently summarized these concepts as follows:

1   Some remodeling is targeted for the replacement of fatigue-microdamaged bone.
2   A substantial amount (70 percent) of the total remodeling is not targeted for this specific purpose.

Non-targeted remodeling is in surplus of load-bearing issues, provides a margin of safety, and may have several purposes or mechanisms:

1   removal of hypermineralized bone;
2   replacement of initially targeted BMUs, which may overshoot their target; and
3   stochastic BMU origination.

Many unsolved issues remain, especially in relation to the signaling mechanisms for bone remodeling. Advances in analytical technology are contributing to recent refinements in bone remodeling theory.

DEVELOPMENTS IN BONE REMODELING THEORY

The general model
The notion that bone remodeling is controlled through mechanical as well as through metabolic influences has been subjected to intense study in recent years. Current

consensus focuses on four fundamental observations or hypotheses. First, bone is thought to contain sensor cells monitoring mechanical strain (or other load-related variables); comparing these levels to a physiologically desirable range; and activating biological processes, if necessary, in order to bring the sensed variable back inside the acceptable range (Frost 1987a, 1989). This representation assumes that bone remodeling removes bone if the mechanical stimulus is too low and adds bone if the stimulus is too high (Carter and Beaupré 2001; Martin 2000). Second, osteocytes have been identified as possible bone mechanosensing cells which produce a signal proportional to the strain on bone surfaces produced by sensitivity to ion channels, interstitial fluid flow, electrical signals, or other perturbations (Mullender and Huiskes 1997).

The third key idea is that osteocytes sense fatigue damage and transmit signals to activate remodeling and to remove the damage. Research has been focused on the cortical bone, showing that an increased activation of remodeling is associated with microdamage (Burr 2002). "It is generally assumed that the same is true in cancellous bone" (Martin 2000: 1). The fourth hypothesis suggests that cells of the osteoblast lineage control the initiation of remodeling. The bone-lining cells are thought to be responsible for activating BMUs in response to osteocytic signals or hormones. These four hypotheses constitute the foundation for a current general model of bone remodeling.

Mechanostat

The modern offspring of Roux's concept of a biological control process (Roesler 1987) is Frost's mechanostat theory (1987a, 1989). This theoretical construction holds that local strains regulate bone mass in the same way in which the local temperature in a room regulates the heater through a thermostat (Frost 1987a). The basic multicellular units maintain local bone mass under control with the help of a mechanical feed-back loop and of a set point, which is the threshold setting for the balance between strain and bone formation/resorption. Frost emphasizes this is a biologically mediated process regulated by mechanical loads. Frost and Jee (1994a, b) have applied this model directly to the endochondral ossification process during ontogeny. This is of relevance to current research directed toward understanding the development of adult skeletal morphology.

Frost's mechanostat theory is credited with distinguishing between modeling and remodeling. The theory is built on the premise that disuse and overload have opposite effects on these two processes. Disuse activates remodeling but inhibits formation-mode modeling, which leads to bone loss. Overload inhibits remodeling and activates formation-mode modeling, which leads to bone gain. Presented in this way, the initial mechanostat model is at odds with the general model described above, as it ignores the activation of remodeling in response to tissue overload and fatigue damage. Experimental data indicates that remodeling is elevated when strains are either excessively low or so excessively high that damage occurs.

The fully elaborated form of Frost's mechanostat theory accounts for these concerns (Burr 1992). It holds that bone adapts through different biological processes which fall within four mechanical usage windows, defined or characterized by minimum effective strains for activating adaptive processes, and called 'set points' (Frost 1987a) Remodeling, which removes or conserves bone, is activated by reduced mechanical usage in the 'trivial loading zone' or by microdamage in the 'pathological loading zone.' Remodeling is suppressed in the 'physiological zone.' Under conditions of disuse, such as immobilization or hypogravity, remodeling on surfaces adjacent to the marrow – that is, the endosteal and trabecular envelopes, but not the Haversian envelope – produces a net bone loss per BMU, which results in overall bone loss.

Modeling, which can add cortical and trabecular bone, reshapes surfaces through resorption or through lamellar formation drift, and is activated by increased mechanical usage in the 'overload zone.' It remains quiescent within or below the physiological zone. The threshold loads for activation – the set points – of these processes may be influenced by various systemic, hormonal, or local factors. For example, the *theoretically perceived* upward shift of the remodeling set point is thought to be associated with the loss of estrogen, which results in activated remodeling and bone loss. Experimental research has provided examples of bone adaptation in adult animals which are consistent with the mechanostat theory (Jee et al. 1990, 1991).

Frost has significantly contributed to an increasing awareness of the mechanical factors involved in the regulation of bone (re)modeling and repair. Recent advances in large-scale computer simulation are driving the research towards integrated quantitative models, which attempt to explain the morphological/biological phenomena occurring in bone. Striving for a unifying paradigm, Martin proposes a theoretical approach, "assuming that the [osteocytic] signal inhibits rather that stimulates remodeling" (2000: 2). Huiskes and colleagues (2000) have developed a unified self-regulating model.

The inhibitory theory of bone remodeling

The concept of an inhibitory osteocytic signal is derived from research which suggests that osteocytes send inhibitory signals to nearby osteoblasts to slow the production of osteoid and to allow contact with the bone surface to be maintained (Marotti 1996). Martin supposes that "this inhibitory osteocytic signal is identical to that which others have hypothesized to be produced by mechanical loading" (2000: 2). Bone-lining cells activate remodeling, unless they are inhibited by the osteocytic signal. In this system the activation of remodeling is increased when the generation or the transmission of the inhibiting signals is diminished. Examples include: a reduced use state (reduction of strain-generated signal); mechanical damage (interrupted signal transmission); osteocyte apoptosis (interrupted signal generation); hormonal alteration of signal generation, transmission, or interpretation. Martin (2000) argues that the essential point of his hypothesis is its 'unifying nature': it accounts for a common signal to guide osteoblasts into bone matrix as osteocytes, it gauges mechanical load and microdamage, and it sends signals to the bone-lining cells to remove or replace bone tissue.

Unified trabecular/cortical bone paradigm

The 'third method of science' is the application of large-scale computer simulation, after 'theory' and 'empiricism' (Kelly 1998). This approach has been used to model a self-regulatory paradigm for cancellous bone adaptation and maintenance (Huiskes et al. 2000) and, more recently, it has been applied to cortical bone (Cadet et al. 2003; Tanck et al. 2006). Trabecular architecture emerges as an optimal mechanical structure adapted to alternative external loads during modeling and remodeling. The central focus of this theory is to provide a framework for the investigative computational explanation of the "effects of mechanical forces on trabecular bone morphogenesis, maintenance and adaptation by relating local mechanical stimuli in the bone matrix to assumed expressions of the cells actually involved in bone metabolism' (Ruimerman et al. 2005).

Bone remodeling involves the formation of cavities by osteoclasts and the subsequent filling of these cavities by osteoblasts. The coupling factor between these two cellular functions in remodeling is mechanical, as it is in modeling. Modeling is thought to be under the control of external forces which change the strains in the mineralized bone at large, while remodeling resorption cavities have a similar strain-enhancing effect locally. Huiskes and co-authors state that "modeling and remodeling could both be described as being governed by strain perturbations, be they generated externally by the load or internally by resorption cavities" (2000: 704). Osteoclastic resorption cavities weaken their trabecula, causing a local elevation of strain, perceived by osteocytes. Osteoblasts are then recruited by the osteocytes to form bone.

This cancellous bone regulatory model involves several key points which have been discussed previously in different contexts. First, the mechanical variable that triggers feed-back from external forces to bone metabolism is a typical rate of strain-energy density (SED) in the bone, as produced by recent loading history. The SED includes loading rate, frequency, and amplitude. Interestingly, relatively few loading cycles per day are required to maintain bone mass (Huiskes et al. 2000). Second, osteocytes respond to loading in their local environments by producing a biochemical messenger in proportion to the typical SED rate. Third, the biochemical signal creates an osteoblastic recruitment stimulus as long as it is above a threshold value. The model links the bone formation stimulus to the SED rate, which is modulated by osteocyte mechanosensitivity and distance attenuation. Fourth, the probability of osteoclast resorption is regulated either through the presence of microcracks within the bone matrix or by disuse.

Osteoclasts are activated by cytokines produced by osteoblasts, including bone lining cells (RANK/RANKL/OPG). The activation process may originate from an osteocyte signal. This theory now merges with Martin's inhibitory concept in that both assume that the osteocytic network normally suppresses osteoclast activation while transporting signals to the surface through mechanical loading. Disuse hampers suppression by reducing the inhibitory signal; microcracks hamper suppression by disconnection of the canaliculi. Parameters in the model can be linked to various metabolic factors.

Iteration of the computer simulation, starting from a generic regular grid, obtains homeostatic trabecular architecture. In homeostasis, the remodeling process continues to renew bone without altering mass or architecture generally. When the external load applied to the homeostatic architecture is rotated 30 degrees, the trabeculae gradually assume a reorientation aligned with the load (which is a demonstration of Wolff's law). This type of computer simulation further indicates that reduced load reduces trabecular thickness; increased load increases bone mass; a new homeostatic configuration results. Huiskes et al. argue that the mechanical feed-back model is a "potent and stable regulator of the complex biochemical metabolic machinery towards lasting optimality of form" (2000: 706). Large-scale finite element modeling (Ruimerman et al. 2005) confirms nineteenth-century speculation about a self-regulating biological system of cancellous bone adaptation (Roux 1881) and trajectorial architecture (Wolff 1986).

This discussion has described the current understanding of skeletal homeostasis through the activity of osteoblasts and osteoclasts, and has related how cell types such as osteocytes and bone-lining cells normally function in two distinct modes, remodeling and modeling. To illustrate these processes at work, the next section will provide an overview of selected aspects of two key age-associated skeletal changes within the human life cycle, namely endochondral ossification and age-associated bone loss.

ONTOGENIC PATTERNS AND MECHANICAL LOADING

The highly regulated multistep process of endochondral ossification sets the basic trabecular bone scaffold upon which all subsequent biologically and mechanically driven modeling and remodeling occurs. From growth plate cartilage down to the secondary spongiosa, trabecular bone morphogenesis is thought to be highly conserved, quantitatively predictable, and very similar among mammalian species (Byers et al. 2000; Salle et al. 2002). Descriptive qualitative and quantitative histomorphometric data on the growth plate and on the associated metaphyseal region of the long bones during human growth and development are well established in the scientific literature and demonstrate in general that trabecular bone mass (BV/TV) increases with age via an increase in trabecular thickness until skeletal maturity (Glorieux et al. 2000; Kneissel et al. 1997; Sontag 1994).

Recent studies of the ontogenetic patterning of human trabecular bone indicate a broad similarity in developmental processes, including modeling and remodeling, across various anatomical sites (humerus, femur, and tibia), while providing evidence that suggests a significant mechanical influence from the initiation and maturation of human bipedal locomotion (Gosman 2007; Gosman and Ketcham 2008; Ryan and Krovitz 2006; Ryan et al. 2007). The bone volume fraction (BV/TV) values for all three bones start out by being very high in the youngest individuals, then reach a minimum in all three bones around one year of age, and then progressively increase again to adult levels throughout development. Most significantly for a locomotor signal is the fact that the BV/TV is higher in the lower limb than in the upper limb. Also, the trabecular thickness results show a divergence between the humerus on the one hand and the femur and tibia on the other. Trabecular thickness increases progressively with age in all three anatomical locations; trabeculae in the tibia and femur are consistently thicker than trabeculae in the humerus. The results indicate that trabecular number (which decreases during ontogeny) and spatially specific anisotropy are more similar across all three bones.

Using finite element models to predict elastic properties of trabecular bone during development, Ryan and colleagues (2007) demonstrated the mechanical significance of the structural differences between the femur and the humerus. The elastic properties of femoral trabecular bone increased at a much faster rate than those of the humerus after the acquisition of unassisted bipedal walking. These results match quite nicely those of Ruff on the development of strength characteristics in the cortical bone of the humerus and femur in humans (Ruff 2003a,b; Sumner and Andriacchi 1996).

Trabecular bone produced at the growth plate is thought to contribute to metaphyseal and diaphyseal cortical bone (endosteal and haversian) through a process of trabecular coalescence, modified by modeling and remodeling (Cadet et al. 2003). This process is important to the longitudinal growth of cortical bone and provides a framework upon which intramembraneous periosteal bone apposition/resorption may work, being regulated in part by the site-specific mechanical environment (Tanck et al. 2006), by genetic patterning and regulatory framework, and by hormonal status.

BONE GAIN/LOSS

Age-associated bone loss is universal among human populations, past and present. Its severity and consequences, as measured by fracture risk, can have a significant impact on mortality and morbidity. While the proximate causes of bone loss include physical activity, inadequate nutrition, or sex hormone deficiency, all bone loss is mediated through remodeling disorders (Parfitt 2003). Bone size, peak bone mass, and architecture (for instance geometry) acquired during growth and development affect the loss of bone in later life. It is generally held that lifestyle in early life is important, and achieving adequate peak bone protects the elderly from fragility fractures (Heaney et al. 2000) Gafni and Baron (2007), however, call this into question, suggesting that bone mass accrual during the subadult years "will have only transient effects" and has little effect on the risk of developing osteoporosis later in life. In addition to bone mass, bone architecture is a determining factor for bone strength. During growth and development and to some extent during adult life, bones are capable of adaptation to patterns of physical activity by altering their geometry through modeling (Ruff et al. 2006). Bones arrive at adulthood with a mass and architecture determined in large part by adaptation to mechanical and other conditions experienced during childhood and adolescence.

The bones of young adults, for example, reflect their adaptation to increased size and muscle strength. Declining muscle strength, which occurs in aging adults, may reduce strain levels to 'trivial loading zone,' causing the loss of bone that is adjacent to marrow (Frost and Schönau 2000). Bone loss can result from changes in any aspect or combination of aspects of bone remodeling, activation, resorption, or formation. An increase in activation frequency can lead to reduced bone mass by decreasing bone volume fraction (that is, the ratio between the area of voids and the total area of bone) by increasing the area of Haversian canals and space occupied by BMUs in process of completion – for instance resorptive bays and refilling BMUs (Martin 1991). Activation frequency is reflected histomorphometrically in the number of BSUs (for example osteons and fragments) per unit area. During the resorptive phase of bone remodeling, osteoclasts may resorb more bone than the amount replaced by osteoblastic formation, or osteoblasts during the formation phase may refill the resorptive cavity incompletely. Both these processes lead to bone loss (Parfitt 2003).

An algorithm suggested by Wu and colleagues (1970) and by Frost (1987b) provides a method to estimate the activation frequency and the bone formation rate by using histomorphometry without requiring *in vivo* labeling. Applications of this algorithm to skeletal remains of various antiquities and to populations (Stout and Paine 1994; Stout and Lueck 1995; Cho and Stout 2003; Cho et al. 2006) suggest that bone remodeling dynamics may vary both among past human societies and among present ones.

CONCLUSIONS

In this chapter we have summarized current mechanobiological concepts and key skeletal cellular and metabolic processes that are essential to our understanding of bone biology and of its applications in biological anthropology. We hope that this summary instills greater appreciation for the increased complexity of our understanding of bone biology, whether viewed from the organ, tissue, cellular, or molecular level of analysis. It is our aspiration, too, to reinforce the value of interdisciplinary communication and the potential for collaborative research, which is indeed necessary.

In the future, research in biological anthropology in general and in skeletal biology in particular will probably require an advanced understanding of what is happening in many related biological and other fields. Topics of interest to skeletal biology include endochondral ossification, hormonal and nutritional influences on skeletal growth and development, population variation in bone metabolism, advanced skeletal and soft tissue imaging, computer simulation modeling, regulatory system biology, and genetic frameworks. The challenge for physical anthropologist is to use these advances not merely as simple tools, but with the aim of generating new research questions and insights and of applying unique approaches to investigate them.

REFERENCES

Agarwal, S., and Stout, S. (eds) (2003) *Bone Loss and Osteoporosis: An Anthropological Perspective*. New York: Kluwer Academic.

Bertram, J., and Biewener, A. (1988) Bone Curvature: Sacrificing Strength for Load Predictability? *Journal of Theoretical Biology* 131: 75–92.

Boyle, W., Simonet, W., and Lacey, D. (2003) Osteoclast Differentiation and Activation. *Nature* 432: 337–342.

Burger, E. H., Klein-Nulend, J., and Smit, T. H. (2003) Strain-Derived Canalicular Fluid Flow Regulates Osteoclast Activity in a Remodeling Osteon: A Proposal. *Journal of Biomechanics* 36: 1453–1459.

Burr, D. B. (1992) Orthopedic Principles of Skeletal Growth, Modeling, and Remodeling. In D. Carlson and S. Goldstein (eds), *Bone Biodynamics in Orthodontic and Orthopedic Treatment* (pp. 15–49). Ann Arbor: Center for Human Growth and Development, The University of Michigan.

Burr, D. B. (2002) Targeted and Nontargeted Remodeling. *Bone* 30: 2–4.

Byers S., Moore, A. J., Byard, R. W., and Fazzalari, N. L. (2000) Quantitative Histomorphometric Analysis of the Human Growth Plate from Birth to Adolescence. *Bone* 27 (4): 495–501.

Cadet, E. R., Gafni, R. I., McCarthy, E. F., McCray, D. R., Bacher, J. D., Barnes, K. M., and Baron, J. (2003) Mechanisms Responsible for Longitudinal Growth of the Cortex: Coalescence of Trabecular Bone into Cortical Bone. *Journal of Bone and Joint Surgery* 85–A: 1739–1748.

Carpenter R., and Carter, D. (2008) The Mechanical Effects of Periosteal Surface Loads. *Biomechanics and Modeling in Mechanobiology* 7: 227–242.

Carter, D., and Beaupré, G. (2001) *Skeletal Function and Form: Mechanobiology of Skeletal Development, Aging, and Regeneration*. Cambridge: Cambridge University Press.

Carter, D., van der Meulen, M., and Beaupré, G. (1996) Mechanical Factors in Bone Growth and Development. *Bone* 18: 5S–10S.

Cho, H., and Stout, S. D. (2003) Bone Remodeling and Age-Associated Bone Loss in the Past: A Histomorphometric Analysis of the Imperial Roman Skeletal Population of Isola Sacra. In S. Agarwal and S. Stout (eds), *Bone Loss and Osteoporosis: An Anthropological Perspective* (pp. 207–228). New York: Kluwer Academic.

Cho, H., Stout, S. D., and Bishop, T. (2006) Cortical Bone Remodeling Rates in a Sample of African American and European American Descent Groups from the American Midwest: Comparisons of Age and Sex in Ribs. *American Journal of Physical Anthropology* 130 (2): 214–226.

Donahue, H., Chen, Q., Saunders, C., and Yellowley, C. (2003) Bone Cells and Mechanotransduction. In R. Rosier and C. Evans (eds), *Molecular Biology in Orthopaedics* (pp. 179–190). Rosemont: American Academy of Orthopedic Surgeons.

Ducy, P., Schinke, T., and Karenty, G. (2000a) The Osteoblast: A Sophisticated Fibroblast under Central Surveillance. *Science* 289: 1501–1504.

Ducy, P., Amling, M., Takeda, S., Priemel, M., Schilling, A., Beil, F., Shen, J., Vinson, C., Reuger, J., and Karsenty, G. (2000b) Leptin Inhibits Bone Formation Through a Hypothalamic Relay: A Central Control of Bone Mass. *Cell* 100: 197–207.

Duong, L., and Rodan, A. (2001) Regulation of Osteoclast Formation and Function. *Reviews in Endocrine and Metabolic Disorders* 2: 95–104.

Frost, H. (1969) Tetracycline-Based Histological Analysis of Bone Remodeling. *Calcified Tissue Research* 3: 211–237.

Frost, H. (1987a) Bone 'Mass' and the 'Mechanostat: A Proposal. *Anatomical Record* 219: 1–9.

Frost, H. (1987b) Secondary Osteon Populations an Algorithm for Estimating the Missing Osteons. *Yearbook of Physical Anthropology* 30: 239–254.

Frost, H. (1989) Skeletal Structural Adaptations to Mechanical Usage (SATMU): 2. Redefining Wolff's Law: The Remodeling Problem. *Anatomical Record* 226: 414–422.

Frost, H. (2003) On Changing Views about Age-Related Bone Loss. In S. Agarwal and S. Stout (eds), *Bone Loss and Osteoporosis: An Anthropological Perspective* (pp. 19–32). New York: Kluwer Academic.

Frost, H., and Jee, W. (1994a) Perspectives: A Vital Biomechanical Model of the Endochondral Ossification Mechanism. *Anatomical Record* 240: 435–446.

Frost H., and Jee, W. (1994b) Perspectives: Applications of a Biomechanical Model of the Endochondral Ossification Mechanism. *Anatomical Record* 240: 447–455.

Frost, H., and Schönau, E. (2000) The 'Muscle-Bone Unit' in Children and Adolescents: A 2000 Overview. *Journal of Pediatric Endochronology and Metabolism* 13: 571–590.

Gafni, R. I., and Baron, J. (2007) Childhood Bone Mass Acquisition and Peak Bone Mass May Not Be Important Determinants of Bone Mass in Late Adulthood. *Pediatrics* 119: S131–S136.

Glorieux, F. H., Travers, R., Taylor, A., Bowen, J. R., Rauch, F., Norman, M., and Parfitt, A. M. (2000) Normative Data for Iliac Bone Histomorphometry in Growing Children. *Bone* 26 (2): 103–109.

Gosman, J. H. (2007) Patterns in Ontogeny of Human Trabecular Bone from Sunwatch Village in the Prehistoric Ohio Valley. PhD dissertation, Ohio State University.

Gosman, J. H., and Ketcham, R. A. (2008) Patterns in Ontogeny of Human Trabecular Bone from SunWatch Village in the Prehistoric Ohio Valley: General Features of Microarchitectural Change. *American Journal of Physical Anthropology*. Published online September 11: doi:10.1002/ajpa.20931.

Harada, S., and Rodan, G. (2003) Control of Osteoblast Function and Regulation of Bone Mass. *Nature* 423: 349–355.

Hauge, E. M., Qvesel, D., Eriksen, E. F., Mosekilde, L., and Melsen, F. (2001) Cancellous Bone Remodeling Occurs in Specialized Compartments Lined by Cells Expressing Osteoblastic Markers. *Journal of Bone and Mineral Research* 16 (9): 1575–1582.

Heaney, R. P., Abrams, S., Dawson-Hughes, B., Looker, A., Marcus, R., Matkovic, V., and Weaver, C. (2000) Peak Bone Mass. *Osteoporosis International* 11 (12): 985–1009.

Hu, H., Hilton, M. J., Tu, X., Yu, K., Ornitz, D. M., and Long, F. (2005) Sequential Roles for Hedgehog and Wnt Signaling in Osteoblast Development. *Development* 132: 49–60.

Huiskes, R. (2000) If Bone Is the Answer, then What Is the Question? *Journal of Anatomy* 197: 145–156.

Huiskes, R., Ruimerman, R., Van Lenthe, G., and Janssen, J. (1998) Indirect Osteoclast–Osteoblast Coupling through Mechanical Stress Relates Trabecular Morphogenesis and Adaptation to Bone Turn-Over. *Second Joint Meeting of The American Society for Bone and Mineral Research and the International Bone and Mineral Society* 23 (Suppl.1): S344.

Huiskes, R., Ruimerman, R., Van Lenthe, G., and Janssen, J. (2000) Effects of Mechanical Forces on Maintenance and Adaptation of Form in Trabecular Bone. *Nature* 405: 704–706.

Jacobs, C. (2000) The Mechanobiology of Cancellous Bone Structural Adaptation. *Journal of Rehabilitation Research and Development* 37: 1–16.

Jee, W. (2001) Integrated Bone Tissue Physiology: Anatomy and Physiology. In S. Cowin (ed.), *Bone Biomechanics Handbook*, 2nd edn (pp. 1–68). Boca Raton: CRC Press.

Jee, W., and Li, X. (1990) Adaptation of Cancellous Bone Overloading in the Adult Rat: A Single Photon Absorptiometry and Histomorphometry Study. *Anatomical Record* 227: 418–426.

Jee, W., Li, X., and Schaffer, M. (1991) Adaptation of Diaphyseal Structure with Aging and Increased Mechanical Usage in the Adult Rat: A Histomorphometrical and Biomechanical Study. *Anatomical Record* 230: 332–338.

Karsenty, G. (2001) Minireview: Transcriptional Control of Osteoblast Differentiation. *Endocrinology* 142: 2731–2733.

Kelly, J. (1998) The Third Culture. *Science* 279: 992–993.

Kneissel, M., Roschger, P., Steiner, W., Schamall, D., Kalchhauser, G., Boyde, A., and Teschler-Nicola, M. (1997) Cancellous Bone Structure in the Growing and Aging Lumbar Spine in a Historic Nubian Population. *Calcified Tissue International* 61: 95–100.

Lanyon, L. (1996) Using Functional Loading to Influence Bone Mass and Architecture Objectives, Mechanisms and Relationship with Estrogen of the Mechanically Adaptive Process in Bone. *Bone* 18: 37S–43S.

Marotti, G. (1996) The Structure of Bone Tissues and the Cellular Control of Their Deposition. *Italian Journal of Anatomy and Embryology* 101: 25–79.

Martin, R. B. (1991) On the Significance of Remodeling Space and Activation Rate Changes in Bone Remodeling. *Bone* 12 (6): 391–400.

Martin, R. B. (1994) On the Histological Measurement of Osteonal BMU Activation Frequency. *Bone* 15: 547–549.

Martin, R. (2000) Toward a Unifying Theory of Bone Remodeling. *Bone* 26: 1–6.

Martin, R. (2003) Functional Adaptation and Fragility of the Skeleton. In S. Agarwal and S. Stout (eds), *Bone Loss and Osteoporosis: An Anthropological Perspective* (pp. 121–138). New York: Kluwer Academic.

Martin, R. (2007) Targeted Bone Remodeling Involves BMU Steering As Well As Activation. *Bone* 40 (6): 1574–1580.

Martin, R., Burr, D., and Sharkey, N. (1998) *Skeletal Tissue Mechanics*. New York: Springer.

Massaro, E., and Rogers, J. (eds) (2004) *The Skeleton*. Totowa, NJ: Humana Press.

Melsen, F., Mosekilde, L., and Eriksen, E. (1995) Spatial Distribution of Sinusoids in Relation to Remodeling Sites: Evidence for Specialized Sinusoidal Structures Associated with Formative Sites. *Journal of Bone and Mineral Research* 10: S209.

Mullender, M., and Huiskes, R. (1997) Osteocytes and Bone Lining Cells: Which are the Best Candidates for Mechano-Sensors in Cancellous Bone? *Bone* 6: 527–532.

Mullender, M., Meer, D., Huiskes, R., and Lips, P. (1996) Osteocyte Density Changes in Aging and Osteoporosis. *Bone* 18: 109–113.

Nashida, S., and Endo, N. (1999) Number of Osteoprogenitor Cells in Human Bone Marrow Markedly Decreases after Skeletal Maturation. *Journal of Bone and Mineral Metabolism* 17: 171–177.

Parfitt, A. M. (1994) Osteonal and Hemi-Osteonal Remodeling: The Spatial and Temporal Framework for Signal Traffic in Adult Human Bone. *Journal of Cellular Biochemistry* 55: 273–286.

Parfitt, A. M. (2000) The Mechanism of Coupling: A Role for the Vasculature. *Bone* 26: 319–323.

Parfitt, A. M. (2002) Targeted and Nontargeted Bone Remodeling: Relationship to Basic Multicellular Unit Origination and Progression. *Bone* 30: 5–7.

Parfitt, A. M. (2003) New Concepts of Bone Remodeling: A Unified Spatial and Temporal Model with Physiologic and Pathophysiologic Implications. In S. Agarwal and S. Stout (eds), *Bone Loss and Osteoporosis: An Anthropological Perspective* (pp. 3–17). New York: Kluwer Academic.

Parfitt, A. M., Drezner, M. K., Glorieux, F. H., Kanis, J. A., Malluche, H., Meunier, P. J., Ott, S. M., and Recker, R. R. (1987) Bone Histomorphometry Nomenclature, Symbols, and Units. Report of the ASBMR Histomorphometry Nomenclature Committee. *Journal of Bone and Mineral Research* 2: 595–610.

Pearson, O., and Lieberman, D. (2004) The Aging of Wolff's 'Law': Ontogeny and Responses to Mechanical Loading in Cortical Bone. *Yearbook of Physical Anthropology* 47: 63–99.

Pettit, A. R., Chang, M. K., and Hume, D. A. (2008) Osteal Macrophages: A New Twist on Coupling during Bone Dynamics. *Bone* 43: 976–982.

Robling, A. G., Castillo, A. B., and Turner, C.H. (2006) Biomechanical and Molecular Regulation of Bone Remodeling. *Annual Review of Biomedical Engineering* 8 (1): 455–498.

Roesler, H. (1987) The History of Some Fundamental Concepts in Bone Biomechanics. *Journal of Biomechanics* 20: 1025–1034.

Rosier, R., and Evans, C. (eds) (2003) *Molecular Biology in Orthopaedics*. Rosemont: American Academy of Orthopedic Surgeons.

Roux, W. (1881) *Der Kampf der Teile im Organismus*. Leipzig: Englemann.

Rubin, J., and Rubin, C. (2008) Functional Adaptation to Loading of a Single Bone Is Neuronally Regulated and Involves Multiple Bones. *Journal of Bone and Mineral Research* 23 (9): 1369–1371.

Ruff, C. (2003a) Growth in Bone Strength, Body Size, and Muscle Size in a Juvenile Longitudinal Sample. *Bone* 33: 317–329.

Ruff, C. (2003b) Ontogenetic Adaptation to Bipedalism: Age Changes in Femoral to Humeral Length and Strength Proportions in Humans, with a Comparison to Baboons. *Journal of Human Evolution* 45: 317–349.

Ruff, C., Holt, B., and Trinkaus, E. (2006) Who's Afraid of the Big Bad? 'Wolff's Law' and Bone Functional Adaptation. *American Journal of Physical Anthropology* 129: 484–498.

Ruimerman, R., Hilbers, P., van Reitbergen, B., and Huiskes, R. (2005) A Theoretical Framework for Strain-Related Trabecular Bone Maintenance and Adaptation. *Journal of Biomechanics* 38: 931–941.

Ryan, T. M., and Krovitz, G. E. (2006) Trabecular Bone Ontogeny in the Human Proximal Femur. *Journal of Human Evolution* 51 (6): 591–602.

Ryan, T. M., van Rietbergen, B., and Krovitz, G. (2007) Mechanical Adaptation of Trabecular Bone in the Growing Human Femur and Humerus. *American Journal of Physical Anthropology* S46: 205.

Salle, B. L., Rauch, F., Travers, R., Bouvier, R., and Glorieux, F. H. (2002) Human Fetal Bone Development: Histomorphometric Evaluation of the Proximal Femoral Metaphysis. *Bone* 30 (6): 823–828.

Sample, S. J., Behan, M., Smith, L., Oldenhoff, W. E., Markel, M. D., Kalscheur, V. L., Hao, Z., Miletic, V., and Muir, P. (2008) Functional Adaptation to Loading of a Single Bone Is

Neuronally Regulated and Involves Multiple Bones. *Journal of Bone and Mineral Research* 23 (9): 1372–1381.

Sommerfeldt, D., and Rubin, C. (2001) Biology of Bone and How It Orchestrates the Form and Function of the Skeleton. *European Spine Journal* 10: S86–S95.

Sontag, W. (1994) Age-Dependent Morphometric Change in the Lumbar Vertebrae of Male and Female Rats: Comparison with the Femur. *Bone* 15 (6): 593–601.

St-Arnaud, R. (2003) Transcriptional Control of the Osteoblast Phenotype. In R. Rosier and C. Evans (eds), *Molecular Biology in Orthopaedics* (pp. 191–209). Rosemont: American Academy of Orthopedic Surgeons.

Stout, S., and Lueck, P. (1995) Bone Remodeling Rates and Skeletal Maturation in Three Archaeological Skeletal Populations. *American Journal of Physical Anthropology* 98: 161–171.

Stout, S., and Paine, R. (1994) Bone Remodeling Rates: A Test of an Algorithm for Estimating Missing Osteons. *American Journal of Physical Anthropology* 93: 123–129.

Sumner, D. R., and Andriacchi, T. P. (1996) Adaptation to Differential Loading: Comparison of Growth-Related Changes in Cross-Sectional Properties of the Human Femur and Humerus. *Bone* 19: 121–126.

Tanck, E., Homminga, J., Van Lenthe, G., and Huiskes, R. (2001) Increase in Bone Volume Fraction Precedes Architectural Adaptation in Growing Bone. *Bone* 28: 650–654.

Tanck, E., Hannink, G., Ruimerman, R., Buma, P., Burger, E. H., and Huiskes, R. (2006) Cortical Bone Development Under the Growth Plate is Regulated by Mechanical Load Transfer. *Journal of Anatomy* 208: 73–79.

Teitelbaum, S. (2000) Bone Resorption by Osteoclasts. *Science* 289: 1504–1508.

van der Meulen, M., and Huiskes, R. (2002) Why Mechanobiology? A Survey Article. *Journal of Biomechanics* 35: 401–414.

van Oers, R. (2008) A Unified Theory for Osteonal and Hemi-Osteonal Remodeling. *Bone* 42 (2): 250–259.

van Oers, R., Ruimerman, R., van Reitbergen, B., Hilbers, A., and Huiskes, R. (2008) Relating Osteon Diameter to Strain. *Bone* 43: 476–482.

Williams, B. O., and Insogna, K. L. (2009) Where Wnts Went: The Exploding Field of Lrp5 and Lrp6 Signaling in Bone. *Journal of Bone and Mineral Research* 24: 171–178.

Wolff, J. (1986) *The Law of Bone Remodeling*, translated by P. Maquet and R. Furlong. Berlin: Springer-Verlag.

Wu, K. K., Schubeck, H. F., and Villanueva, A. (1970) Haversian Bone Formation Rates Determined by a New Method in a Mastadon and in Human Diabetes Mellitus and Osteoporosis. *Calcified Tissue Research* 6: 204–219.

Yellowley, C. E., Li, Z., Zhou, Z., Jacobs, C. R., and Donahue, H. J. (2000) Functional Gap Junctions between Osteocytic and Osteoblastic Cells. *Journal of Bone and Mineral Research* 15: 209–217.

CHAPTER 27

'Growing Planes': Incremental Growth Layers in the Dental Enamel of Human Ancestors

Debbie Guatelli-Steinberg

In 1667, Niels Stensen (also know as 'Steno') had an epiphany while dissecting a shark. Its teeth were uncannily similar to commonly found pieces of rock known as *glossopetrae* or 'tongue stones.' Steno recognized the true identity of these 'tongue stones' as fossilized shark teeth (Maisey 1997). Actually much of the vertebrate fossil record consists of teeth, largely because teeth are the hardest elements of the skeleton (Hillson 1996). The same is true of the human fossil record (although fossilized shark teeth are much more common than those of humans, as sharks lose hundreds of teeth during their lifetime and have been around since the Devonian).

While teeth themselves are hard, their hardest component is enamel, the outer covering of dental crowns, which comes into direct contact with food. Ninety-six percent of mature enamel is mineral, composed of hydroxyapatite – a crystalline calcium phosphate (Ten Cate 1994). No cells are contained in mature enamel, so that, once it is formed, enamel cannot regrow in the way bone can (ibid.). Incremental growth layers in enamel, somewhat analogous to tree-rings, can therefore be preserved for millions of years in fossilized enamel. As enamel in different teeth is formed throughout all the span of time between the prenatal period and late childhood (Hillson 1996), the study of enamel growth in human fossil ancestors provides a window into growth during the early years of life.

In this essay I will describe the basic biology of enamel growth and highlight three areas of paleoanthropological inquiry to which the study of enamel growth contributes important insights. The first of these areas is delimited by the question of life histories of fossil hominins. In an evolutionary context, the phrase 'life history' refers to "a series of growth and maturational phases ultimately related to the scheduling of reproduction and lifetime reproductive output" (Kelley and Smith 2003). These phases include, or are related to, gestation period, age at weaning, age at sexual maturity and first breeding, interbirth intervals, and longevity. Among primates, humans have the most protracted life histories, with particularly long periods of juvenile growth, commonly referred to as 'childhood' (Bogin 1997). Our prolonged periods of juvenile growth are probably related to the very high energy requirements imposed by the growth of our large brains: somatic growth rates are reduced in order to divert energy to brain growth (Leigh and Blomquist 2007; and see Deaner et al. 2003 for a review of this and other hypotheses about the relationship between brain size and growth periods in primates). The study of enamel growth in fossil hominins is making a major contribution to our understanding of *when* our uniquely long human childhood evolved.

While analyzing enamel growth in fossils, researchers have found differences among species (or groups of hominins) in the way in which enamel is formed. Analyzing patterns of enamel growth formation is therefore a second area of inquiry, related to the first, and one which provides insight into differences in growth *processes* among various species. The third area of research which the study of enamel growth addresses is that of physiological stress in fossil hominins. Periods of malnutrition or bouts of disease can disrupt enamel growth, leaving permanent records of these events in fossilized enamel (Hillson 1996). A great deal more has been accomplished in each of these three areas than can be touched upon in this introductory essay. Nevertheless, my essay calls attention to some of the key findings and issues involved in the study of hominin enamel growth.

Background: The Incremental Nature of Enamel Growth

Viewed from inside out, a tooth crown consists of three major tissues: pulp, dentine, and enamel (Figure 27.1, A). Pulp is a soft tissue surrounded by dentine, a hard tissue that is 70 percent mineralized. The harder and more brittle enamel covering of the tooth crown gains some protection from fracture through the shock-absorbing quality of the softer dentine, which underlies it (Ten Cate 1994). The following account of enamel formation is summarized from descriptions by Ten Cate (1994) – except where otherwise noted.

Enamel begins to form at the cusp tip of a crown. In response to the first formed dentine, enamel-forming cells called 'ameloblasts' secrete an organic matrix of proteins which serves the purpose of 'accepting' mineral. Ameloblasts continue to differentiate from epithelial cells *sequentially*, along the presumptive enamel–dentine junction (Figure 27.1, B–C) in response to the sequential formation of dentine along the length of the crown. The rate at which ameloblast differentiation occurs is known as the 'enamel extension rate' (Shellis 1984). As ameloblasts become functional, they migrate away from the enamel–dentine junction and towards what will eventually become the enamel surface, secreting the enamel matrix as they go. During this first step, which is the secretory stage of enamel formation, enamel reaches a state of 30 percent mineralization. After ameloblasts have formed the full thickness of the enamel, they undergo morphological changes associated with the maturation stage of enamel formation, as they cycle between removing water and the organic components of the matrix and introducing additional mineral. Enamel reaches its fully mineralized state at the end of the maturation stage.

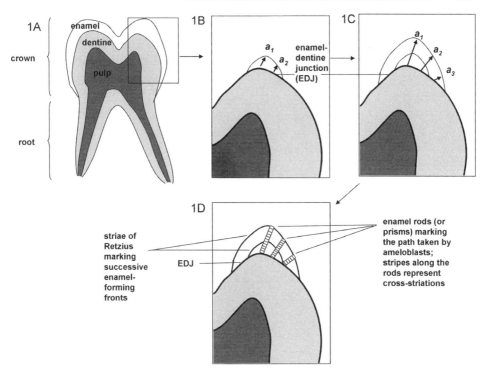

Figure 27.1 Process of enamel formation

A   Dental tissues

B   Enlargement of boxed area in A at the point when enamel first began to form at the cusp tip. The arrows represent the paths of two ameloblasts (a_1 and a_2). At the point in time illustrated here, the first ameloblast has been active secreting enamel for more time than the second. The enamel dome represents a slowing of the enamel-forming front at this particular time

C   A second dome of enamel covers the first and successive ameloblasts (represented by a_3) continue to differentiate along the enamel-dentine junction

D* Striae of Retzius marking the successive enamel-forming fronts are shown. Enamel rods with cross-striations are also shown

The incremental nature of enamel growth is reflected in microstructural details of the enamel formed during the secretory stage. Aside from a small portion of the enamel formed first and last, the enamel formed by each ameloblast attains a rod-like structure (Figure 27.1, D), which is referred to either as an enamel rod (Ten Cate 1994) or as an enamel prism (Dean 1987). Enamel rods reflect the path of the ameloblasts which formed them (Risnes 1986) (Figure 27.1, D). In enamel thin sections inspected through a transmitted light microscope, fine lines known as 'cross-striations' cross-cut the enamel rods. Over the length of the rod cross-striations appear to form at regular intervals (Dean 1987; see Figure 27.1, D). Experimental studies from the 1930s first suggested that cross-striations are formed according to a circadian rhythm (that is, a twenty-four-hour rhythm; for a review, see Dean 1987). Bromage (1991) produced experimental confirmation of this rhythm. The exact physiological mechanism(s) underlying this rhythm are not known, but daily variation in the

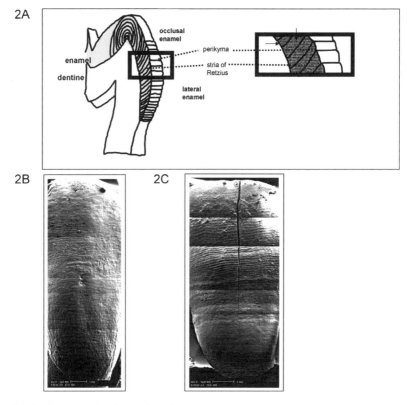

Figure 27.2   Striae of Retzius and perikymata

A   Relationship between striae of Retzius and perikymata. In the inset, the horizontal arrow shows the direction of the enamel rods, while the vertical arrow points to a cross-striation along the rod. Adapted, with alterations, from an illustration in Ten Cate 1994

B   Perikymata on the enamel surface of a Neandertal (Krapina 90) lower lateral incisor. Scanning electron micrograph

C   Perikymata on the enamel surface of an archaeological Inupiaq (Point Hope, Alaska) lateral incisor. Scanning electron micrograph

metabolic activity of ameloblasts may underlie the daily rhythm of cross-striations (Boyde 1979; Dean 1987; Fitzgerald 1998).

Cross-striations are sometimes referred to as short-period increments, so as to be differentiated from a second kind of incremental growth, present in enamel, which is represented by long-period increments (Dean 2000). When viewed under a transmitted light microscope, long-period increments in enamel appear as dark lines traversing a series of enamel rods (Figure 27.2, A is an idealized diagram). More commonly, long-period increments in the enamel are called 'striae of Retzius' (Hillson 1996), after their discoverer Anders Retzius, a Swedish anatomist of the nineteenth century.

Striae of Retzius are actually a series of growth layers in a three-dimensional tooth. These growth layers are formed when all the ameloblasts along the enamel-forming front (Figure 27.1, B–D) simultaneously slow their secretion of the enamel matrix (Dean 1987). The simultaneous slowing of secretory ameloblasts has been shown to occur at regular intervals throughout all of the teeth of an individual (Dean 1987; Fitzgerald 1998), which suggests a systemic physiological cause. The interval varies among individuals, but it is constant for the teeth of any particular individual (Fitzerald 1998). In humans, the interval was for a long time thought to center around seven days; but recent evidence suggests that the average interval in humans is eight or nine days, ranging from a minimum of six to a maximum of twelve days for any one individual (Dean and Reid 2001a; Reid and Dean 2006). To determine this interval, one counts the number of cross-striations that fall between the striae of Retzius. For example, if eight cross-striations are counted between two striae of Retzius, then the interval in question, which is also referred to as the 'periodicity of the striae,' is 9 days.

In a tooth's cuspal or occlusal enamel, the striae of Retzius (layers in three dimensions) cover each other in a series of domes, and so they are not visible from the tooth's surface (Figure 27.2, A). Thus, in cuspal enamel, the striae of Retzius are sometimes called 'hidden' or 'buried' increments. However, on the sides of a tooth, in a tooth's lateral enamel, the striae of Retzius form a series of layered planes in three dimensions, which are called 'Retzius planes.' These 'growing planes' actually emerge onto the surface of enamel (Figure 27.2, A). Here then, in the lateral enamel, the growth layers are no longer buried. The surface manifestations of Retzius planes are known as 'perikymata' (a plural form of the noun 'perikyma'). The name is based on the ancient Greek noun *kuma*, meaning 'wave.' This choice was inspired by the wave-like 'crests' and 'troughs' which perikymata exhibit (Hillson 1996; see Figure 27.2, B–C). With the aid of a microscope, perikymata can be directly observed and counted on fossil enamel surfaces, as long as they haven't been worn or eroded away. Because perikymata are simply surface manifestions of the striae of Retzius, it follows that the periodicity of an individual's striae is exactly the same as the periodicity of his or her perikymata. By counting all the perikymata from the cusp of the tooth to its cervix (the 'bottom' of the tooth), and by considering a range of possible periodicities, an estimated range can be calculated for the time a fossil tooth's lateral enamel took to form.

Although ideally one would want to have a way of looking inside fossil teeth (through natural fractures, through thin-sectioning, or through innovative new synchrotron techniques: Smith and Tafforeau 2008) in order to determine the exact periodicity of the perikymata, doing so is often not possible because of research budget limitations (in the case of new synchrotron techniques) or because of the need to preserve precious fossil remains (in the case of thin-sectioning). Likewise, to determine a tooth's *overall* enamel formation time – in other words, cuspal plus lateral enamel formation time – it would be necessary to look inside a tooth to count the 'buried' or 'hidden' increments in the cuspal enamel. Because this, too, is often not possible, many studies of fossil teeth have focused on counting perikymata on anterior teeth (incisors and canines) rather than on posterior teeth (premolars and molars) – since in the former a much smaller proportion of overall enamel formation time is hidden in the cuspal region (Hillson and Bond 1997).

ENAMEL GROWTH AND THE TEMPO OF FOSSIL HOMININ LIFE HISTORIES

The pace of a primate species' life history is related to its rate of dental development. B. H. Smith (1989, 1991, and 1992) has demonstrated this relationship clearly, particularly with respect to the age at which the first permanent molar erupts. Her analyses of twenty-one species of primates from diverse taxonomic groups showed that the age at which the first molar emerges into the oral cavity is highly correlated with life history variables such as gestation length, weaning age, and age at sexual maturity in females. This relationship exists largely because skeletal growth is slower in species with bigger brains and protracted life histories, so that molars cannot emerge into the jaw until the jaw grows big enough to accommodate them (Smith 1992). Larger-brained species with slow life histories tend to have later first molar eruption ages than smaller-brained species with faster life histories. The first molars erupt in humans at around six years of age (Hillson 1996). Chimpanzees, humans' closest primate relatives, have brains approximately one fourth to one third the size of human brains and an age of first molar eruption that is two to three years earlier than that of humans (Zihlman et al. 2004). The study of fossil hominin tooth enamel addresses the question of when human growth prolongation first began.

Early human ancestors, such as *Australopithecus*, had small brains, not much larger than those of chimpanzees (Smith and Tompkins 1995). Thus, on the basis of the relationship between brain size and first molar eruption, Smith (1991) argued that *Australopithecus* would have had an age of first molar eruption closer to that of chimpanzees than to that of humans. Bromage and Dean (1985) and Beynon and Dean (1988) actually demonstrated that this was true by counting the perikymata on the surfaces of the anterior (incisor and canine) teeth of early hominins. Their analysis of *Australopithecus afarensis* specimen LH2 (from Laetoli, Tanzania, dated to approximately 3.7 mya) illustrates their approach. This ancient hominin died at the point when his/her lower central incisor crown had just completed its growth and when his/her first molar had already erupted into the oral cavity. The lower central incisor had 130 perikymata on its lateral surface. Assuming a seven-day periodicity (which has recently been confirmed as average for early hominins (Lacruz et al. 2008)), these 130 perikymata represent approximately 2.5 years of growth. Adding an estimate for the age at which the first incisor begins to calcify (approximately 0.5 years after birth in humans) and an estimate for the 'buried' Retzius planes in the cuspal enamel (approximately 0.5 years in human teeth), Beynon and Dean (1988) estimated that the LH2 individual was 3.5 years of age at death. Clearly, with a first molar having already erupted at this age, this *Australopithecus afarensis* individual had a rate of dental development which was far more similar to that of chimpanzee than to that of a modern human. This was also the case with the other specimens of *Australopithecus* and *Paranthropus* examined by these two researchers.

Australopithecus (as well as *Paranthropus*) did not only have earlier ages than modern humans at the eruption of the first molar. Counts of perikymata on these early hominins' anterior teeth revealed that these teeth also took, on average, less time to form than those of modern humans (Dean et al. 2001). What is more, the anterior teeth of *Paranthropus* formed in even shorter periods of time than those in *Australopithecus* (ibid.).

The first glimmerings of growth prolongation in our ancestors occurred with *Homo erectus*, a species with a brain which was larger than that of *Australopithecus* but smaller than our own brain (Smith and Tompkins 1995). Dean and colleagues (2001), using more complex histological methods than can be described here on crown and root sections of the Javanese *Homo erectus* specimen Sangiran S-37, estimated that, in this individual, first molar emergence would have occurred around 4.4 years of age. These researchers were also able to count perikymata on the anterior teeth of WT-15000, the 'Nariokotome boy' (an African *Homo erectus* or *Homo ergaster* specimen). Interestingly, for this specimen, estimates of overall crown formation time based on these counts fell well within the estimated range for *Australopithecus*, and below the estimated range for modern humans (ibid.). Furthermore, these researchers determined that enamel formation in the Nariokotome boy's lower canine was completed at the age of 4 years. Dean and colleagues argued that, if the Nariokotome boy was like modern humans in completing enamel formation in his lower canine at the time of M1 emergence, then his first molar would have emerged at approximately 4 years of age. Hence these data on the enamel formation time and on the estimated first molar emergence in *Homo erectus* suggest only a minimal shift towards the prolongation of growth in this species. The small magnitude of this shift was predicted on the basis of the regression of first molar emergence on cranial capacities across modern primate species (Smith and Tompkins 1995).

So, when did growth periods of the same length as those of modern humans evolve? Bermúdez de Castro and colleagues (1999) reported a modern human pattern of dental development in the 0.8-million-year-old hominins from Atapuerca-TD6 (Spain). The state of *relative* development in pairs of each individual's anterior and posterior teeth was similar to that displayed by modern humans. Similarities in relative dental development can, however, belie differences in the absolute time it takes to form the dentition. For example, the nearly simultaneous eruption of first molars and first incisors in both *Paranthropus* and *Homo sapiens* (Bromage 1990) does not necessarily mean that these two taxa shared the same absolute rate of development. It has already been noted that the dental development of *Paranthropus* is accelerated – in absolute time – both with respect to that of *Australopithecus* and with respect to that of modern humans.

The earliest convincing evidence of modern human growth periods occurs with the advent of anatomically modern humans. T. Smith and co-workers used an innovative technique – X-ray synchrotron microtomography – to actually 'look inside' the teeth of the 160,000-year-old *Homo sapiens* dental remains of the Jebel Irhoud specimen from Morocco (Smith et al. 2007b). In so doing, they found this specimen to have the highest periodicity – ten days – among all hominin fossils yet known. These researchers determined that overall enamel formation times in the teeth of this specimen, which were large by modern human standards, were actually *greater* than those of modern humans. Furthermore, Smith and colleagues determined that this individual died at the age of 7.78 years, when its other teeth (premolars and molars) were at stages of development comparable to those of a modern European of the same age.

If early modern humans like Jebel Irhoud had growth periods similar to our own, then were Neandertals, too, like us in this regard? With brain sizes similar to, or greater than, those of modern humans, Neandertals might be expected to have had prolonged juvenile growth periods. Indeed, on the basis of their regression of first molar eruption on brain size across primate species, Smith and Tompkins (1995) predicted that Neandertal first molars would have erupted at around 6.4 years of age.

At the time of writing this chapter, however, the dental evidence bearing on the question of Neandertal life histories is equivocal. Within just the last few years, studies with contradictory findings have been published. First, a study by Ramirez-Rozzi and Bermúdez de Castro (2004) demonstrated that the anterior teeth of Neandertals had fewer perikymata than those of their anatomically modern counterparts from the upper Paleolithic in Europe. On this basis, the two authors suggested that Neandertals had a shorter childhood than modern humans. However, in the following year, my colleagues and I demonstrated that, when compared to a diverse set of today's modern humans, Neandertals actually did *not* have fewer perikymata on their anterior teeth (Guatelli-Steinberg et al. 2005). But our findings still did not settle the question of whether Neandertals had prolonged periods of growth – they simply showed that the number of perikymata on Neandertal anterior teeth does not suggest that Neandertals had shorter childhoods than today's humans. More definitive evidence could be obtained if the age of first molar eruption could be determined in a Neandertal. After all, it is first molar eruption, and not the formation times of anterior tooth enamel, that has been shown to be so closely related to overall developmental rates in non-human primates.

The year after my colleagues and I published our study, another team of researchers estimated the age of first molar eruption in the La Chaise Neandertal from France (Macchiarelli et al. 2006). Their estimate was 6.7 years of age, quite close to the 6.4 years of age which B. H. Smith and Tompkins (1995) had predicted on the basis of Neandertal brain size. Yet, one year later, T. Smith and colleagues analyzed molar development in the Scladina Neandertal from Belgium, which suggested more rapid development than that of modern humans (Smith et al. 2007a). The two studies employed different methods to estimate root formation time, and this may be part of the reason for the contradiction between them. Or it could simply be that Neandertals differed greatly in the amount of time their teeth took to develop, some of them being more like modern humans in this regard. Certainly there is much yet to be learned about Neandertal dental development and about the pace of Neandertal life histories.

VARIATION IN ENAMEL GROWTH PATTERNS

While studying enamel growth in early hominins, Beynon and Dean (1988) noted an interesting difference between *Australopithecus* and *Paranthropus*. In the former, perikymata became much more compact in the final (cervical) third of the crown to form. In the latter perikymata were more evenly distributed, as well as absolutely widely spaced over the entire length of the crown. The authors attributed the wider spacing of perikymata in *Paranthropus* to fast enamel extension rates (the rate at which new ameloblasts along the enamel–dentine junction are recruited to form enamel). Beynon and Wood (1987) had previously examined naturally fractured teeth of *Paranthropus*, finding very rapid extension rates in this genus. These studies shed light on the developmental processes involved in producing the differences in enamel formation time between *Paranthropus* and *Australopithecus* noted earlier. Consistently faster extension rates in *Paranthropus* resulted in more widely spaced, and thus fewer, perikymata on their enamel surfaces. Beynon and Wood (1987) noted that the rapidity with which enamel was formed in *Paranthropus* was especially interesting given the great thickness of this species' enamel.

Although the wide spacing of perikymata in *Paranthropus* reflects its rapid rate of enamel extension, one cannot assume as a general rule that the spacing of perikymata along the surface reflects the enamel extension rate along the enamel–dentine junction.

Other variables such as periodicity, the rate of enamel secretion, enamel thickness, and the course of the striae of Retzius may also affect the absolute spacing of perikymata on the enamel surface (Schwartz and Dean 2001). Further, it is important to note that the absolute spacing of perikymata on the enamel surface (perikymata per mm) is not the same thing as the *distribution pattern* of perikymata over the tooth crown. The distribution pattern of perikymata on any particular tooth reflects variation in the rate of enamel formation as measured along the enamel surface, which could be caused by different enamel growth processes (for instance the enamel extension rate and/or the enamel secretion rate). Is that distribution somewhat uniform, as it is in *Paranthropus*, reflecting a uniform overall rate of enamel formation along the enamel surface? Or is a greater proportion of perikymata present in the cervical portion of the crown, reflecting, as it does in *Australopithecus*, a relative slowing down of enamel formation along the enamel surface?

Dean and Reid (2001b) found that in early *Australopithecus* (*A. afarensis*) there was an even greater proportion of perikymata in the cervical region of the crown than there was in later *Australopithecus* (*A. africanus*). These researchers found that the distribution of perikymata along the length of the crown in early *Australopithecus* was actually somewhat like that found in the modern humans. The teeth of a single *Homo habilis* individual (OH 7), too, showed this more human-like pattern. Yet Dean and Reid (2001b) found that, in *Homo erectus*, the distribution of perikymata more closely resembled the more uniform pattern shown by *Paranthropus*. This may seem a bit strange if *Homo erectus* is a modern human ancestor.

Perhaps, however, the more uniform pattern in which perikymata are distributed in *Homo erectus* is not so strange after all. Ramirez-Rozzi and Bermúdez de Castro (2004) have shown that more uniform perikymata distribution patterns characterized *Homo heidelbergensis*, a species which followed *Homo erectus* in the fossil record but preceded Neandertals. The uniform pattern characterizing the teeth of *Homo erectus*, of *Homo heidelbergensis*, and of Neandertals differed from the more modern human-like patterns exhibited by the Neandertals' contemporaries and successors: upper Paleolithic modern humans (Ramirez-Rozzi and Bermúdez de Castro (2004).

My colleagues and I recently compared the distribution of perikymata on Neandertal teeth to that exhibited by modern human people from disparate regions of the world: Europe, southern Africa, and Alaska (Guatelli-Steinberg et al. 2007; Guatelli-Steinberg and Reid 2008, and Reid et al. 2008). Interestingly, although there are some differences in the way perikymata are distributed in the teeth of these modern people, all of them share a common pattern, in which perikymata become relatively more compact in the cervical half than they are in the cuspal half of the crown. Neandertals show much less of a difference in perikymata compaction between the cuspal and the cervical halves of their crowns (compare the Neandertal and modern human teeth shown in Figures 27.2, B and C). Neandertals are therefore quite distinct in this regard not only from upper Paleolithic modern humans, but also from more recent modern humans.

Thus, although Neandertal anterior teeth were not different from some modern human groups in their total *number* of perikymata, Neandertal anterior teeth did show a considerable difference from those of modern humans in the distribution of perikymata on their crowns. Such a difference in the developmental processes which underlie enamel formation in Neandertals and modern humans should not be so surprising, given that Neandertals and modern humans differ in many other anatomical features and, according to recent DNA analyses, shared their last common ancestor some 400,000–600,000 years ago (Green et al. 2006; Noonan et al. 2006). Other recent studies also find differences between Neandertals and modern humans in enamel formation processes (Macchiarelli et al. 2006; Smith et al. 2007a).

Enamel Growth Disruptions

When systemic physiological stress – induced for instance by malnutrition or illness – is severe enough, it can disturb enamel formation; this results in a particular type of developmental defect, called 'enamel hypoplasia' (Hillson 1996). These stresses disrupt ameloblasts (enamel-producing cells) during the secretory phase of enamel formation (Goodman and Rose 1990; Ten Cate 1994), causing pits or horizontal grooves in the enamel, and occasionally even missing enamel (Fédération Dentaire Internationale 1982, 1992). Once formed, these defects become permanent features of the crown, unless the defects are worn away by abrasion or attrition. For these reasons, and because teeth are the most abundant of skeletal remains, enamel hypoplasias have become one of the most important sources of information about systemic physiological stress in fossil hominins (see for example Bombin 1990; Brennan 1991; Brunet 2002; Guatelli-Steinberg 2003, 2004; Guatelli-Steinberg et al. 2004; Hutchinson et al. 1997; Molnar and Molnar 1985; Ogilvie et al. 1989; White 1978).

Linear enamel hypoplasia (LEH) is the most common type of hypoplastic defect; it takes the form of 'furrows' on the enamel surface (Hillson and Bond 1997). Among the different types of hypoplastic defects, LEH has the greatest potential to reveal information about the duration of enamel growth disturbances. This potential resides in the crucial facts about enamel formation discussed earlier, and in the nature of LEH defects themselves. In a LEH defect, growth disruptions cause ameloblasts to prematurely stop secreting enamel matrix, which results in the exposure of wider than normal portions of the Retzius planes at the enamel surface. Thus perikymata are clearly associated with LEH defects, and can therefore be used to estimate the duration of disruptions in enamel growth (Hillson and Bond 1997; Figure 27.3, A).

In recent studies I have attempted to use the perikymata in LEH defects for estimating the duration of growth disruptions in fossil hominins (Guatelli-Steinberg 2003, 2004; Guatelli-Steinberg et al. 2004). Through microscopic investigation, Hillson and Bond (1997) determined that perikymata are more widely spaced than normal in the occlusal walls of hypoplastic furrows, and that these 'occlusal wall' perikymata therefore reflect the period of disrupted growth. Perikymata in the cervical wall of a defect represent instead a return to normal growth (Hillson and Bond 1997). Figure 27.3, A is a diagram showing a linear defect's occlusal and cervical walls and the perikymata that comprise them. If perikymata can be seen within a defect on an actual tooth crown, then the duration of disrupted growth can be estimated. The Neandertal defect depicted in Figure 27.3, B, with twelve perikymata in its occlusal wall, represents between 84 to 120 days of growth disruption (assuming a perikymata periodicity of seven to ten days).

Enamel hypoplasias in Neandertals are of particular interest because several researchers have argued that Neandertals lived under conditions of nutritional stress (Jelinek 1994) and were inefficient foragers (Trinkaus 1986; Soffer 1994; but see Sorensen

3A

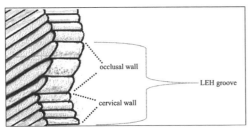

3B

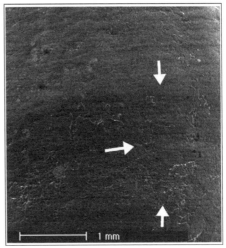

Figure 27.3 Linear enamel hypoplasia
A   Diagram showing perikymata in the occlusal and cervical walls of a linear enamel hypoplasia
B   LEH groove in a Neandertal tooth (Krapina 75). The occlusal wall, representing the
    actual growth disruption, lies between the downward-pointing arrow and the horizontal
    arrow. There are 12 perikymata in the occlusal wall of this defect. The cervical wall is
    delimited by the horizontal arrow and the upward pointing arrow. Based on Hillson and
    Bond 1997

and Leonard 2001). Previous studies of developmental defects in the enamel of
Neandertals indicate that these hominins had relatively high frequencies of enamel
hypoplasia (Brennan 1991; Molnar and Molnar 1985; Ogilvie et al. 1989; Skinner
1996). However, Hutchinson and colleagues (1997) found that these high frequencies are matched by similar frequencies in various prehistoric foraging and horticultural populations.

In my work, I compared the LEH defects of Neandertals to those of Inupiaq inhabitants of Point Hope, Alaska (Guatelli-Steinberg et al. 2004). Many of the Neandertal
specimens included in my study derived from unstable (Hutchinson et al. 1997) or cold
environments (Schwartz and Tattersall 2002), to which the marginal Arctic habitats of
the Point Hope Inupiaq provide a modern analog. Stable isotope analyses also suggest
that Neandertals may have been predominantly meat eaters (Bocherens et al. 1999;
Richards et al. 2000), while the Inupiaq included a large portion of meat and fish in
their diets (Larsen and Rainey 1948). If Neandertals were less efficient foragers than
the Point Hope Inupiaq, then they might be expected to have recorded, in their enamel,
evidence of having withstood stress episodes of longer duration. The evidence I obtained
from counting perikymata within Neandertal defects did not, however, support this
view. In fact, on the basis of counting perikymata within defects, the average estimated
disruption time for Neandertals was slightly shorter than that for the Inupiaq.

It is obvious that Neandertals experienced physiological stress; this is documented
in their high LEH frequencies and in the long duration of stress recorded in some of
their defects (as shown in Figure 27.3, B). The comparison with the Inupiaq, however,

tells us that there may be reason to doubt that Neandertals were *more* stressed (through malnutrition or disease) than some modern human foragers. This is the same conclusion that was reached by Hutchinson and colleagues (1997) in their comparison of LEH frequencies in Neandertals and various modern human foraging groups.

I have also examined linear enamel hypoplasias in early *Homo, Australopithecus,* and *Paranthropus* (Guatelli-Steinberg 2003, 2004). Unfortunately, comparisons across these genera are complicated by the large differences among them in the duration and manner in which they form enamel. Thus it is not at all clear exactly what the LEH differences among them might mean in terms of differences in their experience of stress. For example I found that, of all of these early hominins, *Paranthropus* has fewer average LEH defects per tooth. But I don't think that this result can be clearly interpreted to mean that *Paranthropus* experienced less physiological stress than these other hominin species. In fact, *Paranthropus* would be expected to exhibit fewer defects, simply because its teeth form so quickly, providing a smaller 'window of vulnerability' (Vrijenhoek 1985) to disruption than do the longer-forming teeth of *Australopithecus* or early *Homo.* This in itself suggests that the slower-growing bodily structures of slow-growing species, whatever their advantages, entail an inherent disadvantage in their prolonged exposure to potential disruptive influences on their growth.

Conclusions and Future Directions

The foregoing discussion highlights insights about our ancestors gained from studying incremental growth in fossilized enamel. Analyses of these growth layers have enabled us to trace the evolution of human childhood through the fossil record. It is now clear that a prolonged period of childhood, equal in length to our own, did not evolve until fairly late in human evolutionary history, with the advent of *Homo sapiens* (Smith et al. 2007b). Periods of prolonged childhood growth may also have evolved in Neandertals (Macchiarelli et al. 2006), but further work is necessary to determine if this was so.

In the case of Neandertals, who are so closely related to modern humans, an understanding of dental growth may not be enough to resolve the question. Part of the problem with resolving the question of Neandertal childhood is that the relationship between overall juvenile growth periods and dental development is stronger at higher levels of the taxonomic hierarchy than it is at lower levels (Dirks and Bowman 2007). For example, it is clear that, compared to monkeys, lemurs have a faster dental development, as well as an abbreviated period of juvenile growth (Smith 1989). However, a monkey species with a more rapid rate of dental development than a closely related monkey species may not also have a shorter juvenile growth period than the latter. There may therefore be limits to what the study of dental development can tell us about juvenile growth in our fossil ancestors, particularly in the species which are most closely related to us.

The study of enamel growth increments in our ancestors has also revealed differences in their patterns of enamel growth. In *Paranthropus* (particularly *P. robustus*), enamel extension tended to occur more quickly and in an apparently more uniform manner down the crown than it did in *Australopithecus* or *Homo.* Neandertals and modern humans differed in their enamel growth patterns, as is reflected by differences in perikymata distribution. Exactly why some hominin species had a more uniform distribution of perikymata than others is not clear. The distribution of perikymata along the length of the crown can be related to variation in extension rates, but it is also potentially related to other variables. Are the causes, for example, of the more uniform distribution of perikymata in Neandertals and *Homo heidelbergensis* the same? Are the causes of the compaction of perikymata in the cervical halves of different populations of modern humans the same? Answers to these questions would be interesting to know.

Finally, the study of enamel growth has yielded insights into physiological stress in our ancestors. Neandertals, for example, appear not to have differed from some modern human foragers in their frequencies of linear enamel hyopolasia (Hutchinson et al. 1997) or in the duration of stress episodes which these defects represent (Guatelli-Steinberg et al. 2004). The teeth of *Paranthropus* have fewer defects than those of *Australopithecus* or *Homo* – possibly because, in the former, abbreviated crown formation times prevented the enamel from recording multiple stress episodes (Guatelli-Steinberg 2004). Enamel formation variables, such as the duration of enamel formation, must therefore be considered when one uses linear enamel hypoplasias to try to understand stress in our fossil ancestors.

Although Niels Stensen recognized, in 1667, the fact that teeth fossilized, it is doubtful that he could have anticipated the kinds of information about growth which might be gleaned from them. While many intriguing insights have been gained from the study of enamel growth in our ancestors, there are clearly many more exciting discoveries and refinements to our knowledge on the horizon.

REFERENCES

Bermúdez de Castro, J. M., Rosas, A., Carbonell, E., Nicolás, M. E., Rodríguez, J., and Arsuaga, J. L. (1999) A Modern Pattern of Dental Development In Lower Pleistocene Hominids from Atapuerca-TD6 (Spain). *Proceedings of the National Academy of Science, USA* 96: 4210–4213.

Beynon, D., and Dean, M. C. (1988) Distinct Dental Development Patterns in Early Fossil Hominins. *Nature* 335: 509–514.

Beynon, D., and Wood, B. (1987) Patterns and Rates of Enamel Growth in the Molar Teeth of Early Hominids. *Nature* 326: 493–496.

Bocherens, H., Billiou, D., Mariotti, A., Patou-Mathis, M., Otte, M., Bonjean, D., and Toussaint, M. (1999) Paleoenvironmental and Paleodietary Implications of Isotopic Biogeochemistry of Last Interglacial Neanderthal and Mammal Bones in Scladina Cave (Belgium). *Journal of Archaeological Science* 26: 599–607.

Bogin, B. (1997) Evolutionary Hypotheses for Human Childhood. *Yearbook of Physical Anthropology* 40: 63–89.

Bombin, M. (1990) Transverse Enamel Hypoplasia on Teeth of South African Plio-Pleistocene Hominids. *Naturwissenschaften* 77: 128–129.

Boyde, A. (1979) Carbonate Concentration, Crystal Centres, Core Dissolution, Caries, Cross Striations, Circadian Rhythms, and Compositional Contrast in the SEM. *Journal of Dental Research* (Special Issue) 58: 981–983.

Brennan, M. (1991) Health and Disease in the Middle and Upper Paleolithic of Southwestern France: A Bioarchaeological Study. PhD dissertation, New York University.

Bromage, T. G. (1990) Early Hominid Development and Life History. In C. J. de Rousseau (ed.), *Primate Life History and Evolution* (pp. 105–113). New York: Wiley–Liss.

Bromage, T. G. (1991) Enamel Incremental Periodicity in the Pig-Tailed Macaque: A Poly-chrome Fluorescent Labeling Study of Dental Hard Tissues. *American Journal of Physical Anthropology* 86: 205–214.

Bromage, T. G., and Dean, M. C. (1985) Re-Evaluation of the Age at Death of Immature Fossil Hominids. *Nature* 317: 525–527.

Brunet, M., Fronty, P., Sapanet, M., de Bonis, L., and Viriot, L. (2002) Enamel Hypoplasia in a Pliocene Hominid from Chad. *Connective Tissue Research* 43: 94–97.

Dean, M. C. (1987) Growth Layers and Incremental Markings in Hard Tissues; A Review of the Literature and Some Preliminary Observations about Enamel Structure in *Paranthropus boisei*. *Journal of Human Evolution* 16: 157–172.

Dean, M. C. (2000) Incremental Markings in Enamel and Dentine: What They Can Tell Us about the Way Teeth Grow. In M. F. Teaford, M. M. Smith, and M. W. J. Ferguson (eds), *Development, Function, and Evolution of Teeth* (pp. 119–130). Cambridge: Cambridge University Press.

Dean, M. C., and Reid, D. J. (2001a) Anterior Tooth Formation in *Australopithecus* and *Paranthropus*. In A. Brook (ed.), *Dental Morphology* (pp. 135–143). Sheffield: Sheffield University Press.

Dean, M. C., and Reid, D. J. (2001b) Perikymata Spacing and Distribution on Hominid Anterior Teeth. *American Journal of Physical Anthropology* 116: 209–215.

Dean, M. C., Leakey, M., Reid, D. J., Schrenk, F., Schwartz, G. T., Stringer, C., and Walker, A. (2001) Growth Processes in Teeth Distinguish Modern Humans from *Homo erectus* and Earlier Hominins. *Nature* 414: 628–631.

Deaner, R. O., Barton, R. A., and Van Shaik, C. P. (2003) Primate Brains and Life Histories: Renewing the Connection. In P. M. Kappeler and M. E. Pereira (eds), *Primate Life Histories and Socioecology* (pp. 233–265). Chicago and London: University of Chicago Press.

Dirks, W., and Bowman, J. (2007) Life History Theory and Dental Development in Four Species of Catarrhine Primates. *Journal of Human Evolution* 53: 309–320.

Fédération Dentaire Internationale (1982) An Epidemiological Index of Developmental Defects of Dental Enamel (DDE). *International Dental Journal* 32: 159–167.

Fédération Dentaire Internationale (1992) A Review of the Developmental Defects of Enamel Index (DDE Index). *International Dental Journal* 42: 411–426.

Fitzgerald, C. M. (1998) Do Enamel Microstructures Have Regular Time Dependency? Conclusions from the Literature and a Large Scale Study. *Journal of Human Evolution* 35: 371–386.

Goodman, A. H., and Rose, J. C. (1990) Assessment of Systemic Physiological Perturbations from Dental Enamel Hypoplasias and Associated Histological Structures. *Yearbook of Physical Anthropology* 33: 59–110.

Green, R. E., Krause, J., Ptak, S. E., Briggs, A. W., Ronan, M. T., Simons, J. F., Egholm, M., Rothberg, J. M., Paunovic, M., and Pääbo, S. (2006) Analysis of One Million Base Pairs of Neanderthal DNA. *Nature* 444: 330–336.

Guatelli-Steinberg, D. (2003) Macroscopic and Microscopic Analyses of Linear Enamel Hypoplasia in Plio-Pleistocene Hominins with Respect to Aspects of Enamel Development and Morphology. *American Journal of Physical Anthropology* 120: 309–322.

Guatelli-Steinberg, D. (2004) Analysis and Significance of Linear Enamel Hypoplasia in Plio-Pleistocene Hominins. *American Journal of Physical Anthropology* 125: 199–215.

Guatelli-Steinberg, D., Larsen, C. S., and Hutchinson, D. L. (2004) Prevalence and the Duration of Linear Enamel Hypoplasia: A Comparative Study of Neandertals and Inuit Foragers. *Journal of Human Evolution* 47: 65–84.

Guatelli-Steinberg, D., and Reid, D. J. (2008) What Molars Contribute to an Emerging Understanding of Lateral Enamel Formation in Neandertals vs. Modern Humans. *Journal of Human Evolution* 54: 236–250.

Guatelli-Steinberg, D., Reid, D. J., and Bishop, T. A. (2007) Did the Lateral Enamel of Neandertals Grow Differently from That of Modern Humans? *Journal of Human Evolution* 52: 72–84.

Guatelli-Steinberg, D., Reid, D. J., Bishop, T. A., and Larsen, C. S. (2005) Anterior Tooth Growth Periods in Neandertals Were Comparable to Those of Modern Humans. *Proceedings of the National Academy of Sciences, USA* 102: 14197–14202.

Hillson, S. (1996) *Dental Anthropology*. Cambridge: Cambridge University Press.

Hillson, S., and Bond, S. (1997) The Relationship of Enamel Hypoplasia to the Pattern of Tooth Crown Growth: A Discussion. *American Journal of Physical Anthropology* 104: 89–103.

Hutchinson, D. L., Larsen, C. S., and Choi, I. (1997) Stressed to the Max? Physiological Perturbation in the Krapina Neandertals. *Current Anthropology* 38: 904–914.

Jelinek, A. J. (1994) Hominids, Energy, Environment, and Behavior in the Late Pleistocene. In M. H. Nitecki and D. V. Nitecki (eds), *Origins of Anatomically Modern Humans* (pp. 67–92). New York: Plenum Press.

Kelley, J., and Smith, T. M. (2003) Age at First Molar Emergence in Early Miocene *Afropithecus turkanensis* and Life-History Evolution in the Hominoidea. *Journal of Human Evolution* 44: 307–329.

Lacruz, R., Dean, M. C., Ramirez-Rozzi, F., and Bromage, T. (2008) Patterns of Enamel Secretion and Striae Periodicity in Fossil Hominins. *Journal of Anatomy* 213: 148–158.

Larsen, H., and Rainey, F. (1948) Ipiutak and the Arctic Whale Hunting Culture. *Anthropological Papers of the American Museum of Natural History* 42: 1–276.

Leigh, S. R., and Blomquist, G. E. (2007) Life History. In C. J. Campbell, A. Fuentes, K. C. MacKinnon, M. Panger, and S. K. Bearder (eds), *Primates in Perspective* (pp. 396–407). New York and Oxford: Oxford University Press.

Macchiarelli, R., Bondioli, L., Debéhath, A., Mazurier, A., Tournepiche, J.-F., Birch, W., and Dean, C. (2006) How Neandertal Molar Teeth Grew. *Nature* 444: 748–751.

Maisey, J. G. (1997) *Discovering Fossil Fishes*. New York: Holt.

Molnar, S., and Molnar, I. M. (1985) The Prevalence of Enamel Hypoplasia among the Krapina Neandertals. *American Anthropologist* 87: 536–549.

Noonan, J. P., Coop, G., Kudaravalli, S., Smith, D., Krause, J., Alessi, J., Chen, F., Platt, D., Pääbo, S., Pritchard, J. K., and Rubin, E. M. (2006) Sequencing and Analysis of Neanderthal Genomic DNA. *Science* 314: 1113–1118.

Ogilvie, M. D., Curran, B. K., and Trinkaus, E. (1989) Prevalence and Patterning of Dental Enamel Hypoplasia among the Neandertals. *American Journal of Physical Anthropology* 79: 25–41.

Ramirez-Rozzi, F. V., and Bermúdez de Castro, J. M. (2004) Surprisingly Rapid Growth in Neanderthals. *Nature* 428: 936–939.

Reid, D. J., and Dean, M. C. (2006) Variation in Modern Human Enamel Formation Times. *Journal of Human Evolution* 50: 329–346.

Reid, D. J., Guatelli-Steinberg, D., and Walton, P. (2008) Variation in Modern Human Premolar Enamel Formation Times: Implications for Neandertals. *Journal of Human Evolution* 54: 225–235.

Richards, M. P., Petit, P. B., Trinkaus, E., Smith, F. H., Paunovic, M., and Karonovic, I. (2000) Neanderthal Diet at Vindija and Neanderthal Predation: The Evidence from Stable Isotopes. *Proceedings of the National Academy of Sciences, USA* 97: 7663–7666.

Risnes, S. (1986) Enamel Apposition Rate and the Prism Periodicity in Human Teeth. *Scandanavian Journal of Dental Research* 94: 394–404.

Schwartz, G. T., and Dean, M. C. (2001) Ontogeny of Canine Dimorphism in Extant Hominoids. *American Journal of Physical Anthropology* 115: 269–283.

Schwartz, J., and Tattersall, I. (2002) *The Human Fossil Record*, Vol. 1. New York: Wiley–Liss.

Shellis, R. P. (1984) Variation in Growth of the Enamel Crown in Human Teeth and a Possible Relationship between Growth and Enamel Structure. *Archives of Oral Biology* 29: 697–705.

Skinner, M. (1996) Developmental Stress in Immature Hominines from Late Pleistocene Eurasia: Evidence from Enamel Hypoplasia. *Journal of Archaeological Science* 23: 833–852.

Smith, B. H. (1989) Dental Development as a Measure of Life History in Primates. *Evolution* 43: 683–688.

Smith, B. H. (1991) Dental Development and the Evolution of Life History in Hominidae. *American Journal of Physical Anthropology* 86: 157–174.

Smith, B. H. (1992) Life History and the Evolution of Human Maturation. *Evolutionary Anthropology* 1: 134–142.

Smith, B. H., and Tompkins, R. L. (1995) Toward a Life History of the Hominidae. *Annual Review of Anthropology* 24: 257–279.

Smith, T. M., and Tafforeau, P. (2008) New Visions of Dental Tissue Research: Tooth Development, Chemistry, and Structure. *Evolutionary Anthropology* 17: 213–226.

Smith, T. M., Toussaint, M., Reid, D. J., Olejniczak, A., and Hublin, J.-J. (2007a) Rapid Dental Development in a Middle Paleolithic Belgian Neanderthal. *Proceedings of the National Academy of Science, USA* 104: 20220–20225.

Smith, T. M., Tafforeau, P., Reid, D. J., Grün, R., Eggins, S., Boutakiout, M., and Hublin, J.-J. (2007b) Earliest Evidence of Modern Human Life History in North African Early *Homo sapiens*. *Proceedings of the National Academy of Science, USA* 104: 6128–6133.

Soffer, O. (1994) Ancestral Lifeways in Eurasia: The Middle and Upper Paleolithic Records. In M. H. Nitecki and D. V. Nitecki (eds), *Origins of Anatomically Modern Humans* (pp. 84–109). New York: Plenum Press.

Sorensen, M. V., and Leonard, W. R. (2001) Neandertal Energetics and Foraging Efficiency. *Journal of Human Evolution* 40: 483–495.

Ten Cate, A. R. (1994) *Oral Histology: Development, Structure, and Function*, 4th edn. St Louis: Mosby.

Trinkaus, E. (1986) The Neandertals and Modern Human Origins. *Annual Review of Anthropology* 15: 193–218.

Vrijenhoek, R. C. (1985) Animal Population Genetics and Disturbance: The Effect of Local Extinctions and Recolonizations on Heterozygosity and Fitness. In S. T. A. Picket and P. J. White (eds), *The Ecology of Natural Disturbances on Patch Dynamics* (pp. 266–286). San Diego: Academic Press.

White, T. D. (1978) Early Hominid Enamel Hypoplasia. *American Journal of Physical Anthropology* 49: 79–84.

Zihlman, A., Bolter, D., and Boesch, C. (2004) Wild Chimpanzee Dentition and Its Implications for Assessing Life History in Immature Hominin Fossils. *Proceedings of the National Academy of Sciences, USA* 101: 10541–10543.

28 Understanding
Skull Function from
a Mechanobiological
Perspective

David J. Daegling

Given the premise that natural selection has been an instrumental evolutionary force
in primate and human evolution, the interpretation of skull morphology hinges on
considerations of functional anatomy. As the depth of research on skull function is
beyond the scope of the present contribution, this chapter will focus on the utility and
applicability of a particular perspective for approaching questions of functional and
evolutionary adaptation with respect to the bones of the skull. The mechanobiological approach to bone function is purposefully restrictive in assuming that the structural and material characteristics of bone are shaped by mechanical stimuli during
development. My intention in this chapter is to examine the pervasiveness of this perspective in biological anthropology, to evaluate its application to problems of function
and adaptation, and to consider both its potential and its limitations as a conceptual
foundation for understanding bone biology in the context of the skull as it applies to
humans and other primates.

FUNCTIONAL DEMANDS ON SKULL FORM

The morphology of the skull must be compatible with several functions, most of
which are transparent. The skull must provide protection for the brain and organs of
special sensation. It serves as the supporting structure for the cervical muscles involved
in head posture, for the muscles of mastication, and to a lesser extent for the muscles
supporting the pharynx, the larynx, and the tongue. The skull must function adequately for both food processing and the maintenance of the respiratory airway. It is
probably not productive to try to ascertain which function is historically most important in determining skull form. A simple thought experiment would argue against the
idea that any one of these functions is necessarily primary. If, for example, one imagines

any of these functions as being seriously compromised, it is clear that selection would efficiently remove the dysfunctional variant from the population in short order.

In considering the diversity of functions, it is, however, useful to appreciate that, even though all the ones mentioned above are important in terms of fitness, their individual efficiency may have detrimental effects on other attributes. For example, changes in the relationship of facial and basicranial bones were instrumental in the development of the anatomically modern human upper vocal tract, which in turn facilitates articulate speech. The adaptive value of speech is manifest, but the morphological changes accompanying this adaptation came at a cost: they predisposed people to obstructive sleep apnea (Davidson 2003).

OVERVIEW OF PRIMATE SKULL DIVERSITY

There are systematic differences in the number of bones that comprise the primate skull; prosimians have more bones than anthropoids, on account of different sutural configurations. The metopic suture is patent in prosimians and is usually obliterated in anthropoids; the dentaries are not united in prosimians, and the human premaxilla is 'lost' owing to sutural fusion. The strength of these characters as taxonomic demarcators is overstated: metopic sutures occasionally persist in adult people (Ajmani et al. 1983), symphyseal fusion is documented among prosimians (Ravosa 1996; Ravosa 1991), and premaxillary sutures may persist in people and become obliterated in non-human primates (Ashley-Montagu 1935). There is mounting evidence that sutural morphology (including fusion) is mediated by mechanobiological factors (Byron et al. 2004; Byron et al. 2008; Herring and Teng 2000), although, with the exception of the mandibular symphysis (see below), functional explanations for systematic differences among primates are relatively undeveloped.

Beyond differences in bone number, variations in skull form can be conceived of as differences in:

- the relative proportions of different bones to one another;
- the changing spatial relationships that accompany these changes in proportion.

In some cases there have been persuasive arguments as to adaptive or functional significance; for example, the relatively long faces of certain male anthropoids are probably related to requirements of gape for the display of large canines (Smith 1984). Most systematic differences in skull proportions or spatial relationships have at some point been explained in functional and implicitly adaptationist terms. Mechanobiological arguments that inform these hypotheses necessarily consider skull development as instrumental in driving and constraining skull variation.

ATOMISTIC AND HOLISTIC APPROACHES: CONFLICT OR CONSENSUS?

Historically, there have been two competing theorems of skull growth and development, each having large implications for functional inference. The evolution of the skull is logically dependent on changes in developmental patterns, and thus the interpretation of differences in functional or biomechanical performance in an evolutionary framework requires consideration of ontogenetic process if inferences of process are to have any credibility (Lieberman 1997). A lingering question is what scale of analysis is best for understanding the functional significance of anatomical variation.

The juxtaposition of particularistic versus holistic approaches to the study of skull form is perhaps most sharply illustrated in the literature by the respective works of Melvin Moss and Donald Enlow. The central assumption of 'functional cranial analysis' is that the local environment of soft tissues primarily governs skeletal growth. Independent development of a skeletal unit is governed by its associated unique functional matrix, such that the size, shape, and position of different regions bear no necessary relationship with one another during growth (Moss 1973; Moss and Young 1960). One consequence of this approach is that it argues against the study of formal osteological units. That is, 'the temporal bone' and 'the mandible' have no particular biological significance as structural entities. Under the concept of the functional matrix, it makes more sense to study the petrous or mastoid portions of the temporal on their own terms; similarly, the mandible does not exist *sui generis*, and an examination of the coronoid or angular processes as independent objects of analysis is fully justified. The conceptual underpinnings of functional cranial analysis today are articulated as epigenetic influences on skull growth (Herring 1993; Moss 1997), and the focus of contemporary investigation on local mechanobiology attests to the durability of the functional matrix as a theoretical premise.

Enlow did not deny the concept of functional matrix so much as amend it. He suggested that the functional matrix operates to provide a developmental latitude among skeletal units, so that developmental perturbations in one region could be offset by compensatory activity in an adjacent functional matrix (Enlow 1982). This 'counterpart principle' suggests that events in any one region of the skull necessarily influence growth in others; consequently, a functional equilibrium is maintained (Enlow and Azuma 1975; Enlow and Moyers 1971). The result of this interregional coordination can be discerned as 'craniofacial constants' (Moyers et al. 1979).

Superficially, the perspectives of Moss and Enlow would appear to be conceptually hostile to each other, although the respective proponents did not consider the underlying principles to be incompatible. One apparent nexus of conflict is the nature of independence within the functional matrix model, with particular respect to spatial relationships. It is worth considering that, when Moss invoked independence, it was intended as a heuristic rather than as a statement of the total autonomy of skeletal units. Conversely, it is difficult to envision a context in which Enlow's broader theme of coordinated growth could not be operative to some degree. The existence of craniofacial constants and compensatory growth is, in some sense, reassuring rather than revolutionary. But the ideas of Moss and Enlow had two important things in common: (1) their conceptual focus was on how ontogeny related to function (it was assumed that the skull was a mosaic of adaptation); and (2) they recognized the importance of mechanobiological factors in the determination of morphology.

Tests for the primacy of functional matrices in determining the form of the skull have had mixed results. The general premise now seems inarguable because experimental and environmental manipulations have established that a purely genetic basis for skull development is untenable (Herring 1993). Specific examples of the ontogeny of what are recognizably discrete skeletal units seem to indicate that functional matrices have effects which transcend local morphology. Intentional reshaping of the neurocranium in human populations produces measurable changes in the basicranium and face, including the mandible (Anton 1989; Cheverud and Midkiff 1992). The analysis of angular relations among parts of the cranium in cercopithecoids suggests that hypotheses of either atomistic (independent) or holistic (coordinated) growth may enjoy strong support depending on one's choice of the samples to be examined (Ravosa and Shea 1994).

More recent work on morphological integration has in some ways obviated debate on questions of functional and developmental independence in the skull. The concept emphasizes the interdependence of traits that contribute to particular functions, the correlation among which is an expected outcome of their co-evolution (Cheverud 1995). A model of growth that views mechanobiological factors as proximately causal in determining relationships among parts of the skull essentially blurs the distinction between developmental and functional integration. Sets of features of the skull can be reckoned as functional complexes that – developmentally, genetically, and evolutionary speaking – represent the traits screened by natural selection (Cheverud 1996). This further suggests that concepts of developmental plasticity and independence are relative rather than absolute. For example, the angular process of the mandible is developmentally inseparable from the masseter, as is the coronoid process with respect to the temporalis. These constitute unique functional matrices in the formal sense, but the evidence for developmental integration of these skeletal units in ontogeny and evolution is inarguable (ibid.). Moreover, there is strong evidence for morphological integration of the mandibular ramus and the cranial base (Bastir and Rosas 2005). Thus even components of the skull that emerge from distinct embryological precursors – the basicranium undergoes endochondral ossification, while the facial skeleton ossifies intramembranously – do not apparently enjoy developmental independence (Lieberman et al. 2000). This idea has important implications for a strictly local mechanobiological criterion in understanding skull development: namely, such a model is suspect unless we can demonstrate that local mechanical environments correlate with broader regional mechanical conditions, cross-cutting distinct functional matrices. Such a demonstration is not impossible per se, but at present we do not have the discrimination required to evaluate the possibility (Herring 1993).

DIET, FEEDING BEHAVIOR, AND SKULL FORM

Functional morphological studies of the skull usually focus on the masticatory apparatus. Historically, paleoanthropological interests have accounted for this apparent preoccupation with mastication over and above other functional complexes. Reasons include the vagaries of the fossil record (dental and gnathic elements enjoy preferential preservation for a number of reasons), and also the recognition that dietary reconstruction is central to ecological and behavioral inferences about human evolution.

A well documented example of the connection between masticatory function and skull form is provided by the shift in subsistence strategies in recent human evolution. As human populations have made the transition from a foraging ecology to one involving agriculture (with greater emphasis on cooking), gracilization of the skull is an expected result of reduced masticatory demands (Carlson and Van Gerven 1977);

this hypothesis is supported by observations in the bioarchaeological record. Larsen (1997) argues that the pan-global trend of cranial shortening and gracilization is the direct result of masticatory, dietary, and technological changes among recent human populations.

Both in the recent human record and in broader comparative contexts, the logic behind the idea that diet relates to skull form is straightforward. Food items vary in mechanical properties, and primates vary in dietary preferences. More mechanically challenging foods require greater force to be processed, greater biting forces require higher muscular forces and incur larger temporomandibular joint forces, and a facial skeleton subjected to these forces requires either structural reinforcement or reorganization in order to accommodate masticatory stress. Two distinct but complementary approaches evaluate skull morphology with respect to these structural solutions. Reorganization refers to changes in spatial relationships among parts of the facial skeleton, and is most accessibly inferred by treating the masticatory system as a third-class lever. This perspective treats the masticatory system as undeformable, and considers the effects of muscular leverage (moment arms) against those of the biting forces (load arms). By contrast, the idea of reinforcement is based on the assumption that the mandible behaves as a structural beam or some other deformable body, and inferences of performance are based on how well facial bones resist masticatory forces.

Lever systems measure efficiency (and, in the biological context, presumably adaptation) in terms of relative mechanical advantage. With respect to mastication, the crucial question is how efficiently muscular force is utilized to produce biting force. Such an approach was used to provide a biomechanical framework for distinguishing the ecology of the hominin genera *Australopithecus* and *Paranthropus* (DuBrul 1977). Reconstructing the anatomical relationships among masticatory muscles, dentition, and temporomandibular joint, DuBrul demonstrated that the mechanical advantage for the production of biting forces was greater in the jaws of *Paranthropus* than in those of *Australopithecus*. The configuration of the masticatory apparatus in the former resembled the skulls of obligate herbivores, whereas *Australopithecus* represented a more generalized condition. The analogies drawn are persuasive, but the question looms as to whether lever analyses can systematically discriminate among primates with diets that differ in their fundamental mechanical demands. The application of a constrained lever model to the masticatory configuration of anthropoids has addressed this question (Spencer 1999). The model constraint is that the potential distraction of the temporomandibular joint (that is, the tensile forces which would separate the mandibular condyle and the articular eminence) limits the geometric configuration of the masticatory vectors (Greaves 1978). While Spencer's study was focused on how primates avoided distractive forces at the temporomandibular joint, it also argued that the reorganization of the masticatory apparatus in primates as a whole was fundamentally constrained within narrow phenotypic limits. It does not appear that primates deal with mechanically challenging diets in a consistent fashion; at the very least, with a few important exceptions, they do not increase the mechanical advantage of their masticatory musculature as a routine response to dietary challenges.

The approach that is complementary to lever analysis – and more directly intelligible from a mechanobiological perspective – is the treatment of the facial skeleton as a load-bearing deformable structure. This approach seeks to understand the mechanical consequences of morphological variation in terms of stress and strain. Masticatory stress can be thought of as internal forces in the facial bones – forces which result from the chewing activity. More formally, it is calculated as force per unit area. Strain refers to deformations in bone resulting from the same activity, and is expressed as a dimensionless ratio of change in length over original length. The ratio can be positive (indicating tension) or negative (indicating compression). Since the deformation of bone comes about through the application of force, it follows that stress and strain co-occur.

Hylander's *in vivo* studies of bone strain in macaques were watershed events in the study of the primate skull as a load-bearing structure (Hylander 1979a, 1984). Beyond the observation of strain magnitudes during chewing, the patterns of strain also provided insight into the nature of masticatory loads, which could not be reliably discerned from simple lever analysis. The result was an empirical model of masticatory function that provided information on the types of loads experienced by the mandible during chewing and permitted predictions about how these distinctive loads could be optimally resisted in the primate skull. All this led to an explosion of research on the covariation of feeding behavior, masticatory function, and jaw form in primates (reviewed in Taylor 2002).

With respect to the question of the covariation of diet and skull morphology, there were additional experimental studies that provided justification for comparative work within the discipline. First, it was established that foods differing in hardness and toughness could be reliably associated with increased levels of bone strain (Hylander 1979b; Weijs and de Jongh 1977). Second, the mechanical effects of altered stress and strain magnitudes with respect to dietary variation were shown to translate into developmental changes in bone structure and metabolic activity (Bouvier and Hylander 1981, 1984). Consequently, functional inferences of craniofacial variation proceeded from a simple mechanobiological calculus: hard foods would be associated with large faces. This complemented the optimality criterion of lever models – that is, the understanding that shorter jaws and retracted faces would be more favorably disposed toward the production of large occlusal forces.

For example, the deep, foreshortened faces of folivorous colobine monkeys (in comparison to those of cercopithecines) made sense in a biomechanical framework. Durophagous primates are expected to show a similar suite of features, including relatively large mandibular corpus dimensions, in comparison to appropriate lever-arm proxies. Predicted associations between qualitative dietary categories and craniofacial biomechanical features are, however, inconsistently observed (Daegling and McGraw 2001). The absence of quantitative dietary data and the inaccuracy of models for estimating masticatory stress are contributing factors. Another problem is that the intervening variables between feeding behavior and bone stress are masticatory forces, which are rarely measured directly – both for operational and for theoretical reasons. Despite the fact that the picture is less clear than desired, there is little question that there exists a functional linkage between craniofacial morphology and masticatory forces. In the absence of normal masticatory forces during development, functional occlusion is disrupted and other effects on the facial skeleton accrue (Beecher and Corruccini 1981; Corruccini and Beecher 1982; Corruccini and Beecher 1984). We can logically extrapolate beyond these particular findings to argue that the morphology of the facial skeleton is determined epigenetically, and that a mechanobiological model is the most productive approach for understanding how this occurs.

Another outstanding example of the utility of this perspective with respect to the skull is the work on symphyseal fusion in primates (Ravosa 1999; Ravosa and Hylander 1994). Experimental and comparative data have been recruited in order to argue persuasively that there is a biomechanical basis for the ossification of the mandibular symphysis in relation to specific masticatory loadcases of dorsoventral shear and lateral transverse bending. Thus this diagnostic trait, which separates anthropoids from prosimians, has been shown to have a functional basis related to masticatory mechanics, and there are now data that can be used to link mechanobiological processes with developmental patterns at the symphysis (Ravosa et al. 2008).

One view which challenges this interpretation is the argument that an unfused symphysis is capable of effective transfer of force between the dentaries (Lieberman and Crompton 2000). The implications of this perspective are: (1) that strengthening the symphysis, while a consequence of ossification, is not mechanically necessary; and (2) that enhancing stiffness is the selective basis for symphyseal fusion. While ossification can be expected to enhance stiffness and strength simultaneously, the points of disagreement are not esoteric, because they address the question of adaptive significance in the context of evolutionary history. This 'stiffness over strength' argument implicitly minimizes the influence of masticatory mechanics on symphyseal tissues developmentally – a premise which is at odds with observation (Ravosa et al. 2008).

SUPRAORBITAL MORPHOLOGY

Ideas surrounding the evolutionary significance of the hominin browridge provide an example of unrestrained inference in functional morphology. Both adaptive and non-adaptive explanations for the trait have been offered historically. Adaptive hypotheses have ranged from the sober to the fantastic (Russell 1985); they include suggestions that the supraorbital torus functioned as a rain or sun visor, an object of intimidation, a shield from the venom of spitting snakes, or an extra-cultural means of keeping hair out of one's eyes. Most attention has focused on mechanical explanations for the expression of the torus, which included suggestons that Paleolithic life was sufficiently perilous that the reinforcement afforded by the browridge was selectively important. But perhaps the most credible hypothesis was that the supraorbital torus represented a functional response to masticatory or paramasticatory activity. The synthesis of this hypothesis (Russell 1985) was based on data from *in vitro* experiments as well as on theoretical biomechanical and comparative analyses of hominin skulls. In sum, the torus functioned to relieve stress in skulls with particular configurations of craniofacial hafting. Under this model, modern humans needed a relatively modest development of the torus, as the vertical orientation of the frontal provided structural support which was coincident with the resultant masticatory forces.

Research on facial bone strain in baboons and macaques provided a test of the masticatory stress hypothesis (Hylander and Johnson 1992; Hylander et al. 1991). The reasoning behind the test was that, if facial bone is optimized for stress resistance, then *in vivo* strains during feeding activity should be, by and large, invariant throughout the facial skeleton, as lower strains would imply a waste of skeletal material (needlessly costly) whereas higher strains would indicate an insufficient margin of safety (needlessly risky). These experiments revealed relatively low strains and, by extension, modest stresses in the supraorbital region. From an economy of material point of view, these results suggest that supraorbital buttressing is excessive, because without it the facial skeleton would still enjoy an adequate margin of safety.

These experiments effectively rule out masticatory forces as functionally linked to browridge development – which prompts a re-examination of so-called 'spatial' hypotheses. These assume that the salience of the torus is determined by the spatial relationship of the orbits to the adjacent neurocranium, or, more generally, by the nature of craniofacial hafting (Ravosa 1988). Ravosa's data on cercopithecids indicate that the correlation between biomechanical variables of facial proportions and torus formation is essentially allometric: in other words, size alone is as effective an explanation as models of biomechanical adaptation for supraorbital morphology.

The co-variation of spatial factors and supraorbital torus expression still leaves room for functional explanation. A recent hypothesis is that the torus represents an adaptation "to prevent structural failure due to relatively infrequent non-masticatory external traumatic forces" (Hylander and Johnson 1992: 565). This view complements spatial explanations because the torus could be regarded as a structural response to an intrinsic weakening of the skull that accompanies certain patterns of neuro-orbital relationship. The evaluation of the hypothesis requires two kinds of data:

1   evidence that head trauma occurs with sufficient frequency in natural populations that selection could be expected to be operative to a nontrivial degree; and
2   mechanical analyses to demonstrate that browridge morphology functions to strengthen the cranium in those individuals where it is most strongly expressed.

With respect to the latter point, one cannot assume that simply adding material to a particular structure always confers additional strength (Gordon 1978). In any case, if the hypothesis that infrequent traumatic loading is responsible for torus formation is valid, it is difficult to envision how a developmental mechanobiological model can account for variation in this region.

SPECIAL SENSORY CAPSULES

The skull itself is obviously not responsible for the transmission of special sensation, but it houses the organs that are, and effort has been expended on determining whether skull variation can tell us anything about its possessor's sensory acuity, or at least elucidate the morphological consequences of variation in these capabilities. Some correlations are obvious. The relatively large orbits of tarsiers and owl monkeys have to do with nocturnality in species who lack a *tapetum lucidum*. Allometry of orbital size in euprimates has been marshaled to infer activity patterns (Kay and Cartmill 1977). Other aspects of orbital anatomy may have less to do with vision in the strict sense, but still raise interesting questions of functional significance. All modern primates have postorbital bars, and anthropoids are distinguished by their development of a postorbital septum. A mechanobiological approach takes a teleological view of the septum: its presence in anthropoids fulfills a critical biological role. The most tenable hypotheses posit that the intimate spatial relationship among the temporalis, the eyeball, and the postorbital septum accounts for its development. One view is that the postorbital septum arose as an additional area for the origin of the anterior temporalis, presumably to assist early anthropoids in generating vertical incisal bite forces (Cachel 1978). Alternatively, activity in the anthropoid temporalis is postulated to cause uncoupled movement of the eyes, potentially compromising vision in anthropoids owing to the evolution of the retinal fovea (Cartmill 1980). Anatomical evidence does not support Cachel's hypothesis, while Cartmill's hypothesis is circumstantially supported by the fact that the frontation and convergence of anthropoid orbits have the effect of moving the anterior temporalis and the orbital contents closer together (Ross 1995, 1996). The septum would thus provide a 'kinetic insulation' of the anthropoid eye that strepsirhines presumably do not require. Others have suggested that the septum represents a structural adaptation to the evolution of the anthropoid pattern of mastication; specifically, the septum resists twisting moments arising from mastication (Rosenberger 1986). If one applies the same reasoning used to evaluate supraorbital function, there is little support for this hypothesis (Ross and Hylander 1996). *In vivo* strains arising in the postorbital septum are so modest that it is difficult to argue that the septum plays any significant role in the structural reinforcement of the circumorbital region or of the face as a whole. That is, the absence of a septum places none of the remaining facial bones in danger of failure. Moreover, the twisting load assumed to predispose the facial skeleton to a more unfavorable stress environment does not appear to occur during mastication in anthropoids (ibid.), and strain data suggest that differences in circumorbital morphology between anthropoids and prosimians are due to some functional requirements other than mastication (Ross 2008).

The nasal capsule is spatially associated with olfaction, and differences in the relative size of the cribriform plate are plausibly associated with the development of the olfactory bulbs, but confirmatory data are lacking (Smith and Rossie 2006). A related question is whether the size of the nasal capsule, as it relates to turbinal development, might also be associated with differences in olfactory acuity. Recent anatomical investigation in primates (Smith et al. 2004) indicate that a simple relationship is unlikely. The validity of the premise of an association between olfactory acuity and turbinal development rests on an assumption that there exists a predictable and invariant association of turbinal complexity with the distribution of olfactory epithelium. The use of surface area as a proxy for olfactory receptor distribution is, however, problematic, because the variation in cell densities and in epithelial thickness probably has effects on olfactory capabilities (ibid.). These new data underscore the fact that more data are needed to justify any generalizations about olfactory capacity in fossil primates. In any case, there would seem to be no role for a mechanobiological criterion in informing these questions.

The relationship of the ectotympanic to the auditory bulla in primates is diagnostic for higher taxa. Most of the discussion on middle ear morphology has focused primarily on its phylogenetic valence, with only secondary consideration of functional consequences. Comparative anatomical data do not provide a neat association between morphology and auditory performance; and, again, this is in part due to a paucity of investigations targeting performance specifically. The relatively longer lever arm of the malleus in strepsirhines (relative to anthropoids) is hypothesized to increase impedance matching performance (the ability of the ossicular chain to mitigate the energy loss as sound waves travel from air to the fluid-filled inner ear), but this does not, apparently, result in enhanced auditory sensitivity (Coleman and Ross 2004). Allometry is a necessary focus of future investigation, as scale effects on auditory performance may be as important as morphological details (Heffner 2004). In contrast to the special sense of olfaction, a mechanobiological approach would appear to be a fruitful avenue of inquiry, at least in terms of development of the ossicular chain. The cochlea of the inner ear is functionally associated with hearing; yet, despite interspecific differences that can be documented, there is no clear relationship between gross cochlear morphology and auditory characteristics in primates (Spoor and Zonneveld 1998).

POSTURAL ADAPTATIONS

Obligate bipedality being one defining feature of the human lineage, there has been considerable speculation that the morphology of the human skull is explicable in terms of preserving functional efficiency, given orthograde posture. The relative position of the foramen magnum, its orientation, and the degree of basicranial flexion have all been hypothesized to reflect altered functional requirements imposed by human posture and locomotion. At its most basic, the functional model is in this case a first-class lever, the head's center of gravity (located anteriorly to the occipital condyles) representing the load and the nuchal muscles representing the effort. It is demonstrable that the human foramen magnum is anteriorly situated, in terms of the overall length of the skull, in relation to its position in apes; its position on the basicranium is also distinct, although less obviously so (Ahern 2005). The evolutionary connection between bipedality and basicranial flexion is more tenuous, and there are comparative morphometric data indicating that basicranial flexion is uncorrelated with posture, being instead more plausibly related to brain size (Ross and Ravosa 1993). Basicranial flexion and foramen magnum orientation have also been proposed to reflect necessary changes in orbital axis orientation corresponding to the hominin locomotor shift, but here again, once the appropriate variables are measured in interspecific constrasts, there is little justification for proposing a necessary linkage between skull form and bipedality. Foramen magnum orientation is a poor predictor of head and neck posture in primates (Lieberman et al. 2000; Strait and Ross 1999).

These findings do not preclude a relationship between skull morphology and postural variables, but they underscore the need to identify variables that have clear functional consequences. In this case, the preceding hypotheses can be seen in retrospect to be not so much developed from a biomechanical model per se as motivated by the desire to attribute uniquely human attributes to a common functional basis, namely locomotion. In effect, the association is articulated in such general terms that the mechanobiological underpinnings are never developed.

Yet there is a context in which skull morphology can be more directly related to locomotor biomechanics. Variation in the vestibular apparatus of primates is plausibly linked to the dynamics of locomotion. Modern humans are characterized by a relative enlargement of the anterior and posterior semicircular canals in comparison to that of apes and early hominins, which is potentially linked to an increased sensitivity to angular movement in vertical planes (Spoor et al. 1994). Relative semicircular canal size probably correlates less with broad categories of locomotion (such as quadrupedalism and bipedalism) than with locomotor agility, broadly defined: for example, galagos and tarsiers exhibit relatively large semicircular canals in comparison to lorises

(Spoor et al. 2007). The remaining challenge is to collect quantifiable physical and behavioral data (for instance frequency spectra of head movements) to permit a more fine-grained association between locomotion and labyrinthine variation (Spoor and Zonneveld 1998). Whether a mechanobiological approach would succeed in clarifying outstanding issues in this context is uncertain: can strains in the basicranium that accompany locomotor behavior have anything to do with labyrinthine development? Although, dynamically speaking, bone can be sensitive to low-level strains, the growth of the labyrinth terminates prenatally (Spoor et al. 1994), and the highly specialized function may make the bone substance here immune to the mechanical triggers of bone metabolic activity that operate elsewhere. This would seem to obviate a developmental model based on conventional relationships among stress, strain, modeling, and remodeling (assuming that these were known).

FUTURE DIRECTIONS

The overwhelming majority of anthropological literature on skull function is based on the identification of, and inferences about, patterns of variation. What is of primary interest for inferring the functional consequences of this variation is the morphogenetic processes that lead to these observed patterns (Lieberman 1997). The comparative study of skull form has been effective in determining good morphological candidates for adaptation; the Achilles heel of the comparative approach is that, when there is a poor match between biomechanics (or, more broadly, function) and the ecological variable (however this is defined in physical terms), we do not know what to do other than complain about sampling problems or blame a nebulous phylogenetic issue. We should not delude ourselves into thinking that, because the literature is replete with examples of solid form/function synergy, there are no theoretical difficulties; our file drawers are full of unpublished studies that did not coincide with the adaptationist paradigm we insist we are indifferent to.

We could blame reductionism for our difficulties, in that "if we accept the premise that adaptations are mechanical in nature, then the mechanical variables that need to be considered are unapproachably complex" (Smith 1982: 100), but we could also question our choice of variables. Much in the same way in which parsimony is utilized in phylogenetic analysis, functional morphology proceeds implicitly from a criterion of optimality. This is appropriate as an initial yardstick, but since we fully expect evolutionary outcomes to fall short of the mark, we should not be astonished when our hypotheses 'don't work.'

Consider a general functional premise – the bones of the skull exist for purposes of protection – and a specific biomechanical assertion to the effect that the bones of the skull are optimized for strength, in other words, to resist failure. The second statement could be interpreted as a formal quantitative proof of the first, but the problem is that the first statement is undoubtedly accurate while the second is demonstrably false. It would make our work easier if we could show that the ratio of strength to physiological stress was similar throughout the skull. The data at hand, however, suggest that this is a morphologist's pipe dream (Daegling 2004).

This does not constitute a recommendation that we reject biomechanical criteria as interpretive tools. On the contrary, a mechanobiological approach addresses the

problem that *ad hoc* mechanical explanations fail because they run into biological reality (Smith 1982). Mechanical signals play a certain role in the determination of skull form, but we do not yet know what aspects of stress and strain the bone cells are sensitive to, even though we do know that mechanical signals are instrumental in gene expression. Thus, the distinction between 'genetic' and 'environmental' influences on morphology is blurred. This understanding clarifies the role that a mechanobiological perspective can provide in identifying the processes underlying patterns of variation both in developmental and in evolutionary contexts.

REFERENCES

Ahern, J. C. M. (2005) Foramen Magnum Position Variation in *Pan troglodytes*, Plio-Pleistocene Hominids, and Recent *Homo sapiens*: Implications for Recognizing the Earliest Hominids. *American Journal of Physical Anthropology* 127 (3): 267–276.

Ajmani, M. L., Mittal, R. K., and Jain, S. P. (1983) Incidence of the Metopic Suture in Adult Nigerian Skulls. *Journal of Anatomy* 137 (1): 177–183.

Anton, S. C. (1989) Intentional Cranial Vault Deformation and Induced Changes of the Cranial Base and Face. *American Journal of Physical Anthropology* 79: 253–267.

Ashley-Montagu, M. F. (1935) The Premaxilla in the Primates. *The Quarterly Review of Biology* 10 (1–2): 32–59, 181–208.

Bastir, M., and Rosas, A. (2005) Hierarchical Nature of Morphological Integration and Modularity in the Human Posterior Face. *American Journal of Physical Anthropology* 128 (1): 26–34.

Beecher, R. M., and Corruccini, R. S. (1981) Effect of Dietary Consistency on Craniofacial and Occlusal Development in the Rat. *Angle Orthodontist* 51: 61–69.

Bouvier, M., and Hylander, W. L. (1981) Effect of Bone Strain on Cortical Bone Structure in Macaques (*Macaca mulatta*). *Journal of Morphology* 167 (1): 1–12.

Bouvier, M., and Hylander, W. L. (1984) The Effect of Dietary Consistency on Gross and Histologic Morphology in the Craniofacial Region of Young Rats. *American Journal of Anatomy* 170: 117–126.

Byron, C. D., Borke, J., Yu, J., Pashley, D., Wingard, C. J., and Hamrick, M. (2004) Effects of Increased Muscle Mass on Mouse Sagittal Suture Morphology and Mechanics. *The Anatomical Record Part A: Discoveries in Molecular, Cellular, and Evolutionary Biology* 279A (1): 676–684.

Byron, C. D., Maness, H., Yu, J. C., and Hamrick, M. W. (2008) Enlargement of the Temporalis Muscle and Alterations in the Lateral Cranial Vault. *Integrative and Comparative Biology* 48 (3): 338–344.

Cachel, S. M. (1978) A Functional Analysis of the Primate Masticatory System and the Origin of the Anthropoid Post-Orbital Septum. *American Journal of Physical Anthropology* 50: 1–17.

Carlson, D. S., and Van Gerven, D. P. (1977) Masticatory Function and Post-Pleistocene Evolution in Nubia. *American Journal of Physical Anthropology* 46: 495–506.

Cartmill, M. (1980) Morphology, Function, and Evolution of the Anthropoid Postorbital Septum. In R. L. Ciochon and A. B. Chiarelli (eds), *Evolutionary Biology of the New World Monkeys and Continental Drift* (pp. 243–274). New York: Plenum Press.

Cheverud, J. M. (1995) Morphological Integration in the Saddle-Back Tamarin (*Saguinus fuscicollis*) Cranium. *American Naturalist* 145 (1): 63–89.

Cheverud, J. M. (1996) Developmental Integration and the Evolution of Pleiotropy. *American Zoologist* 36: 44–50.

Cheverud, J. M., and Midkiff, J. E. (1992) Effects of Fronto-Occipital Cranial Reshaping on Mandibular Form. *American Journal of Physical Anthropology* 87: 167–171.

Coleman, M. N., and Ross, C. F. (2004) Primate Auditory Diversity and Its Influence on Hearing Performance. *The Anatomical Record Part A: Discoveries in Molecular, Cellular, and Evolutionary Biology* 281A (1): 1123–1137.

Corruccini, R. S., and Beecher, R. M. (1982) Occlusal Variation Related to Soft Diet in a Non-human Primate. *Science* 218 (4567): 74–76.

Corruccini, R. S., and Beecher, R. M. (1984) Occlusofacial Morphological Integration Lowered in Baboons Raised on Soft Diet. *Journal of Craniofacial Genetics and Developmental Biology* 4: 135–142.

Daegling, D. J. (2004) Relationship of Strain Magnitude to Morphological Variation in the Primate Skull. *American Journal of Physical Anthropology* 124 (4): 346–352.

Daegling, D. J., and McGraw, W. S. (2001) Feeding, Diet, and Jaw Form in West African *Colobus* and *Procolobus*. *International Journal of Primatology* 22: 1033–1055.

Davidson, T. M. (2003) The Great Leap Forward: The Anatomic Basis for the Acquisition of Speech and Obstructive Sleep Apnea. *Sleep Medicine* 4 (3): 185–194.

DuBrul, E. Ll. (1977) Early Hominid Feeding Mechanisms. *American Journal of Physical Anthropology* 47: 305–320.

Enlow, D. H. (1982) *Handbook of Facial Growth*. Philadelphia: Saunders.

Enlow, D. H., and Azuma, M. (1975) Functional Growth Boundaries in the Human and Mammalian Face. In D. Bergsma (ed.), *Morphogenesis and Malformation of Face and Brain* (pp. 217–230). New York: Alan R. Liss.

Enlow, D. H., and Moyers, R. E. (1971) Growth and Architecture of the Face. *Journal of the American Dental Association* 82 (4): 763–774.

Gordon, J. E. (1978) *Structures: Or Why Things Don't Fall Down*. New York: Da Capo.

Greaves, W. S. (1978) The Jaw Lever System in Ungulates: A New Model. *Journal of Zoology* (London) 184: 271–285.

Heffner, R. S. (2004) Primate Hearing from a Mammalian Perspective. *The Anatomical Record Part A: Discoveries in Molecular, Cellular, and Evolutionary Biology* 281A (1): 1111–1122.

Herring, S. W. (1993) Epigenetic and Functional Influences on Skull Growth. In J. Hanken and B.K. Hall (eds), *The Skull: Development*, Vol. 1 (pp. 153–206). Chicago: University of Chicago Press.

Herring, S. W., and Teng, S. (2000) Strain in the Braincase and Its Sutures during Function. *American Journal of Physical Anthropology* 112: 575–593.

Hylander, W. L. (1979a) The Functional Significance of Primate Mandibular Form. *Journal of Morphology* 160 (2): 223–239.

Hylander, W. L. (1979b) Mandibular Function in *Galago crassicaudatus* and *Macaca fascicularis*: An *in vivo* Approach to Stress Analysis of the Mandible. *Journal of Morphology* 159 (2): 253–296.

Hylander, W. L. (1984) Stress and Strain in the Mandibular Symphysis of Primates: A Test of Competing Hypotheses. *American Journal of Physical Anthropology* 64: 1–46.

Hylander, W. L., and Johnson, K. R. (1992) Strain Gradients in the Craniofacial Region of Primates. In Z. Davidovitch (ed.), *The Biological Mechanisms of Tooth Movement and Craniofacial Adaptation* (pp. 559–569). Columbus OH: The Ohio State University College of Dentistry.

Hylander, W. L., Picq, P. G., and Johnson, K. R. (1991) Function of the Supraorbital Region of Primates. *Archives of Oral Biology* 36 (4): 273–281.

Kay, R. F., and Cartmill, M. (1977) Cranial Morphology and Adaptations of *Palaechthon nacimienti* and Other Paromomyidae (Plesiadapoidea, ?Primates), with a Description of a New Genus and Species. *Journal of Human Evolution* 6: 19–35.

Larsen, C. S. (1997) *Bioarchaeology: Interpreting Behavior from the Human Skeleton.* Cambridge: Cambridge University Press.

Lieberman, D. E. (1997) Making Behavioral and Phylogenetic Inferences from Hominid Fossils: Considering the Developmental Influence of Mechanical Forces. *Annual Review of Anthropology* 26 (1): 185–210.

Lieberman, D. E., and Crompton, A. W. (2000) Why Fuse the Mandibular Symphysis? A Comparative Analysis. *American Journal of Physical Anthropology* 112 (4): 517–540.

Lieberman, D. E., Ross, C. F., and Ravosa, M. J. (2000) The Primate Cranial Base: Ontogeny, Function, and Integration. *American Journal of Physical Anthropology* 113(S31): 117–169.

Moss, M. L. (1973) A Functional Cranial Analysis of Primate Craniofacial Growth. In M. Zingeser (ed.), *Fourth International Congress of Primatologists*, Vol. 3 (pp. 191–208). Basel: Karger.

Moss, M. L. (1997) The Functional Matrix Hypothesis Revisited. 1. The Role of Mechanotransduction. *American Journal of Orthodontics and Dentofacial Orthopaedics* 112: 8–11.

Moss, M. L., and Young, R. W. (1960) A Functional Approach to Craniology. *American Journal of Physical Anthropology* 18: 281–292.

Moyers, R. E., Bookstein, F. L., and Guire, K. E. (1979) The Concept of Pattern in Craniofacial Growth. *American Journal of Orthodontics* 76: 136–148.

Ravosa, M. J. (1988) Browridge Development in Cercopithecidae: A Test of Two Models. *American Journal of Physical Anthropology* 76: 535–555.

Ravosa, M. J. (1991) Structural Allometry of the Prosimian Mandibular Corpus and Symphysis. *Journal of Human Evolution* 20 (1): 3–20.

Ravosa, M. J. (1996) Mandibular Form and Function in North American and European Adapidae and Omomyidae. *Journal of Morphology* 229 (2): 171–190.

Ravosa, M. J. (1999) Anthropoid Origins and the Modern Symphysis. *Folia Primatologica* 70: 65–78.

Ravosa, M. J., and Hylander, W. L. (1994) Function and Fusion of the Mandibular Symphysis in Primates: Stiffness or Strength? In J. G. Fleagle and R. F. Kay (eds), *Anthropoid Origins* (pp. 447–468). New York: Plenum Press.

Ravosa, M. J., and Shea, B. T. (1994) Pattern in Craniofacial Biology: Evidence from the Old World Monkeys (Cercopithecidae). *International Journal of Primatology* 15: 801–822.

Ravosa, M. J., Lopez, E. K., Menegaz, R. A., Stock S. R., Stack, M. S., and Hamrick, M. W. (2008) Adaptive Plasticity in the Mammalian Masticatory Complex: You Are What, and How, You Eat. In C. J. Vinyard, M. J. Ravosa, and C. E. Wall (eds), *Primate Craniofacial Function and Biology* (pp. 293–328). New York: Springer.

Rosenberger, A. L. (1986) Platyrrhines, Catarrhines and the Anthropoid Transition. In B. A. Wood, L. Martin, and P. Andrews (eds), *Major Topics in Primate and Human Evolution* (pp. 66–88). Cambridge: Cambridge University Press.

Ross, C. F. (1995) Muscular and Osseous Anatomy of the Primate Anterior Temporal Fossa and the Functions of the Postorbital Septum. *American Journal of Physical Anthropology* 98 (3): 275–306.

Ross, C. F. (1996) Adaptive Explanation for the Origins of the Anthropoidea (Primates). *American Journal of Primatology* 40 (3): 205–230.

Ross, C. F. (2008) Does the Primate Face Torque? In C. J. Vinyard, M. J. Ravosa, and C. E. Wall (eds), *Primate Craniofacial Function and Biology* (pp. 63–81). New York: Springer.

Ross, C. F., and Hylander, W. L. (1996) *In vivo* and *in vitro* Bone Strain in the Owl Monkey Circumorbital Region and the Function of the Postorbital Septum. *American Journal of Physical Anthropology* 101 (2): 183–215.

Ross, C. F., and Ravosa, M. J. (1993) Basicranial Flexion, Relative Brain Size and Facial Kyphosis in Nonhuman Primates. *American Journal of Physical Anthropology* 91: 305–324.

Russell, M. D. (1985) The Supraorbital Torus: 'A Most Remarkable Peculiarity.' *Current Anthropology* 26 (3): 337.

Smith, R. J. (1982) On the Mechanical Reduction of Functional Morphology. *Journal of Theoretical Biology* 96: 99–106.

Smith, R. J. (1984) Comparative Functional Morphology of Maximum Mandibular Opening (Gape) in Primates. In D. J. Chivers, B. A. Wood, and A. Bilsborough (eds), *Food Acquisition and Processing in Primates* (pp. 231–255). New York: Plenum.

Smith, T. D., Bhatnagar, K. P., Tuladar, P., and Burrows, A. M. (2004) Distribution of Olfactory Epithelium in the Primate Nasal Cavity: Are Microsmia and Macrosmia Valid Morphological Concepts? *The Anatomical Record Part A: Discoveries in Molecular, Cellular, and Evolutionary Biology* 281A: 1173–1181.

Smith, T. D., and Rossie, J. (2006) Primate Olfaction: Anatomy and Evolution. In W. Brewer, D. Castle, C. Pantelis, and P. Doherty (eds), *Olfaction and the Brain* (pp. 135–166). Cambridge: Cambridge University Press.

Spencer, M. A. (1999) Constraints on Masticatory System Evolution in Anthropoid Primates. *American Journal of Physical Anthropology* 108 (4): 483–506.

Spoor, F., and Zonneveld, F. (1998) Comparative Review of the Human Bony Labyrinth. *American Journal of Physical Anthropology* 107 (S27): 211–251.

Spoor, F., Wood, B., and Zonneveld, F. (1994) Implications of Early Hominid Labyrinthine Morphology for Evolution of Human Bipedal Locomotion. *Nature* 369 (6482): 645–648.

Spoor, F., Garland, T. Jr., Krovitz, G., Ryan, T. M., Silcox, M. T., and Walker, A. (2007) The Primate Semicircular Canal System and Locomotion. *Proceedings of the National Academy of Sciences, USA* 104 (26): 10808–10812.

Strait, D. S., and Ross, C. F. (1999) Kinematic Data on Primate Head and Neck Posture: Implications for the Evolution of Basicranial Flexion and an Evaluation of Registration Planes Used in Paleoanthropology. *American Journal of Physical Anthropology* 108 (2): 205–222.

Taylor, A. B. (2002) Masticatory Form and Function in the African Apes. *American Journal of Physical Anthropology* 117 (2): 133–156.

Weijs, W. A., and de Jongh, H. J. (1977) Strain in Mandibular Alveolar Bone During Mastication in the Rabbit. *Archives of Oral Biology* 22: 667–675.

CHAPTER **29** Tooth Form and Function in Biological Anthropology

*Peter S. Ungar
and Peter W. Lucas*

Diet is an important key to understanding an animal's place in nature. The biosphere is a giant smorgasbord of sorts, and animals have many options for meeting their basic nutritional needs. The choices they make have important implications for nearly every aspect of their lives. It should come as no surprise, then, that biological anthropologists are interested in food preferences. Changes in diet through time may lead to important insights into the evolution of humans and other primates, and to new understandings of the subsistence and social structures of bioarcheological populations.

How can we uncover information on the diets of extinct animals and past peoples? Perhaps the most direct approach involves the study of teeth. These durable parts of the digestive system are the most commonly preserved elements in most fossil assemblages. They have evolved so as to fracture and to fragment plant and animal tissues, and a great deal of effort has gone into teasing information on diet from them. This chapter will survey the various techniques used by biological anthropologists to reconstruct the diets of fossil primates and early humans. We begin with a consideration of foods and their mechanical defenses. As Aristotle noted in Book 3 of *De Partibus Animalium* more than two thousand years ago, "teeth have one invariable office, namely the reduction of food" (in Ogle's translation of 1912). We cannot really appreciate teeth unless we understand the challenges they face as they function to ingest, fracture and fragment various foods. We then turn to the teeth themselves, examining these structures as tools for ingestion and mastication. Efforts to glean details of diet from tooth shape, size, structure, wear, and chemistry will all be considered. We end with a brief discussion of possible directions for future research – directions that promise to provide even more insights into the diets of past peoples, human ancestors, and other fossil primates.

A Food's Eye View

The food choices that animals make are constrained to a great extent by the defenses of those organisms whose tissues could be targeted as food. Plants do not want to be eaten, and so they construct chemical and mechanical defenses. Stress-limited defenses are those that stiffen or harden; they are intended to prevent a crack from starting, and they are simple and quick to construct. In contrast, displacement-limited defenses toughen to resist the spread or growth of a crack (see Ashby 2005). Each of these phrases has very specific meanings for those who study the science of material properties (Lucas 2004). Primates, like many other animals, tend to avoid plant defenses. They seek out undefended foods that are easy to ingest, chew, and digest, such as fleshy fruits.

Fruit flesh is a wrapping for seeds produced by flowering plants in order to give the seeds a better chance of survival. This is perhaps the major resource on the planet that is intended to be eaten. Fruits are 'seasonal,' a fruiting species often being available just for a few days. Animals attracted to the flesh usually either swallow or spit the contained seeds whole, thus dispersing them. The flesh of ripe fruits is generally weak and fails with little work.

However, some primates specialize in leaves and seeds. It does plants little good to have their seeds destroyed or their leaves eaten; hence these structures are chemically and mechanically defended. Seeds can develop tough or hard outer coverings (Figure 29.1). Leaves, too, are protected from cracks by their tough vascular systems, together with the fact that they are too thin to grow cracks easily. However, these defenses can be avoided by eating unripe seeds and young leaves before their defenses are completely in place. Since these are not available with regularity, primates often fall back on heavily defended items when their preferred foods are unavailable. It is then that the craniodental morphology of a primate begins to make sense in terms of food form.

A Tooth's Eye View

So how can teeth meet the challenges of defended plant (or animal) tissues? We can take as our starting point the fundamental aphorism that natural selection should favor teeth that can efficiently obtain and process the foods a primate is adapted to eat. Like other mammals, most primates maintain high metabolic rates, and the rate of energy intake must match the rate of their energy expenditure. Energy assimilation can be increased by raising acquisition rates; by letting more bulk food pass down elongated guts; by choosing more energy-dense foods; or by improving digestive efficiency. Chewing allows mammals to accomplish the last of these options, as food fracture and fragmentation exposes the protected nutrients and increases the surface area for digestive enzymes to act on. For any given tooth type, the rate of fragmentation depends on food material properties. Species with diets that differ in this respect should evolve tooth sizes, shapes, and structures that give the desired rate of food transfer to the abdominal gut.

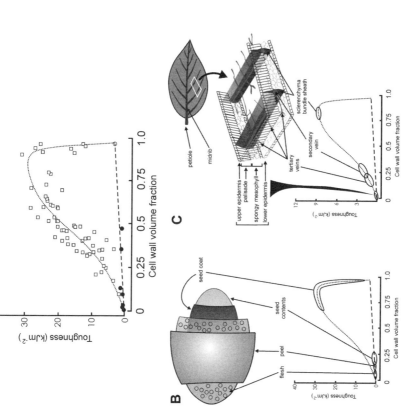

Figure 29.1 Food properties. Most properties of foods can be predicted from examining the amount of cell wall within them, which can be called their 'fiber content' on a volume basis. For example, the stiffness of plant foods increases with fiber. The exceptional property is toughness, plotted here against 'fiber content' (see A). Filled symbols show tissues just with primary cell walls; open symbols also possess a secondary wall; circles represent roughly spherical cells; rectangles denote elongate cells. Note that elongate cells with secondary cell walls are much tougher than other tissues, until fiber content is very high, when toughness drops precipitously. Thus seed coats can be brittle, even if they are built with woody tissue, simply because they are so dense (see B). At lower right, typical toughness values for ripe fruit tissues is low, and often similar to those of young leaves. Mature leaves are composites (see C), with the tough elements usually surrounding veins.

If we can understand tooth–food relationships in living primates with known diets, we can use them to generate a baseline that allows us to infer properties of foods from the teeth of extinct species. We can also use the comparative method to examine durable traces of foods left on or in the teeth of individuals during life. Microscopic use-wear and mineralized tissue chemistry offer important information about diets. This information can be integrated with functional morphology to give us a more complete picture of food preferences and foraging strategies.

Tooth size

Studies of tooth size as it relates to diet have focused mainly on the incisors and their use in ingestion, and on the molars and their use in mastication.

Incisor size   Higher primates have distinctive, bladed, 'spatulate' incisors. They can be used in two ways: either just to grip food objects or to fracture them. Modern primates with the broadest incisors often eat fruits with a rind or a peel. They use these teeth like wedges, to separate the flesh or the seeds of a fruit from its outer covering (Ang et al. 2006; Agrawal et al. 2008). The blade of the incisor controls the fracture, so that it stays on the peel–flesh interface. It is actually very difficult to get into fruits with peels without such a device; its absence fends off birds most effectively (Janson 1983). Broader incisors tend to remove more peel than narrower ones, and primates with narrower incisors are often folivores that use these teeth for little more than to grip and pluck leaves.

So how can we use incisor size to infer aspects of diet and tooth use in fossil species? We can begin by plotting incisor row breadth against body size for a group of closely related primates with differing diets (Hylander 1975). Higher primates that eat larger, husked fruits usually have relatively larger incisors than those that prefer items requiring little incisal preparation, such as leaves or berries (Figure 29.2). By simply placing data points for fossil primates on the graph, we should be able to get a sense of the extents of their incisor adaptations for anterior tooth use by comparisons with data for living primates with known ingestive behaviors.

There is, nevertheless, a strong phylogenetic component to incisor size (e.g. Ungar 1996). While frugivorous New World monkeys and Old World monkeys each have larger incisors than folivores closely related to them, the former have smaller incisors than the latter, independently of diet (Eaglen 1984). The ranges of incisor size are similar but the morphological starting point, or the ancestral form, differed. This suggests that we must choose our comparative baseline series carefully when we attempt to infer ingestive behaviors from incisor size in fossil forms, especially those with uncertainly affinities.

Molar size   The notion of how large the postcanine teeth need to be in order to fulfill their digestive role goes back to Pilbeam and Gould (1974), who reasoned that larger mammals need relatively larger teeth in order to process more food, given the energy requirements of a larger body. This principle is called 'metabolic scaling.' The situation is, however, complicated by the fact that larger mammals need less energy per unit mass than smaller ones do; and, as Kay (1975) pointed out, smaller mammals frequently consume higher-energy foods, which require less chewing than do larger ones. In fact, occlusal area and body size scale 'isometrically,' or at the same rate, when we control for diet. Interestingly, the volume of food processed in a given period of

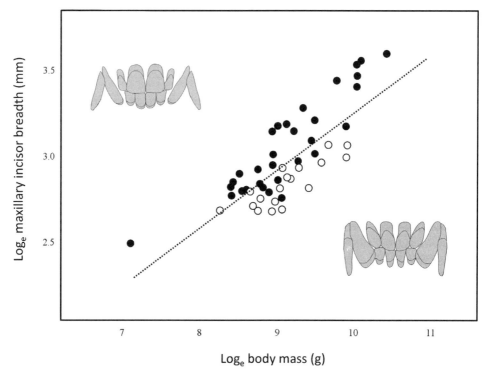

Figure 29.2 Incisor size and diet in cercopithecoid primates. The filled and open circles represent species of cercopithecines and colobines respectively. Note that cercopithecines tend to consume more fruit flesh whereas more colobines ingest and fracture leaves and seeds. Adapted from Hylander 1975

time seems to scale metabolically, given differences in rates of chewing between small and large mammals (Fortelius 1985).

More recently, Lucas (2004) pointed out that tooth size should also relate to the external properties of foods. For example, smaller food particles, or those that form thin sheets or rods should select for larger teeth to increase the probability of fracture. Further, sticky foods that clump should not spread well along the tooth row, and should select for short, wide dental arches. In any case, relationships between tooth size and diet are not simple, as is made obvious by the fact that, while folivorous New World monkeys have larger molars than frugivorous ones, the opposite holds true for Old World monkeys (Kay 1977; Ungar 1998). This makes it difficult to develop sweeping generalizations about food quality, or even about broad diet categories in fossil primates, on the basis of the sizes of their molar teeth alone.

Tooth shape
Most work on the functional aspects of tooth shape has focused on molar teeth and their role in fracturing and fragmenting food during mastication.

Molar shape Imagine a food particle that is large enough to require reduction in size in order to be swallowed, if not also in order to be digested. If we ignore for a moment its properties and structure, the cheapest method of cracking it is to push a point into it. Pointed features on primate tooth crowns are called cusps. A hard particle with stress-limited defenses will be stiff and thus there will be a small 'point' contact. Once a crack is initiated in such a particle, it will run swiftly in the food well ahead of the movement of the cusp. So the particle will break into fragments easily. Due to the small area of contact, a blunt tooth cusp would serve just as well as a sharp one, and it would have the critical advantage of resistance to cracking itself. Most primate molars have a series of cusps surrounding a basin. Food held in that basin reduces quickly, as each chew cycle produces more and more fragments.

But what about foods with displacement-limited defenses? Tough, pliant foods tend to spread across a cusp when they are loaded, thus increasing the contact area with the tooth. This has the effect of suppressing the possible development of cracks in the tooth cusp tip because cracks do not develop in compressive stress fields. This is what protects even a very sharp cusp. However, since tough foods resist crack propagation, cusps are not well suited to the task of fragmenting them. For this we need a blade, a surface in which one dimension is very small. Blades must pass all the way through a tough food in order to propagate a crack. Two similarly oriented opposing blades are best, much like a set of shears.

Clearly, then, natural selection should favor blunt cusped molars in those primates that are adapted to consuming hard, brittle foods with stress-limited defenses, and bladed or crested cheek teeth in primates that need to eat tough foods with displacement-limited defenses. And this division seems indeed to hold up quite well for all the major primate groups. Primates that regularly consume tough leaves or other plant parts, or insects with tough exoskeletons, typically have long blades, called 'shearing crests,' which run the lengths of their teeth up and over the cusps. Soft-fruit eaters tend to lack these long, sharp blades; and primates adapted to hard objects such as some nuts and palm fronds tend to have the flattest occlusal crowns with the bluntest cusps.

Quantifying tooth shape An understanding of the relationships between molar crown shape and food properties in living primates cannot help us to infer the diets of fossil species unless we have a way to characterize and compare functionally relevant aspects of tooth form. Kay's (1977) 'shearing quotient' (SQ) has been the gold standard for measuring crest or blade lengths in primates for more than three decades. First, summed mesiodistal crest lengths of molars are regressed over the straight-line distances between the mesial and distal edges of those teeth for closely related species (say, cercopithecoids) with similar diets (say, frugivores). The resulting regression line represents expected summed shearing crest length for a member of that group with the given diet. Residuals that deviate substantially from zero have either longer or shorter crests than those expected of – in this case, a fruit-eating Old World monkey.

SQ studies in the 1980s and 1990s confirmed relationships between crest length and diet for all major groups of primates. Folivores and insectivores have higher SQs than frugivores, and, among frugivores, hard-object feeders evince the shortest relative shearing crest lengths (see Kay and Covert 1984; Anthony and Kay 1993; Ungar 1998). We must understand, however, that, just as incisor size reflects both function and phylogeny, so too does molar crest length. Cercopithecoids, for example, have longer crest lengths than hominoids or platyrrhines independently of diet – presumably because the first Old World monkey had longer crests than the first ape (Kay and Ungar 1997).

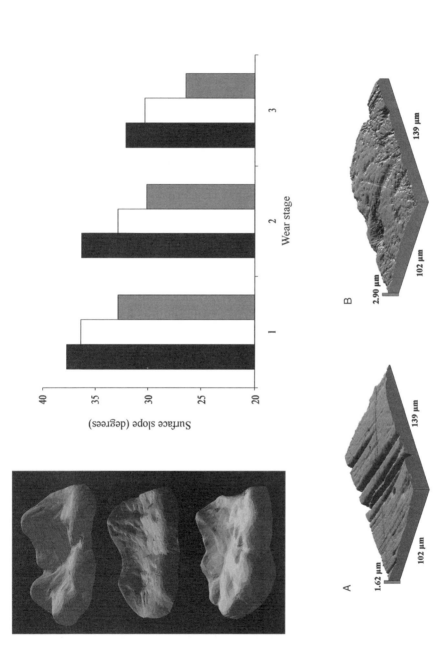

Figure 29.3 Dental topography and microwear. The upper left image presents triangulated irregular network models for lower second molar teeth of a gorilla (top), orangutan (middle), and chimpanzee (bottom). The graph on the upper right illustrates average surface slope values for the lower second molars of gorillas (black), orangutans (white), and chimpanzees (gray) at three stages of wear. (Adapted from Unger 2007.) The lower images are three-dimensional axiomatic representations of microwear surfaces on the molars of *Alouatta palliata* (A) and *Cebus apella* (B). The surface areas represented are 100μm × 140μm each. Adapted from Unger and Scott 2009

Thus, while we can calculate the SQs of fossils from the regression line of living primates in order to infer diet, we should use related species whenever possible.

SQs have proven to be very useful for assessing relationships between diet and the morphology of unworn molars; but the cusp tips used as landmarks for measurement are quickly obliterated with wear. This is a problem for two reasons. First, wear begins as soon as teeth erupt into occlusion, and most primate teeth available for study, living or fossil, are worn. Second, limiting analyses to unworn teeth only gives us a part of the picture. Surely natural selection does not stop when teeth begin to wear. Primate dentitions are literally sculpted with wear, in a manner that keeps them functionally efficient through the reproductive years (Ungar and M'Kirera 2003; King et al. 2005). We need to be able to incorporate worn teeth into our analyses to appreciate this.

Dental topographic analysis was developed with this worn tooth conundrum in mind. A scanning device is used to obtain a point cloud representing the occlusal surface of a tooth, while surface characterization software quantifies functional aspects of crown morphology. One common technique combines a laser scanner with Geographic Information Systems (GIS) software to create virtual models of teeth resembling landscapes (Figure 29.3). Cusps are modeled as mountains, fissures as valleys, and so on. Surface slope, relief, angularity, basin volume and other attributes are calculated without the need to identify specific landmarks that are subjected to wear. Differences between frugivores and folivores are as expected. The lower second molars of leaf-eating *Procolobus badius* and *Gorilla gorilla*, for example, have steeper sloping, more angular surfaces and greater occlusal relief than fruit-eating *Cercocebus torquatus* and *Pan troglodytes* have, respectively, when gross wear stage is controlled for (M'Kirera and Ungar 2003; Ungar and M'Kirera 2003; Ungar and Bunn 2008).

In fact, if we score gross wear, we can actually gauge changes in morphology that come with wear within a species. Some changes and some consistencies are seen through the wear sequence. For example, while average surface slopes tend to decrease with wear, surface angularity or jaggedness tends to remain fairly constant through much of the wear sequence. Primate teeth may lose their functional surface roughness and approach senescence as the last of the occlusal table enamel goes. Similar patterns have been observed for all major groups of primates (M'Kirera and Ungar 2003; Ungar and M'Kirera 2003; Dennis 2004; King et al. 2005; Ungar and Bunn 2008).

Tooth structure

Another functionally relevant aspect of tooth form that can inform us on primate diets is the structure of the tooth, and especially that of its enamel cap. Dental anthropologists consider both gross enamel thickness and the microscopic structure of that enamel.

Enamel thickness   Enamel is a heavily mineralized tissue that, in unworn primate teeth, provides a durable coating to the underlying mineralized dentin, which forms the core of a tooth. Enamel is extremely stiff, and thus, even when the dentin is exposed, enamel will take the load. Primate enamel thickness can range anywhere from 0.05 to 5.0 mm, depending on tooth type, species, and position on the crown where thickness is measured. Species with thin cuspal enamel may have relatively thicker enamel on the sides of the crown, and vice versa.

There are two hypotheses purporting to explain why enamel might be of variable thickness:

1   Thicker enamel strengthens the tooth crown in mammals that feed on objects with stress-limited defenses.
2   Thicker enamel increases wear potential, where 'wear' refers to the abrasion or attrition of enamel surfaces during feeding.

Both hypotheses really refer to feeding on hard objects, albeit items of very different sizes, and both may be correct. Figure 29.1 shows this. Against very small but sufficiently hard particles, such as phyoliths and grit, enamel tends to yield. Depending on the movement involved, this plastic deformation leads to scratching and pitting, which are often precursors to the loss of material through small subsurface cracks. The thickness of the enamel is irrelevant to the forces involved (Lucas et al. 2008). Against large hard particles, enamel is much more vulnerable to cracking rather than yielding. These cracks are predicted to start farther below the enamel surface, and possibly right at the enamel–dentin junction. The propensity to develop these cracks is much reduced through thickening the enamel.

The above trends, suggesting that enamel should be thick, contrast with the patterns that might be expected for eating foods with displacement-limited defenses. A tooth adapted to tough foods can benefit from wear when sharp, blade-like edges form at the boundary between the remaining, harder enamel and the newly exposed, softer dentin. Tooth breakage is not a big problem in this case, as spreading a pliant food over a cusp or ridge effectively protects the edge from cracking. Potential problems develop, however, lower down the crown, where fractures may easily result from hoop stresses (such as those stresses in wooden barrels that require the presence of steel hoops). These stresses can be imagined in terms of the barrel contents (by analogy, the dentin) attempting to escape by inducing cracks in inner enamel. Increasing the bulk of the tooth at the base of the crown protects it in such cases.

To date, few studies have explicitly used enamel thickness to reconstruct the diets of fossil primates. As Kay (1981) has noted, those primates that regularly eat foods with stress-limited defenses do tend to have thicker enamel than closely related ones that do not. It has been rather difficult to build a comparative baseline series for the interpretation of fossil forms, though, as Dumont (1995) has shown, there is no 'thickness threshold' for hard-object feeders across groups of primates.

Enamel microstructure   Enamel is heterogeneous and largely composed of long, thin rods or prisms that run from the inside of the crown outward. Sometimes the rods are straight, but often they wave. Adjacent rods can wave slightly out of phase, a phenomenon called 'decussation' or crossing. Decussation is a marked feature of the enamel of many mammals, with a wide variety of patterns documented:

1   radial enamel, in which rods pass towards the surface without deviating;
2   enamel where decussation is restricted to the region close to the dentin (as in modern humans); and
3   enamel where decussation is pervasive, and extends close to the tooth surface.

More and more evidence suggests that decussation greatly increases enamel toughness – despite the exceptionally high mineral content, which would otherwise make it very brittle.

Non-genetic indicators of diet

The sizes, shapes, and structures of the teeth can teach us a great deal about adaptation, but they tell us more about what an individual in the past was capable of eating what it actually ate on a daily basis. Natural selection should favor teeth that are themselves able to resist and at the same time to inflict fractures in the strongest items a primate eats – regardless of how often such foods are consumed. In fact it is often fallback items, taken only rarely, that have the most significant mechanical defenses and low energy yields. These are the very sorts of foods that require dental specializations. As Kinzey (1978) has written, "when a food item is critical for survival, even though not part of the primary specialization, it will influence the selection of dental features" (378).

Just as most automobiles have the potential to go much faster than the speeds at which they are normally driven, craniodental adaptations may allow an animal to fragment foods that are mechanically more challenging than the ones usually eaten. An animal may actually avoid the very foods to which its teeth are adapted if more nutritious, easier to digest items are available to it. This is a fairly common phenomenon in nature, and it is known as 'Liem's paradox' (Robinson and Wilson 1998). Gorillas, for example, have long shearing crests and strong chewing muscles, capable of processing very tough foods, but they will choose soft fruits over leaves when they are presented with a choice between the two (Remis 2002). It is, however, the leaves and the other tough items consumed as fallback foods at times of resource stress, when soft fruits are unavailable, that the teeth are adapted to.

But how do we know whether a dental adaptation in a fossil species reflects preferred foods, or less commonly eaten but still important fallback items? This question gets to the very nature of the way selection works. In order to answer it, however, we need an independent measure of diet, one that reflects what individuals actually ate in the past on a regular basis. We need some trace left by foods that is preserved in the fossil record. There are two lines of evidence that paleoanthropologists typically look to: dental microwear and tooth tissue chemistry.

Dental microwear Dental microwear analysis is the study of microscopic patterns of scratches and pits that form on a tooth's surface as the result of its use. Primates that consume hard and brittle foods – such as many nuts and palm fronds – typically have microwear surfaces dominated by pits, as opposing teeth approach one another to crush these items. Teeth that fracture tougher foods – such as some leaves and insect exoskeletons – tend to have parallel microwear scratches, which form as abrasives are dragged across tooth surfaces, as these shear past one another to cut those items (see Figure 29.3). Animals with mixed diets, or with diets possessing intermediate fracture properties, tend to have intermediate microwear patterns (Teaford 1988; Ungar 1998).

Conventional dental microwear analysis involves high-magnification imaging of surfaces through the use of a scanning electron microscope. Individual features are then identified by an observer and counted and measured with a mouse-driven cursor on a computer screen. The ratio of pits to scratches on a surface has proved to be valuable, but high observer error rates and limitations to two-dimensional measurements have probably prevented microwear from reaching its ultimate potential in revealing aspects of diet and tooth use.

A new approach, called 'microwear texture analysis,' offers an objective, repeatable, three-dimensional method for surface characterization by combining point clouds generated by using a white-light scanning confocal profiler with scale-sensitive fractal analysis (see Ungar et al. 2007). Results indicate that primates consuming hard, brittle foods tend to have more complex microwear surface textures, with roughness values varying with the scale of observation. Tough food feeders tend to have more anisotropic microwear textures, with surfaces dominated by long, linear, parallel features. These and other texture variables have been shown to distinguish between primates with subtly differing diets.

Individual microwear surface textures can turnover in a matter of days as features are replaced with further tooth wear. A microwear study on many specimens can give us an idea of the feeding preferences of a species by inferring foods eaten a few days before death for several individuals. Microwear texture analysis provides the repeatable measurements for individuals needed to assess within species variation. A hard-object fallback pattern, for example, should have a concentration of specimens with low complexity values, but a few falling outside this pattern, toward the high extreme. Such microwear texture data, when compared with tooth size, shape and structure, may allow us to examine whether adaptations reflect preferred foods or foods consumed only on occasion.

Tooth chemistry   The other 'non-genetic' line of evidence for diet, used especially in studies of fossil hominins, is tooth chemistry. This work is reviewed in greater detail by Schoeninger's contribution in the present volume; but the topic bears a mention here, for completeness. The basic idea is that food provides the raw materials used to form mineralized tissues, so teeth should bear the chemical signatures of the diets adopted during dental development. And concentrations of trace elements and ratios of stable isotopes differ in different types of foods. For example, stable isotopes of oxygen (O), nitrogen (N), and carbon (C) are especially useful for reconstructing diet. Water molecules containing ^{16}O evaporate more quickly than those containing ^{18}O. Water in leaves has more of the latter, and folivores should have relatively high ratios of $^{18}O/^{16}O$ (see Yakir 1992). Ratios of $^{15}N/^{14}N$ increase as one moves up the food chain: carnivores have higher values than herbivores (Schoeninger and DeNiro 1984). Among herbivores, those that consume plants from drier areas tend to be ^{15}N enriched (Murphy and Bowman 2006). Finally, ratios of $^{13}C/^{12}C$ in plants reflect their photosynthetic pathways. C_4 grasses and sedges have lower $^{13}C/^{12}C$ ratios than other plants do, so grass grazers and animals that eat them have lower ratios than browsers do (Sponheimer et al. 2003).

FUTURE DIRECTIONS

Dental anthropologists have made great progress toward understanding relationships between teeth and diet and the ways in which we can use these relationships to make inferences about diet from the teeth of past peoples and of fossilized primates. Nevertheless, much work remains to be done.

From the perspective of food, our current systems of measuring external and internal properties in the field require substantial improvements, so that they may give us the best information on tooth form. Indentation tests look promising (Lucas et al. in press). For example friction is an essential component of feeding, for instance in ingesting leaves by stripping, but has never really been measured. Friction is probably heavily affected by the presence of tannins in foods (Prinz and Lucas 2000).

From the perspective of teeth, much more needs to be done. First we must go beyond measuring whether teeth possess sharp or blunt cusped or ridged features, to an understanding of the arrangement of these features on teeth. Moreover, we must develop better characterizations of functional aspects of tooth form that would be specific to predictions made on the basis of biomechanical expectations. Cusp relief, surface area, angularity or jaggedness, aspect, basin volume, 'drainage patterns,' and just about any other topographic attribute imaginable can be measured (Zuccotti et al. 1998). Such measurements will be key to developing the best possible baseline for the inference of dietary adaptations in fossil species from the shapes of their teeth.

We also need to understand tooth structure better, both as it relates to resisting breakage and as a means by which occlusal surfaces are sculpted with wear. How do teeth weather millions of potentially injurious contacts without disintegrating? One possible approach is through finite element analysis (FEA) – a long-standing method of finding the distribution of stresses in an object of complex geometry by dividing that object into sufficiently small elements of standard volume and shape and then establishing the stress on each. There are several problems with it for this application though. The closer a model imitates reality, the less it can predict anything. More serious is that in dealing with structure and the interfaces between microstructural elements, this method cannot currently model the growth of cracks in structures – and this is serious because forces can rise substantially even as cracks grow (Lucas et al. 2008).

Research is currently progressing towards a better understanding of the details of tooth structure on microscales and nanoscales, by using a variety of new technologies such as X-ray microtomography (Olejniczak et al. 2007). Relationships between enamel crown shape and the shape of the underlying dentin cap, as well as their degrees of hardness in relation to dietary abrasives, will surely provide new insights into the process of enamel sculpting and into the way teeth are adapted to change or to maintain their shape as they wear.

Then there is the question of adaptations for fallback versus preferred resources. How can we know whether a given anatomy relates to the properties of foods taken on a daily, seasonal, or even generation-length basis? The integration of non-genetic indicators, such as microwear and stable isotopes, with tooth size, shape, and structure may offer new insights into food choices and foraging strategies in our ancestors, and perhaps may even help to inform us on the very nature of selection.

ACKNOWLEDGMENTS

We thank Clark Spencer Larsen for his kind invitation for us to contribute to this volume. We acknowledge the US National Science Foundation and LSB Leakey Foundation for their funding over the years.

REFERENCES

Agrawal, K. R., Ang, K., Sui, Z., Tan, H. T. W., and Lucas, P. W. (2008) Methods of Ingestion and Incisal Designs. In J. D. Irish and G. C. Nelson (eds), *Technique and Application in Dental Anthropology* (pp. 349–363). Cambridge: Carmbridge University Press.

Ang, K. Y., Lucas, P. W., and Tan, H. T. W. (2006) Incisal Orientation and Biting Efficiency. *Journal of Human Evolution* 50: 663–672.

Anthony, M. R. L., and Kay, R. F. (1993) Tooth Form and Diet in Ateline and Alouattine Primates: Reflections on the Comparative Method. *American Journal of Science* 293A: 356–382.

Ashby, M. F. (2005) *Materials Selection in Mechanical Design*, 3nd edn. London: Butterworth Heinemann.

Dennis, J. C., Ungar, P. S., Teaford, M. F., and Glander, K. E. (2004) Dental Topography and Molar Wear in *Alouatta palliata* from Costa Rica. *American Journal of Physical Anthropology* 125: 152–161.

Dumont, E. R. (1995) Enamel Thickness and Dietary Adaptation among Extant Primates and Chiropterans. *Journal of Mammalogy* 76: 1127–1136.

Eaglen, R. H. (1984) Incisor Size and Diet Revisited: The View from a Platyrrhine Perspective. *American Journal of Physical Anthropology* 64: 263–275.

Fortelius, M. 1985. Ungulate Cheek Teeth: Developmental, Functional and Evolutionary Interrelations. *Acta Zoologica Fennica* 180: 1–76.

Hylander, W. L. (1975) Incisor Size and Diet in Anthropoids with Special Reference to Cercopithecidae. *Science* 189: 1095–1098.

Janson, C. H. (1983) Adaptation of Fruit Morphology to Dispersal Agents in a Neotropical Forest. *Science* 219: 187–189.

Kay, R. F. (1975) Allometry and Early Hominids (comment). *Science* 189: 63.

Kay, R. F. (1977) Evolution of Molar Occlusion in Cercopithecidae and Early Catarrhines. *American Journal of Physical Anthropology* 46: 327–352.

Kay, R. F. (1981) The Nut-Crackers: A New Theory of the Adaptations of the Ramapithecinae. *American Journal of Physical Anthropology* 55: 141–151.

Kay, R. F., and Covert, H. H. (1984) Anatomy and Behavior of Extinct Primates. In D. J. Chivers, B. A. Wood, and A. Bilsborough (eds), *Food Acquisition and Processing in Primates* (pp. 467–508). New York: Plenum Press.

Kay, R. F., and Ungar, P. S. (1997) Dental Evidence for Diet in Some Miocene Catarrhines with Comments on the Effects of Phylogeny on the Interpretation of Adaptation. In D. R. Begun, C. Ward, and M. Rose (eds), *Function, Phylogeny and Fossils: Miocene Hominoids and Great Ape and Human Origins* (pp. 131–151). New York: Plenum Press.

King, S. J., Arrigo-Nelson, S. J., Pochron, S. T., Semprebon, G. M., Godfrey, L. R., Wright, P. C., and Jernvall J. (2005) Dental Senescence in a Long-Lived Primate Links Infant Survival to Rainfall. *Proceedings of the National Academy of Sciences, USA* 102: 16579–16583.

King, S. J., Blanco, M. B., and Godfrey, L. R. (2005) Dietary Reconstruction of *Archeolemur* Using Dental Topographic Analysis. *American Journal of Physical Anthropology* (Suppl.) 40: 133.

Kinzey, W. G. (1978) Feeding Behavior and Molar Features in Two Species of Titi Monkey. In D. J. Chivers and J. Herbert (eds), *Recent Advances in Primatology*, Vol. 1: *Behavior* (pp. 373–385). New York: Academic Press.

Lucas, P. W. (2004) *Dental Functional Morphology: How Teeth Work*. New York: Cambridge University Press.

Lucas, P., Constantino, P., Wood, B., and Lawn, B. (2008) Dental Enamel as a Dietary Indicator in Mammals. *Bioessays* 30: 374–385.

Lucas, P. W., Constantino, P. J., Chalk, J., Ziscovici, C., Wright, B. W., Fragaszy, D. M., Hill, D. A., Lee, J. J. W, Chai, H., Darvell, B. W., Lee, P. K. D., and Yuen, T. D. B. (in press)

Indentation as a Technique to Assess the Mechanical Properties of Fallback Foods. *American Journal of Physical Anthropology*.

M'Kirera, F., and Ungar, P. S. (2003) Occlusal Relief Changes with Molar Wear in *Pan troglodytes troglodytes* and *Gorilla gorilla gorilla*. *American Journal of Primatology* 60: 31–41.

Murphy, B. P., and Bowman, D. M. J. S. (2006) Kangaroo Metabolism Does Not Cause the Relationship between Bone Collagen $\delta^{15}N$ and water availability. *Functional Ecology* 20: 1062–1069.

Ogle, W. (1912) *The Works of Aristotle Translated into English*. Oxford: Clarendon Press.

Olejniczak, A. J., Tafforeau, P., Smith, T. M., Temming, H., and Hublin, J. -J. (2007) Compatibility of Microtomographic Imaging Systems for Dental Measurements. *American Journal of Physical Anthropology* 134: 130–134.

Pilbeam, D., and Gould. S. F. (1974) Size and Scaling in Human Evolution. *Science* 186: 892-901

Prinz, J. F., and Lucas, P. W. (2000) Saliva Tannin Interactions. *Journal of Oral Rehabilitation* 27: 991–994.

Remis, M. J. (2002) Food Preferences among Captive Western Gorillas (*Gorilla gorilla gorilla*) and Chimpanzees (*Pan troglodytes*). *International Journal of Primatology* 23: 231–249.

Robinson, B. W., and Wilson, D. S. (1998) Optimal Foraging, Specialization, and a Solution to Liem's Paradox. *American Naturalist* 151 (3): 223–235.

Schoeninger, M., and DeNiro, M. (1984) Nitrogen and Carbon Isotopic Composition of Bone Collagen from Marine and Terrestrial Animals. *Geochimica et Cosmochimica Acta* 48: 625–639.

Sponheimer, M., Lee-Thorp, J. A., DeRuiter, D. J., Smith, J. M., van der Merwe, N. J., Reed, K., Grant, C. C., Ayliffe, L. K., Robinson, T. F., Heidelberger, C., and Marcus, W. (2003) Diets of Southern African Bovidae: Stable Isotope Evidence. *Journal of Mammalogy* 84: 471–479.

Teaford, M. F. (1988) A Review of Dental Microwear and Diet in Modern Mammals. *Scanning Microscopy* 2: 1149–1166.

Ungar, P. (1998) Dental Allometry, Morphology, and Wear as Evidence for Diet in Fossil Primates. *Evolutionary Anthropology* 6: 205–217.

Ungar, P. S. (1996) Relationship of Incisor Size to Diet and Anterior Tooth Use in Sympatric Sumatran Anthropoids. *American Journal of Primatology* 38: 145–156.

Ungar, P. S. (2007) Dental Functional Morphology: The Known, the Unknown and the Unknowable. In P. S. Ungar (ed.), *Early Hominin Diets: The Known, the Unknown and the Unknowable* (pp. 39–55). Oxford: Oxford University Press.

Ungar, P. S., and Bunn, J. M. (2008) Primate Dental Topographic Analysis and Functional Morphology. In J. D. Irish and G. C. Nelson (eds), *Technique and Application in Dental Anthropology* (pp. 253–265). New York: Cambridge University Press.

Ungar, P. S., and M'Kirera, F. (2003) A Solution to the Worn Tooth Conundrum in Primate Functional Anatomy. *Proceedings of the National Academy of Sciences, USA* 100: 3874–3877.

Ungar, P. S., and Scott, R. S. (2009) Dental Evidence for Diets of Early *Homo*. In F. E. Grine, J. G. Fleagle, and R. E. Leakey (eds), *The First Humans: Origin and Evolution of the Genus Homo* (pp. 121–134). New York: Springer.

Ungar, P. S., Scott, R. S., Scott, J. R., and Teaford, M. F. (2007) Dental Microwear Analysis: Historical Perspectives and New Approaches. In J. D. Irish and G. C. Nelson (eds), *Dental Anthropology* (pp. 389–425). Cambridge: Cambridge University Press.

Yakir, D. (1992) Variations in the Natural Abundances of Oxygen-18 and Deuterium in Plant Carbohyrates. *Plant Cell Environment* 15: 1005–1020.

Zuccotti, L. F., Williamson, M. D., Limp, W. F., and Ungar, P. S. (1998). Technical Note: Modeling Primate Occlusal Topography Using Geographic Information Systems Technology. *American Journal of Physical Anthropology* 107: 137–142.

CHAPTER 30

Locomotor Function across Primates (Including Humans)

Daniel L. Gebo

INTRODUCTION

The bodies of living primates (including humans) are time capsules of our evolutionary past. All of the major locomotor and postural changes through time are in fact present in our current bodies. This is an important point if you are trying to understand postcranial function since primate movement patterns are among the most varied in any mammalian Order. Primates leap, run along branches or across the ground, arm-swing, hang by their feet, or cling to tree trunks; while we walk on two legs – the most peculiar movement of all. We tend to divide primate movements into quadrupedalism, leaping, climbing, and suspension (usually performed with the feet, but occasionally using hands and forelimbs). Primates as a group are hindlimb-dominated; they utilize a diagonal couplet gait; and they tend to bend their elbows and knees as they move along branches (this is called 'gait compliance'; see Hildebrand 1967; Napier 1967; Martin 1972; Kimura et al. 1979; Rollinson and Martin 1981; Demes et al. 1994; Schmitt 1995; Larson 1998, Larson et al. 2001; Cartmill et al. 2002). All of these characteristics help to maintain balance along a curved surface. Life in the canopy is a constant stream of body adjustments. This is why in general primates have quite mobile joints throughout their body plan. To understand primate postcranial function, you need to be able to place the anatomical structures under study into their true behavioral positions. Grasping hands make little sense in a standard human anatomy position; and this is why understanding primate movements and postural patterns is important if you are trying to examine bones, muscles, and joints for an overall comprehension of postcranial function. In contrast to what is presented in most introductory textbooks of physical anthropology, primate bodies are not 'generalized.' They are in fact quite specialized for life in the trees.

GRASPING

Grasping is the hallmark adaptation among primate limbs (Le Gros Clark 1959; Cartmill 1974, 1985; Szalay and Dagosto 1988; Lewis 1989). The ability to hold onto small curved surfaces (for instance tiny branches) has allowed primates to explore the arboreal canopy in great detail (Figure 30.1). With the rare exception of some marsupials, a few tree shrews, and climbing mice, grasping is an exceedingly rare adaptation among living mammals. Primate grasping differs in most anatomical aspects from that of other mammalian graspers. First, both the hand and the foot in primates are capable of swinging their respective first digit across the palm or sole to oppose the lateral digits. Only humans have lost this ability in the foot, while a few primates (colobines, spider monkeys, and orangutans) have greatly shortened the first digit in their hands. Primates have nails instead of claws, several large intrinsic and extrinsic muscles devoted to digital flexion and grasping, and mobile joint surfaces allowing hand and foot rotations as well as the opposability of the first digit. All are key components in grasping.

Hands come in a variety of postural types, which include palmigrade, digitigrade, knuckle-walking, fist-walking, and suspensory hand positions. All digits can flex at the metacarpal–phalangeal joint and at the interphalangeal joints. Palmigrade hands are most common among primates, who are capable of rotating the hand into pronated or supinated positions. Hand rotation occurs actively at the elbow (the capitulum–radial head joint) rather than at the wrist, in contrast to rotation at the mobile intrinsic joints of the foot. Wrist joints primarily flex and extend the hands of primates. The distal elements of the hand contact a substrate before the proximal elements of the

Figure 30.1   Arboreal grasping in primates.

wrist. Palmigrade hands are the active grasping structures, and thus the active pulling and climbing structures for primates. Their greater surface area of contact with the substrate appears to add stability during arboreal locomotion (Cartmill 1979). Primates have wide fingers and toes with broad palms or soles.

Digitigrade hands are found among Old World monkeys. Digitigrady serves to lengthen the forelimb in these terrestrial quadrupedal taxa. In digitigrade hands the metacarpal–phalangeal joint supports the forelimb, and the proximal hand is well elevated above the surface. Weight transfer does not move onto the palm in digitigrady (Whitehead 1993). The tip of the thumb contacts the substrate only intermittently.

Fist-walking and knuckle-walking hands allow orangutans and the African apes respectively to fold their long fingers underneath as they move quadrupedally, usually terrestrially (Tuttle 1967; Tuttle and Beck 1972; Susman 1974). With these folded fingers, all four proximal phalanges support the forelimb in fist-walkers, while the middle phalangeal shafts bear the weight in knuckle-walking.

Unlike these hand types with compressive and weight-bearing positions, suspensory hands are like hooks, with elongated fingers that facilitate arm-hanging postures as well as arm-swinging movements for the living apes and spider monkeys, as they move through gaps in the canopy. What facilitates hook-grasping and hanging is the long extrinsic finger flexors, which originate from the medial epicondyle of the humerus and insert on the palmar surface of the distal phalanges.

Lastly, hands are also feeding tools among primates. The acts of reaching, grasping, and pulling items to the mouth add another dimension to hand adaptations across primates (Napier 1980; Hamrick 1998, 2001; Schmitt and Lemelin 2002). This adaptation has figured prominently in the visual predation hypothesis formulated by Cartmill (1972).

With the exception of human feet, primate foot anatomy is all about grasping and climbing. Most primates utilize a heel-elevated foot position allowing mid-foot contact first with the substrate. This facilitates great rotational movements at the transverse tarsal joint. In contrast, African apes and humans contact terrestrial surfaces with a heel-strike. Heel-up (semi-plantigrady) or heel-down (heel-strike plantigrady) foot contact is an important distinction when it comes to placing the anatomical structures of the foot in their correct functional alignment. In short, the contact pattern dictates how primate feet work from a mechanical point of view. In semi-plantigrady, weight is borne by the plantar surfaces of the cuboid, navicular, and entocunieform and by the digits. The key foot joint is the transverse tarsal joint, since this joint allows feet to obtain their rotational mobility (or lack thereof in humans). This joint is made up of the calcaneocuboid and the talonavicular joints, and these joints allow for inverted foot positions to be achieved. The inverted, slightly abducted foot position, along with the grasping big toe, are all part of the great adaptive success of primate arboreality. The unusual shape of the distal entocuneiform, with its saddle-shaped joint for the first metatarsal, allows the great swing of the big toe to oppose the lateral digits during grasping. The large extrinsic flexors (*flexor hallucis longus* and *flexor digitorum longus*) as well as the intrinsic *adductor hallucis*, are large and important muscles for digital flexion and for grasping in primates.

The last feature to consider in relation to hands and feet is the secondary evolution of claw-like nails among a variety of different primates. This adaptation is tied to the ecological use of large-diameter trunks – a type of substrate that exceeds the grasping span of hands and feet (Cartmill 1979). *Phaner*, a cheirogaleid, *Euoticus*, a galagid, and callitrichines, New World monkeys, all possess claw-like nails and are considered exudate feeders (Charles-Dominique 1977; Garber 1992).

CLIMBING

All primates climb, even humans – although not very well. Climbing, like grasping, is an ancient arboreal adaptation for primates. Moving up vertical or semi-vertical substrates is well documented across a wide range of primates; but, surprisingly, quantitative studies have shown that climbing is not the most common mode in any locomotor profile (Gebo 1996): leaping, quadrupedalism, or brachiation dominate all such profiles in primates. Primates clearly need to move upward from time to time, but, compared to all other movements, upward climbing is not that frequent relative to the traveling locomotor modes. Thus it is difficult to say that some primates are truly 'better' climbers than others. In fact it is not easy to separate anatomical structures related to grasping from those of climbing. Some primates, like the lorises, seem to be especially mobile ones, who use a variety of body contortions to move arboreally, and often these movements are described as 'climbing.' The body anatomy of lorises, with their highly mobile joint surfaces, reflects their serpentine design (Hill 1953; Grand 1967; Cartmill and Milton 1977; McArdle 1981; MacPhee and Jacobs 1986). On the other hand, Old World monkeys often show frequent use of climbing movements in their overall locomotor pattern, and yet, as a group, they present reduced mobility at the key primate joints (shoulder, elbow, and foot) – an anatomical situation one would not expect to find. Apes have long arms and are known to be frequent vertical climbers, when arboreal, but forelimb lengthening comes from their brachiating ancestry and is not related to an original 'more efficient' climbing adaptation. In sum, climbing and grasping are highly intertwined when one considers limb function across primates.

QUADRUPEDALISM

Arboreal quadrupedalism is a common primate movement pattern. Quadrupedal primates have forelimbs and hindlimbs of relatively equal length. They tend to lower their center of gravity toward the branch (Napier 1967; Larson 1998) by bending their elbows and knees as they move along a curved surface (Schmitt 1995). The use of diagonal couplets allows primates to have only a single limb off the substrate at any given time. Terrestrial quadrupedal primates also have forelimbs and hindlimbs of similar lengths, although many terrestrial taxa possess even longer limbs than arboreal quadrupeds; but these latter primates (often cercopithecids) have greatly reduced joint mobility throughout their limbs. Their joints absorb the pounding forces of the ground rather than being oriented toward mobility and toward dealing with all the unusual substrate sizes and angles in the canopy. Arboreal quadrupedal primates position their hands and feet toward the curve of the support (this is called 'palmigrade support'). In contrast, terrestrial primates use more pronated hand positions. The same is true for the feet.

Most quadrupedal primates, like other quadrupedal mammals, have a thorax that is similar to a cylinder (Figure 30.2). The forelimbs are set below, and the shoulder blades are set along, the sides of the tube. Heads and tails span each end. For these pronograde primates, the backs are essentially long tubes, and the viscera hang down from them away from the dorsal wall. The ribs curve gently to form a cylinder. The lumbar vertebrae are long and flexible. Primates typically have 7 cervical vertebrae, 11–14 thoracic vertebrae, 5–9 lumbar vertebrae, and 3–7 sacral vertebrae (Ankel-Simons 2000). Almost all primates have tails. The centrum, or the large bony joint surface of a vertebra, absorbs and transmits the weight-bearing forces along the horizontally oriented vertebral column. The discs between the joints represent more flexible padding, while the bony processes coming off the vertebrae serve to anchor the ligaments and muscles of the back. Most quadrupedal primates have quite flexible backs (Schultz 1969).

In terms of limbs, quadrupedal primates have near-equal forelimb and hindlimb length and a general pattern of limb mobility throughout the body. Unique aspects include a protracted humerus, limb elongation relative to other mammals, good joint mobility, and greater supraspinal control (Reynolds 1985, 1987; Vilensky 1989; Larson 1998; Larson et al. 2001). A protracted humerus and a compliant gait reduces the peak force in the forelimb, thereby sparing it from high locomotor stress (Schmitt 1995; Larson et al. 2000). Reduced stress allows forelimb mobility to increase, adding improved manipulative skills for primates. The basic quadrupedal body plan is an ancestral inheritance for primates. This body has been further modified toward greater control over the arboreal surfaces it moves across. By reducing forelimb locomotor stress, this limb can also act as a key feeding adaptation.

LEAPING

Primates who leap frequently come in two varieties. Strepsirhine primates (for instance lemurs and galagos) and tarsiers are known for their forceful upward parabolic leaps, while anthropoids tend to leap outward, along a horizontal plane, and then fall downward. Both types can leap frequently, although size tends to be limiting: there are few frequent leapers above ten kilograms. Long legs (or long lever arms) help frequent leapers to increase the height or length of a leap. Long legs produce leaps with less relative muscle force (Hall-Craggs 1965). In terms of hindlimb anatomy, strepsirhines and tarsiers have very narrow, rod-like innominates (Tattersall 1982; Gebo et al. 2008). A short, dorsally projecting ischium relates to the regular use of an extended hip joint for the more specialized vertical clingers and leapers (Fleagle and Anapol 1992). The third trochanter of the femur is proximally located in strepsirhines and tarsiers, and this proximal location helps the *gluteus maximus* to extend the hip joint during active leaping. Most leapers have round femoral heads, but tarsiers and galagos have a very modified cylindrical femoral head shape, which suggests constrained fore and aft movements. In frequent leapers, the greater trochanter often overhangs the anterior aspect of the femoral shaft, the entire proximal part of the femoral shaft being buttressed and curved (Dagosto and Schmid 1996). All leapers have long femora; but it is the anatomy of the knee, with its tall antero-posterior height and the high lateral patellar rim, that separates the occasional leaper from the professional one. As you might expect, the muscles of the quadriceps are huge, especially the *vastus lateralis*, to produce the leg extension force necessary for moving these primates across canopy gaps quickly and efficiently. Most primates have separated and non-fused fibulas, but many have closely apposed fibulas along the distal third of the tibial shaft (Fleagle and Simons 1983; Dagosto 1985). Tarsiers are the most extreme case: they present complete tibio-fibular fusion along the distal half of the tibia. Only tarsiers and galagos obtain significantly increased foot length by elongating their calcaneus and navicular bones, and thereby achieve longer legs and, ultimately, better lever mechanics. Other primates have moderate foot bone lengthening; but most of the primates who leap frequently, including the vertically clinging and leaping indriids, have no extra lengthening. Morton (1924) argued that the reason why primates elongate the calcaneus and the navicular instead of their metatarsals is a morphological compromise between the mechanical demands of leaping and grasping. Although long lever arms (that is, long feet) help to produce better gear ratios for greater leaping distances, the feet of arboreal primates must also be able to grasp. By elongating the calcaneus and the navicular, tarsiers and galagos have been able to maintain mobility in the tarsus while greatly increasing foot length.

Brachiation

The upper body of living apes (including humans) is quite different from that of other primates (see Figures 30.2 and 30.3). All of these features are related to brachiation and arm suspension (Keith 1923; Washburn 1968; Gebo 1996). The thorax is broad and flattened antero-posteriorly rather than being long like a cylinder. The back is an orthograde one (that is, an erect back) in comparison to the more common pronograde backs of primates. The viscera are attached to the dorsal body wall rather than hanging below, as in pronogrady. In this body plan, the lumbar vertebrae are shorter, providing a stiff lower back. Ape and human backs are adapted to vertical and erect postures, in contrast to the pronograde and quadrupedally adapted backs of other primates. The ribs are highly curved in orthogrady, the sternum is broader, and the clavicles are elongated. The shoulders are pushed out to the sides of the body, with scapulae on the back rather than along the sides of the ribcage, as in quadrupedal primates. This new position for the scapula forces the shoulders to the sides and away from the midline of the body, adding rotational mobility in the process. The clavicle is long, to meet the new position of the scapula, and the infraspinous fossa of the scapula increases in size. The acromion is enlarged in orthograde primates, given their deltoid muscularity. The forelimb is long, thereby increasing stride length (or, in this case, arm swinging). The glenoid fossa of the scapula faces laterally outward (instead of anteriorly, as in quadrupedal primates), and this lateral position forces the enlarged humeral head to twist (medial torsion) so as to articulate with the scapula and to allow the elbow to face forward.

Living apes have a very circular capitulum and a spool-shaped trochlea, separated by a large gap (*zona conoidea*). This elbow morphology allows for large rotational movements between the radius and the capitulum and for large flexion–extension movements for the ulna at the trochlea (Rose 1988). In fact the olecranon process is

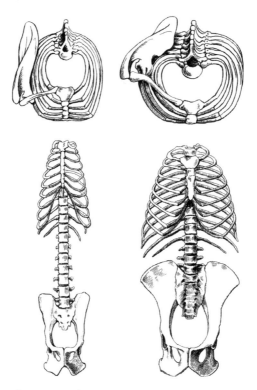

Figure 30.2   Pronograde versus orthograde body plans. Cranial (top) and ventral (bottom) views of a monkey (left) and ape (right) thorax. Redrawn from Schultz 1969

greatly shortened among apes, allowing for full extension at the elbow – an unusual ability relative to any other primate, but a necessary condition for fully extended arm hanging. The ulna and radius are elongated among apes, especially among the gibbons. At the wrist, apes have also increased abduction capabilities, through the shortening of the styloid process of the ulna and the addition of a meniscus (Lewis 1969, 1989). Ape fingers are very long (not so in the case of humans). Many studies have been undertaken to understand muscle function during brachiation in apes and spider monkeys (see for example Ashton and Oxnard 1964; Stern et al. 1977; Jungers and Stern 1980; Stern and Larson 2001).

BIPEDALISM

Over time, the locomotor adaptations for human bipedalism have completely remodeled the lower limb and the back in the human lineage. This is no small evolutionary feat, considering the number of changes needed for it to occur. In fact, one might argue that the lower limb adaptations for human bipedalism exceed those of any other locomotor mode among primates. "Bipedality is a dangerous form of locomotion and limb elongation in a habitual biped carries significant locomotor liabilities" (Lovejoy 2005b: 120).

Instead of a four-limb support system, humans must do with two supporting limbs. Each leg supports 50 percent of our body weight when we stand up and 100 percent during the swing phase of bipedalism. Clearly, lower back and pelvic changes would

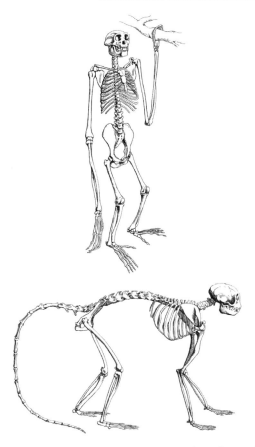

Figure 30.3   The skeletal body of an ape (top) relative to that of a monkey (bottom). Redrawn from Schultz 1969

need to occur to maintain structural support while a subject is standing, walking, or running. Human lumbar vertebrae have enlarged vertebral bodies, to help support upper body weight. Likewise, the promontory of the sacrum is enlarged for structural support, in that this is the last point of contact before weight can be re-distributed to each leg. As one might guess, the articular surface for the sacrum and for the ilium is enlarged in comparison to that of apes – as is the iliac tuberosity, where all of the ligaments that bind these two bones fit together in humans. The sacrum is quite wide and more angled in humans than in apes.

The position of the pelvis in humans versus African apes shows how the alignment of forces, the muscle positions, and the bony changes have been modified between the two (Figure 30.4). In apes, the shorter lumbar region, with a reduced distance between the thorax and the iliac crests, implies an immobile lower spine (Lovejoy 2005a). In humans, the lower spine is quite mobile in comparison to that of the great apes. It is longer, with a shortening and broadening of the ilia and of the sacrum. The widening and shortening of the gluteal plane and the anteromedial bending of the iliac tubercle bring the smaller gluteal muscles (*gluteus medius* and *gluteus minimus*) to the side of the pelvis, where they can act as abductors. The pelvic tilt mechanism, or lateral balance control, is a key innovation in human bipedalism (Lovejoy 1988, 2005b). It allows humans to maintain balance as they swing their pelvis away from the stance leg during

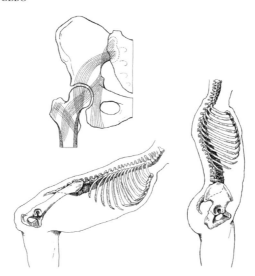

Figure 30.4   Weight distribution in a human pelvis and femur (top left) and pelvic position in an ape (bottom left) and human (right). Redrawn from Kapandji 1987 and Schultz 1969

walking. In short, these two gluteal muscles are responsible for pelvic stabilization during the single support phase of human gait. Weight transfer must go from the sacrum and the sacroiliac joints to the pelvic acetabulum, to the head and neck of the femur, and downward to the foot (Figure 30. 4). These bony areas have internal bony trabecular systems designed to transmit these weight-bearing forces (Kapandji 1987; Aiello and Dean 1990). The pelvis presents one other key innovation in humans: the iliac pillar, which reinforces the ilium in relation to the pull of the gluteal muscles. The large *gluteus maximus* muscle, perhaps the most famous human muscle, is in fact silent during walking activities and is only really active in running or climbing stairs (that is, in cases of extreme extension). The *gluteus maximus* stabilizes the trunk upon the lower limb, bracing the sacroiliac joint. It keeps the trunk from falling forward. The human ilium also has a large anterior inferior iliac spine, where the *rectus femoris* attaches. This muscle, like the other quadriceps ones, is important in leg extension. The quadriceps are the primary muscles of propulsion, while the hamstrings control and decelerate the limbs during the end of a swing phase (Lovejoy 2005b). Humans have more lower limb musculature than African apes do (Zihlman and Brunker 1979; Zihlman 1984).

At the hip, humans possess massive ligaments: the iliofemoral ligament anteriorly and the ishiofemoral ligament posteriorly, which are designed to strengthen the hip joint. The femoral head is larger in humans than in apes, and the internal anatomy of the femoral neck is quite distinct in apes and in humans (Lovejoy 1988). Most of the ligamentous attachments at the hip are critical, since the human leg angles inward (in what is called the 'bicondylar angle'), toward the midline of the body, rather than being oriented straight downward, as in apes. Given our long legs, this is a critical distinction. This bicondylar angle forces the quadricep musculature contractions to pull the patella laterally, away from its midline. In relation to apes, the human knee has a proximal extension for the patellar joint surface, a deeper groove, and a high lateral rim for the lateral condyle. All of these features help to keep the patella from being dislocated as it is pulled upward during leg extension. The distal femoral condyles at the knee are quite flattened in humans, in comparison to those of apes, and they are often described as elliptical. At the human knee, the lateral condyle is elongated anteroposteriorly, allowing greater cartilage contact during the last twenty degrees of extension (Lovejoy 2006). This elongation reduces stress from the ground reaction force during heel-strike and toe-off. Such a reduction is needed, since limb elongation increases torque about the knee and ankle, causing increased loads for ligaments, and both joints commonly have traumatic injuries in humans. The large size of the epicondyles and their change of shape help in weight bearing, since the human knee can be hyperextended and 'locked' in extension for long periods of standing. The anterior cruciate is tensed, as are the collateral ligaments. This is why the *popliteus* muscle is so important in humans: it unlocks the knee. Distally, the angle between the distal fibular joint surface and that of the talus is quite large in apes and quite small in humans. As a consequence, the fibula does not transmit any significant weight to the foot in humans, as it does in apes. Relative to apes, humans also have a small gap between the tibia and the fibula distally.

As noted above, heel-strike plantigrady positions the human foot – and, by extension, the leg – onto a terrestrial substrate. In humans the foot is a platform for weight transfer, since humans have lost their ancestral grasping big toe. Human tarsals are large and restricted in their mobility (especially rotationally), while human toes are shortened and small (in other words, not good for grasping). The one exception is the human big toe, which is hyperenlarged for weight bearing. The loss of a grasping big toe and the subsequent enlargement of the first digit (first metatarsal, proximal and distal phalanges) is one of the most profound anatomical changes related to bipedalism between African apes and humans. The loss of opposability is also evidenced by the flattening of the first metatarsal – entocuneiform joint, which stabilizes this joint in order to transmit walking forces. The size of the first metatarsal also suggests an increase in the transmission of force through this digit. This is evident in the human gait in the sequence of toe-offs, when all of the weight is borne by the distal phalanx of the first digit as the opposite leg swings forward. The human distal phalanx is twisted distally, with a marked lateral rotation. To add to the platform stability of the human foot, the calcaneocuboid joint locks. The talar trochlea is wide, for bearing weight at the upper ankle joint. The heel region of the calcaneus has added an extra lateral plantar tubercle, for greater width and weight support. The human calcaneus is in fact quite robust as a tarsal element. Human metatarsal heads have expanded their dorsoarticular surfaces, and a groove between the head and the shaft allows the hyperextension of the toes during the toe-off phase of bipedalism.

Fossils

The interpretation of bodies of fossil primates and fossil humans depends largely on our understanding of the living primates. Unfortunately, no living primate is a perfect match for any particular fossil taxon. This is especially true for older fossils and suggests that we must blend our imperfect knowledge of different living primates to understand our past.

Biomechanical studies often help our comprehension as well. Let's examine the body and limb anatomy of two fossil primates. One of the best known of all fossil primates is *Notharctus*, a 50-million-year-old fossil adapiform from North America. Gregory's 1920 classic study of the skeleton of *Notharctus* shows that its body compares best with that of lemurs and indriids; he therefore inferred a similar movement pattern for

Notharctus – arboreal quadrupedalism, climbing, and leaping. *Notharctus* clearly possesses a cylindrical body, with long leg and a long tail. Gregory (1920) reports a lemur-like back. The scapula is long, without an unusually wide medial border; the clavicle is short; and the shoulder is mobile, but clearly not adapted for brachiation. The humerus is short and robust, with very large muscle attachments (for instance the brachioradialis flange, the deltoid tuberosity, and the medial epicondyle). The elbow presents a clear separation (a wide *zona conoidea*) between the very round capitulum and the trochlea, which implies a quite mobile rotational joint at the elbow. The ulna has an olecranon process, which indicates a bent forelimb posture. The fingers and hand of *Notharctus* are fairly long, showing a grasping morphology with an abducted first digit, nails, and prominent flexor grooves for the flexor tendons. The ulna has a long styloid process for the wrist. All of these anatomical features support the hypothsis of grasping and climbing and of a quadrupedal body plan for an arboreal primate.

When we move to examine the hindlimb, we observe leaping features in the leg and grasping features in the foot. A long femur and hindlimb, a tall knee joint, with an elevated lateral rim, all suggest frequent leaping. In the foot, which is not elongated, grasping digits, nails, and a robust first metatarsal are meant evidently for grasping. The ankle joint shows a sloping talo-fibular facet, a shift in the groove for the *flexor hallucis longus* tendon, a single tibial spine at the tibial plateau, a tibio-talar mortise with corresponding long fibular side, and a long tibial malleolus. All of these features suggest foot and knee abduction, which in turn implies frequent grasping of vertical supports. All these distinctive features are found among the living strepsirhines as well. The hindlimb of *Notharctus* is anatomically adapted for frequent arboreal leaping and for grasping on vertical supports – movement patterns similar to those of lemurs and indriids (though not a perfect match for any one lemur).

Proconsul, a fossil 'ape,' has had a more controversial history of interpretation (see Walker and Shipman 2005). A phyletic position close to the living apes is less likely today than was acknowledged in earlier studies (for example Pilbeam 1969). There have been many different interpretations, but the consensus today is that the body of *Proconsul* is more monkey-like than ape-like (Rose 1983; Walker and Pickford 1983; Ward 1993; Ward et al. 1991). Its body is pronograde, not orthograde. It has equal limb lengths rather than a long forelimb. The humeral shaft is retroflexed dorsoventrally, as in quadrupedal primates. The ulna possesses a long olecranon process and a long syloid process. Both features make *Proconsul* unsimilar to the brachiating apes. The humeral head in *Proconsul* is not expanded, nor does it display medial torsion. The elbow does show an incipient ape-like trochlear morphology. *Proconsul* does possess a prominent big toe and a wide fibula for grasping and climbing capabilities, features similar to those of living apes. *Proconsul* also lacks a tail – a key ape and human feature. In sum, *Proconsul* shares with apes aspects of its leg and foot anatomy, especially tail-loss, in contrast to its forelimb anatomy, which is very quadrupedally or non-suspensory oriented. Among living primates, *Proconsul* is best compared to the arboreal quadrupedal and climbing monkeys from South America.

NEW TECHNIQUES

The quantitative studies of primate movements pioneered in the 1970s by Fleagle, Morbeck, Ripley, and Rose have made our knowledge of general primate movement patterns more precise. These studies allow us to know what primates actually do and how they use arboreal substrates. Such work helps us to understand primate ecological adaptations, and it allows us to observe how primates use their anatomy in the wild. Unfortunately, this body of work has not been able to provide a synthetic explanation for primate movement patterns.

An alternative approach to field work has been to study primates in the laboratory. A biomechanical examination of primate movements through force plates, electromyography (EMG), gait analyses, beam modeling, and other approaches has added tremendously to our understanding of movements and limb function. With force plate studies, EMG, gait analyses, and biomechanical models approaching fifty years of work (and perhaps more for engineering models), the newest technology to be applied to primate and human anatomy is the laser scanning of specimens, allied with sophisticated statistical analyses designed to assess shape changes (see Aiello et al. 1998; Wood et al. 1998; Harcourt-Smith et al. 2008; Polly 2008). These approaches have been applied to tarsal morphology and have achieved an entire three-dimensional surface of a bone, after which geometric morphometrics are applied to assess morphology, function, and phylogeny.

CONCLUSION

Understanding primate and human anatomy continues at a faster pace than even a few decades ago. Although new work needs to be evaluated over time, progress is steady, thereby enhancing our understanding of primate limb and body adaptations throughout the entire primate order. As we learn more, we can better model primate and human evolution in attempts to understand why certain adaptive events occurred along the different lineages. Of these, the most important still might be the attempt to understand why the human lineage gave up quadrupedalism to become a biped. There are other fascinating radiations to resolve as well. In all, the body holds many of the key secrets of primate success and survival throughout our evolutionary history.

REFERENCES

Aiello, L., and Dean, C. (1990) *An Introduction to Human Evolutionary Anatomy*. New York: Academic Press.

Aiello, L. C., Wood, B. A., Key, C., and Wood, C. (1998) Laser Scanning and Palaeoanthropology: An Example from Olduvai Gorge, Tanzania. In E. Strasser, J. G. Fleagle, A. L. Rosenberger, and H. M. McHenry (eds), *Primate Locomotion: Recent Advances* (pp. 223–236). New York: Plenum Press.

Ankel-Simons, F. (2000) *Primate Anatomy – An Introduction*. New York: Academic Press.

Ashton, E. H., and Oxnard, C. E. (1964) Functional Adaptations of the Primate Shoulder Girdle. *Proceedings of the Zoological Society* (London) 142: 49–66.

Cartmill, M. (1972) Arboreal Adaptations and the Origin of the Order Primates. In R. H. Tuttle (ed.), *The Functional and Evolutionary Biology of Primates* (pp. 97–122). Chicago: Aldine Press.

Cartmill, M. (1974) Pads and Claws in Arboreal Locomotion. In J. A. Jenkins (ed.), *Primate Locomotion* (pp. 45–83). New York: Academic Press.

Cartmill, M. (1979) The Volar Skin of Primates: Its Frictional Characteristics and Their Functional Significance. *American Journal of Physical Anthropology* 50: 497–510.

Cartmill, M. (1985) Climbing. In M. Hildebrand, D. M. Bramble, K. F. Liem, D. B. Wake (eds), *Functional Vertebrate Morphology*. (pp.73–88). Cambridge MA: Belknap Press of Harvard University.

Cartmill, M., and Milton, K. (1977) The Lorisiform Wrist Joint and the Evolution of 'Brachiating' Adaptation in the Hominoidea. *American Journal of Physical Anthropology* 47: 249–272.

Cartmill, M., Lemelin, P., and Schmitt, D. O. (2002) Support Polygons and Symmetrical Gaits in Mammals. *Zoological Journal of the Linnean Society* 136: 401–420.

Charles-Dominique, P. (1977) *Ecology and Behaviour of Nocturnal Primates*. New York: Columbia University Press.

Dagosto, M. (1985) The Distal Tibia of Primates with Special Reference to the Omomyidae. *International Journal of Primatology* 6: 45–75.

Dagosto, M., and Schmid, P. (1996) Proximal Femoral Anatomy of Omomyiform Primates. *Journal of Human Evolution* 30: 29–56.

Demes, B., Larson, S. G., Stern, J. T., Jungers, W. L., Biknevicius, A. R., and Schmitt, D. (1994) The Kinetics of Primate Quadrupedalism: 'Hindlimb Drive' Reconsidered. *Journal of Human Evolution* 26: 353–374.

Fleagle, J. G., and Anapol, F. (1992) The Indriid Ischium and the Hominid Hip. *Journal of Human Evolution* 22: 285–305.

Fleagle, J. G., and Simons, E. L. (1983) The Tibio-Fibular Articulation in *Apidium phiomense*, an Oligocene Anthropoid. *Nature* 301: 238–239.

Garber, P. A. (1992) Vertical Clinging, Small Body Size, and the Evolution of Feeding Adaptation in the Callitrichinae. *American Journal of Physical Anthropology* 88: 469–482.

Gebo, D. L. (1996) Climbing, Brachiation, and Terrestrial Quadrupedalism: Historical Precursors of Hominid Bipedalism. *American Journal of Physical Anthropology* 101: 55–92.

Gebo, D. L., Dagosto, M., Beard, K. C., and Ni, X. (2008) New Hindlimb Elements from the Middle Eocene of China. *Journal of Human Evolution* 55: 999–1014.

Grand, T. I. (1967) The Functional Anatomy of the Ankle and Foot of the Slow Loris (*Nycticebus coucang*). *American Journal of Physical Anthropology* 28: 168–182.

Gregory, W. K. (1920) On the Structure and Relations of *Notharctus*, an American Eocene Primate. *Memoirs of the American Museum of Natural History* 3: 49–243.

Hall-Craggs, E. C. B. (1965) An Analysis of the Jump of the Lesser Galago. *Journal of Zoology* (London) 147: 20–29.

Hamrick, M. W. (1998) Functional and Adaptive Significance of Primate Pads and Claws: Evidence for New World Anthropoids. *American Journal of Physical Anthropology* 106: 113–127.

Hamrick, M. W. (2001) Primate Origins: Evolutionary Change in Digital Ray Patterning and Segmentation. *Journal of Human Evolution* 40: 339–351.

Harcourt-Smith, W. E. H., Tallman, M., Frost, S. R., Wiley, D. F., Rohlf, F. J., and Delson, E. (2008) Analysis of Selected Hominoid Joint Surfaces Using Laser Scanning and Geometric Morphometrics: A Preliminary Report. In E. J. Sargis and M. Dagosto (eds), *Mammalian Evolutionary Morphology* (pp. 373–384). Dordrecht Netherlands: Springer.

Hildebrand, M. (1967) Symmetrical Gaits of Primates. *American Journal of Physical Anthropology* 26: 119–130.

Hill, W. C. O. (1953) *Strepsirhini Primates: Comparative Anatomy and Taxonomy*, Vol. 1. Edinburgh: Edinburgh University Press.

Jungers, W. L., and Stern, J. T. (1980) Telemetered Electromyography of Forelimb Muscle Chains in Gibbons (*Hylobates lar*). *Science* 208: 617–619.

Kapandji, I. A. (1987) *The Physiology of the Joints*, Vol. 2: *Lower Limb*, 5th edn. Edinburgh: Churchill Livingstone.

Keith, A. (1923) Man's Posture: Its Evolution and Disorders. *British Medical Journal* 1: 451–454, 545–548, 587–590, 624–626, 669–672.

Kimura, T., Okada, M., and Ishida, H. (1979) Kinesiological Characteristics of Primate Walking: Its Significance in Human Walking. In M. E. Morbeck, H. Preuschoft, and N. Gomberg (eds), *Environment, Behavior and Morphology: Dynamic Interactions in Primates* (pp. 297–311). New York: Gustav Fischer.

Larson, S. G. (1998) Unique Aspects of Quadrupedal Locomotion in Nonhuman Primates. In E. Strasser, J. G. Fleagle, A. L. Rosenberger, and H. M. McHenry (eds), *Primate Locomotion: Recent Advances* (pp. 157–173). New York: Plenum Press.

Larson, S. G., Schmitt, D., Lemelin, P., and Hamrick, M. (2000) Uniqueness of Primate Fore-limb Posture during Quadrupedal Locomotion. *American Journal of Physical Anthropology* 112: 87–101.

Larson, S. G., Schmitt, D., Lemelin, P., and Hamrick, M. (2001) Limb Excursion during Quadrupedal Walking: How Do Primates Compare to Other Mammals. *Journal of Zoology* (London) 255: 353–365.

Le Gros Clark, W. E. (1959) *The Antecedents of Man: An Introduction to the Evolution of Primates.* Edinburgh: Edinburgh University Press.

Lewis, O. J. (1969) The Hominoid Wrist Joint. *American Journal of Physical Anthropology* 30: 251–268.

Lewis, O. J. (1989) *Functional Morphology of the Evolving Hand and Foot.* Oxford: Oxford Science Publications.

Lovejoy, C. O. (1988) Evolution of Human Walking. *Scientific American* 259: 118–125.

Lovejoy, C. O. (2005a) The Natural History of Human Gait and Posture, Part 1: Spine and Pelvis. *Gait and Posture* 21: 95–112.

Lovejoy, C. O. (2005b) The Natural History of Human Gait and Posture, Part 2: Hip and Thigh. *Gait and Posture* 21: 113–124.

Lovejoy, C. O. (2006) The Natural History of Human Gait and Posture, Part 3: The Knee. *Gait and Posture* 25: 325–341.

MacPhee, R. D. E., and Jacobs, L. L. (1986) *Nycticeboides simpsoni* and the Morphology, Adaptations, and Relationships of Miocene Siwalik Lorisidae. In K. M. Flanagan and J. A. Lillegraven (eds), *Contributions to Geology* (pp. 131–161). Laramie: Univeristy of Wyoming Special Paper 3.

Martin, R. D. (1972) Adaptive Radiation and Behavior of the Malagasy Lemurs. *Philosophical Transactions of the Royal Society – Biology* 264: 295–352.

McArdle, J. E. (1981) The Functional Morphology of the Hip and Thigh of the Lorisiformes. *Contributions to Primatology* 17: 1–132.

Morton, D. J. (1924) The Evolution of the Human Foot, Part II. *American Journal of Physical Anthropology* 1: 1–52.

Napier, J. R. (1967) Evolutionary Aspects of Primate Locomotion. *American Journal of Physical Anthropology* 27: 333–342.

Napier, J. R. (1980) *Hands.* New York: Pantheon Books.

Pilbeam, D. R. (1969) Tertiary Pongidae of East Africa: Evolutionary Relationships and Taxonomy. *Bulletin Peabody Museum of Natural History* 31: 1–185.

Polly, P. D. (2008) Adaptive Zones and the Pinniped Ankle: A Three-Dimensional Quantitative Analysis of Carnivoran Tarsal Evolution. In E. J. Sargis and M. Dagosto (eds), *Mammalian Evolutionary Morphology* (pp. 167–198). Dordrecht Netherlands: Springer.

Reynolds, T. R. (1985) Stresses on the Limbs of Quadrupedal Primates. *American Journal of Physical Anthropology* 67: 351–362.

Reynolds, T. R. (1987) Stride Length and Its Determinants in Humans, Early Hominids, Primates and Mammals. *American Journal of Physical Anthropology* 72: 101–116.

Rollinson, J., and Martin, R. D. (1981) Comparative Aspects of Primate Locomotion, with Special Reference to Arboreal Cercopithecines. *Symposium of the Zoological Society London* 48: 377–427.

Rose, M. D. (1983) Miocene Hominoid Postcranial Morphology: Monkey-Like, Ape-Like, Neither, or Both? In R. L. Ciochon and R. S. Corruccini (eds), *New Interpretations of Ape and Human Ancestry* (pp. 405–420). New York: Plenum Press.

Rose, M. D. (1988) Another Look at the Anthropoid Elbow. *Journal of Human Evolution* 17: 193–224.

Schmitt, D. (1995) A Kinematic and Kinetic Analysis of Forelimb Use during Arboreal and Terrestrial Quadrupedalism in Old World Monkeys. PhD Dissertation, SUNY at Stony Brook.

Schmitt, D., and Lemelin, P. (2002) Origins of Primate Locomotion: Gait Mechanics of the Woolly Opossum. *American Journal of Physical Anthropology* 118: 231–238.

Schultz, A. H. (1969) *The Life of Primates.* London: Weidenfeld and Nicolson.

Stern, J. T., and Larson, S. G. (2001) Telemetered Electromyography of the Supinators and Pronators of the Forearm in Gibbons and Chimpanzees: Implications for the Fundamental Positional Adaptation of Hominoids. *American Journal of Physical Anthropology* 115: 253–268.

Stern, J. T., Wells, J. P., Vangor, A. K., and Fleagle, J. G. (1977) Electromyography of Some Muscles of the Upper Limb in *Ateles* and *Lagothrix*. *Yearbook of Physical Anthropology* 20: 498–507.

Susman, R. L. (1974) Facultative Terrestrial Hand Postures in an Orangutan and Pongid Evolution. *American Journal of Physical Anthropology* 40: 27–38.

Szalay, F. S., and Dagosto, M. (1988) Evolution of Hallucial Grasping in the Primates. *Journal of Human Evolution* 17: 1–33.

Tattersall, I. (1982) *The Primates of Madagascar.* New York: Columbia University.

Tuttle, R. H. (1967) Knuckle-Walking and the Evolution of Hominoid Hands. *American Journal of Physical Anthropology* 26: 171–206.

Tuttle, R. H., and Beck, B. B. (1972) Knuckle-Walking Hand Postures in an Orangutan (*Pongo pygmaeus*). *Nature* 236: 33–34.

Vilensky, J. A. (1989) Primate Quadrupedalism: How and Why Does It Differ from That of Typical Quadrupeds? *Brain, Behavior and Evolution* 34: 357–364.

Walker, A. C., and Pickford, M. (1983) New Postcranial Fossils of *Proconsul africanus* and *Proconsul nyanzae*. In R. L. Ciochon and R. S. Corruccini (eds), *New Interpretations of Ape and Human Ancestry* (pp. 325–351). New York: Plenum Press.

Walker, A., and Shipman, P. (2005) *The Ape in the Tree.* Cambridge: Belknap Press Harvard University.

Ward, C. V. (1993) Torso Morphology and Locomotion in *Proconsul nyanzae*. *American Journal of Physical Anthropology* 92: 291–328.

Ward, C. V., Walker, A. C., and Teaford, M. F. (1991) *Proconsul* Did not Have a Tail. *Journal of Human Evolution* 21: 215–220.

Washburn, S. L. (1968) *The Study of Human Evolution* (Congdon Lectures). Eugene: University of Oregon Books.

Whitehead, P. (1993) Aspects of the Wrist and Hand. In D. L. Gebo (ed.), *Postcranial Adaptation in Nonhuman Primates* (pp. 96–120). DeKalb: Northern Illinois University Press.

Wood, B. A., Aiello, L. C., Wood, C., and Key, C. A. (1998) A Technique for Establishing the Identity of 'Isolated' Fossil Hominid Limb Bones. *Journal of Anatomy* 193: 61–72.

Wood Jones, F. (1916) *Arboreal Man.* New York: Longmans, Green and Co.

Zihlman, A. L. (1984) Body Build and Tissue Composition in *Pan paniscus* and *Pan troglodytes*, with Comparisons to Other Hominoids. In R. L. Susman (ed.), *The Pygmy Chimpanzee* (pp. 179–200). New York: Plenum Press.

Zihlman, A. L., and Brunker, L. (1979) Hominid Bipedalism: Then and Now. *Yearbook of Physical Anthropology* 22: 132–162.

PART V Science and Education

CHAPTER 31

Science Education and Physical Anthropology

Martin K. Nickels

INTRODUCTION

From an interview with Waheed Badawy, a chemistry professor at Cairo University, as reported by Todd Pitock in July 2007:

> What about, say, evolutionary biology or Darwinism? I ask. [...] "If you are asking if Adam came from a monkey, no," Badawy responds. "Man did not come from a monkey. If I am religious, if I agree with Islam, then I have to respect all of the ideas of Islam. And one of these ideas is the creation of the human from Adam and Eve. If I am a scientist, I have to believe that."
>
> But from the point of view of a scientist, is it not just a story? I ask. He tells me that if I were writing an article saying that Adam and Eve is a big lie, it will not be accepted until I can prove it. "Nobody can just write what he thinks without proof. But we have real proof that the story of Adam as the first man is true."
>
> "What proof?"
>
> He looks at me with disbelief: "It's written in the Koran."

And from Henry Morris, the founder of 'scientific creationism,' in *The Remarkable Birth of Planet Earth* (1972: 94):

> The only way we can determine the true age of the earth is for God to tell us what it is. And since He has told us, very plainly, in the Holy Scriptures that it is several thousand years in age, and no more, that ought to settle all basic questions of terrestrial chronology.

In June 2008, the Gallup Poll asked Americans a three-part question regarding evolution and human origins: "Which comes closest to your views: 1) Humans developed over millions of years, God guided (2) Humans developed over millions of years, God had no part, 3) God created humans as is within the last 10,000 years." Gallup has been asking this question since 1982. In 1982 the percentage of adult Americans who agreed with the idea that God created humans within the last 10,000 years was

44 percent – exactly the same percentage as in 2008. Nothing has changed for these people. This is a higher percentage of non-evolution-accepters than the one found in thirty-two other nations around the world. Only Turkey has a higher percentage of people rejecting evolution than the United States (Owen 2006).

A 2007 Harris poll found that 62 percent of Americans believed that the devil exists. So even more Americans believe in the existence of Lucifer than in the fact that 'Lucy' (*Australopithecus afarensis*) was an early African hominin and part of human ancestry (Cole 2007).

An average of 37 percent of respondents over the 1982–2008 time period told Gallup that they think humans evolved over millions of years, but did so with some involvement on God's part (presumably either through direct intervention or according to a divinely preordained pattern). The percentage of adult Americans thinking that humans evolved through strictly natural processes rose from 9 percent to 14 percent. At least the combined percentage of Americans thinking that human evolution has occurred with or without divine intervention or guidance rose slightly from 47 to 50 percent from 1982 to 2008.

Nevertheless, 44 percent of adult Americans still reject the idea that human evolution has occurred in any way, shape, or form. Essentially nothing has changed. Why? Were there no new fossils found between 1982 and 2008 anywhere in Africa, Europe, Asia, Australia, or the Americas? Were there no discoveries made about the genetic similarities and differences between humans and apes? Did we fail to recover genetic material from prehistoric human fossils, to compare it to that of modern humans? Did we completely abandon all scientific research into human biology and prehistory between 1982 and 2008, so that there was no new evidence to contribute to the study of humanity's place and origin in the universe? Is it simply because we had no new evidence to teach about? Is this why 44 percent of the adult Americans still reject the case for human evolution?

The answer to every single one of these questions is an emphatic, resounding, deafening 'No!' Simply scan the publication dates of the citations listed in the bibliography for each of the earlier chapters of this book. How many of them have pre-1982 dates? Stunningly few. This would hardly be surprising for any scientific field, let alone one with as much interest and on-going research as there is in human biology and origins. Since 1982, there have been amazing and wonderful discoveries in genetics that relate to our overall understanding of evolutionary biology, as well as to human evolution. We understand the differences between ourselves and other species – both living and extinct – in greater detail than ever before. Biologists regard these enhanced insights as stunning confirmation of the evolutionary relationships existing between these species. Surely the number of anti-evolutionists would have jumped spectacularly if we had discovered that humans (and other species) had unique genetic compositions, showing no overlap whatsoever with other species. No such discoveries were made.

How many fossil hominoids and early hominins have been discovered since 1982? Too many to list here, but almost all of them have been discussed in earlier chapters of the present book. The pattern of these finds is easy to summarize, however: None of the fossils unearthed since 1982 is older or younger, geologically, than would be expected from what we had already found. None of them was found in unacceptably unexpected places.

Were all of these fossil discoveries kept secret from the general public? Were there no newspaper or magazine articles about them? Were there no television stories or documentaries dealing with these discoveries in human genetics or paleoanthropology? Did textbooks fail to mention them? Has there been, over the last quarter century, any single valid discovery of any pre-*Homo sapiens* hominin fossil anywhere outside of Africa or Eurasia, to challenge our understanding of human evolution? The answer is 'No' to all of the above.

So, did the sheer number and volume of fossil, archaeological, and genetic discoveries made since 1982 about human biology and prehistory contribute to a dramatic increase in the percentage of adults who accept this evidence as valid? Was there a corresponding decrease in the percentage of adult Americans who reject the growing amount of evidence in favor human evolution? No. Forty-four percent still think that modern humans were created as modern humans less than 10,000 years ago.

The situation we face as educators in physical anthropology is clearly not characterized by a lack of material and evidence for us to teach about. It is probably not the case, either, that our students are completely unaware of the existence of hominin fossils. Paleontological and paleoanthropological discoveries make headlines around the world. They are featured regularly in television documentaries. A great many people know that there are lots of fossils and other kinds of evidence which scientists use in arguing for evolution; they simply reject it. Forty-four percent of adult Americans reject all of this and choose to think that the world has existed for just a few thousand years. They reject the validity of every geological dating method, of every astrophysical inference about the age of the solar system and universe, of every fossil sequence interpreted as representing change over geological time. They reject all the evidence of modern organisms showing varying degrees of similarity to each other, in agreement with different times of evolutionary divergence in the past. Apparently none of these Americans will ever read a word of this book, or of any other book about evolution, cosmology, prehistory, paleontology, archaeology or any other science dealing with the past. None of these sciences is real for them.

Do physical anthropologists of the twenty-first century have any obligation to try and educate people who reject all the conclusions of modern science regarding the existence, patterns, and importance of the human past? If so, how can we do this effectively, both in and outside of our classrooms? It should be clear by now that simply including more and more scientific 'facts' is not enough.

PHYSICAL ANTHROPOLOGY AND SCIENCE

The 44 percent of adult Americans who think that God created modern humans 10,000 years ago reject virtually every finding of modern science regarding the natural history of everything, from the universe itself to humans. This position is referred to as 'young-earth creationism.' What reason can such a high percentage of adult Americans have for rejecting the modern scientific evidence for geological antiquity and for embracing such a radical alternative? There is no credible scientific evidence in support of their belief. The answer, of course, is that their belief about human origins is not rooted in scientific research, but in their religious doctrine.

The idea of the supernatural creation of humans and of the entire universe is a foundational belief in all three of the world's largest monotheistic religions: Judaism, Christianity, and Islam. However, not all adherents to these religions think that the creation event they profess belief in occurred as recently as 10,000 years ago. Reform Jews, Catholics, the majority of Protestant Christians, and at least some Muslims do not tie their belief in creation to a specific time. Rather, they are willing to leave the determination of just when creation occurred to scientific research. Many of these religious believers are also willing to regard creation less as a one-time, instantaneous event and more as an on-going process. They view scientific research into the natural history of the world and of humans as fleshing out and enriching their view that God is the creator of the universe. They do not regard science as a rival to their religious beliefs. Young-earth creationists, however, reject any and all conclusions indicating that the universe is billions of years old and that modern species – at least humans – are the evolved descendants of earlier life forms. In short, they reject the modern scientific approach to studying the past.

Scientific literacy must start with a proper understanding of the nature of science. Only a few of our students will actually become scientists themselves. They will, however, become voters of school board members and members of school boards themselves. By that time, they will probably have forgotten many individual scientific facts we taught them in our classes. But we will all benefit if they remember at least the overall evidentiary strength of evolutionary theory and its internally consistent logic and, therefore, why it should be taught as science and creationism should not.

By teaching about evolution as an example of modern scientific thinking, we do more than simply present our students with the latest scientific facts. Rather, we provide a context for them to understand why evolutionary theory is such a robust scientific theory and, therefore, why it is so highly regarded by the scientific community. Students are then better able to judge for themselves the strengths of the evolutionary perspective and, in my experience, they become then much more open to it as a valid explanation.

What is the nature of modern science and of scientific knowledge? Modern science endeavors to understand and explain how the natural world works and how it came to be the way that it is. 'Natural' here refers to our being able to detect or sense the world. Even though the boundaries of the natural world may be somewhat fuzzy on occasion, science is nonetheless limited to studying those phenomena that it can sense. An extension of this limitation is that whatever processes scientists use to explain how the natural world works must themselves be natural. This means that science cannot study or explain 'supernatural' events or beings – which is not to say that they may not exist, or may not be studied by using other approaches.

Scientific knowledge (especially at the level of explanation) is limited by being inherently uncertain to varying degrees – that is, not absolutely, eternally, and infallibly true. This intrinsic uncertainty is due in part to several assumptions and limitations of the scientific process. Two key assumptions are that natural processes are sufficient or adequate for explaining or accounting for natural phenomena or events; and that nature operates uniformly, both in space and in time, unless we have evidence to the contrary. This is known as the 'principle of uniformity' and underlies the 'methodological naturalism' which is intrinsic to scientific inquiry.

In addition to these basic assumptions of science, there are limitations. One limitation is that scientific knowledge is necessarily contingent by its very nature (and, therefore, uncertain), rather than absolute in the sense of being certain and eternally true. One reason for this state of things is that scientists deal with evidence rather than with 'proof,' whereby either our knowledge or our explanations would be indisputable or irrefutable. The distinction is that evidence must be interpreted and made sense of, while 'proof' need not.

Despite the inherent tentativeness or uncertainty of scientific explanations, scientific knowledge is probably the most reliable kind of knowledge we can have about the natural world and its workings. Stronger scientific hypotheses account for more data than weaker ones and utilize known natural processes as explanations. (Compare the Darwinian and the Lamarckian explanations of how evolution occurs.) Stronger theories also account better for previously unexplained phenomena. (For example, biological evolution makes sense of unusual traits or 'oddball' characters such as the skeletal tail and ear muscles of humans, explaining them as retentions from ancestral forms.) Stronger theories also generate more reliable predictions, not just about what will happen in the future in the natural world, but also about what we should expect to find in nature if the theory is accurate. (For example, both previous fossil discoveries and biochemical calibrations about the timing of the evolutionary divergence date of the last common ancestor of humans and apes indicated where – in Africa – and – when – in which geological deposits – we should look for the earliest hominins.)

Providing our students with even this sort of brief overview and characterization of modern science, with all of its limitations and assumptions, should make science teaching less threatening to those who have doubts about some of its claims. One can then teach about evolution as being an example of an especially strong scientific theory without having to claim that it must be absolutely and certainly true. At the same time, by explaining just how reliable scientific knowledge and explanations can be and just how many different lines of evidence can be used to support some explanations and conclusions (for example, that humans have evolved), we allow our students to assess the evidence for themselves.

These lines of evidence, and how they illustrate the characteristics of an especially strong scientific theory, are summarized in the next section.

HUMANS AS A CASE STUDY FOR EVOLUTION AND THE NATURE OF SCIENCE

One of the more important ways for assessing the strength of any scientific theory is to determine how many different lines of evidence support it and, as a corollary, how well and accurately one such line predicts others. In addition to presenting evolution in general and human evolution in particular as examples of strong scientific thinking, physical anthropologists focus on the one organism which is clearly the most problematic, since it is especially difficult for many people to accept that humans have evolved. On the other hand, we deal with a species which is unparalleled in terms of the amount of scientific information and evidence discovered about its past, and also in terms of the deep interest it arouses – for people interested in learning about themselves. This situation provides us with an unparalleled teaching opportunity, as well as with an obligation. The opportunity involves taking advantage of our students' innate interest in human nature and its origin. The obligation consists in ensuring that students learn just how strong the overall case for human evolution is and why evolutionary theory in general is such strong science.

By presenting the evidence for human evolution, we actually make the case for virtually every other species. After all, once you have already dealt with the single most problematic species of all, there cannot be many serious objections to thinking that other organisms have also evolved. Here are the major areas or lines of evidence that we can cite to support the idea that humans have evolved.

Comparative biology of living species (including oddball structures)

In 1758, Linnaeus used overall anatomical similarity to group living humans with apes, monkeys, and lemurs into the order Primates. He thought that God had created the similarities between these forms on purpose. A century later, Darwinian evolutionary theory explained the same pattern of anatomical similarities between these species as having resulted from their shared ancestry and subsequent divergent evolution. The important teaching point here is that organisms supernaturally created *de novo* need not show any degrees of similarity to one another. Each organism clearly could have been created with completely different organizational plans and constructed from very different materials from any other. If they were created supernaturally and independently, humans need not look like apes; yet they do. Of course, they could also have been deliberately created so as to resemble apes. But, if we actually have evolved from a common ancestor with apes, then we must resemble them more than we resemble other species. This high degree of similarity is actually a prediction of evolutionary theory.

A century after Darwin, twentieth century science extended the comparison between apes and humans well beyond anatomy. Biochemical and genetic comparisons revealed an even higher degree of ape–human similarity than indicated by anatomical studies. These deeper biological comparisons actually served as a test of evolutionary theory. If we had discovered that humans and apes were not especially similar, biochemically or genetically, that would have created a significant problem for evolutionary theory. But, instead of having to deal with such a conundrum, our overall confidence in evolutionary theory was enhanced greatly.

One of the more informative areas of evidence for evolution lies not in the pattern of varying degrees of similarity between species, but rather, in what Stephen Jay Gould (1980) deemed to be the 'senseless signs of history.' These consist in biological structures that represent less than optimal 'design' or adaptive compromises. The human pelvis is such an example, in that its configuration is not ideally suited either for supporting our mode of erect bipedalism or for making the birthing process of big-brained babies as easy as the birth process is for smaller-brained apes. The shape of the human pelvis is a compromise between the adaptive pressures of having to anchor an erect and flexible spine, conducive for efficient bipedal striding, and also allowing the birthing of the biggest-brained baby of any primate.

The significance of 'oddball' structures in organisms is that they clearly make more sense as legacies or remnants of ancestral structures than as components of deliberate design or special creation. If humans and all other species have evolved, then we should expect to see that at least some current traits are relatively recent modifications of earlier ones. Structurally, the non-opposable big toe of humans is virtually indistinguishable from the more opposable one of other primates. It is simply aligned differently. Our canine tooth is the most reduced version of those canines that project more prominently in other primates. Our erect vertebral column is similar to that of other vertebrates, but in our case it is a weight-bearing column.

Structures such as these underscore the idea that, if living species do indeed share evolutionary ties reflecting different divergent times from shared ancestors, then they must show occasional vestiges of that ancestry. But there is no intrinsic requirement for any creature who was specially created or designed to share any structures in common at all, let alone to show variation in similar structures.

Biogeography, the fossil record, and fossil intermediates

Biogeography includes the study of the geographical distribution of living species. Its importance as evidence for evolution lies in the fact that similar species tend to live closer to each other geographically. In 1871 Darwin, acknowledging the work of comparative anatomists, concluded that humans resemble most nearly the African apes, and that therefore "[i]t is [...] probable that Africa was formerly inhabited by extinct apes closely allied to the gorilla and chimpanzee; and as these two species are now man's nearest allies [evolutionary cousins], it is somewhat more probable that our early progenitors lived on the African continent than elsewhere."

Keep in mind that, in 1871, this conclusion was based on only two lines of existing evidence, namely comparative anatomy and the biogeography of living species. Not a single fossil was known from Africa at the time Darwin wrote. What Darwin essentially did in 1871 was to make a prediction about what a third line of evidence – the actual human fossil record – should look like if, indeed, the African apes and humans shared a common ancestor more recently than they shared ancestry with any other living species. Darwin predicted that fossils of the earliest more human-like descendants of such an ancestor should be found in Africa, since that was the most probable place where an ancestor of the African apes and humans most likely lived. In essence, Darwin made a prediction that was a test of his evolutionary thinking. Since one measure of the strength of any scientific theory is the congruence of different lines of evidence in support of it, discovering an African fossil record of the earliest stages of human evolution would be a significant boost for evolutionary thinking in general. On the other hand, finding the earliest such fossils in Eurasia would have been problematic, and finding them in Australia or in the Americas would have been devastating for Darwin's idea (since there are no living Australian or American apes, and we have never found any ape fossils whatsoever in these areas).

What was actually eventually found? The first significant human-like fossil from Africa – at Taung – was found in 1924, fifty-three years after Darwin's prediction. It took another twenty-five years of additional fossil finds, however, before they were accepted as early hominins in the early 1950s – three-quarters of a century after Darwin's prediction. To date, no earlier fossils or better candidate ancestors have been found on any other continent. Darwin was vindicated and the idea of human evolution bolstered. The fossil evidence for human evolution has only grown stronger as additional early human-like fossils continued to be found in Africa. This pattern of discovery has also strengthened general evolutionary theory.

One of the most impressive aspects of the fossils from the earlier African hominin fossil record is the mosaic or mixed nature of the forms. Very simply, these early forms are different from apes in the same way in which we are different from apes today. They stood erect and walked bipedally and, eventually, reduced their big front teeth (especially the canines) and acquired bigger and bigger brains. The further back in time we go, the less hominins resemble humans. If the earliest hominins are indeed the evolved descendants of an extinct African ape form who lived 6–8 mya, then we should fully expect them to be increasingly difficult to distinguish from that ancestral form the closer we approach the time when they diverged.

What does the overall human fossil record look like? Early African fossils show more evidence of an erect, bipedal adaptation than of bigger brains or human-sized teeth. Somewhat later fossils, from 2–3 mya, have smaller teeth and bigger brains. Still later fossils, from 1–2 mya, have even bigger brains and have expanded into Eurasia. The biggest-brained humans of all – Neandertals and members of *Homo sapiens* – appeared in the last 200,000 years. This overall pattern is extraordinarily consistent with the conclusion that some earlier ape-like creature evolved into the human species of today.

USING HISTORY TO TEACH ABOUT CREATIONISM

One of the more interesting aspects of modern anti-evolutionist thinking is just how much the alternatives its supporters advocate are the same as the ones proposed in the past. In some cases, these non-evolutionary ideas pre-date Darwin by hundreds of years. By teaching about these ideas in a historical context, one can address them more dispassionately. This tends to make them less provocative and confrontational for some students. Here is a sampling of some historical precedents for today's anti-evolutionist ideas. Many of the earlier authors have their own unique views, as well.

Young earth: 1650, James Ussher, *The Annals of the World*
Using genealogical data from Genesis, Ussher, who was an Irish Protestant Bishop, calculated that "time began at 6 p.m. on the evening of Saturday October 22, 4004 B.C." (Gorst 2001: 39). This chapter's second opening quotation, from Henry Morris in 1972, expresses the identical idea.

Flood geology and catastrophism: 1695, John Woodward, *An Essay Towards a Natural History of the Earth*
Woodward asserted that the earth's geological formations and strata are largely the result of a worldwide flood (invariably thought to be the Noachian deluge – the Flood recounted in Genesis). In modern times, John C. Whitcomb and Henry Morris (1961) authored *The Genesis Flood*, which revived Flood geology as an all-encompassing explanation for the earth's geological and paleontological formations. This book is generally recognized as initiating the modern 'creation science' or 'scientific creationism' movement.

Intelligent design: 1802, William Paley, *Natural Theology; or, Evidence of the Existence and Attributes of the Deity Collected from the Appearances of Nature*
This is the 'classic' presentation of the argument from design, in which Paley uses the metaphor of finding a watch on the ground and concluding that it must have been

intelligently designed. Part of this argument is that, just as partially built watches are dysfunctional, so, too, are organic structures at intermediate stages of development. Michael Behe and William Dembski are modern advocates of this position.

Successive creations: 1812, Georges Cuvier, *Ossemens fossiles (Fossil Bones)*

Cuvier proposed the catastrophist idea that there had actually been a series or a succession of creations ('successive creationism'), in which God periodically and regionally destroyed through flooding previously created forms and replaced them with new ones. The Noachian Flood was the last such catastrophe. Cuvier used the discovery of relatively intact frozen Siberian mammoths as evidence of the suddenness of ancient catastrophes. This curious variation of progressive creationism is rarely advocated today, but modern creationists like Morris and Gish still use frozen Siberian mammoths to argue for the suddenness of the Noachian Flood.

Orthogenesis: 1844, Robert Chambers, *Vestiges of the Natural History of Creation*

Fifteen years before Darwin published *On the Origin of Species*, Chambers argued for evolution, but through a process involving the gradual unfolding of God's predetermined divine plan of development. Chambers thought that God had built a preordained pattern into nature whereby natural processes would occasionally change so as to appear to be of a miraculous sort (Bowler 1989: 145–146).

   Theodor Eimer popularized the idea of 'orthogenesis' or goal-directed evolution at the end of the nineteenth century. This idea accepts evolution as having occurred, but neither as the result of the contingency of natural selection nor through occasional miraculous interventions from God. Rather, the perceived progression of life forms is thought to have derived either from an 'inner perfecting principle' directing evolution (an idea attributed to Carl von Nägeli) or from to the unfolding of God's master plan (Bowler 1989: 268). This is a position held today by those who combine their belief that there is a divinely ordained plan for existence, or their perception of God as a sort of impersonal divine architect, with their acceptance of deep geological time and of the biological evolution of species.

Creation with an appearance of age: 1857, Phillip Gosse, *Omphalos*

Gosse attempted to reconcile the growing evidence for a geologically ancient earth with a literal reading of Genesis by arguing that God created the world with 'an appearance of age.' He argued for example that, even though the biblical Adam had no pre-existing biological mother, he must have had a navel (*omphalos* is the ancient Greek noun for 'navel') because Adam was fully human and all humans possess navels. Adam's having a navel would indicate – falsely – that an earlier existing woman gave birth to him. In essence, the idea here is that when God created the world it could only have looked older than it actually is. This idea has been advocated recently by Henry Morris:

> It is even possible that the 'light' bathing the earth on the first three days [in *Genesis*] was created in space as en route from the innumerable 'light bearers' [stars] which were yet to be constituted on the fourth day. The reason such concepts appear at first strange and

unbelievable is that our minds are so conditioned to think in uniformitarian terms that we cannot easily grasp the meaning of creation. Actually, real creation necessarily involves creation of 'apparent age.' Whatever is truly created – that is, called instantly into existence out of nothing – must certainly look as though it had been there prior to its creation. Thus it has an appearance of age. (Henry Morris 1972: 62)

God formed it [the universe] full-grown in every respect, including even Adam and Eve as mature individuals when they were first formed. The whole universe had an 'appearance of age' right from the start. It could not have been otherwise for true creation to have taken place. (ibid.: 210).

Progressive creation/intelligent design/successive creations: 1859, Louis Agassiz, *An Essay in Classification*

In 1837, Louis Agassiz (a student of Cuvier) proposed that there had been prehistoric ice ages. Like Cuvier, he attributed the succession of life forms to separate divine creations that conformed to a master plan: Humans are "the last term of a series, beyond which there is no material progress possible in accordance with the plan upon which the whole animal kingdom is constructed" (Eiseley 1961: 97). The idea that humans represent the pinnacle of creation (or evolution, for that matter) is widespread even today, both among those who accept evolution and among those who do not. The progressive creation model described in Duane Gish's 1978 book *Evolution? The Fossils Say No!* is built on this thinking. (Curiously, the arguments in Gish's book actually contradict his own beliefs as a young-earth creationist, because so many of his anti-evolution arguments presume the validity of the geological and fossil record.)

Day–age interpretation of Genesis: 1804–1811, James Parkinson, *Organic Remains of a Former World*

This is one of the earliest presentations of the idea that the creation 'days' in Genesis represent vast periods of geological time. This 'day–age' thinking is associated typically with the idea of 'progressive creation,' namely that God did indeed create all life forms, but that creations of different organisms took place at different times during the geological past, not in six consecutive twenty-four-hour days.

Theistic evolution (sort of): 1889, Alfred Wallace, *Darwinism*

As the co-developer of the idea of evolution through natural selection, Wallace emphasized the central role of natural selection, but he disagreed with Darwin's conception of how human evolution occurred. Wallace accepted an ape ancestry for humans, except for the human brain and mind (Milner 1993: 457). He thought that our intellectual and moral faculties "can only find adequate cause in the unseen universe of Spirit." Central to various philosophical and theological positions is the idea of the uniqueness of humans, according to which we are not just animals – we are something more, something different, something special. Recall this chapter's opening quotation.

This is but a sampling of some of the historical ideas that are still adhered to and advocated by anti-evolutionists today. Some of these still reject completely both evolution and a geologically ancient earth. Others accept both, but believe that everything was pre-destined by God to happen as it did. Still others accept both, but believe that God was more active in the past in directing and shaping evolutionary events. Eugenie Scott (2004) has a more detailed discussion of the many permutations of contemporary belief about origins.

'INTELLIGENT DESIGN' THEORY

Biological evolution and any form of creationism refer to processes (supernatural in the case of creationism) that produce organic structures and organisms. 'Intelligent design' (ID), on the other hand, refers to an attribute, trait, or characteristic of something. To say that a structure reflects intelligence in its design is to describe its nature, not the nature of the process through which it came to be. There can be intelligence guiding, or embedded in, any number of different kinds of processes: sculpting, painting, architecture, music, legal systems, organizations, and so on. While the processes and mechanisms used in each of these endeavors may differ radically from one another, what they share is the presence of a detectable intent or blueprint to produce something.

One of the difficulties with ID as an explanation, when it is applied to biological structures, is that it entails the necessity of invoking some form of non-natural process as a necessary alternative to the sufficiency of known natural processes. This is the argument of William Behe, who claims that there are some biochemical structures (for example the flagellum of bacteria) that are too 'irreducibly complex' to have arisen through known natural processes. He implies that an alternative non-natural process must have been involved. This is a variation of the 'God of the Gaps' argument discussed earlier. There are several problems with this argument, though.

One problem is that geneticists have proposed a plausible natural process or mechanism to explain how a structure may arise through a series of even non-functional stages: gene duplication. It is a known fact that there are duplicate copies of many genes in organisms (Ledford 2008). These duplicate genes are able to undergo mutations that would essentially disable the original gene's function, but, because they occur only in the duplicate gene, these mutations allow for novelties to appear and be preserved. Preserving them allows for additional mutational novelties to appear later. Eventually, in some cases, these accumulated novelties produce a functionally new structure or a biochemical pathway. There is evidence that there have been more than 3,500 gene duplications in vertebrates alone (Gross 2005). The ABO blood group system is a prominent example.

A second problem with the claim that some biological structures are too complex to have arisen naturally, through a series of intermediate steps that lack the full functionality of the current structure, is that it ignores the history of scientific discoveries. This history shows that the 'God of the Gaps' approach repeatedly fails as new processes are discovered that are sufficient, or adequate enough, to account for some previously inexplicable structure or species. Darwin himself was aware of this problem with regard to the complexity of the eye. He reasoned that, if less complex eyes – or even merely light sensitive tissues and structures – existed in different organisms, then there would be adaptive advantages associated with earlier intermediate stages of full eye development. Such structures have been found in a variety of living organisms.

A third problem with ID explanations in biology involves actually identifying the intelligent entity or being responsible for the alleged design. The two principal current

ID advocates (Michael Behe and Wiliam Dembski) clearly think that God is the responsible agent, even though they avoid admitting as much in many of their publications. The difficulty with invoking God as the designer, however, is that one may be invoking the wrong god. It is also possible that the alleged 'designer' is not supernatural at all; it may be a more technologically advanced extraterrestrial..

Consider these two quotations: "Any sufficiently advanced technology is indistinguishable from magic" (Clarke 1973); and: "Any sufficiently advanced extraterrestrial intelligence is indistinguishable from God" (Shermer 2002). The point of both of these declarations is that our own advanced scientific knowledge may well be able both to describe and to explain the natural pathway along which the alleged designed structures arose; it may even be able to duplicate them artificially. The implication of Shermer's quotation is that it is theoretically possible that scientifically-advanced alien beings – who themselves evolved – have already done so on previous visits to earth! Absurd as this may seem, we cannot be absolutely, positively sure that it hasn't happened, can we? So, even if there has been deliberate manipulation or intervention in some biological systems in the past in order to produce otherwise unobtainable structures, we cannot be sure who or what was responsible for that intervention.

One additional problem with ID is the pervasiveness of the sort of imperfect or less than optimal structures and adaptive compromises discussed earlier in this chapter. The presence of these design 'flaws' is difficult for many to reconcile with an all-knowing, all-powerful supernatural being, endowed with the power to create anything and everything from nothingness. The 'flaws' are much more consistent with a natural history of modifications of existing structures over long periods of time.

In sum, there really seems no good reason to resort to some unknown supernatural process to explain apparent 'design' when natural processes (including Darwin's original idea of natural selection) exist that are sufficient and adequate to the task. It also seems very risky to identify any specific intelligent designer when there are far too many options – supernatural or extraterrestrial – for us to be able to determine which one might be actually responsible.

BEYOND THE CLASSROOM

Extrapolating from statistics from the United States Bureau of Labor Statistics, many of the 44 percent of Americans who reject evolution clearly did not take a physical anthropology course in college – because they did not go to college. About two-thirds of the nearly 3 million high-school graduates of 2006–2007 entered college in 2007. Clearly, not all of these enroll in physical anthropology courses, either. However, approximately 80 percent of adult Americans have graduated from high school (Henry 2002). If physical anthropologists are interested in reaching the vast majority of Americans who never take our courses, then we have to move out of our classrooms to find them.

Because their high-school science classes are the last formal education in science that many Americans will receive, one of the most effective and easiest ways for us to reach more students is by guest lecturing in high-school biology classes. To judge from its inclusion in textbooks and state science standards, evolution is clearly a part of the high-school biology curriculum, although how extensively and how well it is taught varies greatly across the country. I have found that high-school teachers invariably welcome credible outside experts, who can enliven their classes. Teachers and students alike enjoy someone who can present the basics of human evolution. They enjoy especially actually handling fossil and ape casts. (Even if one's expertise is in genetics and biochemistry, the casts are easier for most students to relate to than molecular data.) Conducting in-service sessions for teachers is also very effective, since many of them simply need updated knowledge and examples of teaching that they can use in their own classrooms. Giving presentations at state and national teachers' conferences of the National Association of Biology Teachers and of the National Science Teachers Association greatly increases the number of teachers – and therefore students – one can reach.

In addition to working with high-school teachers and students, one can participate in broader community teaching opportunities. These include everything, from church forums and Sunday School classes to senior citizen enrichment programs and Elderhostels. One can write op-ed pieces for a newspaper, as well as pen letters to the editor to combat the continual flow of anti-evolutionist letters that seem to appear in newspapers across the country. Not all of these activities may represent ideal teaching opportunities, but they are nevertheless necessary to ensure that the voices of science and rationality are never silent in the presence of ignorance.

REFERENCES

WORKS MENTIONED IN THE TEXT

Bowler, P. J. (1989) *Evolution: The History of an Idea*, rev. edn. Berkeley: University of California Press.

Buckland, W. (1820) *Vindiciae Geologicae, or the Connexion of Geology with Religion Explained*. Oxford: Oxford University Press.

Clarke, A. C. (1973) Hazards of Prophecy: The Failure of Imagination in *Profiles of the Future*, rev. edn). New York: Macmillan.

Cole, E. (2007) Poll: More Americans Believe in Devil than Darwin. Electronic document. Accessed November 14, 2008 at: http://www.christianpost.com/article/20071203/30307_Poll%3A_More_Americans_Believe_in_Devil_than_Darwin.htm.

Eiseley, L. (1961) *Darwin's Century*. New York: Doubleday Anchor Books.

Gallup Poll (2008) Republicans, Democrats Differ on Creationism. Electronic document. Accessed September 26, 2008 at: http://www.gallup.com/poll/108226/Republicans-Democrats-Differ-Creationism.aspx.

Gish, D. (1978) *Evolution? The Fossils Say No!* San Diego: Creation Life Publishers.

Gorst, M. (2001) *Measuring Eternity*. New York: Broadway Books.

Gould, S. J. (1980) Senseless Signs of History. In S. J. Gould, *The Panda's Thumb: More Reflections in Natural History* (pp. 27–34). New York: W. W. Norton.

Gross, L. (2005) Clear Evidence for Two Rounds of Vertebrate Genome Duplication. *PLoS Biology* 3 (10): e344 doi: 10.1371/journal.pbio.0030344.

Henry, T. (2002) Report: Greater Percentage of Americans Educated. *USA Today*, June 5. Electronic document. Accessed October 8, 2008 at: http://www.usatoday.com/news/education/2002-06-05-education-census.htm#more.

Ledford, H. (2008) Human Genes are Multitaskers. Accessed November 4, 2008 at: http://www.nature.com/news/2008/081102/full/news.2008.1199.html.

Mayr, E. (1982) *The Growth of Biological Thought*. Cambridge MA: Harvard University Press.

Milner, R. (1993) *The Encyclopedia of Evolution*. New York: Henry Holt and Company.

Morris, H. (1972) *The Remarkable Birth of Planet Earth*. Minneapolis: Bethany Fellowship.

Morris, H. (1985) *Scientific Creationism*, 2nd edn. San Diego: Creation-Life Publishers.

Owen, J. (2006) Evolution Less Accepted in U.S. Than Other Western Countries, Study Finds. Electronic document. Accessed September 28, 2008 at: http://news.nationalgeographic.com/news/2006/08/060810-evolution.html.

Pitock, T. (2007) Science and Islam in Conflict. *Discover Magazine* 28 (7): 36–45.

Ramm, B. (1954) *The Christian View of Science and Scripture*. Grand Rapids MI: William B. Eerdmans Publishing Company.

Scott, E. C. (2004) *Evolution vs. Creationism*. Westport CT: Greenwood Press.

Shermer, M. (2002) Shermer's Last Law. *Scientific American* 286 (1): 33.

Whitcomb, J. C., and Morris, H. (1961) *The Genesis Flood*. Philadelphia: Presbyterian and Reformed Publishing.

GENERAL BIBLIOGRAPHY AND SOURCEBOOKS

ENSI/SENSI: Evolution and the Nature of Science. Accessed November 13, 2008 at: http://www.indiana.edu/~ensiweb/.

Isaak, M. (2007) *The Counter-Creationism Handbook*. Berkeley: University of California Press.

National Center for Science Education: Defending the Teaching of Evolution in Public Schools. Accessed October 24, 2008 at: http://ncseweb.org/.

Nelson, C. E. (2007) Teaching Evolution Effectively: A Central Dilemma and Alternative Strategies. *McGill Journal of Education* 42 (2): 265–283. Electronic document. Accessed September 6, 2008 at: http://mje.mcgill.ca/article/view,2223/1693.

Nickels, M. (1998) Humans as a Case Study for the Evidence of Evolution. *Reports of the National Center for Science Education* 18 (5): 24–27.

Nickels, M. K., Nelson, C. E., and Beard, J. (1996) Better Biology Teaching by Emphasizing Evolution and the Nature of Science. *The American Biology Teacher* 58 (6): 332–336.

Panda's Thumb. Discussions and Critiques of Evolutionary Theory, Science and Education. Accessed July 10, 2008 at: http://www.pandasthumb.org/.

Pennock, R. T., ed. (2002) *Intelligent Design Creationism and Its Critics*. Cambridge MA: MIT Press.

Skybreak, A. (2006) *The Science of Evolution and the Myth of Creationism*. Chicago: Insight Press.

Index

Page numbers in italics, e.g. *144*, indicate figures or tables.